THE IDEA OF MAN

An Anthology of Literature

ADVENTURES IN GOOD BOOKS
(FOR GRADES 7–12)

Four Famous Adventures

Five American Adventures

Four Adventures in Courage

Four Novels for Adventure

Four Novels for Appreciation

Five World Biographies

Adventures in Fiction

Adventures in Poetry

Four American Novels

Four American Biographies

Four English Novels

Four English Biographies

Five World Plays

Three World Classics

♦ *The Idea of Man*

TEACHER'S MANUAL FOR EACH VOLUME

THE IDEA OF MAN

An Anthology of Literature

Edmund Fuller

O. B. Davis

HARCOURT, BRACE & WORLD, INC.

New York · Chicago · San Francisco · Atlanta · Dallas

EDMUND FULLER, who has taught at Columbia University, Kent School, and St. Stephen's School in Rome, is a literary critic and author of twelve books including *Man in Modern Fiction* and three novels. He is co-author of *Adventures in American Literature*, Laureate Edition, and is General Editor of the Adventures in Good Books Series.

O. B. DAVIS has been head of the English Department at Kent School, Kent, Connecticut, since 1954, and has taught there since 1949. He has contributed to various professional periodicals and collaborated with J. B. Priestley on *Four English Novels* and *Four English Biographies,* and with Edmund Fuller on *Four American Biographies* and *Three World Classics.*

The cover photograph is a Greek sculpture representing Poseidon.

ACKNOWLEDGMENTS: For permission to reprint copyrighted material, grateful acknowledgment is made to the following sources:

DOUBLEDAY & COMPANY, INC.: "The Blue Hotel" from *Complete Short Stories and Sketches* by Stephen Crane, edited by Thomas Gullason. From *Sheppey,* copyright 1933 by W. Somerset Maugham.

HARCOURT, BRACE & WORLD, INC.: *The Oedipus Rex of Sophocles: An English Version by Dudley Fitts and Robert Fitzgerald,* copyright 1949 by Harcourt, Brace & World, Inc.; Footnotes to *Oedipus Rex* by Richard Levin from his volume, *Tragedy: Plays, Theory and Criticism,* © 1960 by Harcourt, Brace & World, Inc. "Aunt Helen" from *Collected Poems 1909–1962* by T. S. Eliot, copyright 1936 by Harcourt, Brace & World, Inc.; copyright © 1963, 1964 by T. S. Eliot. "Florence Nightingale" and an excerpt from the Preface to *Eminent Victorians* by Lytton Strachey.

1428867

Contents

ix

THE IDEA OF MAN

An Anthology of Literature

WHY MAN WRITES

For many generations people have taken for granted the processes of writing and reading. Taking anything for granted is harmful; it makes us lose our fresh and sensitive awareness both of *what* things are and *why* they are. We will have a look at the nature of writing and reading, these familiar and vital acts, taking nothing about them for granted.

Most commonly, people speak of "reading and writing," but we have said "writing and reading." There is no riddle here of "Which came first — the chicken or the egg?" There must be writing before there can be reading. First, then, why do men write?

PART OF WHAT IT MEANS TO BE HUMAN

Perhaps on some of the other planets, in some of the other solar systems that astronomers now believe must be scattered plentifully through our galaxy and the rest of the universe, there may be other kinds of creatures that have developed the art of writing. On our home base, Earth, we creatures who call ourselves human and are fond of giving such flattering titles to ourselves as *Homo sapiens* (wise man) are the only ones who write in any form.

Thus, writing is one of the abilities that set us apart distinctly from the other creatures who share this planet with us. It is one of many factors that give us the advantage over animals whose natural strength and agility exceed our own. Man invented writing because there were certain qualities in his nature that made such invention possible when he found it necessary. By helping him to generate, record, and exchange ideas, writing has been a major factor in his emergence from the primitive.

AN ENORMOUS MEMORY

Do you think it would be possible for a single person, in one lifetime, to learn everything that the human race knows? Indeed, it is not even possible to learn everything about any one main branch of knowledge, such as science, history, or art. It is not possible for one man to keep up with every subdivision of physics; he must know parts of it and work with those who know other parts. It is not possible for any man to read a very large fraction of the books that exist, or even of the new ones published in any given year.

Scientists believe that our brains record permanently every impression of the five senses, and every thought and emotion that we ever experience. At our present level of ability, we can recall in memory only a small portion of that record. Some of us have better memories than others. A distressingly large part of our memory is occupied with things not worth remembering or things that we wish we could forget.

In our education there are certain elementary things that we must remember, beginning with the alphabet and the multiplication tables. But because of the limits of our minds, part of a sound education consists in learning how to use a vast storehouse of knowledge and thought far greater than our individual memories can retain. That storehouse is the product of writing — the cumulative world library of books and documents.

Each animal discovers everything anew in its own lifetime, and passes on no accumulated knowledge or experience to succeeding generations of animals beyond a few primal skills of hunting and self-preservation. But through the storehouse of writing, the human being has laid down layer upon layer of knowledge, discovery, and speculation (often mistaken), upon which generations have built, without the impossible task of having to do the whole job over again in each lifetime. The written word, therefore, is our great, cumulative, human memory. It has made us what we are — for the best and the worst — and it is what makes it possible for you, as an individual, to become whatever you may become that is worthy of remark.

TO GIVE A MESSAGE

When we consider how great is the effect of the process of writing, it is almost astonishing to observe how simple is the basic reason for why we do it. It is to give a message. It is to communicate. The very first person to whom a man ever wished to give a written message may have been himself. He may have put down in pictures — his earliest form of writing — some description of the animal encountered in his day's hunt so that he might remember it; that he might think about it and thus know it better; that he might ponder his feelings about it; and perhaps finally, that he might convey his experience to someone who was not with him at the time.

We still communicate with ourselves in writing. That is what you are doing when you keep a diary or jot down memos. Through the centuries, however, a host of forms of written communication have been developed, from the merely practical or informational to history, philosophy, religious revelations, science, and the various literary media of prose, poetry, and drama.

The means of writing evolved through long, complicated stages. Its most primitive form, picture writing, was too limited to serve man's needs. Simpler, formalized symbols for pictures were developed (hieroglyphs, pictographs), and then symbols for sounds (alphabets), which brought the process of writing and the development of language to maturity.

Still the process exists to give a message — to ourselves or others, whether the content be simple or complex, superficial or profound. A grocery list can be sent to the store for the filling of an order, or the housewife may carry it with her to make sure she does not forget any items. It is useful, but it is not of high importance.

The Bible records the inspired teachings and wisdom of great prophets and holy men. The communication of this message is infinitely more important than the grocery list; the point is that both are messages, and they have this in common with every coherent word ever written.

But unlike grocery lists and memoranda, the Bible is part of a vast body of writing to which we give the comprehensive name, "literature." There are many variations of kind and purpose in literature, but one common thread unites it all — it deals with Man.

MAN THINKS AND WRITES ABOUT HIMSELF

It has always been in the nature of man to wonder about himself — to be conscious of himself in ways that lead him to ask certain questions. For centuries he has been asking these questions and attempting to answer them, yet each generation finds it necessary to ask them over again, to examine the answers that other men have made, and to set forth answers of their own.

Among these enduring questions are: What am I? Who am I? What am I doing here? Whence have I come? Where am I going? Why do I exist? What purposes does life have? What will become of me at the end of my life? What is good? What is evil? How should I live?

From the dawn of writing men have put down their questions and answers about such great matters — earliest of all in the myths. As time passed, these queries and responses were elaborated into many forms, including dramas, poems, novels, histories, and biographies. One of the largest segments of this accumulation of writing is called "story."

There is a curious thing about stories. Their "truth" or value does not depend on whether the events happened in real life or not. Jesus told a parable about two men who built houses. One built his house upon sand, and the winds and the rains came and beat upon the house, and it fell, and great was the fall of it. The other man built his house upon a rock. The winds and the rains beat upon it, but the house stood firm upon its solid foundation.

There is truth in that story. Yet Jesus was not speaking of two specific men and two actual houses. The story is not even about houses at all, as we see quite readily, but is about the question of whether we base our lives upon permanent and profound values, or upon impermanent and superficial ones.

The story you might tell as a witness in a trial must be about what actually happened as you saw it, or else it can have no truth or value as evidence. If the New York *Times* describes an event that occurred to certain people at a certain time and place, it must have happened so, or the story has no truth or value as newspaper reporting. But these are special standards. In the realm of literature — the realm of story in all its possible imaginative and artistic forms — the measure is whether or not the story shows us something that is true about men and women and their experiences of life. What is wholly true about anybody is likely to be partly true about everybody.

It is through reflecting broad truths about human experiences, emotions, and problems that myths, fairy tales, fables, and fantasies of all kinds, including ones about imaginary beings on other planets, can have great value in helping us to understand ourselves and others.

At once the simplest, and in some ways the most difficult, question that we can ask about any piece of literature is, "What does it say about Man?" Deciding for ourselves whether what it says about Man is true or false, in whole or in part, is one of the most important steps in deciding the value of any writing. To be able to make such judgments requires a good bit of experience and wisdom, both in literature and in living.

EXPERIENCE TO IDEA

The experiences and observations of men lead them to that mulling-over in the mind that we call reflection. Reflection begets ideas. To the Greek philosopher Plato, an idea meant the original and eternal pattern of any class of things, from which those things about us are derived — but derived imperfectly, never matching the pure idea. In a crudely material analogy to this, the Bureau of Standards in Washington, D.C., contains the *idea* of a poundweight, a pint, a bushel, an inch, or a yard: standards by which all such weights and measurements can be checked for their deviations from perfection.

But this Platonic idea of an "idea" is much too limited to accommodate all the intellectual freight the word must carry. There are many fascinating gradations of meaning it has known and still knows, as you will discover by investigating the word in the great Oxford English Dictionary. The sense which is of chief concern to us is summed up as "Any product of mental apprehension or activity, existing in the mind as an object of knowledge or thought; a thought, conception, notion; an item of knowledge or belief; a way of thinking."

Originally, experiences generated ideas. Hunger and its satisfaction generated the *idea* of food; intimate associations, at first instinctive, generated the *idea* of love; mystery, wonder, awe at the natural world around us generated the *idea* of God, though it is the teaching of the great religions based on revelation that the idea of God cannot progress beyond superstition without a helping move toward man by God Himself.

Though experience is the origin of ideas, they may yet remain at a most primitive level. The idea of writing opened the way to the flowering of all ideas, and to the realization that the relationship of experience to ideas is reciprocal. For in turn, ideas generate new experience, sometimes utterly alien to man's apparent limitation, such as the idea of flight which, after centuries, became experience.

Writing is the systematic breeder, preserver, explorer, projector, and disseminator of ideas. If those who read books are in pursuit of ideas, how much more so are those who labor to write them? You who read what is in this book are following the trail of those many writers whose varied explorations of ideas are gathered here. They are necessarily a small sampling, but they are selected as representative of some of man's major preoccupations. They are a group of ideas you will be traveling with throughout your life.

The
Idea
of Man

In the first story of this section, someone asks the question, "What do you mean by man?" Later you will find the English poet, Alexander Pope, declaring, "There must be, somewhere, such a rank as Man."

Man is man because he has the *idea* of man. He is a self-conscious creature, aware of both his species and his separate personhood. The general Introduction already has indicated that the idea of man is the theme of this book.

That the volume title is also the particular title of Part I is because each of the three works studied in this section is concerned with defining not this man or that, not one kind or another, but the whole species and its place in the scheme of existing things.

The later sections will examine men in several of their principal aspects. But here, with C. S. Lewis of the twentieth century, John Milton of the seventeenth, and Alexander Pope of the eighteenth, we pursue that primary question, "What do you mean by man?" and further inquire why there should be, anywhere, such a rank as he.

Out of the Silent Planet

by C. S. Lewis (1898–1963)

If we travel from our country for any length of time, we come to look upon home in new perspectives. We may see it quite differently from the way we saw it before. We become more aware of it, more conscious of its real nature and qualities.

In *Out of the Silent Planet,* C. S. Lewis makes us take a look at Earth from another point in space. What he shows us provokes startling thoughts about the planet we inhabit and the kind of creatures we are. The story is a fantasy, but the far reaches of imagination serve just as well as the far reaches of space to give us the beneficial effects of long perspectives. Like the ancient myths, a modern imaginative tale of this kind can tell us important truths through metaphors and symbols, provided the teller of the tale has something to say that is worth thinking about.

Out of the Silent Planet is a first-class adventure story, exuberantly inventive and especially distinguished for its vivid descriptions of an imaginary world. Among its admirers is a noted scholar, Marjorie Hope Nicolson, long-time head of the English Department of Columbia University. In her book *Voyages to the Moon* (Macmillan, 1948), a study of the tradition of space-travel fantasies from ancient times to the present, she pays tribute to the visual richness and lyrical freshness of Lewis's descriptions: *"Out of the Silent Planet* . . . is to me the most beautiful of all cosmic voyages and in some ways the most moving."

Lewis remarks in another of his books, *An Adventure in Criticism* (Cambridge University Press, 1961):

> I am probably one of many who, on a wakeful night, entertain themselves with invented landscapes. I trace the great rivers from where the gulls scream at the estuary, through the windings of ever narrower and more precipitous gorges, up to the barely audible tinkling of their source in a fold of the moors.

It was undoubtedly this intense, absorbed visualizing that created the delights of the Malacandrian scenes you are about to encounter.

The story is both science-fiction and something more. Lewis pictures our world and the rest of the universe as part of an orderly creation with plan and purpose. The great questions are: Whose creation? Whose plan? Whose purpose?

AUTHOR'S NOTE: *Certain slighting references to earlier stories of this type which will be found in the following pages have been put there for purely dramatic purposes. The author would be sorry if any reader supposed he was too stupid to have enjoyed Mr. H. G. Wells's fantasies or too ungrateful to acknowledge his debt to them.*   *C.S.L.*

Chapter 1

The last drops of the thunder-shower had hardly ceased falling when the Pedestrian stuffed his map into his pocket, settled his pack more comfortably on his tired shoulders, and stepped out from the shelter of a large chestnut-tree into the middle of the road. A violent yellow sunset was pouring through a rift in the clouds to westward, but straight ahead over the hills the sky was the colour of dark slate. Every tree and blade of grass was dripping, and the road shone like a river. The Pedestrian wasted no time on the landscape but set out at once with the determined stride of a good walker who has lately realized that he will have to walk farther than he intended. That, indeed, was his situation. If he had chosen to look back, which he did not, he could have seen the spire of Much Nadderby, and, seeing it, might have uttered a malediction on the inhospitable little hotel

which, though obviously empty, had refused him a bed. The place had changed hands since he last went for a walking-tour in these parts. The kindly old landlord on whom he had reckoned had been replaced by someone whom the barmaid referred to as "the lady," and the lady was apparently a British innkeeper of that orthodox school who regard guests as a nuisance. His only chance now was Sterk, on the far side of the hills, and a good six miles away. The map marked an inn at Sterk. The Pedestrian was too experienced to build any very sanguine hopes on this, but there seemed nothing else within range.

He walked fairly fast, and doggedly, without looking much about him, like a man trying to shorten the way with some interesting train of thought. He was tall, but a little round-shouldered, about thirty-five to forty years of age, and dressed with that particular kind of shabbiness which marks a member of the intelligentsia on a holiday. He might easily have been mistaken for a doctor or a schoolmaster at first sight, though he had not the man-of-the-world air of the one or the indefinable breeziness of the other. In fact, he was a philologist, and fellow of a Cambridge college. His name was Ransom.

He had hoped when he left Nadderby that he might find a night's lodging at some friendly farm before he had walked as far as Sterk. But the land this side of the hills seemed almost uninhabited. It was a desolate, featureless sort of country mainly devoted to cabbage and turnip, with poor hedges and few trees. It attracted no visitors like the richer country south of Nadderby and it was protected by the hills from the industrial areas beyond Sterk. As the evening drew in and the noise of the birds came to an end it grew more silent than an English landscape usually is. The noise of his own feet on the metalled [1] road became irritating.

He had walked thus for a matter of two miles when he became aware of a light ahead. He was close under the hills by now and it was nearly dark, so that he still cherished hopes of a substantial farmhouse until he was quite close to the real origin of the light, which proved to be a very small cottage of ugly nineteenth-century brick. A woman darted out of the open doorway as he approached it and almost collided with him.

"I beg your pardon, sir," she said. "I thought it was my Harry."

Ransom asked her if there was any place nearer than Sterk where he might possibly get a bed.

"No, sir," said the woman. "Not nearer than Sterk. I dare say as they might fix you up at Nadderby."

She spoke in a humbly fretful voice as if her mind were intent on something else. Ransom explained that he had already tried Nadderby.

"Then I don't know, I'm sure, sir," she replied. "There isn't hardly any house before Sterk, not what

[1] metalled: (British) hard-surfaced.

you want. There's only The Rise, where my Harry works, and I thought you was coming from that way, sir, and that's why I come out when I heard you, thinking it might be him. He ought to be home this long time."

"The Rise," said Ransom. "What's that? A farm? Would they put me up?"

"Oh no, sir. You see there's no one there now except the Professor and the gentleman from London, not since Miss Alice died. They wouldn't do anything like that, sir. They don't even keep any servants, except my Harry for doing the furnace like, and he's not in the house."

"What's this professor's name?" asked Ransom, with a faint hope.

"I don't know, I'm sure, sir," said the woman. "The other gentleman's Mr. Devine, he is, and Harry says the *other* gentleman is a professor. He don't know much about it, you see, sir, being a little simple, and that's why I don't like him coming home so late, and they said they'd always send him home at six o'clock. It isn't as if he didn't do a good day's work either."

The monotonous voice and the limited range of the woman's vocabulary did not express much emotion, but Ransom was standing sufficiently near to perceive that she was trembling and nearly crying. It occurred to him that he ought to call on the mysterious professor and ask for the boy to be sent home: and it occurred to him just a fraction of a second later that once he were inside the house — among men of his own profession — he might very reasonably accept the offer of a night's hospitality. Whatever the process of thought may have been, he found that the mental picture of himself calling at The Rise had assumed all the solidity of a thing determined upon. He told the woman what he intended to do.

"Thank you very much, sir, I'm sure," she said. "And if you would be so kind as to see him out of the gate and on the road before you leave, if you see what I mean, sir. He's that frightened of the Professor and he wouldn't come away once your back was turned, sir, not if they hadn't sent him home themselves like."

Ransom reassured the woman as well as he could and bade her goodbye, after ascertaining that he would find The Rise on his left in about five minutes. Stiffness had grown upon him while he was standing still, and he proceeded slowly and painfully on his way.

There was no sign of any lights on the left of the road — nothing but the flat fields and a mass of darkness which he took to be a copse. It seemed more than five minutes before he reached it and found that he had been mistaken. It was divided from the road by a good hedge and in the hedge was a white gate; and the trees which rose above him as he examined the gate were not the first line of a copse, but only a belt, and the sky

showed through them. He felt quite sure now that this must be the gate of The Rise and that these trees surrounded a house and garden. He tried the gate and found it locked. He stood for a moment undecided, discouraged by the silence and the growing darkness. His first inclination, tired as he felt, was to continue his journey to Sterk: but he had committed himself to a troublesome duty on behalf of the old woman. He knew that it would be possible, if one really wanted, to force a way through the hedge. He did not want to. A nice fool he would look, blundering in upon some retired eccentric — the sort of a man who kept his gates locked in the country — with this silly story of a hysterical mother in tears because her idiot boy had been kept half an hour late at his work! Yet it was perfectly clear that he would have to get in, and since one cannot crawl through a hedge with a pack on, he slipped his pack off and flung it over the gate. The moment he had done so, it seemed to him that he had not till now fully made up his mind — now that he must break into the garden if only in order to recover the pack. He became very angry with the woman, and with himself, but he got down on his hands and knees and began to worm his way into the hedge.

The operation proved more difficult than he had expected and it was several minutes before he stood up in the wet darkness on the inner side of the hedge smarting from his contact with thorns and nettles. He groped his way to the gate, picked up his pack, and then for the first time turned to take stock of his surroundings. It was lighter on the drive than it had been under the trees and he had no difficulty in making out a large stone house divided from him by a width of untidy neglected lawn. The drive branched into two a little way ahead of him — the right-hand path leading in a gentle sweep to the front door, while the left ran straight ahead, doubtless to the back premises of the house. He noticed that this path was churned up into deep ruts — now full of water — as if it were used to carrying a traffic of heavy lorries.[1] The other, on which he now began to approach the house, was overgrown with moss. The house itself showed no light: some of the windows were shuttered, some gaped blank without shutter or curtain, but all were lifeless and inhospitable. The only sign of occupation was a column of smoke that rose from behind the house with a density which suggested the chimney of a factory, or at least of a laundry, rather than that of a kitchen. The Rise was clearly the last place in the world where a stranger was likely to be asked to stay the night, and Ransom, who had already wasted some time in exploring it, would certainly have turned away if he had not been bound by his unfortunate promise to the old woman.

[1] lorries: (British) trucks.

He mounted the three steps which led into the deep porch, rang the bell, and waited. After a time he rang the bell again and sat down on a wooden bench which ran along one side of the porch. He sat so long that though the night was warm and starlit the sweat began to dry on his face and a faint chilliness crept over his shoulders. He was very tired by now, and it was perhaps this which prevented him from rising and ringing a third time: this, and the soothing stillness of the garden, the beauty of the summer sky, and the occasional hooting of an owl somewhere in the neighbourhood which seemed only to emphasize the underlying tranquillity of his surroundings. Something like drowsiness had already descended upon him when he found himself startled into vigilance. A peculiar noise was going on — a scuffling, irregular noise, vaguely reminiscent of a football scrum. He stood up. The noise was unmistakable by now. People in boots were fighting or wrestling or playing some game. They were shouting too. He could not make out the words but he heard the monosyllabic barking ejaculations of men who are angry and out of breath. The last thing Ransom wanted was an adventure, but a conviction that he ought to investigate the matter was already growing upon him when a much louder cry rang out in which he could distinguish the words, "Let me go. Let me go," and then, a second later, "I'm not going in there. Let me go home."

Throwing off his pack, Ransom sprang down the steps of the porch, and ran round to the back of the house as quickly as his stiff and footsore condition allowed him. The ruts and pools of the muddy path led him to what seemed to be a yard, but a yard surrounded with an unusual number of outhouses. He had a momentary vision of a tall chimney, a low door filled with red firelight, and a huge round shape that rose black against the stars, which he took for the dome of a small observatory: then all this was blotted out of his mind by the figures of three men who were struggling together so close to him that he almost cannoned into them. From the very first Ransom felt no doubt that the central figure, whom the two others seemed to be detaining in spite of his struggles, was the old woman's Harry. He would like to have thundered out, "What are you doing to that boy?" but the words that actually came — in rather an unimpressive voice — were, "Here! I say! . . ."

The three combatants fell suddenly apart, the boy blubbering. "May I ask," said the thicker and taller of the two men, "who the devil you may be and what you are doing here?" His voice had all the qualities which Ransom's had so regrettably lacked.

"I'm on a walking-tour," said Ransom, "and I promised a poor woman —— "

"Poor woman be damned," said the other. "How did you get in?"

"Through the hedge," said Ransom, who felt a little ill-temper coming to his assistance. "I don't know what you're doing to that boy, but —— "

"We ought to have a dog in this place," said the thick man to his companion, ignoring Ransom.

"You mean we should have a dog if you hadn't insisted on using Tartar for an experiment," said the man who had not yet spoken. He was nearly as tall as the other, but slender, and apparently the younger of the two, and his voice sounded vaguely familiar to Ransom.

The latter made a fresh beginning. "Look here," he said. "I don't know what you are doing to that boy, but it's long after hours and it is high time you sent him home. I haven't the least wish to interfere in your private affairs, but —— "

"Who are you?" bawled the thick man.

"My name is Ransom, if that is what you mean. And —— "

"By Jove," said the slender man, "not Ransom who used to be at Wedenshaw?"

"I was at school at Wedenshaw," said Ransom.

"I thought I knew you as soon as you spoke," said the slender man. "I'm Devine. Don't you remember me?"

"Of course. I should think I do!" said Ransom as the two men shook hands with the rather laboured cordiality which is traditional in such meetings. In actual fact Ransom had disliked Devine at school as much as anyone he could remember.

"Touching, isn't it?" said Devine. "The far-flung line even in the wilds of Sterk and Nadderby. This is where we get a lump in our throats and remember Sunday-evening Chapel in the D.O.P.[1] You don't know Weston, perhaps?" Devine indicated his massive and loud-voiced companion. *"The* Weston," he added. "You know. The great physicist. Has Einstein on toast and drinks a pint of Schrödinger's[2] blood for breakfast. Weston, allow me to introduce my old schoolfellow, Ransom. Dr. Elwin Ransom. *The* Ransom, you know. The great philologist. Has Jespersen[3] on toast and drinks a pint —— "

"I know nothing about it," said Weston, who was still holding the unfortunate Harry by the collar. "And if you expect me to say that I am pleased to see this person who has just broken into my garden, you will be disappointed. I don't care twopence what school he was at nor on what unscientific foolery he is at present wasting money that ought to go to research. I want to know what he's doing here: and

---

[1] D.O.P.: Dear Old Place. A mocking use of a cliché of old school sentiment.

[2] Schrödinger: Austrian theoretical physicist (1887–1961), co-winner of 1933 Nobel prize in physics.

[3] Jespersen: Danish philologist (1860–1943).

---

after that I want to see the last of him."

"Don't be an ass, Weston," said Devine in a more serious voice. "His dropping in is delightfully apropos. You mustn't mind Weston's little way, Ransom. Conceals a generous heart beneath a grim exterior, you know. You'll come in and have a drink and something to eat of course?"

"That's very kind of you," said Ransom. "But about the boy —— "

Devine drew Ransom aside. "Balmy," he said in a low voice. "Works like a beaver as a rule but gets these fits. We are only trying to get him into the wash-house and keep him quiet for an hour or so till he's normal again. Can't let him go home in his present state. All done by kindness. You can take him home yourself presently if you like — and come back and sleep here."

Ransom was very much perplexed. There was something about the whole scene suspicious enough and disagreeable enough to convince him that he had blundered on something criminal, while on the other hand he had all the deep, irrational conviction of his age and class that such things could never cross the path of an ordinary person except in fiction and could least of all be associated with professors and old schoolfellows. Even if they had been ill-treating the boy, Ransom did not see much chance of getting him from them by force.

While these thoughts were passing through his head, Devine had been speaking to Weston, in a low voice, but no lower than was to be expected of a man discussing hospitable arrangements in the presence of a guest. It ended with a grunt of assent from Weston. Ransom, to whose other difficulties a merely social embarrassment was now being added, turned with the idea of making some remark. But Weston was now speaking to the boy.

"You have given enough trouble for one night, Harry," he said. "And in a properly governed country I'd know how to deal with you. Hold your tongue and stop sniveling. You needn't go into the wash-house if you don't want——"

"It weren't the wash-house," sobbed the half-wit, "you know it weren't. I don't want to go in *that* thing again."

"He means the laboratory," interrupted Devine. "He got in there and was shut in by accident for a few hours once. It put the wind up him for some reason. Lo, the poor Indian,[1] you know." He turned to the boy. "Listen, Harry," he said. "This kind gentleman is going to take you home as soon as he's had a rest. If you'll come in and sit down quietly in the hall I'll give you something you like." He imitated the noise of a cork being drawn from a bottle — Ransom remembered it had been one of Devine's tricks at school — and a guf-

[1] Lo, the poor Indian: a reference to Alexander Pope's "An Essay on Man," Epistle I, line 99 (page 201).

faw of infantile knowingness broke from Harry's lips.

"Bring him in," said Weston as he turned away and disappeared into the house. Ransom hesitated to follow, but Devine assured him that Weston would be very glad to see him. The lie was barefaced, but Ransom's desire for a rest and a drink were rapidly overcoming his social scruples. Preceded by Devine and Harry, he entered the house and found himself a moment later seated in an arm-chair and awaiting the return of Devine, who had gone to fetch refreshments.

Chapter 2

The room into which he had been shown revealed a strange mixture of luxury and squalor. The windows were shuttered and curtainless, the floor was uncarpeted and strewn with packing-cases, shavings, newspapers and boots, and the wall-paper showed the stains left by the pictures and furniture of the previous occupants. On the other hand, the only two arm-chairs were of the costliest type, and in the litter which covered the tables, cigars, oyster-shells and empty champagne-bottles jostled with tins of condensed milk and opened sardine-tins, with cheap crockery, broken bread, and teacups a quarter full of tea and cigarette-ends.

His hosts seemed to be a long

time away, and Ransom fell to thinking of Devine. He felt for him that sort of distaste we feel for someone whom we have admired in boyhood for a very brief period and then outgrown. Devine had learned just half a term earlier than anyone else that kind of humour which consists in a perpetual parody of the sentimental or idealistic clichés of one's elders. For a few weeks his references to the Dear Old Place and to Playing the Game, to the White Man's Burden and a Straight Bat, had swept everyone, Ransom included, off their feet. But before he left Wedenshaw, Ransom had already begun to find Devine a bore, and at Cambridge he had avoided him, wondering from afar how anyone so flashy and, as it were, ready-made, could be so successful. Then had come the mystery of Devine's election to the Leicester fellowship, and the further mystery of his increasing wealth. He had long since abandoned Cambridge for London, and was presumably something "in the city." [1] One heard of him occasionally and one's informant usually ended either by saying, "A damn clever chap, Devine, in his own way," or else by observing plaintively, "It's a mystery to me how that man has got where he is." As far as Ransom could gather from their brief conversation in the yard, his old schoolfellow had altered very little.

[1] "in the city": in the old city of London, now the financial district of Greater London.

He was interrupted by the opening of the door. Devine entered alone, carrying a bottle of whiskey on a tray with glasses, and a syphon.

"Weston is looking out something to eat," he said as he placed the tray on the floor beside Ransom's chair, and addressed himself to opening the bottle. Ransom, who was very thirsty indeed by now, observed that his host was one of those irritating people who forget to use their hands when they begin talking. Devine started to prise up the silver paper which covered the cork with the point of a corkscrew, and then stopped to ask:

"How do you come to be in this benighted part of the country?"

"I'm on a walking-tour," said Ransom; "slept at Stoke Underwood last night and had hoped to end at Nadderby to-night. They wouldn't put me up, so I was going on to Sterk."

"God!" exclaimed Devine, his corkscrew still idle. "Do you do it for money, or is it sheer masochism?"

"Pleasure, of course," said Ransom, keeping his eye immovably on the still unopened bottle.

"Can the attraction of it be explained to the uninitiate?" asked Devine, remembering himself sufficiently to rip up a small portion of the silver paper.

"I hardly know. To begin with, I like the actual walking ——"

"God! You must have enjoyed the army. Jogging along to Thingummy, eh?"

"No, no. It's just the opposite of the army. The whole point about the army is that you are never alone for a moment and can never choose where you're going or even what part of the road you're walking on. On a walking-tour you are absolutely detached. You stop where you like and go on when you like. As long as it lasts you need consider no one and consult no one but yourself."

"Until one night you find a wire waiting at your hotel saying, 'Come back at once,'" replied Devine, at last removing the silver paper.

"Only if you were fool enough to leave a list of addresses and go to them! The worst that could happen to me would be that man on the wireless saying, 'Will Dr. Elwin Ransom, believed to be walking somewhere in the Midlands ——'"

"I begin to see the idea," said Devine, pausing in the very act of drawing the cork. "It wouldn't do if you were in business. You are a lucky devil! But can even you just disappear like that? No wife, no young, no aged but honest parent or anything of that sort?"

"Only a married sister in India. And then, you see, I'm a don. And a don in the middle of long vacation is almost a non-existent creature, as you ought to remember. College neither knows nor cares where he is, and certainly no one else does."

The cork at last came out of the bottle with a heart-cheering noise.

"Say when," said Devine, as Ran-som held out his glass. "But I feel sure there's a catch somewhere. Do you really mean to say that no one knows where you are or when you ought to get back, and no one can get hold of you?"

Ransom was nodding in reply when Devine, who had picked up the syphon, suddenly swore. "I'm afraid this is empty," he said. "Do you mind having water? I'll have to get some from the scullery. How much do you like?"

"Fill it up, please," said Ransom.

A few minutes later Devine returned and handed Ransom his long-delayed drink. The latter remarked, as he put down the half-emptied tumbler with a sigh of satisfaction, that Devine's choice of residence was at least as odd as his own choice of a holiday.

"Quite," said Devine. "But if you knew Weston you'd realize that it's much less trouble to go where he wants than to argue the matter. What you call a strong colleague."

"Colleague?" said Ransom inquiringly.

"In a sense." Devine glanced at the door, drew his chair closer to Ransom's, and continued in a more confidential tone. "He's the goods all right, though. Between ourselves, I am putting a little money into some experiments he has on hand. It's all straight stuff — the march of progress and the good of humanity and all that, but it has an industrial side."

While Devine was speaking something odd began to happen to

Ransom. At first it merely seemed to him that Devine's words were no longer making sense. He appeared to be saying that he was industrial all down both sides but could never get an experiment to fit him in London. Then he realized that Devine was not so much unintelligible as inaudible, which was not surprising, since he was now so far away — about a mile away, though perfectly clear like something seen through the wrong end of a telescope. From that bright distance where he sat in his tiny chair he was gazing at Ransom with a new expression on his face. The gaze became disconcerting. Ransom tried to move in his chair but found that he had lost all power over his own body. He felt quite comfortable, but it was as if his legs and arms had been bandaged to the chair and his head gripped in a vice; a beautifully padded, but quite immovable vice. He did not feel afraid, though he knew that he ought to be afraid and soon would be. Then, very gradually, the room faded from his sight.

Ransom could never be sure whether what followed had any bearing on the events recorded in this book or whether it was merely an irresponsible dream. It seemed to him that he and Weston and Devine were all standing in a little garden surrrounded by a wall. The garden was bright and sunlit, but over the top of the wall you could see nothing but darkness. They were trying to climb over the wall and Weston asked them to give him a hoist up. Ransom kept on telling him not to go over the wall because it was so dark on the other side, but Weston insisted, and all three of them set about doing so. Ransom was the last. He got astride on the top of the wall, sitting on his coat because of the broken bottles. The other two had already dropped down on the outside into the darkness, but before he followed them a door in the wall — which none of them had noticed — was opened from without and the queerest people he had ever seen came into the garden bringing Weston and Devine back with them. They left them in the garden and retired into the darkness themselves, locking the door behind them. Ransom found it impossible to get down from the wall. He remained sitting there, not frightened but rather uncomfortable because his right leg, which was on the outside, felt so dark and his left leg felt so light. "My leg will drop off if it gets much darker," he said. Then he looked down into the darkness and asked, "Who are you?" and the Queer People must still have been there for they all replied, "Hoo — Hoo — Hoo?" just like owls.

He began to realize that his leg was not so much dark as cold and stiff, because he had been resting the other on it for so long: and also that he was in an arm-chair in a lighted room. A conversation was going on near him and had, he now realized, been going on for some time. His head was comparatively clear. He realized that he had been drugged or hypnotized, or both, and he felt that some control over his own body was returning to him though he was still very weak. He listened intently without trying to move.

"I'm getting a little tired of this, Weston," Devine was saying, "and specially as it's my money that is being risked. I tell you he'll do quite as well as the boy, and in some ways better. Only, he'll be coming round very soon now and we must get him on board at once. We ought to have done it an hour ago."

"The boy was ideal," said Weston sulkily. "Incapable of serving humanity and only too likely to propagate idiocy. He was the sort of boy who in a civilized community would be automatically handed over to a state laboratory for experimental purposes."

"I dare say. But in England he is the sort of boy in whom Scotland Yard might conceivably feel an interest. This busybody, on the other hand, will not be missed for months, and even then no one will know where he was when he disappeared. He came alone. He left no address. He has no family. And finally he has poked his nose into the whole affair of his own accord."

"Well, I confess I don't like it. He is, after all, human. The boy was really almost a — a preparation. Still, he's only an individual, and probably a quite useless one. We're risking our own lives too. In a great cause —— "

"For the Lord's sake don't start all that stuff now. We haven't time."

"I dare say," replied Weston, "he would consent if he could be made to understand."

"Take his feet and I'll take his head," said Devine.

"If you really think he's coming round," said Weston, "you'd better give him another dose. We can't start till we get the sunlight. It wouldn't be pleasant to have him struggling in there for three hours or so. It would be better if he didn't wake up till we were under weigh."[1]

"True enough. Just keep an eye on him while I run upstairs and get another."

Devine left the room. Ransom saw through his half-closed eyes that Weston was standing over him. He had no means of foretelling how his own body would respond, if it responded at all, to a sudden attempt of movement, but he saw at once that he must take his chance. Almost before Devine had closed the door he flung himself with all his force at Weston's feet. The scientist fell forward across the chair, and Ransom, flinging him off with an agonizing effort, rose and dashed out into the hall. He was very weak and fell as he entered it: but terror was behind him and in a couple of seconds he had found the hall door and was working desperately to master the bolts. Darkness and his

[1] under weigh: underway.

trembling hands were against him. Before he had drawn one bolt, booted feet were clattering over the carpetless floor behind him. He was gripped by the shoulders and the knees. Kicking, writhing, dripping with sweat, and bellowing as loud as he could in the faint hope of rescue, he prolonged the struggle with a violence of which he would have believed himself incapable. For one glorious moment the door was open, the fresh night air was in his face, he saw the reassuring stars and even his own pack lying in the porch. Then a heavy blow fell on his head. Consciousness faded, and the last thing of which he was aware was the grip of strong hands pulling him back into the dark passage, and the sound of a closing door.

Chapter **3**

When Ransom came to his senses he seemed to be in bed in a dark room. He had a pretty severe headache, and this, combined with a general lassitude, discouraged him at first from attempting to rise or to take stock of his surroundings. He noticed, drawing his hand across his forehead, that he was sweating freely, and this directed his attention to the fact that the room (if it was a room) was re-

markably warm. Moving his arms to fling off the bedclothes, he touched a wall at the right side of the bed: it was not only warm, but hot. He moved his left hand to and fro in the emptiness on the other side and noticed that there the air was cooler — apparently the heat was coming from the wall. He felt his face and found a bruise over the left eye. This recalled to his mind the struggle with Weston and Devine, and he instantly concluded that they had put him in an outhouse behind their furnace. At the same time he looked up and recognized the source of the dim light in which, without noticing it, he had all along been able to see the movements of his own hands. There was some kind of skylight immediately over his head — a square of night sky filled with stars. It seemed to Ransom that he had never looked out on such a frosty night. Pulsing with brightness as with some unbearable pain or pleasure, clustered in pathless and countless multitudes, dreamlike in clarity, blazing in perfect blackness, the stars seized all his attention, troubled him, excited him, and drew him up to a sitting position. At the same time they quickened the throb of his headache, and this reminded him that he had been drugged. He was just formulating to himself the theory that the stuff they had given him might have some effect on the pupil and that this would explain the unnatural splendour and fullness of the sky, when a disturbance of silver light, almost a pale and miniature sunrise, at one corner of the skylight, drew his eyes upward again. Some minutes later the orb of the full moon was pushing its way into the field of vision. Ransom sat still and watched. He had never seen such a moon — so white, so blinding and so large. "Like a great football just outside the glass," he thought, and then, a moment later, "No — it's bigger than that." By this time he was quite certain that something was seriously wrong with his eyes: no moon could possibly be the size of the thing he was seeing.

The light of the huge moon — if it was a moon — had by now illuminated his surroundings almost as clearly as if it were day. It was a very strange room. The floor was so small that the bed and a table beside it occupied the whole width of it: the ceiling seemed to be nearly twice as wide and the walls sloped outwards as they rose, so that Ransom had the impression of lying at the bottom of a deep and narrow wheelbarrow. This confirmed his belief that his sight was either temporarily or permanently injured. In other respects, however, he was recovering rapidly and even beginning to feel an unnatural lightness of heart and a not disagreeable excitement. The heat was still oppressive, and he stripped off everything but his shirt and trousers before rising to explore. His rising was disastrous and raised graver apprehensions in his mind about the effects

of being drugged. Although he had been conscious of no unusual muscular effort, he found himself leaping from the bed with an energy which brought his head into sharp contact with the skylight and flung him down again in a heap on the floor. He found himself on the other side against the wall — the wall that ought to have sloped outwards like the side of a wheelbarrow, according to his previous reconnaissance. But it didn't. He felt it and looked at it: it was unmistakably at right angles to the floor. More cautiously this time, he rose again to his feet. He felt an extraordinary lightness of body: it was with difficulty that he kept his feet on the floor. For the first time a suspicion that he might be dead and already in the ghost-life crossed his mind. He was trembling, but a hundred mental habits forbade him to consider this possibility. Instead, he explored his prison. The result was beyond doubt: all the walls looked as if they sloped outwards so as to make the room wider at the ceiling than it was at the floor, but each wall as you stood beside it turned out to be perfectly perpendicular — not only to sight but to touch also if one stooped down and examined with one's fingers the angle between it and the floor. The same examination revealed two other curious facts. The room was walled and floored with metal, and was in a state of continuous faint vibration — a silent vibration with a strangely life-like and unmechanical quality about it — but if the vibration was silent, there was plenty of noise going on — a series of musical raps or percussions at quite irregular intervals which seemed to come from the ceiling. It was as if the metal chamber in which he found himself was being bombarded with small, tinkling missiles. Ransom was by now thoroughly frightened — not with the prosaic fright that a man suffers in a war, but with a heady, bounding kind of fear that was hardly distinguishable from his general excitement: he was poised on a sort of emotional watershed from which, he felt, he might at any moment pass either into delirious terror or into an ecstasy of joy. He knew now that he was not in a house, but in some moving vessel. It was clearly not a submarine: and the infinitesimal quivering of the metal did not suggest the motion of any wheeled vehicle. A ship then, he supposed, or some kind of airship . . . but there was an oddity in all his sensations for which neither supposition accounted. Puzzled, he sat down again on the bed, and stared at the portentous moon.

An airship, some kind of flying-machine . . . but why did the moon look so big? It was larger than he had thought at first. No moon could really be that size; and he realized now that he had known this from the first but had repressed the knowledge through terror. At the same moment a thought came into his head which stopped his breath — there could be no full moon at all that night. He remembered distinctly that he had walked from Nadderby in a moonless night. Even if the thin crescent of a new moon had escaped his notice, it could not have grown to this in a few hours. It could not have grown to this at all — this megalomaniac disk, far larger than the football he had at first compared it to, larger than a child's hoop, filling almost half the sky. And where was the old "man in the moon" — the familiar face that had looked down on all the generations of men? The thing wasn't the Moon at all; and he felt his hair move on his scalp.

At that moment the sound of an opening door made him turn his head. An oblong of dazzling light appeared behind him and instantly vanished as the door closed again, having admitted the bulky form of a naked man whom Ransom recognized as Weston. No reproach, no demand for an explanation, rose to Ransom's lips or even to his mind; not with that monstrous orb above them. The mere presence of a human being, with its offer of at least some companionship, broke down the tension in which his nerves had long been resisting a bottomless dismay. He found, when he spoke, that he was sobbing.

"Weston! Weston!" he gasped. "What is it? It's not the moon, not that size. It can't be, can it?"

"No," replied Weston, "it's the Earth."

Chapter 4

Ransom's legs failed him, and he must have sunk back upon the bed, but he only became aware of this many minutes later. At the moment he was unconscious of everything except his fear. He did not even know what he was afraid of: the fear itself possessed his whole mind, a formless, infinite misgiving. He did not lose consciousness, though he greatly wished that he might do so. Any change — death or sleep, or, best of all, a waking which should show all this for a dream — would have been inexpressibly welcome. None came. Instead, the lifelong self-control of social man, the virtues which are half hypocrisy or the hypocrisy which is half a virtue, came back to him and soon he found himself answering Weston in a voice not shamefully tremulous.

"Do you mean that?" he asked.

"Certainly."

"Then where are we?"

"Standing out from Earth about eighty-five thousand miles."

"You mean we're — in space." Ransom uttered the word with difficulty as a frightened child speaks of ghosts or a frightened man of cancer.

Weston nodded.

"What for?" said Ransom. "And what on earth have you kidnapped me for? And how have you done it?"

For a moment Weston seemed disposed to give no answer; then, as if on a second thought, he sat down on the bed beside Ransom and spoke as follows:

"I suppose it will save trouble if I deal with these questions at once, instead of leaving you to pester us with them every hour for the next month. As to how we do it — I suppose you mean how the space-ship works — there's no good your asking that. Unless you were one of the four or five real physicists now living you couldn't understand: and if there were any chance of your understanding you certainly wouldn't be told. If it makes you happy to repeat words that don't mean anything — which is, in fact, what unscientific people want when they ask for an explanation — you may say we work by exploiting the less observed properties of solar radiation. As to why we are here, we are on our way to Malacandra. . . ."

"Do you mean a star called Malacandra?"

"Even you can hardly suppose we are going out of the solar system. Malacandra is much nearer than that: we shall make it in about twenty-eight days."

"There isn't a planet called Malacandra," objected Ransom.

"I am giving it its real name, not the name invented by terrestrial astronomers," said Weston.

"But surely this is nonsense," said Ransom. "How the deuce did you find out its real name, as you call it?"

"From the inhabitants."

It took Ransom some time to digest this statement. "Do you mean to tell me you claim to have been to this star before, or this planet, or whatever it is?"

"Yes."

"You can't really ask me to believe that," said Ransom. "Damn it all, it's not an everyday affair. Why has no one heard of it? Why has it not been in all the papers?"

"Because we are not perfect idiots," said Weston gruffly.

After a few moments' silence Ransom began again. "Which planet is it in our terminology?" he asked.

"Once and for all," said Weston, "I am not going to tell you. If you know how to find out when we get there, you are welcome to do so: I don't think we have much to fear from your scientific attainments. In the meantime, there is no reason for you to know."

"And you say this place is inhabited?" said Ransom.

Weston gave him a peculiar look and then nodded. The uneasiness which this produced in Ransom rapidly merged in an anger which he had almost lost sight of amidst the conflicting emotions that beset him.

"And what has all this to do with me?" he broke out. "You have assaulted me, drugged me, and are apparently carrying me off as a prisoner in this infernal thing. What have I done to you? What do you say for yourself?"

"I might reply by asking you why you crept into my backyard like a thief. If you had minded your own business you would not be here. As it is, I admit that we have had to infringe your rights. My only defense is that small claims must give way to great. As far as we know, we are doing what has never been done in the history of man, perhaps never in the history of the universe. We have learned how to jump off the speck of matter on which our species began; infinity, and therefore perhaps eternity, is being put into the hands of the human race. You cannot be so small-minded as to think that the rights or the life of an individual or of a million individuals are of the slightest importance in comparison with this."

"I happen to disagree," said Ransom, "and I always have disagreed, even about vivisection. But you haven't answered my question. What do you want me for? What good am I to do you on this — on Malacandra?"

"That I don't know," said Weston. "It was no idea of ours. We are only obeying orders."

"Whose?"

There was another pause. "Come," said Weston at last, "there is really no use in continuing this cross-examination. You keep on asking me questions I can't answer: in some cases because I don't know the answers, in others because you wouldn't understand them. It will make things very much pleasanter during the voyage if you can only resign your mind to your fate and stop bothering yourself and us. It would be easier if your philosophy of life were not so insufferably narrow and individualistic. I had thought no one could fail to be inspired by the role you are being asked to play: that even a worm, if it could understand, would rise to the sacrifice. I mean, of course, the sacrifice of time and liberty, and some little risk. Don't misunderstand me."

"Well," said Ransom, "you hold all the cards, and I must make the best of it. I consider *your* philosophy of life raving lunacy. I suppose all that stuff about infinity and eternity means that you think you are justified in doing anything—absolutely anything—here and now, on the off chance that some creatures or other descended from man as we know him may crawl about a few centuries longer in some part of the universe."

"Yes—anything whatever," returned the scientist sternly, "and all educated opinion—for I do not call classics and history and such trash education—is entirely on my side. I am glad you raised the point, and I advise you to remember my answer. In the meantime, if you will follow me into the next room, we will have breakfast. Be careful how you get up: your weight here is hardly appreciable compared with your weight on Earth."

Ransom rose and his captor opened the door. Instantly the room was flooded with a dazzling golden light which completely eclipsed the pale earthlight behind him.

"I will give you darkened glasses in a moment," said Weston as he preceded him into the chamber whence the radiance was pouring. It seemed to Ransom that Weston went up a hill towards the doorway and disappeared suddenly downwards when he had passed it. When he followed—which he did with caution—he had the curious impression that he was walking up to the edge of a precipice: the new room beyond the doorway seemed to be built on its side so that its farther wall lay almost in the same plane as the floor of the room he was leaving. When, however, he ventured to put forward his foot, he found that the floor continued flush and as he entered the second room the walls suddenly righted themselves and the rounded ceiling was over his head. Looking back, he perceived that the bedroom in its turn was now heeling over—its roof a wall and one of its walls a roof.

"You will soon get used to it," said Weston, following his gaze. "The ship is roughly spherical, and now that we are outside the gravitational field of the Earth 'down' means—and feels—towards the centre of our own little metal world. This, of course, was foreseen and we built her accordingly. The core of the ship is a hollow globe—we keep our stores inside it—and the surface of that globe is the floor we are walking on. The cabins are arranged all round this, their walls supporting an outer globe which from our point of view is the roof. As the centre is always 'down,' the piece of floor you are standing on always feels flat or horizontal and the wall you are standing against always seems vertical. On the other hand, the globe of floor is so small that you can always see over the edge of it — over what would be the horizon if you were a flea — and then you see the floors and wall of the next cabin in a different plane. It is just the same on Earth, of course, only we are not big enough to see it."

After this explanation he made arrangements in his precise, ungracious way for the comfort of his guest or prisoner. Ransom, at his advice, removed all his clothes and substituted a little metal girdle hung with enormous weights to reduce, as far as possible, the unmanageable lightness of his body. He also assumed tinted glasses, and soon found himself seated opposite Weston at a small table laid for breakfast. He was both hungry and thirsty and eagerly attacked the meal which consisted of tinned meat, biscuit, butter and coffee.

But all these actions he had performed mechanically. Stripping, eating and drinking passed almost unnoticed, and all he ever remembered of his first meal in the spaceship was the tyranny of heat and light. Both were present in a degree which would have been intolerable on Earth, but each had a new qual-

ity. The light was paler than any light of comparable intensity that he had ever seen; it was not pure white but the palest of all imaginable golds, and it cast shadows as sharp as a floodlight. The heat, utterly free from moisture, seemed to knead and stroke the skin like a gigantic masseur: it produced no tendency to drowsiness: rather intense alacrity. His headache was gone: he felt vigilant, courageous and magnanimous as he had seldom felt on Earth. Gradually he dared to raise his eyes to the skylight. Steel shutters were drawn across all but a chink of the glass, and that chink was covered with blinds of some heavy and dark material; but still it was too bright to look at.

"I always thought space was dark and cold," he remarked vaguely.

"Forgotten the sun?" said Weston contemptuously.

Ransom went on eating for some time. Then he began, "If it's like this in the early morning," and stopped, warned by the expression on Weston's face. Awe fell upon him: there were no mornings here, no evenings, and no night — nothing but the changeless noon which had filled for centuries beyond history so many millions of cubic miles. He glanced at Weston again, but the latter held up his hand.

"Don't talk," he said. "We have discussed all that is necessary. The ship does not carry oxygen enough for any unnecessary exertion; not even for talking."

Shortly afterwards he rose, without inviting the other to follow him, and left the room by one of the many doors which Ransom had not yet seen opened.

Chapter **5**

The period spent in the space-ship ought to have been one of terror and anxiety for Ransom. He was separated by an astronomical distance from every member of the human race except two whom he had excellent reasons for distrusting. He was heading for an unknown destination, and was being brought thither for a purpose which his captors steadily refused to disclose. Devine and Weston relieved each other regularly in a room which Ransom was never allowed to enter and where he supposed the controls of their machine must be. Weston, during his watches off, was almost entirely silent. Devine was more loquacious and would often talk and guffaw with the prisoner until Weston rapped on the wall of the control-room and warned them not to waste air. But Devine was secretive after a certain point. He was quite ready to laugh at Weston's solemn scientific idealism. He didn't give a damn, he said, for the future of the species or the meeting of two worlds.

"There's more to Malacandra than that," he would add with a

wink. But when Ransom asked him what more, he would lapse into satire and make ironical remarks about the white man's burden [1] and the blessings of civilization.

"It *is* inhabited, then?" Ransom would press.

"Ah — there's always a native question in these things," Devine would answer. For the most part his conversation ran on the things he would do when he got back to Earth: ocean-going yachts, the most expensive women and a big place on the Riviera figured largely in his plans. "I'm not running all these risks for fun."

Direct questions about Ransom's own role were usually met with silence. Only once, in reply to such a question, Devine, who was then in Ransom's opinion very far from sober, admitted that they were rather "handing him the baby."

"But I'm sure," he added, "you'll live up to the old school tie."

All this, as I have said, was sufficiently disquieting. The odd thing was that it did not very greatly disquiet him. It is hard for a man to brood on the future when he is feeling so extremely well as Ransom now felt. There was an endless night on one side of the ship and an endless day on the other: each was marvellous and he moved from the

[1] **the white man's burden:** (from a poem with this title by Rudyard Kipling, written in 1899) the supposed duty of the white peoples to manage the affairs of the undeveloped colored races.

one to the other at his will, delighted. In the nights, which he could create by turning the handle of a door, he lay for hours in contemplation of the skylight. The Earth's disk was nowhere to be seen; the stars, thick as daisies on an uncut lawn, reigned perpetually with no cloud, no moon, no sunrise to dispute their sway. There were planets of unbelievable majesty, and constellations undreamed of: there were celestial sapphires, rubies, emeralds and pin-pricks of burning gold; far out on the left of the picture hung a comet, tiny and remote: and between all and behind all, far more emphatic and palpable than it showed on Earth, the undimensioned, enigmatic blackness. The lights trembled: they seemed to grow brighter as he looked. Stretched naked on his bed, a second Danaë,[1] he found it night by night more difficult to disbelieve in old astrology: almost he felt, wholly he imagined, "sweet influence" pouring or even stabbing into his surrendered body. All was silence but for the irregular tinkling noises. He knew now that these were made by meteorites, small, drifting particles of the world-stuff that smote continually on their hollow drum of steel; and he guessed that at any moment they might meet something large enough to make mete-

[1] Danaë: in Greek mythology, Perseus' mother, who was visited by Zeus in the guise of a shower of gold, and kept captive in a chamber as a safeguard against such visitations.

orites of ship and all. But he could not fear. He now felt that Weston had justly called him little-minded in the moment of his first panic. The adventure was too high, its circumstance too solemn, for any emotion save a severe delight. But the days — that is, the hours spent in the sunward hemisphere of their microcosm — were the best of all. Often he rose after only a few hours' sleep to return, drawn by an irresistible attraction, to the regions of light; he could not cease to wonder at the noon which always awaited you however early you went to seek it. There, totally immersed in a bath of pure ethereal colour and of unrelenting though unwounding brightness, stretched his full length and with eyes half closed in the strange chariot that bore them, faintly quivering, through depth after depth of tranquillity far above the reach of night, he felt his body and mind daily rubbed and scoured and filled with new vitality. Weston, in one of his brief, reluctant answers, admitted a scientific basis for these sensations: they were receiving, he said, many rays that never penetrated the terrestrial atmosphere.

But Ransom, as time wore on, became aware of another and more spiritual cause for his progressive lightening and exultation of heart. A nightmare, long engendered in the modern mind by the mythology that follows in the wake of science, was falling off him. He had read of "Space": at the back of his thinking for years had lurked the dismal fancy of the black, cold vacuity, the utter deadness, which was supposed to separate the worlds. He had not known how much it affected him till now — now that the very name "Space" seemed a blasphemous libel for this empyrean ocean of radiance in which they swam. He could not call it "dead"; he felt life pouring into him from it every moment. How indeed should it be otherwise, since out of this ocean the worlds and all their life had come? He had thought it barren: he saw now that it was the womb of worlds, whose blazing and innumerable offspring looked down nightly even upon the earth with so many eyes — and here, with how many more! No: Space was the wrong name. Older thinkers had been wiser when they named it simply the heavens — the heavens which declared the glory — the

> "happy climes that ly
> Where day never shuts his eye
> Up in the broad fields of the sky."

He quoted Milton's words to himself lovingly, at this time and often.

He did not, of course, spend all his time in basking. He explored the ship (so far as he was allowed), passing from room to room with those slow movements which Weston enjoined upon them lest exertion should overtax their supply of air. From the necessity of its shape, the space-ship contained a good many more chambers than were in regular use: but Ransom was also inclined to think that its owners — or at least Devine — intended these to be filled with cargo of some kind on the return voyage. He also became, by an insensible process, the steward and cook of the company; partly because he felt it natural to share the only labours he could share — he was never allowed into the control-room — and partly in order to anticipate a tendency which Weston showed to make him a servant whether he would or no. He preferred to work as a volunteer rather than in admitted slavery: and he liked his own cooking a good deal more than that of his companions.

It was these duties that made him at first the unwilling, and then the alarmed, hearer of a conversation which occurred about a fortnight (he judged) after the beginning of their voyage. He had washed up the remains of their evening meal, basked in the sunlight, chatted with Devine — better company than Weston, though in Ransom's opinion much the more odious of the two — and retired to bed at his usual time. He was a little restless, and after an hour or so it occurred to him that he had forgotten one or two small arrangements in the galley which would facilitate his work in the morning. The galley opened off the saloon or day-room, and its door was close to that of the control-room. He rose and went there at once. His feet, like the rest of him, were bare.

The galley skylight was on the

dark side of the ship, but Ransom did not turn on the light. To leave the door ajar was sufficient, as this admitted a stream of brilliant sunlight. As everyone who has "kept house" will understand, he found that his preparations for the morning had been even more incomplete than he supposed. He did his work well, from practice, and therefore quietly. He had just finished and was drying his hands on the roller-towel behind the galley door when he heard the door of the control-room open and saw the silhouette of a man outside the galley — Devine's, he gathered. Devine did not come forward into the saloon, but remained standing and talking — apparently into the control-room. It thus came about that while Ransom could hear distinctly what Devine said he could not make out Weston's answers.

"I think it would be dam' silly," said Devine. "If you could be sure of meeting the brutes where we alight there might be something in it. But suppose we have to trek? All we'd gain by your plan would be having to carry a drugged man and his pack instead of letting a live man walk with us and do his share of the work."

Weston apparently replied.

"But he *can't* find out," returned Devine. "Unless someone is fool enough to tell him. Anyway, even if he suspects, do you think a man like that would have the guts to run away on a strange planet? Without food? Without weapons?

You'll find he'll eat out of your hand at the first sight of a *sorn*."

Again Ransom heard the indistinct noise of Weston's voice.

"How should I know?" said Devine. "It may be some sort of chief: much more likely a mumbo-jumbo."

This time came a very short utterance from the control-room: apparently a question. Devine answered at once.

"It would explain why he was wanted."

Weston asked him something more.

"Human sacrifice, I suppose. At least it wouldn't be human from *their* point of view; you know what I mean."

Weston had a good deal to say this time, and it elicited Devine's characteristic chuckle.

"Quite, quite," he said. "It is understood that you are doing it all from the highest motives. So long as they lead to the same actions as *my* motives, you are quite welcome to them."

Weston continued; and this time Devine seemed to interrupt him.

"You're not losing your own nerve, are you?" he said. He was then silent for some time, as if listening. Finally, he replied:

"If you're so fond of the brutes as that you'd better stay and interbreed — if they have sexes, which we don't yet know. Don't you worry. When the time comes for cleaning the place up we'll save one or two for you, and you can keep them as pets or vivisect them or sleep with them or all three — whichever way it takes you. . . . Yes, I know. Perfectly loathsome. I was only joking. Good night."

A moment later Devine closed the door of the control-room, crossed the saloon and entered his own cabin. Ransom heard him bolt the door of it according to his invariable, though puzzling, custom. The tension with which he had been listening relaxed. He found that he had been holding his breath, and breathed deeply again. Then cautiously he stepped out into the saloon.

Though he knew that it would be prudent to return to his bed as quickly as possible, he found himself standing still in the now familiar glory of the light and viewing it with a new and poignant emotion. Out of this heaven, these happy climes, they were presently to descend — into *what? Sorns,* human sacrifice, loathsome sexless monsters. What was a *sorn?* His own role in the affair was now clear enough. Somebody or something had sent for him. It could hardly be for him personally. The somebody wanted a victim — any victim — from Earth. He had been picked because Devine had done the picking; he realized for the first time — in all circumstances a late and startling discovery — that Devine had hated him all these years as heartily as he hated Devine. But what was a *sorn?* "When he saw them he would eat out of Devine's

hands." His mind, like so many minds of his generation, was richly furnished with bogies. He had read his H. G. Wells and others. His universe was peopled with horror such as ancient and mediæval mythology could hardly rival. No insect-like, vermiculate or crustacean Abominable, no twitching feelers, rasping wings, slimy coils, curling tentacles, no monstrous union of superhuman intelligence and insatiable cruelty seemed to him anything but likely on an alien world. The *sorns* would be . . . would be . . . he dared not think what the *sorns* would be. And he was to be given to them. Somehow this seemed more horrible than being caught by them. Given, handed over, offered. He saw in imagination various incompatible monstrosities — bulbous eyes, grinning jaws, horns, stings, mandibles. Loathing of insects, loathing of snakes, loathing of things that squashed and squelched, all played their horrible symphonies over his nerves. But the reality would be worse: it would be an extraterrestrial Otherness — something one had never thought of, never could have thought of. In that moment Ransom made a decision. He could face death, but not the *sorns.* He must escape when they got to Malacandra, if there were any possibility. Starvation, or even to be chased by *sorns,* would be better than being handed over. If escape were impossible, then it must be suicide. Ransom was a pious man. He hoped he would be forgiven. It was no more in his power, he thought, to decide otherwise than to grow a new limb. Without hesitation he stole back into the galley and secured the sharpest knife: henceforward he determined never to be parted from it.

Such was the exhaustion produced by terror that when he regained his bed he fell instantly into stupefied and dreamless sleep.

Chapter 6

He woke much refreshed, and even a little ashamed of his terror on the previous night. His situation was, no doubt, very serious: indeed the possibility of returning alive to Earth must be almost discounted. But death could be faced, and rational fear of death could be mastered. It was only the irrational, the biological, horror of monsters that was the real difficulty: and this he faced and came to terms with as well as he could while he lay in the sunlight after breakfast. He had the feeling that one sailing in the heavens, as he was doing, should not suffer abject dismay before any earthbound creature. He even reflected that the knife could pierce other flesh as well as his own. The bellicose mood was a very rare one with Ransom. Like many men of his own age, he rather underestimated than overestimated his own

courage; the gap between boyhood's dreams and his actual experience of the War had been startling, and his subsequent view of his own unheroic qualities had perhaps swung too far in the opposite direction. He had some anxiety lest the firmness of his present mood should prove a short-lived illusion; but he must make the best of it.

As hour followed hour and waking followed sleep in their eternal day, he became aware of a gradual change. The temperature was slowly falling. They resumed clothes. Later, they added warm underclothes. Later still, an electric heater was turned on in the centre of the ship. And it became certain, too — though the phenomenon was hard to seize — that the light was less overwhelming than it had been at the beginning of the voyage. It became certain to the comparing intellect, but it was difficult to *feel* what was happening as a diminution of light and impossible to think of it as "darkening" because, while the radiance changed in degree, its unearthly quality had remained exactly the same since the moment he first beheld it. It was not, like fading light upon the Earth, mixed with the increasing moisture and phantom colours of the air. You might halve its intensity, Ransom perceived, and the remaining half would still be what the whole had been — merely less, not other. Halve it again, and the residue would still be the same. As long as it was at all, it would be itself — out even to that unimagined distance where its last force was spent. He tried to explain what he meant to Devine.

"Like thingummy's soap!" grinned Devine. "Pure soap to the last bubble, eh?"

Shortly after this the even tenor of their life in the space-ship began to be disturbed. Weston explained that they would soon begin to feel the gravitational pull of Malacandra.

"That means," he said, "that it will no longer be 'down' to the centre of the ship. It will be 'down' towards Malacandra — which from our point of view will be under the control-room. As a consequence, the floors of most of the chambers will become wall or roof, and one of the walls a floor. You won't like it."

The result of this announcement, so far as Ransom was concerned, was hours of heavy labour in which he worked shoulder to shoulder now with Devine and now with Weston as their alternating watches liberated them from the control-room. Water-tins, oxygen-cylinders, guns, ammunition and foodstuffs had all to be piled on the floors alongside the appropriate walls and lying on their sides so as to be upright when the new "downwards" came into play. Long before the work was finished disturbing sensations began. At first Ransom supposed that it was the toil itself which so weighted his limbs: but rest did not alleviate the symptom,

and it was explained to him that their bodies, in response to the planet that had caught them in its field, were actually gaining weight every minute and doubling in weight with every twenty-four hours. They had the experiences of a pregnant woman, but magnified almost beyond endurance.

At the same time their sense of direction — never very confident on the space-ship — became continuously confused. From any room on board, the next room's floor had always looked downhill and felt level: now it looked downhill and felt a little, a very little, downhill as well. One found oneself running as one entered it. A cushion flung aside on the floor of the saloon would be found hours later to have moved an inch or so towards the wall. All of them were afflicted with vomiting, headache and palpitations of the heart. The conditions grew worse hour by hour. Soon one could only grope and crawl from cabin to cabin. All sense of direction disappeared in a sickening confusion. Parts of the ship were definitely below in the sense that their floors were upside down and only a fly could walk on them: but no part seemed to Ransom to be indisputably the right way up. Sensations of intolerable height and of falling — utterly absent in the heavens — recurred constantly. Cooking, of course, had long since been abandoned. Food was snatched as best they could, and drinking presented great difficulties: you could never be sure that you were really holding your mouth below, rather than beside, the bottle. Weston grew grimmer and more silent than ever. Devine, a flask of spirits ever in his hand, flung out strange blasphemies and coprologies [1] and cursed Weston for bringing them. Ransom ached, licking his dry lips, nursed his bruised limbs and prayed for the end.

A time came when one side of the sphere was unmistakably down. Clamped beds and tables hung useless and ridiculous on what was now wall or roof. What had been doors became trapdoors, opened with difficulty. Their bodies seemed made of lead. There was no more work to be done when Devine had set out the clothes — their Malacandrian clothes — from their bundles and squatted down on the end wall of the saloon (now its floor) to watch the thermometer. The clothes, Ransom noticed, included heavy woollen underwear, sheepskin jerkins, fur gloves and eared caps. Devine made no reply to his questions. He was engaged in studying the thermometer and in shouting down to Weston in the control-room.

"Slower, slower," he kept shouting. "Slower, you damned fool. You'll be in air in a minute or two." Then sharply and angrily, "Here! Let me get at it."

Weston made no replies. It was unlike Devine to waste his advice: Ransom concluded that the man

[1] coprologies: filthy expressions.

was almost out of his senses, whether with fear or excitement.

Suddenly the lights of the Universe seemed to be turned down. As if some demon had rubbed the heaven's face with a dirty sponge, the splendour in which they had lived for so long blenched to a pallid, cheerless and pitiable grey. It was impossible from where they sat to open the shutters or roll back the heavy blind. What had been a chariot gliding in the fields of heaven became a dark steel box dimly lighted by a slit of window, and falling. They were falling out of the heaven, into a world. Nothing in all his adventures bit so deeply into Ransom's mind as this. He wondered how he could ever have thought of planets, even of the Earth, as islands of life and reality floating in a deadly void. Now, with a certainty which never after deserted him, he saw the planets — the "earths" he called them in his thought — as mere holes or gaps in the living heaven — excluded and rejected wastes of heavy matter and murky air, formed not by addition to, but by subtraction from, the surrounding brightness. And yet, he thought, beyond the solar system the brightness ends. Is that the real void, the real death? Unless . . . he groped for the idea . . . unless visible light is also a hole or gap, a mere diminution of something else. Something that is to bright unchanging heaven as heaven is to the dark, heavy earths. . . .

Things do not always happen as

a man would expect. The moment of his arrival in an unknown world found Ransom wholly absorbed in a philosophical speculation.

For Study

1. Near the end of Chapter 1, Weston says to the boy Harry, "And in a properly governed country I'd know how to deal with you." Toward the end of Chapter 2, Weston speaks of Harry's probable fate in "a civilized community." What do you think would be Weston's idea of a properly governed country? of a civilized community? Had England been such a country or community, how do you think Weston would have dealt with Harry?

2. In Chapter 2, what are the first clear indications that Devine is beginning to scheme against Ransom?

3. In their discussion of kidnapping Ransom (which he faintly overhears, toward the end of Chapter 2), do you detect any difference in ethics between Weston and Devine? If so, point it out. What are the implications of Weston's statement, "Still, he's only an individual, and probably a quite useless one"?

4. In Chapter 4, attempting to justify himself to Ransom, Weston says, "My only defense is that small claims must give way to great." Do you think Weston's defense is a valid one? What limits should there be on the principle that small claims must give way to great? Look up the meaning of *eminent domain* and the related meaning of the verb *condemn*.

Why is consideration of these terms pertinent to a discussion of how far that principle should be carried? Consider this exchange between Weston and Ransom through the sentence containing Weston's remark, "I do not call classics and history and such trash education," and explain the differences between the two men on the moral-ethical questions raised in their talk.

5. Early in Chapter 5, speaking of his emotions in the space-ship, Ransom uses the phrase "a severe delight." This is a strikingly fresh juxtaposition of words. Use your dictionary to explore both denotations and connotations of the words *severe* and *delight*. Discuss the meaning of Ransom's phrase.

6. Further in the same passage, Ransom reflects on the difference between the concept of "space" and that of "the heavens." What is this difference? Modern science suggests that the radiations in space from our sun and other sources have had a part in the development of life, even though many of them, if we were not screened from them by Earth's atmosphere and magnetic field, would be fatal to us. Does this deadliness of some radiations necessarily conflict with Ransom's view of "the heavens" as "the womb of worlds," teeming with life?

7. On the long space voyage, Ransom considers Devine "better company" than Weston, though "much the more odious of the two." Why do you think Ransom holds this view? Do you agree with him?

For Writing

1. At the beginning of Chapter 4 occur these words: ". . . the lifelong self-control of social man, the virtues which are half hypocrisy or the hypocrisy which is half a virtue. . . ." Write a brief paper developing ideas suggested by these phrases.

2. Explore in a brief paper Ransom's new perspectives, described in the next-to-the-last paragraph of Chapter 6 (page 35), as the spaceship enters the atmosphere of the strange planet. He achieves a mind-stretching freshness of vision. What new ways of thinking does Ransom's experience suggest to you?

Chapter **7**

"Having a doze?" said Devine. "A bit blasé about new planets by now?"

"Can you see anything?" interrupted Weston.

"I can't manage the shutters, damn them," returned Devine. "We may as well get to the manhole."

Ransom awoke from his brown study. The two partners were working together close beside him in the semi-darkness. He was cold and his body, though in fact much lighter than on Earth, still felt intolerably heavy. But a vivid sense of his situation returned to him; some fear, but more curiosity. It might mean death, but what a scaffold! Already

cold air was coming in from without, and light. He moved his head impatiently to catch some glimpse between the labouring shoulders of the two men. A moment later the last nut was unscrewed. He was looking out through the manhole.

Naturally enough all he saw was the ground — a circle of pale pink, almost of white: whether very close and short vegetation or very wrinkled and granulated rock or soil he could not say. Instantly the dark shape of Devine filled the aperture, and Ransom had time to notice that he had a revolver in his hand — "For me or for *sorns* or for both?" he wondered.

"You next," said Weston curtly.

Ransom took a deep breath and his hand went to the knife beneath his belt. Then he got his head and shoulders through the manhole, his two hands on the soil of Malacandra. The pink stuff was soft and faintly resilient, like india-rubber; clearly vegetation. Instantly Ransom looked up. He saw a pale blue sky — a fine winter-morning sky it would have been on Earth — a great billowy cumular mass of rose-colour lower down which he took for a cloud, and then ——

"Get out," said Weston from behind him.

He scrambled through and rose to his feet. The air was cold but not bitterly so, and it seemed a little rough at the back of his throat. He gazed about him, and the very intensity of his desire to take in the new world at a glance defeated itself. He saw nothing but colours — colours that refused to form themselves into things. Moreover, he knew nothing yet well enough to see it: you cannot see things till you know roughly what they are. His first impression was of a bright, pale world — a water-colour world out of a child's paint-box; a moment later he recognized the flat belt of light blue as a sheet of water, or of something like water, which came nearly to his feet. They were on the shore of a lake or river.

"Now then," said Weston, brushing past him. He turned and saw to his surprise a quite recognizable object in the immediate foreground — a hut of unmistakably terrestrial pattern though built of strange materials.

"They're human," he gasped. "They build houses?"

"*We* do," said Devine. "Guess again," and, producing a key from his pocket, proceeded to unlock a very ordinary padlock on the door of the hut. With a not very clearly defined feeling of disappointment or relief Ransom realized that his captors were merely returning to their own camp. They behaved as one might have expected. They walked into the hut, let down the slats which served for windows, sniffed the close air, expressed surprise that they had left it so dirty, and presently re-emerged.

"We'd better see about the stores," said Weston.

Ransom soon found that he was to have little leisure for observation and no opportunity of escape. The monotonous work of transferring food, clothes, weapons and many unidentifiable packages from the ship to the hut kept him vigorously occupied for the next hour or so, and in the closest contact with his kidnappers. But something he learned. Before anything else he learned that Malacandra was beautiful; and he even reflected how odd it was that this possibility had never entered into his speculations about it. The same peculiar twist of imagination which led him to people the universe with monsters had somehow taught him to expect nothing on a strange planet except rocky desolation or else a network of nightmare machines. He could not say why, now that he came to think of it. He also discovered that the blue water surrounded them on at least three sides: his view in the fourth direction was blotted out by the vast steel football [1] in which they had come. The hut, in fact, was built either on the point of a peninsula or on the end of an island. He also came little by little to the conclusion that the water was not merely blue in certain lights like terrestrial water but "really" blue. There was something about its behaviour under the very gentle breeze which puzzled him — something wrong or unnatural about the waves. For one thing, they were too big for such a wind, but that

[1] **football**: a soccer ball — hence, a sphere.

was not the whole secret. They reminded him somehow of the water that he had seen shooting up under the impact of shells in pictures of naval battles. Then suddenly realization came to him: they were the wrong shape, out of drawing, far too high for their length, too narrow at the base, too steep in the sides. He was reminded of something he had read in one of those modern poets about a sea rising in "turreted walls."

"Catch!" shouted Devine. Ransom caught and hurled the parcel on to Weston at the hut door.

On one side the water extended a long way — about a quarter of a mile, he thought, but perspective was still difficult in the strange world. On the other side it was much narrower, not wider than fifteen feet perhaps, and seemed to be flowing over a shallow — broken and swirling water that made a softer and more hissing sound than water on Earth; and where it washed the hither bank — the pinkish-white vegetation went down to the very brink — there was a bubbling and sparkling which suggested effervescence. He tried hard, in such stolen glances as the work allowed him, to make out something of the farther shore. A mass of something purple, so huge that he took it for a heather-covered mountain, was his first impression: on the other side, beyond the larger water, there was something of the same kind. But there, he could see over the top of it. Beyond were strange upright shapes of whitish green: too jagged and irregular for buildings, too thin and steep for mountains. Beyond and above these again was the rose-coloured cloud-like mass. It might really be a cloud, but it was very solid-looking and did not seem to have moved since he first set eyes on it from the manhole. It looked like the top of a gigantic red cauliflower — or like a huge bowl of red soapsuds — and it was exquisitely beautiful in tint and shape.

Baffled by this, he turned his attention to the nearer shore beyond the shallows. The purple mass looked for a moment like a plump of organ-pipes, then like a stack of rolls of cloth set up on end, then like a forest of gigantic umbrellas blown inside out. It was in faint motion. Suddenly his eyes mastered the object. The purple stuff was vegetation: more precisely it was vegetables, vegetables about twice the height of English elms, but apparently soft and flimsy. The stalks — one could hardly call them trunks — rose smooth and round, and surprisingly thin, for about forty feet: above that, the huge plants opened into a sheaf-like development, not of branches but of leaves, leaves large as lifeboats but nearly transparent. The whole thing corresponded roughly to his idea of a submarine forest: the plants, at once so large and so frail, seemed to need water to support them, and he wondered that they could hang in the air. Lower down, between the stems, he saw the vivid purple twilight, mottled with paler sunshine, which made up the internal scenery of the wood.

"Time for lunch," said Devine suddenly. Ransom straightened his back: in spite of the thinness and coldness of the air, his forehead was moist. They had been working hard and he was short of breath. Weston appeared from the door of the hut and muttered something about "finishing first." Devine, however, overruled him. A tin of beef and some biscuits were produced, and the men sat down on the various boxes which were still plentifully littered between the space-ship and the hut. Some whiskey — again at Devine's suggestion and against Weston's advice — was poured into the tin cups and mixed with water; the latter, Ransom noticed, was drawn from their own water-tins and not from the blue lakes.

As often happens, the cessation of bodily activity drew Ransom's attention to the excitement under which he had been labouring ever since their landing. Eating seemed almost out of the question. Mindful, however, of a possible dash for liberty, he forced himself to eat very much more than usual, and appetite returned as he ate. He devoured all that he could lay hands on either of food or drink: and the taste of that first meal was ever after associated in his mind with the first unearthly strangeness (never fully recaptured) of the bright, still, sparkling, unintelligible landscape — with nee-

dling shapes of pale green, thousands of feet high, with sheets of dazzling blue sodawater, and acres of rose-red soapsuds. He was a little afraid that his companions might notice, and suspect, his new achievements as a trencherman; but their attention was otherwise engaged. Their eyes never ceased roving the landscape; they spoke abstractedly and often changed position, and were ever looking over their shoulders. Ransom was just finishing his protracted meal when he saw Devine stiffen like a dog, and lay his hand in silence on Weston's shoulder. Both nodded. They rose. Ransom, gulping down the last of his whiskey, rose too. He found himself between his two captors. Both revolvers were out. They were edging him to the shore of the narrow water, and they were looking and pointing across it.

At first he could not see clearly what they were pointing at. There seemed to be some paler and slenderer plants than he had noticed before amongst the purple ones: he hardly attended to them, for his eyes were busy searching the ground — so obsessed was he with the reptile fears and insect fears of modern imagining. It was the reflections of the new white objects in the water that sent his eyes back to them: long, streaky, white reflections motionless in the running water — four or five, no, to be precise, six of them. He looked up. Six white things *were* standing there. Spindly and flimsy things, twice or three times the height of a man. His first idea was that they were images of men, the work of savage artists; he had seen things like them in books of archæology. But what could they be made of, and how could they stand? — so crazily thin and elongated in the leg, so top-heavily pouted in the chest, such stalky, flexible-looking distortions of earthly bipeds . . . like something seen in one of those comic mirrors. They were certainly not made of stone or metal, for now they seemed to sway a little as he watched; now with a shock that chased the blood from his cheeks he saw that they were alive, that they were moving, that they were coming at him. He had a momentary, scared glimpse of their faces, thin and unnaturally long, with long, drooping noses and drooping mouths of half-spectral, half-idiotic solemnity. Then he turned wildly to fly and found himself gripped by Devine.

"Let me go," he cried.

"Don't be a fool," hissed Devine, offering the muzzle of his pistol. Then, as they struggled, one of the things sent its voice across the water to them: an enormous horn-like voice far above their heads.

"They want us to go across," said Weston.

Both the men were forcing him to the water's edge. He planted his feet, bent his back and resisted donkey-fashion. Now the other two were both in the water, pulling him, and he was still on the land. He found that he was screaming.

Suddenly a second, much louder and less articulate noise broke from the creatures on the far bank. Weston shouted too, relaxed his grip on Ransom and suddenly fired his revolver not across the water but up it. Ransom saw why at the same moment.

A line of foam like the track of a torpedo was speeding towards them, and in the midst of it some large, shining beast. Devine shrieked a curse, slipped and collapsed into the water. Ransom saw a snapping jaw between them, and heard the deafening noise of Weston's revolver again and again beside him and, almost as loud, the clamour of the monsters on the far bank, who seemed to be taking the water too. He had had no need to make a decision. The moment he was free he had found himself automatically darting behind his captors, then behind the space-ship and on as fast as his legs could carry him into the utterly unknown beyond it. As he rounded the metal sphere a wild confusion of blue, purple and red met his eyes. He did not slacken his pace for a moment's inspection. He found himself splashing through water and crying out not with pain but with surprise because the water was warm. In less than a minute he was climbing out on to dry land again. He was running up a steep incline. And now he was running through purple shadow between the stems of another forest of the huge plants.

Chapter 8

A month of inactivity, a heavy meal and an unknown world do not help a man to run. Half an hour later, Ransom was walking, not running, through the forest, with a hand pressed to his aching side and his ears strained for any noise of pursuit. The clamour of revolver-shots and voices behind him (not all human voices) had been succeeded first by rifle-shots and calls at long intervals and then by utter silence. As far as eye could reach he saw nothing but the stems of the great plants about him receding in the violet shade, and far overhead the multiple transparency of huge leaves filtering the sunshine to the solemn splendour of twilight in which he walked. Whenever he felt able he ran again; the ground continued soft and springy, covered with the same resilient weed which was the first thing his hands had touched in Malacandra. Once or twice a small red creature scuttled across his path, but otherwise there seemed to be no life stirring in the wood; nothing to fear — except the fact of wandering unprovisioned and alone in a forest of unknown vegetation thousands of millions of miles beyond the reach or knowledge of man.

But Ransom was thinking of sorns — for doubtless those were the sorns, those creatures they had tried to give him to. They were quite un-like the horrors his imagination had conjured up, and for that reason had taken him off his guard. They appealed away from the Wellsian fantasies to an earlier, almost an infantile, complex of fears. Giants — ogres — ghosts — skeletons: those were its key words. Spooks on stilts, he said to himself; surrealistic bogy-men with their long faces. At the same time, the disabling panic of the first moments was ebbing away from him. The idea of suicide was now far from his mind; instead, he was determined to back his luck to the end. He prayed, and he felt his knife. He felt a strange emotion of confidence and affection towards himself — he checked himself on the point of saying, "We'll stick to one another."

The ground became worse and interrupted his meditation. He had been going gently upwards for some hours with steeper ground on his right, apparently half scaling, half skirting a hill. His path now began to cross a number of ridges, spurs doubtless of the higher ground on the right. He did not know why he should cross them, but for some reason he did; possibly a vague memory of earthly geography suggested that the lower ground would open out to bare places between wood and water where *sorns* would be more likely to catch him. As he continued crossing ridges and gullies he was struck with their extreme steepness; but somehow they were not very difficult to cross. He noticed, too, that even the smallest hummocks of earth were of an unearthly shape — too narrow, too pointed at the top and too small at the base. He remembered that the waves on the blue lakes had displayed a similar oddity. And glancing up at the purple leaves he saw the same theme of perpendicularity — the same rush to the sky — repeated there. They did not tip over at the ends; vast as they were, air was sufficient to support them so that the long aisles of the forest all rose to a kind of fan tracery. And the *sorns*, likewise — he shuddered as he thought it — they too were madly elongated.

He had sufficient science to guess that he must be on a world lighter than the Earth, where less strength was needed and nature was set free to follow her skyward impulse on a superterrestrial scale. This set him wondering where he was. He could not remember whether Venus was larger or smaller than Earth, and he had an idea that she would be hotter than this. Perhaps he was on Mars; perhaps even on the Moon. The latter he at first rejected on the ground that, if it were so, he ought to have seen the Earth in the sky when they landed; but later he remembered having been told that one face of the Moon was always turned away from the Earth. For all he knew he was wandering on the Moon's outer side; and, irrationally enough, this idea brought about him a bleaker sense of desolation than he had yet felt.

Many of the gullies which he crossed now carried streams, blue hissing streams, all hastening to the lower ground on his left. Like the lake they were warm, and the air was warm above them, so that as he climbed down and up the sides of the gullies he was continually changing temperatures. It was the contrast, as he crested the farther bank of one such small ravine, which first drew his attention to the growing chilliness of the forest; and as he looked about him he became certain that the light was failing too. He had not taken night into his calculations. He had no means of guessing what night might be on Malacandra. As he stood gazing into the deepening gloom a sigh of cold wind crept through the purple stems and set them all swaying, revealing once again the startling contrast between their size and their apparent flexibility and lightness. Hunger and weariness, long kept at bay by the mingled fear and wonder of his situation, smote him suddenly. He shivered and forced himself to proceed. The wind increased. The mighty leaves danced and dipped above his head, admitting glimpses of a pale and then a paler sky; and then, discomfortingly, of a sky with one or two stars in it. The wood was no longer silent. His eyes darted hither and thither in search of an approaching enemy and discovered only how quickly the darkness grew upon him. He welcomed the streams now for their warmth.

It was this that first suggested to him a possible protection against the increasing cold. There was really no use in going farther; for all he knew he might as well be walking towards danger as away from it. All was danger; he was no safer travelling than resting. Beside some stream it might be warm enough to lie. He shuffled on to find another gully, and went so far that he began to think he had got out of the region of them. He had almost determined to turn back when the ground began falling steeply; he slipped, recovered and found himself on the bank of a torrent. The trees — for as "trees" he could not help regarding them — did not quite meet overhead, and the water itself seemed to have some faintly phosphorescent quality, so that it was lighter here. The fall from right to left was steep. Guided by some vague picnicker's hankering for a "better" place, he went a few yards upstream. The valley grew steeper, and he came to a little cataract. He noticed dully that the water seemed to be descending a little too slowly for the incline, but he was too tired to speculate about it. The water was apparently hotter than that of the lake — perhaps nearer its subterranean source of heat. What he really wanted to know was whether he dared drink it. He was very thirsty by now; but it looked very poisonous, very un-

watery. He would try not to drink it; perhaps he was so tired that thirst would let him sleep. He sank on his knees and bathed his hands in the warm torrent; then he rolled over in a hollow close beside the fall, and yawned.

The sound of his own voice yawning — the old sound heard in night-nurseries, school dormitories and in so many bedrooms — liberated a flood of self-pity. He drew his knees up and hugged himself; he felt a sort of physical, almost a filial, love for his own body. He put his wrist-watch to his ear and found that it had stopped. He wound it. Muttering, half whimpering to himself, he thought of men going to bed on the far-distant planet Earth — men in clubs, and liners, and hotels, married men, and small children who slept with nurses in the room, and warm, tobacco-smelling men tumbled together in forecastles and dug-outs. The tendency to talk to himself was irresistible. . . . "We'll look after you, Ransom . . . we'll stick together, old man." It occurred to him that one of those creatures with snapping jaws might live in the stream. "You're quite right, Ransom," he answered mumblingly. "It's not a safe place to spend the night. We'll just rest a bit till you feel better, then we'll go on again. Not now. Presently."

Chapter 9

It was thirst that woke him. He had slept warm, though his clothes were damp, and found himself lying in sunlight, the blue waterfall at his side dancing and coruscating with every transparent shade in the whole gamut of blue and flinging strange lights far up to the underside of the forest leaves. The realization of his position, as it rolled heavily back upon consciousness, was unbearable. If only he hadn't lost his nerve the *sorns* would have killed him by now. Then he remembered with inexpressible relief that there was a man wandering in the wood — poor devil — he'd be glad to see him. He would come up to him and say, "Hullo, Ransom," — he stopped, puzzled. No, it was only himself: he *was* Ransom. Or was he? Who was the man whom he had led to a hot stream and tucked up in bed, telling him not to drink the strange water? Obviously some new-comer who didn't know the place as well as he. But whatever Ransom had told him, he was going to drink now. He lay down on the bank and plunged his face in the warm rushing liquid. It was good to drink. It had a strong mineral flavour, but it was very good. He drank again and found himself greatly refreshed and steadied. All that about the other Ransom was nonsense. He was quite aware of the danger of madness,

and applied himself vigorously to his devotions and his toilet. Not that madness mattered much. Perhaps he was mad already, and not really on Malacandra but safe in bed in an English asylum. If only it might be so! He would ask Ransom — curse it! there his mind went playing the same trick again. He rose and began walking briskly away.

The delusions recurred every few minutes as long as this stage of his journey lasted. He learned to stand still mentally, as it were, and let them roll over his mind. It was no good bothering about them. When they were gone you could resume sanity again. Far more important was the problem of food. He tried one of the "trees" with his knife. As he expected, it was toughly soft like a vegetable, not hard like wood. He cut a little piece out of it, and under this operation the whole gigantic organism vibrated to its top — it was like being able to shake the mast of a full-rigged ship with one hand. When he put it in his mouth he found it almost tasteless but by no means disagreeable, and for some minutes he munched away contentedly. But he made no progress. The stuff was quite unswallowable and could only be used as a chewing-gum. As such he used it, and after it many other pieces; not without some comfort.

It was impossible to continue yesterday's flight as a flight — inevitably it degenerated into an endless ramble, vaguely motivated by the search for food. The search was necessarily vague, since he did not know whether Malacandra held food for him nor how to recognize it if it did. He had one bad fright in the course of the morning when, passing through a somewhat more open glade, he became aware first of a huge, yellow object, then of two, and then of an indefinite multitude coming towards him. Before he could fly he found himself in the midst of a herd of enormous pale furry creatures more like giraffes than anything else he could think of, except that they could and did raise themselves on their hind legs and even progress several paces in that position. They were slenderer, and very much higher, than giraffes, and were eating the leaves off the tops of the purple plants. They saw him and stared at him with their big liquid eyes, snorting in *basso profondissimo*,[1] but had apparently no hostile intentions. Their appetite was voracious. In five minutes they had mutilated the tops of a few hundred "trees" and admitted a new flood of sunlight into the forest. Then they passed on.

This episode had an infinitely comforting effect on Ransom. The planet was not, as he had begun to fear, lifeless except for *sorns*. Here was a very presentable sort of animal, an animal which man could probably tame, and whose food

[1] *basso profondissimo:* (Italian) deepest bass.

man could possibly share. If only it were possible to climb the "trees"! He was staring about him with some idea of attempting this feat, when he noticed that the devastation wrought by the leaf-eating animals had opened a vista overhead beyond the plant-tops to a collection of the same greenish-white objects which he had seen across the lake at their first landing. This time they were much closer. They were enormously high, so that he had to throw back his head to see the top of them. They were something like pylons in shape, but solid; irregular in height and grouped in an apparently haphazard and disorderly fashion. Some ended in points that looked from where he stood as sharp as needles, while others, after narrowing towards the summit, expanded again into knobs or platforms that seemed to his terrestrial eyes ready to fall at any moment. He noticed that the sides were rougher and more seamed with fissures than he had realized at first, and between two of them he saw a motionless line of twisting blue brightness — obviously a distant fall of water. It was this which finally convinced him that the things, in spite of their improbable shape, were mountains; and with that discovery the mere oddity of the prospect was swallowed up in the fantastic sublime. Here, he understood, was the full statement of that *perpendicular* theme which beast and plant and earth all played on Malacandra — here in this riot of rock, leaping and surging skyward like solid jets from some rock-fountain, and hanging by their own lightness in the air, so shaped, so elongated, that all terrestrial mountains must ever after seem to him to be mountains lying on their sides. He felt a lift and lightening at the heart.

But next moment his heart stood still. Against the pallid background of the mountains and quite close to him — for the mountains themselves seemed but a quarter of a mile away — a moving shape appeared. He recognized it instantly as it moved slowly (and, he thought, stealthily) between two of the denuded plant-tops — the giant stature, the cadaverous leanness, the long, drooping, wizard-like profile of a *sorn*. The head appeared to be narrow and conical; the hands or paws with which it parted the stems before it as it moved were thin, mobile, spidery and almost transparent. He felt an immediate certainty that it was looking for him. All this he took in in an infinitesimal time. The ineffaceable image was hardly stamped on his brain before he was running as hard as he could into the thickest of the forest.

He had no plan save to put as many miles as he could between himself and the *sorn*. He prayed fervently that there might be only one; perhaps the wood was full of them — perhaps they had the intelligence to make a circle round him. No matter — there was noth-ing for it now but sheer running, running knife in hand. The fear had all gone into action; emotionally he was cool and alert, and ready — as ready as he ever would be — for the last trial. His flight led him downhill at an ever-increasing speed; soon the incline was so steep that if his body had had terrestrial gravity he would have been compelled to take to his hands and knees and clamber down. Then he saw something gleaming ahead of him. A minute later he had emerged from the wood altogether; he was standing, blinking in the light of sun and water, on the shore of a broad river, and looking out on a flat landscape of intermingled river, lake, island and promontory — the same sort of country on which his eyes had first rested in Malacandra.

There was no sound of pursuit. Ransom dropped down on his stomach and drank, cursing a world where *cold* water appeared to be unobtainable. Then he lay still to listen and to recover his breath. His eyes were upon the blue water. It was agitated. Circles shuddered and bubbles danced ten yards away from his face. Suddenly the water heaved and a round, shining, black thing like a cannon-ball came into sight. Then he saw eyes and mouth — a puffing mouth bearded with bubbles. More of the thing came up out of the water. It was gleaming black. Finally it splashed and wallowed to the shore and rose, steaming, on its hind legs

— six or seven feet high and too thin for its height, like everything in Malacandra. It had a coat of thick black hair, lucid as seal-skin, very short legs with webbed feet, a broad beaver-like or fish-like tail, strong forelimbs with webbed claws or fingers, and some complication half-way up the belly which Ransom took to be its genitals. It was something like a penguin, something like an otter, something like a seal; the slenderness and flexibility of the body suggested a giant stoat. The great round head, heavily whiskered, was mainly responsible for the suggestion of seal; but it was higher in the forehead than a seal's and the mouth was smaller.

There comes a point at which the actions of fear and precaution are purely conventional, no longer felt as terror or hope by the fugitive. Ransom lay perfectly still, pressing his body as well down into the weed as he could, in obedience to a wholly theoretical idea that he might thus pass unobserved. He felt little emotion. He noted in a dry, objective way that this was apparently to be the end of his story — caught between a *sorn* from the land and a big, black animal from the water. He had, it is true, a vague notion that the jaws and mouth of the beast were not those of a carnivore; but he knew that he was too ignorant of zoology to do more than guess.

Then something happened which completely altered his state of mind.

The creature, which was still steaming and shaking itself on the bank and had obviously not seen him, opened its mouth and began to make noises. This in itself was not remarkable; but a lifetime of linguistic study assured Ransom almost at once that these were articulate noises. The creature was *talking*. It had language. If you are not yourself a philologist, I am afraid you must take on trust the prodigious emotional consequences of this realization in Ransom's mind. A new world he had already seen — but a new, an extra-terrestrial, a non-human language was a different matter. Somehow he had not thought of this in connection with the *sorns;* now it flashed upon him like a revelation. The love of knowledge is a kind of madness. In the fraction of a second which it took Ransom to decide that the creature was really talking, and while he still knew that he might be facing instant death, his imagination had leaped over every fear and hope and probability of his situation to follow the dazzling project of making a Malacandrian grammar. *An Introduction to the Malacandrian language — The Lunar verb — A Concise Martian-English Dictionary* . . . the titles flitted through his mind. And what might one not discover from the speech of a non-human race? The very form of language itself, the principle behind all possible languages, might fall into his hands.

Unconsciously he raised himself on his elbow and stared at the black beast. It became silent. The huge bullet head swung round and lustrous amber eyes fixed him. There was no wind on the lake or in the wood. Minute after minute in utter silence the representatives of two so far-divided species stared each into the other's face.

Ransom rose to his knees. The creature leaped back, watching him intently, and then became motionless again. Then it came a pace nearer, and Ransom jumped up and retreated, but not far; curiosity held him. He summoned up his courage and advanced, holding out his hand; the beast misunderstood the gesture. It backed into the shallows of the lake and he could see the muscles tightened under its sleek pelt, ready for sudden movement. But there it stopped; it, too, was in the grip of curiosity. Neither dared let the other approach, yet each repeatedly felt the impulse to do so himself, and yielded to it. It was foolish, frightening, ecstatic and unbearable all in one moment. It was more than curiosity. It was like a courtship — like the meeting of the first man and the first woman in the world; it was like something beyond that; so natural is the contact of sexes, so limited the strangeness, so shallow the reticence, so mild the repugnance to be overcome, compared with the first tingling intercourse of two different, but rational, species.

The creature suddenly turned and began walking away. A disappointment like despair smote Ransom.

"Come back," he shouted in English. The thing turned, spread out its arms and spoke again in its unintelligible language; then it resumed its progress. It had not gone more than twenty yards away when Ransom saw it stoop down and pick something up. It returned. In its hand (he was already thinking of its webbed fore-paw as a hand) it was carrying what appeared to be a shell — the shell of some oyster-like creature, but rounder and more deeply domed. It dipped the shell in the lake and raised it full of water. Then it held the shell to its own middle and seemed to be pouring something into the water. Ransom thought with disgust that it was urinating in the shell. Then he realized that the protuberances on the creature's belly were not genital organs nor organs at all; it was wearing a kind of girdle hung with various pouch-like objects, and it was adding a few drops of liquid from one of these to the water in the shell. This done it raised the shell to its black lips and drank — not throwing back its head like a man but bowing it and sucking like a horse. When it had finished it refilled the shell and once again added a few drops from the receptacle — it seemed to be some kind of skin bottle — at its waist. Supporting the shell in its two arms, it extended them towards Ransom.

The intention was unmistakable. Hesitantly, almost shyly, he advanced and took the cup. His finger-tips touched the webbed membrane of the creature's paws and an indescribable thrill of mingled attraction and repulsion ran through him; then he drank. Whatever had been added to the water was plainly alcoholic; he had never enjoyed a drink so much.

"Thank you," he said in English. "Thank you very much."

The creature struck itself on the chest and made a noise. Ransom did not at first realize what it meant. Then he saw that it was trying to teach him its name — presumably the name of the species.

"*Hross*," it said, "*Hross*," and flapped itself.

"*Hross*," repeated Ransom, and pointed at it; then "Man," and struck his own chest.

"*Hmā — hmā — hmān*," imitated the *hross*. It picked up a handful of earth, where earth appeared between weed and water at the bank of the lake.

"*Handra*," it said. Ransom repeated the word. Then an idea occurred to him.

"*Malacandra?*" he said in an inquiring voice. The *hross* rolled its eyes and waved its arms, obviously in an effort to indicate the whole landscape. Ransom was getting on well. *Handra* was earth the element; *Malac-andra* the "earth" or planet as a whole. Soon he would find out what *Malac* meant. In the meantime "H disappears after C" he noted, and made his first step in Malacandrian phonetics. The *hross* was now trying to teach him the meaning of *handramit*. He recognized the root *handra*– again (and noted "They have suffixes as well as prefixes"), but this time he could make nothing of the *hross's* gestures, and remained ignorant what a *handramit* might be. He took the initiative by opening his mouth, pointing to it and going through the pantomime of eating. The Malacandrian word for *food* or *eat* which he got in return proved to contain consonants unreproducible by a human mouth, and Ransom, continuing the pantomime, tried to explain that his interest was practical as well as philological. The *hross* understood him, though he took some time to understand from its gestures that it was inviting him to follow it. In the end, he did so.

It took him only as far as where it had got the shell, and here, to his not very reasonable astonishment, Ransom found that a kind of boat was moored. Man-like, when he saw the artifact he felt more certain of the *hross's* rationality. He even valued the creature the more because the boat, allowing for the usual Malacandrian height and flimsiness, was really very like an earthly boat; only later did he set himself the question, "What else could a boat be like?" The *hross* produced an oval platter of some tough but slightly flexible material, covered it with strips of spongy, orange-coloured substance and gave it to Ransom. He cut a convenient length off with his knife and began to eat; doubtfully at first and then ravenously. It had a bean-like taste but sweeter; good enough for a starving man. Then, as his hunger ebbed, the sense of his situation returned with dismaying force. The huge, seal-like creature seated beside him became unbearably ominous. It seemed friendly; but it was very big, very black, and he knew nothing at all about it. What were its relations to the *sorns?* And was it really as rational as it appeared?

It was only many days later that Ransom discovered how to deal with these sudden losses of confidence. They arose when the rationality of the *hross* tempted you to think of it as a man. Then it became abominable — a man seven feet high, with a snaky body, covered, face and all, with thick black animal hair, and whiskered like a cat. But starting from the other end you had an animal with everything an animal ought to have — glossy coat, liquid eye, sweet breath and whitest teeth — and added to all these, as though Paradise had never been lost and earliest dreams were true, the charm of speech and reason. Nothing could be more disgusting than the one impression; nothing more delightful than the other. It all depended on the point of view.

Chapter 10

When Ransom had finished his meal and drunk again of the strong waters of Malacandra, his host rose and entered the boat. He did this head-first like an animal, his sinuous body allowing him to rest his hands on the bottom of the boat while his feet were still planted on the land. He completed the operation by flinging rump, tail and hind legs all together about five feet into the air and then whisking them neatly on board with an agility which would have been quite impossible to an animal of his bulk on Earth.

Having got into the boat, he proceeded to get out again and then pointed to it. Ransom understood that he was being invited to follow his example. The question which he wanted to ask above all others could not, of course, be put. Were the *hrossa* (he discovered later that this was the plural of *hross*) the dominant species on Malacandra, and the *sorns,* despite their more man-like shape, merely a semi-intelligent kind of cattle? Fervently he hoped that it might be so. On the other hand, the *hrossa* might be the domestic animals of the *sorns,* in which case the latter would be superintelligent. His whole imaginative training somehow encouraged him to associate superhuman intelligence with monstrosity of form and ruthlessness of will. To step on board the *hross's* boat might mean surrendering himself to *sorns* at the other end of the journey. On the other hand, the *hross's* invitation might be a golden opportunity of leaving the *sorn*-haunted forests for ever. And by this time the *hross* itself was becoming puzzled at his apparent inability to understand it. The urgency of its signs finally determined him. The thought of parting from the *hross* could not be seriously entertained; its animality shocked him in a dozen ways, but his longing to learn its language, and, deeper still, the shy, ineluctable fascination of unlike for unlike, the sense that the key to prodigious adventure was being put in his hands — all this had really attached him to it by bonds stronger than he knew. He stepped into the boat.

The boat was without seats. It had a very high prow, an enormous expanse of free-board, and what seemed to Ransom an impossibly shallow draught. Indeed, very little of it even rested on the water; he was reminded of a modern European speed-boat. It was moored by something that looked at first like rope; but the *hross* cast off not by untying but by simply pulling the apparent rope in two as one might pull in two a piece of soft toffee or a roll of plasticine. It then squatted down on its rump in the stern-sheets and took up a paddle — a paddle of such enormous blade that

Ransom wondered how the creature could wield it, till he again remembered how light a planet they were on. The length of the *hross's* body enabled him to work freely in the squatting position despite the high gunwale. It paddled quickly.

For the first few minutes they passed between banks wooded with the purple trees, upon a waterway not more than a hundred yards in width. Then they doubled a promontory, and Ransom saw that they were emerging on to a much larger sheet of water — a great lake, almost a sea. The *hross,* now taking great care and often changing direction and looking about it, paddled well out from the shore. The dazzling blue expanse grew moment by moment wider around them; Ransom could not look steadily at it. The warmth from the water was oppressive; he removed his cap and jerkin, and by so doing surprised the *hross* very much.

He rose cautiously to a standing position and surveyed the Malacandrian prospect which had opened on every side. Before and behind them lay the glittering lake, here studded with islands, and there smiling uninterruptedly at the pale blue sky; the sun, he noticed, was almost immediately overhead — they were in the Malacandrian tropics. At each end the lake vanished into more complicated groupings of land and water, softly, featherily embossed in the purple giant weed. But this marshy land or chain of archipelagoes, as he now beheld it, was bordered on each side with jagged walls of the pale green mountains, which he could still hardly call mountains, so tall they were, so gaunt, sharp, narrow and seemingly unbalanced. On the starboard they were not more than a mile away and seemed divided from the water only by a narrow strip of forest; to the left they were far more distant, though still impressive — perhaps seven miles from the boat. They ran on each side of the watered country as far as he could see, both onwards and behind them; he was sailing, in fact, on the flooded floor of a majestic canyon nearly ten miles wide and of unknown length. Behind and sometimes above the mountain peaks he could make out in many places great billowy piles of the rose-red substance which he had yesterday mistaken for cloud. The mountains, in fact, seemed to have no fall of ground behind them; they were rather the serrated bastion of immeasurable tablelands, higher in many places than themselves, which made the Malacandrian horizon left and right as far as eye could reach. Only straight ahead and straight astern was the planet cut with the vast gorge, which now appeared to him only as a rut or crack in the tableland.

He wondered what the cloud-like red masses were and endeavoured to ask by signs. The question was, however, too particular for sign-language. The *hross,* with a wealth of gesticulation — its arms or fore-limbs were more flexible than his and in quick motion almost whip-like — made it clear that it supposed him to be asking about the high ground in general. It named this *harandra.* The low, watered country, the gorge or canyon, appeared to be *handramit.* Ransom grasped the implications, *handra* earth, *harandra* high earth, mountain, *handramit,* low earth, valley. Highland and lowland, in fact. The peculiar importance of the distinction in Malacandrian geography he learned later.

By this time the *hross* had attained the end of its careful navigation. They were a couple of miles from land when it suddenly ceased paddling and sat tense with its paddle poised in the air; at the same moment the boat quivered and shot forward as if from a catapult. They had apparently availed themselves of some current. In a few seconds they were racing forward at some fifteen miles an hour and rising and falling on the strange, sharp, perpendicular waves of Malacandra with a jerky motion quite unlike that of the choppiest sea that Ransom had ever met on Earth. It reminded him of disastrous experiences on a trotting horse in the army; and it was intensely disagreeable. He gripped the gunwale with his left hand and mopped his brow with his right — the damp warmth from the water had become very troublesome. He wondered if the Malacandrian food, and still more the Malacandrian drink, were really digestible by a human stomach. Thank heaven he was a good sailor! At least a fairly good sailor. At least ——

Hastily he leaned over the side. Heat from blue water smote up to his face; in the depth he thought he saw eels playing: long, silver eels. The worst happened not once but many times. In his misery he remembered vividly the shame of being sick at a children's party . . . long ago in the star where he was born. He felt a similar shame now. It was not thus that the first representative of humanity would choose to appear before a new species. Did *hrossa* vomit too? Would it know what he was doing? Shaking and groaning, he turned back into the boat. The creature was keeping an eye on him, but its face seemed to him expressionless; it was only long after that he learned to read the Malacandrian face.

The current meanwhile seemed to be gathering speed. In a huge curve they swung across the lake to within a furlong of the farther shore, then back again, and once more onward, in giddy spirals and figures of eight, while purple wood and jagged mountain raced backwards and Ransom loathingly associated their sinuous course with the nauseous curling of the silver eels. He was rapidly losing all interest in Malacandra: the distinction between Earth and other planets seemed of no importance compared with the awful distinction of earth and water. He wondered despairingly whether the *hross* habitually lived on water. Perhaps they were going to spend the night in this detestable boat. . . .

His sufferings did not, in fact, last long. There came a blessed cessation of the choppy movement and a slackening of speed, and he saw that the *hross* was backing water rapidly. They were still afloat, with shores close on each side; between them a narrow channel in which the water hissed furiously — apparently a shallow. The *hross* jumped overboard, splashing abundance of warm water into the ship; Ransom, more cautiously and shakily, clambered after it. He was about up to his knees. To his astonishment, the *hross,* without any appearance of effort, lifted the boat bodily on to the top of its head, steadied it with one forepaw, and proceeded, erect as a Grecian caryatid, to the land. They walked forward — if the swinging movement of the *hross's* short legs from its flexible hips could be called walking — beside the channel. In a few minutes Ransom saw a new landscape.

The channel was not only a shallow but a rapid — the first, indeed, of a series of rapids by which the water descended steeply for the next half-mile. The ground fell away before them and the canyon — or *handramit* — continued at a very much lower level. Its walls, however, did not sink with it, and from his present position Ransom got a clearer notion of the lie of the land. Far more of the highlands to left and right were visible, sometimes covered with the cloudlike red swellings, but more often level, pale and barren to where the smooth line of their horizon marched with the sky. The mountain peaks now appeared only as the fringe or border of the true highland, surrounding it as the lower teeth surround the tongue. He was struck by the vivid contrast between *harandra* and *handramit*. Like a rope of jewels the gorge spread beneath him, purple, sapphire blue, yellow and pinkishwhite, a rich and variegated inlay of wooded land and disappearing, reappearing, ubiquitous water. Malacandra was less like Earth than he had been beginning to suppose. The *handramit* was no true valley rising and falling with the mountain chain it belonged to. Indeed, it did not belong to a mountain chain. It was only an enormous crack or ditch, of varying depth, running through the high and level *harandra;* the latter, he now began to suspect, was the true "surface" of the planet — certainly would appear as surface to a terrestrial astronomer. To the *handramit* itself there seemed no end; uninterrupted and very nearly straight, it ran before him, a narrowing line of colour, to where it clove the horizon with a V-shaped indenture. There must be a hundred miles of it in view, he thought; and he reckoned that he had put some

thirty or forty miles of it behind him since yesterday.

All this time they were descending beside the rapids to where the water was level again and the *hross* could relaunch its skiff. During this walk Ransom learned the words for boat, rapid, water, sun and carry; the latter, as his first verb, interested him particularly. The *hross* was also at some pains to impress upon him an association or relation which it tried to convey by repeating the contrasted pairs of words *hrossa-handramit* and *séroni-harandra*. Ransom understood him to mean the *hrossa* lived down in the *handramit* and the *séroni* up on the *harandra*. What the deuce were *séroni,* he wondered. The open reaches of the *harandra* did not look as if anything lived up there. Perhaps the *hrossa* had a mythology — he took it for granted they were on a low cultural level — and the *séroni* were gods or demons.

The journey continued, with frequent, though decreasing recurrences of nausea for Ransom. Hours later he realized that *séroni* might very well be the plural of *sorn*.

The sun declined, on their right. It dropped quicker than on Earth, or at least on those parts of Earth that Ransom knew, and in the cloudless sky it had little sunset pomp about it. In some other queer way which he could not specify it differed from the sun he knew; but even while he speculated the needle-like mountain-tops stood out black against it and the *handramit* grew dark, though eastward (to their left) the high country of the *harandra* still shone pale rose, remote and smooth and tranquil, like another and more spiritual world.

Soon he became aware that they were landing again, that they were treading solid ground, were making for the depth of the purple forest. The motion of the boat still worked in his fantasy and the earth seemed to sway beneath him; this, with weariness and twilight, made the rest of the journey dream-like. Light began to glare in his eyes. A fire was burning. It illuminated the huge leaves overhead, and he saw stars beyond them. Dozens of *hrossa* seemed to have surrounded him; more animal, less human, in their multitude and their close neighborhood to him, than his solitary guide had seemed. He felt some fear, but more a ghastly inappropriateness. He wanted men — any men, even Weston and Devine. He was too tired to do anything about these meaningless bullet heads and furry faces — could make no response at all. And then, lower down, closer to him, more mobile, came in throngs the whelps, the puppies, the cubs, whatever you called them. Suddenly his mood changed. They were jolly little things. He laid his hand on one black head and smiled; the creature scurried away.

He never could remember much of that evening. There was more eating and drinking, there was continual coming and going of black

forms, there were strange eyes luminous in the firelight; finally, there was sleep in some dark, apparently covered place.

For Study and Writing

1. Early in Chapter 7, when Ransom is trying to distinguish shapes on the strange planet, the observation is made that "you cannot see things till you know roughly what they are." This is a simple truth not often thought about. Have you ever looked at a landscape with unfamiliar vegetation, colors, or shapes and found that time was required for your eyes to distinguish and identify details? This difficulty is the basis of picture puzzles of several kinds. What is a common military application of this principle?

2. What facts about the planet can you deduce from the vegetation and the waves as described in the first part of Chapter 7?

3. What clues are given us, early in both Chapter 8 and Chapter 9, that Ransom is religious in more than a merely nominal sense?

4. At several points during Ransom's first experiences on the planet, there is conflict between fear and intellectual curiosity (e.g., at the start of Chapter 7, when he is about to leave the space-ship; in Chapter 9, when he has encountered the *hross* and we are told that "the love of knowledge is a kind of madness"). In the light of these incidents, discuss the interplay of these two motivations. With regard to fear, why is one's point of view im-

portant? (In answering that question, be sure to consider Ransom's experience as told in the last paragraph of Chapter 9, page 51.)

5. In Chapter 10 we are told that it took Ransom a long time to learn "to read the Malacandrian face." Discuss this difficulty as an analogy to the problem of not being able to see things well until you know roughly what they are.

6. Why does Ransom take it for granted that the *hrossa* are on a low cultural level? Do you think this assumption is sound?

7. By this time have you picked up any clues as to which planet Ransom has reached? Which one do you think it is? Why?

Chapter **11**

Ever since he awoke on the spaceship Ransom had been thinking about the amazing adventure of going to another planet, and about his chances of returning from it. What he had not thought about was *being* on it. It was with a kind of stupefaction each morning that he found himself neither arriving in, nor escaping from, but simply living on, Malacandra; waking, sleeping, eating, swimming and even, as the days passed, talking. The wonder of it smote him most strongly when he found himself, about three weeks after his arrival, actually going for a walk. A few weeks later

he had his favourite walks, and his favourite foods; he was beginning to develop habits. He knew a male from a female *hross* at sight, and even individual differences were becoming plain. Hyoi who had first found him — miles away to the north — was a very different person from the grey-muzzled, venerable Hnohra who was daily teaching him the language; and the young of the species were different again. They were delightful. You could forget all about the rationality of *hrossa* in dealing with them. Too young to trouble him with the baffling enigma of reason in an inhuman form, they solaced his loneliness, as if he had been allowed to bring a few dogs with him from the Earth. The cubs, on their part, felt the liveliest interest in the hairless goblin which had appeared among them. With them, and therefore indirectly with their dams, he was a brilliant success.

Of the community in general his earlier impressions were all gradually being corrected. His first diagnosis of their culture was what he called "old stone age." The few cutting instruments they possessed were made of stone. They seemed to have no pottery but a few clumsy vessels used for boiling, and boiling was the only cookery they attempted. Their common drinking vessel, dish and ladle all in one, was the oyster-like shell in which he had first tasted *hross* hospitality; the fish which it contained was their only animal food. Vegetable fare they had in great plenty and variety, some of it delicious. Even the pinkish-white weed which covered the whole *handramit* was edible at a pinch, so that if he had starved before Hyoi found him he would have starved amidst abundance. No *hross,* however, ate the weed (*honodraskrud*) for choice, though it might be used *faute de mieux* [1] on a journey. Their dwellings were beehive-shaped huts of stiff leaf and the villages — there were several in the neighbourhood — were always built beside rivers for warmth and well upstream towards the walls of the *handramit* where the water was hottest. They slept on the ground. They seemed to have no arts except a kind of poetry and music which was practised almost every evening by a team or troupe of four *hrossa*. One recited half chanting at great length while the other three, sometimes singly and sometimes antiphonally, interrupted him from time to time with song. Ransom could not find out whether these interruptions were simply lyrical interludes or dramatic dialogue arising out of the leader's narrative. He could make nothing of the music. The voices were not disagreeable and the scale seemed adapted to human ears, but the time-pattern was meaningless to his sense of rhythm. The occupations of the tribe or family were at first mysterious.

[1] *faute de mieux:* (French) for want of something better.

People were always disappearing for a few days and reappearing again. There was a little fishing and much journeying in boats of which he never discovered the object. Then one day he saw a kind of caravan of *hrossa* setting out by land each with a load of vegetable food on its head. Apparently there was some kind of trade in Malacandra.

He discovered their agriculture in the first week. About a mile down the *handramit* one came to broad lands free of forest and clothed for many miles together in low pulpy vegetation in which yellow, orange and blue predominated. Later on, there were lettuce-like plants about the height of a terrestrial birch-tree. Where one of these overhung the warmth of water you could step into one of the lower leaves and lie deliciously as in a gently moving, fragrant hammock. Elsewhere it was not warm enough to sit still for long out of doors; the general temperature of the *handramit* was that of a fine winter's morning on Earth. These food-producing areas were worked communally by the surrounding villages, and division of labour had been carried to a higher point than he expected. Cutting, drying, storing, transport and something like manuring were all carried on, and he suspected that some at least of the water channels were artificial.

But the real revolution in his understanding of the *hrossa* began when he had learned enough of their language to attempt some satisfaction of their curiosity about himself. In answer to their questions he began by saying that he had come out of the sky. Hnohra immediately asked from which planet or earth (*handra*). Ransom, who had deliberately given a childish version of the truth in order to adapt it to the supposed ignorance of his audience, was a little annoyed to find Hnohra painfully explaining to him that he could not live in the sky because there was no air in it; he might have come through the sky but he must have come from a *handra*. He was quite unable to point Earth out to them in the night sky. They seemed surprised at his inability, and repeatedly pointed out to him a bright planet low on the western horizon — a little south of where the sun had gone down. He was surprised that they selected a planet instead of a mere star and stuck to their choice; could it be possible that they understood astronomy? Unfortunately he still knew too little of the language to explore their knowledge. He turned the conversation by asking them the name of the bright southern planet, and was told that it was Thulcandra — the silent world or planet.

"Why do you call it *Thulc?*" he asked. "Why silent?" No one knew. "The *séroni* know," said Hnohra. "That is the sort of thing they know."

Then he was asked how he had come, and made a very poor attempt at describing the space-ship — but again:

"The *séroni* would know."

Had he come alone? No, he had come with two others of his kind — bad men ("bent" men was the nearest *hrossian* equivalent) who tried to kill him, but he had run away from them. The *hrossa* found this very difficult, but all finally agreed that he ought to go to Oyarsa. Oyarsa would protect him. Ransom asked who Oyarsa was. Slowly, and with many misunderstandings, he hammered out the information that Oyarsa (1) lived at Meldilorn; (2) knew everything and ruled everyone; (3) had always been there; and (4) was not a *hross,* nor one of the *séroni.* Then Ransom, following his own idea, asked if Oyarsa had made the world. The *hrossa* almost barked in the fervour of their denial. Did people in Thulcandra not know that Maleldil the Young had made and still ruled the world? Even a child knew that. Where did Maleldil live, Ransom asked.

"With the Old One."

And who was the Old One? Ransom did not understand the answer. He tried again.

"Where was the Old One?"

"He is not that sort," said Hnohra, "that he has to live anywhere," and proceeded to a good deal which Ransom did not follow. But he followed enough to feel once more a certain irritation. Ever since he had discovered the rationality of the *hrossa* he had been haunted by a conscientious scruple as to whether it might not be his duty to undertake their religious instruction; now, as a result of his tentative efforts, he found himself being treated as if *he* were the savage and being given a first sketch of civilized religion — a sort of *hrossian* equivalent of the shorter catechism. It became plain that Maleldil was a spirit without body, parts or passions.

"He is not a *hnau*," said the *hrossa.*

"What is *hnau?*" asked Ransom.

"You are *hnau*. I am *hnau*. The *séroni* are *hnau*. The *pfifltriggi* are *hnau.*"

"*Pfifltriggi?*" said Ransom.

"More than ten days' journey to the west," said Hnohra. "The *harandra* sinks down not into a *handramit* but into a broad place, an open place, spreading every way. Five days' journey from the north to the south of it; ten days' journey from the east to the west. The forests are of other colours there than here, they are blue and green. It is very deep there, it goes to the roots of the world. The best things that can be dug out of the earth are there. The *pfifltriggi* live there. They delight in digging. What they dig they soften with fire and make things of it. They are little people, smaller than you, long in the snout, pale, busy. They have long limbs in front. No *hnau* can match them

in making and shaping things as none can match us in singing. But let *Hmān* see."

He turned and spoke to one of the younger *hrossa* and presently, passed from hand to hand, there came to him a little bowl. He held it close to the firelight and examined it. It was certainly of gold, and Ransom realized the meaning of Devine's interest in Malacandra.

"Is there much of this thing?" he asked.

Yes, he was told, it was washed down in most of the rivers; but the best and most was among the *pfifltriggi,* and it was they who were skilled in it. *Arbol hru,* they called it — Sun's blood. He looked at the bowl again. It was covered with fine etching. He saw pictures of *hrossa* and of smaller, almost frog-like animals; and then, of *sorns*. He pointed to the latter inquiringly.

"*Séroni,*" said the *hrossa,* confirming his suspicions. "They live up almost on the *harandra*. In the big caves."

The frog-like animals — or tapir-headed, frog-bodied animals — were *pfifltriggi*. Ransom turned it over in his mind. On Malacandra, apparently, three distinct species had reached rationality, and none of them had yet exterminated the other two. It concerned him intensely to find out which was the real master.

"Which of the *hnau* rule?" he asked.

"Oyarsa rules," was the reply.

"Is he *hnau?*"

This puzzled them a little. The *séroni,* they thought, would be better at that kind of question. Perhaps Oyarsa was *hnau,* but a very different *hnau.* He had no death and no young.

"These *séroni* know more than the *hrossa?*" asked Ransom.

This produced more a debate than an answer. What emerged finally was that the *séroni* or *sorns* were perfectly helpless in a boat, and could not fish to save their lives, could hardly swim, could make no poetry, and even when *hrossa* had made it for them could understand only the inferior sorts; but they were admittedly good at finding out things about the stars and understanding the darker utterances of Oyarsa and telling what happened in Malacandra long ago — longer ago than anyone could remember.

"Ah — the intelligentsia," thought Ransom. "They must be the real rulers, however it is disguised."

He tried to ask what would happen if the *sorns* used their wisdom to make the *hrossa* do things — this was as far as he could get in his halting Malacandrian. The question did not sound nearly so urgent in this form as it would have done if he had been able to say "used their scientific resources for the exploitation of their uncivilized neighbours." But he might have spared his pains. The mention of the *sorns'* inadequate appreciation of poetry had diverted the whole conversation into literary channels. Of the heated, and apparently technical, discussion which followed he understood not a syllable.

Naturally his conversations with the *hrossa* did not all turn on Malacandra. He had to repay them with information about Earth. He was hampered in this by both the humiliating discoveries which he was constantly making of his own ignorance about his native planet, and partly by his determination to conceal some of the truth. He did not want to tell them too much of our human wars and industrialisms. He remembered how H. G. Wells' Cavor had met his end on the Moon; [1] also he felt shy. A sensation akin to that of physical nakedness came over him whenever they questioned him too closely about men — the *hmāna* as they called them. Moreover, he was determined not to let them know that he had been brought there to be given to the *sorns;* for he was becoming daily more certain that these were the dominant species. What he did tell them fired the imagination of the *hrossa;* they all began making poems about the strange *handra* where the plants were hard like stone and the earth-

[1] A reference to *The First Men in the Moon* (1901), a science-fiction novel by the English author H. G. Wells (1866–1946). In it, Cavor is slain by the lunar inhabitants after he has told them of the warlike characteristics of man and of the possibility that more men might come to the Moon.

weed green like rock and the waters cold and salt, and *hmāna* lived out on top, on the *harandra*.

They were even more interested in what he had to tell them of the aquatic animal with snapping jaws which he had fled from in their own world and even in their own *handramit*. It was a *hnakra*, they all agreed. They were intensely excited. There had not been a *hnakra* in the valley for many years. The youth of the *hrossa* got out their weapons — primitive harpoons with points of bone — and the very cubs began playing at *hnakra*-hunting in the shallows. Some of the mothers showed signs of anxiety and wanted the cubs to be kept out of the water, but in general the news of the *hnakra* seemed to be immensely popular. Hyoi set off at once to do something to his boat, and Ransom accompanied him. He wished to make himself useful, and was already beginning to have some vague capacity with the primitive *hrossian* tools. They walked together to Hyoi's creek, a stone's throw through the forest.

On the way, where the path was single and Ransom was following Hyoi, they passed a little she-*hross*, not much more than a cub. She spoke as they passed, but not to them: her eyes were on a spot about five yards away.

"Who do you speak to, Hrikki?" said Ransom.

"To the *eldil*."

"Where?"

"Did you not see him?"

"I saw nothing."

"There! There!" she cried suddenly. "Ah! He is gone. Did you not see him?"

"I saw no one."

"Hyoi!" said the cub, "the *hmān* cannot see the *eldil*."

But Hyoi, continuing steadily on his way, was already out of earshot, and had apparently noticed nothing. Ransom concluded that Hrikki was "pretending" like the young of his own species. In a few moments he rejoined his companion.

Chapter **12**

They worked hard at Hyoi's boat till noon and then spread themselves on the weed close to the warmth of the creek, and began their midday meal. The war-like nature of their preparations suggested many questions to Ransom. He knew no word for war, but he managed to make Hyoi understand what he wanted to know. Did *séroni* and *hrossa* and *pfifltriggi* ever go out like this, with weapons, against each other?

"What for?" asked Hyoi.

It was difficult to explain. "If both wanted one thing and neither would give it," said Ransom, "would the other at last come with force? Would they say, give it or we kill you?"

"What sort of thing?"

"Well — food, perhaps."

"If the other *hnau* wanted food, why should we not give it to them? We often do."

"But how if we had not enough for ourselves?"

"But Maleldil will not stop the plants growing."

"Hyoi, if you had more and more young, would Maleldil broaden the *handramit* and make enough plants for them all?"

"The *séroni* know that sort of thing. But why should we have more young?"

Ransom found this difficult. At last he said:

"Is the begetting of young not a pleasure among the *hrossa?*"

"A very great one, *Hmān*. This is what we call love."

"If a thing is a pleasure, a *hmān* wants it again. He might want the pleasure more often than the number of young that could be fed."

It took Hyoi a long time to get the point.

"You mean," he said slowly, "that he might do it not only in one or two years of his life but again?"

"Yes."

"But why? Would he want his dinner all day or want to sleep after he had slept? I do not understand."

"But a dinner comes every day. This love, you say, comes only once while the *hross* lives."

"But it takes his whole life. When he is young he has to look for his mate; and then he has to court her; then he begets young; then he rears them; then he remembers all this, and boils it inside him and makes it into poems and wisdom."

"But the pleasure he must be content only to remember?"

"That is like saying 'My food I must be content only to eat.'"

"I do not understand."

"A pleasure is full grown only when it is remembered. You are speaking, *Hmān,* as if the pleasure were one thing and the memory another. It is all one thing. The *séroni* could say it better than I say it now. Not better than I could say it in a poem. What you call remembering is the last part of the pleasure, as the *crah* is the last part of a poem. When you and I met, the meeting was over very shortly, it was nothing. Now it is growing something as we remember it. But still we know very little about it. What it will be when I remember it as I lie down to die, what it makes in me all my days till then — that is the real meeting. The other is only the beginning of it. You say you have poets in your world. Do they not teach you this?"

"Perhaps some of them do," said Ransom. "But even in a poem does a *hross* never long to hear one splendid line over again?"

Hyoi's reply unfortunately turned on one of those points in their language which Ransom had not mastered. There were two verbs which both, as far as he could see, meant to *long* or *yearn;* but the *hrossa* drew a sharp distinction, even an opposition, between them. Hyoi seemed to him merely to be saying that everyone would long for it (*wondelone*) but no one in his senses could long for it (*hluntheline*).

"And indeed," he continued, "the poem is a good example. For the most splendid line becomes fully splendid only by means of all the lines after it; if you went back to it you would find it less splendid than you thought. You would kill it. I mean in a good poem."

"But in a bent poem, Hyoi?"

"A bent poem is not listened to, *Hmān.*"

"And how of love in a bent life?"

"How could the life of a *hnau* be bent?"

"Do you say, Hyoi, that there are no bent *hrossa?*"

Hyoi reflected. "I have heard," he said at last, "of something like what you mean. It is said that sometimes here and there a cub of certain age gets strange twists in him. I have heard of one that wanted to eat earth; there might, perhaps, be somewhere a *hross* likewise that wanted to have the years of love prolonged. I have not heard of it, but it might be. I have heard of something stranger. There is a poem about a *hross* who lived long ago, in another *handramit,* who saw things all made two — two suns in the sky, two heads on a neck; and last of all they say that he fell into such a frenzy that he desired two mates. I do not ask you to believe it, but that is the story: that he loved two *hressni.*"

Ransom pondered this. Here, un-less Hyoi was deceiving him, was a species naturally continent, naturally monogamous. And yet, was it so strange? Some animals, he knew, had regular breeding seasons; and if nature could perform the miracle of turning the sexual impulse outward at all, why could she not go further and fix it, not morally but instinctively, to a single object. He even remembered dimly having heard that some terrestrial animals, some of the "lower" animals, were naturally monogamous. Among the *hrossa,* anyway, it was obvious that unlimited breeding and promiscuity were as rare as the rarest perversions. At last it dawned upon him that it was not they, but his own species, that were the puzzle. That the *hrossa* should have such instincts was mildly surprising; but how came it that the instincts of the *hrossa* so closely resembled the unattained ideals of that far-divided species Man whose instincts were so deplorably different? What was the history of Man? But Hyoi was speaking again.

"Undoubtedly," he said. "Maleldil made us so. How could there ever be enough to eat if everyone had twenty young? And how could we endure to live and let time pass if we were always crying for one day or one year to come back — if we did not know that every day in a life fills the whole life with expectation and memory and that these *are* that day?"

"All the same," said Ransom, unconsciously nettled on behalf of his own world, "Maleldil has let in the *hnakra.*"

"Oh, but that is so different. I long to kill this *hnakra* as he also longs to kill me. I hope that my ship will be the first and I first in my ship with my straight spear when the black jaws snap. And if he kills me, my people will mourn and my brothers will desire still more to kill him. But they will not wish that there were no *hnéraki;* nor do I. How can I make you understand, when you do not understand the poets? The *hnakra* is our enemy, but he is also our beloved. We feel in our hearts his joy as he looks down from the mountain of water in the north where he was born; we leap with him when he jumps the falls; and when winter comes, and the lake smokes higher than our heads, it is with his eyes that we see it and know that his roaming time is come. We hang images of him in our houses, and the sign of all the *hrossa* is a *hnakra.* In him the spirit of the valley lives; and our young play at being *hnéraki* as soon as they can splash in the shallows."

"And then he kills them?"

"Not often them. The *hrossa* would be bent *hrossa* if they let him get so near. Long before he had come down so far we should have sought him out. No, *Hmān,* it is not a few deaths roving the world around him that make a *hnau* miserable. It is a bent *hnau* that would blacken the world. And I say also this. I do not think the forest would be so bright, nor the water so warm, nor love so sweet, if there were no danger in the lakes. I will tell you a day in my life that has shaped me; such a day as comes only once, like love, or serving Oyarsa in Meldilorn. Then I was young, not much more than a cub, when I went far, far up the *handramit* to the land where stars shine at midday and even water is cold. A great waterfall I climbed. I stood on the shore of Balki the pool, which is the place of most awe in all worlds. The walls of it go up for ever and ever, and huge and holy images are cut in them, the work of old times. There is the fall called the Mountain of Water. Because I have stood there alone, Maleldil and I, for even Oyarsa sent me no word, my heart has been higher, my song deeper, all my days. But do you think it would have been so unless I had known that in Balki *hnéraki* dwelled? There I drank life because death was in the pool. That was the best of drinks save one."

"What one?" asked Ransom.

"Death itself in the day I drink it and go to Maleldil."

Shortly after that they rose and resumed their work. The sun was declining as they came back through the wood. It occurred to Ransom to ask Hyoi a question.

"Hyoi," he said, "it comes into my head that when I first saw you, and before you saw me, you were already speaking. That was how I knew that you were *hnau,* for otherwise I should have thought you a beast, and run away. But who were you speaking to?"

"To an *eldil.*"

"What is that? I saw no one."

"Are there no *eldila* in your world, *Hmān?* That must be strange."

"But what are they?"

"They come from Oyarsa — they are, I suppose, a kind of *hnau.*"

"As we came out to-day I passed a child who said she was talking to an *eldil,* but I could see nothing."

"One can see by looking at your eyes, *Hmān,* that they are different from ours. But *eldila* are hard to see. They are not like us. Light goes through them. You must be looking in the right place and the right time; and that is not likely to come about unless the *eldil* wishes to be seen. Sometimes you can mistake them for a sunbeam or even a moving of the leaves; but when you look again you see that it was an *eldil* and that it is gone. But whether your eyes can ever see them I do not know. The *séroni* would know that."

Chapter **13**

The whole village was astir next morning before the sunlight — already visible on the *harandra* — had penetrated the forest. By the light of the cooking-fires Ransom saw an incessant activity of *hrossa.* The females were pouring out steaming food from clumsy pots; Hnohra was directing the transportation of piles of spears to the boats; Hyoi, in the midst of a group of the most experienced hunters, was talking too rapidly and too technically for Ransom to follow; parties were arriving from the neighbouring villages; and the cubs, squealing with excitement, were running hither and thither among their elders.

He found that his own share in the hunt had been taken for granted. He was to be in Hyoi's boat, with Hyoi and Whin. The two *hrossa* would take it in turns to paddle, while Ransom and the disengaged *hross* would be in the bows. He understood the *hrossa* well enough now to know that they were making him the noblest offer in their power, and that Hyoi and Whin were each tormented by the fear lest he should be paddling when the *hnakra* appeared. A short time ago, in England, nothing would have seemed more impossible to Ransom than to accept the post of honour and danger in an attack upon an unknown but certainly deadly aquatic monster. Even more recently, when he had first fled from the *sorns,* or when he had lain pitying himself in the forest by night, it would hardly have been in his power to do what he was intending to do to-day. For his intention was clear. Whatever happened, he must show that the human species also were *hnau.* He was only too well aware that such resolutions might look very different when the moment came, but he felt an unwonted assurance that somehow or other he would be able to go through with it. It was necessary, and the necessary was always possible. Perhaps, too, there was something in the air he now breathed, or in the society of the *hrossa,* which had begun to work a change in him.

The lake was just giving back the first rays of the sun when he found himself kneeling side by side with Whin, as he had been told to, in the bows of Hyoi's ship, with a little pile of throwing-spears between his knees and one in his right hand, stiffening his body against the motion as Hyoi paddled them out into their place. At least a hundred boats were taking part in the hunt. They were in three parties. The central, and far the smallest, was to work its way up the current by which Hyoi and Ransom had descended after their first meeting. Longer ships than he had yet seen, eight-paddled ships, were used for this. The habit of the *hnakra* was to float down the current whenever he could; meeting the ships, he would presumably dart out of it into the still water to left or right. Hence while the central party slowly beat up the current, the light ships, paddling far faster, would cruise at will up and down either side of it to receive the quarry as soon as he broke what might be called his "cover." In this game numbers and intelligence were on the side of the

hrossa; the *hnakra* had speed on his side, and also invisibility, for he could swim under water. He was nearly invulnerable except through his open mouth. If the two hunters in the bows of the boat he made for muffed their shots, this was usually the last of them and of their boat.

In the light skirmishing parties there were two things a brave hunter could aim at. He could keep well back and close to the long-ships where the *hnakra* was most likely to break out, or he could get as far forward as possible in the hope of meeting the *hnakra* going at its full speed and yet untroubled by the hunt, and of inducing it, by a well-aimed spear, to leave the current then and there. One could thus anticipate the beaters and kill the beast — if that was how the matter ended — on one's own. This was the desire of Hyoi and Whin; and almost — so strongly they infected him — of Ransom. Hence, hardly had the heavy craft of the beaters begun their slow progress up-current amid a wall of foam when he found his own ship speeding northward as fast as Hyoi could drive her, already passing boat after boat and making for the freest water. The speed was exhilarating. In the cold morning the warmth of the blue expanse they were clearing was not unpleasant. Behind them arose, re-echoed from the remote rock pinnacles on either side of the valley, the bell-like, deep-mouthed voices of more than two hundred *hrossa,* more musical than a cry of hounds but closely akin to it in quality as in purport. Something long sleeping in the blood awoke in Ransom. It did not seem impossible at this moment that even he might be the *hnakra*-slayer; that the fame of **Hmān hnakrapunt** might be handed down to posterity in this world that knew no other man. But he had had such dreams before, and knew how they ended. Imposing humility on the newly risen riot of his feelings, he turned his eyes to the troubled water of the current which they were skirting, without entering, and watched intently.

For a long time nothing happened. He became conscious of the stiffness of his attitude and deliberately relaxed his muscles. Presently Whin reluctantly went aft to paddle, and Hyoi came forward to take his place. Almost as soon as the change had been effected, Hyoi spoke softly to him and said, without taking his eyes off the current:

"There is an *eldil* coming to us over the water."

Ransom could see nothing — or nothing that he could distinguish from imagination and the dance of sunlight on the lake. A moment later Hyoi spoke again, but not to him.

"What is it, sky-born?"

What happened next was the most uncanny experience Ransom had yet had on Malacandra. He heard the voice. It seemed to come out of the air, about a yard above his head, and it was almost an octave higher than the *hross's* — higher even than his own. He realized that a very little difference in his ear would have made the *eldil* as inaudible to him as it was invisible.

"It is the Man with you, Hyoi," said the voice. "He ought not to be there. He ought to be going to Oyarsa. Bent *hnau* of his own kind from Thulcandra are following him; he should go to Oyarsa. If they find him anywhere else there will be evil."

"He hears you, sky-born," said Hyoi. "And have you no message for my wife? You know what she wishes to be told."

"I have a message for Hleri," said the *eldil*. "But you will not be able to take it. I go to her now myself. All that is well. Only—let the Man go to Oyarsa."

There was a moment's silence.

"He is gone," said Whin. "And we have lost our share in the hunt."

"Yes," said Hyoi with a sigh. "We must put *Hmān* ashore and teach him the way to Meldilorn."

Ransom was not so sure of his courage but that one part of him felt an instant relief at the idea of any diversion from their present business. But the other part of him urged him to hold on to his new-found manhood; now or never — with such companions or with none — he must leave a deed on his memory instead of one more broken dream. It was in obedience to something like conscience that he exclaimed:

"No, no. There is time for that after the hunt. We must kill the *hnakra* first."

"Once an *eldil* has spoken," began Hyoi, when suddenly Whin gave a great cry (a "bark" Ransom would have called it three weeks ago) and pointed. There, not a furlong away, was the torpedo-like track of foam; and now, visible through a wall of foam, they caught the metallic glint of the monster's sides. Whin was paddling furiously. Hyoi threw and missed. As his first spear smote the water his second was already in the air. This time it must have touched the *hnakra*. He wheeled right out of the current. Ransom saw the great black pit of his mouth twice open and twice shut with its snap of shark-like teeth. He himself had thrown now — hurriedly, excitedly, with unpractised hand.

"Back," shouted Hyoi to Whin who was already backing water with every pound of his vast strength. Then all became confused. He heard Whin shout "Shore!" There came a shock that flung him forward almost into the *hnakra's* jaws and he found himself at the same moment up to his waist in water. It was at him the teeth were snapping. Then as he flung shaft after shaft into the great cavern of the gaping brute he saw Hyoi perched incredibly on its back — on its nose — bending forward and hurling from there. Almost at once the *hross* was dislodged and fell with a wide splash nearly ten yards away. But the *hnakra* was killed. It was wallowing on its side, bubbling out its black life. The water around him was dark and stank.

When he recollected himself they were all on shore, wet, steaming, trembling with exertion and embracing one another. It did not now seem strange to him to be clasped to a breast of wet fur. The breath of the *hrossa* which, though sweet, was not human breath, did not offend him. He was one with them. That difficulty which they, accustomed to more than one rational species, had perhaps never felt, was now overcome. They were all *hnau*. They had stood shoulder to shoulder in the face of an enemy, and the shapes of their heads no longer mattered. And he, even Ransom, had come through it and not been disgraced. He had grown up.

They were on a little promontory free of forest, on which they had run aground in the confusion of the fight. The wreckage of the boat and the corpse of the monster lay confused together in the water beside them. No sound from the rest of the hunting party was audible; they had been almost a mile ahead when they met the *hnakra*. All three sat down to recover their breath.

"So," said Hyoi, "we are *hnakra-punti*. This is what I have wanted all my life."

At that moment Ransom was deafened by a loud sound — a perfectly familiar sound which was the last thing he expected to hear. It was a terrestrial, human and civilized sound; it was even European. It was the crack of an English rifle; and Hyoi, at his feet, was struggling to rise and gasping. There was blood on the white weed where he struggled. Ransom dropped on his knees beside him. The huge body of the *hross* was too heavy for him to turn round. Whin helped him.

"Hyoi, can you hear me?" said Ransom with his face close to the round seal-like head. "Hyoi, it is through me that this has happened. It is the other *hmāna* who have hit you, the bent two that brought me to Malacandra. They can throw death at a distance with a thing they have made. I should have told you. We are all a bent race. We have come here to bring evil on Malacandra. We are only half *hnau* — Hyoi . . ." His speech died away into the inarticulate. He did not know the words for "forgive," or "shame," or "fault," hardly the word for "sorry." He could only stare into Hyoi's distorted face in speechless guilt. But the *hross* seemed to understand. It was trying to say something, and Ransom laid his ear close to the working mouth. Hyoi's dulling eyes were fixed on his own, but the expression of a *hross* was not even now perfectly intelligible to him.

"*Hnā — hmā,*" it muttered and then, at last, "*Hmān hnakrapunt.*" Then there came a contortion of the whole body, a gush of blood and saliva from the mouth; his arms gave way under the sudden dead weight of the sagging head, and Hyoi's face became as alien and animal as it had seemed at their first meeting. The glazed eyes and the slowly stiffening, bedraggled fur were like those of any dead beast found in an earthly wood.

Ransom resisted an infantile impulse to break out into imprecations on Weston and Devine. Instead he raised his eyes to meet those of Whin who was crouching — *hrossa* do not kneel — on the other side of the corpse.

"I am in the hands of your people, Whin," he said. "They must do as they will. But if they are wise they will kill me and certainly they will kill the other two."

"One does not kill *hnau,*" said Whin. "Only Oyarsa does that. But these other, where are they?"

Ransom glanced around. It was open on the promontory but thick wood came down to where it joined the mainland, perhaps two hundred yards away.

"Somewhere in the wood," he said. "Lie down, Whin, here where the ground is lowest. They may throw from their thing again."

He had some difficulty in making Whin do as he suggested. When both were lying in dead ground, their feet almost in the water, the *hross* spoke again.

"Why did they kill him?" he asked.

"They would not know he was *hnau,*" said Ransom. "I have told you that there is only one kind of *hnau* in our world. They would think he was a beast. If they thought that, they would kill him for pleasure, or in fear, or" (he hesitated) "because they were hungry. But I must tell you the truth, Whin. They would kill even a *hnau,* knowing it to be *hnau,* if they thought its death would serve them."

There was a short silence.

"I am wondering," said Ransom, "if they saw me. It is for me they are looking. Perhaps if I went to them they would be content and come no farther into your land. But why do they not come out of the wood to see what they have killed?"

"Our people are coming," said Whin, turning his head. Ransom looked back and saw the lake black with boats. The main body of the hunt would be with them in a few minutes.

"They are afraid of the *hrossa,*" said Ransom. "That is why they do not come out of the wood. I will go to them, Whin."

"No," said Whin. "I have been thinking. All this has come from not obeying the *eldil.* He said you were to go to Oyarsa. You ought to have been already on the road. You must go now."

"But that will leave the bent *hmāna* here. They may do more harm."

"They will not set on the *hrossa.* You have said they are afraid. It is more likely that we will come upon them. Never fear — they will not

see us or hear us. We will take them to Oyarsa. But you must go now, as the *eldil* said."

"Your people will think I have run away because I am afraid to look in their faces after Hyoi's death."

"It is not a question of thinking but of what an *eldil* says. This is cubs' talk. Now listen, and I will teach you the way."

The *hross* explained to him that five days' journey to the south the *handramit* joined another *handramit;* and three days' up this other *handramit* to west and north was Meldilorn and the seat of Oyarsa. But there was a shorter way, a mountain road, across the corner of the *harandra* between the two canyons, which would bring him down to Meldilorn on the second day. He must go into the wood before them and through it till he came to the mountain wall of the *handramit;* and he must work south along the roots of the mountains till he came to a road cut up between them. Up this he must go, and somewhere beyond the tops of the mountains he would come to the tower of Augray. Augray would help him. He could cut weed for his food before he left the forest and came into the rock country. Whin realized that Ransom might meet the other two *hmāna* as soon as he entered the wood.

"If they catch you," he said, "then it will be as you say, they will come no farther into our land. But it is better to be taken on your way to

Oyarsa than to stay here. And once you are on the way to him, I do not think he will let the bent ones stop you."

Ransom was by no means convinced that this was the best plan either for himself or for the *hrossa*. But the stupor of humiliation in which he had lain ever since Hyoi fell forbade him to criticize. He was anxious only to do whatever they wanted him to do, to trouble them as little as was now possible, and above all to get away. It was impossible to find out how Whin felt; and Ransom sternly repressed an insistent, whining impulse to renewed protestations and regrets, self-accusations that might elicit some word of pardon. Hyoi with his last breath had called him *hnakra*-slayer; that was forgiveness generous enough and with that he must be content. As soon as he had mastered the details of his route he bade farewell to Whin and advanced alone towards the forest.

For Study

1. In Chapter 11 we discover that the *hrossa* have no word for "bad" or "evil" and that their nearest equivalent for those terms is "bent." What insight into their world does this fact about their language give you? When does Ransom first pronounce his own kind to be bent?

2. In Ransom's discussion with the *hrossa* in Chapter 11, we learn of someone called "Maleldil the Young" and of someone with whom he lives

called "the Old One." In terms of the Christian religion, who would they be? On what evidence in the discussion do you base your answer?

3. What attributes constitute what the *hrossa* call *hnau*? Give reasons for your answer.

4. What is "sun's blood"? What has it to do with Ransom's being on Malacandra?

5. Discuss the distribution of skills among the *hnau* of Malacandra. Compare this with the distribution of skills among men.

6. Why is Ransom reluctant to tell a great deal about his own planet?

7. In Chapters 12 and 13, what has the author done, subtly, to prepare us for Hyoi's death and to help make this saddening event acceptable to us?

8. Discuss the ironies in this sentence in Chapter 13: "It was a terrestrial, human and civilized sound; it was even European."

9. At the close of Chapter 13, how is it suggested that even guilt and remorse can be self-indulgent?

For Writing

1. Discuss in a paper why Ransom is so astonished that there are three distinct rational species on Malacandra "and none of them had yet exterminated the other two." Why does he persist in assuming that one of the species must be master of the others?

2. Early in Chapter 12, Hyoi says, "A pleasure is full grown only when it is remembered." After considering the context of this statement, write a paper on the concepts it involves.

Chapter 14

Until he reached the wood Ransom found it difficult to think of anything except the possibility of another rifle bullet from Weston or Devine. He thought that they probably still wanted him alive rather than dead, and this, combined with the knowledge that a *hross* was watching him, enabled him to proceed with at least external composure. Even when he had entered the forest he felt himself in considerable danger. The long branchless stems made "cover" only if you were very far away from the enemy; and the enemy in this case might be very close. He became aware of a strong impulse to shout out to Weston and Devine and give himself up; it rationalized itself in the form that this would remove them from the district, as they would probably take him off to the *sorns* and leave the *hrossa* unmolested. But Ransom knew a little psychology and had heard of the hunted man's irrational instinct to give himself up — indeed, he had felt it himself in dreams. It was some such trick, he thought, that his nerves were now playing him. In any case he was determined henceforward to obey the *hrossa* or *eldila*. His efforts to rely on his own judgment in Malacandra had so far ended tragically enough. He made a strong resolution, defying in advance all changes of mood, that he

would faithfully carry out the journey to Meldilorn if it could be done.

This resolution seemed to him all the more certainly right because he had the deepest misgivings about that journey. He understood that the *harandra*, which he had to cross, was the home of the *sorns*. In fact he was walking of his own free will into the very trap that he had been trying to avoid ever since his arrival on Malacandra. (Here the first change of mood tried to raise its head. He thrust it down.) And even if he got through the *sorns* and reached Meldilorn, who or what might Oyarsa be? Oyarsa, Whin had ominously observed, did not share the *hrossa's* objection to shedding the blood of a *hnau*. And again, Oyarsa ruled *sorns* as well as *hrossa* and *pfifltriggi*. Perhaps he was simply the arch-*sorn*.[1] And now came the second change of mood. Those old terrestrial fears of some alien, cold intelligence, superhuman in power, sub-human in cruelty, which had utterly faded from his mind among the *hrossa*,

[1] arch-*sorn*: the prefix *arch-*, from Greek, means "chief." *Architect*, combining the Greek *archi* and *tektōn*, means "chief of the builders." The prefix occurs with the same meaning in *archbishop* and *archangel*. It is pronounced with the hard "k" sound before a vowel, with the soft "k" sound before a consonant. *Arch* occurs also as a suffix, as in *patriarch* and *matriarch*. Use your dictionary to find another important and common meaning for this prefix, as in *archaic* and *archaeology*. Do you see a relationship between these meanings?

rose clamouring for readmission. But he strode on. He was going to Meldilorn. It was not possible, he told himself, that the *hrossa* should obey any evil or monstrous creature; and they had told him — or had they? he was not quite sure — that Oyarsa was not a *sorn*. Was Oyarsa a god? — perhaps that very idol to whom the *sorns* wanted to sacrifice him. But the *hrossa*, though they said strange things about him, clearly denied that he was a god. There was one God, according to them, Maleldil the Young; nor was it possible to imagine Hyoi or Hnohra worshipping a bloodstained idol. Unless, of course, the *hrossa* were after all under the thumb of the *sorns*, superior to their masters in all the qualities that human beings value, but intellectually inferior to them and dependent on them. It would be a strange but not an inconceivable world; heroism and poetry at the bottom, cold scientific intellect above it, and overtopping all some dark superstition which scientific intellect, helpless against the revenge of the emotional depths it had ignored, had neither will nor power to remove. A mumbo-jumbo . . . but Ransom pulled himself up. He knew too much now to talk that way. He and all his class would have called the *eldila* a superstition if they had been merely described to them, but now he had heard the voice himself. No, Oyarsa was a real person if he was a person at all.

He had now been walking for about an hour, and it was nearly midday. No difficulty about his direction had yet occurred; he had merely to keep going uphill and he was certain of coming out of the forest to the mountain wall sooner or later. Meanwhile he felt remarkably well, though greatly chastened in mind. The silent, purple half-light of the woods spread all around him as it had spread on the first day he spent in Malacandra, but everything else was changed. He looked back on that time as on a nightmare, on his own mood at that time as a sort of sickness. Then all had been whimpering, unanalysed, self-nourishing, self-consuming dismay. Now, in the clear light of an accepted duty, he felt fear indeed, but with it a sober sense of confidence in himself and in the world, and even an element of pleasure. It was the difference between a landsman in a sinking ship and a horseman on a bolting horse: either may be killed, but the horseman is an agent as well as a patient.

About an hour after noon he suddenly came out of the wood into bright sunshine. He was only twenty yards from the almost perpendicular bases of the mountain spires, too close to them to see their tops. A sort of valley ran up in the re-entrant between two of them at the place where he had emerged: an unclimbable valley consisting of a single concave sweep of stone, which in its lower parts ascended steeply as the roof of a house and farther up seemed almost vertical.

At the top it even looked as if it hung over a bit, like a tidal wave of stone at the very moment of breaking; but this, he thought, might be an illusion. He wondered what the *hrossa's* idea of a road might be.

He began to work his way southward along the narrow, broken ground between wood and mountain. Great spurs of the mountains had to be crossed every few moments, and even in that lightweight world it was intensely tiring. After about half an hour he came to a stream. Here he went a few paces into the forest, cut himself an ample supply of the groundweed, and sat down beside the water's edge for lunch. When he had finished he filled his pockets with what he had not eaten and proceeded.

He began soon to be anxious about his road, for if he could make the top at all he could do it only by daylight, and the middle of the afternoon was approaching. But his fears were unnecessary. When it came it was unmistakable. An open way through the wood appeared on the left — he must be somewhere behind the *hross* village now — and on the right he saw the road, a single ledge or, in places, a trench, cut sidewise and upwards across the sweep of such a valley as he had seen before. It took his breath away — the insanely steep, hideously narrow staircase without steps, leading up and up from where he stood to where it was an almost invisible thread on the pale green surface of the rock. But there was no time to stand and look at it. He was a poor judge of heights, but he had no doubt that the top of the road was removed from him by a more than Alpine distance. It would take him at least till sundown to reach it. Instantly he began the ascent.

Such a journey would have been impossible on earth; the first quarter of an hour would have reduced a man of Ransom's build and age to exhaustion. Here he was at first delighted with the ease of his movement, and then staggered by the gradient and length of the climb which, even under Malacandrian conditions, soon bowed his back and gave him an aching chest and trembling knees. But this was not the worst. He heard already a singing in his ears, and noticed that despite his labour there was no sweat on his forehead. The cold, increasing at every step, seemed to sap his vitality worse than any heat could have done. Already his lips were cracked; his breath, as he panted, showed like a cloud; his fingers were numb. He was cutting his way up into a silent arctic world, and had already passed from an English to a Lapland winter. It frightened him, and he decided that he must rest here or not at all; a hundred paces more and if he sat down he would sit for ever. He squatted on the road for a few minutes, slapping his body with his arms. The landscape was terrifying. Already the *handramit* which had made his world for so many weeks was only a thin purple cleft sunk amidst the boundless level desolation of the *harandra* which now, on the farther side, showed clearly between and above the mountain peaks. But long before he was rested he knew that he must go on or die.

The world grew stranger. Among the *hrossa* he had almost lost the feeling of being on a strange planet; here it returned upon him with desolating force. It was no longer "the world," scarcely even "a world": it was a planet, a star, a waste place in the universe, millions of miles from the world of men. It was impossible to recall what he had felt about Hyoi, or Whin, or the *eldila,* or Oyarsa. It seemed fantastic to have thought he had duties to such hobgoblins — if they were not hallucinations — met in the wilds of space. He had nothing to do with them: he was a man. Why had Weston and Devine left him like this?

But all the time the old resolution, taken when he could still think, was driving him up the road. Often he forgot where he was going, and why. The movement became a mechanical rhythm — from weariness to stillness, from stillness to unbearable cold, from cold to motion again. He noticed that the *handramit* — now an insignificant part of the landscape — was full of a sort of haze. He had never seen a fog while he was living there. Perhaps that was what the air of the *handramit* looked like from above; certainly it was different air from this. There was something more wrong with his lungs and heart than even the cold and the exertion accounted for. And though there was no snow, there was an extraordinary brightness. The light was increasing, sharpening and growing whiter; and the sky was a much darker blue than he had ever seen on Malacandra. Indeed, it was darker than blue; it was almost black, and the jagged spires of rock standing against it were like his mental picture of a lunar landscape. Some stars were visible.

Suddenly he realized the meaning of these phenomena. There was very little air above him: he was near the end of it. The Malacandrian atmosphere lay chiefly in the *handramits;* the real surface of the planet was naked or thinly clad. The stabbing sunlight and the black sky above him were that "heaven" out of which he had dropped into the Malacandrian world, already showing through the last thin veil of air. If the top were more than a hundred feet away, it would be where no man could breathe at all. He wondered whether the *hrossa* had different lungs and had sent him by a road that meant death for man. But even while he thought of this he took note that those jagged peaks blazing in sunlight against an almost black sky were level with him. He was no longer ascending. The road ran on before him in a kind of shallow ravine bounded on his left by the tops of the highest rock pinnacles and on his right by a smooth ascending swell of stone that ran up to the true *harandra*. And where he was he could still breathe, though gasping, dizzy and in pain. The blaze in his eyes was worse. The sun was setting. The *hrossa* must have foreseen this; they could not live, any more than he, on the *harandra* by night. Still staggering forward, he looked about him for any sign of Augray's tower, whatever Augray might be.

Doubtless he exaggerated the time during which he thus wandered and watched the shadows from the rocks lengthening towards him. It cannot really have been long before he saw a light ahead — a light which showed how dark the surrounding landscape had become. He tried to run but his body would not respond. Stumbling in haste and weakness, he made for the light; thought he had reached it and found that it was far farther off than he had supposed; almost despaired; staggered on again, and came at last to what seemed a cavern mouth. The light within was an unsteady one and a delicious wave of warmth smote on his face. It was firelight. He came into the mouth of the cave and then, unsteadily, round the fire and into the interior, and stood still blinking in the light. When at last he could see, he discerned a smooth chamber of green rock, very lofty. There were two things in it. One of them, dancing on the wall and roof, was the

huge, angular shadow of a *sorn;* the other, crouched beneath it, was the *sorn* himself.

Chapter **15**

"Come in, Small One," boomed the *sorn*. "Come in and let me look at you."

Now that he stood face to face with the spectre that had haunted him ever since he set foot on Malacandra, Ransom felt a surprising indifference. He had no idea what might be coming next, but he was determined to carry out his programme; and in the meantime the warmth and more breathable air were a heaven in themselves. He came in, well in past the fire, and answered the *sorn*. His own voice sounded to him a shrill treble.

"The *hrossa* have sent me to look for Oyarsa," he said.

The *sorn* peered at him. "You are not from this world," it said suddenly.

"No," replied Ransom, and sat down. He was too tired to explain.

"I think you are from Thulcandra, Small One," said the *sorn*.

"Why?" said Ransom.

"You are small and thick and that is how the animals ought to be made in a heavier world. You cannot come from Glundandra, for it is so heavy that if any animals could live there they would be flat like plates — even you, Small One, would break if you stood up on that world. I do not think you are from Perelandra, for it must be very hot; if any came from there they would not live when they arrived here. So I conclude you are from Thulcandra."

"The world I come from is called Earth by those who live there," said Ransom. "And it is much warmer than this. Before I came into your cave I was nearly dead with cold and thin air."

The *sorn* made a sudden movement with one of its long fore-limbs. Ransom stiffened (though he did not allow himself to retreat), for the creature might be going to grab him. In fact, its intentions were kindly. Stretching back into the cave, it took from the wall what looked like a cup. Then Ransom saw that it was attached to a length of flexible tube. The *sorn* put it into his hands.

"Smell on this," it said. "The *hrossa* also need it when they pass this way."

Ransom inhaled and was instantly refreshed. His painful shortness of breath was eased and the tension of chest and temples was relaxed. The *sorn* and the lighted cavern, hitherto vague and dream-like to his eyes, took on a new reality.

"Oxygen?" he asked; but naturally the English word meant nothing to the *sorn*.

"Are you called Augray?" he asked.

"Yes," said the *sorn*. "What are you called?"

"The animal I am is called Man, and therefore the *hrossa* call me *Hmān*. But my own name is Ransom."

"Man — Ren-soom," said the *sorn*. He noticed that it spoke differently from the *hrossa*, without any suggestion of their persistent initial H.

It was sitting on its long, wedge-shaped buttocks with its feet drawn close up to it. A man in the same posture would have rested his chin on his knees, but the *sorn's* legs were too long for that. Its knees rose high above its shoulders on each side of its head — grotesquely suggestive of huge ears — and the head, down between them, rested its chin on the protruding breast. The creature seemed to have either a double chin or a beard; Ransom could not make out which in the firelight. It was mainly white or cream in colour and seemed to be clothed down to the ankles in some soft substance that reflected the light. On the long fragile shanks, where the creature was closest to him, he saw that this was some natural kind of coat. It was not like fur but more like feathers. In fact it was almost exactly like feathers. The whole animal, seen at close quarters, was less terrifying than he had expected, and even a little smaller. The face, it was true, took a good deal of getting used to — it was too long, too solemn and too colourless, and it was much more unpleasantly like a human face than any inhuman creature's face ought to be. Its eyes, like those of all very large creatures, seemed too small for it. But it was more grotesque than horrible. A new conception of the *sorns* began to arise in his mind: the ideas of "giant" and "ghost" receded behind those of "goblin" and "gawk."

"Perhaps you are hungry, Small One," it said.

Ransom was. The *sorn* rose with strange spidery movements and began going to and fro about the cave, attended by its thin goblin shadow. It brought him the usual vegetable foods of Malacandra, and strong drink, with the very welcome addition of a smooth brown substance which revealed itself to nose, eye and palate, in defiance of all probability, as cheese. Ransom asked what it was.

The *sorn* began to explain painfully how the female of some animals secreted a fluid for the nourishment of its young, and would have gone on to describe the whole process of milking and cheese-making, if Ransom had not interrupted it.

"Yes, yes," he said. "We do the same on Earth. What is the beast you use?"

"It is a yellow beast with a long neck. It feeds on the forests that grow in the *handramit*. The young ones of our people who are not yet fit for much else drive the beasts down there in the mornings and follow them while they feed; then before night they drive them back and put them in the caves."

For a moment Ransom found something reassuring in the thought that the *sorns* were shepherds. Then he remembered that Cyclops in Homer [1] plied the same trade.

"I think I have seen one of your people at this very work," he said. "But the *hrossa* — they let you tear up their forests?"

"Why should they not?"

"Do you rule the *hrossa?*"

"Oyarsa rules them."

"And who rules you?"

"Oyarsa."

"But you know more than the *hrossa?*"

"The *hrossa* know nothing except about poems and fish and making things grow out of the ground."

"And Oyarsa — is he a *sorn?*"

"No, no, Small One. I have told you he rules all *nau*" (so he pronounced *hnau*), "and everything in Malacandra."

"I do not understand this Oyarsa," said Ransom. "Tell me more."

"Oyarsa does not die," said the *sorn*. "And he does not breed. He is the one of his kind who was put into Malacandra to rule it when Malacandra was made. His body is not like ours, nor yours; it is hard to see and the light goes through it."

[1] **Cyclops in Homer:** In ancient Greek religion, a Cyclops was one of a group of one-eyed giants. In the *Odyssey* by Homer (perhaps c. 900 B.C.), Odysseus and his friends were captured by Polyphemus, a Cyclops.

"Like an *eldil?*"

"Yes, he is the greatest of *eldila* who ever came to a *handra.*"

"What are these *eldila?*"

"Do you tell me, Small One, that there are no *eldila* in your world?"

"Not that I know of. But what are *eldila,* and why can I not see them? Have they no bodies?"

"Of course they have bodies. There are a great many bodies you cannot see. Every animal's eyes see some things but not others. Do you not know of many kinds of body in Thulcandra?"

Ransom tried to give the *sorn* some idea of the terrestrial terminology of solids, liquids and gases. It listened with great attention.

"That is not the way to say it," it replied. "Body is movement. If it is at one speed, you smell something; if at another, you hear a sound; if at another, you see a sight; if at another, you neither see nor hear nor smell, nor know the body in any way. But mark this, Small One, that the two ends meet."

"How do you mean?"

"If movement is faster, then that which moves is more nearly in two places at once."

"That is true."

"But if the movement were faster still — it is difficult, for you do not know many words — you see that if you made it faster and faster, in the end the moving thing would be in all places at once, Small One."

"I think I see that."

"Well, then, that is the thing at the top of all bodies — so fast that it is at rest, so truly body that it has ceased being body at all. But we will not talk of that. Start from where we are, Small One. The swiftest thing that touches our senses is light. We do not truly see light, we only see slower things lit by it, so that for us light is on the edge — the last thing we know before things become too swift for us. But the body of an *eldil* is a movement swift as light; you may say its body is made of light, but not of that which is light for the *eldil.* His 'light' is a swifter movement which for us is nothing at all; and what we call light is for him a thing like water, a visible thing, a thing he can touch and bathe in — even a dark thing when not illumined by the swifter. And what we call firm things — flesh and earth — seem to him thinner, and harder to see, than our light, and more like clouds, and nearly nothing. To us the *eldil* is a thin, half-real body that can go through walls and rocks: to himself he goes through them because he is solid and firm and they are like cloud. And what is true light to him and fills the heaven, so that he will plunge into the rays of the sun to refresh himself from it, is to us the black nothing in the sky at night. These things are not strange, Small One, though they are beyond our senses. But it is strange that the *eldila* never visit Thulcandra."

"Of that I am not certain," said Ransom. It had dawned on him that the recurrent human tradition of bright, elusive people sometimes appearing on the Earth — *albs, devas* and the like — might after all have another explanation than the anthropologists had yet given. True, it would turn the universe rather oddly inside out; but his experiences in the space-ship had prepared him for some such operation.

"Why does Oyarsa send for me?" he asked.

"Oyarsa has not told me," said the *sorn*. "But doubtless he would want to see any stranger from another *handra*."

"We have no Oyarsa in my world," said Ransom.

"That is another proof," said the *sorn*, "that you come from Thulcandra, the silent planet."

"What has that to do with it?"

The *sorn* seemed surprised. "It is not very likely if you had an Oyarsa that he would never speak to ours."

"Speak to yours? But how could he — it is millions of miles away."

"Oyarsa would not think of it like that."

"Do you mean that he ordinarily receives messages from other planets?"

"Once again, he would not say it that way. Oyarsa would not say that he lives on Malacandra and that another Oyarsa lives on another earth. For him Malacandra is only a place in the heavens; it is in the heavens that he and the others live. Of course they talk together. . . ."

Ransom's mind shied away from the problem; he was getting sleepy and thought he must be misunderstanding the *sorn*.

"I think I must sleep, Augray," he said. "And I do not know what you are saying. Perhaps, too, I do not come from what you call Thulcandra."

"We will both sleep presently," said the *sorn*. "But first I will show you Thulcandra."

It rose and Ransom followed it into the back of the cave. Here he found a little recess and running up within it a winding stair. The steps, hewn for *sorns,* were too high for a man to climb with any comfort, but using hands and knees he managed to hobble up. The *sorn* preceded him. Ransom did not understand the light, which seemed to come from some small round object which the creature held in its hand. They went up a long way, almost as if they were climbing up the inside of a hollow mountain. At last, breathless, he found himself in a dark but warm chamber of rock, and heard the *sorn* saying:

"She is still well above the southern horizon." It directed his attention to something like a small window. Whatever it was, it did not appear to work like an earthly telescope, Ransom thought; though an attempt, made next day, to explain the principles of the telescope to the *sorn* threw grave doubts on his own ability to discern the difference. He leaned forward with his elbows on the sill of the aperture and looked. He saw perfect blackness and, floating in the centre of it, seemingly an arm's length away, a bright disk about the size of a half-crown. Most of its surface was featureless, shining silver; towards the bottom markings appeared, and below them a white cap, just as he had seen the polar caps in astronomical photographs of Mars. He wondered for a moment if it was Mars he was looking at; then, as his eyes took in the markings better, he recognized what they were — Northern Europe and a piece of North America. They were upside down with the North Pole at the bottom of the picture and this somehow shocked him. But it was Earth he was seeing — even, perhaps, England, though the picture shook a little and his eyes were quickly getting tired, and he could not be certain that he was not imagining it. It was all there in that little disk — London, Athens, Jerusalem, Shakespeare. There everyone had lived and everything had happened; and there, presumably, his pack was still lying in the porch of an empty house near Sterk.

"Yes," he said dully to the *sorn*. "That is my world." It was the bleakest moment in all his travels.

Chapter **16**

Ransom awoke next morning with the vague feeling that a great weight had been taken off his mind. Then he remembered that he was the guest of a *sorn* and that the creature he had been avoiding ever since he landed had turned out to be as amicable as the *hrossa,* though he was far from feeling the same affection for it. Nothing then remained to be afraid of in Malacandra except Oyarsa . . . "The last fence," thought Ransom.

Augray gave him food and drink.

"And now," said Ransom, "how shall I find my way to Oyarsa?"

"I will carry you," said the *sorn*. "You are too small a one to make the journey yourself and I will gladly go to Meldilorn. The *hrossa* should not have sent you this way. They do not seem to know from looking at an animal what sort of lungs it has and what it can do. It is just like a *hross*. If you died on the *harandra* they would have made a poem about the gallant *hmān* and how the sky grew black and the cold stars shone and he journeyed on and journeyed on; and they would have put in a fine speech for you to say as you were dying . . . and all this would seem to them just as good as if they had used a little forethought and saved your life by sending you the easier way round."

"I like the *hrossa*," said Ransom a little stiffly. "And I think the way they talk about death is the right way."

"They are right not to fear it, Ren-soom, but they do not seem to look at it reasonably as part of the very nature of our bodies — and therefore often avoidable at times when they would never see how to avoid it. For example, this has saved the life of many a *hross*, but a *hross* would not have thought of it."

He showed Ransom a flask with a tube attached to it, and at the end of the tube a cup, obviously an apparatus for administering oxygen to oneself.

"Smell on it as you have need, Small One," said the *sorn*. "And close it up when you do not."

Augray fastened the thing on his back and gave the tube over his shoulder into his hand. Ransom could not restrain a shudder at the touch of the *sorn's* hands upon his body; they were fan-shaped, seven-fingered, mere skin over bone like a bird's leg, and quite cold. To divert his mind from such reactions he asked where the apparatus was made, for he had as yet seen nothing remotely like a factory or a laboratory.

"We thought it," said the *sorn*, "and the *pfifltriggi* made it."

"Why do they make them?" said Ransom. He was trying once more, with his insufficient vocabulary, to find out the political and economic framework of Malacandrian life.

"They like making things," said Augray. "It is true they like best the making of things that are only good to look at and of no use. But sometimes when they are tired of that they will make things for us, things we have thought, provided they are difficult enough. They have not patience to make easy things however useful they would be. But let us begin our journey. You shall sit on my shoulder."

The proposal was unexpected and alarming, but seeing that the *sorn* had already crouched down, Ransom felt obliged to climb on to the plume-like surface of its shoulder, to seat himself beside the long, pale face, casting his right arm as far as it would go round the huge neck, and to compose himself as well as he could for this precarious mode of travel. The giant rose cautiously to a standing position and he found himself looking down on the landscape from a height of about eighteen feet.

"Is all well, Small One?" it asked.

"Very well," Ransom answered, and the journey began.

Its gait was perhaps the least human thing about it. It lifted its feet very high and set them down very gently. Ransom was reminded alternately of a cat stalking, a strutting barn-door fowl, and a high-stepping carriage horse; but the movement was not really like that of any terrestrial animal. For the passenger it was surprisingly comfortable. In a few minutes he had lost all sense of what was dizzying or unnatural in his position. Instead, ludicrous and even tender associations came crowding into his mind. It was like riding an elephant at the zoo in boyhood — like riding on his father's back at a still earlier age. It was fun. They seemed to be doing between six and seven miles an hour. The cold, though severe, was endurable; and thanks to the oxygen he had little difficulty with his breathing.

The landscape which he saw from his high, swaying post of observation was a solemn one. The *handramit* was nowhere to be seen. On each side of the shallow gully in which they were walking, a world of naked, faintly greenish rock, interrupted with wide patches of red, extended to the horizon. The heaven, darkest blue where the rock met it, was almost black at the zenith, and looking in any direction where sunlight did not blind him, he could see the stars. He learned from the *sorn* that he was right in thinking they were near the limits of the breathable. Already on the mountain fringe that borders the *harandra* and walls the *handramit,* or in the narrow depression along which their road led them, the air is of Himalayan rarity, ill breathing for a *hross,* and a few hundred feet higher, on the *harandra* proper, the true surface of the planet, it admits no life. Hence the brightness through which they walked was almost that of heaven — celestial light hardly at all tempered with an atmospheric veil.

The shadow of the *sorn,* with Ransom's shadow on its shoulder, moved over the uneven rock unnaturally distinct like the shadow of a tree before the headlights of a car; and the rock beyond the shadow hurt his eyes. The remote horizon seemed but an arm's length away. The fissures and moulding of distant slopes were clear as the background of a primitive picture made before men learned perspective. He was on the very frontier of that heaven he had known in the space-ship, and rays that the air-enveloped worlds cannot taste were once more at work upon his body. He felt the old lift of the heart, the soaring solemnity, the sense, at once sober and ecstatic, of life and power offered in masked and unmeasured abundance. If there had been air enough in his lungs he would have laughed aloud. And now, even in the immediate landscape, beauty was drawing near. Over the edge of the valley, as if it had frothed down from the true *harandra,* came great curves of the rose-tinted cumular stuff which he had seen so often from a distance. Now on a nearer view they appeared hard as stone in substance, but puffed above and stalked beneath like vegetation. His original simile of giant cauliflower turned out to be surprisingly correct — stone cauliflowers the size of cathedrals and the colour of pale rose. He asked the *sorn* what it was.

"It is the old forests of Malacandra," said Augray. "Once there was air on the *harandra* and it was warm. To this day, if you could get up there and live, you would see it all covered with the bones of ancient creatures; it was once full of life and noise. It was then these forests grew, and in and out among their stalks went a people that have vanished from the world these many thousand years. They were covered not with fur but with a coat like mine. They did not go in the water swimming or on the ground walking; they glided in the air on broad flat limbs which kept them up. It is said they were great singers, and in those days the red forests echoed with their music. Now the forests have become stone and only *eldila* can go among them."

"We still have such creatures in our world," said Ransom. "We call them birds. Where was Oyarsa when all this happened to the *harandra?*"

"Where he is now."

"And he could not prevent it?"

"I do not know. But a world is not made to last for ever, much less a race; that is not Maleldil's way."

As they proceeded the petrified forests grew more numerous, and often for half an hour at a time the whole horizon of the lifeless, almost airless, waste blushed like an English garden in summer. They passed many caves where, as Augray told him, *sorns* lived; sometimes a high cliff would be perforated with countless holes to the very top and unidentifiable noises came hollowly from within. "Work" was in progress, said the *sorn,* but of what kind it could not make him understand. Its vocabulary was very different from that of the *hrossa.* Nowhere did he see anything like a village or city of *sorns,* who were apparently solitary not social creatures. Once or twice a long pallid face would show from a cavern mouth and exchange a horn-like greeting with the travel-lers, but for the most part the long valley, the rock-street of the silent people, was still and empty as the *harandra* itself.

Only towards afternoon, as they were about to descend into a dip of the road, they met three *sorns* together coming towards them down the opposite slope. They seemed to Ransom to be rather skating than walking. The lightness of their world and the perfect poise of their bodies allowed them to lean forward at right angles to the slope, and they came swiftly down like full-rigged ships before a fair wind. The grace of their movement, their lofty stature, and the softened glancing of the sunlight on their feathery sides, effected a final transformation in Ransom's feelings towards their race. "Ogres" he had called them when they first met his eyes as he struggled in the grip of Weston and Devine; "Titans" or "Angels" he now thought would have been a better word. Even the faces, it seemed to him, he had not then seen aright. He had thought them spectral when they were only august, and his human reaction to their lengthened severity of line and profound stillness of expression now appeared to him not so much cowardly as vulgar. So might Parmenides [1] or Confucius [2] look to the eyes of a Cockney schoolboy! The great white creatures sailed to-

[1] **Parmenides:** Greek philosopher of the fifth century B.C.

[2] **Confucius:** Chinese philosopher (c. 551–479? B.C.).

wards Ransom and Augray and dipped like trees and passed.

In spite of the cold — which made him often dismount and take a spell on foot — he did not wish for the end of the journey; but Augray had his own plans and halted for the night long before sundown at the home of an older *sorn*. Ransom saw well enough that he was brought there to be shown to a great scientist. The cave, or, to speak more correctly, the system of excavations, was large and many-chambered, and contained a multitude of things that he did not understand. He was specially interested in a collection of rolls seemingly of skin, covered with characters, which were clearly books; but he gathered that books were few in Malacandra.

"It is better to remember," said the *sorns*.

When Ransom asked if valuable secrets might not thus be lost, they replied that Oyarsa always remembered them and would bring them to light if he thought fit.

"The *hrossa* used to have many books of poetry," they added. "But now they have fewer. They say that the writing of books destroys poetry."

Their host in these caverns was attended by a number of other *sorns* who seemed to be in some way subordinate to him; Ransom thought at first that they were servants but decided later that they were pupils or assistants.

The evening's conversation was not such as would interest a terrestrial reader, for the *sorns* had determined that Ransom should not ask, but answer, questions. Their questioning was very different from the rambling, imaginative inquiries of the *hrossa*. They worked systematically from the geology of Earth to its present geography, and thence in turn to flora, fauna, human history, languages, politics and arts. When they found that Ransom could tell them no more on a given subject — and this happened pretty soon in most of their inquiries — they dropped it at once and went on to the next. Often they drew out of him indirectly much more knowledge than he consciously possessed, apparently working from a wide background of general science. A casual remark about trees when Ransom was trying to explain the manufacture of paper would fill up for them a gap in his sketchy answers to their botanical questions; his account of terrestrial navigation might illuminate mineralogy; and his description of the steam-engine gave them a better knowledge of terrestrial air and water than Ransom had ever had. He had decided from the outset that he would be quite frank, for he now felt that it would be not *hnau,* and also that it would be unavailing, to do otherwise. They were astonished at what he had to tell them of human history — of war, slavery and prostitution.

"It is because they have no Oyarsa," said one of the pupils.

"It is because every one of them wants to be a little Oyarsa himself," said Augray.

"They cannot help it," said the old *sorn*. "There must be rule, yet how can creatures rule themselves? Beasts must be ruled by *hnau* and *hnau* by *eldila* and *eldila* by Maleldil. These creatures have no *eldila*. They are like one trying to lift himself by his own hair — or one trying to see over a whole country when he is on a level with it — like a female trying to beget young on herself."

Two things about our world particularly stuck in their minds. One was the extraordinary degree to which problems of lifting and carrying things absorbed our energy. The other was the fact that we had only one kind of *hnau:* they thought this must have far-reaching effects in the narrowing of sympathies and even of thought.

"Your thought must be at the mercy of your blood," said the old *sorn*. "For you cannot compare it with thought that floats on a different blood."

It was a tiring and very disagreeable conversation for Ransom. But when at last he lay down to sleep it was not of the human nakedness nor of his own ignorance that he was thinking. He thought only of the old forests of Malacandra and of what it might mean to grow up seeing always so few miles away a land of colour that could never be reached and had once been inhabited.

Chapter 17

Early next day Ransom again took his seat on Augray's shoulder. For more than an hour they travelled through the same bright wilderness. Far to the north the sky was luminous with a cloud-like mass of dull red or ochre; it was very large and drove furiously westward about ten miles above the waste. Ransom, who had yet seen no cloud in the Malacandrian sky, asked what it was. The *sorn* told him it was sand caught up from the great northern deserts by the winds of that terrible country. It was often thus carried, sometimes at a height of seventeen miles, to fall again, perhaps in a *handramit,* as a choking and blinding duststorm. The sight of it moving with menace in the naked sky served to remind Ransom that they were indeed on the *outside* of Malacandra — no longer dwelling in a world but crawling the surface of a strange planet. At last the cloud seemed to drop and burst far on the western horizon, where a glow, not unlike that of a conflagration, remained visible until a turn of the valley hid all that region from his view.

The same turn opened a new prospect to his eyes. What lay before him looked at first strangely like an earthly landscape — a landscape of grey downland ridges rising and falling like waves of the sea. Far beyond, cliffs and spires of the familiar green rock rose against the dark blue sky. A moment later he saw that what he had taken for downlands was but the ridged and furrowed surface of a blue-grey valley mist — a mist which would not appear a mist at all when they descended into the *handramit*. And already, as their road began descending, it was less visible and the many-coloured pattern of the low country showed vaguely through it. The descent grew quickly steeper; like the jagged teeth of a giant — a giant with very bad teeth — the topmost peaks of the mountain wall down which they must pass loomed up over the edge of their gully. The look of the sky and the quality of the light were infinitesimally changed. A moment later they stood on the edge of such a slope as by earthly standards would rather be called a precipice; down and down this face, to where it vanished in a purple blush of vegetation, ran their road. Ransom refused absolutely to make the descent on Augray's shoulder. The *sorn,* though it did not fully understand his objection, stooped for him to dismount, and proceeded, with that same skating and forward-sloping motion, to go down before him. Ransom followed, using gladly but stiffly his numb legs.

The beauty of this new *handramit* as it opened before him took his breath away. It was wider than that in which he had hitherto lived and right below him lay an almost circular lake — a sapphire twelve miles in diameter set in a border of purple forest. Amidst the lake there rose like a low and gently sloping pyramid, or like a woman's breast, an island of pale red, smooth to the summit, and on the summit a grove of such trees as man had never seen. Their smooth columns had the gentle swell of the noblest beech-trees: but these were taller than a cathedral spire on earth, and at their tops, they broke rather into flower than foliage; into golden flower bright as tulips, still as rock, and huge as summer cloud. Flowers indeed they were, not trees, and far down among their roots he caught a pale hint of slab-like architecture. He knew before his guide told him that this was Meldilorn. He did not know what he had expected. The old dreams which he had brought from Earth of some more than American complexity of offices or some engineers' paradise of vast machines had indeed been long laid aside. But he had not looked for anything quite so classic, so virginal, as this bright grove — lying so still, so secret, in its coloured valley, soaring with inimitable grace so many hundred feet into the wintry sunlight. At every step of his descent the comparative warmth of the valley came up to him more deliciously. He looked above — the sky was turning to a paler blue. He looked below — and sweet and faint the thin fragrance of the giant blooms came up to him. Distant crags were growing less sharp in outline, and surfaces less bright. Depth, dimness, softness and perspective were returning to the landscape. The lip or edge of rock from which they had started their descent was already far overhead; it seemed unlikely that they had really come from there. He was breathing freely. His toes, so long benumbed, could move delightfully inside his boots. He lifted the earflaps of his cap and found his ears instantly filled with the sound of falling water. And now he was treading on soft ground-weed over level earth and the forest roof was above his head. They had conquered the *harandra* and were on the threshold of Meldilorn.

A short walk brought them into a kind of forest "ride" — a broad avenue running straight as an arrow through the purple stems to where the vivid blue of the lake danced at the end of it. There they found a gong and hammer hung on a pillar of stone. These objects were all richly decorated, and the gong and hammer were of a greenish blue metal which Ransom did not recognize. Augray struck the gong. An excitement was rising in Ransom's mind which almost prevented him from examining as coolly as he wished the ornamentation of the stone. It was partly pictorial, partly pure decoration. What chiefly struck him was a certain balance of packed and empty surfaces. Pure line drawings, as bare as the prehistoric pictures of reindeer on Earth, alternated with patches of

design as close and intricate as Norse or Celtic jewellery; and then, as you looked at it, these empty and crowded areas turned out to be themselves arranged in larger designs. He was struck by the fact that the pictorial work was not confined to the emptier spaces; quite often large arabesques included as a subordinate detail intricate pictures. Elsewhere the opposite plan had been followed — and this alternation, too, had a rhythmical or patterned element in it. He was just beginning to find out that the pictures, though stylized, were obviously intended to tell a story, when Augray interrupted him. A ship had put out from the island shore of Meldilorn.

As it came towards them Ransom's heart warmed to see that it was paddled by a *hross*. The creature brought its boat up to the shore where they were waiting, stared at Ransom and then looked inquiringly at Augray.

"You may well wonder at this *hnau*, Hrinha," said the *sorn*, "for you have never seen anything like it. It is called Ren-soom and has come through heaven from Thulcandra."

"It is welcome, Augray," said the *hross* politely. "Is it coming to Oyarsa?"

"He has sent for it."

"And for you also, Augray?"

"Oyarsa has not called me. If you will take Ren-soom over the water, I will go back to my tower."

The *hross* indicated that Ransom

should enter the boat. He attempted to express his thanks to the *sorn* and after a moment's consideration unstrapped his wrist-watch and offered it to him; it was the only thing he had which seemed a suitable present for a *sorn*. He had no difficulty in making Augray understand its purpose; but after examining it the giant gave it back to him, a little reluctantly, and said:

"This gift ought to be given to a *pfifltrigg*. It rejoices my heart, but they would make more of it. You are likely to meet some of the busy people in Meldilorn: give it to them. As for its use, do your people not know except by looking at this thing how much of the day has worn?"

"I believe there are beasts that have a sort of knowledge of that," said Ransom, "but our *hnau* have lost it."

After this, his farewells to the *sorn* were made and he embarked. To be once more in a boat and with a *hross*, to feel the warmth of water on his face and to see a blue sky above him, was almost like coming home. He took off his cap and leaned back luxuriously in the bows, plying his escort with questions. He learned that the *hrossa* were not specially concerned with the service of Oyarsa, as he had surmised from finding a *hross* in charge of the ferry: all three species of *hnau* served him in their various capacities, and the ferry was naturally entrusted to those who understood boats. He learned that his

own procedure on arriving in Meldilorn must be to go where he liked and do what he pleased until Oyarsa called for him. It might be an hour or several days before this happened. He would find huts near the landing-place where he could sleep if necessary and where food would be given him. In return he related as much as he could make intelligible of his own world and his journey from it; and he warned the *hross* of the dangerous bent men who had brought him and who were still at large on Malacandra. As he did so, it occurred to him that he had not made this sufficiently clear to Augray; but he consoled himself with the reflection that Weston and Devine seemed to have already some liaison with the *sorns* and that they would not be likely to molest things so large and so comparatively man-like. At any rate, not yet. About Devine's ultimate designs he had no illusions; all he could do was to make a clean breast of them to Oyarsa. And now the ship touched land.

Ransom rose, while the *hross* was making fast, and looked about him. Close to the little harbour which they had entered, and to the left, were low buildings of stone — the first he had seen in Malacandra — and fires were burning. There, the *hross* told him, he could find food and shelter. For the rest the island seemed desolate, and its smooth slopes empty up to the grove that crowned them, where, again, he saw stonework. But this appeared to be neither temple nor house in the human sense, but a broad avenue of monoliths — a much larger Stonehenge, stately, empty and vanishing over the crest of the hill into the pale shadow of the flower-trunks. All was solitude; but as he gazed upon it he seemed to hear, against the background of morning silence, a faint, continual agitation of silvery sound — hardly a sound at all, if you attended to it, and yet impossible to ignore.

"The island is all full of *eldila,*" said the *hross* in a hushed voice.

He went ashore. As though half expecting some obstacle, he took a few hesitant paces forward and stopped, and then went on again in the same fashion.

Though the ground-weed was unusually soft and rich and his feet made no noise upon it, he felt an impulse to walk on tiptoes. All his movements became gentle and sedate. The width of water about this island made the air warmer than any he had yet breathed in Malacandra; the climate was almost that of a warm earthly day in late September — a day that is warm but with a hint of frost to come. The sense of awe which was increasing upon him deterred him from approaching the crown of the hill, the grove and the avenue of standing stones.

He ceased ascending about halfway up the hill and began walking to his right, keeping a constant distance from the shore. He said to himself that he was having a look at the island, but his feeling was rather that the island was having a look at him. This was greatly increased by a discovery he made after he had been walking for about an hour, and which he ever afterwards found great difficulty in describing. In the most abstract terms it might be summed up by saying that the surface of the island was subject to tiny variations of light and shade which no change in the sky accounted for. If the air had not been calm and the ground-weed too short and firm to move in the wind, he would have said that a faint breeze was playing with it, and working such slight alterations in the shading as it does in a corn-field on the Earth. Like the silvery noises in the air, these footsteps of light were shy of observation. Where he looked hardest they were least to be seen: on the edges of his field of vision they came crowding as though a complex arrangement of them were there in progress. To attend to any one of them was to make it invisible, and the minute brightness seemed often to have just left the spot where his eyes fell. He had no doubt that he was "seeing" — as much as he ever would see — the *eldila.* The sensation it produced in him was curious. It was not exactly uncanny, not as if he were surrounded by ghosts. It was not even as if he were being spied upon; he had rather the sense of being looked at by things that had a right to look. His feeling was less than fear; it had in it something of embarrassment, something of shyness, something of submission, and it was profoundly uneasy.

He felt tired and thought that in this favoured land it would be warm enough to rest out of doors. He sat down. The softness of the weed, the warmth and the sweet smell which pervaded the whole island, reminded him of Earth and gardens in summer. He closed his eyes for a moment; then he opened them again and noticed buildings below him, and over the lake he saw a boat approaching. Recognition suddenly came to him. That was the ferry, and these buildings were the guest-house beside the harbour; he had walked all round the island. A certain disappointment succeeded this discovery. He was beginning to feel hungry. Perhaps it would be a good plan to go down and ask for some food; at any rate it would pass the time.

But he did not do so. When he rose and looked more closely at the guest-house he saw a considerable stir of creatures about it, and while he watched he saw that a full load of passengers was landing from the ferry-boat. In the lake he saw some moving objects which he did not at first identify but which turned out to be *sorns* up to their middles in the water and obviously wading to Meldilorn from the mainland. There were about ten of them. For some reason or other the island was receiving an influx of visitors. He no longer supposed that any harm would be done to him if he went down and mixed in the crowd, but he felt a reluctance to do so. The situation brought vividly back to his mind his experience as a new boy at school — new boys came a day early — hanging about and watching the arrival of the old hands. In the end he decided not to go down. He cut and ate some of the ground-weed and dozed for a little.

In the afternoon, when it grew colder, he resumed his walking. Other *hnau* were roaming about the island by this time. He saw *sorns* chiefly, but this was because their height made them conspicuous. There was hardly any noise. His reluctance to meet these fellow-wanderers, who seemed to confine themselves to the coast of the island, drove him half consciously upwards and inwards. He found himself at last on the fringes of the grove and looking straight up the monolithic avenue. He had intended, for no very clearly defined reason, not to enter it, but he fell to studying the stone nearest to him, which was richly sculptured on all its four sides, and after that curiosity led him on from stone to stone.

The pictures were very puzzling. Side by side with representations of *sorns* and *hrossa* and what he supposed to be *pfifltriggi* there occurred again and again an upright wavy figure with only the suggestion of a face, and with wings. The wings were perfectly recognizable, and this puzzled him very much. Could it be that the traditions of

Malacandrian art went back to that earlier geological and biological era when, as Augray had told him, there was life, including bird-life, on the *harandra?* The answer of the stones seemed to be Yes. He saw pictures of the old red forests with unmistakable birds flying among them, and many other creatures that he did not know. On another stone many of these were represented lying dead, and a fantastic *hnakra*-like figure, presumably symbolizing the cold, was depicted in the sky above them shooting at them with darts. Creatures still alive were crowding round the winged, wavy figure, which he took to be Oyarsa, pictured as a winged flame. On the next stone Oyarsa appeared, followed by many creatures, and apparently making a furrow with some pointed instrument. Another picture showed the furrow being enlarged by *pfifltriggi* with digging tools. *Sorns* were piling the earth up in pinnacles on each side, and *hrossa* seemed to be making water channels. Ransom wondered whether this were a mythical account of the making of *handramits* or whether they were conceivably artificial in fact.

Many of the pictures he could make nothing of. One that particularly puzzled him showed at the bottom a segment of a circle, behind and above which rose three-quarters of a disk divided into concentric rings. He thought it was a picture of the sun rising behind a hill; certainly the segment at the bottom

was full of Malacandrian scenes — Oyarsa in Meldilorn, *sorns* on the mountain edge of the *harandra,* and many other things both familiar to him and strange. He turned from it to examine the disk which rose behind it. It was not the sun. The sun was there, unmistakably, at the centre of the disk: round this the concentric circles revolved. In the first and smallest of these was pictured a little ball, on which rode a winged figure something like Oyarsa, but holding what appeared to be a trumpet. In the next, a similar ball carried another of the flaming figures. This one, instead of even the suggested face, had two bulges which after long inspection he decided were meant to be the udders or breasts of a female mammal. By this time he was quite sure that he was looking at a picture of the solar system. The first ball was Mercury, the second Venus — "And what an extraordinary coincidence," thought Ransom, "that their mythology, like ours, associates some idea of the female with Venus." The problem would have occupied him longer if a natural curiosity had not drawn his eyes on to the next ball which must represent the Earth. When he saw it, his whole mind stood still for a moment. The ball was there, but where the flamelike figure should have been, a deep depression of irregular shape had been cut as if to erase it. Once then — but his speculations faltered and became silent before a series of unknowns. He looked at the next circle. Here there was no ball. Instead, the bottom of this circle touched the top of the big segment filled with Malacandrian scenes, so that Malacandra at this point touched the solar system and came out of it in perspective towards the spectator. Now that his mind had grasped the design, he was astonished at the vividness of it all. He stood back and drew a deep breath preparatory to tackling some of the mysteries in which he was engulfed. Malacandra, then, was Mars. The Earth — but at this point a sound of tapping or hammering, which had been going on for some time without gaining admission to his consciousness, became too insistent to be ignored. Some creature, and certainly not an *eldil,* was at work, close to him. A little startled — for he had been deep in thought — he turned around. There was nothing to be seen. He shouted out, idiotically, in English:

"Who's there?"

The tapping instantly stopped and a remarkable face appeared from behind a neighbouring monolith.

It was hairless like a man's or a *sorn's.* It was long and pointed like a shrew's, yellow and shabby-looking, and so low in the forehead that but for the heavy development of the head at the back and behind the ears (like a bag-wig) it could not have been that of an intelligent creature. A moment later the whole of the thing came into view with a startling jump. Ransom guessed that it was a *pfifltrigg* — and was glad that he had not met one of this third race on his first arrival in Malacandra. It was much more insect-like or reptilian than anything he had yet seen. Its build was distinctly that of a frog, and at first Ransom thought it was resting, frog-like, on its "hands." Then he noticed that that part of its forelimbs on which it was supported was really, in human terms, rather an elbow than a hand. It was broad and padded and clearly made to be walked on; but upwards from it, at an angle of about forty-five degrees, went the true fore-arms — thin, strong fore-arms, ending in enormous, sensitive, many-fingered hands. He realized that for all manual work from mining to cutting cameos this creature had the advantage of being able to work with its full strength from a supported elbow. The insect-like effect was due to the speed and jerkiness of its movements and to the fact that it could swivel its head almost all the way around like a mantis; and it was increased by a kind of dry, rasping jingling quality in the noise of its moving. It was rather like a grasshopper, rather like one of Arthur Rackham's [1] dwarfs, rather like a frog, and rather like a little, old taxidermist whom Ransom knew in London.

[1] **Arthur Rackham:** English artist (1867–1939), especially noted as illustrator of children's books.

"I come from another world," began Ransom.

"I know, I know," said the creature in a quick, twittering, rather impatient voice. "Come here, behind the stone. This way, this way. Oyarsa's orders. Very busy. Must begin at once. Stand there."

Ransom found himself on the other side of the monolith, staring at a picture which was still in process of completion. The ground was liberally strewn with chips and the air was full of dust.

"There," said the creature. "Stand still. Don't look at me. Look over there."

For a moment Ransom did not quite understand what was expected of him; then, as he saw the *pfifltrigg* glancing to and fro at him and at the stone with the unmistakable glance of artist from model to work which is the same in all worlds, he realized and almost laughed. He was standing for his portrait! From his position he could see that the creature was cutting the stone as if it were cheese and the swiftness of its movements almost baffled his eyes, but he could get no impression of the work done, though he could study the *pfifltrigg*. He saw that the jingling and metallic noise was due to the number of small instruments which it carried about its body. Sometimes, with an exclamation of annoyance, it would throw down the tool it was working with and select one of these; but the majority of those in immediate use it kept in its mouth. He realized also that this was an animal artificially clothed like himself, in some bright scaly substance which appeared richly decorated though coated in dust. It had folds of furry clothing about its throat like a comforter, and its eyes were protected by dark bulging goggles. Rings and chains of a bright metal — not gold, he thought — adorned its limbs and neck. All the time it was working it kept up a sort of hissing whisper to itself; and when it was excited — which it usually was — the end of its nose wrinkled like a rabbit's. At last it gave another startling leap, landed about ten yards away from its work, and said:

"Yes, yes. Not so good as I hoped. Do better another time. Leave it now. Come and see yourself."

Ransom obeyed. He saw a picture of the planets, not now arranged to make a map of the solar system, but advancing in a single procession towards the spectator, and all, save one, bearing its fiery charioteer. Below lay Malacandra and there, to his surprise, was a very tolerable picture of the space-ship. Beside it stood three figures for all of which Ransom had apparently been the model. He recoiled from them in disgust. Even allowing for the strangeness of the subject from a Malacandrian point of view and for the stylization of their art, still, he thought, the creature might have made a better attempt at the human form than these stocklike dummies, almost as thick as they were tall, and sprouting about the head and neck into something that looked like fungus.

He hedged. "I expect it is like me as I look to your people," he said. "It is not how they would draw me in my own world."

"No," said the *pfifltrigg*. "I do not mean it to be too like. Too like, and they will not believe it — those who are born after." He added a good deal more which was difficult to understand; but while he was speaking it dawned upon Ransom that the odious figures were intended as an *idealization* of humanity. Conversation languished for a little. To change the subject Ransom asked a question which had been in his mind for some time.

"I cannot understand," he said, "how you and the *sorns* and the *hrossa* all come to speak the same speech. For your tongues and teeth and throats must be very different."

"You are right," said the creature. "Once we all had different speeches and we still have at home. But everyone has learned the speech of the *hrossa*."

"Why is that?" said Ransom, still thinking in terms of terrestrial history. "Did the *hrossa* once rule the others?"

"I do not understand. They are our great speakers and singers. They have more words and better. No one learns the speech of my people, for what we have to say is said in stone and suns' blood and stars'

milk and all can see them. No one learns the *sorns'* speech, for you can change their knowledge into any words and it is still the same. You cannot do that with the songs of the *hrossa*. Their tongue goes all over Malacandra. I speak it to you because you are a stranger. I would speak it to a *sorn*. But we have our old tongues at home. You can see it in the names. The *sorns* have big-sounding names like Augray and Arkal and Belmo and Falmay. The *hrossa* have furry names like Hnoh and Hnihi and Hyoi and Hlith-nahi."

"The best poetry, then, comes in the roughest speech?"

"Perhaps," said the *pfifltrigg*. "As the best pictures are made in the hardest stone. But my people have names like Kalakaperi and Para-kataru and Tafalakeruf. I am called Kanakaberaka."

Ransom told it his name.

"In our country," said Kanaka-beraka, "it is not like this. We are not pinched in a narrow *handramit*. There are the true forests, the green shadows, the deep mines. It is warm. It does not blaze with light like this, and it is not silent like this. I could put you in a place there in the forests where you could see a hundred fires at once and hear a hundred hammers. I wish you had come to our country. We do not live in holes like the *sorns* nor in bundles of weed like the *hrossa*. I could show you houses with a hundred pillars, one of suns' blood and the next of stars' milk, all the way . . . and all the world painted on the walls."

"How do you rule yourselves?" asked Ransom. "Those who are digging in the mines — do they like it as much as those who paint the walls?"

"All keep the mines open; it is a work to be shared. But each digs for himself the thing he wants for his work. What else would he do?"

"It is not so with us."

"Then you must make very bent work. How would a maker understand working in suns' blood unless he went into the home of suns' blood himself and knew one kind from another and lived with it for days out of the light of the sky till it was in his blood and his heart, as if he thought it and ate it and spat it?"

"With us it lies very deep and hard to get and those who dig it must spend their whole lives on the skill."

"And they love it?"

"I think not . . . I do not know. They are kept at it because they are given no food if they stop."

Kanakaberaka wrinkled his nose. "Then there is not food in plenty on your world?"

"I do not know," said Ransom. "I have often wished to know the answer to that question but no one can tell me. Does no one keep your people at their work, Kanakaberaka?"

"Our females," said the pfifltrigg with a piping noise which was apparently his equivalent for a laugh.

"Are your females of more account among you than those of the other hnau among them?"

"Very greatly. The sorns make least account of females and we make most."

For Study

1. Have you realized what the eldila are in Biblical terminology? As an eldil of high rank and authority, what would Oyarsa be in that terminology? (For a clue, see the first footnote in Chapter 14, page 73.)

2. On page 80, in discussing the eldila, the sorn says, "Body is movement." Compare this idea, as developed by the sorn, with a modern physicist's concept of matter.

3. In Chapter 16, the sorn remarks that the pfifltriggi "like best the making of things that are only good to look at and of no use." Discuss the implications of this statement with regard to art. Does this statement suggest a limit in the perceptions of the sorn? Describe the characteristic abilities of each of the three types of Malacandrian hnau.

4. There are few books in Malacandra. The sorns say that "it is better to remember." The hrossa feel that "the writing of books destroys poetry." Discuss these two attitudes toward books. Do you think the author of Out of the Silent Planet is opposed to books? Anti-intellectual? Anti-artistic?

5. Why is the conversation that closes Chapter 16 "very disagreeable" for Ransom?

For Writing

1. In a brief paper, discuss these words of the *sorn* near the end of Chapter 16: "There must be rule, yet how can creatures rule themselves?"

2. At the end of Chapter 16, having learned that there is only one kind of *hnau* on Earth, the *sorn* says to Ransom: "Your thought must be at the mercy of your blood. . . . For you cannot compare it with thought that floats on a different blood." Can you think of a sense in which man might be said to compare his thought with "thought that floats on a different blood"? Answer in a brief paper.

Chapter **18**

That night Ransom slept in the guest-house, which was a real house built by *pfifltriggi* and richly decorated.

His pleasure at finding himself, in this respect, under more human conditions was qualified by the discomfort which, despite his reason, he could not help feeling in the presence, at close quarters, of so many Malacandrian creatures. All three species were represented. They seemed to have no uneasy feelings towards each other, though there were some differences of the kind that occur in a railway carriage on Earth — the *sorns* finding the house too hot and the *pfifltriggi* finding it too cold. He learned more

of Malacandrian humour and of the noises that expressed it in this one night than he had learned during the whole of his life on the strange planet hitherto. Indeed, nearly all Malacandrian conversations in which he had yet taken part had been grave. Apparently the comic spirit arose chiefly from the meeting of the different kinds of *hnau*. The jokes of all three were equally incomprehensible to him. He thought he could see differences in kind — as that the *sorns* seldom got beyond irony, while the *hrossa* were extravagant and fantastic, and the *pfifltriggi* were sharp and excelled in abuse — but even when he understood all the words he could not see the points. He went early to bed.

It was at the time of early morning, when men on Earth go out to milk the cows, that Ransom was wakened. At first he did not know what had roused him. The chamber in which he lay was silent, empty and nearly dark. He was preparing himself to sleep again when a high-pitched voice close beside him said, "Oyarsa sends for you." He sat up, staring about him. There was no one there, and the voice repeated, "Oyarsa sends for you." The confusion of sleep was now clearing in his head, and he recognized that there was an *eldil* in the room. He felt no conscious fear, but while he rose obediently and put on such of his clothes as he had laid aside he found that his heart was beating rather fast. He was thinking less of the invisible creature in the room than of the interview that lay before him. His old terrors of meeting some monster or idol had quite left him: he felt nervous as he remembered feeling on the morning of an examination when he was an undergraduate. More than anything in the world he would have liked a cup of good tea.

The guest-house was empty. He went out. The bluish smoke was rising from the lake and the sky was bright behind the jagged eastern wall of the canyon; it was a few minutes before sunrise. The air was still very cold, the ground weed drenched with dew, and there was something puzzling about the whole scene which he presently identified with the silence. The *eldil* voices in the air had ceased and so had the shifting network of small lights and shades. Without being told, he knew that it was his business to go up to the crown of the island and the grove. As he approached them he saw with a certain sinking of heart that the monolithic avenue was full of Malacandrian creatures, and all silent. They were in two lines, one on each side, and all squatting or sitting in the various fashions suitable to their anatomies. He walked on slowly and doubtfully, not daring to stop, and ran the gauntlet of all those inhuman and unblinking eyes. When he had come to the very summit, at the middle of the avenue where the biggest of the stones rose, he stopped — he never could

remember afterwards whether an *eldil* voice had told him to do so or whether it was an intuition of his own. He did not sit down, for the earth was too cold and wet and he was not sure if it would be decorous. He simply stood — motionless like a man on parade. All the creatures were looking at him and there was no noise anywhere.

He perceived, gradually, that the place was full of *eldila*. The lights, or suggestions of light, which yesterday had been scattered over the island, were now all congregated in this one spot, and were all stationary or very faintly moving. The sun had risen by now, and still no one spoke. As he looked up to see the first, pale sunlight upon the monoliths, he became conscious that the air above him was full of a far greater complexity of light than the sunrise could explain, and light of a different kind, *eldil*-light. The sky, no less than the earth, was full of them; the visible Malacandrians were but the smallest part of the silent consistory which surrounded him. He might, when the time came, be pleading his cause before thousands or before millions: rank behind rank about him, and rank above rank over his head, the creatures that had never yet seen man, and whom man could not see, were waiting for his trial to begin. He licked his lips, which were quite dry, and wondered if he would be able to speak when speech was demanded of him. Then it occurred to him that perhaps this —

this waiting and being looked at — *was* the trial; perhaps even now he was unconsciously telling them all they wished to know. But afterwards — a long time afterwards — there was a noise of movement. Every visible creature in the grove had risen to its feet and was standing, more hushed than ever, with its head bowed; and Ransom saw (if it could be called seeing) that Oyarsa was coming up between the long lines of sculptured stones. Partly he knew it from the faces of the Malacandrians as their lord passed them; partly he saw — he could not deny that he saw — Oyarsa himself. He never could say what it was like. The merest whisper of light — no, less than that, the smallest diminution of shadow — was travelling along the uneven surface of the ground-weed; or rather some difference in the look of the ground, too slight to be named in the language of the five senses, moved slowly towards him. Like a silence spreading over a room full of people, like an infinitesimal coolness on a sultry day, like a passing memory of some long-forgotten sound or scent, like all that is stillest and smallest and most hard to seize in nature, Oyarsa passed between his subjects and drew near and came to rest, not ten yards away from Ransom in the centre of Meldilorn. Ransom felt a tingling of his blood and a pricking on his fingers as if lightning were near him; and his heart and body seemed to him to be made of water.

Oyarsa spoke — a more unhuman voice than Ransom had yet heard, sweet and seemingly remote; an unshaken voice; a voice, as one of the *hrossa* afterwards said to Ransom, "with no blood in it. Light is instead of blood for them." The words were not alarming.

"What are you so afraid of, Ransom of Thulcandra?" it said.

"Of you, Oyarsa, because you are unlike me and I cannot see you."

"Those are not great reasons," said the voice. "You are also unlike me, and, though I see you, I see you very faintly. But do not think we are utterly unlike. We are both copies of Maleldil. These are not the real reasons."

Ransom said nothing.

"You began to be afraid of me before you set foot in my world. And you have spent all your time since then in flying from me. My servants saw your fear when you were in your ship in heaven. They saw that your own kind treated you ill, though they could not understand their speech. Then to deliver you out of the hands of those two I stirred up a *hnakra* to try if you would come to me of your own will. But you hid among the *hrossa,* and though they told you to come to me, you would not. After that I sent my *eldil* to fetch you, but still you would not come. And in the end your own kind have chased you to me, and *hnau's* blood has been shed."

"I do not understand, Oyarsa. Do you mean that it was you who sent for me from Thulcandra?"

"Yes. Did not the other two tell you this? And why did you come with them unless you meant to obey my call? My servants could not understand their talk to you when your ship was in heaven."

"Your servants . . . I cannot understand," said Ransom.

"Ask freely," said the voice.

"Have you servants out in the heavens?"

"Where else? There is nowhere else."

"But you, Oyarsa, are here on Malacandra, as I am."

"But Malacandra, like all worlds, floats in heaven. And I am not 'here' altogether as you are, Ransom of Thulcandra. Creatures of your kind must drop out of heaven into a world; for us the worlds are places in heaven. But do not try to understand this now. It is enough to know that I and my servants are even now in heaven; they were around you in the sky-ship no less than they are around you here."

"Then you knew of our journey before we left Thulcandra?"

"No. Thulcandra is the world we do not know. It alone is outside the heaven, and no message comes from it."

Ransom was silent, but Oyarsa answered his unspoken questions.

"It was not always so. Once we knew the Oyarsa of your world — he was brighter and greater than I — and then we did not call it Thulcandra. It is the longest of all stories and the bitterest. He became bent.

That was before any life came on your world. Those were the Bent Years of which we still speak in the heavens, when he was not yet bound to Thulcandra but free like us. It was in his mind to spoil other worlds besides his own. He smote your moon with his left hand and with his right he brought the cold death on my *harandra* before its time; if by my arm Maleldil had not opened the *handramits* and let out the hot springs, my world would have been unpeopled. We did not leave him so at large for long. There was great war, and we drove him back out of the heavens and bound him in the air of his own world as Maleldil taught us. There doubtless he lies to this hour, and we know no more of that planet: it is silent. We think that Maleldil would not give it up utterly to the Bent One, and there are stories among us that He has taken strange counsel and dared terrible things, wrestling with the Bent One in Thulcandra. But of this we know less than you; it is a thing we desire to look into."

It was some time before Ransom spoke again and Oyarsa respected his silence. When he had collected himself he said:

"After this story, Oyarsa, I may tell you that our world is very bent. The two who brought me knew nothing of you, but only that the *sorns* had asked for me. They thought you were a false *eldil*, I think. There are false *eldila* in the wild parts of our world; men kill other men before them — they think the *eldil* drinks blood. They thought the *sorns* wanted me for this or for some other evil. They brought me by force. I was in terrible fear. The tellers of tales in our world make us think that if there is any life beyond our own air it is evil."

"I understand," said the voice. "And this explains things that I have wondered at. As soon as your journey had passed your own air and entered heaven, my servants told me that you seemed to be coming unwillingly and that the others had secrets from you. I did not think any creature could be so bent as to bring another of its own kind here by force."

"They did not know what you wanted me for, Oyarsa. Nor do I know yet."

"I will tell you. Two years ago — and that is about four of your years — this ship entered the heavens from your world. We followed its journey all the way hither and *eldila* were with it as it sailed over the *harandra,* and when at last it came to rest in the *handramit* more than half my servants were standing round it to see the strangers come out. All beasts we kept back from the place, and no *hnau* yet knew of it. When the strangers had walked to and fro on Malacandra and made themselves a hut and their fear of a new world ought to have worn off, I sent certain *sorns* to show themselves and to teach the strangers our language. I chose

sorns because they are most like your people in form. The Thulcandrians feared the *sorns* and were very unteachable. The *sorns* went to them many times and taught them a little. They reported to me that the Thulcandrians were taking suns' blood wherever they could find it in the streams. When I could make nothing of them by report, I told the *sorns* to bring them to me, not by force but courteously. They would not come. I asked for one of them, but not even one of them would come. It would have been easy to take them; but though we saw they were stupid we did not know yet how bent they were, and I did not wish to stretch my authority beyond the creatures of my own world. I told the *sorns* to treat them like cubs, to tell them that they would be allowed to pick up no more of the suns' blood until one of their race came to me. When they were told this they stuffed as much as they could into the sky-ship and went back to their own world. We wondered at this, but now it is plain. They thought I wanted one of your race to eat and went to fetch one. If they had come a few miles to see me I would have received them honourably; now they have twice gone a voyage of millions of miles for nothing and will appear before me none the less. And you also, Ransom of Thulcandra, you have taken many vain troubles to avoid standing where you stand now."

"That is true, Oyarsa. Bent creatures are full of fears. But I am here now and ready to know your will with me."

"Two things I wanted to ask of your race. First I must know why you come here — so much is my duty to my world. And secondly I wish to hear of Thulcandra and of Maleldil's strange wars there with the Bent One; for that, as I have said, is a thing we desire to look into."

"For the first question, Oyarsa, I have come here because I was brought. Of the others, one cares for nothing but the suns' blood, because in our world he can exchange it for many pleasures and powers. But the other means evil to you. I think he would destroy all your people to make room for our people; and then he would do the same with other worlds again. He wants our race to last for always, I think, and he hopes they will leap from world to world . . . always going to a new sun when an old one dies . . . or something like that."

"Is he wounded in his brain?"

"I do not know. Perhaps I do not describe his thoughts right. He is more learned than I."

"Does he think he could go to the great worlds? [1] Does he think Maleldil wants a race to live for ever?"

"He does not know there is any Maleldil. But what is certain, Oyarsa, is that he means evil to your world. Our kind must not be allowed to come here again. If you

[1] the great worlds: the great planets, Jupiter and Saturn.

can prevent it only by killing all three of us, I am content."

"If you were my own people I would kill them now, Ransom, and you soon; for they are bent beyond hope, and you, when you have grown a little braver, will be ready to go to Maleldil. But my authority is over my own world. It is a terrible thing to kill someone else's *hnau*. It will not be necessary."

"They are strong, Oyarsa, and they can throw death many miles and can blow killing airs at their enemies."

"The least of my servants could touch their ship before it reached Malacandra, while it was in the heaven, and make it a body of different movements — for you, no body at all. Be sure that no one of your race will come into my world again unless I call him. But enough of this. Now tell me of Thulcandra. Tell me all. We know nothing since the day when the Bent One sank out of heaven into the air of your world, wounded in the very light of his light. But why have you become afraid again?"

"I am afraid of the lengths of time, Oyarsa . . . or perhaps I do not understand. Did you not say this happened before there was life on Thulcandra?"

"Yes."

"And you, Oyarsa? You have lived . . . and that picture on the stone where the cold is killing them on the *harandra*? Is that a picture of something that was before my world began?"

"I see you are *hnau* after all," said the voice. "Doubtless no stone that faced the air then would be a stone now. The picture has begun to crumble away and been copied again more times than there are *eldila* in the air above us. But it was copied right. In that way you are seeing a picture that was finished when your world was still half-made. But do not think of these things. My people have a law never to speak much of sizes or numbers to you others, not even to *sorns*. You do not understand, and it makes you do reverence to nothings and pass by what is really great. Rather tell me what Maleldil has done in Thulcandra."

"According to our traditions——" Ransom was beginning, when an unexpected disturbance broke in upon the solemn stillness of the assembly. A large party, almost a procession, was approaching the grove from the direction of the ferry. It consisted entirely, as far as he could see, of *hrossa*, and they appeared to be carrying something.

Chapter **19**

As the procession drew nearer Ransom saw that the foremost *hrossa* were supporting three long and narrow burdens. They carried them on their heads, four *hrossa* to each. After these came a number of others armed with harpoons and apparently guarding two creatures which he did not recognize. The light was behind them as they entered between the two farthest monoliths. They were much shorter than any animal he had yet seen on Malacandra, and he gathered that they were bipeds, though the lower limbs were so thick and sausage-like that he hesitated to call them legs. The bodies were a little narrower at the top than at the bottom so as to be very slightly pear-shaped, and the heads were neither round like those of *hrossa* nor long like those of *sorns*, but almost square. They stumped along on narrow, heavy-looking feet which they seemed to press into the ground with unnecessary violence. And now their faces were becoming visible as masses of lumped and puckered flesh of variegated colour fringed in some bristly, dark substance. . . . Suddenly, with an indescribable change of feeling, he realized that he was looking at men. The two prisoners were Weston and Devine and he, for one privileged moment, had seen the human form with almost Malacandrian eyes.

The leaders of the procession had now advanced to within a few yards of Oyarsa and laid down their burdens. These, he now saw, were three dead *hrossa* laid on biers of some unknown metal; they were on their backs and their eyes, not closed as we close the eyes of human dead, stared disconcertingly up at the far-off golden canopy of the grove. One of them he took to be Hyoi, and it was certainly Hyoi's brother, Hyahi, who now came forward, and after an obeisance to Oyarsa began to speak.

Ransom at first did not hear what he was saying, for his attention was concentrated on Weston and Devine. They were weaponless and vigilantly guarded by the armed *hrossa* about them. Both of them, like Ransom himself, had let their beards grow ever since they landed on Malacandra, and both were pale and travel-stained. Weston was standing with folded arms, and his face wore a fixed, even an elaborate, expression of desperation. Devine, with his hands in his pockets, seemed to be in a state of furious sulks. Both clearly thought that they had good reason to fear, though neither was by any means lacking in courage. Surrounded by their guards as they were, and intent on the scene before them, they had not noticed Ransom.

He became aware of what Hyoi's brother was saying.

"For the death of these two, Oyarsa, I do not so much complain, for when we fell upon the *hmāna* by night they were in terror. You may say it was a hunt and these two were killed as they might have been by a *hnakra*. But Hyoi they hit from afar with a coward's weapon when he had done nothing to frighten them. And now he lies there (and I do not say it because he was my brother, but all the *handramit* knows it) and he was a

hnakrapunt and a great poet and the loss of him is heavy."

The voice of Oyarsa spoke for the first time to the two men.

"Why have you killed my *hnau?*" it said.

Weston and Devine looked anxiously about them to identify the speaker.

"God!" exclaimed Devine in English. "Don't tell me they've got a loud-speaker."

"Ventriloquism," replied Weston in a husky whisper. "Quite common among savages. The witch-doctor or medicine-man pretends to go into a trance and he does it. The thing to do is to identify the medicine-man and address your remarks to *him* wherever the voice seems to come from; it shatters his nerve and shows you've seen through him. Do you see any of the brutes in a trance? By Jove — I've spotted him."

Due credit must be given to Weston for his powers of observation: he had picked out the only creature in the assembly which was not standing in an attitude of reverence and attention. This was an elderly *hross* close beside him. It was squatting; and its eyes were shut. Taking a step towards it, he struck a defiant attitude and exclaimed in a loud voice (his knowledge of the language was elementary):

"Why you take our puff-bangs away? We very angry with you. We not afraid."

On Weston's hypothesis his action ought to have been impressive.

Unfortunately for him, no one else shared his theory of the elderly *hross's* behaviour. The *hross* — who was well known to all of them, including Ransom — had not come with the funeral procession. It had been in its place since dawn. Doubtless it intended no disrespect to Oyarsa; but it must be confessed that it had yielded, at a much earlier stage of the proceedings, to an infirmity which attacks elderly *hnau* of all species, and was by this time enjoying a profound and refreshing slumber. One of its whiskers twitched a little as Weston shouted in its face, but its eyes remained shut.

The voice of Oyarsa spoke again. "Why do you speak to him?" it said. "It is I who ask you. Why have you killed my *hnau?*"

"You let us go, then we talkee-talkee," bellowed Weston at the sleeping *hross.* "You think we no power, think you do all you like. You no can. Great big head-man in sky he send us. You no do what I say, he come, blow you all up — Pouff! Bang!"

"I do not know what *bang* means," said the voice. "But why have you killed my *hnau?*"

"Say it was an accident," muttered Devine to Weston in English.

"I've told you before," replied Weston in the same language, "You don't understand how to deal with natives. One sign of yielding and they'll be at our throats. The only thing is to intimidate them."

"All right! Do your stuff, then," growled Devine. He was obviously losing faith in his partner.

Weston cleared his throat and again rounded on the elderly *hross.*

"We kill him," he shouted. "Show what we can do. Every one who no do all we say — pouff! bang! — kill him same as that one. You do all we say and we give you much pretty things. See! See!" To Ransom's intense discomfort, Weston at this point whipped out of his pocket a brightly coloured necklace of beads, the undoubted work of Mr. Woolworth, and began dangling it in front of the faces of his guards, turning slowly round and round and repeating, "Pretty, pretty! See! See!"

The result of this manœuvre was more striking than Weston himself had anticipated. Such a roar of sounds as human ears had never heard before — baying of *hrossa,* piping of *pfifltriggi,* booming of *sorns* — burst out and rent the silence of that august place, waking echoes from the distant mountain walls. Even in the air above them there was a faint ringing of the *eldil* voices. It is greatly to Weston's credit that though he paled at this he did not lose his nerve.

"You no roar at me," he thundered. "No try make me afraid. Me no afraid of you."

"You must forgive my people," said the voice of Oyarsa — and even it was subtly changed — "but they are not roaring at you. They are only laughing."

But Weston did not know the

Malacandrian word for *laugh:* indeed, it was not a word he understood very well in any language. He looked about him with a puzzled expression. Ransom, biting his lips with mortification, almost prayed that one experiment with the beads would satisfy the scientist; but that was because he did not know Weston. The latter saw that the clamour had subsided. He knew that he was following the most orthodox rules for frightening and then conciliating primitive races; and he was not the man to be deterred by one or two failures. The roar that went up from the throats of all spectators as he again began revolving like a slow-motion picture of a humming-top, occasionally mopping his brow with his left hand and conscientiously jerking the necklace up and down with his right, completely drowned anything he might be attempting to say; but Ransom saw his lips moving and had little doubt that he was working away at "Pretty, pretty!" Then suddenly the sound of laughter almost redoubled its volume. The stars in their courses were fighting against Weston. Some hazy memory of efforts made long since to entertain an infant niece had begun to penetrate his highly trained mind. He was bobbing up and down from the knees and holding his head on one side; he was almost dancing; and he was by now very hot indeed. For all Ransom knew he was saying "Diddle, diddle, diddle."

It was sheer exhaustion which ended the great physicist's performance — the most successful of its kind ever given on Malacandra — and with it the sonorous raptures of his audience. As silence returned Ransom heard Devine's voice in English:

"For God's sake stop making a buffoon of yourself, Weston," it said. "Can't you see it won't work?"

"It *doesn't* seem to be working," admitted Weston, "and I'm inclined to think they have even less intelligence than we supposed. Do you think, perhaps, if I tried it just once again — or would you like to try this time?"

"Oh, Hell!" said Devine, and, turning his back on his partner, sat down abruptly on the ground, produced his cigarette-case and began to smoke.

"I'll give it to the witch-doctor," said Weston during the moment of silence which Devine's action had produced among the mystified spectators; and before anyone could stop him he took a step forward and attempted to drop the string of beads round the elderly *hross's* neck. The *hross's* head was, however, too large for this operation and the necklace merely settled on its forehead like a crown, slightly over one eye. It shifted its head a little, like a dog worried with flies, snorted gently, and resumed its sleep.

Oyarsa's voice now addressed Ransom. "Are your fellow-creatures hurt in their brains, Ransom of

Thulcandra?" it said. "Or are they too much afraid to answer my questions?"

"I think, Oyarsa," said Ransom, "that they do not believe you are there. And they believe that all these *hnau* are — are like very young cubs. The thicker *hmān* is trying to frighten them and then to please them with gifts."

At the sound of Ransom's voice the two prisoners turned sharply around. Weston was about to speak when Ransom interrupted him hastily in English:

"Listen, Weston. It is not a trick. There really is a creature there in the middle — there where you can see a kind of light, or a kind of something, if you look hard. And it is at least as intelligent as a man — they seem to live an enormous time. Stop treating it like a child and answer its questions. And if you take my advice, you'll speak the truth and not bluster."

"The brutes seem to have intelligence enough to take you in, anyway," growled Weston; but it was in a somewhat modified voice that he turned once more to the sleeping *hross* — the desire to wake up the supposed witch-doctor was becoming an obsession — and addressed it.

"We sorry we kill him," he said, pointing to Hyoi. "No go to kill him. *Sorns* tell us bring man, give him your big head. We go away back into sky. *He* come (here he indicated Ransom) with us. He very bent man, run away, no do

what *sorns* say like us. We run after him, get him back for *sorns,* want to do what we say and *sorns* tell us, see? He not let us. Run away, run, run. We run after. See big black one, think he kill us, we kill him — pouff! bang! All for bent man. He no run away, he be good, we no run after, no kill big black one, see? You have bent man — bent man make all trouble — you plenty keep him, let us go. He afraid of you, we no afraid. Listen —— "

At this moment Weston's continual bellowing in the face of the *hross* at last produced the effect he had striven for so long. The creature opened its eyes and stared mildly at him in some perplexity. Then, gradually realizing the impropriety of which it had been guilty, it rose slowly to its standing position, bowed respectfully to Oyarsa, and finally waddled out of the assembly still carrying the necklace draped over its right ear and eye. Weston, his mouth still open, followed the retreating figure with his gaze till it vanished among the stems of the grove.

It was Oyarsa who broke the silence. "We have had mirth enough," he said, "and it is time to hear true answers to our questions. Something is wrong in your head, *hnau* from Thulcandra. There is too much blood in it. Is Firikitekila here?"

"Here, Oyarsa," said a *pfifltrigg*.

"Have you in your cisterns water that has been made cold?"

"Yes, Oyarsa."

"Then let this thick *hnau* be taken to the guest-house and let them bathe his head in cold water. Much water and many times. Then bring him again. Meanwhile I will provide for my killed *hrossa*."

Weston did not clearly understand what the voice said — indeed, he was still too busy trying to find out where it came from — but terror smote him as he found himself wrapped in the strong arms of the surrounding *hrossa* and forced away from his place. Ransom would gladly have shouted out some reassurance, but Weston himself was shouting too loud to hear him. He was mixing English and Malacandrian now, and the last that was heard was a rising scream of "Pay for this — pouff! bang! — Ransom, for God's sake — Ransom! Ransom!"

"And now," said Oyarsa, when silence was restored, "let us honour my dead *hnau*."

At his words ten of the *hrossa* grouped themselves about the biers. Lifting their heads, and with no signal given as far as Ransom could see, they began to sing.

To every man, in his acquaintance with a new art, there comes a moment when that which before was meaningless first lifts, as it were, one corner of the curtain that hides its mystery, and reveals, in a burst of delight which later and fuller understanding can hardly ever equal, one glimpse of the in-definite possibilities within. For Ransom, this moment had now come in his understanding of Malacandrian song. Now first he saw that its rhythms were based on a different blood from ours, on a heart that beat more quickly, and a fiercer internal heat. Through his knowledge of the creatures and his love for them he began, ever so little, to hear it with their ears. A sense of great masses moving at visionary speeds, of giants dancing, of eternal sorrows eternally consoled, of he knew not what and yet what he had always known, awoke in him with the very first bars of the deep-mouthed dirge, and bowed down his spirit as if the gate of heaven had opened before him.

"Let it go hence," they sang. "Let it go hence, dissolve and be no body. Drop it, release it, drop it gently, as a stone is loosed from fingers drooping over a still pool. Let it go down, sink, fall away. Once below the surface there are no divisions, no layers in the water yielding all the way down; all one and all unwounded is that element. Send it voyaging where it will not come again. Let it go down; the *hnau* rises from it. This is the second life, the other beginning. Open, oh coloured world, without weight, without shore. You are second and better; this was first and feeble. Once the worlds were hot within and brought forth life, but only the pale plants, the dark plants. We see their children when they grow to-day, out of the sun's light in the sad places. After, the heaven made grow another kind on worlds: the high climbers, the bright-haired forests, cheeks of flowers. First were the darker, then the brighter. First was the worlds' blood, then the suns' brood."

This was as much of it as he con-trived later to remember and could translate. As the song ended Oyarsa said:

"Let us scatter the movements which were their bodies. So will Maleldil scatter all worlds when the first and feeble is worn."

He made a sign to one of the *pfifltriggi*, who instantly arose and approached the corpses. The *hrossa*, now singing again but very softly, drew back at least ten paces. The *pfifltrigg* touched each of the three dead in turn with some small ob-ject that appeared to be made of glass or crystal — and then jumped away with one of his frog-like leaps. Ransom closed his eyes to protect them from a blinding light and felt something like a very strong wind blowing in his face, for a fraction of a second. Then all was calm again, and the three biers were empty.

"God! That would be a trick worth knowing on earth," said De-vine to Ransom. "Solve the mur-derers' problem about the disposal of the body, eh?"

But Ransom, who was thinking of Hyoi, did not answer him; and before he spoke again everyone's attention was diverted by the re-turn of the unhappy Weston among his guards.

Chapter **20**

The *hross* who headed this pro-cession was a conscientious crea-ture and began at once explaining itself in a rather troubled voice.

"I hope we have done right, Oyarsa," it said. "But we do not know. We dipped his head in the cold water seven times, but the seventh time something fell off it. We had thought it was the top of his head, but now we saw it was a covering made of the skin of some other creature. Then some said we had done your will with the seven dips, and others said not. In the end we dipped it seven times more. We hope that was right. The creature talked a lot between the dips, and most between the second seven, but we could not understand it."

"You have done very well, Hnoo," said Oyarsa. "Stand away that I may see it, for now I will speak to it."

The guards fell away on each side. Weston's usually pale face, un-der the bracing influence of the cold water, had assumed the colour of a ripe tomato, and his hair, which had naturally not been cut since he reached Malacandra, was plastered in straight lank masses across his forehead. A good deal of water was still dripping over his nose and ears. His expression — unfortunately wasted on an audience ignorant of terrestrial physiognomy — was that of a brave man suffering in a great cause, and rather eager than reluctant to face the worst or even to provoke it. In explanation of his conduct it is only fair to remember that he had already that morning endured all the terrors of an expected martyrdom and all the anticlimax of fourteen compulsory cold douches. Devine, who knew his man, shouted out to Weston in English:

"Steady, Weston. These devils can split the atom or something pretty like it. Be careful what you say to them and don't let's have any of your bloody nonsense."

"Huh!" said Weston. "So you've gone native too?"

"Be silent," said the voice of Oyarsa. "You, thick one, have told me nothing of yourself, so I will tell it to you. In your own world you have attained great wisdom concerning bodies and by this you have been able to make a ship that can cross the heaven; but in all other things you have the mind of an animal. When first you came here, I sent for you, meaning you nothing but honour. The darkness in your own mind filled you with fear. Because you thought I meant evil to you, you went as a beast goes against a beast of some other kind, and snared this Ransom. You would give him up to the evil you feared.

To-day, seeing him here, to save your own life, you would have given him to me a second time, still thinking I meant him hurt. These are your dealings with your own kind. And what you intend to my people, I know. Already you have killed some. And you have come here to kill them all. To you it is nothing whether a creature is *hnau* or not. At first I thought this was because you cared only whether a creature had a body like your own; but Ransom has that and you would kill him as lightly as any of my *hnau*. I did not know that the Bent One had done so much in your world and still I do not understand it. If you were mine, I would unbody you even now. Do not think follies; by my hand Maleldil does greater things than this, and I can unmake you even on the borders of your own world's air. But I do not yet resolve to do this. It is for you to speak. Let me see if there is anything in your mind besides fear and death and desire."

Weston turned to Ransom. "I see," he said, "that you have chosen the most momentous crisis in the history of the human race to betray it." Then he turned in the direction of the voice.

"I know you kill us," he said. "Me not afraid. Others come, make it our world ——"

But Devine had jumped to his feet, and interrupted him.

"No, no, Oyarsa," he shouted. "You no listen him. He very foolish man, he have dreams. We little people, only want pretty sun-bloods. You give us plenty sun-bloods, we go back into sky, you never see us no more. All done, see?"

"Silence," said Oyarsa. There was an almost imperceptible change in the light, if it could be called light, out of which the voice came, and Devine crumpled up and fell back on the ground. When he resumed his sitting position he was white and panting.

"Speak on," said Oyarsa to Weston.

"Me, no . . . no," began Weston in Malacandrian and then broke off. "I can't say what I want in their accursed language," he said in English.

"Speak to Ransom and he shall turn it into our speech," said Oyarsa.

Weston accepted the arrangement at once. He believed that the hour of his death was come and he was determined to utter the thing — almost the only thing outside his own science — which he had to say. He cleared his throat, almost he struck a gesture, and began:

"To you I may seem a vulgar robber, but I bear on my shoulders the destiny of the human race. Your tribal life with its stone-age weapons and bee-hive huts, its primitive coracles and elementary social structure, has nothing to compare with our civilization — with our science, medicine and law, our armies, our architecture, our commerce, and our transport system which is rapidly annihilating space and time. Our

right to supersede you is the right of the higher over the lower. Life——"

"Half a moment," said Ransom in English. "That's about as much as I can manage at one go." Then, turning to Oyarsa, he began translating as well as he could. The process was difficult and the result — which he felt to be rather unsatisfactory — was something like this:

"Among us, Oyarsa, there is a kind of *hnau* who will take other *hnau's* food and — and things, when they are not looking. He says he is not an ordinary one of that kind. He says what he does now will make very different things happen to those of our people who are not yet born. He says that, among you, *hnau* of one kindred all live together and the *hrossa* have spears like those we used a very long time ago and your huts are small and round and your boats small and light and like our old ones, and you have only one ruler. He says it is different with us. He says we know much. There is a thing happens in our world when the body of a living creature feels pains and becomes weak, and he says we sometimes know how to stop it. He says we have many bent people and we kill them or shut them in huts and that we have people for settling quarrels between the bent *hnau* about their huts and mates and things. He says we have many ways for the *hnau* of one land to kill those of another and some are trained to do it. He says we build very big and strong huts of stones and other things — like the *pfifltriggi*. And he says we exchange many things among ourselves and can carry heavy weights very quickly a long way. Because of all this, he says it would not be the act of a bent *hnau* if our people killed all your people."

As soon as Ransom had finished, Weston continued.

"Life is greater than any system of morality; her claims are absolute. It is not by tribal taboos and copybook maxims that she has pursued her relentless march from the amœba to man and from man to civilization."

"He says," began Ransom, "that living creatures are stronger than the question whether an act is bent or good — no, that cannot be right — he says it is better to be alive and bent than to be dead — no — he says, he says — I cannot say what he says, Oyarsa, in your language. But he goes on to say that the only good thing is that there should be very many creatures alive. He says there were many other animals before the first men and the later ones were better than the earlier ones; but he says the animals were not born because of what is said to the young about bent and good action by their elders. And he says these animals did not feel any pity."

"She —— " began Weston.

"I'm sorry," interrupted Ransom, "but I've forgotten who She is."

"Life, of course," snapped Weston. "She has ruthlessly broken down all obstacles and liquidated all failures and to-day in her highest form — civilized man — and in me as his representative, she presses forward to that interplanetary leap which will, perhaps, place her forever beyond the reach of death."

"He says," resumed Ransom, "that these animals learned to do many difficult things, except those who could not; and those ones died and the other animals did not pity them. And he says the best animal now is the kind of man who makes the big huts and carries the heavy weights and does all the other things I told you about; and he is one of these and he says that if the others all knew what he was doing they would be pleased. He says that if he could kill you all and bring our people to live in Malacandra, then they might be able to go on living here after something had gone wrong with our world. And then if something went wrong with Malacandra they might go and kill all the *hnau* in another world. And then another — and so they would never die out."

"It is in her right," said Weston, "the right, or, if you will, the might of Life herself, that I am prepared without flinching to plant the flag of man on the soil of Malacandra: to march on, step by step, superseding, where necessary, the lower forms of life that we find, claiming planet after planet, system after system, till our posterity — whatever strange form and yet unguessed mentality they have assumed — dwell in the universe wherever the universe is habitable."

"He says," translated Ransom, "that because of this it would *not* be a bent action — or else, he says, it *would* be a possible action — for him to kill you all and bring us here. He says he would feel no pity. He is saying again that perhaps they would be able to keep moving from one world to another and wherever they came they would kill everyone. I think he is now talking about worlds that go round other suns. He wants the creatures born from us to be in as many places as they can. He says he does not know what kind of creatures they will be."

"I may fall," said Weston. "But while I live I will not, with such a key in my hand, consent to close the gates of the future on my race. What lies in that future, beyond our present ken, passes imagination to conceive: it is enough for me that there is a Beyond."[1]

[1] An allusion to the last line of George Bernard Shaw's play, *Back to Methuselah* (1920), which extends in time from the Garden of Eden to the far future. The character Lilith says: "Of Life only is there no end; and though of its million starry mansions many are empty and many still un-built, and though its vast domain is as yet unbearably desert, my seed shall one day fill it and master its matter to its uttermost confines. And for what may be beyond, the eyesight of Lilith is too short. It is enough that there is a beyond." The harmony of this vision with Weston's is obvious.

"He is saying," Ransom trans-lated, "that he will not stop trying to do all this unless you kill him. And he says that though he doesn't know what will happen to the crea-tures sprung from us, he wants it to happen very much."

Weston, who had now finished his statement, looked round instinc-tively for a chair to sink into. On Earth he usually sank into a chair as the applause began. Finding none — he was not the kind of man to sit on the ground like Devine — he folded his arms and stared with a certain dignity about him.

"It is well that I have heard you," said Oyarsa. "For though your mind is feebler, your will is less bent than I thought. It is not for yourself that you would do all this."

"No," said Weston proudly in Malacandrian. "Me die. Man live."

"Yet you know that these crea-tures would have to be made quite unlike you before they lived on other worlds."

"Yes, yes. All new. No one know yet. Strange! Big!"

"Then it is not the shape of body that you love?"

"No. Me no care how they shaped."

"One would think, then, that it is for the mind you care. But that can-not be, or you would love *hnau* wherever you met it."

"No care for *hnau*. Care for man."

"But if it is neither man's mind, which is as the mind of all other *hnau* — is not Maleldil maker of them all? — nor his body, which will change — if you care for neither of these, what do you mean by man?"

This had to be translated to Weston. When he understood it, he replied:

"Me care for man — care for our race — what man begets —— " He had to ask Ransom the words for *race* and *beget*.

"Strange!" said Oyarsa. "You do not love any one of your race — you would have let me kill Ransom. You do not love the mind of your race, nor the body. Any kind of creature will please you if only it is begotten by your kind as they now are. It seems to me, Thick One, that what you really love is no completed creature but the very seed itself: for that is all that is left."

"Tell him," said Weston when he had been made to understand this, "that I don't pretend to be a metaphysician. I have not come here to chop logic. If he cannot understand — as apparently you can't either — anything so fundamental as a man's loyalty to humanity, I can't make him understand it."

But Ransom was unable to translate this and the voice of Oyarsa continued:

"I see now how the lord of the silent world has bent you. There are laws that all *hnau* know, of pity and straight dealing and shame and the like, and one of these is the love of kindred. He has taught you to break all of them except this one, which is not one of the greatest

laws; this one he has bent till it becomes folly and has set it up, thus bent, to be a little, blind Oyarsa in your brain. And now you can do nothing but obey it, though if we ask you why it is a law you can give no other reason for it than for all the other and greater laws which it drives you to disobey. Do you know why he has done this?"

"Me think no such person — me wise, new man — no believe all that old talk."

"I will tell you. He has left you this one because a bent *hnau* can do more evil than a broken one. He has only bent you; but this Thin One who sits on the ground he has broken, for he has left him nothing but greed. He is now only a talking animal and in my world he could do no more evil than an animal. If he were mine I would unmake his body for the *hnau* in it is already dead. But if you were mine I would try to cure you. Tell me, Thick One, why did you come here?"

"Me tell you. Make man live all the time."

"But are your wise men so ignorant as not to know that Malacandra is older than your own world and nearer its death? Most of it is dead already. My people live only in the *handramits;* the heat and the water have been more and will be less. Soon now, very soon, I will end my world and give back my people to Maleldil."

"Me know all that plenty. This only first try. Soon they go on another world."

"But do you not know that all worlds will die?"

"Men go jump off each before it deads — on and on, see?"

"And when all are dead?"

Weston was silent. After a time Oyarsa spoke again.

"Do you not ask why my people, whose world is old, have not rather come to yours and taken it long ago?"

"Ho! Ho!" said Weston. "You not know how."

"You are wrong," said Oyarsa. "Many thousands of thousand years before this, when nothing yet lived on your world, the cold death was coming on my *harandra*. Then I was in deep trouble, not chiefly for the death of my *hnau* — Maleldil does not make them long-livers — but for the things which the lord of your world, who was not yet bound, put into their minds. He would have made them as your people are now — wise enough to see the death of their kind approaching but not wise enough to endure it. Bent counsels would soon have risen among them. They were well able to have made sky-ships. By me Maleldil stopped them. Some I cured, some I unbodied —— "

"And see what come!" interrupted Weston. "You now very few — shut up on *handramits* — soon all die."

"Yes," said Oyarsa, "but one thing we left behind us on the *harandra*: fear. And with fear, murder and rebellion. The weakest of my people does not fear death. It is the Bent One, the lord of your world, who wastes your lives and befouls them with flying from what you know will overtake you in the end. If you were subjects of Maleldil you would have peace."

Weston writhed in the exasperation born of his desire to speak and his ignorance of the language.

"Trash! Defeatist trash!" he shouted at Oyarsa in English; then, drawing himself up to his full height, he added in Malacandrian, "You say your Maleldil let all go dead. Other one, Bent One, he fight, jump, live — not all talkee-talkee. Me no care Maleldil. Like Bent One better: me on his side."

"But do you not see that he never will nor can," began Oyarsa, and then broke off, as if recollecting himself. "But I must learn more of your world from Ransom, and for that I need till night. I will not kill you, not even the Thin One, for you are out of my world. To-morrow you shall go hence again in your ship."

Devine's face suddenly fell. He began talking rapidly in English.

"For God's sake, Weston, make him understand. We've been here for months — the Earth is not in opposition now. Tell him it can't be done. He might as well kill us at once."

"How long will your journey be to Thulcandra?" asked Oyarsa.

Weston, using Ransom as his interpreter, explained that the journey, in the present position of the two planets, was almost impossible.

The distance had increased by millions of miles. The angle of their course to the solar rays would be totally different from that which he had counted upon. Even if by a hundredth chance they could hit the Earth, it was almost certain that their supply of oxygen would be exhausted long before they arrived.

"Tell him to kill us now," he added.

"All this I know," said Oyarsa. "And if you stay in my world I must kill you: no such creature will I suffer in Malacandra. I know there is small chance of your reaching your world; but small is not the same as none. Between now and the next moon choose which you will take. In the meantime, tell me this. If you reach it at all, what is the most time you will need?"

After a prolonged calculation, Weston, in a shaken voice, replied that if they had not made it in ninety days they would never make it, and they would, moreover, be dead of suffocation.

"Ninety days you shall have," said Oyarsa. "My *sorns* and *pfifltriggi* will give you air (we also have that art) and food for ninety days. But they will do something else to your ship. I am not minded that it should return into the heaven if once it reaches Thulcandra. You, Thick One, were not here when I unmade my dead *hrossa* whom you killed: the Thin One will tell you. This I can do, as Maleldil has taught me, over a gap of time or a gap of place. Before

your sky-ship rises, my *sorns* will have so dealt with it that on the ninetieth day it will unbody, it will become what you call nothing. If that day finds it in heaven your death will be no bitterer because of this; but do not tarry in your ship if once you touch Thulcandra. Now lead these two away, and do you, my children, go where you will. But I must talk with Ransom."

Chapter **21**

All that afternoon Ransom remained alone answering Oyarsa's questions. I am not allowed to record this conversation, beyond saying that the voice concluded it with the words:

"You have shown me more wonders than are known in the whole of heaven."

After that they discussed Ransom's own future. He was given full liberty to remain in Malacandra or to attempt the desperate voyage to Earth. The problem was agonizing to him. In the end he decided to throw in his lot with Weston and Devine.

"Love of our own kind," he said, "is not the greatest of laws, but you, Oyarsa, have said it is a law. If I cannot live in Thulcandra, it is better for me not to live at all."

"You have chosen rightly," said Oyarsa. "And I will tell you two things. My people will take all the strange weapons out of the ship, but they will give one to you. And the *eldila* of deep heaven will be about your ship till it reaches the air of Thulcandra, and often in it. They will not let the other two kill you."

It had not occurred to Ransom before that his own murder might be one of the first expedients for economizing food and oxygen which would occur to Weston and Devine. He was now astonished at his obtuseness, and thanked Oyarsa for his protective measures. Then the great *eldil* dismissed him with these words:

"You are guilty of no evil, Ransom of Thulcandra, except a little fearfulness. For that, the journey you go on is your pain, and perhaps your cure: for you must be either mad or brave before it is ended. But I lay also a command on you; you must watch this Weston and this Devine in Thulcandra if ever you arrive there. They may yet do much evil in, and beyond, your world. From what you have told me, I begin to see that there are *eldila* who go down into your air, into the very stronghold of the Bent One; your world is not so fast shut as was thought in these parts of heaven. Watch those two bent ones. Be courageous. Fight them. And when you have need, some of our people will help you. Maleldil will show them to you. It may even be that you and I shall meet again while you are still in the body; for it is not without the wisdom of Malel-

dil that we have met now and I have learned so much of your world. It seems to me that this is the beginning of more comings and goings between the heavens and the worlds and between one world and another — though not such as the Thick One hoped. I am allowed to tell you this. The year we are now in — but heavenly years are not as yours — has long been prophesied as a year of stirrings and high changes and the siege of Thulcandra may be near its end. Great things are on foot. If Maleldil does not forbid me, I will not hold aloof from them. And now farewell."

It was through vast crowds of all the Malacandrian species that the three human beings embarked next day on their terrible journey. Weston was pale and haggard from a night of calculations intricate enough to tax any mathematician even if his life did not hang on them. Devine was noisy, reckless and a little hysterical. His whole view of Malacandra had been altered overnight by the discovery that the "natives" had an alcoholic drink, and he had even been trying to teach them to smoke. Only the *pfifltriggi* had made much of it. He was now consoling himself for an acute headache and the prospect of a lingering death by tormenting Weston. Neither partner was pleased to find that all weapons had been removed from the space-ship, but in other respects everything was as they wished it. At about an hour after noon Ransom took a last, long look at the blue waters, purple forest and remote green walls of the familiar *handramit,* and followed the other two through the manhole. Before it was closed Weston warned them that they must economize air by absolute stillness. No unnecessary movement must be made during their voyage; even talking must be prohibited.

"I shall speak only in an emergency," he said.

"Thank God for that, anyway," was Devine's last shot. Then they screwed themselves in.

Ransom went at once to the lower side of the sphere, into the chamber which was now most completely upside down, and stretched himself on what would later become its skylight. He was surprised to find that they were already thousands of feet up. The *handramit* was only a straight purple line across the rose-red surface of the *harandra.* They were above the junction of two *handramits.* One of them was doubtless that in which he had lived, the other that which contained Meldilorn. The gully by which he had cut off the corner between the two, on Augray's shoulders, was quite invisible.

Each minute more *handramits* came into view — long straight lines, some parallel, some intersecting, some building triangles. The landscape became increasingly geometrical. The waste between the purple lines appeared perfectly flat. The rosy colour of the petrified forests accounted for its tint immedi-

ately below him; but to the north and east the great sand deserts of which the *sorns* had told him were now appearing as illimitable stretches of yellow and ochre. To the west a huge discoloration began to show. It was an irregular patch of greenish blue that looked as if it were sunk below the level of the surrounding *harandra.* He concluded it was the forest lowland of the *pfifltriggi* — or rather one of their forest lowlands, for now similar patches were appearing in all directions, some of them mere blobs at the intersection of *handramits,* some of vast extent. He became vividly conscious that his knowledge of Malacandra was minute, local, parochial. It was as if a *sorn* had journeyed forty million miles to the Earth and spent his stay there between Worthing and Brighton. He reflected that he would have very little to show for his amazing voyage if he survived it: a smattering of the language, a few landscapes, some half-understood physics—but where were the statistics, the history, the broad survey of extra-terrestrial conditions, which such a traveller ought to bring back? Those *handramits,* for example. Seen from the height which the space-ship had now attained, in all their unmistakable geometry, they put to shame his original impression that they were natural valleys. They were gigantic feats of engineering, about which he had learned nothing; feats accomplished, if all were true, before human history began . . . before animal history began. Or was that only mythology? He knew it would seem like mythology when he got back to Earth (if he ever got back), but the presence of Oyarsa was still too fresh a memory to allow him any real doubts. It even occurred to him that the distinction between history and mythology might be itself meaningless outside the Earth.

The thought baffled him, and he turned again to the landscape below — the landscape which became every moment less of a landscape and more of a diagram. By this time, to the east, a much larger and darker patch of discoloration than he had yet seen was pushing its way into the reddish ochre of the Malacandrian world — a curiously shaped patch with long arms or horns extended on each side and a sort of bay between them, like the concave side of a crescent. It grew and grew. The wide dark arms seemed to be spread out to engulf the whole planet. Suddenly he saw a bright point of light in the middle of this dark patch and realized that it was not a patch on the surface of the planet at all, but the black sky showing behind her. The smooth curve was the edge of her disk. At this, for the first time since their embarkation, fear took hold of him. Slowly, yet not too slowly for him to see, the dark arm spread farther and even farther round the lighted surface till at last they met. The whole disk, framed in blackness, was before him. The faint percussions of the meteorites had long been audible; the window through which he was gazing was no longer definitely beneath him. His limbs, though already very light, were almost too stiff to move, and he was very hungry. He looked at his watch. He had been at his post, spell-bound, for nearly eight hours.

He made his way with difficulty to the sunward side of the ship and reeled back almost blinded with the glory of the light. Groping, he found his darkened glasses in his old cabin and got himself food and water: Weston had rationed them strictly in both. He opened the door of the control-room and looked in. Both the partners, their faces drawn with anxiety, were seated before a kind of metal table; it was covered with delicate, gently vibrating instruments in which crystal and fine wire were the predominant materials. Both ignored his presence. For the rest of the silent journey he was free of the whole ship.

When he returned to the dark side, the world they were leaving hung in the star-strewn sky not much bigger than our earthly moon. Its colours were still visible — a reddish-yellow disk blotched with greenish-blue and capped with white at the poles. He saw the two tiny Malacandrian moons — their movement quite perceptible — and reflected that they were among the thousand things he had not noticed during his sojourn there. He slept, and woke, and saw the disk still hanging in the sky. It was smaller than the Moon now. Its colours were gone except for a faint, uniform tinge of redness in its light; even the light was not now incomparably stronger than that of the countless stars which surrounded it. It had ceased to be Malacandra; it was only Mars.

He soon fell back into his old routine of sleeping and basking, punctuated with the making of some scribbled notes for his Malacandrian dictionary. He knew that there was very little chance of his being able to communicate his new knowledge to man, that unrecorded death in the depth of space would almost certainly be the end of their adventure. But already it had become impossible to think of it as "space." Some moments of cold fear he had; but each time they were shorter and more quickly swallowed up in a sense of awe which made his personal fate seem wholly insignificant. He could not feel that they were an island of life journeying through an abyss of death. He felt almost the opposite — that life was waiting outside the little iron egg-shell in which they rode, ready at any moment to break in, and that, if it killed them, it would kill them by excess of its vitality. He hoped passionately that if they were to perish they would perish by the "unbodying" of the space-ship and not by suffocation within it. To be let out, to be set free, to dissolve into the ocean of eternal noon, seemed to him at certain moments a consummation even more desirable than their return to Earth. And if he had felt some such lift of the heart when first he passed through heaven on their outward journey, he felt it now tenfold, for now he was convinced that the abyss was full of life in the most literal sense, full of living creatures.

His confidence in Oyarsa's words about the *eldila* increased rather than diminished as they went on. He saw none of them; the intensity of light in which the ship swam allowed none of the fugitive variations which would have betrayed their presence. But he heard, or thought he heard, all kinds of delicate sound, or vibrations akin to sound, mixed with the tinkling rain of meteorites, and often the sense of unseen presences even within the space-ship became irresistible. It was this, more than anything else, that made his own chances of life seem so unimportant. He and all his race showed small and ephemeral against a background of such immeasurable fullness. His brain reeled at the thought of the true population of the universe, the three-dimensional infinitude of their territory, and the unchronicled æons of their past; but his heart became steadier than it had ever been.

It was well for him that he had reached this frame of mind before the real hardships of their journey began. Ever since their departure from Malacandra, the thermometer had steadily risen; now it was higher than it had stood at any time on their outward journey. And it still rose. The light also increased. Under his glasses he kept his eyes habitually tight shut, opening them only for the shortest time for necessary movements. He knew that if he reached Earth it would be with permanently damaged sight. But all this was nothing to the torment of heat. All three of them were awake for twenty-four hours out of the twenty-four, enduring with dilated eyeballs, blackened lips and froth-flecked cheeks the agony of thirst. It would be madness to increase their scanty rations of water: madness even to consume air in discussing the question.

He saw well enough what was happening. In his last bid for life Weston was venturing inside the Earth's orbit, leading them nearer the Sun than man, perhaps than life, had ever been. Presumably this was unavoidable; one could not follow a retreating Earth round the rim of its own wheeling course. They must be trying to meet it — to cut across . . . it was madness! But the question did not much occupy his mind; it was not possible for long to think of anything but thirst. One thought of water; then one thought of thirst; then one thought of thinking of thirst; then of water again. And still the thermometer rose. The walls of the ship were too hot to touch. It was obvious that a crisis was approaching. In the next few hours it must kill them or get less.

It got less. There came a time when they lay exhausted and shivering in what seemed the cold, though it was still hotter than any terrestrial climate. Weston had so far succeeded; he had risked the highest temperature at which human life could theoretically survive, and they had lived through it. But they were not the same men. Hitherto Weston had slept very little even in his watches off; always after an hour or so of uneasy rest, he had returned to his charts and to his endless, almost despairing, calculations. You could see him fighting the despair — pinning his terrified brain down, and again down, to the figures. Now he never looked at them. He even seemed careless in the control-room. Devine moved and looked like a somnambulist. Ransom lived increasingly on the dark side and for long hours he thought of nothing. Although the first great danger was past, none of them, at this time, had any serious hope of a successful issue to their journey. They had now been fifty days, without speech, in their steel shell, and the air was already very bad.

Weston was so unlike his old self that he even allowed Ransom to take his share in the navigation. Mainly by signs, but with the help of a few whispered words, he taught him all that was necessary at this stage of the journey. Apparently they were racing home — but with little chance of reaching it in time — before some sort of cosmic "trade-wind." [1] A few rules of thumb enabled Ransom to keep the star which Weston pointed out to him in its position at the centre of the skylight, but always with his left hand on the bell to Weston's cabin.

This star was not the Earth. The days — the purely theoretical "days" which bore such a desperately practical meaning for the travellers — mounted to fifty-eight before Weston changed course, and a different luminary was in the centre. Sixty days, and it was visibly a planet. Sixty-six, and it was like a planet seen through field-glasses. Seventy and it was like nothing that Ransom had ever seen — a little dazzling disk too large for a planet and far too small for the Moon. Now that he was navigating, his celestial mood was shattered. Wild, animal thirst for life, mixed with homesick longing for the free airs and the sights and smells of earth — for grass and meat and beer and tea and the human voice — awoke in him. At first his chief difficulty on watch had been to resist drowsiness; now, though the air was worse, feverish excitement kept him

[1] **cosmic "trade-wind"**: The Mariner II space probe, launched toward Venus by the United States in 1962, verified the suspected existence of a so-called solar wind, a wholly metaphorical name for a constant stream of particles of energy streaming out into space from the sun. This fact of science makes an interesting parallel to the author's imaginative phrase.

vigilant. Often when he came off duty he found his right arm stiff and sore; for hours he had been pressing it unconsciously against the control-board as if his puny thrust could spur the space-ship to yet greater speed.

Now they had twenty days to go. Nineteen — eighteen — and on the white terrestrial disk, now a little larger than a sixpence, he thought he could make out Australia and the south-east corner of Asia. Hour after hour, though the markings moved slowly across the disk with the Earth's diurnal revolution, the disk itself refused to grow larger. "Get on! Get on!" Ransom muttered to the ship. Now ten days were left and it was like the Moon and so bright that they could not look steadily at it. The air in their little sphere was ominously bad, but Ransom and Devine risked a whisper as they changed watches.

"We'll do it," they said. "We'll do it yet."

On the eighty-seventh day, when Ransom relieved Devine, he thought there was something wrong with the Earth. Before his watch was done, he was sure. It was no longer a true circle, but bulging a little on one side; it was almost pear-shaped. When Weston came on duty he gave one glance at the skylight, rang furiously on the bell for Devine, thrust Ransom aside, and took the navigating seat. His face was the colour of putty. He seemed to be about to do something to the controls, but as Devine entered the room he looked up and shrugged his shoulders with a gesture of despair. Then he buried his face in his hands and laid his head down on the control-board.

Ransom and Devine exchanged glances. They bundled Weston out of the seat — he was crying like a child — and Devine took his place. And now at last Ransom understood the mystery of the bulging Earth. What had appeared as a bulge on one side of her disk was becoming increasingly distinct as a second disk, a disk almost as large in appearance as her own. It was covering more than half of the Earth. It was the moon — between them and the Earth, and two hundred and forty thousand miles nearer. Ransom did not know what fate this might mean for the space-ship. Devine obviously did, and never had he appeared so admirable. His face was as pale as Weston's but his eyes were clear and preternaturally bright; he sat crouched over the controls like an animal about to spring and he was whistling very softly between his teeth.

Hours later Ransom understood what was happening. The Moon's disk was now larger than the Earth's and very gradually it became apparent to him that both disks were diminishing in size. The space-ship was no longer approaching either the Earth or the Moon; it was farther away from them than it had been half an hour ago, and that was the meaning of Devine's feverish activity with the controls. It was not merely that the Moon was crossing their path and cutting them off from the Earth; apparently for some reason — probably gravitational — it was dangerous to get too close to the Moon, and Devine was standing off into space. In sight of harbour they were being forced to turn back to the open sea. He glanced up at the chronometer. It was the morning of the eighty-eighth day. Two days to make the Earth, and they were moving away from her.

"I suppose this finishes us?" he whispered.

"Expect so," whispered Devine, without looking round.

Weston presently recovered sufficiently to come back and stand beside Devine. There was nothing for Ransom to do. He was sure now, that they were soon to die. With this realizaton, the agony of his suspense suddenly disappeared. Death, whether it came now or some thirty years later on Earth, rose up and claimed his attention. There were preparations a man likes to make. He left the control-room and returned into one of the sunward chambers, into the indifference of the moveless light, the warmth, the silence and the sharp-cut shadows. Nothing was farther from his mind than sleep. It must have been the exhausted atmosphere which made him drowsy. He slept.

He awoke in almost complete darkness in the midst of a loud continuous noise, which he could not at first identify. It reminded him of something — something he seemed to have heard in a previous existence. It was a prolonged drumming noise close above his head. Suddenly his heart gave a great leap.

"Oh God," he sobbed. "Oh God! It's *rain.*"

He was on Earth. The air was heavy and stale about him, but the choking sensations he had been suffering were gone. He realized that he was still in the space-ship. The others, in fear of its threatened "unbodying," had characteristically abandoned it the moment it touched Earth and left him to his fate. It was difficult in the dark, and under the crushing weight of terrestrial gravity, to find his way out. But he managed it. He found the manhole and slithered, drinking great draughts of air, down the outside of the sphere; slipped in mud, blessed the smell of it, and at last raised the unaccustomed weight of his body to its feet. He stood in pitch-black night under torrential rain. With every pore of his body he drank it in; with every desire of his heart he embraced the smell of the field about him — a patch of his native planet where grass grew, where cows moved, where presently he would come to hedges and a gate.

He had walked about half an hour when a vivid light behind him and a strong, momentary wind informed him that the space-ship was no more. He felt very little interest.

He had seen dim lights, the lights of men, ahead. He contrived to get into a lane, then into a road, then into a village street. A lighted door was open. There were voices from within and they were speaking English. There was a familiar smell. He pushed his way in, regardless of the surprise he was creating, and walked to the bar.

"A pint of bitter, please," said Ransom.

Chapter **22**

At this point, if I were guided by purely literary considerations, my story would end, but it is time to remove the mask and to acquaint the reader with the real and practical purpose for which this book has been written. At the same time he will learn how the writing of it became possible at all.

Dr. Ransom — and at this stage it will become obvious that that is not his real name — soon abandoned the idea of his Malacandrian dictionary and indeed all idea of communicating his story to the world. He was ill for several months, and when he recovered he found himself in considerable doubt as to whether what he remembered had really occurred. It looked very like a delusion produced by his illness, and most of his apparent adventures could, he saw, be explained psychoanalytically. He did not lean very heavily on this fact himself, for he had long since observed that a good many "real" things in the fauna and flora of our own world could be accounted for in the same way if you started with the assumption that they were illusions. But he felt that if he himself half doubted his own story the rest of the world would disbelieve it completely. He decided to hold his tongue, and there the matter would have rested but for a very curious coincidence.

This is where I come into the story. I had known Dr. Ransom slightly for several years and corresponded with him on literary and philological subjects, though we very seldom met. It was, therefore, quite in the usual order of things that I should write him a letter some months ago, of which I will quote the relevant paragraph. It ran like this:

"I am now working at the Platonists[1] of the twelfth century and incidentally discovering that they wrote damnably difficult Latin. In one of them, Bernardus Silvestris, there is a word I should particularly like your views on — the word *Oyarses*. It occurs in the description of a voyage through the heavens, and an *Oyarses* seems to be the "in-

[1] **Platonists:** followers of the Greek philosopher Plato (427?–347? B.C.); in this instance, a school of medieval Christian philosophers who used Platonic methods in writing about theological matters.

telligence" or tutelary spirit of a heavenly sphere, i.e. in our language, of a planet. I asked C. J. about it and he says it ought to be *Ousiarches*. That, of course, would make sense, but I do not feel quite satisfied. Have you by any chance ever come across a word like *Oyarses,* or can you hazard any guess as to what language it may be?"

The immediate result of this letter was an invitation to spend a week-end with Dr. Ransom. He told me his whole story, and since then he and I have been almost continuously at work on the mystery. A good many facts, which I have no intention of publishing at present, have fallen into our hands; facts about planets in general and about Mars in particular, facts about mediæval Platonists, and (not least in importance) facts about the Professor to whom I am giving the fictitious name of Weston. A systematic report of these facts might, of course, be given to the civilized world: but that would almost certainly result in universal incredulity and in a libel action from "Weston." At the same time, we both feel that we cannot be silent. We are being daily confirmed in our belief that the *oyarses* of Mars was right when it said that the present "celestial year" was to be a revolutionary one, that the long isolation of our own planet is nearing its end, and that great doings are on foot. We have found reason to believe that the mediæval Platonists were living in the same celestial year as ourselves — in fact, that it began in the twelfth century of our era — and that the occurrence of the name Oyarsa (Latinized as *oyarses*) in Bernardus Silvestris is not an accident. And we have also evidence — increasing almost daily — that "Weston," or the force or forces behind "Weston," will play a very important part in the events of the next few centuries, and, unless we prevent them, a very disastrous one. We do not mean that they are likely to invade Mars — our cry is not merely "Hands off Malacandra." The dangers to be feared are not planetary but cosmic, or at least solar, and they are not temporal but eternal. More than this it would be unwise to say.

It was Dr. Ransom who first saw that our only chance was to publish in the form of *fiction* what would certainly not be listened to as fact. He even thought — greatly overrating my literary powers — that this might have the incidental advantage of reaching a wider public, and that, certainly, it would reach a great many people sooner than "Weston." To my objection that if accepted as fiction it would for that very reason be regarded as false, he replied that there would be indications enough in the narrative for the few readers — the very few — who *at present* were prepared to go further into the matter.

"And they," he said, "will easily find out you, or me, and will easily identify Weston. Anyway," he continued, "what we need for the moment is not so much a body of belief as a body of people familiarized with certain ideas. If we could even effect in one per cent of our readers a change-over from the conception of Space to the conception of Heaven we should have made a beginning."

What neither of us foresaw was the rapid march of events which was to render the book out of date before it was published. These events have already made it rather a prologue to our story than the story itself. But we must let it go as it stands. For the later stages of the adventure — well, it was Aristotle, long before Kipling, who taught us the formula, "That is another story."

POSTSCRIPT

(*Being extracts from a letter written by the original of "Dr. Ransom" to the author.*)

. . . I think you are right, and after the two or three corrections (marked in red) the MS. will have to stand. I won't deny that I am disappointed, but then any attempt to tell such a story is bound to disappoint the man who has really been there. I am not now referring to the ruthless way in which you have cut down all the philological part, though, as it now stands, we are giving our readers a mere caricature of the Malacandrian language. I mean something more difficult — something which I couldn't possibly express. How can one "get across" the Malacandrian *smells?* Nothing comes back to me more vividly in my dreams . . . especially the early morning smell in those purple woods, where the very mention of "early morning" and "woods" is misleading because it must set you thinking of earth and moss and cobwebs and the smell of our own planet, but I'm thinking of something totally different. More "aromatic" . . . yes, but then it is not hot or luxurious or exotic as that word suggests. Something aromatic, spicy, yet very cold, very thin, tingling at the back of the nose — something that did to the sense of smell what high, sharp violin notes do to the ear. And mixed with that I always hear the sound of the singing — great hollow hound-like music from enormous throats, deeper than Chaliapin,[1] a "warm, dark noise." I am homesick for my old Malacandrian valley when I think of it; yet God knows when I heard it there I was homesick enough for the Earth.

Of course you are right; if we are to treat it as a story you *must* telescope the time I spent in the village during which "nothing happened." But I grudge it. Those quiet weeks, the mere living among the *hrossa,* are to me the main thing that happened. I *know* them, Lewis; that's

[1] **Feodor Chaliapin:** Russian operatic basso (1873–1938).

what you can't get into a mere story. For instance, because I always take a thermometer with me on a holiday (it has saved many a one from being spoiled) I know that the normal temperature of a *hross* is 103°. I know — though I can't remember learning it — that they live about 80 Martian years, or 160 earth years; that they marry at about 20 (= 40); that their droppings, like those of the horse, are not offensive to themselves, or to me, and are used for agriculture; that they don't shed tears, or blink; that they do get (as you would say) "elevated" but not drunk on a gaudy night — of which they have many. But what can one do with these scraps of information? I merely analyse them out of a whole living memory that can never be put into words, and no one in this world will be able to build up from such scraps quite the right picture. For example, can I make even you understand how I know, beyond all question, why it is that the Malacandrians don't keep pets and, in general, don't feel about their "lower animals" as we do about ours? Naturally it is the sort of thing they themselves could never have told me. One just sees why when one sees the three species together. Each of them is to the others *both* what a man is to us *and* what an animal is to us. They can talk to each other, they can co-operate, they have the same ethics; to that extent a *sorn* and a *hross* meet like two men. But then each finds the other different, funny, attractive as an animal is attractive. Some instinct starved in us, which we try to soothe by treating irrational creatures almost as if they were rational, is really satisfied in Malacandra. They don't need pets.

By the way, while we are on the subject of species, I am rather sorry that the exigencies of the story have been allowed to simplify the biology so much. Did I give you the impression that each of the three species was perfectly homogeneous? If so, I misled you. Take the *hrossa;* my friends were black *hrossa,* but there are also silver *hrossa,* and in some of the western *handramits* one finds the great crested *hross* — ten feet high, a dancer rather than a singer, and the noblest animal, after man, that I have ever seen. Only the males have the crest. I also saw a pure white *hross* at Meldilorn, but like a fool I never found out whether he represented a sub-species or was a mere freak like our terrestrial *albino.* There is at least one other kind of *sorn* besides the kind I saw — the *soroborn* or red *sorn* of the desert, who lives in the sandy north. He's a corker by all accounts.

I agree, it is a pity I never saw the *pfifltriggi* at home. I know nearly enough about them to "fake" a visit to them as an episode in the story, but I don't think we ought to introduce any mere fiction. "True in substance" sounds all very well on earth, but I can't imagine myself explaining it to Oyarsa, and I have a shrewd suspicion (see my last letter) that I have not heard the end of *him.* Anyway, why should our "readers" (you seem to know the devil of a lot about them!), who are so determined to hear nothing about the language, be so anxious to know more of the *pfifltriggi?* But if you can work it in, there is, of course, no harm in explaining that they are oviparous and matriarchal, and short-lived compared with the other species. It is pretty plain that the great depressions which they inhabit are the old ocean-beds of Malacandra. *Hrossa,* who have visited them, describe themselves as going down into deep forests over sand, "the bone-stones (fossils) of ancient wave-borers about them." No doubt these are the dark patches seen on the Martian disk from Earth. And that reminds me — the "maps" of Mars which I have consulted since I got back are so inconsistent with one another that I have given up the attempt to identify my own *handramit.* If you want to try your hand, the desideratum is a "roughly north-east and south-west 'canal' cutting a north and south 'canal' not more than twenty miles from the equator." But astronomers differ very much as to what they can see.

Now as to your most annoying question: "Did Augray, in describing the *eldila,* confuse the ideas of a subtler body and a superior being?" No. The confusion is entirely your own. He said two things: that the *eldila* had bodies different from those of planetary animals, and that they were superior in intelligence. Neither he nor anyone else in Malacandra ever confused the one statement with the other or deduced the one from the other. In fact, I have reasons for thinking that there are also irrational animals with the *eldil* type of body (you remember Chaucer's "airish beasts"?).

I wonder are you wise to say nothing about the problem of *eldil* speech? I agree that it would spoil the narrative to raise the question during the trial-scene at Meldilorn, but surely many readers will have enough sense to ask how the *eldila,* who obviously don't breathe, can talk. It is true that we should have to admit we don't know, but oughtn't the readers to be told that? I suggested to J. — the only scientist here who is in my confidence — your theory that they might have instruments, or even organs, for manipulating the air around them and thus producing sounds indirectly, but he didn't seem to think much of it. He thought it probable that they directly manipulated the ears of those they were "speaking" to. That sounds pretty difficult . . . of course one must remember that we have really no knowledge of the shape or size of an *eldil,* or even of its relations to space (*our* space) in general. In fact, one wants to keep on insisting that we really know next to nothing about them. Like you, I can't help trying to fix their relation to the things that appear in

terrestrial tradition — gods, angels, fairies. But we haven't the data. When I attempted to give Oyarsa some idea of our own Christian angelology, he certainly seemed to regard our "angels" as different in some way from himself. But whether he meant that they were a different species, or only that they were some special military caste (since our poor old earth turns out to be a kind of Ypres Salient [1] in the universe), I don't know.

Why must you leave out my account of how the shutter jammed just before our landing on Malacandra? Without this, your description of our sufferings from excessive light on the return journey raises the very obvious question, "Why didn't they close their shutters?" I don't believe your theory that "readers never notice that sort of thing." I'm sure I should.

There are two scenes that I wish you could have worked into the book; no matter — they are worked into me. One or other of them is always before me when I close my eyes.

In one of them I see the Malacandrian sky at morning; pale blue, so pale that now, when I have grown once more accustomed to terrestrial skies, I think of it as almost white. Against it the nearer tops of the giant weeds — the "trees" as you call them — show black, but far away, across miles of that blind-

[1] **Ypres Salient:** Ypres, a town in Flanders (Belgium), was the scene of crucial battles in World War I.

ing blue water, the remoter woods are water-colour purple. The shadows all around me on the pale forest-floor are like shadows on snow. There are figures walking before me; slender yet gigantic forms, black and sleek as animated tall hats; their huge round heads, poised on their sinuous stalk-like bodies, give them the appearance of black tulips. They go down, singing, to the edge of the lake. The music fills the wood with its vibration, though it is so soft that I can hardly hear it: it is like dim organ music. Some of them embark, but most remain. It is done slowly; this is no ordinary embarkation, but some ceremony. It is, in fact, a *hross* funeral. Those three with the grey muzzles whom they have helped into the boat are going to Meldilorn to die. For in that world, except for some few whom the *hnakra* gets, no one dies before his time. All live out the full span allotted to their kind, and a death with them is as predictable as a birth with us. The whole village has known that those three will die this year, this month; it was an easy guess that they would die even this week. And now they are off, to receive the last counsel of Oyarsa, to die, and to be by him "unbodied." The corpses, as corpses, will exist only for a few minutes: there are no coffins in Malacandra, no sextons, churchyards, or undertakers. The valley is solemn at their departure, but I see no signs of passionate grief. They do not doubt their immortality, and friends of the same generation are not torn apart. You leave the world, as you entered it, with the "men of your own year." Death is not preceded by dread nor followed by corruption.

The other scene is a nocturne. I see myself bathing with Hyoi in the warm lake. He laughs at my clumsy swimming; accustomed to a heavier world, I can hardly get enough of me under the water to make any headway. And then I see the night sky. The greater part of it is very like ours, though the depths are blacker and the stars brighter; but something that no terrestrial analogy will enable you fully to picture is happening in the west. Imagine the Milky Way magnified — the Milky Way seen through our largest telescope on the clearest night. And then imagine this, not painted across the zenith, but rising like a constellation behind the mountain-tops — a dazzling necklace of lights brilliant as planets, slowly heaving itself up till it fills a fifth of the sky and now leaves a belt of blackness between itself and the horizon. It is too bright to look at for long, but it is only a preparation. Something else is coming. There is a glow like moonrise on the *harandra*. *Ahihra!* cries Hyoi, and other baying voices answer him from the darkness all about us. And now the true king of night is set up, and now he is threading his way through that strange western galaxy and making its lights dim by comparison with his own. I turn my eyes away, for the little disk is far brighter than the Moon in her greatest splendour. The whole *handramit* is bathed in colourless light; I could count the stems of the forest on the far side of the lake: I see that my finger-nails are broken and dirty. And now I guess what it is that I have seen — Jupiter rising beyond the Asteroids and forty million miles nearer than he has ever been to earthly eyes. But the Malacandrians would say "within the Asteroids," for they have an odd habit, some-times, of turning the solar system inside out. They call the Asteroids the "dancers before the threshold of the Great Worlds." The Great Worlds are the planets, as we should say, "beyond" or "outside" the Asteroids. Glundandra (Jupi-ter) is the greatest of these and has some importance in Malacandrian thought which I cannot fathom. He is "the centre," "great Meldilorn," "throne" and "feast." They are, of course, well aware that he is unin-habitable, at least by animals of the planetary type; and they certainly have no pagan idea of giving a lo-cal habitation to Maleldil. But somebody or something of great importance is connected with Jupi-ter; as usual "The *séroni* would know." But they never told me. Per-haps the best comment is in the au-thor whom I mentioned to you: "For as it was well said of the great Africanus that he was never less alone than when alone, so, in our philosophy, no parts of this univer-sal frame are less to be called soli-tarie than those which the vulgar

esteem most solitarie, since the withdrawing of men and beasts sig-nifieth but the greater frequency of more excellent creatures."

More of this when you come. I am trying to read every old book on the subject that I can hear of. Now that "Weston" has shut the door, the way to the planets lies through the past; if there is to be any more space-travelling, it will have to be time-travelling as well . . . !

For Study

1. At the start of Chapter 18, in the discussion of Malacandrian humor, this statement is made: "Apparently the comic spirit arose chiefly from the meeting of the different kinds of *hnau*." Difference is a natural source of humor. Why is it that among men difference is often a cause of malice and hostility? Do we lose something if we let occasional vicious laughter at differences deprive us of a proper kind of humor arising out of our dif-ferences?

2. Humans sometimes fear differ-ences. Discuss Oyarsa's answer to Ransom when the latter, on page 100 in Chapter 18, tries to explain his fear by saying "you are unlike me."

3. In Chapter 18, what are the per-sons and events Oyarsa tells about in discussing the history of the two plan-ets, Malacandra and Thulcandra? What is alluded to when Oyarsa re-fers to Maleldil as having "dared ter-rible things, wrestling with the Bent

One in Thulcandra"? Who and what is "the Bent One"? Who and what are the "false *eldila* in the wild parts of our world," of which Ransom speaks?

4. In Chapter 19, after Weston's attempt to impress the Malacandrians has failed, why is he "inclined to think they have even less intelligence than we supposed"? What assumptions govern his approach to them?

5. Earlier in Chapter 15, a *sorn* said, "Body is movement." At the end of Chapter 19, Oyarsa says of the dead *hrossa*, "Let us scatter the movements which were their bodies." What does this mean in terms of physics?

6. Immediately after this "unbodying," what further insight into Devine's character are we given?

7. Discuss the distinction which Oyarsa draws between Weston and Devine (page 115).

8. Summarize Oyarsa's statements to Weston on what is wrong with man (page 116). Contrast the state of mind and spirit of the Malacandrian *hnau* with that of man. What does Oyarsa teach about the deaths of individuals and of species? In Chapter 16, what was the attitude of the *sorn* toward death? As told near the end of the Postscript, how do the *hrossa* handle deaths and funerals?

9. Discuss the point which Oyarsa makes in Chapter 20 about the folly of exaggerating one sound principle or law at the expense of other sound principles or laws. What examples of such exaggerations can you mention?

10. In the long scene with Oyarsa (Chapters 19–20), C. S. Lewis displays a talent for combining humor with solemnity. Here, as indeed throughout the story, Weston is shown as humorless. Why is this characteristic a part of his nature? What trait has killed his sense of humor?

11. At the beginning of Chapter 21, Oyarsa says to Ransom, "You have shown me more wonders than are known in the whole of heaven." To what "wonders" is Oyarsa referring?

12. What narrative purpose is served by Chapter 22 and the Postscript? What effect do they create? Discuss the meaning of the word *verisimilitude*. To what extent do you consider this story to be verisimilar?

For Writing

Write an essay on the aims of Weston as expounded by him to Oyarsa on pages 111–16. In your essay, explain these aims, discuss their importance in human history, and make clear your opinions about them.

Looking Back at the Story as a Whole

1. In the light of information gained from Ransom's scene with Oyarsa, reconsider the second paragraph of Chapter 10 (page 51). Why do you think that Ransom's "whole imaginative training somehow encouraged him to associate superhuman intelligence with monstrosity of form and ruthlessness of will"?

2. Now that you have seen the great difference between Malacandra and Thulcandra, the "silent planet," what early clue to the meaning of the story can you find planted at the close of Chapter 9 (page 51)?

3. In Chapter 12, disturbed by his conversation with Hyoi, Ransom is led to wonder, "What was the history of man?" What is the story's ultimate answer to this question? What is the significance of the alterations in the stone carvings that Ransom sees in Chapter 17?

4. In varying degrees, Ransom dreads in advance, or is nervous about, his encounter with each species or order of being on Malacandra. Yet after each encounter he finds his fears to have been groundless. Indeed, it is his own kind and his own world he has best cause to fear. Why does Oyarsa refer to Ransom's fears as a form of bentness? (Several passages in the story touch this question.)

5. One of the sensations captured in this story is the feeling we call awe. Look up *awe* in a large dictionary (in the *Oxford English Dictionary*, if available). Discuss the source and the quality of the awe that Ransom feels

in Meldilorn, especially at the approach and the presence of Oyarsa. Why is it that Ransom feels awe but Weston and Devine feel no more than anger and common fear?

6. What is meant by Oyarsa's words to Ransom in Chapter 18: "We are both copies of Maleldil?" In the Bible (Genesis 1:26) we are told "And God said, Let us make man in our image, after our likeness. . . ." Clearly the image or likeness there spoken of is not physical. What is the attribute that God is said to share with Oyarsa and the other *eldila,* as well as with man and the various Malacandrian *hnau?*

For Writing

1. Write a paper on this statement of Hyoi in Chapter 12: ". . . it is not a few deaths roving the world around him that make a *hnau* miserable. It is a bent *hnau* that would blacken the world."

2. Write a paper on this statement, which appears in the second paragraph of Chapter 13: "It was necessary, and the necessary was always possible."

Paradise Lost

by *John Milton* (*1608-1674*)

An epic is a long narrative poem that relates great events about heroic personages of tradition or history. John Milton had cherished the ambition to write an epic in English many years before he made up his mind about a specific subject. He achieved his ambition so well that he stands beside Chaucer and Shakespeare as one of the foremost poets in our language. The great eighteenth-century critic, Samuel Johnson, said of *Paradise Lost* that it "is not the greatest of heroic poems only because it is not the first."

An epic requires events and characters on a grand scale. No one could have chosen a frame more vast and awesome than that of war in Heaven, the casting out of rebellious angels, the creation of Earth and man, the temptation and fall of man, and the ongoing consequences. The opening lines declare a purpose which in itself carries literary ambition to the point of peril: to "assert Eternal Providence" and to "justify the ways of God to men." The poet's staggering breadth of subject, superhuman cast of characters, and challenging aim justify his boast that he is pursuing "Things unattempted yet in prose or rhyme."

Bear in mind that the events here narrated are the same as many which C. S. Lewis has told about, in strikingly different terms, in *Out of the Silent Planet*. We will consider the relationships between these works at the end of this section. As you read, look for correspondences yourself. You will find that Milton's epic is an older version of the story of Thulcandra, the "silent planet."

THE VERSE

The measure is English heroic verse without rhyme, as that of Homer in Greek, and of Virgil in Latin — rhyme being no necessary adjunct or true ornament of poem or good verse, in longer works especially, but the invention of a barbarous age, to set off wretched matter and lame metre; graced indeed since by the use of some famous modern poets,[1] carried away by custom, but much to their own vexation, hindrance, and constraint to express many things

---

[1] Milton here makes a thrust at John Dryden (1631–1700), one of the chief literary figures of the day, a defender and user of rhyme. Dryden, for his part, spoke generously of Milton's achievement in *Paradise Lost,* saying, "This man cuts us all out, and the ancients too."

otherwise, and for the most part worse, than else they would have expressed them. Not without cause, therefore, some both Italian and Spanish poets of prime note have rejected rhyme both in longer and shorter works, as have also long since our best English tragedies, as a thing of itself, to all judicious ears, trivial and of no true musical delight; which consists only in apt numbers, fit quantity of syllables, and the sense variously drawn out from one verse into another, not in the jingling sound of like endings — a fault avoided by the learned ancients both in poetry and all good oratory. This neglect then of rhyme so little is to be taken for a defect, though it may seem so perhaps to vulgar readers, that it rather is to be esteemed an example set — the first in English — of ancient liberty recovered to heroic poem from the troublesome and modern bondage of riming.

Book I

THE ARGUMENT

The First Book proposes, first in brief, the whole subject — Man's disobedience, and the loss thereupon of Paradise, wherein he was placed; then touches the prime cause of his fall — the Serpent, or rather Satan in the Serpent; who, revolting from God, and drawing to his side many legions of Angels, was, by the command of God, driven out of Heaven, with all his crew, into the great Deep. Which action passed over, the Poem hastens into the midst of things, presenting Satan, with his Angels, now fallen into Hell — described here not in the Centre [1] (for heaven and

[1] **not in the Centre:** Even in Milton's time, the seventeenth century, the Copernican astronomy had placed the Earth in its right relation to the sun and removed any simple, mythical sense of Heaven as *up* and Hell as *down* (or as any part of Earth). Thus Milton himself regards all questions of *place* or *location* in his poem as metaphorical. As to where Hell is, lines from Christopher Marlowe's drama *Dr. Faustus* (c. 1588) go directly to the point. There the fiend Mephistophilis, in answer to Faustus's question, says:

> Why, this is hell, nor am I out of it.
> Think'st thou that I, who saw the face of God
> And tasted the eternal joys of heaven,
> Am not tormented with ten thousand hells
> In being depriv'd of everlasting bliss?

And in a later passage:

> . . . when all the world dissolves,
> And every creature shall be purified,
> All places shall be hell that are not heaven.

earth may be supposed as yet not made, certainly not yet accursed), but in a place of utter darkness, fitliest called Chaos. Here Satan, with his Angels lying on the burning lake, thunderstruck and astonished, after a certain space recovers, as from confusion; calls up him who, next in order and dignity, lay by him: they confer of their miserable fall. Satan awakens all his legions, who lay till then in the same manner confounded. They rise: their numbers; array of battle; their chief leaders named, according to the idols known afterwards in Canaan and the countries adjoining. To these Satan directs his speech; comforts them with hope yet of regaining Heaven; but tells them, lastly, of a new world and new kind of creature to be created, according to an ancient prophecy, or report, in Heaven — for that Angels were long before this visible creation was the opinion of many ancient Fathers. To find out the truth of this prophecy, and what to determine thereon, he refers to a full council. What his associates thence attempt. Pandemonium, the palace of Satan, rises, suddenly built out of the Deep; the infernal Peers there sit in council.

Of Man's first disobedience and the fruit
Of that forbidden tree whose mortal taste
Brought death into the world and all our woe,
With loss of Eden, till one greater Man°
Restore us and regain the blissful seat,   5
Sing, Heavenly Muse,° that on the secret top
Of Oreb or of Sinai° didst inspire
That shepherd° who first taught the chosen seed°
In the beginning how the heavens and earth
Rose out of Chaos; or, if Sion hill   10
Delight thee more, and Siloa's brook° that flowed
Fast by° the oracle of God,° I thence
Invoke thy aid to my adventurous song,
That with no middle flight intends to soar
Above the Aonian mount,° while it pursues   15
Things unattempted yet in prose or rhyme.

4. one greater Man: Christ. 6. Heavenly Muse: in Greek literature the patron goddess of poetry, whom Milton invokes in conventional classic style but whom he equates with the Holy Spirit, the Third Person of the Christian Trinity, as inspirer of the arts. 7. Oreb . . . Sinai: Mount Oreb (or Horeb) or Mount Sinai, where Moses spoke with God. 8. That shepherd: Moses; the chosen seed: Israel. 10–11. Sion hill . . . Siloa's brook: in Jerusalem. 12. Fast by: close by; the oracle of God: Solomon's temple. 15. Aonian mount: Helicon, where the Muses dwelt.

And chiefly Thou, O Spirit,° that dost prefer
Before all temples the upright heart and pure,
Instruct me, for Thou know'st; Thou from the first
Wast present, and, with mighty wings outspread,   20
Dovelike sat'st brooding on the vast Abyss
And mad'st it pregnant: what in me is dark
Illumine, what is low raise and support,
That, to the height of this great argument,
I may assert Eternal Providence,   25
And justfy the ways of God to men.
   Say first — for Heaven hides nothing from thy view,
Nor the deep tract of Hell — say first what cause
Moved our grand Parents, in that happy state,
Favoured of Heaven so highly, to fall off   30
From their Creator and transgress his will,
For one restraint, lords of the world besides?°
Who first seduced them to that foul revolt?
The infernal Serpent;° he it was whose guile,
Stirred up with envy and revenge, deceived   35
The mother of mankind, what time° his pride
Had cast him out from Heaven, with all his host
Of rebel Angels, by whose aid aspiring
To set himself in glory above his peers,°
He trusted to have equalled the Most High,   40
If he opposed, and with ambitious aim
Against the throne and monarchy of God
Raised impious war in Heaven and battle proud,
With vain attempt. Him the Almighty Power
Hurled headlong flaming from the ethereal sky,   45
With hideous ruin and combustion down
To bottomless perdition,° there to dwell
In adamantine° chains and penal fire,
Who durst defy the Omnipotent to arms.
Nine times the space that measures day and night   50
To mortal men, he with his horrid crew
Lay vanquished, rolling in the fiery gulf,

---

17. **O Spirit:** again the Holy Spirit. The allusion that follows in lines 19–22 is
to the account of creation in the first chapter of Genesis: "And the Spirit of God
moved upon the face of the waters." 32. **For . . . besides:** Everything about them
was theirs, except the single tree whose fruit they were forbidden. 34. **infernal
Serpent:** Satan in the form he assumed when tempting Eve. 36. **what time:** when.
39. **his peers:** his equals among the angels. 47. **perdition:** complete loss or ruin;
here, Hell. 48. **adamantine:** hard as steel, unbreakable.

Confounded, though immortal;° but his doom
Reserved him to more wrath, for now the thought
Both of lost happiness and lasting pain   55
Torments him: round he throws his baleful eyes,
That witnessed huge affliction and dismay,
Mixed with obdúrate° pride and steadfast hate;
At once, as far as angel's ken,° he views
The dismal situation waste and wild;   60
A dungeon horrible, on all sides round,
As one great furnace flamed, yet from those flames
No light, but rather darkness visible
Served only to discover sights of woe,
Regions of sorrow, doleful shades, where peace   65
And rest can never dwell, hope never comes
That comes to all, but torture without end
Still urges,° and a fiery deluge, fed
With ever-burning sulphur unconsumed.
Such place Eternal Justice had prepared   70
For those rebellious, here their prison ordained
In utter darkness, and their portion set,
As far removed from God and light of Heaven
As from the centre thrice to the utmost pole.
Oh, how unlike the place from whence they fell!   75
There the companions of his fall, o'erwhelmed
With floods and whirlwinds of tempestuous fire,
He soon discerns, and, weltering by his side,
One next himself in power, and next in crime,
Long after known in Palestine, and named   80
Beëlzebub. To whom the Arch-Enemy,
And thence in Heaven called Satan,° with bold words
Breaking the horrid silence, thus began:
  "If thou beest he — but oh, how fallen! how changed
From him who, in the happy realms of light,   85
Clothed with transcendent brightness, didst outshine
Myriads, though bright! — if he whom mutual league,
United thoughts and counsels, equal hope
And hazard in the glorious enterprise,
Joined with me once, now misery hath joined   90

53. Confounded, though immortal: defeated in their rebellion, though they cannot die. **58. obdúrate:** here accented on the second rather than the first syllable to make the line scan. **59. as far as angel's ken:** as far as an angel can see or know. **68. Still urges:** keeps on. **82. Satan:** The word, in Hebrew, means "adversary."

In equal ruin; into what pit thou seest
From what height fallen: so much the stronger proved
He° with his thunder — and till then who knew
The force of those dire arms?° Yet not for those,
Nor what the potent Victor in his rage   95
Can else inflict, do I repent or change,
Though changed in outward lustre, that fixed mind,
And high disdain from sense of injured merit,
That with the Mightiest raised me to contend,
And to the fierce contention brought along   100
Innumerable force of Spirits armed
That durst dislike his reign, and, me preferring,
His utmost power with adverse power opposed
In dubious battle on the plains of Heaven,
And shook his throne. What though the field be lost?   105
All is not lost — the unconquerable will,
And study of revenge, immortal hate,
And courage never to submit or yield —
And what is else not to be overcome.
That glory never shall his wrath or might   110
Extort from me. To bow and sue for grace
With suppliant knee, and deify his power
Who, from the terror of this arm, so late
Doubted his empire — that were low indeed;
That were an ignominy and shame beneath   115
This downfall; since by fate the strength of Gods
And this empyreal° substance cannot fail;°
Since, through experience of this great event,
In arms not worse, in foresight much advanced,
We may with more successful hope resolve   120
To wage by force or guile eternal war
Irreconcilable, to our grand Foe,
Who now triúmphs, and in the excess of joy
Sole reigning holds the tyranny of Heaven."
    So spake the apostate Angel, though in pain,   125
Vaunting aloud, but racked with deep despair;
And him thus answered soon his bold compeer:°
"O Prince, O Chief of many thronèd Powers

93. He: God. 93–94. and . . . arms?: This question might well be applied to
the explosion of the first atom bomb over Hiroshima, Japan, at the end of World
War II. 117. empyreal: heavenly; fail: die, or be destroyed. 127. compeer: companion and equal.

That led the embattled Seraphim° to war
Under thy conduct, and, in dreadful deeds   130
Fearless, endangered Heaven's perpetual King,
And put to proof his high supremacy,
Whether upheld by strength, or chance, or fate!
Too well I see and rue the dire event
That, with sad overthrow and foul defeat,   135
Hath lost us Heaven, and all this mighty host
In horrible destruction laid thus low,
As far as Gods and Heavenly Essences°
Can perish: for the mind and spirit remains
Invincible and vigour soon returns,   140
Though all our glory extinct, and happy state
Here swallowed up in endless misery.
But what if he our Conqueror (whom I now
Of force believe almighty, since no less
Than such could have o'erpowered such force as ours)   145
Have left us this our spirit and strength entire
Strongly to suffer and support our pains,
That we may so suffice his vengeful ire
Or do him mightier service as his thralls
By right of war, whate'er his business be,   150
Here in the heart of Hell to work in fire,
Or do his errands in the gloomy Deep?
What can it then avail though yet we feel
Strength undiminished, or eternal being
To undergo eternal punishment?"   155
    Whereto with speedy words the Arch-Fiend replied:
"Fallen Cherub,° to be weak is miserable,
Doing or suffering — but of this be sure:
To do aught good never will be our task,
But ever to do ill our sole delight,   160
As being the contrary to his high will
Whom we resist. If then his providence
Out of our evil seek to bring forth good,
Our labour must be to pervert that end,
And out of good still to find means of evil;   165
Which oft-times may succeed so as perhaps
Shall grieve him, if I fail not, and disturb

129. **Seraphim:** plural of *Seraph*, an angel of a high order. Milton uses terms for ranks of angels without adhering strictly to the distinctions of medieval angelology. 138. **Essences:** beings. 157. **Cherub:** like Seraph, an angel of a high order.

His inmost counsels from their destined aim.
But see! the angry Victor hath recalled
His ministers of vengeance and pursuit   170
Back to the gates of Heaven: the sulphurous hail,
Shot after us in storm, o'erblown hath laid
The fiery surge that from the precipice
Of Heaven received us falling; and the thunder,
Winged with red lightning and impetuous rage,   175
Perhaps hath spent his shafts, and ceases now
To bellow through the vast and boundless Deep.
Let us not slip° the occasion, whether scorn
Or satiate° fury yield it from our Foe.
Seest thou yon dreary plain, forlorn and wild,   180
The seat of desolation, void of light,
Save what the glimmering of these livid flames
Casts pale and dreadful? Thither let us tend
From off the tossing of these fiery waves;
There rest, if any rest can harbour there;   185
And, reassembling our afflicted powers,
Consult how we may henceforth most offend
Our Enemy, our own loss how repair,
How overcome this dire calamity,
What reinforcement we may gain from hope,   190
If not, what resolution from despair."
    Thus Satan, talking to his nearest mate,
With head uplift above the wave, and eyes
That sparkling blazed; his other parts besides
Prone on the flood, extended long and large,   195
Lay floating many a rood,° in bulk as huge
As whom the fables name of monstrous size,
Titanian or Earth-born, that warred on Jove,°
Briareos or Typhon,° whom the den
By ancient Tarsus° held, or that sea-beast   200
Leviathan,° which God of all his works
Created hugest that swim the ocean-stream.
Him, haply slumbering on the Norway foam,

178. slip: let slip or lose. 179. satiate: satiated, satisfied to the full. 196. rood:
rod, a measure of length. 198. Titanian . . . Jove: The Titans, giant in size, were
the older deities of Greek mythology, who unsuccessfully waged war against the
usurper Zeus (or Jove). They were children of Ge (Earth). 199. Briareos or Typhon: gigantic monsters who, like the Titans, were offspring of Ge. 200. ancient
Tarsus: city in what is now Turkey. 201. Leviathan: sea monster referred to in
the Old Testament.

The pilot of some small night-foundered skiff
Deeming some island, oft, as seamen tell,   205
With fixèd anchor in his scaly rind
Moors by his side under the lee, while night
Invests° the sea and wishèd morn delays.
So stretched out huge in length the Arch-Fiend lay,
Chained on the burning lake; nor ever thence   210
Had risen or heaved his head but that the will
And high permission of all-ruling Heaven
Left him at large to his own dark designs,
That with reiterated crimes he might
Heap on himself damnation, while he sought   215
Evil to others, and enraged might see
How all his malice served but to bring forth
Infinite goodness, grace, and mercy, shown
On Man by him seduced, but on himself
Treble confusion, wrath, and vengeance poured.   220
    Forthwith upright he rears from off the pool
His mighty stature; on each hand the flames,
Driven backward, slope their pointing spires, and, rolled
In billows, leave i' the midst a horrid vale.
Then with expanded wings he steers his flight   225
Aloft, incumbent on° the dusky air,
That felt unusual weight, till on dry land
He lights — if it were land that ever burned
With solid, as the lake with liquid fire,
And such appeared in hue as when the force   230
Of subterranean wind transports a hill
Torn from Pelorus,° or the shattered side
Of thundering Aetna,° whose combustible
And fuelled entrails, thence conceiving fire,
Sublimed° with mineral fury, aid the winds,   235
And leave a singèd bottom all involved
With stench and smoke: such resting found the sole
Of unblest feet. Him followed his next mate,
Both glorying to have 'scaped the Stygian° flood
As gods, and by their own recovered strength,   240
Not by the sufferance° of Supernal° Power.
    "Is this the region, this the soil, the clime,"

208. Invests: covers. 226. incumbent on: lying upon. 232. Pelorus: promontory
in Sicily. 233. Aetna: volcano in Sicily. 235. Sublimed: set aflame. 239. Stygian: infernal, hellish. 241. sufferance: permission; Supernal: heavenly, divine.

Said then the lost Archangel, "this the seat
That we must change for Heaven, this mournful gloom
For that celestial light? Be it so, since he   245
Who now is sovran can dispose and bid
What shall be right: farthest from him is best,
Whom reason hath equalled, force hath made supreme
Above his equals. Farewell, happy fields,
Where joy for ever dwells! Hail, horrors! hail,   250
Infernal World! and thou, profoundest Hell,
Receive thy new possessor — one who brings
A mind not to be changed by place or time.
The mind is its own place, and in itself
Can make a Heaven of Hell, a Hell of Heaven.°   255
What matter where, if I be still the same,
And what I should be, all but less than he
Whom thunder hath made greater? Here at least
We shall be free; the Almighty hath not built
Here for his envy, will not drive us hence: 260
Here we may reign secure, and, in my choice,
To reign is worth ambition, though in Hell:
Better to reign in Hell than serve in Heaven.
But wherefore let we then our faithful friends,
The associates and co-partners of our loss,   265
Lie thus astonished° on the oblivious° pool,
And call them not to share with us their part
In this unhappy mansion, or once more
With rallied arms to try what may be yet
Regained in Heaven, or what more lost in Hell?"°   270
     So Satan spake; and him Beëlzebub
Thus answered: "Leader of those armies bright
Which, but the Omnipotent, none could have foiled,
If once they hear that voice, their liveliest pledge
Of hope in fears and dangers, heard so oft   275
In worst extremes, and on the perilous edge
Of battle, when it raged, in all assaults
Their surest signal, they will soon resume
New courage and revive, though now they lie
Grovelling and prostrate on yon lake of fire,   280
As we erewhile, astounded and amazed;

254–56. Compare these lines to the quotations from Marlowe's *Dr. Faustus*,
footnote, page 136. 266. astonished: dazed; oblivious: causing forgetfulness.
270. Satan is saying, in effect, "We have everything to gain and nothing to lose."

No wonder, fallen such a pernicious° highth!"
He scarce had ceased when the superior Fiend
Was moving toward the shore; his ponderous shield,
Ethereal temper,° massy,° large, and round,   285
Behind him cast. The broad circumference
Hung on his shoulders like the moon, whose orb
Through optic glass° the Tuscan artist° views
At evening, from the top of Fesole,°
Or in Valdarno,° to descry new lands,   290
Rivers, or mountains, in her spotty globe.
His spear, to equal which the tallest pine
Hewn on Norwegian hills to be the mast
Of some great ammiral° were but a wand,
He walked with, to support uneasy steps   295
Over the burning marl,° not like those steps
On Heaven's azure; and the torrid clime
Smote on him sore besides, vaulted with fire.
Nathless° he so endured till on the beach
Of that inflamèd sea he stood and called   300
His legions, Angel forms, who lay entranced°
Thick as autumnal leaves that strew the brooks
In Vallombrosa,° where the Etrurian shades
High overarched embower; or scattered sedge
Afloat, when with fierce winds Orion° armed   305
Hath vexed the Red Sea coast, whose waves o'erthrew
Busiris° and his Memphian chivalry°
While with perfidious hatred they pursued
The sojourners of Goshen° who beheld
From the safe shore their floating carcasses   310
And broken chariot-wheels — so thick bestrewn,
Abject° and lost, lay these, covering the flood,
Under amazement of their hideous change.

282. pernicious: ruinous, destructive. 285. Ethereal temper: His shield was tempered (that is, hardened) in Heaven; massy: massive. 288. optic glass: telescope; Tuscan artist: Galileo, whom Milton, when a young man, had visited. 289. Fesole: Fiesole, a town on a hill near Florence, Italy. 290. Valdarno: valley of the Arno, where Florence lies. 294. ammiral (admiral): flagship. 296. marl: crumbly soil. 299. Nathless: nevertheless. 301. entranced: in a trance. 303. Vallombrosa: "shady valley," a place in old Etruria, now Tuscany, in Italy. 305. Orion: a constellation, the rising and setting of which were associated with storms. 307. Busiris: Egyptian Pharaoh; Memphian chivalry: cavalry from Memphis, a capital city of ancient Egypt. 309. sojourners of Goshen: Israelites. This passage refers to the Old Testament story of the exodus of the Jews from Egypt and the loss of their pursuers in the Red Sea (see Exodus 14). 312. Abject: cast down.

He called so loud that all the hollow deep
Of Hell resounded: "Princes, Potentates,   315
Warriors, the Flower of Heaven, once yours, now lost,
If such astonishment as this can seize
Eternal Spirits; or have ye chosen this place
After the toil of battle to repose
Your wearied virtue, for the ease you find   320
To slumber here, as in the vales of Heaven?
Or in this abject posture have ye sworn
To adore the Conqueror? who now beholds
Cherub and Seraph rolling in the flood
With scattered arms and ensigns, till anon   325
His swift pursuers from Heaven-gates discern
The advantage, and, descending, tread us down
Thus drooping, or with linkèd thunderbolts
Transfix us to the bottom of his gulf?
Awake, arise, or be for ever fallen!"   330
   They heard and were abashed,° and up they sprung
Upon the wing, as when men wont to watch
On duty, sleeping found by whom they dread,
Rouse and bestir themselves ere well awake.
Nor did they not perceive the evil plight   335
In which they were, or the fierce pains not feel,
Yet to their General's voice they soon obeyed
Innumerable. As when the potent rod
Of Amram's son,° in Egypt's evil day,
Waved round the coast, up-called a pitchy cloud   340
Of locusts, warping on the eastern wind,
That o'er the realm of impious Pharaoh hung
Like Night, and darkened all the land of Nile,
So numberless were those bad Angels seen
Hovering on wing under the cope° of Hell,   345
'Twixt upper, nether, and surrounding fires;
Till, at a signal given, the uplifted spear
Of their great Sultan waving to direct
Their course, in even balance down they light
On the firm brimstone and fill all the plain: 350
A multitude like which the populous North
Poured never from her frozen loins to pass

---

331. abashed: ashamed. **339. Amram's son:** Moses. The allusion that follows is to one of the ten plagues that Moses called down upon Egypt when Pharaoh refused to release the Israelites from slavery (see Exodus 10). **345. cope:** covering.

Rhene or the Danaw,° when her barbarous sons
Came like a deluge on the South and spread
Beneath Gibraltar to the Libyan sands.   355
Forthwith, from every squadron and each band,
The heads and leaders thither haste where stood
Their great Commander; godlike shapes, and forms
Excelling human; princely Dignities;
And Powers that erst in Heaven sat on thrones,   360
Though of their names in Heavenly records now
Be no memorial, blotted out and rased
By their rebellion from the Books of Life.
Nor had they yet among the sons of Eve
Got them new names, till, wandering o'er the earth,   365
Through God's high sufferance for the trial of man,
By falsities and lies the greatest part
Of mankind they corrupted to forsake
God their Creator, and the invisible
Glory of him that made them to transform   370
Oft to the image of a brute, adorned
With gay religions full of pomp and gold,
And devils to adore for deities:°
Then were they known to men by various names,
And various idols through the heathen world.   375
    Say, Muse, their names then known, who first, who last,
Roused from the slumber on that fiery couch
At their great Emperor's call, as next in worth
Came singly where he stood on the bare strand,
While the promiscuous° crowd stood yet aloof?   380
    The chief were those who, from the pit of Hell°
Roaming to seek their prey on Earth, durst fix
Their seats, long after, next the seat of God,
Their altars by his altar, gods adored
Among the nations round, and durst abide   385
Jehovah thundering out of Sion, throned
Between the Cherubim; yea, often placed

353. Rhene . . . Danaw: the Rhine and the Danube, boundaries of the Roman empire. Barbaric Teutonic tribes crossed these rivers to swoop down upon southern Europe and north Africa. **373.** Milton, following the tradition of the early Christian Fathers, identifies all the heathen gods of the past with fallen angels who have deluded men into serving and worshiping them as gods. Viewed thus, they are real demons but false gods. **380. promiscuous:** mingled without being sorted out. **381–91.** These lines tell how the false gods later dared to push their altars close to those of God and even to invade His temples.

Within his sanctuary itself their shrines,
Abominations; and with cursèd things
His holy rites and solemn feasts profaned,   390
And with their darkness durst affront his light.

[Lines 392–587 catalogue the chief demons, giving them the
names by which they were worshiped as gods and telling of their
places of influence and their rites. The passage is impressive but
filled with obscure references; it can be omitted without loss for
our present purposes of study. The major demonic personages will
be identified as they take part in the council that follows. We
pick up the thread when the whole host has recovered from its
confusion and stands in order before Satan. He surveys his followers with mingled feelings of pride and anguish, and then addresses them.]

     . . . Thus far these beyond
Compare of mortal prowess, yet observed
Their dread Commander. He, above the rest
In shape and gesture proudly eminent,   590
Stood like a tower; his form had yet not lost
All her original brightness, nor appeared
Less than Archangel ruined, and the excess
Of glory obscured — as when the sun new-risen
Looks through the horizontal misty air   595
Shorn of his beams, or, from behind the moon,
In dim eclipse, disastrous° twilight sheds
On half the nations, and with fear of change
Perplexes monarchs. Darkened so, yet shone
Above them all the Archangel; but his face   600
Deep scars of thunder had intrenched, and care
Sat on his faded cheek, but under brows
Of dauntless courage, and considerate pride
Waiting revenge: cruel his eye, but cast
Signs of remorse and passion, to behold   605
The fellows of his crime — the followers rather
(Far other once beheld in bliss), condemned
For ever now to have their lot in pain,
Millions of Spirits for his fault amerced°
Of Heaven, and from eternal splendours flung   610

---

597. **disastrous:** portending disaster. The lines allude to the superstitious dread
of eclipses and other natural signs in the sky. 609. **amerced:** punished by loss.

For his revolt; yet faithful how they stood,
Their glory withered, as, when Heaven's fire
Hath scathed the forest oaks or mountain pines,
With singèd top their stately growth, though bare,
Stands on the blasted heath. He now prepared   615
To speak; whereat their doubled ranks they bend
From wing to wing, and half enclose him round
With all his peers: attention held them mute.
Thrice he assayed,° and thrice, in spite of scorn,
Tears, such as Angels weep, burst forth; at last   620
Words interwove with sighs found out their way:
    "O myriads of immortal Spirits! O Powers
Matchless, but with the Almighty! — and that strife
Was not inglorious, though the event was dire,
As this place testifies, and this dire change,   625
Hateful to utter. But what power of mind,
Foreseeing or presaging,° from the depth
Of knowledge past or present could have feared
How such united force of gods, how such
As stood like these, could ever know repulse?   630
For who can yet believe, though after loss,
That all these puissant° legions, whose exile
Hath emptied Heaven,° shall fail to reascend,
Self-raised, and repossess their native seat?
For me, be witness all the host of Heaven,   635
If counsels different° or danger shunned
By me have lost our hopes. But he who reigns
Monarch in Heaven till then as one secure
Sat on his throne, upheld by old repute,
Consent or custom, and his regal state   640
Put forth at full, but still his strength concealed,
Which tempted our attempt, and wrought our fall.
Henceforth his might we know, and know our own,
So as not either to provoke or dread
New war, provoked: our better part remains   645
To work in close design, by fraud or guile,
What force effected not; that he no less
At length from us may find, who overcomes

619. assayed: tried. He is trying to speak but his emotions at first are too
much for him, even though he scorns his own feelings. 627. presaging: foreknowing. 632. puissant: powerful. 633. Hath emptied Heaven: a boastful exaggeration,
for they are a minority. 636. counsels different: He is saying that he is not guilty
of having ignored better advice.

By force hath overcome but half his foe.
Space may produce new Worlds; whereof so rife   650
There went a fame in Heaven that he ere long
Intended to create, and therein plant
A generation whom his choice regard
Should favour equal to the Sons of Heaven.°
Thither, if but to pry, shall be perhaps   655
Our first eruption — thither, or elsewhere:
For this infernal pit shall never hold
Celestial Spirits in bondage, nor the Abyss
Long under darkness cover. But these thoughts
Full counsel must mature. Peace is despaired,   660
For who can think submission? War then, war
Open or understood, must be resolved."
  He spake; and, to confirm his words, out flew
Millions of flaming swords, drawn from the thighs
Of mighty Cherubim; the sudden blaze   665
Far round illumined Hell. Highly they raged
Against the Highest, and fierce with graspèd arms
Clashed on their sounding shields the din of war,
Hurling defiance toward the vault of Heaven.
  There stood a hill not far whose grisly top   670
Belched fire and rolling smoke; the rest entire
Shone with a glossy scurf° — undoubted sign
That in his womb was hid metallic ore,
The work of sulphur. Thither, winged with speed,
A numerous brigade hastened, as when bands   675
Of pioneers, with spade and pickaxe armed,
Forerun the royal camp to trench a field
Or cast a rampart. Mammon° led them on,
Mammon, the least erected° Spirit that fell
From Heaven; for even in Heaven his looks and thoughts   680
Were always downward bent, admiring more
The riches of Heaven's pavement, trodden gold,
Than aught divine or holy else enjoyed
In vision beatific; by him first
Men also, and by his suggestion taught,   685

650–54. Satan is speaking of Earth and the creation of man. 672. scurf: crust.
678. Mammon: The word for "riches" in ancient Chaldean. Milton here personi-
fies the word as a demon of greed and love of gold. In Matthew 6:24, in the
Sermon on the Mount, Jesus says, "Ye cannot serve God and mammon." Milton
goes on to say that Mammon taught men to mine for gold and other precious metals
and gems. 679. least erected: standing least erect.

Ransacked the Centre, and with impious hands
Rifled the bowels of their mother Earth
For treasures better hid. Soon had his crew
Opened into the hill a spacious wound,
And digged out ribs of gold. Let none admire   690
That riches grow in Hell; that soil may best
Deserve the precious bane.° And here let those
Who boast in mortal things, and wondering tell
Of Babel,° and the works of Memphian kings,°
Learn how their greatest monuments of fame,   695
And strength, and art, are easily outdone
By Spirits reprobate, and in an hour
What in an age they, with incessant toil
And hands innumerable, scarce perform.
Nigh on the plain, in many cells prepared,   700
That underneath had veins of liquid fire
Sluiced from the lake, a second multitude
With wondrous art founded° the massy ore,
Severing° each kind, and scummed the bullion-dross;°
A third as soon had formed within the ground   705
A various° mould, and from the boiling cells
By strange conveyance filled each hollow nook —
As in an organ, from one blast of wind,
To many a row of pipes the sound-board breathes.
Anon out of the earth a fabric huge   710
Rose like an exhalation, with the sound
Of dulcet symphonies and voices sweet,
Built like a temple, where pilasters° round°
Were set, and Doric pillars overlaid
With golden architrave;° nor did there want   71;
Cornice or frieze, with bossy° sculptures graven:
The roof was fretted° gold. Not Babylon
Nor great Alcairo° such magnificence
Equalled in all their glories, to enshrine
Belus° or Serapis° their gods, or seat   720

692. bane: evil, something harmful. 694. Babel: the tower of Babel (see Genesis 11); Memphian kings: kings of Egypt in the capital of Memphis, where great monuments were built. 703. founded: melted. 704. Severing: separating; bullion-dross: the slag on the molten gold. 706. various: complex. 713. pilasters: rectangular columns; round: The columns were set all about. 715. architrave: beam over the tops of columns. 716. bossy: embossed. 717. fretted: intricately decorated. 718. Alcairo: Cairo, Egypt. 720. Belus: Bel or Baal, a Babylonian god often mentioned in the Old Testament; Serapis: an Egyptian god.

Their kings, when Egypt with Assyria strove
In wealth and luxury. The ascending pile
Stood fixed° her stately height, and straight° the doors,
Opening their brazen folds, discover, wide
Within, her ample spaces o'er the smooth   725
And level pavement: from the archèd roof,
Pendent by subtle magic, many a row
Of starry lamps and blazing cressets,° fed
With naphtha and asphaltus,° yielded light
As from a sky. The hasty multitude   730
Admiring entered; and the work some praise,
And some the architect:° his hand was known
In Heaven by many a towered structure high,
Where sceptred Angels held their residence
And sat as Princes, whom the supreme King   735
Exalted to such power, and gave to rule,
Each in his hierarchy, the Orders bright.
Nor was his name unheard or unadored
In ancient Greece, and in Ausonian° land
Men called him Mulciber,° and how he fell   740
From Heaven they fabled, thrown by angry Jove
Sheer o'er the crystal battlements: from morn
To noon he fell, from noon to dewy eve,
A summer's day, and with the setting sun
Dropped from the zenith, like a falling star,   745
On Lemnos, the Aegaean isle. Thus they relate,
Erring; for he with this rebellious rout
Fell long before; nor aught availed him now
To have built in Heaven high towers; nor did he scape
By all his engines,° but was headlong sent,   750
With his industrious crew, to build in Hell.
    Meanwhile the wingèd Heralds, by command
Of sovran power, with awful ceremony
And trumpet's sound throughout the host proclaim
A solemn council forthwith to be held   755

723. **fixed:** finished; **straight:** straightway, at once. 728. **cressets:** hanging lamps.
729. **naphtha and asphaltus:** Naphtha is an oily liquid derived from petroleum;
asphalt is a tarry substance from the same source. 732. **the architect:** as named
in line 740, Mulciber, another name for the classic god of the forge, Hephaestus
(Greek) or Vulcan (Latin). In the Greek myths, Zeus in anger threw Hephaestus
down from Olympus; hence he was lame. Milton here treats this myth as a confusion of the angels' fall from Heaven. 739. **Ausonian:** Italian. 740. **Mulciber:** See
footnote for line 732. 750. **engines:** contrivances.

At Pandemonium,° the high capital
Of Satan and his peers.° Their summons called
From every band and squarèd regiment
By place or choice the worthiest; they anon
With hundreds and with thousands trooping came   760
Attended: all access was thronged; the gates
And porches wide, but chief the spacious hall
(Though like a covered field, where champions bold
Wont° ride in armed, and at the Soldan's° chair
Defied the best of Paynim° chivalry   765
To mortal combat, or career with lance)
Thick swarmed, both on the ground and in the air,
Brushed with the hiss of rustling wings. As bees
In springtime, when the Sun with Taurus° rides,
Pour forth their populous youth about the hive   770
In clusters; they among fresh dews and flowers
Fly to and fro, or on the smoothed plank,
The suburb of their straw-built citadel,
New rubbed with balm, expatiate, and confer°
Their state-affairs: so thick the aery crowd   775
Swarmed and were straitened; till, the signal given,
Behold a wonder! they but now who seemed
In bigness to surpass Earth's giant sons,°
Now less than smallest dwarfs, in narrow room
Throng numberless, like that pygmean race°   780
Beyond the Indian mount; or faery elves,
Whose midnight revels by a forest-side
Or fountain some belated peasant sees,
Or dreams he sees, while overhead the Moon
Sits arbitress,° and nearer to the Earth   785
Wheels her pale course: they, on their mirth and dance
Intent, with jocund music charm his ear;
At once with joy and fear his heart rebounds.

756. **Pandemonium:** the name appropriately coined by Milton for this impressive, quickly built capital of Hell. It means, literally, the place of all demons. By metaphorical extension the word often is used for a hellish noise, a frightful tumult of noises such as might be associated with an assembly of devils. 757. **peers:** here, the nobles of his court, no longer his equals but subject to him by their own consent. 764. **Wont:** were accustomed to; **Soldan's:** Sultan's. 765. **Paynim:** pagan (in this context, Moslem). 769. **Taurus:** the sign of the bull, a sign of the Zodiac referred to in astrology. 774. **expatiate, and confer:** spread out and discuss (the word *expatiate* by itself means "to speak at length"). 778. **Earth's giant sons:** the Titans. 780. **pygmean race:** legendary pygmies in Asia. 785. **arbitress:** witness.

Thus incorporeal Spirits to smallest forms
Reduced their shapes immense, and were at large,   790
Though without number still, amidst the hall
Of that infernal court. But far within,
And in their own dimensions like themselves,
The great Seraphic Lords and Cherubim
In close recess and secret conclave sat,   795
A thousand demi-gods on golden seats,
Frequent° and full. After short silence then,
And summons read, the great consúlt° began.

    797. **Frequent:** crowded. 798. **consúlt:** consultation.

For Study

1. In line 127, who is the "bold compeer" who answers Satan? Why is this compeer now persuaded that God is almighty? What suspicion does he state about the purposes that God may have for the defeated rebellious angels? What is Satan's response to this conjecture?

2. In lines 248–49, what is Satan's boast? Is it true? Consider this passage through line 263. What connection with Satan's downfall does this attitude have? Discuss the meaning of line 256: "What matter where, if I be still the same. . . ."

3. What has happened in Heaven to the very names of the rebel angels? Find a parallel in Chapter 17 of *Out of the Silent Planet.*

4. What is the significance of the statement (lines 364–65) that the fallen angels had not yet "among the sons of Eve/Got them new names

. . . ."? With what are they identified?

5. What is the one thing that causes Satan some remorse and regret for his actions? Cite lines.

6. Wherein does Satan claim that God positively tempted the angels to revolt? Cite lines. Is this a valid claim?

7. Who is called "the least erected Spirit that fell/From Heaven"? Why?

8. Why is the capital built in Hell called "Pandemonium"? Explain that term.

9. Who was architect of Pandemonium? With whom in classical mythology is he identified?

For Writing

Write an essay discussing the meaning of this sentence in lines 690–93: "Let none admire/That riches grow in Hell; that soil may best/Deserve the precious bane." Do you agree that riches are an evil? Support your view.

Book II

The consultation begun, Satan debates whether another battle be to be hazarded for the recovery of Heaven: some advise it, others dissuade. A third proposal is preferred, mentioned before by Satan, to search the truth of that prophecy or tradition in Heaven concerning another world, and another kind of creature, equal, or not much inferior, to themselves, about this time to be created. Their doubt who shall be sent on this difficult search: Satan, their chief, undertakes alone the voyage; is honoured and applauded. The council thus ended, the rest betake them several ways and to several employments, as their inclinations lead them, to entertain the time till Satan return. He passes on his journey to Hell-gates; finds them shut, and who sat there to guard them; by whom at length they are opened, and discover to him the great gulf between Hell and Heaven; with what difficulty he passes through, directed by Chaos, the Power of that place, to the sight of this new World which he sought.

> High on a throne of royal state, which far
> Outshone the wealth of Ormus° and of Ind,°
> Or where the gorgeous East with richest hand
> Showers on her kings barbaric pearl and gold,
> Satan exalted sat, by merit raised   5
> To that bad eminence; and, from despair
> Thus high uplifted beyond hope, aspires
> Beyond thus high, insatiate° to pursue
> Vain war with Heaven; and, by success° untaught,
> His proud imaginations thus displayed: 10
>   "Powers and Dominions, Deities of Heaven!
> For, since no deep within her gulf can hold
> Immortal vigour, though oppressed and fallen,
> I give not Heaven for lost: from this descent
> Celestial Virtues° rising will appear   15
> More glorious and more dread° than from no fall,
> And trust themselves to fear no second fate:
> Me though just right, and the fixed laws of Heaven,

2. **Ormus:** city on the Persian Gulf where diamonds were traded; **Ind:** India. 8. **insatiate:** never satisfied. 9. **success:** outcome, whether good or bad. The meaning here is that he has not learned his lesson from his defeat. 15. **Virtues:** one of the orders of angels; used here in a general sense. 16. **dread:** to be dreaded.

Did first create your leader, next, free choice,
With what besides, in council or in fight, 20
Hath been achieved of merit, yet this loss,
Thus far at least recovered, hath much more
Established in a safe, unenvied throne,
Yielded with full consent. The happier state
In Heaven, which follows dignity, might draw 25
Envy from each inferior, but who here
Will envy° whom the highest place exposes
Foremost to stand against the Thunderer's aim
Your bulwark, and condemns to greatest share
Of endless pain? Where there is, then, no good 30
For which to strive, no strife can grow up there
From faction, for none sure will claim in Hell
Precedence, none, whose portion is so small
Of present pain that with ambitious mind
Will covet more. With this advantage, then, 35
To union, and firm faith, and firm accord,
More than can be in Heaven, we now return
To claim our just inheritance of old,
Surer to prosper than prosperity
Could have assured us,° and by what best way, 40
Whether of open war or covert guile,
We now debate; who can advise, may speak."
    He ceased; and next him Moloch,° sceptred king,
Stood up, the strongest and the fiercest Spirit
That fought in Heaven, now fiercer by despair. 45
His trust was with the Eternal to be deemed
Equal in strength, and rather than be less
Cared not to be at all; with that care lost
Went all his fear: of God, or Hell, or worse,
He recked not,° and these words thereafter spake: 50
    "My sentence is for open war. Of wiles,
More unexpert, I boast not: them let those
Contrive who need, or when they need, not now;
For, while they sit contriving, shall the rest —
Millions that stand in arms, and longing wait 55
The signal to ascend — sit lingering here,

26–27. who here/Will envy: These and the following lines are boastful.
39–40. In effect he says there is nowhere to go but up. 43. Moloch: a god of the
ancient Canaanites (Phoenicians) and Ammonites, often mentioned in the Old
Testament. Children were sacrificed to him by burning. 50. recked not: did not care.

Heaven's fugitives, and for their dwelling-place
Accept this dark opprobrious° den of shame,
The prison of his tyranny who reigns
By our delay? No! let us rather choose,   60
Armed with Hell-flames and fury, all at once
O'er Heaven's high towers to force resistless way,
Turning our tortures into horrid arms
Against the Torturer; when, to meet the noise
Of his almighty engine, he shall hear   65
Infernal thunder, and, for lightning, see
Black fire and horror shot with equal rage
Among his Angels, and his throne itself
Mixed with Tartarean° sulphur and strange fire,
His own invented torments. But perhaps   70
The way seems difficult, and steep to scale
With upright wing against a higher foe.
Let such bethink them, if the sleepy drench°
Of that forgetful lake benumb not still,
That in our proper motion we ascend   75
Up to our native seat; descent and fall
To us is adverse. Who but felt of late,
When the fierce foe hung on our broken rear
Insulting, and pursued us through the Deep,
With what compulsion and laborious flight   80
We sunk thus low? The ascent is easy, then;
The event is feared! Should we again provoke
Our stronger, some worse way his wrath may find
To our destruction, if there be in Hell
Fear to be worse destroyed! What can be worse   85
Than to dwell here, driven out from bliss, condemned
In this abhorrèd deep to utter woe;
Where pain of unextinguishable fire
Must exercise us without hope of end
The vassals of his anger, when the scourge   90
Inexorably, and the torturing hour,
Calls us to penance? More destroyed than thus,
We should be quite abolished, and expire.
What fear we then? what doubt we to incense
His utmost ire? which, to the height enraged,   95

58. opprobrious: disgraceful. 69. Tartarean: from *Tartarus*, meaning Hell.
Moloch remarks the irony that these things made by God should be turned against
Him. 73. sleepy drench: sleep-causing drink.

Will either quite consume us, and reduce
To nothing this essential° — happier far
Than miserable to have eternal being —
Or, if our substance be indeed divine,
And cannot cease to be, we are at worst   100
On this side nothing;° and by proof we feel
Our power sufficient to disturb his Heaven,
And with perpetual inroads to alarm,
Though inaccessible, his fatal° throne:
Which, if not victory, is yet revenge."   105
    He ended frowning, and his look denounced°
Desperate revenge and battle dangerous
To less than gods. On the other side up rose
Belial,° in act more graceful and humane;
A fairer person lost not Heaven; he seemed   110
For dignity composed, and high exploit,
But all was false and hollow, though his tongue
Dropped manna, and could make the worse appear
The better reason, to perplex and dash°
Maturest counsels: for his thoughts were low,   115
To vice industrious, but to nobler deeds
Timorous and slothful; yet he pleased the ear,
And with persuasive accent thus began:
    "I should be much for open war, O Peers,
As not behind in hate, if what was urged   120
Main reason to persuade immediate war
Did not dissuade me most, and seem to cast
Ominous conjecture on the whole success;
When he who most excels in fact of arms,
In what he counsels and in what excels   125
Mistrustful, grounds his courage on despair
And utter dissolution as the scope
Of all his aim, after some dire revenge.
First, what revenge? The towers of Heaven are filled
With armèd watch, that render all access   130
Impregnable: oft on the bordering Deep
Encamp their legions, or with obscure wing
Scout far and wide into the realm of Night,

---

97. **essential:** essence. **100–01. we . . . nothing:** At worst we are just short of
being annihilated. **104. fatal:** ordained by fate. **106. denounced:** proclaimed.
109. Belial: a Hebrew word meaning "worthlessness" or "baseness," here personified as a demon of lazy insolence, glibly fluent and persuasive. **114. dash:** frustrate.

Scorning surprise. Or could we break our way
By force, and at our heels all Hell should rise   135
With blackest insurrection, to confound
Heaven's purest light, yet our great Enemy,
All incorruptible, would on his throne
Sit unpolluted, and the ethereal mould,°
Incapable of stain, would soon expel   140
Her mischief, and purge off the baser fire,
Victorious. Thus repulsed, our final hope
Is flat despair: we must exasperate
The Almighty Victor to spend all his rage,
And that must end us, that must be our cure,   145
To be no more — sad cure, for who would lose,
Though full of pain, this intellectual being,
Those thoughts that wander through eternity,
To perish rather, swallowed up and lost
In the wide womb of uncreated Night,   150
Devoid of sense and motion? And who knows,
Let° this be good, whether our angry Foe
Can give it, or will ever? How he can
Is doubtful; that he never will is sure.
Will he, so wise, let loose at once his ire,   155
Belike° through impotence or unaware,
To give his enemies their wish, and end
Them in his anger whom his anger saves
To punish endless? 'Wherefore cease we, then?'
Say they who counsel war; 'we are decreed,   160
Reserved, and destined to eternal woe;
Whatever doing, what can we suffer more,
What can we suffer worse?' Is this, then, worst —
Thus sitting, thus consulting, thus in arms?
What when we fled amain, pursued and struck   165
With Heaven's afflicting thunder, and besought
The Deep to shelter us? this Hell then seemed
A refuge from those wounds. Or when we lay
Chained on the burning lake? that sure was worse.
What if the breath that kindled those grim fires,   170
Awaked, should blow them into sevenfold rage,
And plunge us in the flames, or from above
Should intermitted vengeance arm again
His red right hand to plague us? What if all

139. mould: substance. 152. Let: granted. 156. Belike: doubtless (ironical).

Her stores were opened, and this firmament 175
Of Hell should spout her cataracts of fire,
Impendent° horrors, threatening hideous fall
One day upon our heads, while we perhaps,
Designing or exhorting glorious war,
Caught in a fiery tempest, shall be hurled, 180
Each on his rock transfixed, the sport and prey
Of racking whirlwinds, or forever sunk
Under yon boiling ocean, wrapt in chains,
There to converse with everlasting groans,
Unrespited, unpitied, unreprieved, 185
Ages of hopeless end? This would be worse.
War, therefore, open or concealed, alike
My voice dissuades; for what can force or guile
With him, or who deceive his mind, whose eye
Views all things at one view? He from Heaven's height 190
All these our motions vain° sees and derides,
Not more almighty to resist our might
Than wise to frustrate all our plots and wiles.
Shall we, then, live thus vile, the race of Heaven,
Thus trampled, thus expelled, to suffer here 195
Chains and these torments? Better these than worse,
By my advice; since fate inevitable
Subdues us, and omnipotent decree,
The Victor's will. To suffer, as to do,
Our strength is equal, nor the law unjust 200
That so ordains; this was at first resolved,
If we were wise, against so great a foe
Contending, and so doubtful what might fall.°
I laugh when those who at the spear are bold
And venturous, if that fail them, shrink, and fear 205
What yet they know must follow — to endure
Exile, or ignominy, or bonds, or pain,
The sentence of their conqueror. This is now
Our doom, which if we can sustain and bear,
Our Supreme Foe in time may much remit 210
His anger, and perhaps, thus far removed,
Not mind us not offending,° satisfied
With what is punished; whence these raging fires
Will slacken, if his breath stir not their flames.

177. Impendent: overhanging. 191. motions vain: vain schemes. 203. fall: befall. 212. Not . . . not offending: Pay no attention to us if we offend Him no more.

Our purer essence then will overcome   215
Their noxious vapour, or, inured, not feel;
Or, changed at length, and to the place conformed
In temper and in nature, will receive
Familiar the fierce heat, and void of pain;
This horror will grow mild, this darkness light;   220
Besides what hope the never-ending flight
Of future days may bring, what chance, what change
Worth waiting, since our present lot appears
For happy though but ill, for ill not worst,
If we procure not to ourselves more woe."   225
    Thus Belial, with words clothed in reason's garb,
Counselled ignoble ease and peaceful sloth,
Not peace; and after him thus Mammon spake:
    "Either to disenthrone the King of Heaven
We war, if war be best, or to regain   230
Our own right lost. Him to unthrone we then
May hope when everlasting Fate shall yield
To fickle Chance, and Chaos judge the strife.
The former° vain to hope argues as vain
The latter,° for what place can be for us   235
Within Heaven's bound unless Heaven's Lord Supreme
We overpower? Suppose he should relent,
And publish grace to all, on promise made
Of new subjection; with what eyes could we
Stand in his presence humble and receive   240
Strict laws imposed, to celebrate his throne
With warbled hymns and to his Godhead sing
Forced Halleluiahs, while he lordly sits
Our envied sovran and his altar breathes
Ambrosial° odours and ambrosial flowers,   245
Our servile offerings? This must be our task
In Heaven, this our delight. How wearisome
Eternity so spent in worship paid
To whom we hate! Let us not then pursue,
By force impossible, by leave obtained   250
Unacceptable, though in Heaven, our state
Of splendid vassalage, but rather seek
Our own good from ourselves, and from our own
Live to ourselves, though in this vast recess,

234. former: to dethrone God. 235. latter: to regain our rights. 245. Ambrosial:
referring to ambrosia, the food of the gods, and by extension to delicious odors.

Free and to none accountable, preferring   255
Hard liberty before the easy yoke
Of servile pomp. Our greatness will appear
Then most conspicuous when great things of small,
Useful of hurtful, prosperous of adverse,
We can create, and in what place soe'er   260
Thrive under evil, and work ease out of pain
Through labour and endurance. This deep world
Of darkness do we dread? How oft amidst
Thick clouds and dark doth Heaven's all-ruling Sire
Choose to reside, his glory unobscured,   265
And with the majesty of darkness round
Covers his throne, from whence deep thunders roar,
Mustering their rage, and Heaven resembles Hell!
As he our darkness, cannot we his light
Imitate when we please? This desert soil   270
Wants° not her hidden lustre, gems and gold,
Nor want we skill or art from whence to raise
Magnificence — and what can Heaven show more?
Our torments also may, in length of time,
Become our elements,° these piercing fires   275
As soft as now severe, our temper changed
Into their temper; which must needs remove
The sensible° of pain. All things invite
To peaceful counsels, and the settled state
Of order, how in safety best we may   280
Compose our present evils, with regard
Of what we are and where, dismissing quite
All thoughts of war. Ye have what I advise."
    He scarce had finished, when such murmur filled
The assembly as when hollow rocks retain   285
The sound of blustering winds, which all night long
Had roused the sea, now with hoarse cadence lull
Seafaring men o'erwatched,° whose bark by chance,
Or pinnace, anchors in a craggy bay
After the tempest. Such applause was heard   290
As Mammon ended, and his sentence° pleased,
Advising peace, for such another field°
They dreaded worse than Hell, so much the fear

271. Wants: lacks. 275. elements: the four elements — earth, air, water, and fire.
278. sensible: sense, sensation. 288. o'erwatched: weary with watching. 291. sentence: opinion. 292. field: battlefield.

Of thunder and the sword of Michael°
Wrought still within them, and no less desire   295
To found this nether empire, which might rise,
By policy and long procéss of time,
In emulation opposite to Heaven.
Which when Beëlzebub perceived — than whom,
Satan except, none higher sat — with grave   300
Aspect he rose, and in his rising seemed
A pillar of state; deep on his front engraven
Deliberation sat, and public care,
And princely counsel in his face yet shone,
Majestic, though in ruin; sage he stood,   305
With Atlantean° shoulders, fit to bear
The weight of mightiest monarchies; his look
Drew audience and attention still as night
Or summer's noontide air, while thus he spake:
  "Thrones and Imperial Powers, Offspring of Heaven,   310
Ethereal Virtues! or these titles now
Must we renounce, and, changing style, be called
Princes of Hell? for so the popular vote
Inclines, here to continue, and build up here
A growing empire — doubtless! while we dream,   315
And know not that the King of Heaven hath doomed
This place our dungeon, not our safe retreat
Beyond his potent arm, to live exempt
From Heaven's high jurisdiction in new league
Banded against his throne, but to remain   320
In strictest bondage, though thus far removed,
Under the inevitable curb, reserved
His captive multitude. For he, be sure,
In height or depth, still first and last will reign
Sole king, and of his kingdom lose no part   325
By our revolt, but over Hell extend
His empire, and with iron sceptre rule
Us here, as with his golden those in Heaven.
What° sit we then projecting peace and war?
War hath determined us and foiled with loss   330
Irreparable, terms of peace yet none
Vouchsafed or sought; for what peace will be given
To us enslaved, but custody severe,

294. **Michael:** archangel who led the hosts of God. 306. **Atlantean:** Atlas, a Titan, was condemned to bear the sky on his shoulders. 329. **What:** for what?

And stripes, and arbitrary punishment
Inflicted? and what peace can we return,   335
But, to° our power, hostility and hate,
Untamed reluctance, and revenge, though slow,
Yet ever plotting how the Conqueror least
May reap his conquest, and may least rejoice
In doing what we most in suffering feel?   340
Nor will occasion want, nor shall we need
With dangerous expedition to invade
Heaven, whose high walls fear no assault or siege,
Or ambush from the Deep. What if we find
Some easier enterprise? There is a place   345
(If ancient and prophetic fame in Heaven
Err not), another World, the happy seat
Of some new race, called Man, about this time
To be created like to us, though less
In power and excellence, but favoured more   350
Of him who rules above; so was his will
Pronounced among the Gods, and by an oath
That shook Heaven's whole circumference confirmed.
Thither let us bend all our thoughts, to learn
What creatures there inhabit, of what mould   355
Or substance, how endued,° and what their power,
And where their weakness, how attempted° best,
By force or subtlety. Though Heaven be shut,
And Heaven's high Arbitrator sit secure
In his own strength, this place may lie exposed,   360
The utmost border of his kingdom, left
To their defence who hold it; here, perhaps,
Some advantageous act may be achieved
By sudden onset, either with Hell-fire
To waste his whole creation, or possess   365
All as our own, and drive, as we were driven,
The puny habitants, or, if not drive,
Seduce them to our party, that their God
May prove their foe, and with repenting hand
Abolish his own works. This would surpass   370
Common revenge, and interrupt his joy
In our confusion, and our joy upraise
In his disturbance, when his darling sons,
Hurled headlong to partake with us, shall curse

336. **to:** to the utmost of. 356. **endued:** endowed. 357. **attempted:** attacked.

Their frail originals,° and faded bliss,   375
Faded so soon! Advise if this be worth
Attempting, or to sit in darkness here
Hatching vain empires." Thus Beëlzebub
Pleaded his devilish counsel, first devised
By Satan, and in part proposed — for whence   380
But from the author of all ill could spring
So deep a malice, to confound the race
Of mankind in one root, and Earth with Hell
To mingle and involve, done all to spite
The great Creator? But their spite still serves   385
His glory to augment. The bold design
Pleased highly those Infernal States,° and joy
Sparkled in all their eyes: with full assent
They vote, whereat his speech he thus renews:
    "Well have ye judged, well ended long debate,   390
Synod of Gods, and, like to what ye are,
Great things resolved, which from the lowest deep
Will once more lift us up, in spite of fate,
Nearer our ancient seat — perhaps in view
Of those bright confines, whence, with neighbouring arms,   395
And opportune excursion, we may chance
Re-enter Heaven, or else in some mild zone
Dwell, not unvisited of Heaven's fair light
Secure, and at the brightening orient beam
Purge off this gloom: the soft delicious air,   400
To heal the scar of these corrosive fires,
Shall breathe her balm. But, first, whom shall we send
In search of this new world? whom shall we find
Sufficient? who shall tempt° with wandering feet
The dark, unbottomed, infinite abyss,   405
And through the palpable obscure° find out
His uncouth way, or spread his aery flight,
Upborne with indefatigable wings
Over the vast abrupt,° ere he arrive
The happy isle?° What strength, what art, can then   410
Suffice, or what evasion bear him safe
Through the strict senteries° and stations thick
Of Angels watching round? Here he had need

375. originals: progenitors (Adam and Eve). 387. States: peers. 404. tempt: attempt. 406. palpable obscure: darkness that can be felt. 409. vast abrupt: the abyss of Chaos. 410. The happy isle: the created universe. 412. senteries: sentries.

All circumspection, and we now° no less
Choice in our suffrage,° for on whom we send   415
The weight of all, and our last hope, relies."
    This said, he sat, and expectation held
His look suspense,° awaiting who appeared
To second, or oppose, or undertake
The perilous attempt. But all sat mute,   420
Pondering the danger with deep thoughts, and each
In other's countenance read his own dismay,
Astonished. None among the choice and prime
Of those Heaven-warring champions could be found
So hardy as to proffer or accept,   425
Alone, the dreadful voyage; till, at last,
Satan, whom now transcendent glory raised
Above his fellows, with monarchal pride
Conscious of highest worth, unmoved thus spake:
    "O Progeny of Heaven! Empyreal Thrones!   430
With reason hath deep silence and demur°
Seized us, though undismayed: long is the way
And hard that out of Hell leads up to light;
Our prison strong, this huge convex° of fire,
Outrageous to devour, immures us round   435
Ninefold; and gates of burning adamant,
Barred over us, prohibit all egress.
These passed, if any pass, the void profound
Of unessential° Night receives him next,
Wide-gaping, and with utter loss of being   440
Threatens him, plunged in that abortive gulf.
If thence he scape, into whatever world,
Or unknown region, what remains° him less
Than unknown dangers, and as hard escape?
But I should ill become this throne, O Peers,   445
And this imperial sovranty, adorned
With splendour, armed with power, if aught proposed
And judged of public moment in the shape
Of difficulty or danger could deter
Me from attempting. Wherefore do I assume   450
These royalties, and not refuse to reign,
Refusing to accept as great a share

414. **we now:** we now need. 415. **Choice in our suffrage:** care in our voting.
418. **suspense:** in suspense. 431. **demur:** hesitation, delay. 434. **convex:** vault.
439. **unessential:** without substance. 443. **remains:** awaits.

Of hazard as of honour, due alike
To him who reigns, and so much to him due
Of hazard more as he above the rest   455
High honoured sits? Go, therefore, mighty Powers,
Terror of Heaven, though fallen; intend° at home,
While here shall be our home, what best may ease
The present misery, and render Hell
More tolerable, if there be cure or charm   460
To respite, or deceive, or slack the pain
Of this ill mansion; intermit no watch
Against a wakeful foe, while I abroad
Through all the coasts of dark destruction seek
Deliverance for us all: this enterprise   465
None shall partake with me." Thus saying, rose
The Monarch, and prevented all reply;
Prudent, lest, from his resolution raised,°
Others among the chief might offer now,
Certain to be refused, what erst° they feared,   470
And, so refused, might in opinion stand
His rivals, winning cheap the high repute
Which he through hazard huge must earn. But they
Dreaded not more the adventure than his voice
Forbidding; and at once with him they rose.   475
Their rising all at once was as the sound
Of thunder heard remote. Towards him they bend
With awful reverence prone, and as a God
Extol him equal to the Highest in Heaven.
Nor failed they to express how much they praised   480
That for the general safety he despised
His own; for neither do the Spirits damned
Lose all their virtue, lest bad men should boast
Their specious° deeds on earth, which glory excites,
Or close° ambition varnished o'er with zeal.   485
Thus they their doubtful consultations dark
Ended, rejoicing in their matchless chief:
As when from mountain-tops the dusky clouds
Ascending, while the north wind sleeps, o'erspread
Heaven's cheerful face, the louring element   490
Scowls o'er the darkened landscape snow, or shower,
If chance the radiant sun, with farewell sweet,

457. **intend:** consider. 468. **from . . . raised:** encouraged by his fortitude.
470. **erst:** at first. 484. **specious:** seemingly good. 485. **close:** secret.

Extend his evening beam, the fields revive,
The birds their notes renew, and bleating herds
Attest their joy, that hill and valley rings.   495
O shame to men! Devil with devil damned
Firm concord holds; men only disagree
Of creatures rational, though under hope
Of heavenly grace, and, God proclaiming peace,
Yet live in hatred, enmity, and strife   500
Among themselves, and levy cruel wars,
Wasting the earth, each other to destroy —
As if (which might induce us to accord)
Man had not hellish foes enough besides,
That day and night for his destruction wait.   505
    The Stygian council thus dissolved, and forth
In order came the grand Infernal Peers;
Midst came their mighty Paramount,° and seemed
Alone the antagonist of Heaven. . . .

508. Paramount: highest of all, supreme in power.

For Study

1. The fallen angels have tacitly given consent to Satan's leadership; but, as if not content with this election, he makes a claim early in Book II. What is that claim? Cite lines. Has it any sound basis?

2. Wherein does Satan say that his Hellish throne is more secure than a Heavenly one might be? Why does he believe no one will envy him his place? Cite lines.

3. Who is called "the strongest and the fiercest Spirit/That fought in Heaven"?

4. Who is meant by "A fairer person lost not Heaven"?

5. Who is it "than whom,/Satan except, none higher sat" (lines 299–300)?

6. Why does Satan sharply cut off further discussions after he has announced that he will undertake the scouting trip to Earth? Cite lines.

For Writing

1. Paraphrase briefly and clearly each of the four major addresses to the Council in Pandemonium prior to Satan's announcement of the action he will take.

2. Paraphrase and discuss Milton's rebuke to men in lines 496–505. Whatever the merits or justification that you find in what he says, can you show a sense in which these lines are inconsistent with the poem thus far?

Book III

THE ARGUMENT

God, sitting on his throne, sees Satan flying towards this World, then newly created; shows him to the Son, who sat at his right hand; foretells the success of Satan in perverting mankind; clears his own justice and wisdom from all imputation, having created Man free and able enough to have withstood his Tempter; yet declares his purpose of grace towards him, in regard he fell not of his own malice, as did Satan, but by him seduced. The Son of God renders praises to his Father for the manifestation of his gracious purpose towards Man; but God again declares that grace cannot be extended towards Man without the satisfaction of Divine Justice; Man hath offended the majesty of God by aspiring to Godhead, and therefore, with all his progeny, devoted to death, must die, unless someone can be found sufficient to answer for his offence, and undergo his punishment. The Son of God freely offers himself a ransom for Man; the Father accepts him, ordains his incarnation, pronounces his exaltation above all names in Heaven and Earth, commands all the Angels to adore him; they obey, and, hymning to their harps in full choir, celebrate the Father and the Son. Meanwhile, Satan alights upon the bare convex of this World's outermost orb; where wandering he first finds a place since called the Limbo of Vanity; what persons and things fly up thither; thence comes to the gate of Heaven, described ascending by stairs, and the waters above the firmament that flow about it. His passage thence to the orb of the Sun; he finds there Uriel, the regent of that orb, but first changes himself into the shape of a meaner Angel, and, pretending a zealous desire to behold the new Creation, and Man whom God had placed here, inquires of him the place of his habitation, and is directed; alights first on Mount Niphates.[1]

---

[1] Before going further, read the Biblical account of man's creation, temptation, and fall (pages 194–96). In all questions and discussions that follow, your familiarity with the Biblical version will be assumed.

Book IV

Satan, now in prospect of Eden, and nigh the place where he must now attempt the bold enterprise which he undertook alone against God and Man, falls into many doubts with himself, and many passions, fear, envy, and despair; but at length confirms himself in evil; journeys on to Paradise, whose outward prospect and situation is described; overleaps the bounds; sits, in the shape of a cormorant, on the Tree of Life, as highest in the Garden, to look about him. The Garden described; Satan's first sight of Adam and Eve; his wonder at their excellent form and happy state, but with resolution to work their fall; overhears their discourse; thence gathers that the Tree of Knowledge was forbidden them to eat of under penalty of death, and thereon intends to found his temptation by seducing them to transgress; then leaves them a while, to know further of their state by some other means. Meanwhile Uriel, descending on a sunbeam, warns Gabriel, who had in charge the gate of Paradise, that some evil Spirit had escaped the Deep, and passed at noon by his Sphere, in the shape of a good Angel, down to Paradise, discovered after by his furious gestures in the mount. Gabriel promises to find him ere morning. Night coming on, Adam and Eve discourse of going to their rest: their bower described; their evening worship. Gabriel, drawing forth his bands of night-watch to walk the round of Paradise, appoints two strong Angels to Adam's bower, lest the evil Spirit should be there doing some harm to Adam or Eve sleeping: there they find him at the ear of Eve, tempting her in a dream, and bring him, though unwilling, to Gabriel: by whom questioned, he scornfully answers; prepares resistance; but, hindered by a sign from Heaven, flies out of Paradise.

Book V

Morning approached, Eve relates to Adam her troublesome dream; he likes it not, yet comforts her; they come forth to their day labours; their morning hymn at the door of their bower.

God, to render Man inexcusable,[1] sends Raphael to admonish him of his obedience, of his free estate, of his enemy near at hand, who he is, and why his enemy, and whatever else may avail Adam to know. Raphael comes down to Paradise; his appearance described; his coming discerned by Adam afar off, sitting at the door of his bower; he goes out to meet him, brings him to his lodge, entertains him with the choicest fruits of Paradise, got together by Eve; their discourse at table. Raphael performs his message, minds Adam of his state and of his enemy; relates, at Adam's request, who that enemy is, and how he came to be so, beginning from his first revolt in Heaven, and the occasion thereof; how he drew his legions after him to the parts of the North, and there incited them to rebel with him, persuading all but only Abdiel, a seraph, who in argument dissuades and opposes him, then forsakes him.

Book VI

THE ARGUMENT

Raphael continues to relate how Michael and Gabriel were sent forth to battle against Satan and his Angels. The first fight described: Satan and his Powers retire under night. He calls a council; invents devilish engines, which, in the second day's fight, put Michael and his Angels to some disorder, but they at length, pulling up mountains, overwhelmed both the force and machines of Satan. Yet, the tumult not so ending, God, on the third day, sends Messiah his Son, for whom he had reserved the glory of that victory. He, in the power of his Father, coming to the place, and causing all his legions to stand still on either side, with his chariot and thunder driving into the midst of his enemies, pursues them, unable to resist, towards the wall of Heaven, which opening, they leap down with horror and confusion into the place of punishment prepared for them in the Deep. Messiah returns with triumph to his Father.

---

[1] inexcusable: God explains the situation to them so that if they fall it will not be through ignorance of His wishes or of the dangers. Thus their fall will be their own responsibility.

Book VII

THE ARGUMENT

Raphael, at the request of Adam, relates how and wherefore this world was first created: that God, after the expelling of Satan and his Angels out of Heaven, declared his pleasure to create another world, and other creatures to dwell therein; sends his Son with glory, and attendance of Angels, to perform the work of creation in six days; the Angels celebrate with hymns the performance thereof, and his reascension into Heaven.

Book VIII

THE ARGUMENT

Adam inquires concerning celestial motions, is doubtfully answered,[1] and exhorted to search rather things more worthy of knowledge. Adam assents, and, still desirous to detain Raphael, relates to him what he remembered since his own creation: his placing in Paradise; his talk with God concerning solitude and fit society; his first meeting and nuptials with Eve. His discourse with the Angel thereupon; who, after admonitions repeated, departs.

Book IX

THE ARGUMENT

Satan having compassed the Earth, with meditated guile returns as a mist by night into Paradise; enters into the Serpent sleeping. Adam and Eve in the morning go forth to their labours, which Eve proposes to divide in several places, each labouring apart; Adam consents not, alleging the danger lest that enemy of whom they were forewarned should attempt her found alone. Eve, loth

---

[1] **doubtfully answered:** not that Raphael does not know the answer, but that he doubts that this knowledge is necessary or appropriate for Adam or even that Adam is equipped to comprehend it.

to be thought not circumspect or firm enough, urges her going apart, the rather desirous to make trial of her strength; Adam at last yields. The Serpent finds her alone: his subtle approach, first gazing, then speaking, with much flattery extolling Eve above all other creatures. Eve, wondering to hear the Serpent speak, asks how he attained to human speech and such understanding not till now; the Serpent answers that by tasting of a certain tree in the garden he attained both to speech and reason, till then void of both. Eve requires him to bring her to that tree, and finds it to be the Tree of Knowledge forbidden; the Serpent, now grown bolder, with many wiles and arguments induces her at length to eat. She, pleased with the taste, deliberates a while whether to impart thereof to Adam or not; at last brings him of the fruit; relates what persuaded her to eat thereof. Adam, at first amazed, but perceiving her lost, resolves, through vehemence of love, to perish with her, and, extenuating the trespass, eats also of the fruit. The effects thereof in them both; they seek to cover their nakedness; then fall to variance and accusation of one another.

> So spake the Enemy of mankind, enclosed
> In serpent, inmate bad, and toward Eve   495
> Addressed his way, not with indented wave,
> Prone on the ground, as since, but on his rear,
> Circular base of rising folds, that towered
> Fold above fold a surging maze; his head
> Crested aloft, and carbuncle° his eyes;   500
> With burnished neck of verdant gold, erect
> Amidst his circling spires, that on the grass
> Floated redundant. Pleasing was his shape,
> And lovely, never since of serpent kind
> Lovelier; not those that in Illyria changed   505
> Hermione and Cadmus,° or the god
> In Epidaurus;° nor to which transformed
> Ammonian Jove,° or Capitoline was seen,
> He with Olympias, this with her who bore

500. **carbuncle:** deep red. **505–06. changed . . . Cadmus:** those that Hermione (more commonly Harmonia) and Cadmus became, when metamorphosed at their own desire. **506–07. god . . . Epidaurus:** Aesculapius, god of medicine, whose chief shrine was at Epidaurus and who appeared in serpent form. **508–09.** Plutarch records the legend that Jupiter Ammon was the father of Alexander the Great by Olympias, the queen of Philip of Macedon.

Scipio, the highth of Rome.° With tract oblique°   510
At first, as one who sought access but feared
To interrupt, sidelong he works his way.
As when a ship, by skillful steersman wrought
Nigh river's mouth or foreland, where the wind
Veers oft, as oft so steers and shifts her sail,   515
So varied he, and of his tortuous train
Curled many a wanton wreath in sight of Eve
To lure her eye; she, busied, heard the sound
Of rustling leaves but minded not, as used
To such disport before her through the field   520
From every beast, more duteous at her call
Than at Circean call the herd disguised.°
He, bolder now, uncalled before her stood,
But as in gaze admiring. Oft he bowed
His turret° crest and sleek enamelled neck,   525
Fawning, and licked the ground whereon she trod.
His gentle dumb expression turned at length
The eye of Eve to mark his play; he, glad
Of her attention gained, with serpent-tongue
Organic, or impulse of vocal air,°   530
His fraudulent temptation thus began:
   'Wonder not, sovran mistress, if perhaps
Thou canst who art sole wonder, much less arm
Thy looks, the heaven of mildness, with disdain,
Displeased that I approach thee thus, and gaze   535
Insatiate, I thus single, nor have feared
Thy awful brow, more awful thus retired.
Fairest resemblance of thy Maker fair,
Thee all things living gaze on, all things thine
By gift, and thy celestial beauty adore,   540
With ravishment beheld, there best beheld
Where universally admired. But here,
In this enclosure wild, these beasts among,
Beholders rude, and shallow to discern
Half what in thee is fair, one man except,   545

508–10. Capitoline . . . Rome: according to the tale that Scipio Africanus, the conqueror of Hannibal, was the son of Sempronia and Jupiter (called Capitoline from his temple on the Capitoline hill). 522. Circean . . . disguised: In Homer's *Odyssey*, the enchantress Circe transformed men into beasts. 525. turret: towerlike. 530. The serpent could not speak, but Satan speaks through him by some ingenious trick.

Who sees thee? (and what is one?) who shouldst be seen
A Goddess among Gods, adored and served
By Angels numberless, thy daily train?"
    So glozed° the Tempter, and his proem° tuned.
Into the heart of Eve his words made way,   55c
Though at the voice much marvelling; at length,
Not unamazed, she thus in answer spake:
    "What may this mean? Language of Man pronounced
By tongue of brute, and human sense expressed?
The first at least of these I thought denied   555
To beasts, whom God on their creation-day
Created mute to all articulate sound;
The latter I demur,° for in their looks
Much reason, and in their actions, oft appears.
Thee, Serpent, subtlest beast of all the field   560
I knew, but not with human voice endued;
Redouble, then, this miracle, and say,
How cam'st thou speakable of mute,° and how
To me so friendly grown above the rest
Of brutal kind that daily are in sight: 565
Say, for such wonder claims attention due."
    To whom the guileful Tempter thus replied:
"Empress of this fair World, resplendent Eve,
Easy to me it is to tell thee all
What thou command'st, and right thou shouldst be obeyed.   570
I was at first as other beasts that graze
The trodden herb, of abject thoughts and low,
As was my food, nor aught but food discerned
Or sex, and apprehended nothing high,
Till on a day, roving the field, I chanced   575
A goodly tree far distant to behold,
Loaden with fruit of fairest colours mixed,
Ruddy and gold; I nearer drew to gaze,
When from the boughs a savoury odour blown,
Grateful to appetite, more pleased my sense   580
Than smell of sweetest fennel, or the teats
Of ewe or goat dropping with milk at even,
Unsucked of lamb or kid, that tend their play.
To satisfy the sharp desire I had
Of tasting those fair apples, I resolved   585

549. glozed: flattered; proem: preface. 558. demur: doubt (that the beasts cannot reason). 563. of mute: from being mute.

Not to defer; hunger and thirst at once,
Powerful persuaders, quickened at the scent
Of that alluring fruit, urged me so keen.
About the mossy trunk I wound me soon,
For, high from ground, the branches would require   590
Thy utmost reach, or Adam's: round the tree
All other beasts that saw, with like desire
Longing and envying stood, but could not reach.
Amid the tree now got, where plenty hung
Tempting so nigh, to pluck and eat my fill   595
I spared not, for such pleasure till that hour
At feed or fountain never had I found.
Sated at length, ere long I might perceive
Strange alteration in me, to degree
Of reason in my inward powers, and speech   600
Wanted not long, though to this shape retained.
Thenceforth to speculations high or deep
I turned my thoughts, and with capacious mind
Considered all things visible in Heaven,
Or Earth, or Middle,° all things fair and good.   605
But all that fair and good in thy divine
Semblance, and in thy beauty's heavenly ray,
United I beheld — no fair° to thine
Equivalent or second, which compelled
Me thus, though importune° perhaps, to come   610
And gaze, and worship thee of right declared
Sovran of creatures, universal Dame."°
    So talked the spirited sly Snake, and Eve,
Yet more amazed, unwary thus replied:
    "Serpent, thy overpraising leaves in doubt   615
The virtue of that fruit, in thee first proved.
But say, where grows the tree? from hence how far?
For many are the trees of God that grow
In Paradise, and various, yet unknown
To us; in such abundance lies our choice   620
As leaves a greater store of fruit untouched,
Still hanging incorruptible, till men
Grow up to their provision,° and more hands

605. Middle: the air. 608. fair: fairness, beauty. 610. importune: troublesome.
612. universal Dame: mistress of the universe. From first to last, Satan grossly
flatters Eve, appealing to her vanity. 622–23. till men . . . provision: until there
are more men on Earth to use its plenty.

Help to disburden Nature of her birth."

To whom the wily Adder, blithe and glad: 625
"Empress, the way is ready, and not long:
Beyond a row of myrtles, on a flat,
Fast by a fountain, one small thicket past
Of blowing° myrrh and balm; if thou accept
My conduct, I can bring thee thither soon."   630

"Lead, then," said Eve. He, leading, swiftly rolled
In tangles, and made intricate seem straight,
To mischief swift. Hope elevates, and joy
Brightens his crest, as when a wandering fire,°
Compact of unctuous° vapour, which the night   635
Condenses, and the cold environs round,
Kindled through agitation to a flame
(Which oft, they say, some evil spirit attends),
Hovering and blazing with delusive light,
Misleads the amazed night-wanderer from his way   640
To bogs and mires, and oft through pond or pool,
There swallowed up and lost, from succour far,
So glistered° the dire Snake, and into fraud
Led Eve, our credulous mother, to the Tree
Of Prohibition, root of all our woe;   645
Which when she saw, thus to her guide she spake:

"Serpent, we might have spared our coming hither,
Fruitless to me, though fruit be here to excess,
The credit of whose virtue rest with thee —
Wondrous, indeed, if cause of such effects.   650
But of this tree we may not taste nor touch;
God so commanded, and left that command
Sole daughter of his voice: the rest, we live
Law to our selves; our reason is our law."

To whom the Tempter guilefully replied: 655
"Indeed? Hath God then said that of the fruit
Of all these garden-trees ye shall not eat,
Yet lords declared of all in earth or air?"

To whom thus Eve, yet sinless: "Of the fruit
Of each tree in the garden we may eat,   660
But of the fruit of this fair tree, amidst
The garden, God hath said, 'Ye shall not eat

629. **blowing:** blossoming. 634. **wandering fire:** will-o'-the-wisp. 635. **Compact of unctuous:** composed of oily. Milton's explanation of the phenomenon is not correct. 643. **glistered:** glittered.

Thereof, nor shall ye touch it, lest ye die.' "

    She scarce had said, though brief, when now more bold
The Tempter, but with show of zeal and love   665
To Man, and indignation at his wrong,
New part puts on,° and, as to passion moved,
Fluctuates° disturbed, yet comely, and in act
Raised as of some great matter to begin.
As when of old some orator renowned   670
In Athens or free Rome, where eloquence
Flourished, since mute, to some great cause addressed,
Stood in himself collected, while each part,
Motion, each act, won audience ere the tongue
Sometimes in height° began, as no delay   675
Of preface brooking° through his zeal of right:
So standing, moving, or to height upgrown,
The Tempter, all impassioned, thus began:
    "O sacred, wise, and wisdom-giving Plant,
Mother of science,° now I feel thy power   680
Within me clear, not only to discern
Things in their causes, but to trace the ways
Of highest agents,° deemed however wise.
Queen of this Universe, do not believe
Those rigid threats of death; ye shall not die.   685
How should ye? by the fruit? it gives you life
To knowledge;° by the Threatener? look on me,
Me who have touched and tasted, yet both live
And life more perfect have attained than Fate
Meant me, by venturing higher than my lot.   690
Shall that be shut to Man which to the beast
Is open? or will God incense his ire°
For such a petty trespass, and not praise
Rather your dauntless virtue, whom the pain
Of death denounced,° whatever thing Death be,   695
Deterred not from achieving what might lead
To happier life, knowledge of good and evil?
Of good, how just? of evil, if what is evil

---

   667. **New part puts on**: begins to play a new part. 668. **Fluctuates**: sways.
675. **height**: height of feeling. 676. **brooking**: enduring, tolerating. 680. **science**:
knowledge. 683. **highest agents**: The Serpent is claiming to have the power not
only to understand natural causes and effects but also to understand the minds and
intentions of higher beings, such as angels or even God. 686–87. **it . . . knowledge**: it enlarges your life by knowledge. 692. **incense his ire**: stir up his anger.
695. **denounced**: threatened.

Be real, why not known, since easier shunned?
God, therefore, cannot hurt ye, and be just;   700
Not just, not God; not feared then, nor obeyed:
Your fear itself of death removes the fear.
Why, then, was this forbid? Why but to awe,
Why but to keep ye low and ignorant,
His worshippers? He knows that in the day   705
Ye eat thereof your eyes, that seem so clear
Yet are but dim, shall perfectly be then
Opened and cleared, and ye shall be as Gods,°
Knowing both good and evil, as they know.
That ye should be as Gods, since I as Man,   710
Internal Man,° is but proportion meet;°
I, of brute, human; ye, of human, Gods.
So ye shall die perhaps, by putting off
Human, to put on° Gods — death to be wished,
Though threatened, which no worse than this can bring.   715
And what are Gods, that Man may not become
As they, participating godlike food?
The Gods are first, and that advantage use
On our belief, that all from them proceeds.
I question it, for this fair Earth I see,   720
Warmed by the Sun, producing every kind,
Them nothing.° If they all° things, who enclosed
Knowledge of good and evil in this tree,
That whoso eats thereof forthwith attains
Wisdom without their leave? and wherein lies   725
The offence, that Man should thus attain to know?
What can your knowledge hurt him, or this tree
Impart against his will, if all be his?
Or is it envy? and can envy dwell
In heavenly breasts? These, these and many more   730
Causes import your need of this fair fruit.
Goddess° humane, reach, then, and freely taste."

708. as Gods: Subtly Satan has begun to speak of plural Gods rather than of the
one God. Eve, misled by him, later speaks in the same way. 711. Internal Man:
like a man internally, in my abilities, though still outwardly in serpent's form; is
but proportion meet: It is fitting that, if the fruit makes a serpent like a man, it
should make men like Gods. 714. to put on: to take on the nature of. 722. Them
nothing: He says, in effect, "I see the Earth producing many things, but I do not
see the Gods producing anything." If they all: if they produced all. 732. Goddess:
Already his flattering tongue is elevating her to this status, which is the heart of
the temptation.

He ended, and his words, replete with guile,
Into her heart too easy entrance won:
Fixed on the fruit she gazed, which to behold   735
Might tempt alone, and in her ears the sound
Yet rung of his persuasive words, impregned°
With reason, to her seeming, and with truth.
Meanwhile the hour of noon drew on, and waked
An eager appetite, raised by the smell   740
So savoury of that fruit, which with desire,
Inclinable now grown to touch or taste,
Solicited her longing eye; yet first,
Pausing a while, thus to herself she mused:
    "Great are thy virtues, doubtless, best of fruits,   745
Though kept from Man, and worthy to be admired,
Whose taste, too long forborne,° at first assay°
Gave elocution to the mute, and taught
The tongue not made for speech to speak thy praise.
Thy praise he also who forbids thy use   750
Conceals not from us, naming thee the Tree
Of Knowledge, knowledge both of good and evil;
Forbids us then to taste; but his forbidding
Commends thee more, while it infers° the good
By thee communicated, and our want;   755
For good unknown sure is not had, or, had
And yet unknown, is as not had at all.
In plain,° then, what forbids he but to know,
Forbids us good, forbids us to be wise?
Such prohibitions bind not. But, if Death   760
Bind us with after-bands, what profits then
Our inward freedom? In the day we eat
Of this fair fruit, our doom is we shall die.
How dies the Serpent? He hath eaten, and lives,
And knows, and speaks, and reasons, and discerns,   765
Irrational till then. For us alone
Was death invented? or to us denied
This intellectual food, for beasts reserved?
For beasts it seems, yet that one beast which first
Hath tasted envies not, but brings with joy   770
The good befallen him, author unsuspect,°

737. impregned: impregnated, filled with. 747. forborne: done without; at first
assay: at first trial. 754. infers: implies. 758. In plain: in plain terms. 771. author
unsuspect: She considers the Serpent to be trustworthy, above suspicion.

Friendly to Man, far from deceit or guile,
What fear I, then? rather, what know to fear
Under this ignorance of good and evil,
Of God or Death, of law or penalty? 775
Here grows the cure of all, this fruit divine,
Fair to the eye, inviting to the taste,
Of virtue to make wise. What hinders, then,
To reach, and feed at once both body and mind?"
 So saying, her rash hand in evil hour 780
Forth-reaching to the fruit, she plucked, she eat;°
Earth felt the wound, and Nature from her seat,
Sighing through all her works, gave signs of woe
That all was lost. Back to the thicket slunk
The guilty Serpent, and well might, for Eve, 785
Intent now wholly on her taste, naught else
Regarded; such delight till then, as seemed,
In fruit she never tasted, whether true
Or fancied so through expectation high
Of knowledge; nor was Godhead from her thought. 790
Greedily she engorged without restraint,
And knew not eating° death. Satiate at length,
And heightened as with wine, jocund and boon,°
Thus to herself she pleasingly began:
 "O sovran, virtuous, precious of all trees 795
In Paradise, of operation blest
To sapience,° hitherto obscured, infamed,°
And thy fair fruit let hang, as to no end
Created, but henceforth my early care,
Not without song, each morning, and due praise, 800
Shall tend thee, and the fertile burden ease
Of thy full branches, offered free to all,
Till, dieted by thee, I grow mature
In knowledge, as the Gods who all things know,
Though others envy what they cannot give — 805
For, had the gift been theirs, it had not here
Thus grown. Experience, next to thee I owe,
Best guide: not following thee, I had remained
In ignorance; thou open'st Wisdom's way,
And giv'st access, though secret she retire. 810

781. **eat:** past tense (pronounced *ĕt*). 792. **knew not eating:** knew not that she was eating. 793. **jocund and boon:** joyous and merry. 796–97. **of . . . sapience:** blessed with power to give wisdom; **infamed:** not known (or, perhaps, defamed).

And I perhaps am secret:° Heaven is high —
High, and remote to see from thence distinct
Each thing on Earth; and other care perhaps
May have diverted from continual watch
Our great Forbidder, safe with all his spies   815
About him. But to Adam in what sort
Shall I appear? Shall I to him make known
As yet my change, and give him to partake
Full happiness with me, or rather not,
But keep the odds of knowledge in my power   820
Without co-partner? so to add what wants
In female sex, the more to draw his love,
And render me more equal, and perhaps,
A thing not undesirable, sometime
Superior° — for, inferior, who is free?   825
This may be well; but what if God have seen,
And death ensue? Then I shall be no more,
And Adam, wedded to another Eve,
Shall live with her enjoying, I extinct —
A death to think.° Confirmed, then, I resolve   830
Adam shall share with me in bliss or woe.
So dear I love him that with him all deaths
I could endure, without him live no life."
    So saying, from the tree her step she turned,
But first low reverence done, as to the Power   835
That dwelt within,° whose presence had infused
Into the plant sciential° sap, derived
From nectar, drink of Gods. Adam the while,
Waiting desirous her return, had wove
Of choicest flowers a garland, to adorn   840
Her tresses and her rural labours crown,
As reapers oft are wont their harvest-queen.
Great joy he promised to his thoughts, and new
Solace in her return, so long delayed;

---

811. **am secret:** am unseen. 816–25. Eve's reflections after eating show at once
the effects of the fall. She thinks with pride that the tree is hers to control; she
hopes her act may be unobserved by God; she considers keeping her "change" a
secret from Adam to gain advantage and power over him, but then she goes on to
reject this plan for a motive that is anything but lofty. 830. **A death to think:** The
thought seems to her as bad as death. 835–36. **the Power . . . within:** Eve is now
moving toward worshiping the tree instead of its Creator, and, in so doing, she
manifests the beginning of idolatry. 837. **sciential:** knowledge-giving.

Yet oft his heart, divine of° something ill,   845
Misgave him. He the faltering measure° felt,
And forth to meet her went, the way she took
That morn when first they parted; by the Tree
Of Knowledge he must pass; there he her met,
Scarce from the tree returning, in her hand   850
A bough of fairest fruit, that downy smiled,
New gathered, and ambrosial smell diffused.
To him she hasted; in her face excuse
Came prologue, and apology to prompt,
Which, with bland words at will, she thus addressed: 855
    "Hast thou not wondered, Adam, at my stay?
Thee I have missed, and thought it long, deprived
Thy presence, agony of love till now
Not felt, nor shall be twice, for never more
Mean I to try, what rash untried I sought,   860
The pain of absence from thy sight. But strange
Hath been the cause, and wonderful to hear:
This tree is not, as we are told, a tree
Of danger tasted, nor to evil unknown
Opening the way, but of divine effect   865
To open eyes, and make them Gods who taste;
And hath been tasted such.° The Serpent wise,
Or not restrained as we or not obeying,
Hath eaten of the fruit, and is become,
Not dead, as we are threatened, but thenceforth   870
Endued with human voice and human sense,
Reasoning to admiration, and with me
Persuasively hath so prevailed that I
Have also tasted, and have also found
The effects to correspond — opener mine eyes,   875
Dim erst, dilated spirits, ampler heart,
And growing up to Godhead; which for thee
Chiefly I sought,° without thee can despise.
For bliss, as thou hast part, to me is bliss,
Tedious, unshared with thee, and odious soon.   880
Thou, therefore, also taste, that equal lot
May join us, equal joy, as equal love,
Lest, thou not tasting, different degree

845. **divine of:** divining, foreseeing. 846. **faltering measure:** irregular beat (of his heart). 867. **tasted such:** proved to be such by tasting. 878. **Chiefly I sought:** her first outright lie, misrepresenting her motive as unselfish.

Disjoin us, and I then too late renounce
Deity for thee, when Fate will not permit."   885
    Thus Eve, with countenance blithe, her story told,
But in her cheek distemper flushing glowed.
On the other side, Adam, soon as he heard
The fatal trespass done by Eve, amazed,
Astonied stood and blank, while horror chill   890
Ran through his veins, and all his joints relaxed.
From his slack hand the garland wreathed for Eve
Down dropped, and all the faded roses shed.
Speechless he stood and pale, till thus at length
First to himself he inward silence broke: 895
    "O fairest of creation, last and best
Of all God's works, creature in whom excelled
Whatever can to sight or thought be formed,
Holy, divine, good, amiable, or sweet!
How art thou lost, how on a sudden lost,   900
Defaced, deflowered, and now to death devote?°
Rather, how hast thou yielded to transgress
The strict forbiddance, how to violate
The sacred fruit forbidden? Some cursèd fraud
Of enemy hath beguiled thee, yet unknown,   905
And me with thee hath ruined; for with thee
Certain my resolution is to die.
How can I live without thee? how forgo
Thy sweet converse and love so dearly joined,
To live again in these wild woods forlorn?   910
Should God create another Eve, and I
Another rib afford, yet loss of thee
Would never from my heart. No, no! I feel
The link of nature draw me: flesh of flesh,
Bone of my bone thou art, and from thy state   915
Mine never shall be parted, bliss or woe."
    So having said, as one from sad dismay
Recomforted, and, after thoughts disturbed,
Submitting to what seemed remediless,
Thus in calm mood his words to Eve he turned: 920
    "Bold deed thou hast presumed, adventurous Eve,
And peril great provoked, who thus hast dared,
Had it been only coveting to eye
That sacred fruit, sacred to abstinence,

901. **to death devote:** given over to death.

Much more to taste it, under ban to touch. 925
But past who can recall, or done undo?
Not God Omnipotent, nor Fate; yet so
Perhaps thou shalt not die; perhaps the fact
Is not so heinous now, foretasted fruit,
Profaned first by the Serpent, by him first 930
Made common and unhallowed ere our taste,
Nor yet on him found deadly; he yet lives —
Lives, as thou saidst, and gains to live, as Man,
Higher degree of life: inducement strong
To us, as likely, tasting, to attain 935
Proportional ascent; which cannot be
But to be Gods, or Angels, demi-gods.°
Nor can I think that God, Creator wise,
Though threatening, will in earnest so destroy
Us, his prime creatures, dignified so high, 940
Set over all his works; which, in our fall,
For us created, needs with us must fail,
Dependent made. So God shall uncreate,
Be frustrate, do, undo, and labour lose,
Not well conceived of God, who, though his power 945
Creation could repeat, yet would be loth
Us to abolish, lest the Adversary
Triumph and say: 'Fickle their state whom God
Most favours; who can please him long? Me first
He ruined, now Mankind; whom will he next?' — 950
Matter of scorn not to be given the Foe.
However, I with thee have fixed my lot,
Certain to undergo like doom; if death
Consort with thee, death is to me as life,
So forcible within my heart I feel 955
The bond of Nature draw me to my own;
My own in thee, for what thou art is mine.
Our state cannot be severed; we are one,
One flesh; to lose thee were to lose myself."
    So Adam; and thus Eve to him replied: 960
"O glorious trial of exceeding love,
Illustrious evidence, example high!
Engaging me to emulate; but, short
Of thy perfection, how shall I attain,
Adam, from whose dear side I boast me sprung, 965

937. Adam has fallen in quickly with Eve's thinking, despite his shock.

And gladly of our union hear thee speak,
One heart, one soul in both; whereof good proof
This day affords, declaring thee resolved,
Rather than death, or aught than death more dread,
Shall separate us, linked in love so dear,   970
To undergo with me one guilt, one crime,
If any be, of tasting this fair fruit,
Whose virtue (for of good still good proceeds,
Direct, or by occasion) hath presented
This happy trial of thy love, which else   975
So eminently never had been known.
Were it I thought death menaced would ensue
This my attempt, I would sustain alone
The worst, and not persuade thee — rather die
Deserted than oblige thee with a fact   980
Pernicious to thy peace, chiefly assured
Remarkably so late of thy so true,
So faithful, love unequalled. But I feel
Far otherwise the event: not death, but life
Augmented, opened eyes, new hopes, new joys,   985
Taste so divine that what of sweet before
Hath touched my sense flat seems to this and harsh.
On my experience, Adam, freely taste,
And fear of death deliver to the winds."
    So saying, she embraced him, and for joy   990
Tenderly wept, much won that he his love
Had so ennobled as of choice to incur
Divine displeasure for her sake, or death.
In recompense (for such compliance bad
Such recompense best merits), from the bough   995
She gave him of that fair enticing fruit
With liberal hand. He scrupled not to eat,
Against his better knowledge, not deceived,
But fondly overcome with female charm.
Earth trembled from her entrails, as again   1000
In pangs, and Nature gave a second groan;
Sky lowered, and, muttering thunder, some sad drops
Wept at completing of the mortal sin
Original;°. . . .

1003–04. the mortal sin/Original: In Christian doctrine the fall from innocence
(Original Sin) means that man is partly alienated from his Creator and can never
be wholly free of sin; his redemption is possible through belief in Jesus Christ.

[Almost as soon as Adam has eaten of the fruit, he and Eve, like guilty partners immemorial, have second thoughts and start to blame each other.]

"Would thou hadst hearkened to my words, and stayed
With me, as I besought thee, when that strange   1135
Desire of wandering, this unhappy morn,
I know not whence possessed thee; we had then
Remained still happy, not, as now, despoiled
Of all our good, shamed, naked, miserable.
Let none henceforth seek needless cause to approve°   1140
The faith they owe; when earnestly they seek
Such proof, conclude they then begin to fail."
    To whom, soon moved with touch of blame, thus Eve:
"What words have passed thy lips, Adam severe,
Imput'st thou that to my default, or will   1145
Of wandering, as thou call'st it, which who knows
But might as ill have happened thou being by,
Or to thyself perhaps: hadst thou been there,
Or here the attempt, thou couldst not have discerned
Fraud in the Serpent, speaking as he spake;   1150
No ground of enmity between us known
Why he should mean me ill or seek to harm.
Was I to have never parted from thy side?
As good have grown there still, a lifeless rib.
Being as I am, why didst not thou, the head,   1155
Command me absolutely not to go,
Going into such danger, as thou saidst?
Too facile then, thou didst not much gainsay,
Nay, didst permit, approve, and fair dismiss.
Hadst thou been firm and fixed in thy dissent,   1160
Neither had I transgressed, nor thou with me."
    To whom, then first incensed, Adam replied:
"Is this the love, is this the recompense
Of mine to thee, ingrateful Eve, expressed
Immutable° when thou wert lost, not I,   1165
Who might have lived, and joyed° immortal bliss,
Yet willingly chose rather death with thee?
And am I now upbraided as the cause

1140. approve: prove, test. Eve had wished to go off by herself to prove that she could defend herself against the wiles of the enemy. 1164–65. expressed/Immutable: shown to be unchangeable. 1166. joyed: enjoyed.

Of thy transgressing? not enough severe,
It seems, in thy restraint. What could I more?   1170
I warned thee, I admonished thee, foretold
The danger and the lurking enemy
That lay in wait; beyond this had been force,
And force upon free will hath here no place.°
But confidence then bore thee on, secure   1175
Either to meet no danger or to find
Matter of glorious trial; and perhaps
I also erred in overmuch admiring
What seemed in thee so perfect that I thought
No evil durst attempt thee — but I rue   1180
That error now, which is become my crime,
And thou the accuser. Thus it shall befall
Him who, to worth in women overtrusting,
Lets her will rule: restraint she will not brook,
And, left to herself, if evil thence ensue,   1185
She first his weak indulgence will accuse."
    Thus they in mutual accusation spent
The fruitless hours, but neither self-condemning,°
And of their vain contést appeared no end.

1174. force . . . place: Adam states the same principle by which God had
left them both free to disobey Him. 1188. neither self-condemning: In their fallen
state, both tend to overlook their individual responsibilities.

For Study

1. Why did Eve wish to go off by
herself on the morning of the temptation? What was Adam's opinion
about her wish?

2. What is the first basic appeal
Satan employs in tempting Eve?

3. What is the subtlety in lines
590–91?

4. How does the Serpent explain
his power of speech? What other
powers does he say have increased in
him? Why does he say these powers
drew him to her?

5. What reservation does Eve express about the fruit in her first response after the Serpent has told of
eating it?

6. What is Eve's first reaction when
the Serpent leads her to the tree?

7. What desire is the ultimate lure
of the temptation? Cite lines. (There
are several that make the decisive motive quite clear.) Look up and be
ready to discuss the Greek tragic sin
of *hubris,* which the Judeo-Christian
tradition also recognizes as the primary sin.

8. Since later she explains to Adam
what she has done, why does not Eve
suspect the Serpent's motive or realize that he is the enemy against whom
they have been warned?

9. Point out several signs of Eve's "fall" from her sinless state of grace immediately after she has eaten the fruit. Cite passages. What familiar faults of humanity does she at once begin to exhibit? Consider her vacillation over whether or not to persuade Adam to eat the fruit, and appraise the motives of her decision. What does she tell Adam was her motive for eating?

10. Discuss Adam's reactions when he learns what Eve has done. Appraise his decision to eat also. In what ways does he go beyond his stated desire to share whatever fate awaits Eve and seem to match her rationalizations? Do you think Adam would have resisted the temptation better than Eve?

11. When both Adam and Eve have eaten, how does their fallen state manifest itself in them jointly?

For Writing

1. Paraphrase succinctly the Serpent's reasoning as to why Eve should eat the fruit. The argument is subtle. Attempt to include all its major points.

2. Turn to a dictionary and study the meaning, in psychology, of the verb *rationalize*. Then paraphrase Eve's rationalization before she plucks and eats the fruit.

Book X

THE ARGUMENT

Man's transgression known, the guardian Angels forsake Paradise and return up to Heaven to approve [1] their vigilance, and are approved, God declaring that the entrance of Satan could not be by them prevented. He sends his Son to judge the transgressors, who descends and gives sentence accordingly; then, in pity, clothes them both, and reascends. Sin and Death sitting till then at the gates of Hell, by wondrous sympathy feeling the success of Satan in this new World, and the sin by Man there committed, resolve to sit no longer confined in Hell, but to follow Satan, their sire, up to the place of Man; to make the way easier from Hell to this World to and fro, they pave a broad highway or bridge over Chaos, according to the track that Satan first made; then, preparing for Earth, they meet him, proud of his success, returning to Hell; their mutual gratulation.[2] Satan arrives at Pandemonium, in full assembly relates with boasting his success against Man; instead of applause is entertained with a general hiss by all his audi-

[1] **approve:** prove. [2] **gratulation:** congratulation.

ence, transformed, with himself also, suddenly into Serpents, according to his doom given in Paradise; then, deluded with a show of the Forbidden Tree springing up before them, they, greedily reaching to take of the fruit, chew dust and bitter ashes. The proceedings of Sin and Death: God foretells the final victory of his Son over them, and the renewing of all things, but, for the present, commands his Angels to make several alterations in the Heavens and Elements. Adam, more and more perceiving his fallen condition, heavily bewails, rejects the condolement of Eve; she persists, and at length appeases him; then, to evade the curse likely to fall on their offspring, proposes to Adam violent ways; which he approves not, but, conceiving better hope, puts her in mind of the late promise made them that her seed should be revenged on the Serpent, and exhorts her, with him, to seek peace of the offended Deity by repentance and supplication.

Book XI

THE ARGUMENT

The Son of God presents to his Father the prayers of our first parents now repenting, and intercedes for them. God accepts them, but declares that they must no longer abide in Paradise; sends Michael with a band of Cherubim to dispossess them, but first to reveal to Adam future things; Michael's coming down. Adam shows to Eve certain ominous signs: he discerns Michael's approach; goes out to meet him; the Angel denounces [1] their departure. Eve's lamentation. Adam pleads, but submits; the Angel leads him up to a high hill; sets before him in vision what shall happen till the Flood.

Book XII

THE ARGUMENT

The Angel Michael continues, from the Flood, to relate what shall succeed: then, in the mention of Abraham, comes by degrees to explain who that Seed of the Woman shall be which was

[1] denounces: announces.

promised Adam and Eve in the Fall: [1] his incarnation, death, resurrection, and ascension; the state of the Church till his second coming. Adam, greatly satisfied and recomforted by these relations and promises, descends the hill with Michael; wakens Eve, who all this while had slept, but with gentle dreams composed to quietness of mind and submission. Michael in either hand leads them out of Paradise, the fiery sword waving behind them, and the Cherubim taking their stations to guard the place.

> . . . He° ended; and thus Adam last° replied:
> "How soon hath thy prediction, Seer blest,
> Measured this transient World, the race of Time,
> Till Time stand fixed: beyond is all abyss,   555
> Eternity, whose end no eye can reach.
> Greatly instructed I shall hence depart,
> Greatly in peace of thought, and have my fill
> Of knowledge, what this vessel can contain,
> Beyond which was my folly to aspire.   560
> Henceforth I learn that to obey is best,
> And love with fear the only God, to walk
> As in his presence, ever to observe
> His providence, and on him sole depend,
> Merciful over all his works, with good   565
> Still overcoming evil, and by small
> Accomplishing great things, by things deemed weak
> Subverting worldly-strong, and worldly-wise
> By simply meek; that suffering for Truth's sake
> Is fortitude to highest victory,   570
> And to the faithful death the gate of life;
> Taught this by his example whom I now
> Acknowledge my Redeemer ever blest."
> To whom thus also the Angel last replied:
> "This having learned, thou hast attained the sum   575
> Of wisdom; hope no higher, though all the stars
> Thou knew'st by name, and all the ethereal powers,
> All secrets of the deep, all Nature's works,
> Or works of God in heaven, air, earth, or sea,
> And all the riches of this world enjoy'dst,   580
> And all the rule, one empire. Only add
> Deeds to thy knowledge answerable; add faith;
> Add virtue, patience, temperance; add love,

[1] Jesus Christ. 552. He: the Angel Michael; last: for the last time.

By name to come called Charity, the soul
Of all the rest: then wilt thou not be loth   585
To leave this Paradise, but shalt possess
A Paradise within thee, happier far.
Let us descend now, therefore, from this top
Of speculation;° for the hour precise
Exacts our parting hence; and see, the guards,   590
By me encamped on yonder hill, expect
Their motion, at whose front a flaming sword,
In signal of remove, waves fiercely round.
We may no longer stay: go, waken Eve;
Her also I with gentle dreams have calmed,   595
Portending good, and all her spirits composed
To meek submission: thou, at season fit,
Let her with thee partake what thou hast heard,
Chiefly what may concern her faith to know,
The great deliverance by her seed to come   600
(For by the Woman's Seed) on all mankind,
That ye may live, which will be many days,
Both in one faith unanimous, though sad
With cause for evils past, yet much more cheered
With meditation on the happy end."   605
    He ended, and they both descend the hill;
Descended, Adam to the bower where Eve
Lay sleeping ran before, but found her waked,
And thus with words not sad she him received:
    "Whence thou return'st and whither went'st I know;   610
For God is also in sleep, and dreams advise,
Which he hath sent propitious, some great good
Presaging, since, with sorrow and heart's distress
Wearied, I fell asleep: but now lead on;
In me is no delay; with thee to go   615
Is to stay here; without thee here to stay
Is to go hence unwilling; thou to me
Art all things under Heaven, all places thou,
Who for my wilful crime art banished hence.
This further consolation yet secure   620
I carry hence: though all by me is lost,
Such favour I unworthy am vouchsafed,
By me the Promised Seed shall all restore."
    So spake our Mother Eve; and Adam heard

588–89. this . . . speculation: these high discussions.

Well pleased, but answered not, for now too nigh   625
The Archangel stood, and from the other hill
To their fixed station, all in bright array
The Cherubim descended, on the ground
Gliding meteorous,° as evening mist,
Risen from a river, o'er the marish° glides,   630
And gathers ground fast at the labourer's heel
Homeward returning. High in front advanced,
The brandished sword of God before them blazed,
Fierce as a comet, which with torrid heat,
And vapour as the Libyan air adust,   635
Began to parch that temperate clime; whereat
In either hand the hastening Angel caught
Our lingering parents, and to the eastern gate
Led them direct, and down the cliff as fast
To the subjected° plain; then disappeared.   640
They, looking back, all the eastern side beheld
Of Paradise, so late their happy seat,
Waved over by that flaming brand,° the gate
With dreadful faces thronged and fiery arms:
Some natural tears they dropped, but wiped them soon;   645
The world was all before them, where to choose
Their place of rest, and Providence their guide;
They, hand in hand, with wandering steps and slow,
Through Eden took their solitary way.

629. meteorous: like meteors. 630. marish: marsh. 640. subjected: lower-lying.
643. brand: sword.

For Study and Writing

1. Compare lines 361–63 of Book I of *Paradise Lost* (page 147) and the passage in which Ransom examines the carvings in Meldilorn (pages 93–94) in Chapter 17 of *Out of the Silent Planet.*

2. Wherein might it be said that Weston, as we hear him speak before Oyarsa (Chapter 20), expresses parallels to the attitudes of Satan in Book I? Point to comparative passages.

3. Consider lines 480–85 of Book II (page 167) and Oyarsa's appraisals of the three men in Chapter 20. Has all virtue been lost by the damned spirits of *Paradise Lost?* by the bent men of *Out of the Silent Planet?*

4. Write an essay pointing out the coincidence of materials in Lewis's novel and Milton's epic. Contrast the novelist's and the poet's treatments of the same materials. Express and explain your views about the comparative merits of those treatments.

Man's Creation, Temptation, and Fall

*from Chapters 2 and 3 of the Book of Genesis —
Authorized, or King James, Version*

And the Lord God formed man of the dust of the ground, and breathed into his nostrils the breath of life; and man became a living soul.[1]

And the Lord God planted a garden eastward in Eden; and there he put the man whom he had formed.

And out of the ground made the Lord God to grow every tree that is pleasant to the sight, and good for food; the tree of life also in the midst of the garden, and the tree of knowledge of good and evil. . . .

And the Lord God took the man, and put him into the garden of Eden to dress it and to keep it. And the Lord God commanded the man, saying, Of every tree of the garden thou mayest freely eat: but of the tree of the knowledge of good and evil, thou shalt not eat of it: for in the day that thou eatest thereof thou shalt surely die.

And the Lord God said, It is not good that the man should be alone; I will make him an help meet for him.

And out of the ground the Lord God formed every beast of the field, and every fowl of the air; and

---

[1] There is an earlier brief Biblical statement about the creation of man in Genesis 1:26–27: "And God said, Let us make man in our image, after our likeness. . . . So God created man in his own image, in the image of God created he him; male and female created he them."

brought them unto Adam to see what he would call them: and whatsoever Adam called every living creature, that was the name thereof. And Adam gave names to all cattle, and to the fowl of the air, and to every beast of the field; but for Adam there was not found an help meet for him.

And the Lord God caused a deep sleep to fall upon Adam, and he slept: and he took one of his ribs, and closed up the flesh instead thereof; and the rib, which the Lord God had taken from man, made he a woman, and brought her unto the man.

And Adam said, This is now bone of my bones, and flesh of my flesh: she shall be called Woman, because she was taken out of Man. Therefore shall a man leave his father and his mother, and shall cleave unto his wife: and they shall be one flesh. And they were both naked, the man and his wife, and were not ashamed.

Now the serpent was more subtil than any beast of the field which the Lord God had made. And he said unto the woman, Yea, hath God said, Ye shall not eat of every tree of the garden?

And the woman said unto the serpent, We may eat of the fruit of the trees of the garden: but of the fruit of the tree which is in the midst of the garden, God hath said, Ye shall not eat of it, neither shall ye touch it, lest ye die.

And the serpent said unto the woman, Ye shall not surely die: for God doth know that in the day ye eat thereof, then your eyes shall be opened, and ye shall be as gods, knowing good and evil.

And when the woman saw that the tree was good for food, and that it was pleasant to the eyes, and a tree to be desired to make one wise, she took of the fruit thereof, and did eat, and gave also unto her husband with her; and he did eat.

And the eyes of them both were opened, and they knew that they were naked; and they sewed fig leaves together, and made themselves aprons. And they heard the voice of the Lord God walking in the garden in the cool of the day: and Adam and his wife hid themselves from the presence of the Lord God amongst the trees of the garden.

And the Lord God called unto Adam, and said unto him, Where art thou?

And he said, I heard thy voice in the garden, and I was afraid, because I was naked; and I hid myself.

And he said, Who told thee that thou wast naked? Hast thou eaten of the tree, whereof I commanded thee that thou shouldest not eat?

And the man said, The woman whom thou gavest to be with me, she gave me of the tree, and I did eat.

And the Lord God said unto the woman, What is this that thou hast done? And the woman said, The serpent beguiled me, and I did eat.

And the Lord God said unto the serpent, Because thou hast done this, thou art cursed above all cattle, and above every beast of the field; upon thy belly shalt thou go, and dust shalt thou eat all the days of thy life: and I will put enmity between thee and the woman, and between thy seed and her seed; it shall bruise thy head, and thou shalt bruise his heel.

Unto the woman he said, I will greatly multiply thy sorrow and thy conception; in sorrow shalt thou bring forth children; and thy desire shall be to thy husband, and he shall rule over thee.

And unto Adam he said, Because thou hast hearkened unto the voice of thy wife, and hast eaten of the tree, of which I commanded thee, saying, Thou shalt not eat of it: cursed is the ground for thy sake; in sorrow shalt thou eat of it all the days of thy life; thorns also and thistles shall it bring forth to thee; and thou shalt eat the herb of the field; in the sweat of thy face shalt thou eat bread, till thou return unto the ground; for out of it wast thou taken: for dust thou art, and unto dust shalt thou return.

And Adam called his wife's name Eve; because she was the mother of all living. Unto Adam also and to his wife did the Lord God make coats of skins and clothed them.

And the Lord God said, Behold,

the man is become as one of us, to know good and evil: and now, lest he put forth his hand, and take also of the tree of life, and eat, and live for ever: therefore the Lord God sent him forth from the garden of Eden, to till the ground from whence he was taken. So he drove out the man; and he placed at the east of the garden of Eden Cherubims, and a flaming sword which turned every way, to keep the way of the tree of life.

For Study

1. Why do you think God forbade Adam and Eve the fruit of one tree? Would not everything have been much simpler (as many have complained) if He had not put the tree there at all? What difference would adoption of that alternative have made in the relationship between man and God?

2. Point out the chief element in common between the fall of the angels and the fall of man, and also the chief difference between those falls (other than that angels and man are creatures of a different order of being). Consider Book I of *Paradise Lost,* lines 210–20 (page 143). What is the difference between God's attitude toward fallen angels in *Paradise Lost* and His attitude toward fallen man in *Paradise Lost* and Genesis?

For Writing

1. Write a paper showing characteristic details, embellishments, and enlargements that Milton has added to the sparse narrative of Genesis, Chapters 2 and 3. Do you think he has added to the value of the story? If so, in what ways? Has he violated the spirit of the Biblical account? If so, in what ways? Be sure to take into account the arguments of the omitted books.

2. Write a character study of Satan based on what you have read in *Paradise Lost*. Give what credit you think due to his impressive qualities, but be cautious about his statements. Make use of quotations, identifying each by Book and line number. To what extent is Milton's Satan suggested in the serpent of Genesis?

An Essay on Man

by Alexander Pope (1688–1744)

We have read two works based on similar views of what man is and of why he behaves as he does. Milton and Lewis, separated by almost three centuries, present dramatic narratives which make certain assertions related to Biblical tradition about God and man. *Paradise Lost* and *Out of the Silent Planet* show man as part of the creation of a loving God, a creation that includes other orders of beings capable of reason and free will. Both stories are concerned with the relations between God and these reasonable beings, and both explore the causes for breakdowns in this relationship as well as God's response to such disasters. Both, in short, presume to "justify the ways of God to men." The century that followed Milton's took, on the whole, a skeptical view of such a presumption. Its thinkers had generally a more optimistic faith in human reason as a source of solutions for man's problems than did the thinkers of the seventeenth century or than do those of our own time.

Alexander Pope is one of the brilliant lights of eighteenth-century poetry. His famous rhymed *Essay on Man,* published in 1733–34, is a didactic, not a dramatic, speculation about man. It is written in the mode known as heroic couplets, which, in the hands of one as skillful and witty as Pope, is a lively form. His *Essay* is occasionally forced or obscure, but its defects are much outweighed by its merits. It is one of the most frequently quoted poems in the English language. Numerous passages are familiar to many persons who have forgotten the rest of the poem or have never even read it. The *Essay* was written under the influence of Pope's friend, Henry St. John, Lord Bolingbroke. Dr. Samuel Johnson (1709–1784) praised "the splendid amplifications and sparkling sentences," but added, "Never were penury of knowledge and vulgarity of sentiment so happily disguised."

The basic viewpoint in the poem is known as Deism. It acknowledges a god as creator and regards him as wise and benevolent but remote from man and not intervening directly in his affairs.

We are reading Pope's *Essay* not only for itself but also for the ideas that relate it to *Out of the Silent Planet* and *Paradise Lost.* Be alert for both agreements and differences between Pope's views and those of Milton and C. S. Lewis.

TO

H. St. John Lord Bolingbroke

Argument of Epistle I

OF THE NATURE AND STATE OF MAN

WITH RESPECT TO THE UNIVERSE

Of Man in the abstract. I. That we can judge only with regard to our own system, being ignorant of the relations of systems and things. II. That Man is not to be deemed imperfect, but a Being suited to his place and rank in the creation, agreeable to the general Order of things, and conformable to Ends and Relations to him unknown. III. That it is partly upon his ignorance of future events, and partly upon the hope of a future state, that all his happiness in the present depends. IV. The pride of aiming at more knowledge, and pretending to more Perfection, the cause of Man's error and misery. The impiety of putting himself in the place of God, and judging of the fitness or unfitness, perfection or imperfection, justice or injustice of his dispensations. V. The absurdity of conceiting himself the final cause of the creation, or expecting that perfection in the moral world, which is not in the natural. VI. The unreasonableness of his complaints against Providence, while on the one hand he demands the Perfections of the Angels, and on the other the bodily qualifications of the Brutes; though, to possess any of the sensitive faculties in a higher degree, would render him miserable. VII. That throughout the whole visible world, an universal order and gradation in the sensual and mental faculties is observed, which causes a subordination of creature to creature, and of all creatures to Man. The gradations of sense, instinct, thought, reflection, reason; that Reason alone countervails all the other faculties. VIII. How much further this order and subordination of living creatures may extend, above and below us; were any part of which broken, not that part only, but the whole connected creation must be destroyed. IX. The extravagance, madness, and pride of such a desire. X. The consequence of all, the absolute submission due to Providence, both as to our present and future state.

Epistle I

Awake, my St. John!° leave all meaner things
To low ambition, and the pride of Kings.
Let us (since Life can little more supply
Than just to look about us and to die)
Expatiate free o'er all this scene of Man;   5
A mighty maze! but not without a plan;
A Wild, where weeds and flow'rs promiscuous shoot;
Or Garden, tempting with forbidden fruit.
Together let us beat this ample field,°
Try what the open, what the covert yield;   10
The latent tracts, the giddy heights, explore
Of all who blindly creep, or sightless soar;
Eye Nature's walks, shoot Folly as it flies,
And catch the Manners living as they rise;
Laugh where we must, be candid where we can;   15
But vindicate the ways of God to man.
    I. Say first, of God above, or Man below,
What can we reason, but from what we know?
Of Man, what see we but his station here,
From which to reason, or to which refer?   20
Thro' worlds unnumber'd tho' the God be known,
'Tis ours to trace him only in our own.
He, who thro' vast immensity can pierce,
See worlds on worlds compose one universe,
Observe how system into system runs,   25
What other planets circle other suns,
What vary'd Being peoples ev'ry star,
May tell why Heav'n has made us as we are.
But of this frame the bearings, and the ties,
The strong connexions, nice dependencies,   30
Gradations just, has thy pervading soul
Look'd thro'? or can a part contain the whole?
    Is the great chain, that draws all to agree,
And drawn supports, upheld by God, or thee?
    II. Presumptuous Man! the reason wouldst thou find,   35
Why form'd so weak, so little, and so blind?

1. St. John: pronounced *sin-jun.* Henry St. John Bolingbroke (1678–1751), statesman and philosopher, from whom Pope derived many of the views in this poem. 9–14. This metaphor of the hunt refers especially to the shooting of partridge or pheasant, which are beaten out of cover and shot on the wing.

First, if thou canst, the harder reason guess,
Why form'd no weaker, blinder, and no less?
Ask of thy mother earth, why oaks are made
Taller or stronger than the weeds they shade?   40
Or ask of yonder argent fields above,
Why Jove's satellites are less than Jove?
　　Of Systems possible, if 'tis confest
That Wisdom infinite must form the best,
Where all must full or not coherent be,   45
And all that rises, rise in due degree;
Then, in the scale of reas'ning life, 'tis plain,
There must be, somewhere, such a rank as Man:
And all the question (wrangle e'er so long)
Is only this, if God has plac'd him wrong?   50
　　Respecting Man, whatever wrong we call,
May, must be right, as relative to all.
In human works, tho' labour'd on with pain,
A thousand movements scarce one purpose gain;
In God's, one single can its end produce;   55
Yet serves to second too some other use.
So Man, who here seems principal alone,
Perhaps acts second to some sphere unknown,
Touches some wheel, or verges to some goal;
'Tis but a part we see, and not a whole.   60
　　When the proud steed shall know why Man restrains
His fiery course, or drives him o'er the plains:
When the dull Ox, why now he breaks the clod,
Is now a victim, and now Ægypt's God:°
Then shall Man's pride and dulness comprehend   65
His actions', passions', being's, use and end;
Why doing, suff'ring, check'd, impell'd; and why
This hour a slave, the next a deity.
　　Then say not Man's imperfect, Heav'n in fault;
Say rather, Man's as perfect as he ought: 70
His knowledge measur'd to his state and place;
His time a moment, and a point his space.
If to be perfect in a certain sphere,
What matter, soon or late, or here or there?
The blest to-day is as completely so,   75
As who began a thousand years ago.

64. An allusion to the worship of numerous animal gods in Egypt and elsewhere in the ancient world.

III. Heav'n from all creatures hides the book of Fate,
All but the page prescrib'd, their present state:
From brutes what men, from men what spirits know:
Or who could suffer Being here below?   80
The lamb thy riot° dooms to bleed to-day,
Had he thy Reason, would he skip and play?
Pleas'd to the last, he crops the flow'ry food,
And licks the hand just rais'd to shed his blood.
Oh blindness to the future! kindly giv'n,   85
That each may fill the circle mark'd by Heav'n:
Who sees with equal eye, as God of all,
A hero perish, or a sparrow fall,
Atoms or systems into ruin hurl'd,
And now a bubble burst, and now a world.   90
  Hope humbly then; with trembling pinions soar;
Wait the great teacher Death; and God adore.
What future bliss, he gives not thee to know,
But gives that Hope to be thy blessing now.
Hope springs eternal in the human breast: 95
Man never Is, but always To be blest:°
The soul, uneasy and confin'd from home,
Rests and expatiates in a life to come.
  Lo, the poor Indian! whose untutor'd mind
Sees God in clouds, or hears him in the wind: 100
His soul, proud Science never taught to stray
Far as the solar walk,° or milky way;
Yet simple Nature to his hope has giv'n,
Behind the cloud-topt hill, an humbler heav'n;
Some safer world in depth of woods embrac'd,   105
Some happier island in the wat'ry waste,
Where slaves once more their native land behold,
No fiends torment, no Christians thirst for gold.
To Be, contents his natural desire,
He asks no Angel's wing, no Seraph's fire;   110
But thinks, admitted to that equal sky,
His faithful dog shall bear him company.
  IV. Go, wiser thou! and, in thy scale of sense,
Weigh thy Opinion against Providence;
Call imperfection what thou fancy'st such,   115

81. riot: feasting and revelry. 96. This line finds a lightly mocking echo in Lewis
Carroll's *Through the Looking Glass:* "The rule is, jam tomorrow and jam yesterday — but never jam *today.*" 102. solar walk: sun's path.

Say, here he gives too little, there too much:
Destroy all Creatures for thy sport or gust,°
Yet cry, If Man's unhappy, God's unjust;
If Man alone engross not Heav'n's high care,
Alone made perfect here, immortal there: 120
Snatch from his hand the balance and the rod,
Re-judge his justice, be the GOD of GOD.
　　In Pride, in reas'ning Pride, our error lies;
All quit their sphere, and rush into the skies.
Pride still is aiming at the blest abodes,   125
Men would be Angels, Angels would be Gods.
Aspiring to be Gods, if Angels fell,
Aspiring to be Angels, Men rebel:
And who but wishes to invert the laws
Of ORDER, sins against th' Eternal Cause.   130
　　v.　Ask for what end the heav'nly bodies shine,
Earth for whose use? Pride answers, " 'Tis for mine:
For me kind Nature wakes her genial Pow'r,
Suckles each herb, and spreads out ev'ry flow'r;
Annual for me, the grape, the rose renew   135
The juice nectareous, and the balmy dew;
For me, the mine a thousand treasures brings;
For me, health gushes from a thousand springs;
Seas roll to waft me, suns to light me rise;
My foot-stool earth, my canopy the skies."   140
　　But errs not Nature from this gracious end,
From burning suns when livid deaths descend,
When earthquakes swallow, or when tempests sweep
Towns to one grave, whole nations to the deep?
"No, ('tis reply'd) the first Almighty Cause   145
Acts not by partial, but by gen'ral laws;
Th' exceptions few; some change since all began:
And what created perfect?"° — Why then Man?
If the great end be human Happiness,
Then Nature deviates; and can Man do less?   150
As much that end a constant course requires
Of show'rs and sun-shine, as of Man's desires;
As much eternal springs and cloudless skies,
As Men for ever temp'rate, calm, and wise.
If plagues or earthquakes break not Heav'n's design,   155

117. gust: taste, appetite. 148. "And . . . perfect?": i.e., everything created is by definition imperfect, God alone being perfect.

Why then a Borgia,° or a Catiline?°
Who knows but he, whose hand the lightning forms,
Who heaves old Ocean, and who wings the storms;
Pours fierce Ambition in a Cæsar's mind,
Or turns young Ammon° loose to scourge mankind?   160
From pride, from pride, our very reas'ning springs;
Account for moral, as for nat'ral things:
Why charge we Heav'n in those, in these acquit?
In both, to reason right is to submit.

    Better for Us, perhaps, it might appear,   165
Were there all harmony, all virtue here;
That never air or ocean felt the wind;
That never passion discompos'd the mind.
But ALL subsists by elemental strife;
And Passions are the elements of Life.   170
The gen'ral ORDER, since the whole began,
Is kept in Nature, and is kept in Man.

    VI. What would this Man? Now upward will he soar,
And little less than Angel, would be more;
Now looking downwards, just as griev'd appears   175
To want the strength of bulls, the fur of bears.
Made for his use all creatures if he call,
Say what their use, had he the pow'rs of all?
Nature to these, without profusion, kind,
The proper organs, proper pow'rs assign'd;   180
Each seeming want compensated of course,
Here with degrees of swiftness, there of force;
All in exact proportion to the state;
Nothing to add, and nothing to abate.
Each beast, each insect, happy in its own: 185
Is Heav'n unkind to Man, and Man alone?
Shall he alone, whom rational we call,
Be pleas'd with nothing, if not bless'd with all?

    The bliss of Man (could Pride that blessing find)
Is not to act or think beyond mankind;   190
No pow'rs of body or of soul to share,

---

156. **Borgia:** member of a noble family prominent in Italy during the Renaissance, some of whom were reputed to have committed great crimes; **Catiline:** a
conspirator against the Roman republic in the first century B.C., who rendered
himself infamous by his cruelty and duplicity. 160. **Ammon:** Alexander the Great
(356–323 B.C.), so called from one of the names of Zeus, whose son he was sometimes said to be.

But what his nature and his state can bear.
Why has not Man a microscopic eye?
For this plain reason, Man is not a Fly.
Say what the use, were finer optics giv'n,   195
T' inspect a mite, not comprehend the heav'n?
Or touch, if tremblingly alive all o'er,
To smart and agonize at every pore?
Or quick effluvia° darting thro' the brain,
Die of a rose in aromatic pain?   200
If nature thunder'd in his op'ning ears,
And stunn'd him with the music of the spheres,°
How would he wish that Heav'n had left him still
The whisp'ring Zephyr, and the purling rill?
Who finds not Providence all good and wise,   205
Alike in what it gives, and what denies?
   VII.   Far as Creation's ample range extends,
The scale of sensual, mental pow'rs ascends:
Mark how it mounts, to Man's imperial race,
From the green myriads in the peopled grass: 210
What modes of sight betwixt each wide extreme,
The mole's dim curtain, and the lynx's beam:
Of smell, the headlong lioness between,
And hound sagacious° on the tainted° green:
Of hearing, from the life that fills the Flood,   215
To that which warbles thro' the vernal wood:
The spider's touch, how exquisitely fine!
Feels at each thread, and lives along the line:
In the nice° bee, what sense so subtly true
From pois'nous herbs extracts the healing dew?   220
How Instinct varies in the grov'ling swine,
Compar'd, half-reas'ning elephant, with thine!
'Twixt that, and Reason, what a nice barrier,
For ever sep'rate, yet for ever near!
Remembrance and Reflection how ally'd;   225
What thin partitions Sense from Thought divide:
And Middle natures, how they long to join,
Yet never pass th' insuperable line!
Without this just gradation, could they be
Subjected, these to those, or all to thee?   230

   199. effluvia: a flowing out, as of odors. 202. music of the spheres: in Pythago-
rean philosophy, a harmony produced by the movements of the planets. 214. sagacious: quick of scent; tainted: having odors. 219. nice: delicately discriminating.

The pow'rs of all subdu'd by thee alone,
Is not thy Reason all these pow'rs in one?
   VIII. See, thro' this air, this ocean, and this earth,
All matter quick, and bursting into birth.
Above, how high, progressive life may go!   235
Around, how wide! how deep extend below!
Vast chain of Being! which from God began,
Natures ethereal, human, angel, man,
Beast, bird, fish, insect, what no eye can see,
No glass can reach; from Infinite to thee,   240
From thee to Nothing. — On superior pow'rs
Were we to press, inferior might on ours:
Or in the full creation leave a void,
Where, one step broken, the great scale's destroy'd:
From Nature's chain whatever link you strike,   245
Tenth or ten thousandth, breaks the chain alike.
   And, if each system in gradation roll
Alike essential to th' amazing Whole,
The least confusion but in one, not all
That system only, but the Whole must fall.   250
Let Earth unbalanc'd from her orbit fly,
Planets and Suns run lawless thro' the sky;
Let ruling angels from their spheres be hurl'd,
Being on Being wreck'd, and world on world;
Heav'n's whole foundations to their centre nod,   255
And Nature tremble to the throne of God.
All this dread ORDER break — for whom? for thee?
Vile worm! — Oh Madness! Pride! Impiety!
   IX. What if the foot, ordain'd the dust to tread,
Or hand, to toil, aspir'd to be the head?   260
What if the head, the eye, or ear repin'd
To serve mere engines to the ruling Mind?
Just as absurd for any part to claim
To be another, in this gen'ral frame:
Just as absurd, to mourn the tasks or pains,   265
The great directing MIND of ALL ordains.
   All are but parts of one stupendous whole,
Whose body Nature is, and God the soul;
That, chang'd thro' all, and yet in all the same;
Great in the earth, as in th' ethereal frame;   270
Warms in the sun, refreshes in the breeze,
Glows in the stars, and blossoms in the trees,

Lives thro' all life, extends thro' all extent,
Spreads undivided, operates unspent;
Breathes in our soul, informs our mortal part,   275
As full, as perfect, in a hair as heart:
As full, as perfect, in vile Man that mourns,
As the rapt Seraph that adores and burns:°
To him no high, no low, no great, no small;
He fills, he bounds, connects, and equals all.   280
    x. Cease then, nor ORDER Imperfection name:
Our proper bliss depends on what we blame.
Know thy own point: This kind, this due degree
Of blindness, weakness, Heav'n bestows on thee.
Submit.—In this, or any other sphere,   285
Secure to be as blest as thou canst bear:
Safe in the hand of one disposing Pow'r,
Or in the natal, or the mortal hour.
All Nature is but Art, unknown to thee;
All Chance, Direction, which thou canst not see;   290
All Discord, Harmony not understood;
All partial Evil, universal Good:
And, spite of Pride, in erring Reason's spite,
One truth is clear, WHATEVER IS, IS RIGHT.

278. burns: shines with dazzling light.

For Study and Writing

1. Show where, in the early lines of the *Essay,* Pope may be said to pay his respects to Milton.

2. Consider lines 47–50. Why must there "be, somewhere, such a rank as Man"? Do you agree with Pope? What does this statement imply about the existence of other ranks?

3. Relate line 71 ("His knowledge measur'd to his state and place") both to the scene with Oyarsa in *Out of the Silent Planet* (Chapter 18) and to the instructions given Adam and Eve by angels in *Paradise Lost.*

4. Relate lines 119–30 to Weston's endeavors. Wherein, according to Pope, is it that "our error lies"? Relate Pope's idea to Milton's Satan and, if you can, to themes in Greek drama. (*Oedipus the King,* page 547, presents a case in point.)

5. After careful reading of the paragraph closed by lines 162–64, discuss those lines.

6. In the Bible, read Psalm 8:5. Compare that verse to line 174.

7. What does Pope specify as "the bliss of Man"?

8. What are "the green myriads in the peopled grass" (line 210)?

9. Pope is much preoccupied with "just gradation" (line 229) and the "vast chain of Being" (line 237). What is the meaning of line 232? of lines 241–42?

10. Relate line 253 to both C. S. Lewis's story and to Milton's.

11. In the Bible, read I Corinthians 12:14–26. Discuss parallels in this passage and lines 259–66.

12. In lines 267–68 Pope's Deism seems to embrace Pantheism. After checking both *Deism* and *Pantheism* in a dictionary, discuss this apparent change.

13. Discuss the summing up of Epistle I in lines 289–94. Do you agree? In the light of lines 51–52, discuss Pope's meaning in "Whatever is, is right."

Argument of Epistle II

OF THE NATURE AND STATE OF MAN WITH RESPECT TO HIMSELF, AS AN INDIVIDUAL

I. The Business of Man not to pry into God, but to study himself. His Middle Nature; his Powers and Frailties. The Limits of his Capacity. II. The two Principles of Man, Self-love and Reason, both necessary. Self-love the stronger, and why. Their end the same. III. The Passions, and their use. The predominant Passion, and its force. Its Necessity, in directing Men to different purposes. Its providential Use, in fixing our Principle, and ascertaining our Virtue. IV. Virtue and Vice joined in our mixed Nature; the limits near, yet the things separate and evident: What is the Office of Reason. V. How odious Vice in itself, and how we deceive ourselves into it. VI. That, however, the Ends of Providence and general Good are answered in our Passions and Imperfections. How usefully these are distributed to all Orders of Men. How useful they are to Society. And to the Individuals. In every state, and every age of life.

Epistle II

1. Know then thyself, presume not God to scan;
The proper study of Mankind is Man.
Plac'd on this isthmus of a middle state,
A Being darkly wise, and rudely great:
With too much knowledge for the Sceptic° side,   5
With too much weakness for the Stoic's° pride,
He hangs between; in doubt to act, or rest;
In doubt to deem himself a God, or Beast;
In doubt his Mind or Body to prefer;
Born but to die, and reas'ning but to err;   10
Alike in ignorance, his reason such,
Whether he thinks too little, or too much:
Chaos of Thought and Passion, all confus'd;
Still by himself abus'd, or disabus'd;
Created half to rise, and half to fall;   15
Great lord of all things, yet a prey to all;
Sole judge of Truth, in endless Error hurl'd:
The glory, jest, and riddle of the world!
    Go, wond'rous creature! mount where Science guides,
Go, measure earth, weigh air, and state the tides;   20
Instruct the planets in what orbs to run,
Correct old Time, and regulate the Sun;
Go, soar with Plato° to th' empyreal sphere,
To the first good, first perfect, and first fair;
Or tread the mazy round his follow'rs trod,   25
And quitting sense call° imitating God;
As Eastern priests in giddy circles run,
And turn their heads to imitate the Sun.
Go, teach Eternal Wisdom how to rule —
Then drop into thyself, and be a fool!   30
    Superior beings,° when of late they saw
A mortal Man unfold all Nature's law,
Admir'd such wisdom in an earthly shape,
And shew'd° a NEWTON° as we shew an Ape.

---

5. **Sceptic**: one who doubts or questions, especially religious or philosophical views. 6. **Stoic**: a member of a Greek school of philosophy that urges man to be free from passion, joy, pain, grief, and all other such feelings. 23. **Plato**: Greek philosopher (427?–347? B.C.). 26. **call**: identify as. 31. **Superior beings**: angels. 34. **shew'd**: showed; **Newton**: Sir Isaac Newton (1642–1727), whose great mathematical and scientific advances were still fresh wonders when Pope wrote.

Could he, whose rules the rapid Comet bind,   35
Describe or fix one movement of his Mind?
Who saw its fires here rise, and there descend,
Explain his own beginning, or his end?
Alas what wonder! Man's superior part
Uncheck'd may rise, and climb from art to art;   40
But when his own great work is but begun,
What Reason weaves, by Passion is undone.
　　Trace Science then, with Modesty thy guide;
First strip off all her equipage of Pride;
Deduct what is but Vanity, or Dress,   45
Or Learning's Luxury, or Idleness;
Or tricks to shew the stretch of human brain,
Mere curious pleasure, or ingenious pain;
Expunge the whole, or lop th' excrescent° parts
Of all our Vices have created Arts;   50
Then see how little the remaining sum,
Which serv'd the past, and must the times to come!
　　II.　Two Principles in human nature reign;
Self-love, to urge, and Reason, to restrain;
Nor this a good, nor that a bad we call,   55
Each works its end, to move or govern all:
And to their proper operation still,
Ascribe all Good; to their improper, Ill.
　　Self-love, the spring of motion, acts° the soul;
Reason's comparing balance rules the whole.   60
Man, but for that, no action could attend,
And but for this, were active to no end:
Fix'd like a plant on his peculiar spot,
To draw nutrition, propagate, and rot;
Or, meteor-like, flame lawless thro' the void,   65
Destroying others, by himself destroy'd.
　　Most strength the moving principle requires;
Active its task, it prompts, impels, inspires.
Sedate and quiet the comparing lies,
Form'd but to check, delib'rate, and advise.   70
Self-love still stronger, as its objects nigh;
Reason's at distance, and in prospect lie:
That sees immediate good by present sense;
Reason, the future and the consequence.
Thicker than arguments, temptations throng,   75

49. excrescent: superfluous. 59. acts: actuates.

At best more watchful this, but that more strong.
The action of the stronger to suspend,
Reason still use, to Reason still attend.
Attention, habit and experience gains;
Each strengthens Reason, and Self-love restrains.   80
    Let subtle schoolmen teach these friends to fight,
More studious to divide than to unite;
And Grace and Virtue, Sense and Reason split,
With all the rash dexterity of wit.
Wits, just like Fools, at war about a name,   85
Have full as oft no meaning, or the same.
Self-love and Reason to one end aspire,
Pain their aversion, Pleasure their desire;
But greedy That, its object would devour,
This taste the honey, and not wound the flow'r;   90
Pleasure, or wrong or rightly understood,
Our greatest evil, or our greatest good.
    iii.   Modes of Self-love the Passions we may call;
'Tis real good, or seeming, moves them all:
But since not ev'ry good we can divide,   95
And Reason bids us for our own provide;
Passions, tho' selfish, if their means be fair,
List° under Reason, and deserve her care;
Those, that imparted,° court a nobler aim,
Exalt their kind, and take some Virtue's name.   100
    In lazy Apathy let Stoics boast
Their Virtue fix'd; 'tis fix'd as in a frost;
Contracted all, retiring to the breast;
But strength of mind is Exercise, not Rest:
The rising tempest puts in act the soul,   105
Parts it may ravage, but preserves the whole.
On life's vast ocean diversely we sail,
Reason the card,° but Passion is the gale;
Nor God alone in the still calm we find,
He mounts the storm, and walks upon the wind.   110
    Passions, like Elements, tho' born to fight,
Yet, mix'd and soften'd, in his work unite:
These 'tis enough to temper and employ;
But what composes Man, can Man destroy?
Suffice that Reason keep to Nature's road,   115

98. List: enlist. 99. that imparted: after reason has been imparted to them.
108. card: compass-card.

Subject, compound them, follow her and God.
Love, Hope, and Joy, fair Pleasure's smiling train,
Hate, Fear, and Grief, the family of Pain,
These mix'd with art, and to due bounds confin'd,
Make and maintain the balance of the mind: 120
The lights and shades, whose well accorded strife
Gives all the strength and colour of our life.

    Pleasures are ever in our hands or eyes;
And when in act they cease, in prospect rise:
Present to grasp, and future still to find,   125
The whole employ of body and of mind.
All spread their charms, but charm not all alike;
On diff'rent senses diff'rent objects strike;
Hence diff'rent Passions more or less inflame,
As strong or weak, the organs of the frame;   130
And hence one MASTER PASSION in the breast,
Like Aaron's serpent,° swallows up the rest.

    As Man, perhaps, the moment of his breath,
Receives the lurking principle of death;
The young disease, that must subdue at length,   135
Grows with his growth, and strengthens with his strength:
So, cast and mingled with his very frame,
The Mind's disease, its RULING PASSION came;
Each vital humour° which should feed the whole,
Soon flows to this, in body and in soul: 140
Whatever warms the heart, or fills the head,
As the mind opens, and its functions spread,
Imagination plies her dang'rous art,
And pours it all upon the peccant° part.

    Nature its mother, Habit is its nurse;   145
Wit, Spirit, Faculties, but make it worse;
Reason itself but gives it edge and pow'r;
As Heav'n's blest beam turns vinegar more sour.°

    We, wretched subjects, tho' to lawful sway,
In this weak queen some fav'rite still obey: 150
Ah! if she lend not arms, as well as rules,
What can she more than tell us we are fools?

---

132. **Aaron's serpent:** the rod of Aaron, high priest of Israel, was turned into
a serpent (see Exodus 7:8–13). 139. **humour:** in medieval physiology, one of four
supposed principal body fluids believed to influence health and temperament.
144. **peccant:** offending, sinning. 148. **As . . . sour:** Wine left in sunlight becomes
vinegar that is exceptionally sour.

Teach us to mourn our Nature, not to mend,
A sharp accuser, but a helpless friend!
Or from a judge turn pleader, to persuade   155
The choice we make, or justify it made;
Proud of an easy conquest all along,
She but removes weak passions for the strong:
So, when small humours gather to a gout,
The doctor fancies he has driv'n them out.   160

    Yes, Nature's road must ever be preferr'd;
Reason is here no guide, but still a guard:
'Tis hers to rectify, not overthrow,
And treat this passion more as friend than foe:
A mightier Pow'r the strong direction sends,   165
And sev'ral Men impels to sev'ral ends:
Like varying winds, by other passions tost,
This drives them constant to a certain coast.
Let pow'r or knowledge, gold or glory, please,
Or (oft more strong than all) the love of ease;   170
Thro' life 'tis follow'd, ev'n at life's expense;
The merchant's toil, the sage's indolence,
The monk's humility, the hero's pride,
All, all alike, find Reason on their side.

    Th' Eternal Art educing° good from ill,   175
Grafts on this Passion our our best principle:
'Tis thus the Mercury of Man° is fix'd;
Strong grows the Virtue with his nature mix'd;
The dross cements what else were too refin'd,
And in one int'rest body acts with mind.   180

    As fruits, ungrateful to the planter's care,
On savage stocks inserted, learn to bear;
The surest Virtues thus from Passions shoot,
Wild Nature's vigour working at the root.
What crops of wit and honesty appear   185
From spleen, from obstinacy, hate, or fear!
See anger, zeal and fortitude supply;
Ev'n av'rice, prudence; sloth, philosophy;
Lust, thro' some certain strainers well refin'd,
Is gentle love, and charms all womankind;   190
Envy, to which th' ignoble mind's a slave,
Is emulation in the learn'd or brave;

175. educing: leading out. **177. the Mercury of Man:** man's mercurial (changeable, inconstant) character.

Nor Virtue, male or female, can we name,
But what will grow on Pride, or grow on Shame.
    Thus Nature gives us (let it check our pride)   195
The virtue nearest to our vice ally'd:
Reason the bias turns to good from ill,
And Nero° reigns a Titus,° if he will.
The fiery soul abhorr'd in Catiline,
In Decius° charms, in Curtius° is divine: 200
The same ambition can destroy or save,
And makes a patriot as it makes a knave.
    iv. This light and darkness in our chaos join'd,
What shall divide? The God within the mind:
Extremes in Nature equal ends produce,   205
In Man they join to some mysterious use;
Tho' each by turns the other's bound invade,
As, in some well-wrought picture, light and shade,
And oft so mix, the diff'rence is too nice°
Where ends the Virtue, or begins the Vice.   210
    Fools! who from hence into the notion fall,
That Vice or Virtue there is none at all.
If white and black blend, soften, and unite
A thousand ways, is there no black or white?
Ask your own heart, and nothing is so plain;   215
'Tis to mistake them costs the time and pain.
    v. Vice is a monster of so frightful mien,
As, to be hated, needs but to be seen;
Yet seen too oft, familiar with her face,
We first endure, then pity, then embrace.   220
But where th' Extreme of Vice, was ne'er agreed:
Ask where's the North? at York,° 'tis on the Tweed;°
In Scotland, at the Orcades;° and there,
At Greenland, Zembla,° or the Lord knows where.
No creature owns it° in the first degree,   225
But thinks his neighbour further gone than he;

198. Nero: Roman emperor A.D. 54–68, notorious for vice and cruelty; Titus: Roman emperor A.D. 79–81, said to have sighed to see a day pass without its good deed. 200. Decius: Roman consul said to have "devoted" himself to destruction in battle and charged into the enemy's ranks to certain death (probably in 295 B.C.); Curtius: Marcus Curtius, a hero who sacrificed himself for Rome. (362 B.C.). Curtius's legend is worth looking up. 209. too nice: too subtle a distinction. 222. York: a county and city in England; Tweed: a river north of York. 223. Orcades: the Orkneys, islands off the north coast of Scotland. 224. Zembla: in modern times Novaya Zemlya, two islands in the Arctic Ocean, north of Russia. 225. owns it: acknowledges it (vice).

Ev'n those who dwell beneath its very zone,°
Or never feel the rage, or° never own;
What happier natures shrink at with affright,
The hard inhabitant contends is right.   230
    VI. Virtuous and vicious ev'ry Man must be,
Few in th' extreme, but all in the degree;
The rogue and fool by fits is fair and wise;
And ev'n the best, by fits, what they despise.
'Tis but by parts we follow good or ill;   235
For, Vice or Virtue, Self directs it still;
Each individual seeks a sev'ral° goal;
But HEAV'N's great view is One, and that the Whole.
That counter-works each folly and caprice;
That disappoints th' effect of ev'ry vice;   240
That, happy frailties to all ranks apply'd,
Shame to the virgin, to the matron pride,
Fear to the statesman, rashness to the chief,
To kings presumption, and to crowds belief:
That, Virtue's ends from Vanity can raise,   245
Which seeks no int'rest, no reward but praise;
And build on wants, and on defects of mind,
The joy, the peace, the glory of Mankind.
    Heav'n forming each on other to depend,
A master, or a servant, or a friend,   250
Bids each on other for assistance call,
Till one Man's weakness grows the strength of all.
Wants, frailties, passions, closer still ally
The common int'rest, or endear the tie.
To these we owe true friendship, love sincere,   255
Each home-felt joy that life inherits here;
Yet from the same we learn, in its decline,
Those joys, those loves, those int'rests to resign;
Taught half by Reason, half by mere decay,
To welcome death, and calmly pass away.   260
    Whate'er the Passion, knowledge, fame, or pelf,
Not one will change his neighbour with himself.
The learn'd is happy nature to explore,
The fool is happy that he knows no more;
The rich is happy in the plenty giv'n,   265
The poor contents him with the care of Heav'n.
See the blind beggar dance, the cripple sing,

227. zone: belt or girdle. 228. Or ... or: either ... or. 237. sev'ral: separate.

The sot a hero, lunatic a king;
The starving chemist in his golden views°
Supremely blest, the poet in his Muse.   270
    See some strange comfort ev'ry state attend,
And Pride bestow'd on all, a common friend;
See some fit Passion ev'ry age supply,
Hope travels thro', nor quits us when we die.
    Behold the child, by Nature's kindly law,   275
Pleas'd with a rattle, tickled with a straw:
Some livelier play-thing gives his youth delight,
A little louder, but as empty quite:
Scarfs, garters, gold, amuse his riper stage,
And beads and pray'r-books are the toys of age: 280
Pleas'd with this bauble still, as that before;
'Till tir'd he sleeps, and Life's poor play is o'er.
    Mean-while Opinion gilds with varying rays
Those painted clouds that beautify our days;
Each want of happiness by hope supply'd,   285
And each vacuity of sense by Pride:
These build as fast as knowledge can destroy;
In Folly's cup still laughs the bubble, joy;
One prospect lost, another still we gain;
And not a vanity is giv'n in vain;   290
Ev'n mean Self-love becomes, by force divine,
The scale to measure others' wants by thine.
See! and confess, one comfort still must rise,
'Tis this, Tho' Man's a fool, yet God is Wise.

269. chemist in his golden views: the alchemist seeking means to change base metals into gold.

For Study and Writing

1. Read carefully lines 1–18. What does Pope mean by "this isthmus of a middle state"? With the help of a good dictionary if necessary, tell the precise meaning of the adverbs *darkly* and *rudely* in line 4. Starting at line 5, explain each of the statements that follow. Compare line 13 to line 42, then compare both these lines to the following, attributed to the ghost of Virgil in Thornton Wilder's novel, *The Cabala:* "Are you still alive? Alive? How can you endure it? All your thoughts are guesses, all your body is shaken with breath, all your senses are infirm, and your mind ever full of the fumes of some passion or another." Compare that passage to

the *sorn's* statement near the close of Chapter 16 of *Out of the Silent Planet* (page 87).

2. Read lines 131–44. How does this concept of a "master" or "ruling" passion apply to Lewis's Weston and Devine and to Milton's Satan? What is the "master passion" of each?

3. Discuss the idea in lines 195–96.

4. It is sometimes argued that good and evil are only relative matters. Discuss Pope's opinion of this argument as expressed in lines 211–16.

5. Lines 217–20 are often quoted. What is the warning expressed in them? The American journalist Finley Peter Dunne created a satirical character called Mr. Dooley, who once

offered this variation on Pope's lines: "Vice, as Hogan says, is a monster of so hideous mien as the more ye see av it the better ye like it." Do you think Mr. Dooley renders Pope's thought accurately?

6. Relate the thought in lines 231–32 to C. S. Lewis's concept of the "bentness" of man. Do you think Milton would have agreed with Pope and Lewis in this matter?

7. Do you think lines 261–62 are true? Explain your answer.

8. Compare the thought in lines 275–82 with that in the seven-ages-of-man speech by Jaques in Shakespeare's *As You Like It*, Act II, Scene vii, lines 139–66.

Argument of Epistle III

OF THE NATURE AND STATE OF MAN
WITH RESPECT TO SOCIETY

I. The whole Universe one system of Society. Nothing made wholly for itself, nor yet wholly for another. The happiness of Animals mutual. II. Reason or Instinct operate alike to the good of each Individual. Reason or Instinct operate also to Society, in all animals. III. How far Society carried by Instinct. How much farther by Reason. IV. Of that which is called the State of Nature. Reason instructed by Instinct in the invention of Arts, and in the Forms of Society. V. Origin of Political Societies. Origin of Monarchy, Patriarchal government. VI. Origin of true Religion and Government, from the same principle, of Love. Origin of Superstition and Tyranny, from the same principle, of Fear. The Influence of Self-love operating to the social and public Good. Restoration of true Religion and Government on their first principle. Mixt Government. Various Forms of each, and the true end of all.

Epistle III

Here then we rest: "The Universal Cause
Acts to one end, but acts by various laws."
In all the madness of superfluous health,
The trim of pride, the impudence of wealth,
Let this great truth be present night and day;   5
But most be present, if we preach or pray.
   I. Look round our World; behold the chain of Love
Combining all below and all above.
See plastic Nature working to this end,
The single atoms each to other tend,   10
Attract, attracted to, the next in place
Form'd and impell'd its neighbour to embrace.
See Matter next, with various life endu'd
Press to one centre still, the gen'ral Good.
See dying vegetables life sustain,   15
See life dissolving vegetate again:
All forms that perish other forms supply,
(By turns we catch the vital breath, and die)
Like bubbles on the sea of Matter born,
They rise, they break, and to that sea return.   20
Nothing is foreign: Parts relate to Whole;
One all-extending, all-preserving Soul
Connects each being, greatest with the least;
Made Beast in aid of Man, and Man of Beast;
All serv'd, all serving: nothing stands alone;   25
The chain holds on, and where it ends, unknown.
   Has God, thou fool! work'd solely for thy good,
Thy joy, thy pastime, thy attire, thy food?
Who for thy table feeds the wanton fawn,
For him as kindly spread the flow'ry lawn: 30
Is it for thee the lark ascends and sings?
Joy tunes his voice, joy elevates his wings.
Is it for thee the linnet pours his throat?
Loves of his own and raptures swell the note.
The bounding steed you pompously bestride,   35
Shares with his lord the pleasure and the pride.
Is thine alone the seed that strews the plain?
The birds of heav'n shall vindicate their grain.
Thine the full harvest of the golden year?
Part pays, and justly, the deserving steer: 40

The hog, that ploughs not nor obeys thy call,
Lives on the labours of this lord of all.
    Know, Nature's children all divide her care;
The fur that warms a monarch, warm'd a bear.
While Man exclaims, "See all things for my use!"   45
"See man for mine!" replies a pamper'd goose:
And just as short of reason he must fall,
Who thinks all made for one, not one for all.
    Grant that the pow'rful still the weak control;
Be Man the Wit° and Tyrant of the whole: 50
Nature that Tyrant checks; he only knows,
And helps, another creature's wants and woes.
Say, will the falcon, stooping from above,
Smit with her varying plumage, spare the dove?
Admires the jay the insect's gilded wings?   55
Or hears the hawk when Philomela° sings?
Man cares for all: to birds he gives his woods,
To beasts his pastures, and to fish his floods;
For some his Int'rest prompts him to provide,
For more his pleasure, yet for more his pride: 60
All feed on one vain Patron, and enjoy
Th' extensive blessing of his luxury.
That very life his learned hunger craves,
He saves from famine, from the savage saves;
Nay, feasts the animal he dooms his feast,   65
And, 'till he ends the being, makes it blest;
Which sees no more the stroke, or feels the pain,
Than favour'd Man by touch ethereal slain.
The creature had his feast of life before;
Thou too must perish, when thy feast is o'er!   70
    To each unthinking being Heav'n, a friend,
Gives not the useless knowledge of its end:
To Man imparts it; but with such a view
As, while he dreads it, makes him hope it too:
The hour conceal'd, and so remote the fear,   75
Death still draws nearer, never seeming near.
Great standing miracle! that Heav'n assign'd
Its only thinking thing this turn of mind.
    II. Whether with Reason, or with Instinct blest,
Know, all enjoy that pow'r which suits them best;   80
To bliss alike by that direction tend,

50. the Wit: the rational being. 56. Philomela: the nightingale.

And find the means proportion'd to their end.
Say, where full Instinct is th' unerring guide,
What Pope or Council can they need beside?
Reason, however able, cool at best,   85
Cares not for service, or but serves when prest,
Stays 'till we call, and then not often near;
But honest Instinct comes a volunteer,
Sure never to o'er-shoot, but just to hit;
While still too wide or short is human Wit;   90
Sure by quick Nature happiness to gain,
Which heavier Reason labours at in vain,
This too serves always, Reason never long;
One must go right, the other may go wrong.
See then the acting and comparing pow'rs   95
One in their nature, which are two in ours;
And Reason raise o'er Instinct as you can,
In this 'tis God directs, in that 'tis Man.

   Who taught the nations of the field and flood
To shun their poison, and to choose their food?   100
Prescient,° the tides or tempests to withstand,
Build on the wave, or arch beneath the sand?
Who made the spider parallels design,
Sure as Demoivre,° without rule or line?
Who did the stork, Columbus-like, explore   105
Heav'ns not his own, and worlds unknown before?
Who calls the council, states the certain day,
Who forms the phalanx, and who points the way?

   III. God in the nature of each being founds
Its proper bliss, and sets its proper bounds: 110
But as he fram'd a Whole, the Whole to bless,
On mutual Wants built mutual Happiness:
So from the first, eternal ORDER ran,
And creature link'd to creature, man to man.
Whate'er of life all-quick'ning æther keeps,   115
Or breathes thro' air, or shoots beneath the deeps,
Or pours profuse on earth, one nature feeds
The vital flame, and swells the genial° seeds.
Not Man alone, but all that roam the wood,
Or wing the sky, or roll along the flood,   120

101. **Prescient:** foreknowing. 104. **Demoivre:** Abraham de Moivre (1667–1754), English mathematician of French Huguenot extraction. 118. **genial:** generative.

Each loves itself, but not itself alone,
Each sex desires alike, 'till two are one.
Nor ends the pleasure with the fierce embrace;
They love themselves, a third time, in their race.
Thus beast and bird their common charge attend,   125
The mothers nurse it, and the sires defend;
The young dismiss'd to wander earth or air,
There stops the Instinct, and there ends the care;
The link dissolves, each seeks a fresh embrace,
Another love succeeds, another race.   130
A longer care Man's helpless kind demands;
That longer care contracts more lasting bands:
Reflection, Reason, still the ties improve,
At once extend the int'rest, and the love;
With choice we fix, with sympathy we burn;   135
Each Virtue in each Passion takes its turn;
And still new needs, new helps, new habits rise,
That graft benevolence on charities.
Still as one brood, and as another rose,
These nat'ral love maintain'd, habitual those: 140
The last, scarce ripen'd into perfect Man,
Saw helpless him from whom their life began:
Mem'ry and fore-cast just returns engage,
That pointed back to youth, this on to age;
While pleasure, gratitude, and hope, combin'd,   145
Still spread the int'rest, and preserv'd the kind.
   IV.   Nor think, in NATURE's STATE they blindly trod;
The state of Nature was the reign of God:
Self-love and Social at her birth began,
Union the bond of all things, and of Man.   150
Pride then was not; nor Arts, that Pride to aid;
Man walk'd with beast, joint tenant of the shade;
The same his table, and the same his bed;
No murder cloth'd him, and no murder fed.
In the same temple, the resounding wood,   155
All vocal beings hymn'd their equal God:
The shrine with gore unstain'd, with gold undrest,
Unbrib'd, unbloody, stood the blameless priest:
Heav'n's attribute was Universal Care,
And Man's prerogative to rule, but spare.   160
Ah! how unlike the man of times to come!
Of half that live the butcher and the tomb;

Who, foe to Nature, hears the gen'ral groan,
Murders their species, and betrays his own.
But just disease to luxury succeeds,   165
And ev'ry death its own avenger breeds;
The Fury-passions from that blood began,
And turn'd on Man a fiercer savage, Man.
　　See him from Nature rising slow to Art!
To copy Instinct then was Reason's part;   170
Thus then to Man the voice of Nature spake —
"Go, from the Creatures thy instructions take:
Learn from the birds what food the thickets yield;
Learn from the beasts the physic of the field;°
Thy arts of building from the bee receive;   175
Learn of the mole to plough, the worm to weave;
Learn of the little Nautilus to sail,°
Spread the thin oar, and catch the driving gale.
Here too all forms of social union find,
And hence let Reason, late, instruct Mankind: 180
Here subterranean works and cities see;
There towns aerial on the waving tree.
Learn each small People's genius, policies,
The Ant's republic, and the realm of Bees;
How those in common all their wealth bestow,   185
And Anarchy without confusion know;
And these for ever, tho' a Monarch reign,
Their sep'rate cells and properties maintain.
Mark what unvary'd laws preserve each state,
Laws wise as Nature, and as fix'd as Fate.   190
In vain thy Reason finer webs shall draw,
Entangle Justice in her net of Law,
And right, too rigid, harden into wrong;
Still for the strong too weak, the weak too strong.
Yet go! and thus o'er all the creatures sway,   195
Thus let the wiser make the rest obey;
And, for those Arts mere Instinct could afford,
Be crown'd as Monarchs, or as Gods ador'd."
　　v.　Great Nature spoke; observant Men obey'd;
Cities were built, Societies were made: 200
Here rose one little state; another near

174. the physic of the field: the plant an animal will eat when sick. 177. The
paper nautilus, a mollusk, has sail-like arms which it was believed to use like the
sails of a boat.

Grew by like means, and join'd, thro' love or fear.
Did here the trees with ruddier burdens bend,
And there the streams in purer rills descend?
What War could ravish, Commerce could bestow,   205
And he return'd a friend, who came a foe.
Converse and Love mankind might strongly draw,
When Love was Liberty, and Nature Law.
Thus States were form'd; the name of King unknown,
'Till common int'rest plac'd the sway in one.   210
'Twas VIRTUE ONLY (or in arts or arms,
Diffusing blessings, or averting harms)
The same which in a Sire the Sons obey'd,
A Prince the Father of a People made.
   VI. 'Till then, by Nature crown'd, each Patriarch sate,   215
King, priest, and parent of his growing state;
On him, their second Providence, they hung,
Their law his eye, their oracle his tongue.
He from the wond'ring furrow call'd the food,
Taught to command the fire, control the flood,   220
Draw forth the monsters of th' abyss profound,
Or fetch th' aerial eagle to the ground.
'Till drooping, sick'ning, dying they began
Whom they rever'd as God to mourn as Man:
Then, looking up from sire to sire, explor'd   225
One great first Father, and that first ador'd.
Or plain tradition that this All begun,
Convey'd unbroken faith from sire to son;
The worker from the work distinct was known,
And simple Reason never sought but one: 230
Ere Wit oblique had broke that steady light,
Man, like his Maker, saw that all was right;
To Virtue, in the paths of Pleasure, trod,
And own'd a Father when he own'd a God.
Love all the faith, and all th' allegiance then;   235
For Nature knew no right divine in Men,
No ill could fear in God; and understood
A sov'reign being but a sov'reign good.
True faith, true policy, united ran,
This was but love of God, and this of Man.   240
   Who first taught souls enslav'd, and realms undone,
Th' enormous faith of many made for one;
That proud exception to all Nature's laws,

T' invert the world, and counter-work its Cause?
Force first made Conquest, and that conquest, Law;   245
'Till Superstition taught the tyrant awe,
Then shar'd the Tyranny, then lent it aid,
And Gods of Conqu'rors, Slaves of Subjects made:
She 'midst the lightning's blaze, and thunder's sound,
When rock'd the mountains, and when groan'd the ground,   250
She taught the weak to bend, the proud to pray,
To Pow'r unseen, and mightier far than they:
She, from the rending earth and bursting skies,
Saw Gods descend, and fiends infernal rise:
Here fix'd the dreadful, there the blest abodes;   255
Fear made her Devils, and weak Hope her Gods;
Gods partial, changeful, passionate, unjust,
Whose attributes were Rage, Revenge, or Lust;
Such as the souls of cowards might conceive,
And, form'd like tyrants, tyrants would believe.   260
Zeal then, not charity, became the guide;
And hell was built on spite, and heav'n on pride,
Then sacred seem'd th' ethereal vault no more;
Altars grew marble then, and reek'd with gore:
Then first the Flamen ° tasted living food;   265
Next his grim idol smear'd with human blood;
With Heav'n's own thunders shook the world below,
And play'd the God an engine on his foe.
    So drives Self-love, thro' just and thro' unjust,
To one Man's pow'r, ambition, lucre, lust: 270
The same Self-love, in all, becomes the cause
Of what restrains him, Government and Laws.
For, what one likes if others like as well,
What serves one will, when many wills rebel?
How shall he keep, what, sleeping or awake,   275
A weaker may surprise, a stronger take?
His safety must his liberty restrain:
All join to guard what each desires to gain.
Forc'd into virtue thus by Self-defence,
Ev'n Kings learn'd justice and benevolence: 280
Self-love forsook the path it first pursu'd,
And found the private in the public good.
    'Twas then, the studious head or gen'rous mind,
Follow'r of God or friend of human-kind,

265. Flamen: in ancient Rome, a priest serving one particular deity.

Poet or Patriot, rose but to restore   285
The Faith and Moral, Nature gave before;
Re-lum'd her ancient light, not kindled new;
If not God's image, yet his shadow drew:
Taught Pow'r's due use to People and to Kings,
Taught not to slack, nor strain its tender strings,   290
The less, or greater, set so justly true,
That touching one must strike the other too; °
'Till jarring int'rests, of themselves create
Th' according music of a well-mix'd State.
Such is the World's great harmony, that springs   295
From Order, Union, full Consent of things:
Where small and great, where weak and mighty, made
To serve, not suffer, strengthen, not invade;
More pow'rful each as needful to the rest,
And, in proportion as it blesses, blest;   300
Draw to one point, and to one centre bring
Beast, Man, or Angel, Servant, Lord, or King.
    For Forms of Government let fools contest;
Whate'er is best administer'd is best:
For Modes of Faith let graceless zealots fight;   305
His can't be wrong whose life is in the right:
In Faith and Hope the world will disagree,
But all Mankind's concern is Charity:
All must be false that thwart this One great End;
And all of God, that bless Mankind or mend.   310
    Man, like the gen'rous vine, supported lives;
The strength he gains is from th' embrace he gives.
On their own Axis as the Planets run,
Yet make at once their circle round the Sun;
So two consistent motions act ° the Soul;   315
And one regards Itself, and one the Whole.
    Thus God and Nature link'd the gen'ral frame,
And bade Self-love and Social be the same.

292. strike . . . too: make the other sound too. 315. act: actuate.

For Study and Writing

1. In stating his theme in the first lines of this Epistle, why does Pope make the special emphasis of line 5?

2. Explain lines 15–16.

3. In lines 22–23 we find an anticipation of the American Transcendentalism of the mid-nineteenth century. Pope's "one all-extending, all-pre-

serving Soul" is almost precisely the "Over-Soul" of Ralph Waldo Emerson's essay of that name. What opinion do you think Lewis or Milton would have of this concept of the Over-Soul?

4. What basic caution is given to man in this Epistle about assessing his place in the scheme of Creation? Support your answer by citing lines from the text.

5. Discuss the concept in lines 71–78. Explain the distinction drawn here between man and the lower orders of beings.

6. State Pope's contrast between the nature and the function of Reason and of Instinct. Cite lines.

7. Consider line 124. What is the relation of the idea expressed here to the "bentness" of Weston as explained by Oyarsa? On this point, cite an illuminating passage from *Out of the Silent Planet*.

8. Explain line 154.

9. Point out the passages that show Pope's rationalistic concept of Eden. What is his equivalent of the fall of man? To what does he attribute this fall? What does he count upon to bring the harmful element of man's nature under control? Do you think that history since the eighteenth century has shown Pope to have been too optimistic? Support your opinion with reasons and examples.

Argument of Epistle IV

OF THE NATURE AND STATE OF MAN
WITH RESPECT TO HAPPINESS

I. False Notions of Happiness, Philosophical and Popular, answered. II. It is the End of all Men, and attainable by all. God intends Happiness to be equal; and to be so, it must be social, since all particular happiness depends on general, and since he governs by general, not particular Laws. As it is necessary for Order, and the peace and welfare of Society, that external goods should be unequal, Happiness is not made to consist in these. But, notwithstanding that inequality, the balance of Happiness among Mankind is kept even by Providence, by the two Passions of Hope and Fear. III. What the Happiness of Individuals is, as far as is consistent with the constitution of this world; and that the good Man has here the advantage. The error of imputing to Virtue what are only the calamities of Nature, or of Fortune. IV. The folly of expecting that God should alter his general Laws in favour of particulars. V. That we are not judges who are good; but that, who-

ever they are, they must be happiest. vi. That external goods are
not the proper rewards, but often inconsistent with, or destructive
of Virtue. That even these can make no Man happy without Virtue: Instanced in Riches; Honours; Nobility; Greatness; Fame;
Superior Talents. With pictures of human Infelicity in Men
possessed of them all. vii. That Virtue only constitutes a Happiness, whose object is universal, and whose prospect eternal. That
the perfection of Virtue and Happiness consists in a conformity
to the ORDER OF PROVIDENCE here, and a Resignation to it here
and hereafter.

Epistle IV

Oh Happiness! our being's end and aim!
Good, Pleasure, Ease, Content! whate'er thy name:
That something still which prompts th' eternal sign,
For which we bear to live, or dare to die,
Which still so near us, yet beyond us lies,   5
O'er-look'd, seen double, by the fool, and wise.
Plant of celestial seed! if dropt below,
Say, in what mortal soil thou deign'st to grow?
Fair op'ning to some Court's propitious shine,
Or deep with di'monds in the flaming mine?   10
Twin'd with the wreaths Parnassian laurels ° yield,
Or reap'd in iron harvests of the field?
Where grows? — where grows it not? If vain our toil,
We ought to blame the culture, not the soil:
Fix'd to no spot in Happiness sincere,°   15
'Tis nowhere to be found, or ev'rywhere;
'Tis never to be bought, but always free,
And fled from monarchs, ST. JOHN! dwells with thee.
    I. Ask of the Learn'd the way? The Learn'd are blind;
This bids to serve, and that to shun mankind;   20
Some place the bliss in action, some in ease,
Those call it Pleasure, and Contentment these;
Some sunk to Beasts, find pleasure end in pain;
Some swell'd to Gods, confess ev'n Virtue vain;

---

11. **Parnassian laurels**: Sacred to Apollo and the Muses, Mount Parnassus, in
Greece, was considered the poets' mountain. The ancient Greeks and Romans
crowned victors with wreaths of laurel. **15. sincere**: pure.

Or indolent, to each extreme they fall,   25
To trust in ev'ry thing, or doubt of all.
  Who thus define it, say they more or less
Than this, that Happiness is Happiness?
  II. Take Nature's path, and mad Opinion's leave;
All states can reach it, and all heads conceive;   30
Obvious her goods, in no extreme they dwell;
There needs but thinking right, and meaning well;
And mourn our various portions as we please,
Equal is Common Sense, and Common Ease.
  Remember, Man, "the Universal Cause   35
Acts not by partial, but by gen'ral laws";
And makes what Happiness we justly call
Subsist not in the good of one, but all.
There's not a blessing Individuals find,
But some way leans and hearkens to the kind: 40
No Bandit fierce, no Tyrant mad with pride,
No cavern'd Hermit, rests self-satisfy'd:
Who most to shun or hate Mankind pretend,
Seek an admirer, or would fix a friend:
Abstract what others feel, what others think,   45
All pleasures sicken, and all glories sink:
Each has his share; and who would more obtain,
Shall find, the pleasure pays not half the pain.
  ORDER is Heav'n's first law; and this confest,
Some are, and must be, greater than the rest,   50
More rich, more wise; but who infers from hence
That such are happier, shocks all common sense.
Heav'n to Mankind impartial we confess,
If all are equal in their Happiness:
But mutual wants this Happiness increase;   55
All Nature's diff'rence keeps all Nature's peace.
Condition, circumstance is not the thing;
Bliss is the same in subject or in king,
In who obtain defence, or who defend,
In him who is, or him who finds a friend: 60
Heav'n breathes thro' ev'ry member of the whole
One common blessing, as one common soul.
But Fortune's gifts if each alike possest,
And each were equal, must not all contest?
If then to all Men Happiness was meant,   65
God in Externals could not place Content.

Fortune her gifts may variously dispose,
And these be happy call'd, unhappy those;
But Heav'n's just balance equal will appear,
While those are plac'd in Hope, and these in Fear: 70
Nor present good or ill, the joy or curse,
But future views of better, or of worse.
    Oh sons of earth! attempt ye still to rise,
By mountains pil'd on mountains, to the skies?
Heav'n still with laughter the vain toil surveys,   75
And buries madmen in the heaps they raise.
    III. Know, all the good that individuals find,
Or God and Nature meant to mere Mankind,
Reason's whole pleasure, all the joys of Sense,
Lie in three words, Health, Peace, and Competence.°   80
But Health consists with Temperance alone;
And Peace, oh Virtue! Peace is all thy own.
The good or bad the gifts of Fortune gain;
But these less taste them, as they worse obtain.
Say, in pursuit of profit or delight,   85
Who risk the most, that take wrong means, or right?
Of Vice or Virtue, whether blest or curst,
Which meets contempt, or which compassion first?
Count all th' advantage prosp'rous Vice attains,
'Tis but what Virtue flies from and disdains: 90
And grant the bad what happiness they would,
One they must want, which is, to pass for good.
    Oh blind to Truth, and God's whole scheme below,
Who fancy Bliss to Vice, to Virtue Woe! °
Who sees and follows that great scheme the best,   95
Best knows the blessing, and will most be blest.
But fools the Good alone unhappy call,
For ills or accidents that chance to all.
See FALKLAND ° dies, the virtuous and the just!
See god-like TURENNE ° prostrate on the dust!   100
See SIDNEY ° bleeds amid the martial strife!
Was this their Virtue, or Contempt of Life?
Say, was it Virtue, more tho' Heav'n ne'er gave,

---

80. Competence: sufficient means. **94. Bliss . . . Woe:** that bliss goes with
vice, and woe with virtue. **99. Falkland:** English nobleman killed in battle (1643).
100. Turenne: French marshal killed in battle (1675). **101. Sidney:** Sir Philip Sidney, English soldier, statesman, and author, famed as a model of chivalry, killed in
battle (1586).

Lamented Digby!° sunk thee to the grave?
Tell me, if Virtue made the Son expire,   105
Why, full of days and honour, lives the Sire?°
Why drew Marseille's good bishop° purer breath,
When Nature sicken'd, and each gale was death?
Or why so long (in life if long can be)
Lent Heav'n a parent to the poor and me?°   110
    What makes all physical or moral ill?
There deviates Nature, and here wanders Will.
God sends not ill; if rightly understood,
Or partial Ill is universal Good,
Or Change admits, or Nature lets it fall;   115
Short, and but rare, till Man improv'd it all.
We just as wisely might of Heav'n complain
That righteous Abel was destroy'd by Cain,
As that the virtuous son is ill at ease
When his lewd father gave the dire disease.   120
Think we, like some weak Prince, th' Eternal Cause
Prone for his fav'rites to reverse his laws?
    IV. Shall burning Ætna,° if a sage requires,
Forget to thunder, and recall her fires?
On air or sea new motions be imprest,   125
Oh blameless Bethel! to relieve thy breast?°
When the loose mountain trembles from on high,
Shall gravitation cease, if you go by?
Or some old temple, nodding to its fall,
For Chartres' head° reserve the hanging wall?   130
    V. But still this world (so fitted for the knave)
Contents us not. A better shall we have?
A kingdom of the Just then let it be:
But first consider how those Just agree.
The good must merit God's peculiar care;   135
But who, but God, can tell us who they are?
One thinks on Calvin° Heav'n's own spirit fell;

Another deems him instrument of hell;
If Calvin feel Heav'n's blessing, or its rod,
This cries there is, and that, there is no God.   140
What shocks one part will edify the rest,
Nor with one system can they all be blest.
The very best will variously incline,
And what rewards your Virtue, punish mine.
WHATEVER IS, IS RIGHT. — This world, 'tis true,   145
Was made for Cæsar — but for Titus° too:
And which more blest? who chain'd his country, say,
Or he whose Virtue sigh'd to lose a day?
    "But sometimes Virtue starves, while Vice is fed."
What then? Is the reward of Virtue bread?   150
That, Vice may merit, 'tis the price of toil;
The knave deserves it, when he tills the soil,
The knave deserves it, when he tempts the main,
Where Folly fights for kings, or dives for gain.
The good man may be weak, be indolent;   155
Nor is his claim to plenty, but content.
But grant him Riches, your demand is o'er?
"No — shall the good want Health, the good want Pow'r?"
Add Health, and Pow'r, and ev'ry earthly thing,
"Why bounded Pow'r? why private? why no king?"   160
Nay, why external for internal giv'n?
Why is not Man a God, and Earth a Heav'n?
Who ask and reason thus, will scarce conceive
God gives enough, while he has more to give:
Immense the pow'r, immense were the demand;   165
Say, at what part of nature will they stand?
    VI.   What nothing earthly gives, or can destroy,
The soul's calm sunshine, and the heart-felt joy,
Is Virtue's prize: A better would you fix?
Then give humility a coach and six,   170
Justice a Conq'ror's sword, or Truth a gown,
Or Public Spirit its great cure, a Crown.
Weak, foolish man! will Heav'n reward us there
With the same trash mad mortals wish for here?
The Boy and Man an individual makes,   175
Yet sigh'st thou now for apples and for cakes?
Go, like the Indian,° in another life

146. **Titus:** See Epistle II, line 198, fn. (page 213). 177. **like the Indian:** See
Epistle I, lines 99–112 (page 201).

Expect thy dog, thy bottle, and thy wife:
As well as dream such trifles are assign'd,
As toys and empires, for a god-like mind.   180
Rewards, that either would to Virtue bring
No joy, or be destructive of the thing:
How oft by these at sixty are undone
The Virtues of a saint at twenty-one!
To whom can Riches give Repute, or Trust,   185
Content, or Pleasure, but the Good and Just?
Judges and Senates have been bought for gold,
Esteem and Love were never to be sold.
Oh fool! to think God hates the worthy mind,
The lover and the love of human-kind,   190
Whose life is healthful, and whose conscience clear,
Because he wants a thousand pounds a year.
    Honour and shame from no Condition° rise;
Act well your part, there all the honour lies.
Fortune in Men has some small diff'rence made,   195
One flaunts in rags, one flutters in brocade;
The cobbler apron'd, and the parson gown'd,
The friar hooded, and the monarch crown'd.
"What differ more (you cry) than crown and cowl?"
I'll tell you, friend! a wise man and a Fool.   200
You'll find, if once the monarch acts the monk,
Or, cobbler-like, the parson will be drunk,
Worth makes the man, and want of it, the fellow;
The rest is all but leather or prunella.°
    Stuck o'er with titles and hung round with strings,   205
That thou may'st be by kings, or whores of kings.
Boast the pure blood of an illustrious race,
In quiet flow from Lucrece° to Lucrece:
But by your fathers' worth if yours you rate,
Count me those only who were good and great.   210
Go! if your ancient, but ignoble blood
Has crept thro' scoundrels ever since the flood,
Go! and pretend your family is young;
Nor own, your fathers have been fools so long.
What can ennoble sots, or slaves, or cowards?   215

193. **Condition:** rank. 204. **leather or prunella:** materials, one being used for such things as cobblers' aprons. Leather was prunella, for such things as clergymen's gowns. 208. **Lucrece:** Lucretia, a lady of ancient Rome who was renowned for virtue.

Alas! not all the blood of all the HOWARDS.°

Look next on Greatness; say where Greatness lies?
"Where, but among the Heroes and the wise?"
Heroes are much the same, the point's agreed,
From Macedonia's madman to the Swede;°   220
The whole strange purpose of their lives, to find
Or make, an enemy of all mankind!
Not one looks backward, onward still he goes,
Yet ne'er looks forward farther than his nose.
No less alike the Politic and Wise;   225
All sly slow things, with circumspective° eyes:
Men in their loose unguarded hours they take,
Not that themselves are wise, but others weak.
But grant that those can conquer, these can cheat;
'Tis phrase absurd to call a Villain Great: 230
Who wickedly is wise, or madly brave,
Is but the more a fool, the more a knave.
Who noble ends by noble means obtains,
Or failing, smiles in exile or in chains,
Like good Aurelius° let him reign, or bleed   235
Like Socrates,° that Man is great indeed.

What's Fame? a fancy'd life in others' breath,
A thing beyond us, ev'n before our death.
Just what you hear, you have, and what's unknown
The same (my Lord) if Tully's,° or your own.   240
All that we feel of it begins and ends
In the small circle of our foes or friends;
To all beside as much an empty shade
An Eugene° living, as a Cæsar dead;
Alike or when, or where, they shone, or shine,   245
Or on the Rubicon, or on the Rhine.
A Wit's a feather, and a Chief a rod;
An honest Man's the noblest work of God.
Fame but from death a villain's name can save,

216. Howards: one of the proudest of the English noble families. 220. From
. . . Swede: from Alexander the Great (356–23 B.C.) to Charles XII of Sweden
(1682–1718), whose military exploits amazed Europe. 226. circumspective: circumspect, cautious. 235. Aurelius: Marcus Aurelius (121–180), Roman emperor and
philosopher, author of a famous little book called *Meditations*. 236. Socrates: Greek
philosopher (469–399 B.C.), put to death by the government of Athens.
240. Tully: Marcus Tullius Cicero (106–43 B.C.), greatest Roman orator, also politician and philosopher. 244. Eugene: Prince Eugene of Savoy (1663–1736), a
noted general, alive when Pope wrote this line.

As Justice tears his body from the grave;   250
When what t' oblivion better were resign'd,
Is hung on high, to poison half mankind.
All fame is foreign, but of true desert;
Plays round the head, but comes not to the heart:
One self-approving hour whole years out-weighs   255
Of stupid starers, and of loud huzzas;
And more true joy Marcellus exil'd feels,
Than Cæsar with a senate at his heels.°
    In Parts superior what advantage lies?
Tell (for You° can) what is it to be wise?   260
'Tis but to know how little can be known;
To see all others' faults, and feel our own:
Condemn'd in bus'ness or in arts to drudge,
Without a second, or without a judge:
Truths would you teach, or save a sinking land   265
All fear, none aid you, and few understand.
Painful pre-eminence! yourself to view
Above life's weakness, and its comforts too.
    Bring then these blessings to a strict account;
Make fair deductions; see to what they mount: 270
How much of other each is sure to cost;
How each for other oft is wholly lost;
How inconsistent greater goods with these;
How sometimes life is risk'd, and always ease:
Think, and if still the things thy envy call,°   275
Say, would'st thou be the Man to whom they fall?
To sigh for ribbands if thou art so silly,
Mark how they grace Lord Umbra,° or Sir Billy:°
Is yellow dirt the passion of thy life?
Look but on Gripus° or on Gripus' wife: 280
If Parts allure thee, think how Bacon° shin'd,
The wisest, brightest, meanest° of mankind:
Or ravish'd with the whistling of a Name,

257–58. Marcus Claudius Marcellus was a Roman consul who died in 46 B.C.
An inveterate opponent of Cæsar, he was for a time in exile from Rome. 260. You:
Bolingbroke, to whom Pope addressed this poem. 275. call: demand. 278. Lord
Umbra: "Lord Hollow" (from *umbra*, Latin for "shadow"); Sir Billy: any silly
gentleman of minor rank. 280. Gripus: a name suitable for a miser. 281. Bacon:
Francis Bacon (1561–1626), English statesman, philosopher, and essayist.
282. meanest: Bacon showed a failure of character in striking contrast with the
majesty of his intellect. While Lord Chancellor, he was convicted of corrupt dealings and the taking of bribes and was removed from office.

See Cromwell, damn'd to everlasting fame!° 285
If all, united, thy ambition call,
From ancient story learn to scorn them all.
There, in the rich, the honour'd, fam'd, and great,
See the false scale of Happiness complete!
In hearts of Kings, or arms of Queens who lay,
How happy! those to ruin, these betray.° 290
Mark by what wretched steps their glory grows,
From dirt and sea-weed as proud Venice rose;
In each how guilt and greatness equal ran,
And all that rais'd the Hero, sunk the Man:
Now Europe's laurels on their brows behold, 295
But stain'd with blood, or ill exchang'd for gold:
Then see them broke with toils, or sunk in ease,
Or infamous for plunder'd provinces.
Oh wealth ill-fated! which no act of fame
E'er taught to shine, or sanctify'd from shame! 300
What greater bliss attends their close of life?
Some greedy minion, or imperious wife.
The trophy'd arches, story'd halls invade
And haunt their slumbers in the pompous shade.
Alas! not dazzled with their noon-tide ray, 305
Compute the morn and ev'ning to the day;
The whole amount of that enormous fame,
A Tale, that blends their glory with their shame!
    VII.   Know then this truth (enough for Man to know)
"Virtue alone is Happiness below." 310
The only point where human bliss stands still,
And tastes the good without the fall to ill;°
Where only Merit constant pay receives,
Is blest in what it takes, and what it gives;
The joy unequall'd, if its end it gain, 315
And if it lose, attended with no pain:
Without satiety, tho' e'er so bless'd,
And but more relish'd as the more distress'd:
The broadest mirth unfeeling Folly wears,
Less pleasing far than Virtue's very tears: 320
Good, from each object, from each place acquir'd,

284. See . . . fame: Oliver Cromwell (1599–1658), Puritan general who became Lord Protector of the Commonwealth. Pope calls him "damn'd" because of his part in Charles I's execution. 290. those . . . betray: those to ruin the kings, these to betray the queens. 312. without . . . ill: without tending toward ill.

For ever exercis'd, yet never tir'd;
Never elated, while one man's oppress'd;
Never dejected, while another's bless'd;
And where no wants, no wishes can remain,   325
Since but to wish more Virtue, is to gain.
   See the sole bliss Heav'n could on all bestow!
Which who but feels can taste, but thinks can know:
Yet poor with fortune, and with learning blind,
The bad must miss; the good, untaught, will find;   330
Slave to no sect, who takes no private road,
But looks thro' Nature up to Nature's God;
Pursues that Chain which links th' immense design,
Joins heav'n and earth, and mortal and divine;
Sees, that no Being any bliss can know,   335
But touches some above, and some below;
Learns, from this union of the rising Whole,
The first, last purpose of the human soul;
And knows, where Faith, Law, Morals, all began,
All end, in LOVE OF GOD, and LOVE OF MAN.   340
   For him alone, Hope leads from goal to goal,
And opens still, and opens on his soul;
'Till lengthen'd on to Faith, and unconfin'd,
It pours the bliss that fills up all the mind.
He sees, why Nature plants in Man alone   345
Hope of known bliss, and Faith in bliss unknown:
(Nature, whose dictates to no other kind
Are giv'n in vain, but what they seek they find)
Wise in her present; she connects in this
His greatest Virtue with his greatest Bliss;   350
At once his own bright prospect to be blest,
And strongest motive to assist the rest.
   Self-love thus push'd to social, to divine,
Gives thee to make thy neighbour's blessing thine.
Is this too little for the boundless heart?   355
Extend it, let thy enemies have part:
Grasp the whole worlds of Reason, Life, and Sense,
In one close system of Benevolence:
Happier as kinder, in whate'er degree,
And height of Bliss but height of Charity.   360
   God loves from Whole to Parts: but human soul
Must rise from Individual to the Whole.
Self-love but serves the virtuous mind to wake,

As the small pebble stirs the peaceful lake;
The centre mov'd, a circle straight succeeds,   365
Another still, and still another spreads;
Friend, parent, neighbour, first it will embrace;
His country next; and next all human race;
Wide and more wide, th' o'erflowings of the mind
Take ev'ry creature in, of ev'ry kind;   370
Earth smiles around, with boundless bounty blest,
And Heav'n beholds its image in his breast.
    Come then, my Friend! my Genius!° come along;
Oh master of the poet, and the song!
And while the Muse now stoops, or now ascends,   375
To Man's low passions, or their glorious ends,
Teach me, like thee, in various nature wise,
To fall with dignity, with temper rise;
Form'd by thy converse, happily to steer
From grave to gay, from lively to severe;   380
Correct with spirit, eloquent with ease,
Intent to reason, or polite to please.
Oh! while along the stream of Time thy name
Expanded flies, and gathers all its fame,
Say, shall my little bark attendant sail,   385
Pursue the triumph, and partake the gale?
When statesmen, heroes, kings, in dust repose,
Whose sons shall blush their fathers were thy foes,
Shall then this verse to future age pretend°
Thou wert my guide, philosopher, and friend?   390
That urg'd by thee, I turn'd the tuneful art
From sounds to things, from fancy to the heart;
For Wit's false mirror held up Nature's light;
Shew'd erring Pride, WHATEVER IS, IS RIGHT;
That REASON, PASSION, answer one great aim;   395
That true SELF-LOVE and SOCIAL are the same;
That VIRTUE only makes our Bliss below;
And all our Knowledge is, OURSELVES TO KNOW.

373. Genius: guardian spirit (Bolingbroke). 389. pretend: assert.

For Study and Writing

1. Some thirty-odd years after Pope's death, the American Declaration of Independence asserted "the pursuit of happiness" to be among the unalienable rights of man. Discuss Pope's views on happiness, citing passages. What is the poet's opinion about the relationship between man's happi-

ness and his virtues and vices? What role in man's happiness does he give to Fortune?

2. Relate lines 49–50 to Pope's concern over "just gradation" in Epistle I.

3. What does he say about simple concepts of rewards in a future life?

4. Explain line 203, after checking a good dictionary to establish the appropriate meaning of *fellow* in this context.

5. Discuss line 230 and relate it to specific cases, ancient and modern (such as that of Hitler). According to Pope, what is a great man?

6. Explain lines 361–62.

7. Often in our time the phrase "enlightened self-interest" is used. In the closing lines of the *Essay,* what parallel term is used? Discuss the concept. Do you think it valid? Do you see possible perils in it?

For Writing

1. Write a paper comparing and contrasting Pope's views of man with those of C. S. Lewis and John Milton. Be concrete: cite evidence and use quotations freely.

2. With special but not exclusive reference to Epistle I, write a paper about Pope's attitude toward a man-centered view of the universe.

AFTERWORD

Out of the Silent Planet is part of a twentieth-century variation on the theme of *Paradise Lost:* the myth of the fall of man. Calling it a myth is not to be taken as an implication that it does not contain truth. It states its truths in a symbolic story, which in this case is the most satisfactory way to express them. Both Milton and Lewis dramatize, and thereby clarify for us, the Judeo-Christian tradition about man's peculiar status in the order of creation. Man is shown as being other than he was intended to be. The deep springs of his will have been tainted so that he cannot consistently do the good that he would like to do but sometimes does instead the evil that he would prefer not to do.

An important clue to the meaning of *Out of the Silent Planet* is these words that come to Ransom's mind as he ponders the characteristics of the *hross* (page 51): ". . . as though Paradise had never been lost. . . ." Malacandra is an "unfallen" world. As such, it illuminates by contrast the conditions in our world. Malacandra's three species of *hnau* (intelligent creatures with souls) live in harmony, whereas Earth's one kind of *hnau* is involved in constant hostility and warfare.

In Lewis's scheme, our planet ("Thulcandra" in the Malacandrian language) figures uniquely as enemy-occupied territory, cut off as by an iron curtain from the rest of the harmonious creation. An archangel (Oyarsa) is in charge of each of the planets. As in Milton's account, the Oyarsa of Earth (Satan), with a host of followers, has alienated himself from God by the sin of pride, having sought to overthrow God and seize the powers of Heaven. He and his rebel band are exiled from deep Heaven. He who was to have been shepherd of the planet has seduced his charges into rebellion and evil. His influence has "bent" them, leading to their fall.

In Lewis's version, the Incarnation (the promise of which is the sole comfort for Milton's exiled Adam and Eve) is a beachhead for the reconquest of the planet and the redemption of man. The Oyarsa of Malacandra refers to the Incarnation when he says of Maleldil (God) in Chapter 18: ". . . there are stories among us that he has taken strange counsel and dared terrible things, wrestling with the Bent One in Thulcandra." He refers to it again when, after Ransom has told him details, he says, in Chapter 21: "You have shown me more wonders than are known in the whole of heaven." [1]

Among the wonders of Milton's treatment of the story in *Paradise Lost,* along with the superb, rolling energy of his blank verse, are his abundant, memorable images, wherein the sound of words joins with the conjured visions to evoke vivid scenes: Satan crying to his prostrate band,

Awake, arise, or be for ever fallen!

Their swirling flight and descent, like those of planes directed to their landing on an aircraft carrier,

---

[1] If you enjoyed *Out of the Silent Planet,* you may wish to read the other two volumes in the trilogy of which it is the beginning: *Perelandra* and *That Hideous Strength. Perelandra* is of particular interest, for in it we see a new temptation in a new Garden of Eden, on the planet we call Venus. Lewis's account of another Eve gives us an even deeper understanding of the temptation so skillfully elaborated by Milton from the Biblical version. There is a fascinating difference: on Perelandra there are two voices from Earth, which has already experienced the tragedy of "man's first disobedience." These are the voices of the tempter, who occupies the body of our old acquaintance Weston (as he had occupied that of the serpent), and of Ransom, who must attempt to counteract the Bent One's influence upon Perelandra's first woman. Intellectually, *Perelandra* is more demanding than *Out of the Silent Planet.* Imaginatively and descriptively, it is an even more soaring flight. It is the apex of the trilogy.

Another splendid telling of the Eden story is in the short novel *Adam,* by David Bolt.

> 'Twixt upper, nether, and surrounding fires;
> Till, at a signal given, the uplifted spear
> Of their great Sultan waving to direct
> Their course, in even balance down they light
> On the firm brimstone and fill all the plain. . . .

Their blazing response to his exhortations in a fearsome moment of defiance when,

> . . . to confirm his words, out flew
> Millions of flaming swords, drawn from the thighs
> Of mighty Cherubim; the sudden blaze
> Far round illumined Hell. Highly they raged
> Against the Highest, and fierce with graspèd arms
> Clashed on their sounding shields the din of war,
> Hurling defiance toward the vault of Heaven.

Perhaps most memorable of all, inescapably moving, Adam and Eve when, no longer of lordly estate and dignity, after their expulsion from Paradise,

> They, hand in hand, with wandering steps and slow,
> Through Eden took their solitary way.

They were going forth to begin the existence that we recognize as ours.

It is often remarked that the poem is overshadowed by the figure of Satan, who is its villain, not its hero. The great "Archangel ruined," his splendor still visible though marred and warped, dominates the first two books and gains a dramatic ascendancy over our imaginations that he never quite loses, even when he slinks guiltily, almost unnoticed, from the Garden, his evil goal achieved. It is no doubt an inclination toward defiance of authority (an inclination present to some extent in all of us — C. S. Lewis would say it was "bentness") that makes us feel vibrations of sympathy for the embattled Prince of Hell as he cries "All is not lost" and in obstinate ambition insists "Better to reign in Hell than serve in Heaven." Evil is easier to dramatize than good, just as hate is easier to rouse than love.

There is a romantic tendency in human nature to idealize the rebel and the fighter against hopeless odds. To keep Satan in perspective, we must remember how wanton was his rebellion and against whom, and also that a base and vengeful vandalism is the sole aim and fruit of this demonic struggle against impossible odds. Much of his loftiest, most beguiling rhetoric turns out, when scrutinized, to be boasts and lies. A contemporary English critic, David Daiches, praises Milton for "exposing and castigating all those false romantic notions . . . of heroism as egotistical magnificence . . . the idea that heroic energy in a bad cause is admirable, the dressing up of spite and vanity in grandiose language."

The sin of Satan is the primary sin of pride: an arrogance of spirit that, in its extreme form, acknowledges no superiors and accepts no curb on the will. The *sorn* Augray remarks of men, ". . . every one of them wants to be a little Oyarsa himself." The pagan Greeks considered this arrogance to be the greatest sin against their gods. They called it *hubris,* and in their tragedies it is the cause of most of the disastrous falls from high place.

Satan wishes to overthrow God and usurp His place. Significantly, the temptation by which he corrupts man is of the same kind as that to which he himself has succumbed. His first persuasions of Eve are crude flatterings of vanity, which is less than pride. But he leads her on from vanity to pride, calling her a "Goddess" and assuring her that "ye shall be as Gods." And when Eve at last eats, we are told, ". . . nor was Godhead from her thought." To Adam she speaks of

> . . . growing up to Godhead; which for thee
> Chiefly I sought . . .

All the great religions agree that pride is the fountainhead of sin. With it begins the corruption of will and intention which is the true nature of sin. The wrong occurs in will and intention; an evil act is the consequence of sin, not its beginning.

Milton emphasizes this truth about pride. So, too, does Lewis, through Oyarsa, who underlines Weston's pride by asking: "Does he think he could go to the great worlds? Does he think Maleldil wants a race to live forever?" Weston, for the sake of his vision of man's seed colonizing countless planets, would commit any crime and call it good. His "bent-ness" can be summed up as the desire to affirm man as God or as godlike: the ambition for man to dominate the universe, to supersede other species, and to live forever.

The word *bent,* used by Malacandrians as their nearest approximation for *sinful* or *evil,* was ingeniously chosen by Lewis. *Bent* is never used to describe anything in its original state; hence the word tells us there was a previous condition. It suggests the possibility (but not the certainty) of future developments: the bent thing may be restored to its original state, or it may be bent further, to the point of breaking. When an object is bent, it is misshapen; it malfunctions, or fails to function at all. A bent arrow will veer in its course. By analogy, all these things are true of bent man — man guilty of sin. Judeo-Christian tradition regards evil not as man's original state but as the corruption of something good, which remains susceptible of redemption.

Although Alexander Pope lived in an age of skepticism and questioning — for which it is perhaps too flatteringly called "The Age of Reason" — he nevertheless agrees to a considerable extent with the visions of Milton before him and of Lewis long after him. His *Essay* rounds out this book's first part, of which the chief purpose has been to examine various explanations of man and his complex, paradoxical nature.

His nature is paradoxical in that it contains elements that seem mutually exclusive. Can he be as wicked as he has often shown himself to be and still be any good at all? As noble as he often is and yet contemptible? As foolish as we commonly see him and yet wise?

> Virtuous and vicious ev'ry Man must be,
> Few in th' extreme, but all in the degree. . . .

The *Essay* asserts that we must reason about both God and man from what we can observe of them. Obviously, we can grasp much more about man than about God by such means; hence, says Pope,

> Know then thyself, presume not God to scan;
> The proper study of Mankind is Man.

Both Milton and Lewis would have agreed with Pope that man can find out little about God by his own efforts. The premise of the traditional Judeo-Christian view is that God came in search of man and that we know of Him only what He chooses to reveal to us. In that "proper study of Mankind," which Milton and Lewis pursue as diligently as Pope, they consider the relationship between God and man to be the major clue to understanding man's nature.

In view of the different premises of these three writers, it is remarkable how much their ideas about man agree. With variations, including the pagan Greek views, these are man's concepts of himself that have shaped the Western civilization in which we live. Unless you understand them, you cannot understand our civilization's history and its great works of literature and art, nor can you understand and evaluate the challenges hurled against these concepts today perhaps more massively than ever in the past.

Milton's, Pope's, and Lewis's ideas on man should help to make us aware of the sweeping range of our natures, from bestiality to saintliness. We know that we share some attributes with the animals but differ from them in intellectual capacity. How can we explain the fact that, despite our knowledge of good and evil, we sometimes do horrible things no animal would do?

From his earliest consciousness of himself, man has realized that something is wrong with him and has sought to understand what it is and to ascertain what can be done about it. Seldom has the claim been made that everything is fine with him, and never has such a claim lasted long. In our own time, many writers go to the opposite extreme and express despair of man, regarding him as a hopeless mess.

A huge volume could be compiled of statements defining or appraising man. The Psalmist of the Bible says of him (Psalms 8:5):

> . . . Thou hast made him a little lower than the angels. . . .

Milton and Lewis reflect this view. Protagoras, a Greek philosopher of the fifth century B.C., said:

> Man is the measure of all things.

Shakespeare presents contrasting views. In *Hamlet* occur these lines:

> What a piece of work is a man! How noble in reason! How infinite in faculty! In form and moving how express and admirable! In action how like an angel! In apprehension how like a god! The beauty of the world! The paragon of animals!

In *Measure for Measure* it is said:

> . . . but man, proud man,
> Dress'd in a little brief authority,
> Most ignorant of what he's most assur'd —
> His glassy essence — like an angry ape,
> Plays such fantastic tricks before high heaven
> As make the angels weep. . . .

Pope's opening lines of Epistle II of his *Essay* are among the finest summations of man's paradoxical nature:

> Plac'd on this isthmus of a middle state,
> A Being darkly wise, and rudely great:
> With too much knowledge for the Sceptic side,
> With too much weakness for the Stoic's pride,
> He hangs between; in doubt to act, or rest;
> In doubt to deem himself a God, or Beast;

In doubt his Mind or Body to prefer;
Born but to die, and reas'ning but to err;
Alike in ignorance, his reason such,
Whether he thinks too little, or too much:
Chaos of Thought and Passion, all confus'd;
Still by himself abus'd, or disabus'd;
Created half to rise, and half to fall;
Great lord of all things, yet a prey to all;
Sole judge of Truth, in endless Error hurl'd:
The glory, jest, and riddle of the world!

Socrates, another Greek philosopher of the fifth century B.C., felt that man's chief problem was to know what was good and that if he knew the good he would do it. An early Christian, St. Paul, more realistically lamented something that each of us experiences (Romans 7:19):

For the good that I would I do not; but the evil
which I would not, that I do.

Herman Melville, in *Moby Dick,* writes with caustic irony of man, his state and institutions, but still he says: "Men may seem detestable as joint stock-companies and nations; knaves, fools, and murderers there may be; men may have mean and meager faces; but man, in the ideal, is so noble and so sparkling, such a grand and glowing creature, that over any ignominious blemish in him all his fellows should run to throw their costliest robes." In contrast to this thought, the vogue in much literature of our time is to strip man down to the bone, expose every blemish, but ignore, deny, or conceal whatever is noble and sparkling.

Milton and Lewis offer us, from a common conviction, a concept of man big enough to contain everything that we know of him. Pope's concept, less orthodox (though, ironically, he was a Roman Catholic in predominantly Protestant England), nevertheless agrees largely with theirs. Milton's and Lewis's man is both debased and exalted: debased by his self-wrought evil; exalted through having been created by God in His own image and through God's having become man for his salvation. Pope's man is dignified by being specifically set apart by God from the animal creation to understand, through reason, himself and his relation to his Maker.

The concept that man was created in God's image is not to be taken as meaning that man is a bodily image of God. It means that man resembles God in his possession of free will. According to this view, man was not created helpless to deviate from an imposed pattern but was created free to make choices and, having made a fatal choice, was compelled to accept its consequences, though not abandoned by God without aid or help. We can say this much, at least, for this concept: it gives man an inherent dignity of the highest order, and it makes understandable all his behavior, however noble or base. If we accept this view, we should not be surprised at anything man may do, whether good or evil. It sets limits to man's capacities and expectations, yet it gives meaning and direction to all he does.

Of the countless ideas by which man has struggled forward in the long evolutionary process of awakening and awareness — a process that has come far but is not yet ended — the most important has been this concept of himself as a free, self-conscious, responsible being. We will take this concept as a working hypothesis and see how far it can encompass and illuminate the creature in action that the rest of the literature in this book presents to us.

A PRACTICE TEST

I. Read the following poem carefully before taking up the questions:

Pied Beauty

by Gerard Manley Hopkins
(1844–1889)

Glory be to God for dappled things —
    For skies of couple-colour as a brinded cow;
      For rose-moles all in stipple upon trout that swim;
Fresh-firecoal chestnut-falls; finches' wings;
    Landscape plotted and pieced — fold, fallow, and plough;   5
    And áll trádes, their gear and tackle and trim.

All things counter, original, spare, strange;
    Whatever is fickle, freckled (who knows how?)
      With swift, slow; sweet, sour; adazzle, dim;
He fathers-forth whose beauty is past change: 10
        Praise him.

1. This poem is about God, man, and certain aspects of visible creation. What is the poet's point of view toward each of these subjects? How does he relate them to one another?

2. Discuss, giving specific examples, Hopkins's use of alliteration in this poem. What is the main effect of this device here?

3. What do the four adjectives at the end of line 7 mean? Discuss their similarities and differences in meaning.

4. Note that line 1 and lines 10–11 are religious statements. What is the relation of each of these statements to the rest of the poem?

5. What is the effect of the parenthetical question in line 8?

6. Discuss the metrical pattern of this poem. (You will note that the poet sometimes indicates syllables to be accented, as in line 6.)

II. Write a well-planned essay in which you consider works of fantasy you have read (*Out of the Silent Planet* and *Paradise Lost* are recommended possibilities) in the light of this quotation from Edmund Fuller's *Books with Men Behind Them* (Random House, 1962):

. . . across the range of time and type of story, the so-called fantastic has . . . served to illuminate our understanding of the so-called real.

III. The following is from John Milton's *The Tenure of Kings and Magistrates* (1649):

No man, who knows aught, can be so stupid to deny that all men naturally were born free, being the image and resemblance of God himself, and were, by privilege above all the creatures, born to command, and not to obey: and that they lived so, till from the root of Adam's transgression falling among themselves to do wrong and violence, and foreseeing that such courses must needs tend to the destruction of them all, they agreed by common league to bind each other from mutual injury, and jointly to defend themselves against any that gave disturbance or opposition to such agreement. Hence came cities, towns, and commonwealths. And because no faith in all was found sufficiently binding, they saw it needful to ordain some authority that might restrain by force and punishment what was violated against peace and common right.

1. Construct an outline demonstrating how Milton develops his thesis in the passage. Be sure to make clear the relationship between each point or idea and the following one.

2. What devices, other than an orderly, logical arrangement of ideas, does Milton use to make this passage persuasive?

Part **II**

Mirrors
of
Man

The concept of the arts — of literature and the stage in particular — as mirrors of man is much older than what may be its most familiar text, from *Hamlet,* about "the purpose of playing, whose end, both at the first and now, was and is, to hold, as 't were, the mirror up to nature." More than eighteen centuries ago, Plutarch, discussing the value of writing biography, spoke of "the virtues of these great men serving me as a sort of looking glass, in which I may see how to adjust and adorn my own life."

The reflections or — to use a still more useful word — images of man offered us by the arts cover the full range of his nature and behavior. In this part of our course, we are going to concentrate on three types of images, immensely comprehensive and ideally suited for literary study: affirmative, ironic, and tragic images of man.

In Thornton Wilder's novel *The Ides of March* (Harper & Row, 1948), Julius Caesar reflects at the bedside of a dying poet:

> I am no stranger to deathbeds. To those in pain one talks about themselves, to those of clear mind one praises the world that they are quitting. There is no dignity in leaving a despicable world, and the dying are often fearful life was not worth the effort it had cost them. I am never short of subjects to praise.

Affirmative images are reflections of the belief that life has value irrespective of man's good or bad character or of good or bad fortune. Always there have been some men ready to challenge the inherent value of life; today their challenge may be more clamorous than ever before. But most men struggle to hold to the belief that this hard life is worth living. The works by C. S. Lewis, Milton, and Pope that we have read so far are all powerfully affirmative of this belief.

The affirmations in the widely varied works that follow, however, are not always simple or obvious. A few are ringingly clear. In other instances you will find it challenging to determine how a given image of life is to be considered affirmative at all.

The Tall Men

by William Faulkner (1897–1962)

They passed the dark bulk of the cotton gin. Then they saw the lamplit house and the other car, the doctor's coupé, just stopping at the gate, and they could hear the hound baying.

"Here we are," the old deputy marshal said.

"What's that other car?" the younger man said, the stranger, the state draft investigator.

"Doctor Schofield's," the marshal said. "Lee McCallum asked me to send him out when I telephoned we were coming."

"You mean you warned them?" the investigator said. "You telephoned ahead that I was coming out with a warrant for these two evaders? Is this how you carry out the orders of the United States Government?"

The marshal was a lean, clean old man who chewed tobacco, who had been born and lived in the county all his life.

"I understood all you wanted was to arrest these two McCallum boys and bring them back to town," he said.

"It was!" the investigator said. "And now you have warned them, given them a chance to run. Possibly put the Government to the expense of hunting them down with troops. Have you forgotten that you are under a bond yourself?"

"I ain't forgot it," the marshal said. "And ever since we left Jefferson [1] I been trying to tell you something for you not to forget. But I reckon it will take these McCallums to impress that on you. . . . Pull in behind the other car. We'll try to find out first just how sick whoever it is that is sick is."

The investigator drew up behind the other car and switched off and blacked out his lights. "These people," he said. Then he thought, *But this doddering, tobacco-chewing old man is one of them, too, despite the honor and pride of his office, which should have made him different.* So

[1] **Jefferson**: county seat of Yoknapatawpha County, famous as the setting for many of Faulkner's stories. The county is an imaginary one, but Jefferson can be identified with Faulkner's home town, Oxford, Mississippi.

he didn't speak it aloud, removing the keys and getting out of the car, and then locking the car itself, rolling the windows up first, thinking, *These people who lie about and conceal the ownership of land and property in order to hold relief jobs which they have no intention of performing, standing on their constitutional rights against having to work, who jeopardize the very job itself through petty and transparent subterfuge to acquire a free mattress which they intend to attempt to sell; who would relinquish even the job, if by so doing they could receive free food and a place, any rathole, in town to sleep in; who, as farmers, make false statements to get seed loans which they will later misuse, and then react in loud vituperative outrage and astonishment when caught at it. And then, when at long last a suffering and threatened Government asks one thing of them in return, one thing simply, which is to put their names down on a selective-service list, they refuse to do it.*

The old marshal had gone on. The investigator followed, through a stout paintless gate in a picket fence, up a broad brick walk between two rows of old shabby cedars, toward the rambling and likewise paintless sprawl of the two-story house in the open hall of which the soft lamplight glowed and the lower story of which, as the investigator now perceived, was of logs.

He saw a hall full of soft lamplight beyond a stout paintless gallery running across the log front, from beneath which the same dog which they had heard, a big hound, came booming again, to stand foursquare facing them in the walk, bellowing, until a man's voice spoke to it from the house. He followed the marshal up the stairs onto the gallery. Then he saw the man standing in the door, waiting for them to approach — a man of about forty-five, not tall, but blocky, with a brown, still face and horseman's hands, who looked at him once, brief and hard, and then no more, speaking to the marshal, "Howdy, Mr. Gombault. Come in."

"Howdy, Rafe," the marshal said. "Who's sick?"

"Buddy," the other said. "Slipped and caught his leg in the hammer mill this afternoon."

"Is it bad?" the marshal said.

"It looks bad to me," the other said. "That's why we sent for the doctor instead of bringing him in to town. We couldn't get the bleeding stopped."

"I'm sorry to hear that," the marshal said. "This is Mr. Pearson." Once more the investigator found the other looking at him, the brown eyes still, courteous enough in the brown face, the hand he offered hard enough, but the clasp quite limp, quite cold. The marshal was still speaking. "From Jackson. From the draft board." Then he said, and the investigator could discern no change whatever in his tone: "He's got a warrant for the boys."

The investigator could discern no change whatever anywhere. The limp hard hand merely withdrew from his, the still face now looking at the marshal. "You mean we have declared war?"

"No," the marshal said.

"That's not the question, Mr. McCallum," the investigator said. "All required of them was to register. Their numbers might not even be drawn this time; under the law of averages, they probably would not be. But they refused — failed, anyway — to register."

"I see," the other said. He was not looking at the investigator. The investigator couldn't tell certainly if he was even looking at the marshal, although he spoke to him, "You want to see Buddy? The doctor's with him now."

"Wait," the investigator said. "I'm sorry about your brother's accident, but I —— " The marshal glanced back at him for a moment, his shaggy gray brows beetling, with something at once courteous yet a little impatient about the glance, so that during the instant the investigator sensed from the old marshal the same quality which had been in the other's brief look. The investigator was a man of better than average intelligence; he was already becoming aware of something a little different here from what he had expected. But he had been in relief work in the state several years, dealing almost exclusively with country people, so he still believed he knew them. So he looked at the old marshal, thinking, *Yes. The same sort of people, despite the office, the authority and responsibility which should have changed him.* Thinking again, *These people. These people.* "I intend to take the night train back to Jackson," he said. "My reservation is already made. Serve the warrant and we will——"

"Come along," the old marshal said. "We are going to have plenty of time."

So he followed — there was nothing else to do — fuming and seething, attempting in the short length of the hall to regain control of himself in order to control the situation, because he realized now that if the situation were controlled, it would devolve upon him to control it; that if their departure with their prisoners were expedited, it must be himself and not the old marshal who would expedite it. He had been right. The doddering old officer was not only at bottom one of these people, he had apparently been corrupted anew to his old, inherent, shiftless sloth and unreliability merely by entering the house. So he followed in turn, down the hall and into a bedroom; whereupon he looked about him not only with amazement but with something very like terror. The room was a big room, with a bare unpainted floor, and besides the bed, it contained only a chair or two and one other piece of old-fashioned furniture. Yet to the investigator it seemed so filled with tremendous

men cast in the same mold as the man who had met them that the very walls themselves must bulge. Yet they were not big, not tall, and it was not vitality, exuberance, because they made no sound, merely looking quietly at him where he stood in the door, with faces bearing an almost identical stamp of kinship — a thin, almost frail old man of about seventy, slightly taller than the others; a second one, white-haired, too, but otherwise identical with the man who had met them at the door; a third one about the same age as the man who had met them, but with something delicate in his face and something tragic and dark and wild in the same dark eyes; the two absolutely identical blue-eyed youths; and lastly the blue-eyed man on the bed over which the doctor, who might have been any city doctor, in his neat city suit, leaned — all of them turning to look quietly at him and the marshal as they entered. And he saw, past the doctor, the slit trousers of the man on the bed and the exposed, bloody, mangled leg, and he turned sick, stopping just inside the door under that quiet, steady regard while the marshal went up to the man who lay on the bed, smoking a cob pipe, a big, old-fashioned, wicker-covered demijohn, such as the investigator's grandfather had kept his whisky in, on the table beside him.

"Well, Buddy," the marshal said, "this is bad."

"Ah, it was my own damn fault,"

the man on the bed said. "Stuart kept warning me about that frame I was using."

"That's correct," the second old one said.

Still the others said nothing. They just looked steadily and quietly at the investigator until the marshal turned slightly and said, "This is Mr. Pearson. From Jackson. He's got a warrant for the boys."

Then the man on the bed said, "What for?"

"That draft business, Buddy," the marshal said.

"We're not at war now," the man on the bed said.

"No," the marshal said. "It's that new law. They didn't register."

"What are you going to do with them?"

"It's a warrant, Buddy. Swore out."

"That means jail."

"It's a warrant," the old marshal said. Then the investigator saw that the man on the bed was watching him, puffing steadily at the pipe.

"Pour me some whisky, Jackson," he said.

"No," the doctor said. "He's had too much already."

"Pour me some whisky, Jackson," the man on the bed said. He puffed steadily at the pipe, looking at the investigator. "You come from the Government?" he said.

"Yes," the investigator said. "They should have registered. That's all required of them yet. They did not ——" His voice ceased, while the seven pairs of eyes contemplated him, and the man on the bed puffed steadily.

"We would have still been here," the man on the bed said. "We wasn't going to run." He turned his head. The two youths were standing side by side at the foot of the bed. "Anse, Lucius," he said.

To the investigator it sounded as if they answered as one. "Yes, father."

"This gentleman has come all the way from Jackson to say the Government is ready for you. I reckon the quickest place to enlist will be Memphis. Go upstairs and pack."

The investigator started, moved forward. "Wait!" he cried.

But Jackson, the eldest, had forestalled him. He said, "Wait," also, and now they were not looking at the investigator. They were looking at the doctor.

"What about his leg?" Jackson said.

"Look at it," the doctor said. "He almost amputated it himself. It won't wait. And he can't be moved now. I'll need my nurse to help me, and some ether, provided he hasn't had too much whisky to stand the anesthetic too. One of you can drive to town in my car. I'll telephone —— "

"Ether?" the man on the bed said. "What for? You just said yourself it's pretty near off now. I could whet up one of Jackson's butcher knives and finish it myself, with another drink or two. Go on. Finish it."

"You couldn't stand any more

shock," the doctor said. "This is whisky talking now."

"Shucks," the other said. "One day in France we was running through a wheat field and I saw the machine gun, coming across the wheat, and I tried to jump it like you would jump a fence rail somebody was swinging at your middle, only I never made it. And I was on the ground then, and along toward dark that begun to hurt, only about that time something went whang on the back of my helmet, like when you hit a anvil, so I never knowed nothing else until I woke up. There was a heap of us racked up along a bank outside a field dressing station, only it took a long time for the doctor to get around to all of us, and by that time it was hurting bad. This here ain't hurt none to speak of since I got a-holt of this johnny-jug. You go on and finish it. If it's help you need, Stuart and Rafe will help you. . . . Pour me a drink, Jackson."

This time the doctor raised the demijohn and examined the level of the liquor. "There's a good quart gone," he said. "If you've drunk a quart of whisky since four o'clock, I doubt if you could stand the anesthetic. Do you think you could stand it if I finished it now?"

"Yes, finish it. I've ruined it; I want to get shut of it."

The doctor looked about at the others, at the still, identical faces watching him. "If I had him in town, in the hospital, with a nurse to watch him, I'd probably wait un-til he got over his first shock and got the whisky out of his system. But he can't be moved now, and I can't stop the bleeding like this, and even if I had ether or a local anesthetic —— "

"Shucks," the man on the bed said. "God never made no better local nor general comfort or anesthetic neither than what's in this johnny-jug. And this ain't Jackson's leg nor Stuart's nor Rafe's nor Lee's. It's mine. I done started it; I reckon I can finish cutting it off any way I want to."

But the doctor was still looking at Jackson. "Well, Mr. McCallum?" he said. "You're the oldest."

But it was Stuart who answered. "Yes," he said. "Finish it. What do you want? Hot water, I reckon."

"Yes," the doctor said. "Some clean sheets. Have you got a big table you can move in here?"

"The kitchen table," the man who had met them at the door said. "Me and the boys —— "

"Wait," the man on the bed said. "The boys won't have time to help you." He looked at them again. "Anse, Lucius," he said.

Again it seemed to the investigator that they answered as one, "Yes, father."

"This gentleman yonder is beginning to look impatient. You better start. Come to think of it, you won't need to pack. You will have uniforms in a day or two. Take the truck. There won't be nobody to drive you to Memphis and bring the truck back, so you can leave it at the Gayoso Feed Company until we can send for it. I'd like for you to enlist into the old Sixth Infantry, where I used to be. But I reckon that's too much to hope, and you'll just have to chance where they send you. But it likely won't matter, once you are in. The Government done right by me in my day, and it will do right by you. You just enlist wherever they want to send you, need you, and obey your sergeants and officers until you find out how to be soldiers. Obey them, but remember your name and don't take nothing from no man. You can go now."

"Wait!" the investigator cried again; again he started, moved forward into the center of the room. "I protest this! I'm sorry about Mr. McCallum's accident. I'm sorry about the whole business. But it's out of my hands and out of his hands now. This charge, failure to register according to law, has been made and the warrant issued. It cannot be evaded this way. The course of the action must be completed before any other step can be taken. They should have thought of this when these boys failed to register. If Mr. Gombault refuses to serve this warrant, I will serve it myself and take these men back to Jefferson with me to answer this charge as made. And I must warn Mr. Gombault that he will be cited for contempt!"

The old marshal turned, his shaggy eyebrows beetling again, speaking down to the investigator as if he were a child, "Ain't you found out yet that me or you neither ain't going nowhere for a while?"

"What?" the investigator cried. He looked about at the grave faces once more contemplating him with that remote and speculative regard. "Am I being threatened?" he cried.

"Ain't anybody paying any attention to you at all," the marshal said. "Now you just be quiet for a while, and you will be all right, and after a while we can go back to town."

So he stopped again and stood while the grave, contemplative faces freed him once more of that impersonal and unbearable regard, and saw the two youths approach the bed and bend down in turn and kiss their father on the mouth, and then turn as one and leave the room, passing him without even looking at him. And sitting in the lamplit hall beside the old marshal, the bedroom door closed now, he heard the truck start up and back and turn and go down the road, the sound of it dying away, ceasing, leaving the still, hot night — the Mississippi Indian summer, which had already outlasted half of November — filled with the loud last shrilling of the summer's cicadas, as though they, too, were aware of the imminent season of cold weather and of death.

"I remember old Anse," the marshal said pleasantly, chattily, in that tone in which an adult addresses a strange child. "He's been dead fifteen-sixteen years now. He was about sixteen when the old war broke out, and he walked all the way to Virginia to get into it. He could have enlisted and fought right here at home, but his ma was a Carter, so wouldn't nothing do him but to go all the way back to Virginia to do his fighting, even though he hadn't never seen Virginia before himself; walked all the way back to a land he hadn't never even seen before and enlisted in Stonewall Jackson's army and stayed in it all through the Valley, and right up to Chancellorsville, where them Carolina boys shot Jackson by mistake, and right on up to that morning in 'Sixty-five when Sheridan's cavalry blocked the road from Appomattox to the Valley, where they might have got away again. And he walked back to Mississippi with just about what he had carried away with him when he left, and he got married and built the first story of this house — this here log story we're in right now — and started getting them boys — Jackson and Stuart and Raphael and Lee and Buddy.

"Buddy come along late, late enough to be in the other war, in France in it. You heard him in there. He brought back two medals, an American medal and a French one, and no man knows till yet how he got them, just what he done. I don't believe he even told Jackson and Stuart and them. He hadn't hardly got back home, with them numbers on his uniform and the wound stripes and them two med-als, before he had found him a girl, found her right off, and a year later them twin boys was born, the livin', spittin' image of old Anse McCallum. If old Anse had just been above seventy-five years younger, the three of them might have been thriblets. I remember them — two little critters exactly alike, and wild as spikehorn bucks, running around here day and night both with a pack of coon dogs until they got big enough to help Buddy and Stuart and Lee with the farm and the gin, and Rafe with the horses and mules, when he would breed and raise and train them and take them to Memphis to sell, right on up to three, four years back, when they went to the agricultural college for a year to learn more about whiteface cattle.

"That was after Buddy and them had quit raising cotton. I remember that too. It was when the Government first begun to interfere with how a man farmed his own land, raised his cotton. Stabilizing the price, using up the surplus, they called it, giving a man advice and help, whether he wanted it or not. You may have noticed them boys in yonder tonight; curious folks almost, you might call them. That first year, when county agents was trying to explain the new system to farmers, the agent come out here and tried to explain it to Buddy and Lee and Stuart, explaining how they would cut down the crop, but that the Government would pay farmers the difference, and so they would actually be better off than trying to farm by themselves.

"'Why, we're much obliged,' Buddy says. 'But we don't need no help. We'll just make the cotton like we always done; if we can't make a crop of it, that will just be our lookout and our loss, and we'll try again.'

"So they wouldn't sign no papers nor no cards nor nothing. They just went on and made the cotton like old Anse had taught them to; it was like they just couldn't believe that the Government aimed to help a man whether he wanted help or not, aimed to interfere with how much of anything he could make by hard work on his own land, making the crop and ginning it right here in their own gin, like they had always done, and hauling it to town to sell, hauling it all the way into Jefferson before they found out they couldn't sell it because, in the first place, they had made too much of it and, in the second place, they never had no card to sell what they would have been allowed. So they hauled it back. The gin wouldn't hold all of it, so they put some of it under Rafe's mule shed and they put the rest of it right here in the hall where we are setting now, where they would have to walk around it all winter and keep themselves reminded to be sho and fill out that card next time.

"Only next year they didn't fill out no papers neither. It was like they still couldn't believe it, still be-lieved in the freedom and liberty to make or break according to a man's fitness and will to work, guaranteed by the Government that old Anse had tried to tear in two once and failed, and admitted in good faith he had failed and taken the consequences, and that had give Buddy a medal and taken care of him when he was far away from home in a strange land and hurt.

"So they made that second crop. And they couldn't sell it to nobody neither because they never had no cards. This time they built a special shed to put it under, and I remem-ber how in that second winter Buddy come to town one day to see Lawyer Gavin Stevens. Not for legal advice how to sue the Gov-ernment or somebody into buying the cotton, even if they never had no card for it, but just to find out why. 'I was for going ahead and signing up for it,' Buddy says. 'If that's going to be the new rule. But we talked it over, and Jackson ain't no farmer, but he knowed father longer than the rest of us, and he said father would have said no, and I reckon now he would have been right.'

"So they didn't raise any more cotton; they had a plenty of it to last a while — twenty-two bales, I think it was. That was when they went into whiteface cattle, putting old Anse's cotton land into pasture, because that's what he would have wanted them to do if the only way they could raise cotton was by the Government telling them how much they could raise and how much they could sell it for, and where, and when, and then pay them for not doing the work they didn't do. Only even when they didn't raise cotton, every year the county agent's young fellow would come out to measure the pasture crops they planted so he could pay them for that, even if they never had no not-cotton to be paid for. Except that he never measured no crop on this place. 'You're welcome to look at what we are doing,' Buddy says. 'But don't draw it down on your map.'

" 'But you can get money for this,' the young fellow says. 'The Government wants to pay you for planting all this.'

" 'We are aiming to get money for it,' Buddy says. 'When we can't, we will try something else. But not from the Government. Give that to them that want to take it. We can make out.'

"And that's about all. Them twenty-two bales of orphan cotton are down yonder in the gin right now, because there's room for it in the gin now because they ain't using the gin no more. And them boys grew up and went off a year to the agricultural college to learn right about whiteface cattle, and then come back to the rest of them — these here curious folks living off here to themselves, with the rest of the world all full of pretty neon lights burning night and day both, and easy, quick money scattering itself around everywhere for any man

to grab a little, and every man with a shiny new automobile already wore out and throwed away and the new one delivered before the first one was even paid for, and everywhere a fine loud grabble and snatch of AAA and WPA [1] and a dozen other three-letter reasons for a man not to work. Then this here draft comes along, and these curious folks ain't got around to signing that neither, and you come all the way up from Jackson with your paper all signed and regular, and we come out here, and after a while we can go back to town. A man gets around, don't he?"

"Yes," the investigator said. "Do you suppose we can go back to town now?"

"No," the marshal told him in that same kindly tone, "not just yet. But we can leave after a while. Of course you will miss your train. But there will be another one tomorrow."

He rose, though the investigator had heard nothing. The investigator watched him go down the hall and open the bedroom door and enter and close it behind him. The investigator sat quietly, listening to the night sounds and looking at the closed door until it opened presently and the marshal came

[1] AAA and WPA: Agricultural Adjustment Administration and Works Progress Administration. These were federal agencies established in President Franklin D. Roosevelt's administration, in the economic depression of the 1930's, to help farmers and unemployed persons.

back, carrying something in a bloody sheet, carrying it gingerly.

"Here," he said. "Hold it a minute."

"It's bloody," the investigator said.

"That's all right," the mashal said. "We can wash when we get through." So the investigator took the bundle and stood holding it while he watched the old marshal go back down the hall and on through it and vanish and return presently with a lighted lantern and a shovel. "Come along," he said. "We're pretty near through now."

The investigator followed him out of the house and across the yard, carrying gingerly the bloody, shattered, heavy bundle in which it still seemed to him he could feel some warmth of life, the marshal striding on ahead, the lantern swinging against his leg, the shadow of his striding scissoring and enormous along the earth, his voice still coming back over his shoulder, chatty and cheerful, "Yes, sir. A man gets around and he sees a heap; a heap of folks in a heap of situations. The trouble is, we done got into the habit of confusing the situations with the folks. Take yourself, now," he said in that same kindly tone, chatty and easy; "you mean all right. You just went and got yourself all fogged up with rules and regulations. That's our trouble. We done invented ourselves so many alphabets and rules and recipes that we can't see anything else; if what we see can't be

fitted to an alphabet or a rule, we are lost. We have come to be like critters doctor folks might have created in laboratories, that have learned how to slip off their bones and guts and still live, still be kept alive indefinite and forever maybe even without even knowing the bones and the guts are gone. We have slipped our backbone; we have about decided a man don't need a backbone any more; to have one is old-fashioned. But the groove where the backbone used to be is still there, and the backbone has been kept alive, too, and someday we're going to slip back onto it. I don't know just when nor just how much of a wrench it will take to teach us, but someday."

They had left the yard now. They were mounting a slope; ahead of them the investigator could see another clump of cedars, a small clump, somehow shaggily formal against the starred sky. The marshal entered it and stopped and set the lantern down and, following with the bundle, the investigator saw a small rectangle of earth enclosed by a low brick coping. Then he saw the two graves, or the headstones — two plain granite slabs set upright in the earth.

"Old Anse and Mrs. Anse," the marshal said. "Buddy's wife wanted to be buried with her folks. I reckon she would have been right lonesome up here with just McCallums. Now, let's see." He stood for a moment, his chin in his hand; to the investigator he looked exactly like an old lady trying to decide where to set out a shrub. "They was to run from left to right, beginning with Jackson. But after the boys was born, Jackson and Stuart was to come up here by their pa and ma, so Buddy could move up some and make room. So he will be about here." He moved the lantern nearer and took up the shovel. Then he saw the investigator still holding the bundle. "Set it down," he said. "I got to dig first."

"I'll hold it," the investigator said. "Nonsense, put it down," the marshal said. "Buddy won't mind."

So the investigator put the bundle down on the brick coping and the marshal began to dig, skillfully and rapidly, still talking in that cheerful, interminable voice, "Yes, sir. We done forgot about folks. Life has done got cheap, and life ain't cheap. Life's a pretty durn valuable thing. I don't mean just getting along from one WPA relief check to the next one, but honor and pride and discipline that make a man worth preserving, make him of any value. That's what we got to learn again. Maybe it takes trouble, bad trouble, to teach it back to us; maybe it was the walking to Virginia because that's where his ma come from, and losing a war and then walking back, that taught it to old Anse. Anyway, he seems to learned it, and to learned it good enough to bequeath it to his boys. Did you notice how all Buddy had to do was to tell them boys of his it was time to go, because the Gov-

ernment had sent them word? And how they told him good-by? Growned men kissing one another without hiding and without shame. Maybe that's what I am trying to say. . . . There," he said. "That's big enough."

He moved quickly, easily; before the investigator could stir, he had lifted the bundle into the narrow trench and was covering it, covering it as rapidly as he had dug, smoothing the earth over it with the shovel. Then he stood up and raised the lantern — a tall, lean old man, breathing easily and lightly.

"I reckon we can go back to town now," he said.

For Study and Writing

1. Analyze the character of the old marshal, paying particular attention to his way of handling the draft investigator and to his attitude toward the McCallums. Do you think he fails in his duty in this case? Support your opinion. Note the significance of the fact that he "had been born and lived in the county all his life." Early in the story the marshal tells the investigator: "And ever since we left Jefferson I been trying to tell you something for you not to forget. But I reckon it will take these McCallums to impress that on you." What do you think "that" is?

2. As the marshal and the investigator approach the McCallum house, the younger man reflects bitterly about "these people." What about "these people" cause his bitterness? Are

there such people? What keeps the McCallums from being like them? Do you think the government may be helping to produce the qualities that the investigator complains about? Support your opinion.

3. Trace the full range of the investigator's attitude toward the marshal, from first to last.

4. Several times during the investigator's first encounters with the McCallums, Faulkner stresses that they were "not big, not tall." Why, then, is the story called "The Tall Men"?

5. Rafe McCallum, on first meeting the investigator, "looked at him once, brief and hard, and then no more. . . ." Interpret the quoted words. What implications about Rafe's character do they carry?

6. Soon after his arrival at the McCallum house, the investigator realizes "that if the situation were controlled, it would devolve upon him to control it. . . ." Does he ever control it? Justify your answer.

7. On first entering the bedroom, why does the investigator feel "something very like terror"?

8. What subtle significance can you find in the casual, oblique reference to the investigator's grandfather and his demijohn, as the investigator is surveying the bedroom?

9. What inferences about Buddy's character may be drawn from his remark about his leg: "I've ruined it; I want to get shut of it"?

10. Show the relation between the McCallums' attitude toward government authority and Buddy's dealings with the doctor. Make a generaliza-

tion to link these two matters to the McCallums' character in general.

11. Discuss in detail the meaning of Buddy's instructions to the two boys, his sons: "Obey them, but remember your name and don't take nothing from no man."

12. What is ironical about the investigator's threat to the marshal that "he will be cited for contempt"?

13. In the paragraph describing the departure of the boys (page 255), explain the words "impersonal and unbearable regard."

14. What complex meanings lie in the reference to "the loud last shrilling of the summer's cicadas, as though they, too, were aware of the imminent season of cold weather and of death" (page 255)?

15. What significance do you find in the names of the elder McCallum brothers?

16. What bearing do the McCallums' relations with the government about farming have upon their attitude toward the investigator?

17. Why do you think Buddy once told the county agent's representative, "You're welcome to look at what we are doing. . . . But don't draw it down on your map"?

18. What evidence is there that the McCallums' attitude of noncooperation with the government's agricultural agents is not simply invincible ignorance?

19. Explain both the tone and the meaning of the marshal's repeated allusion to the McCallums as "curious folks."

20. What is the significance of these

words from the marshal, when he has finished sketching the McCallums' history: "A man gets around, don't he?"

21. Sum up your opinion of the McCallums. Are they misfits? What is your opinion of the standard of values that is summed up by the marshal, the standard that seems prevalent in our time, and the standard to which the McCallums adhere?

22. Discuss the legal issues raised by the story. Should the McCallum boys be pursued, prosecuted, and punished? If you think not, are you supporting a dangerously anarchic principle? If you think the law should be strictly applied, are you supporting the penalizing of people for qualities a country needs? What do you think the investigator will do? What would you do?

Comparison of Demosthenes and Cicero

by Plutarch (A.D. c. 46 – c. 120)

You are now about to make a shift from Faulkner's story to Plutarch's lives comparing a man from ancient Greece with another from ancient Rome — a shift from modern fiction to classical biography. This shift is not as drastic as it may at first appear to be. "The Tall Men" and the following biographical essay have some themes in common. Be alert for these as you read.

The arts of history and biography are cousins. History, which attempts to record and explain man's past, must examine closely the lives of influential individuals; biography, which attempts to present a comprehensive account of an individual's life, must show how he has been shaped by, and has helped to shape, the history of his time. Both arts are major branches of the great tree of literature — branches that are sometimes regrettably neglected because of our preoccupation with other literary forms.

The father of the art of biography is Plutarch, a Greek who lived in the first and second centuries A.D. (The exact date of his birth and death are unknown.) He lived in Greece, but he traveled to Egypt and at least once visited Rome, where he gave lectures.

He is one of the foremost figures in classical literature. For centuries, practically all educated Europeans were nurtured intellectually by his *Parallel Lives.* His works have been a prime source of material for other writers. Shakespeare, for instance, derived from Plutarch many of the incidents in *Julius Caesar, Antony and Cleopatra, Coriolanus, Pericles,* and *Timon of Athens.* A distinguished classical scholar of our time, Moses Hadas, says in his *Ancilla to Classical Reading* (Columbia University Press, 1954):

> . . . if today a curious reader should ask for a single author who might communicate the fullest sense of the totality of classical culture, the answer would have to be Plutarch. . . . He has indubitably had more European readers than any other pagan Greek and has been the greatest single channel for communicating to Europe a general sense of the men and manners of antiquity.

Through a series of translations, the most famous of which came from Sir Thomas North in 1579, Plutarch became an important figure in

English literature. The text used here was published by an English poet, Arthur Hugh Clough, in 1859. It is a revision of a seventeenth-century translation that has been commonly attributed to John Dryden but was actually made "by several hands." (Dryden wrote a life of Plutarch to accompany the then-new edition.)

Plutarch's characteristic method was to present the life of a notable Greek with that of a notable Roman whose career was similar in some ways to the Greek's, then to compare the two men in a brief, separate afterword.

Following is the comparison afterword on the lives of two great orators, Demosthenes, a Greek, and Cicero, a Roman. Their biographies are set against backgrounds of major events in the histories of ancient Greece and Rome. But the historical material is subordinate to the elements for which we read these lives now: subtlety and depth of character analysis; simplicity and clarity of presentation; an affirmation that, despite a man's shortcomings, honor and nobility can make him memorable, whether in failure or success. It is for this persistent assertion that Plutarch's masterpiece traditionally bears in English the title, *Lives of the Noble Grecians and Romans.*

These are the most memorable circumstances recorded in history of Demosthenes and Cicero which have come to our knowledge. But omitting an exact comparison of their respective faculties in speaking, yet thus much seems fit to be said; that Demosthenes, to make himself a master in rhetoric, applied all the faculties he had, natural or acquired, wholly that way that he far surpassed in force and strength of eloquence all his contemporaries in political and judicial speaking, in grandeur and majesty all the panegyrical orators, and in accuracy and science all the logicians and rhetoricians of his day; that Cicero was highly educated, and by his diligent study became a most accomplished general scholar in all these branches, having left behind him numerous philosophical treatises of his own on Academic principles; as, indeed, even in his written speeches, both political and judicial, we see him continually trying to show his learning by the way. And one may discover the different temper of each of them in their speeches. For Demosthenes's oratory was without all embellishment and jesting, wholly composed for real effect and seriousness; not smelling of the lamp, as Pytheas scoffingly said, but of the temperance, thoughtfulness, austerity, and grave earnestness of his temper. Whereas Cicero's love of mockery often ran him into scurrility; and in his love of laughing away serious arguments in judicial cases by jests and facetious remarks, with a view to the advantage of his clients, he paid too little regard to what was decent: saying, for example, in his defence of Caelius, that he had done no absurd thing in such plenty and affluence to indulge himself in pleasures, it being a kind of madness not to enjoy the things we possess, especially since the most eminent philosophers have asserted pleasures to be the chiefest good. So also we are told that when Cicero, being consul, undertook the defence of Murena against Cato's prosecution, by way of bantering Cato, he made a long series of jokes upon the absurd paradoxes, as they are called, of the Stoic set; so that a loud laughter passing from the crowd to the judges, Cato, with a quiet smile, said to those that sat next him, "My friends, what an amusing consul we have."

And, indeed, Cicero was by natural temper very much disposed to mirth and pleasantry, and always appeared with a smiling and serene countenance. But Demosthenes had constant care and thoughtfulness in his look, and a serious anxiety, which he seldom, if ever, laid aside; and therefore, was accounted by his enemies, as he himself confessed, morose and ill-mannered.

Also, it is very evident, out of their several writings, that Demosthenes never touched upon his own praises but decently and without offence when there was need of it, and for some weightier end; but upon other occasions modestly and sparingly. But Cicero's immeasurable boasting of himself in his orations argues him guilty of an uncontrollable appetite for distinction, his cry being evermore that arms should give place to the gown, and the soldier's laurel to the tongue. And at last we find him extolling not only his deeds and actions, but his orations also, as well those that were only spoken, as those that were published; as if he were engaged in a boyish trial of skill, who should speak best, with the rhetoricians, Isocrates and Anaximenes, not as one who could claim the task to guide and instruct the Roman nation, the —

Soldier full-armed, terrific to the foe.

It is necessary, indeed, for a political leader to be an able speaker; but it is an ignoble thing for any man to admire and relish the glory of his own eloquence. And, in this matter, Demosthenes had a more than ordinary gravity and magnificence of mind, accounting his talent in speaking nothing more than a mere accomplishment and matter of practice, the success of which must depend greatly on the goodwill and candour of his hearers, and regarding those who pride themselves on such accounts to be men of a low and petty disposition.

The power of persuading and governing the people did, indeed, equally belong to both, so that those who had armies and camps at command stood in need of their assistance; as Charas, Diopithes, and Leosthenes of Demosthenes's, Pompey and young Caesar of Cicero's, as the latter himself admits in his Memoirs addressed to Agrippa and Maecenas. But what are thought and commonly said most to demonstrate and try the tempers of men, namely, authority and place, by moving every passion, and discovering every frailty, these are things which Demosthenes never received; nor was he ever in a position to give such proof of himself, having never obtained any eminent office, nor led any of those armies into the field against Philip which he raised by his eloquence. Cicero, on the other hand, was sent quaestor into Sicily, and proconsul into Cilicia and Cappadocia, at a time when avarice was at the height, and the commanders and governors who were employed abroad, as though they thought it a mean thing to steal, set themselves to seize by open force; so that it seemed no heinous matter to take bribes, but he that did it most moderately was in good esteem. And yet he, at this time, gave the most abundant proofs alike of his contempt of riches and of his humanity and good-nature. And at Rome, when he was created consul in name, but indeed received sovereign and dictatorial authority against Catiline and his conspirators, he attested the truth of Plato's prediction, that then the miseries of states would be at an end when, by a happy fortune, supreme power, wisdom, and justice should be united in one.

It is said, to the reproach of Demosthenes, that his eloquence was mercenary; that he privately made orations for Phormion and Apollodorus, though adversaries in the same cause; that he was charged with moneys received from the King of Persia, and condemned for bribes from Harpalus. And should we grant that all those (and they are not few) who have made these statements against him have spoken what is untrue, yet that Demosthenes was not the character to look without desire on the presents offered him out of respect and gratitude by royal persons, and that one who lent money on maritime usury was likely to be thus indifferent, is what we cannot assert. But that Cicero refused, from the Sicilians when he was quaestor, from the King of Cappadocia when he was proconsul, and from his friends at Rome when he was in exile, many presents, though urged to receive them, has been said already.

Moreover, Demosthenes's banishment was infamous, upon conviction for bribery; Cicero's very honorable, for ridding his country of a set of villains. Therefore, when Demosthenes fled his country, no man regarded it; for Cicero's sake the senate changed their habit, and put on mourning, and would not be persuaded to make any act before Cicero's return was decreed. Cicero, however, passed his exile idly in Macedonia. But the very exile of Demosthenes made up a great part of the services he did for his country; for he went through the cities of Greece, and everywhere, as we have said, joined in the conflict on behalf of the Grecians, driving out the Macedonian ambassadors, and approving himself a much better citizen than Themistocles and Alcibiades did in the like fortune. And, after his return, he again devoted himself to the same public service, and continued firm to his opposition to Antipater and the Macedonians. Whereas Laelius reproached Cicero in the senate for sitting silent when Caesar, a beardless youth, asked leave to come forward, contrary to the law, as a candidate for the consulship; and Brutus, in his epistles, charges him with nursing and rearing a greater and more heavy tyranny than that they had removed.

Finally, Cicero's death excites our pity; for an old man to be miserably carried up and down by his servants, flying and hiding himself from that death which was, in the course of nature, so near at hand; and yet at last to be murdered. De-mosthenes, though he seemed at first a little to supplicate, yet, by his preparing and keeping the poison by him, demands our admiration; and still more admirable was his using it. When the temple of the god no longer afforded him a sanctuary, he took refuge, as it were, at a mightier altar, freeing himself from arms and soldiers, and laughing to scorn the cruelty of Antipater.

For Study and Writing

1. Compare and contrast the two orators with respect to their techniques of delivery and argument.

2. Compare and contrast their qualities of character, noting both strengths and weaknesses. Which of them seems to you the greater? Support your view. Weigh their services to the state, their firmness of principle, and the manner in which each faced death.

3. Write a paper establishing some common themes between the lives of these two men and "The Tall Men." You will find a primary clue in the marshal's concluding words about the value of life at the close of the Faulkner story.

AFTERWORD

In his life of the Greek general Timoleon, Plutarch explains his motives for writing biography:

> It was for the sake of others that I first commenced writing biographies; but I find myself proceeding and attaching myself to it for my own, the virtues of these great men serving me as a sort of looking-glass, in which I may see how to adjust and adorn my own life. Indeed, it can be compared to nothing but daily living and associating together; we receive, as it were, in our inquiry, and entertain each successive guest, view — "Their stature and their qualities," and select from their actions all that is noblest and worthiest to know. . . . My method . . . is, by the study of history, and by the familiarity acquired in writing, to habituate my memory to receive and retain images of the best and worthiest characters. I am thus enabled to free myself from any ignoble, base, or vicious impressions, contracted from the contagion of ill company that I may be unavoidably engaged in; by the remedy of turning my thoughts in a happy and calm temper to view these noble examples.

The rallying power of eloquent oratory often has been a decisive force in crises of history from the times described by Plutarch down to the present. For examples we have only to remember America's Patrick Henry crying "I know not what course others may take; but as for me, give me liberty or give me death!" and England's Winston Churchill proclaiming ". . . we shall defend our island, whatever the cost may be: we shall fight on the beaches; we shall fight on the landing grounds; we shall fight in the fields and in the streets; we shall fight in the hills — we shall never surrender!"

In such instances it is not only the ringing words but also the powerful emanation of great character that produce the effect achieved by the oration. In the portrayal of character, Plutarch is paramount. He brings before us vividly the orators Demosthenes and Cicero. Both were leaders and statesmen. Both were fated to live at a time when freedom was waning in their countries and government ceased to rest upon the consent of the governed and became subject to the wills of strong men. One saw the end of Athenian democracy; the other saw the end of Roman republicanism.

Plutarch's short biographies anticipated another mode of literature. The essay, as a recognized form under that name, was created in the sixteenth century by the French writer Montaigne. It became an immensely popular form in the English language. Plutarch's lives may be called biographical essays, models for many who used the form centuries after him. (In Lytton Strachey's "Florence Nightingale," which you will study later in this course, you will see Plutarch's influence.)

As the father of biography, Plutarch contributes enormously to the study of man and to our awareness of his nature and the wide range and variation of his character. Plutarch does not present his subjects as *either* good *or* bad, but as complex men with *both* good *and* bad qualities. *Both . . . and* is a deeper way of appraising almost anything than is *either . . . or*. Plutarch's genius for seeing all aspects of a man, for praising and blaming him freely without tending to do solely either one or the other, is carried to a high point in the skillful comparison that he draws of his two subjects. Here the art of sifting and weighing evidence and reaching a balanced, objective conclusion is admirably demonstrated. Innovator of a branch of literature, Plutarch remains unsurpassed in it.

For Further Reading

For further reading in and about Plutarch:

Plutarch. *Lives of the Noble Grecians and Romans* (complete). New York: The Modern Library, Random House, 1932.

Plutarch. *Lives of the Noble Greeks* (selections). (Laurel Books.) New York: Dell Publishing Co., 1959.

Plutarch. *Lives of the Noble Romans* (selections). (Laurel Books.) New York: Dell Publishing Co., 1959.

Plutarch. *On Love, the Family, and the Good Life.* Translated by Moses Hadas. New York: Mentor Books, New American Library of World Literature, 1957.

Hadas, Moses. *Ancilla to Classical Reading.* New York: Columbia University Press, 1954.

For further reading in biography:

Fuller, Edmund and Davis, O. B. *Four American Biographies.* (Adventures in Good Books.) New York: Harcourt, Brace & World, 1961.

Priestley, J. B. and Davis, O. B. *Four English Biographies.* (Adventures in Good Books.) New York: Harcourt, Brace & World, 1961.

Edel, Leon, White, Elizabeth S., and Brown, Madolyn W. *Five World Biographies.* (Adventures in Good Books.) New York: Harcourt, Brace & World, 1961.

The Taming of the Shrew

by William Shakespeare (1564–1616)

A test of wills between man and woman is an ancient and ever-popular theme of comedy. Borrowing from the treasure house of Italian comedy of the Renaissance, Shakespeare gave us this delightful tale of a shrew who meets her match.

Critics have not always given this play its due. One of Shakespeare's early works, it does not contain the soaring splendors of his poetry. Of all his comedies, it is the simplest in structure, the least complicated. Nonetheless, in it the voice of his genius is clear and unmistakable.

Proof of the comedy's appeal and vitality is that it has always been popular on the stage. It is candidly theatrical, frankly frolicsome. Its main play is set within another play, and it opens with a practical joke. In recent years it was adapted for musical comedy: *Kiss Me, Kate*,[1] its title taken from Shakespeare's lines, was a smash hit for both Broadway and Hollywood.

DRAMATIS PERSONAE

A LORD
CHRISTOPHER SLY, *a tinker*
HOSTESS, PAGE, PLAYERS, HUNTSMEN, *and* SERVANTS
} *persons in the Induction*

BAPTISTA MINOLA, *a gentleman of Padua*
VINCENTIO, *a merchant of Pisa*
LUCENTIO, *son to Vincentio, in love with Bianca*
PETRUCHIO, *a gentleman of Verona, a suitor to Katharine*

GREMIO
HORTENSIO
} *suitors to Bianca*

TRANIO
BIONDELLO
} *servants to Lucentio*

GRUMIO
CURTIS
} *servants to Petruchio*

A PEDANT

KATHARINE
BIANCA
} *daughters to Baptista*

A WIDOW
TAILOR, HABERDASHER, *and* SERVANTS

SCENE: *Padua, and* PETRUCHIO'*s house in the country.*

[1] *Kiss Me, Kate* (1948), book by Bella and Samuel Spewack, music and lyrics by Cole Porter (1893–1964).

INDUCTION

SCENE I. *Before an alehouse on a heath.*

Enter HOSTESS *and* SLY.

SLY. I'll pheeze you,° in faith.

HOSTESS. A pair of stocks,° you rogue!

SLY. Y'are a baggage, the Slys are no rogues. Look in the Chronicles, we
came in with Richard Conqueror. Therefore paucas pallabris,° let
the world slide. Sessa!°   5

HOSTESS. You will not pay for the glasses you have burst?

SLY. No, not a denier. Go by Saint Jeronimy, go to thy cold bed, and
warm thee.

HOSTESS. I know my remedy; I must go fetch the thirdborough.°   *Exit.*

SLY. Third, or fourth, or fifth borough, I'll answer him by law. I'll   10
not budge an inch, boy. Let him come, and kindly.

[*Lies down on the ground and falls asleep. Horns winded.*
Enter LORD *from hunting, with* HUNTSMEN *and* SERVANTS.]

LORD. Huntsman, I charge thee, tender well my hounds.
Breathe Merriman, the poor cur is embossed,°
And couple Clowder with the deep-mouthed brach.°
Saw'st thou not, boy, how Silver made it good   15
At the hedge-corner, in the coldest fault?°
I would not lose the dog for twenty pound.

FIRST HUNTSMAN. Why, Belman is as good as he, my lord.
He cried upon it at the merest loss,
And twice to-day picked out the dullest scent.   20
Trust me, I take him for the better dog.

LORD. Thou art a fool. If Echo were as fleet,
I would esteem him worth a dozen such.
But sup them well, and look unto them all.
To-morrow I intend to hunt again.   25

FIRST HUNTSMAN. I will, my lord.

LORD. What's here? One dead, or drunk? See, doth he breathe?

---

1. **pheeze you:** drive you away. 2. **stocks:** a threat to have him set in the stocks.
4. **paucas pallabris:** few words. 5. **Sessa!:** a contemptuous expression. 9. **thirdborough:** constable. 13. **embossed:** foaming. 14. **brach:** a bitch hound. 16. **coldest
fault:** faintest scent.

SECOND HUNTSMAN. He breathes, my lord. Were he not warmed with ale,
    This were a bed but cold to sleep so soundly.
LORD. O monstrous beast, how like a swine he lies.   30
    Grim death, how foul and loathsome is thine image.
    Sirs, I will practise° on this drunken man.
    What think you, if he were conveyed to bed,
    Wrapped in sweet clothes, rings put upon his fingers,
    A most delicious banquet by his bed,   35
    And brave attendants near him when he wakes,
    Would not the beggar then forget himself?
FIRST HUNTSMAN. Believe me, lord, I think he cannot choose.
SECOND HUNTSMAN. It would seem strange unto him when he waked.
LORD. Even as a flattering dream, or worthless fancy.   40
    Then take him up, and manage well the jest.
    Carry him gently to my fairest chamber,
    And hang it round with all my wanton pictures.
    Balm his foul head in warm distilled waters,
    And burn sweet wood to make the lodging sweet.   45
    Procure me music ready when he wakes,
    To make a dulcet° and a heavenly sound;
    And if he chance to speak, be ready straight
    And with a low submissive reverence
    Say, what is it your honour will command?   50
    Let one attend him with a silver basin
    Full of rose-water, and bestrewed with flowers;
    Another bear the ewer, the third a diaper,°
    And say, will't please your lordship cool your hands?
    Some one be ready with a costly suit,   55
    And ask him what apparel he will wear.
    Another tell him of his hounds and horse,
    And that his lady mourns at his disease.
    Persuade him that he hath been lunatic;
    And when he says he is Sly, say that he dreams,   60
    For he is nothing but a mighty lord.
    This do, and do it kindly, gentle sirs.
    It will be pastime passing excellent,
    If it be husbanded with modesty.
FIRST HUNTSMAN. My lord, I warrant you we'll play our part,   65

    32. practise: play a trick. **47. dulcet:** sweet. **53. diaper:** towel.

As he shall think by our true diligence
He is no less than what we say he is.
LORD. Take him up gently, and to bed with him,
And each one to his office when he wakes.

[SLY *is borne out. Trumpets sound.*]

Sirrah,° go see what trumpet 'tis that sounds.   *Exit* SERVANT.   70
Belike° some noble gentleman that means,
Travelling some journey, to repose him here.

Enter SERVANT.

How now? Who is it?
SERVANT.   An it please your honour,
Players that offer service to your lordship.
LORD. Bid them come near.

Enter PLAYERS.

Now, fellows, you are welcome.   75
PLAYERS. We thank your honour.
LORD. Do you intend to stay with me to-night?
FIRST PLAYER. So please your lordship to accept our duty.
LORD. With all my heart. This fellow I remember,
Since once he played a farmer's eldest son.   80
'Twas where you wooed the gentlewoman so well.
I have forgot your name; but sure that part
Was aptly fitted, and naturally performed.
FIRST PLAYER. I think 'twas Soto that your honour means.
LORD. 'Tis very true, thou didst it excellent.   85
Well you are come to me in happy time,
The rather for I have some sport in hand,
Wherein your cunning can assist me much.
There is a lord will hear you play to-night;
But I am doubtful of your modesties,   90
Lest over-eyeing of his odd behaviour —
For yet his honour never heard a play —
You break into some merry passion,
And so offend him; for I tell you, sirs,

70. **Sirrah:** term of address used to an inferior. 71. **Belike:** probably.

If you should smile, he grows impatient.   95
FIRST PLAYER. Fear not, my lord, we can contain ourselves,
  Were he the veriest antic° in the world.
LORD. Go sirrah, take them to the buttery,°
  And give them friendly welcome every one.
  Let them want nothing that my house affords.   100

         Exit SERVANT *with the* PLAYERS.

  [*To another* SERVANT] Sirrah, go you to Barthol'mew my page,
  And see him dressed in all suits like a lady.
  That done, conduct him to the drunkard's chamber,
  And call him madam, do him obeisance.
  Tell him from me, as he will win my love,   105
  He bear himself with honourable action,
  Such as he hath observed in noble ladies
  Unto their lords, by them accomplished;
  Such duty to the drunkard let him do,
  With soft low tongue and lowly courtesy,   110
  And say, what is't your honour will command,
  Wherein your lady, and your humble wife,
  May show her duty, and make known her love?
  And then with kind embracements, tempting kisses,
  And with declining head into his bosom,   115
  Bid him shed tears, as being overjoyed
  To see her noble lord restored to health,
  Who for twice seven years hath esteemed him
  No better than a poor and loathsome beggar.
  And if the boy have not a woman's gift   120
  To rain a shower of commanded tears,
  An onion will do well for such a shift,
  Which in a napkin being close conveyed,
  Shall in despite enforce a watery eye.
  See this dispatched with all the haste thou canst,   125
  Anon I'll give thee more instructions.   *Exit* SERVANT.
  I know the boy will well usurp the grace,
  Voice, gait, and action of a gentlewoman.
  I long to hear him call the drunkard husband,

  97. antic: ludicrous fellow. 98. buttery: pantry, a place where food and drink
may be had.

And how my men will stay themselves from laughter,   130
When they do homage to this simple peasant.
I'll in to counsel them; haply my presence
May well abate the over-merry spleen,
Which otherwise would grow into extremes.   *Exeunt.*

SCENE II. *A bedchamber in the* LORD's *house.* SLY *discovered,*
with ATTENDANTS; *some with apparel, basin, ewer, and other*
appurtenances; and LORD.

SLY. For God's sake, a pot of small ale.

FIRST SERVANT. Will't please your lordship drink a cup of sack?°

SECOND SERVANT. Will't please your honour taste of these conserves?

THIRD SERVANT. What raiment will your honour wear to-day?

SLY. I am Christophero Sly, call not me honour nor lordship. I ne'er   5
drank sack in my life. And if you give me any conserves, give me
conserves of beef. Ne'er ask me what raiment I'll wear, for I have
no more doublets than backs, no more stockings than legs, nor no
more shoes than feet, nay sometime more feet than shoes, or such
shoes as my toes look through the overleather.   10

LORD. Heaven cease this idle humour in your honour.
O that a mighty man of such descent,
Of such possessions, and so high esteem,
Should be infused with so foul a spirit!

SLY. What would you make me mad? Am not I Christopher Sly, old   15
Sly's son of Burton-heath, by birth a pedlar, by education a card-
maker, by transmutation a bear-herd, and now by present profession a tinker? Ask Marian Hacket, the fat ale-wife of Wincot,
if she know me not. If she say I am not fourteen pence on the
score for sheer ale, score me up for the lying'st knave in Chris-   20
tendom. What, I am not bestraught;° here's —

FIRST SERVANT. O this it is that makes your lady mourn.

SECOND SERVANT. O this it is that makes your servants droop.

LORD. Hence comes it, that your kindred shuns your house,
As beaten hence by your strange lunacy.   25
O noble lord, bethink thee of thy birth,
Call home thy ancient thoughts from banishment,
And banish hence these abject lowly dreams.

2. **sack:** wine. 21. **bestraught:** distraught, crazed.

Look how thy servants do attend on thee,
Each in his office ready at thy beck. 30
Wilt thou have music? Hark, Apollo plays,

[*Music.*]

And twenty caged nightingales do sing.
Or wilt thou sleep? We'll have thee to a couch
Softer and sweeter than the lustful bed
On purpose trimmed up for Semiramis.° 35
Say thou wilt walk; we will bestrew the ground.
Or wilt thou ride? Thy horses shall be trapped,°
Their harness studded all with gold and pearl.
Dost thou love hawking? Thou hast hawks will soar
Above the morning lark. Or wilt thou hunt, 40
Thy hounds shall make the welkin° answer them,
And fetch shrill echoes from the hollow earth.

FIRST SERVANT. Say thou wilt course,° thy greyhounds are as swift
As breathed° stags, ay, fleeter than the roe.

SECOND SERVANT. Dost thou love pictures? We will fetch thee straight 45
Adonis° painted by a running brook,
And Cytherea° all in sedges° hid,
Which seem to move and wanton with her breath,
Even as the waving sedges play with wind.

LORD. We'll show thee Io,° as she was a maid, 50
And how she was beguiled and surprised,
As lively painted as the deed was done.

THIRD SERVANT. Or Daphne° roaming through a thorny wood,
Scratching her legs, that one shall swear she bleeds,
And at that sight shall sad Apollo weep, 55
So workmanly the blood and tears are drawn.

LORD. Thou art a lord, and nothing but a lord.
Thou hast a lady far more beautiful,

35. **Semiramis:** legendary Assyrian queen, founder of Babylon and wife of Ninus, with whom she founded Nineveh. **37. trapped:** adorned. **41. welkin:** vault of heaven. **43. course:** hunt with hounds that follow by sight rather than scent. **44. breathed:** exercised in the chase. **46. Adonis:** in mythology, a handsome youth loved by Venus. **47. Cytherea:** another name for Venus, or Aphrodite, derived from the island where she arose from the sea; **sedges:** tall marsh grasses. **50. Io:** in mythology, a maiden whom Zeus loved and pursued; she was turned into a heifer because of the jealousy of Hera. **53. Daphne:** in mythology, a nymph turned into a laurel tree to escape the amorous pursuit of Apollo.

Than any woman in this waning age.

FIRST SERVANT. And till the tears that she hath shed for thee   60
Like envious floods o'er-run her lovely face,
She was the fairest creature in the world,
And yet she is inferior to none.

SLY. Am I a lord, and have I such a lady?
Or do I dream? Or have I dreamed till now?   65
I do not sleep. I see, I hear, I speak.
I smell sweet savours, and I feel soft things.
Upon my life, I am a lord indeed,
And not a tinker, nor Christopher Sly.
Well, bring our lady hither to our sight,   70
And once again a pot o' th' smallest ale.

SECOND SERVANT. Will't please your mightiness to wash your hands?

[SERVANTS *present basin, etc.*]

O how we joy to see your wit restored!
O that once more you knew but what you are!
These fifteen years you have been in a dream,   75
Or when you waked, so waked as if you slept.

SLY. These fifteen years! By my fay, a goodly nap.
But did I never speak of all that time?

FIRST SERVANT. O yes, my lord, but very idle words,
For though you lay here in this goodly chamber,   80
Yet would you say, ye were beaten out of door,
And rail upon the hostess of the house,
And say you would present her at the leet,°
Because she brought stone jugs, and no sealed quarts.°
Sometimes you would call out for Cicely Hacket.   85

SLY. Ay, the woman's maid of the house.

THIRD SERVANT. Why, sir, you know no house, nor no such maid,
Nor no such men as you have reckoned up,
As Stephen Sly, and old John Naps of Greece,
And Peter Turph, and Henry Pimpernell,   90
And twenty more such names and men as these,
Which never were, nor no man ever saw.

SLY. Now Lord be thanked for my good amends.°

83. leet: a court for small offenses. 84. sealed quarts: officially stamped as containing a quart. 93. amends: recovery.

ALL. Amen.

SLY. I thank thee: thou shalt not lose by it.   95

Enter PAGE *as a lady, with* ATTENDANTS.

PAGE. How fares my noble lord?

SLY. Marry° I fare well, for here is cheer enough.
    Where is my wife?

PAGE. Here, noble lord, what is thy will with her?

SLY. Are you my wife, and will not call me husband?   100
    My men should call me lord, I am your good-man.

PAGE. My husband and my lord, my lord and husband.
    I am your wife in all obedience.

SLY. I know it well. What must I call her?

LORD. Madam.   105

SLY. Al'ce madam, or Joan madam?

LORD. Madam, and nothing else, so lords call ladies.

SLY. Madam wife, they say that I have dreamed,
    And slept above some fifteen year or more.

PAGE. Ay, and the time seems thirty unto me,   110
    Being all this time abandoned from your bed.

SLY. 'Tis much. Servants, leave me and her alone.
    Madam, undress you, and come now to bed.

PAGE. Thrice-noble lord, let me entreat of you
    To pardon me yet for a night or two.   115
    Or if not so, until the sun be set.
    For your physicians have expressly charged,
    In peril to incur your former malady,
    That I should yet absent me from your bed.
    I hope this reason stands for my excuse.   120

SLY. Ay, it stands so that I may hardly tarry so long.
    But I would be loth to fall into my dreams again.
    I will therefore tarry in despite of the flesh and the blood.

Enter MESSENGER.

MESSENGER. Your honour's players, hearing your amendment,
    Are come to play a pleasant comedy.   125
    For so your doctors hold it very meet,
    Seeing too much sadness hath congealed your blood,

97. **Marry**: Mary, by the Virgin.

And melancholy is the nurse of frenzy;
Therefore they thought it good you hear a play,
And frame your mind to mirth and merriment, 130
Which bars a thousand harms, and lengthens life.

SLY. Marry, I will, let them play it. Is not a comonty° a
Christmas gambol, or a tumbling-trick?

PAGE. No, my good lord, it is more pleasing stuff.

SLY. What, household stuff? 135

PAGE. It is a kind of history.

SLY. Well, we'll see't. Come, madam wife, sit by my side, and let the
world slip, we shall ne'er be younger.

[*Flourish.**]

132. comonty: Sly means "comedy." * Flourish: stage direction for notes on a
trumpet to draw attention to the entrance of the actors.

ACT I

SCENE I. *Padua. A Square.*

Enter LUCENTIO *and* TRANIO.

LUCENTIO. Tranio, since for the great desire I had
To see fair Padua, nursery of arts,
I am arrived for fruitful Lombardy,
The pleasant garden of great Italy,
And by my father's love and leave am armed 5
With his good will, and thy good company,
My trusty servant, well approved in all,
Here let us breathe, and haply institute
A course of learning, and ingenious studies.
Pisa renowned for grave citizens 10
Gave me my being and my father first,
A merchant of great traffic through the world,
Vincentio, come of the Bentivolii.
Vincentio's son, brought up in Florence,
It shall become to serve all hopes conceived 15
To deck his fortune with his virtuous deeds.

And therefore Tranio, for the time I study,
Virtue and that part of philosophy
Will I apply that treats of happiness
By virtue specially to be achieved.   20
Tell me thy mind, for I have Pisa left,
And am to Padua come, as he that leaves
A shallow plash,° to plunge him in the deep,
And with satiety seeks to quench his thirst.
TRANIO. *Mi perdonato,*° gentle master mine.   25
I am in all affected as yourself,
Glad that you thus continue your resolve
To suck the sweets of sweet philosophy.
Only, good master, while we do admire
This virtue, and this moral discipline,   30
Let's be no stoics, nor no stocks,° I pray,
Or so devote to Aristotle's checks,°
As Ovid° be an outcast quite abjured.
Balk logic with acquaintance° that you have,
And practise rhetoric in your common talk;   35
Music and poesy use, to quicken you;
The mathematics, and the metaphysics,
Fall to them, as you find your stomach serves you.
No profit grows, where is no pleasure ta'en.
In brief, sir, study what you most affect.   40
LUCENTIO. Gramercies,° Tranio, well dost thou advise.
If, Biondello, thou wert come ashore,
We could at once put us in readiness,
And take a lodging fit to entertain
Such friends as time in Padua shall beget.   45

Enter BAPTISTA *with* KATHARINE *and* BIANCA, GREMIO, *and*
HORTENSIO. LUCENTIO *and* TRANIO *stand aside.*

But stay awhile, what company is this?
TRANIO. Master, some show to welcome us to town.

23. plash: pool. 25. *Mi perdonato:* Pardon me. 31. stocks: without feeling.
32. Aristotle's checks: rules or critical restraints set up by the Greek critic and
philosopher. 33. Ovid: Latin poet of love. The emperor Augustus banished Ovid
in A.D. 8 because of his *Ars Amatoria,* which challenged Augustus's policy of moral
reform. 34. Balk . . . acquaintance: practice logic on your friends. 41. Gramercies: an expression of thanks.

BAPTISTA.   Gentlemen, importune me no further,
            For how I firmly am resolved you know.
            That is, not to bestow my youngest daughter,   50
            Before I have a husband for the elder.
            If either of you both love Katharina,
            Because I know you well, and love you well,
            Leave shall you have to court her at your pleasure.
GREMIO.   To cart her rather. She's too rough for me.   55
            There, there, Hortensio, will you any wife?
KATHARINE.   [*To* BAPTISTA] I pray you sir, is it your will
            To make a stale of me amongst these mates?°
HORTENSIO.   Mates, maid, how mean you that? No mates for you,
            Unless you were of gentler, milder mould.   60
KATHARINE.   I' faith, sir, you shall never need to fear.
            Iwis° it is not half way to her heart.
            But if it were, doubt not, her care should be
            To comb your noddle with a three-legged stool,
            And paint your face, and use you like a fool.   65
HORTENSIO.   From all such devils, good Lord deliver us.
GREMIO.   And me too, good Lord.
TRANIO.   [*Aside to* LUCENTIO] Hush, master, here's some good pastime
            toward.
            That wench is stark mad, or wonderful froward.°
LUCENTIO.   [*Aside to* TRANIO] But in the other's silence do I see   70
            Maid's mild behaviour and sobriety.
            Peace, Tranio.
TRANIO.   [*Aside to* LUCENTIO] Well said, master, mum! And gaze your fill.
BAPTISTA.   Gentlemen, that I may soon make good
            What I have said, Bianca get you in,   75
            And let it not displease thee, good Bianca,
            For I will love thee ne'er the less my girl.
KATHARINE.   A pretty peat,° it is best put finger in the eye, an she knew
            why.°
BIANCA.   Sister, content you, in my discontent.   80
            Sir, to your pleasure humbly I subscribe.
            My books and instruments shall be my company,

---

58. To . . . mates: to make me cheap before your companions. Hortensio proceeds to pun on the word *mates*. 62. Iwis: surely. 69. froward: intractable, unmanageable. 78. peat: pet. 78–79. put . . . why: She is calling Bianca a crybaby.

On them to look, and practise by myself.
LUCENTIO. [*Aside to* TRANIO] Hark, Tranio, thou mayst hear Minerva°
    speak.
HORTENSIO. Signior Baptista, will you be so strange?   85
    Sorry am I that our good will effects
    Bianca's grief.
GREMIO.   Why will you mew her up,°
    Signior Baptista, for this fiend of hell,
    And make her bear the penance of her tongue?
BAPTISTA. Gentlemen, content ye. I am resolved.   90
    Go in, Bianca.   *Exit* BIANCA.
    And for I know she taketh most delight
    In music, instruments, and poetry,
    Schoolmasters will I keep within my house,
    Fit to instruct her youth. If you, Hortensio,   95
    Or Signior Gremio, you, know any such,
    Prefer them hither; for to cunning men
    I will be very kind, and liberal
    To mine own children in good bringing-up.
    And so farewell. Katharina, you may stay,   100
    For I have more to commune with Bianca.   *Exit.*
KATHARINE. Why, and I trust I may go too, may I not? What, shall I
    be appointed hours, as though belike, I knew not what to take,
    and what to leave, ha?   *Exit.*
GREMIO. You may go to the devil's dam. Your gifts are so good   105
    here's none will hold you there. Love is not so great Hortensio,
    but we may blow our nails together, and fast it fairly out.° Our
    cake's dough on both sides.° Farewell; yet for the love I bear my
    sweet Bianca, if I can by any means light on a fit man to teach
    her that wherein she delights, I will wish him° to her father.   110
HORTENSIO. So will I, Signior Gremio. But a word, I pray. Though the
    nature of our quarrel yet never brooked parle,° know now upon
    advice, it toucheth us both — that we may yet again have access
    to our fair mistress, and be happy rivals in Bianca's love — to
    labour and effect one thing specially.   115

---

84. **Minerva:** goddess of wisdom. 87. **mew her up:** pen her up. 107. **we . . .
out:** We may stand in the cold and starve. 107–08. **Our . . . sides:** equivalent of
"Our goose is cooked." 110. **wish him:** commend him. 112. **brooked parle:** allowed
talk (i.e., allowed us to discuss our rivalry).

GREMIO. What's that I pray?

HORTENSIO. Marry sir to get a husband for her sister.

GREMIO. A husband? A devil.

HORTENSIO. I say a husband.

GREMIO. I say, a devil. Think'st thou, Hortensio, though her father   129
be very rich, any man is so very a fool to be married to hell?

HORTENSIO. Tush, Gremio. Though it pass your patience and mine to
endure her loud alarums, why man, there be good fellows in the
world, an a man could light on them, would take her with all
faults, and money enough.   125

GREMIO. I cannot tell; but I had as lief take her dowry with this condition — to be whipped at the high-cross° every morning.

HORTENSIO. Faith, as you say, there's small choice in rotten apples. But
come, since this bar in law makes us friends, it shall be so far forth
friendly maintained, till by helping Baptista's eldest daughter   130
to a husband, we set his youngest free for a husband, and then
have to't afresh. Sweet Bianca! Happy man be his dole. He that
runs fastest, gets the ring. How say you, Signior Gremio?

GREMIO. I am agreed, and would I had given him the best horse in
Padua to begin his wooing that would thoroughly woo her,   135
wed her, and bed her, and rid the house of her. Come on.

                                    Exeunt GREMIO *and* HORTENSIO.

TRANIO. I pray, sir, tell me, is it possible
That love should of a sudden take such hold?

LUCENTIO. O Tranio, till I found it to be true,
I never thought it possible or likely.   140
But see, while idly I stood looking on,
I found the effect of love in idleness,
And now in plainness do confess to thee,
That art to me as secret and as dear
As Anna to the Queen of Carthage was—°   145
Tranio, I burn, I pine, I perish, Tranio,
If I achieve not this young modest girl.
Counsel me, Tranio, for I know thou canst.
Assist me, Tranio, for I know thou wilt.

TRANIO. Master, it is no time to chide you now;   150
Affection is not rated from the heart.

127. high-cross: center of the marketplace. 145. Anna . . . was: Anna was
sister and confidante of Dido, legendary Queen of Carthage.

If love have touched you, naught remains but so,
Redime te captum quam queas minimo.°
LUCENTIO. Gramercies, lad. Go forward, this contents.
The rest will comfort, for thy counsel's sound. 155
TRANIO. Master, you looked so longly on the maid,
Perhaps you marked not what's the pith of all.
LUCENTIO. O yes, I saw sweet beauty in her face,
Such as the daughter of Agenor° had,
That made great Jove to humble him to her hand, 160
When with his knees he kissed the Cretan strand.
TRANIO. Saw you no more? Marked you not how her sister
Began to scold, and raise up such a storm,
That mortal ears might hardly endure the din?
LUCENTIO. Tranio, I saw her coral lips to move, 165
And with her breath she did perfume the air.
Sacred and sweet was all I saw in her.
TRANIO. Nay, then, 'tis time to stir him from his trance.
I pray awake sir. If you love the maid,
Bend thoughts and wits to achieve her. Thus it stands. 170
Her elder sister is so curst and shrewd,
That till the father rid his hands of her,
Master, your love must live a maid at home,
And therefore has he closely mewed her up,
Because she will not be annoyed with suitors. 175
LUCENTIO. Ah, Tranio, what a cruel father's he.
But art thou not advised, he took some care
To get her cunning schoolmasters to instruct her?
TRANIO. Ay, marry, am I, sir, and now 'tis plotted.
LUCENTIO. I have it, Tranio.
TRANIO.   Master, for my hand, 180
Both our inventions meet and jump in one.
LUCENTIO. Tell me thine first.
TRANIO.   You will be schoolmaster,
And undertake the teaching of the maid.
That's your device.
LUCENTIO.   It is. May it be done?

---

153. **Redime . . . minimo:** Ransom yourself as cheaply as you can. 159. **daugh-ter of Agenor:** Europa, another of the sweethearts of Zeus. To win her, he transformed himself into a white bull and knelt before her.

TRANIO. Not possible; for who shall bear your part, 185
    And be in Padua here Vincentio's son,
    Keep house, and ply his book, welcome his friends,
    Visit his countrymen, and banquet them?
LUCENTIO. Basta,° content thee, for I have it full.
    We have not yet been seen in any house, 190
    Nor can we be distinguished by our faces,
    For man or master. Then it follows thus —
    Thou shalt be master, Tranio, in my stead,
    Keep house, and port, and servants, as I should.
    I will some other be, some Florentine, 195
    Some Neapolitan, or meaner man of Pisa.
    'Tis hatched, and shall be so. Tranio, at once
    Uncase thee; take my coloured hat and cloak.
    When Biondello comes, he waits on thee,
    But I will charm him first to keep his tongue. 200
TRANIO. So had you need.

[They exchange habits.]

    In brief, sir, sith° it your pleasure is,
    And I am tied to be obedient —
    For so your father charged me at our parting,
    Be serviceable to my son, quoth he, 205
    Although I think 'twas in another sense —
    I am content to be Lucentio,
    Because so well I love Lucentio.
LUCENTIO. Tranio, be so, because Lucentio loves,
    And let me be a slave, t' achieve that maid, 210
    Whose sudden sight hath thralled my wounded eye.

Enter BIONDELLO.

    Here comes the rogue. Sirrah, where have you been?
BIONDELLO. Where have I been? Nay, how now, where are you? Master,
    has my fellow Tranio stolen your clothes, or you stolen his, or
    both? Pray what's the news? 215
LUCENTIO. Sirrah, come hither, 'tis no time to jest,
    And therefore frame your manners to the time.
    Your fellow Tranio here, to save my life,

189. Basta: enough. **202. sith:** since.

Puts my apparel and my countenance on,
And I for my escape have put on his.   220
For in a quarrel since I came ashore,
I killed a man, and fear I was descried.
Wait you on him, I charge you, as becomes,
While I make way from hence to save my life.
You understand me?

BIONDELLO.   I, sir? Ne'er a whit.   225
LUCENTIO.   And not a jot of Tranio in your mouth.
Tranio is changed into Lucentio.

BIONDELLO.   The better for him, would I were so too.
TRANIO.   So could I faith boy, to have the next wish after,
That Lucentio indeed had Baptista's youngest daughter. 230
But, sirrah, not for my sake, but your master's, I advise
You use your manners discreetly in all kind of companies.
When I am alone, why then I am Tranio,
But in all places else, your master Lucentio.

LUCENTIO.   Tranio, let's go.   235
One thing more rests, that thyself execute,
To make one among these wooers. If thou ask me why,
Sufficeth, my reasons are both good and weighty.   *Exeunt.*

[*The* PRESENTERS * *above speak.*]

FIRST SERVANT.   My lord, you nod, you do not mind the play.
SLY.   Yes, by Saint Anne do I. A good matter surely.   240
Comes there any more of it?

PAGE.   My lord, 'tis but begun.
SLY.   'Tis a very excellent piece of work, madam lady.
Would 'twere done.

* **Presenters**: actors who commented on the play for the audience's benefit.

SCENE II. *The same. Before* HORTENSIO'*s house.*

Enter PETRUCHIO *and* GRUMIO.

PETRUCHIO.   Verona, for awhile I take my leave,
To see my friends in Padua; but of all
My best beloved and approved friend,

Hortensio; and I trow° this is his house.

Here, sirrah Grumio, knock I say.   5

GRUMIO. Knock, sir? Whom should I knock? Is there any man has
    rebused° your worship?

PETRUCHIO. Villain, I say, knock me° here soundly.

GRUMIO. Knock you here, sir? Why, sir, what am I, sir, that I should
    knock you here, sir?   10

PETRUCHIO. Villain, I say, knock me at this gate,
    And rap me well, or I'll knock your knave's pate.

GRUMIO. My master is grown quarrelsome. I should knock you first,
    And then I know after who comes by the worst.

PETRUCHIO. Will it not be?   15
    Faith, sirrah, an you'll not knock, I'll ring it,
    I'll try how you can sol, fa,° and sing it.

[Wrings him by the ears.]

GRUMIO. Help, masters, help! My master is mad.

PETRUCHIO. Now knock when I bid you, sirrah villain.

Enter HORTENSIO.

HORTENSIO. How now, what's the matter? My old friend Grumio,   20
    and my good friend Petruchio! How do you all at Verona?

PETRUCHIO. Signior Hortensio, come you to part the fray?
    Con tutto il cuore ben trovato,° may I say.

HORTENSIO. *Alla nostra casa ben venuto, molto honorato signior mio*
    Petruchio.°   25
    Rise, Grumio, rise, we will compound° this quarrel.

GRUMIO. [*Rising*] Nay, 'tis no matter, sir, what he 'leges in Latin. If this
    be not a lawful cause for me to leave his service, look you, sir. He
    bid me knock him, and rap him soundly sir. Well, was it fit for a
    servant to use his master so, being perhaps, for aught I see,   30
    two and thirty, a pip out?
    Whom would to God I had well knocked at first,
    Then had not Grumio come by the worst.

PETRUCHIO. A senseless villain. Good Hortensio,

4. trow: think. 7. rebused: abused. 8. me: for me (a construction frequent in
Elizabethan English). 17. sol, fa: syllables for tones in the musical scale. 23. Con
. . . trovato: With all my heart, well met. 24–25. Alla . . . Petruchio: Welcome
to our house, much honored Signior Petruchio. 26. compound: settle.

I bade the rascal knock upon your gate, 35
And could not get him for my heart to do it.
GRUMIO. Knock at the gate? O heavens! Spake you not these words
plain, sirrah, knock me here; rap me here; knock me well; and
knock me soundly? And come you now with knocking at the
gate? 40
PETRUCHIO. Sirrah, be gone, or talk not, I advise you.
HORTENSIO. Petruchio, patience, I am Grumio's pledge.
Why, this's a heavy chance 'twixt him and you,
Your ancient, trusty, pleasant servant Grumio.
And tell me now, sweet friend, what happy gale 45
Blows you to Padua here, from old Verona?
PETRUCHIO. Such wind as scatters young men through the world,
To seek their fortunes further than at home,
Where small experience grows. But in a few,
Signior Hortensio, thus it stands with me. 50
Antonio, my father is deceased,
And I have thrust myself into this maze,
Haply to wive and thrive, as best I may.
Crowns in my purse I have, and goods at home,
And so am come abroad to see the world. 55
HORTENSIO. Petruchio, shall I then come roundly to thee,
And wish thee to a shrewd° ill-favoured wife?
Thou'dst thank me but a little for my counsel.
And yet I'll promise thee she shall be rich,
And very rich. But thou'rt too much my friend, 60
And I'll not wish thee to her.
PETRUCHIO. Signior Hortensio, 'twixt such friends as we,
Few words suffice; and therefore, if thou know
One rich enough to be Petruchio's wife —
As wealth is burthen of my wooing dance — 65
Be she as foul as was Florentius' love,°
As old as Sibyl,° and as curst and shrewd
As Socrates' Xanthippe,° or a worse,

---

57. **shrewd:** shrewish. 66. **Florentius' love:** In an ancient story, Florentius sought
the answer to the riddle, "What do women most love?" An old hag promised to tell
him if he married her. After their marriage, she became a beautiful woman.
67. **Sibyl:** the Sibyl of Cumae, who was promised by Apollo as many years of life
as the grains of sand she could hold in her hand. 68. **Xanthippe:** wife of Socrates.

She moves me not, or not removes at least
Affection's edge in me, were she as rough   70
As are the swelling Adriatic seas.
I come to wive it wealthily in Padua;
If wealthily, then happily in Padua.

GRUMIO. Nay, look you, sir, he tells you flatly what his mind is. Why
give him gold enough, and marry him to a puppet or an aglet-   75
baby;° or an old trot with ne'er a tooth in her head, though she
have as many diseases as two and fifty horses. Why, nothing comes
amiss, so money comes withal.

HORTENSIO. Petruchio, since we are stepped thus far in,
I will continue that I broached in jest.   80
I can, Petruchio, help thee to a wife
With wealth enough, and young and beauteous,
Brought up as best becomes a gentlewoman.
Her only fault, and that is faults enough,
Is, that she is intolerable curst,   85
And shrewd, and froward, so beyond all measure,
That, were my state far worser than it is,
I would not wed her for a mine of gold.

PETRUCHIO. Hortensio, peace. Thou know'st not gold's effect.
Tell me her father's name, and 'tis enough.   90
For I will board her, though she chide as loud
As thunder, when the clouds in autumn crack.

HORTENSIO. Her father is Baptista Minola,
An affable and courteous gentleman.
Her name is Katharina Minola,   95
Renowned in Padua for her scolding tongue.

PETRUCHIO. I know her father, though I know not her,
And he knew my deceased father well.
I will not sleep, Hortensio, till I see her,
And therefore let me be thus bold with you,   100
To give you over at this first encounter,
Unless you will accompany me thither.

GRUMIO. I pray you, sir, let him go while the humour lasts. O' my word,
an she knew him as well as I do, she would think scolding would
do little good upon him. She may perhaps call him half a   105
score knaves, or so. Why, that's nothing; an he begin once, he'll

75–76. aglet-baby: metal tag at the end of laces for tying hose or stockings.

rail in his rhetricks.° I'll tell you what, sir, an she stand him but
a little, he will throw a figure° in her face, and so disfigure her
with it, that she shall have no more eyes to see withal than a cat.
You know him not, sir.   110

HORTENSIO. Tarry, Petruchio, I must go with thee,
For in Baptista's keep my treasure is.
He hath the jewel of my life in hold,
His youngest daughter, beautiful Bianca,
And her withholds from me and other more,   115
Suitors to her and rivals in my love.
Supposing it a thing impossible,
For those defects I have before rehearsed,
That ever Katharina will be wooed.
Therefore this order hath Baptista ta'en,   120
That none shall have access unto Bianca,
Till Katharine the curst have got a husband.

GRUMIO. Katharine the curst,
A title for a maid, of all titles the worst.

HORTENSIO. Now shall my friend Petruchio do me grace,   125
And offer me, disguised in sober robes,
To old Baptista as a schoolmaster
Well seen in music, to instruct Bianca;
That so I may by this device at least
Have leave and leisure to make love to her,   130
And unsuspected court her by herself.

GRUMIO. Here's no knavery! See, to beguile the old folks, how the
young folks lay their heads together.

Enter GREMIO, *and* LUCENTIO *disguised as* CAMBIO, *a schoolmaster.*

Master, master, look about you. Who goes there, ha?

HORTENSIO. Peace, Grumio, it is the rival of my love.   135
Petruchio, stand by awhile.

GRUMIO. A proper stripling and an amorous.

[They stand aside.]

GREMIO. O very well; I have perused the note.

107. rhetricks: Grumio's mispronunciation of *rhetoric.* 108. figure: He means
figure of speech, name-calling.

Hark you, sir. I'll have them very fairly bound—
All books of love, see that at any hand—   140
And see you read no other lectures to her.
You understand me. Over and beside
Signior Baptista's liberality,
I'll mend it with a largess. Take your paper too,
And let me have them very well perfumed;   145
For she is sweeter than perfume itself,
To whom they go to. What will you read to her?
LUCENTIO.   Whate'er I read to her, I'll plead for you,
As for my patron, stand you so assured,
As firmly as yourself were still in place;   150
Yea, and perhaps with more successful words
Than you—unless you were a scholar, sir.
GREMIO.   O this learning, what a thing it is!
GRUMIO.   [*Aside*] O this woodcock, what an ass it is!
PETRUCHIO.   [*Aside*] Peace, sirrah.   155
HORTENSIO.   Grumio, mum! [*Comes forward*] God save you, Signior
        Gremio.
GREMIO.   And you are well met, Signior Hortensio.
        Trow you whither I am going? To Baptista Minola.
        I promised to enquire carefully
        About a schoolmaster for the fair Bianca,   160
        And by good fortune I have lighted well
        On this young man; for learning and behaviour
        Fit for her turn, well read in poetry
        And other books, good ones, I warrant ye.
HORTENSIO.   'Tis well; and I have met a gentleman   165
        Hath promised me to help me to another,
        A fine musician to instruct our mistress;
        So shall I no whit be behind in duty
        To fair Bianca, so beloved of me.
GREMIO.   Beloved of me, and that my deeds shall prove.   170
GRUMIO.   [*Aside*] And that his bags shall prove.
HORTENSIO.   Gremio, 'tis now no time to vent our love.
        Listen to me, and if you speak me fair,
        I'll tell you news indifferent good for either.
        Here is a gentleman whom by chance I met,   175
        Upon agreement from us to his liking,

Will undertake to woo curst Katharine,
Yea, and to marry her, if her dowry please.
GREMIO. So said, so done, is well.
    Hortensio, have you told him all her faults? 180
PETRUCHIO. I know she is an irksome brawling scold:
    If that be all masters, I hear no harm.
GREMIO. No, sayst me so, friend? What countryman?
PETRUCHIO. Born in Verona, old Antonio's son.
    My father dead, my fortune lives for me, 185
    And I do hope, good days and long to see.
GREMIO. O sir, such a life, with such a wife, were strange.
    But if you have a stomach, to't a God's name,°
    You shall have me assisting you in all.
    But will you woo this wild-cat?
PETRUCHIO.   Will I live? 190
GRUMIO. Will he woo her? Ay, or I'll hang her.
PETRUCHIO. Why came I hither, but to that intent?
    Think you a little din can daunt mine ears?
    Have I not in my time heard lions roar?
    Have I not heard the sea, puffed up with winds, 195
    Rage like an angry boar, chafed with sweat?
    Have I not heard great ordnance in the field,
    And heaven's artillery thunder in the skies?
    Have I not in a pitched battle heard
    Loud 'larums, neighing steeds, and trumpet's clang? 200
    And do you tell me of a woman's tongue,
    That gives not half so great a blow to hear,
    As will a chestnut in a farmer's fire?
    Tush, tush, fear° boys with bugs.
GRUMIO.   For he fears none.
GREMIO. Hortensio, hark. 205
    This gentleman is happily arrived,
    My mind presumes, for his own good, and yours.
HORTENSIO. I promised we would be contributors,
    And bear his charge of wooing whatsoe'er.
GREMIO. And so we will, provided that he win her. 210
GRUMIO. I would I were as sure of a good dinner.

    188. if . . . name: If you have the nerve or courage for it, go to it, in God's name. 204. fear: frighten.

Enter TRANIO *dressed as* LUCENTIO, *and* BIONDELLO.

TRANIO. Gentlemen, God save you. If I may be bold,
    Tell me I beseech you, which is the readiest way
    To th' house of Signior Baptista Minola?
BIONDELLO. He that has the two fair daughters — is't he you mean? 215
TRANIO. Even he, Biondello.
GREMIO. Hark you, sir, you mean not her to —
TRANIO. Perhaps him and her sir, what have you to do?
PETRUCHIO. Not her that chides, sir, at any hand I pray.
TRANIO. I love no chiders, sir. Biondello, let's away. 220
LUCENTIO. [*Aside*] Well begun, Tranio.
HORTENSIO.   Sir, a word ere you go.
    Are you a suitor to the maid you talk of, yea or no?
TRANIO. An if I be, sir, is it any offence?
GREMIO. No; if without more words you will get you hence.
TRANIO. Why, sir, I pray are not the streets as free 225
    For me, as for you?
GREMIO.   But so is not she.
TRANIO. For what reason I beseech you?
GREMIO.   For this reason if you'll know,
    That she's the choice love of Signior Gremio.
HORTENSIO. That she's the chosen of Signior Hortensio.
TRANIO. Softly, my masters! If you be gentlemen, 230
    Do me this right; hear me with patience.
    Baptista is a noble gentleman,
    To whom my father is not all unknown,
    And were his daughter fairer than she is,
    She may more suitors have, and me for one. 235
    Fair Leda's daughter° had a thousand wooers,
    Then well one more may fair Bianca have;
    And so she shall. Lucentio shall make one,
    Though Paris° came, in hope to speed alone.
GREMIO. What, this gentleman will out-talk us all. 240
LUCENTIO. Sir, give him head, I know he'll prove a jade.°
PETRUCHIO. Hortensio, to what end are all these words?
HORTENSIO. Sir, let me be so bold as ask you,

236. **Leda's daughter:** Helen of Troy. 239. **Paris:** prince of Troy, who abducted Helen. 241. **jade:** an old worn-out horse, hence one that will soon tire.

Did you yet ever see Baptista's daughter?

TRANIO.   No, sir, but hear I do that he hath two;   245
    The one as famous for a scolding tongue,
    As is the other, for beauteous modesty.

PETRUCHIO.   Sir, sir, the first's for me, let her go by.

GREMIO.   Yea, leave that labour to great Hercules,
    And let it be more than Alcides' twelve.°   250

PETRUCHIO.   Sir, understand you this of me, in sooth.
    The youngest daughter whom you hearken for,
    Her father keeps from all access of suitors,
    And will not promise her to any man
    Until the elder sister first be wed.   255
    The younger then is free, and not before.

TRANIO.   If it be so, sir, that you are the man
    Must stead us all, and me amongst the rest.
    And if you break the ice, and do this feat,
    Achieve the elder, set the younger free   260
    For our access, whose hap shall be to have her
    Will not so graceless be, to be ingrate.

HORTENSIO.   Sir, you say well, and well you do conceive,
    And since you do profess to be a suitor,
    You must, as we do, gratify this gentleman,   265
    To whom we all rest generally beholding.

TRANIO.   Sir, I shall not be slack; in sign whereof,
    Please ye we may contrive° this afternoon,
    And quaff carouses to our mistress' health,
    And do as adversaries do in law,   270
    Strive mightily, but eat and drink as friends.

GRUMIO *and* BIONDELLO.   O excellent motion! Fellows let's be gone.

HORTENSIO.   The motion's good indeed, and be it so,
    Petruchio, I shall be your ben venuto.°   *Exeunt.*

---

250. **Alcides' twelve:** the twelve heroic labors that Hercules was compelled to
perform. (Alcides is a variation of his name, meaning son of Alcmene.) 268. **contrive:** spend lavishly, waste. 274. **ben venuto:** welcome.

ACT II

Enter KATHARINE, *and* BIANCA *with her hands bound.*

BIANCA. Good sister, wrong me not, nor wrong yourself,
To make a bondmaid and a slave of me —
That I disdain. But for these other gauds,°
Unbind my hands, I'll put them off myself,
Yea, all my raiment, to my petticoat,   5
Or what you will command me, will I do,
So well I know my duty to my elders.
KATHARINE. Of all thy suitors, here I charge thee, tell
Whom thou lov'st best. See thou dissemble not.
BIANCA. Believe me, sister, of all the men alive,   10
I never yet beheld that special face,
Which I could fancy more than any other.
KATHARINE. Minion thou liest. Is't not Hortensio?
BIANCA. If you affect him, sister, here I swear
I'll plead for you myself, but you shall have him.   15
KATHARINE. O then belike you fancy riches more;
You will have Gremio to keep you fair.
BIANCA. Is it for him you do envy me so?
Nay then you jest, and now I well perceive
You have but jested with me all this while.   20
I prithee, sister Kate, untie my hands.
KATHARINE. If that be jest, then all the rest was so.

[*Strikes her.*]

Enter BAPTISTA.

BAPTISTA. Why, how now, dame, whence grows this insolence?
Bianca, stand aside. Poor girl, she weeps.
Go ply thy needle, meddle not with her.   25
For shame thou hilding° of a devilish spirit,
Why dost thou wrong her, that did ne'er wrong thee?
When did she cross thee with a bitter word?
KATHARINE. Her silence flouts me, and I'll be revenged.

3. gauds: trifles (i.e., articles of ornament). **26. hilding:** worthless person.

[*Makes for* BIANCA.]

BAPTISTA. [*Holds her back.*] What, in my sight? Bianca, get thee in.   30
Exit BIANCA.

KATHARINE.   What will you not suffer me? Nay, now I see
She is your treasure, she must have a husband;
I must dance barefoot on her wedding-day,
And for your love to her, lead apes in hell.°
Talk not to me, I will go sit and weep,   35
Till I can find occasion of revenge.   *Exit.*

BAPTISTA.   Was ever gentleman thus grieved as I?

Enter GREMIO, *with* LUCENTIO *as* CAMBIO; PETRUCHIO, *with*
HORTENSIO *as* LICIO *the musician; and* TRANIO *as* LUCENTIO,
with BIONDELLO *bearing a lute and books.*

But who comes here?

GREMIO.   Good morrow, neighbour Baptista.

BAPTISTA.   Good morrow, neighbour Gremio. God save you, gentle-   40
men.

PETRUCHIO.   And you, good sir. Pray have you not a daughter
Called Katharina, fair and virtuous?

BAPTISTA.   I have a daughter, sir, called Katharina.

GREMIO.   You are too blunt, go to it orderly.   45

PETRUCHIO.   You wrong me, Signior Gremio, give me leave.
I am a gentleman of Verona, sir,
That hearing of her beauty, and her wit,
Her affability and bashful modesty,
Her wondrous qualities, and mild behaviour,   50
Am bold to show myself a forward guest
Within your house, to make mine eye the witness
Of that report which I so oft have heard.
And for an entrance to my entertainment,
I do present you with a man of mine,   55

[*Presents* HORTENSIO.]

Cunning in music and the mathematics,
To instruct her fully in those sciences,
Whereof I know she is not ignorant.

34. lead . . . hell: proverbial fate of old maids.

Accept of him, or else you do me wrong.
His name is Licio, born in Mantua. 60
BAPTISTA. You're welcome, sir, and he, for your good sake.
But for my daughter Katharine, this I know,
She is not for your turn, the more my grief.
PETRUCHIO. I see you do not mean to part with her,
Or else you like not of my company. 65
BAPTISTA. Mistake me not, I speak but as I find.
Whence are you, sir? What may I call your name?
PETRUCHIO. Petruchio is my name, Antonio's son,
A man well known throughout all Italy.
BAPTISTA. I knew him well; you are welcome for his sake. 70
GREMIO. Saving your tale, Petruchio, I pray
Let us that are poor petitioners speak too.
Baccare!° You are marvellous forward.
PETRUCHIO. O, pardon me, Signior Gremio, I would fain be doing.
GREMIO. I doubt it not, sir, but you will curse your wooing. 75
Neighbour, this is a gift very grateful, I am sure of it. To express
the like kindness myself, that have been more kindly beholding
to you than any, I freely give unto you this young scholar [*Presents*
LUCENTIO], that hath been long studying at Rheims; as cunning
in Greek, Latin, and other languages, as the other in music 80
and mathematics — his name is Cambio°; pray accept his service.
BAPTISTA. A thousand thanks, Signior Gremio. Welcome good Cambio.
[*To* TRANIO] But, gentle sir, methinks you walk like a stranger.
May I be so bold to know the cause of your coming?
TRANIO. Pardon me, sir, the boldness is mine own, 85
That being a stranger in this city here,
Do make myself a suitor to your daughter,
Unto Bianca, fair and virtuous.
Nor is your firm resolve unknown to me,
In the preferment of the eldest sister. 90
This liberty is all that I request,
That upon knowledge of my parentage,
I may have welcome 'mongst the rest that woo,
And free access and favour as the rest.
And toward the education of your daughters, 95
I here bestow a simple instrument,

73. **Baccare!**: Back! 81. **Cambio**: (Italian) The name means "change."

And this small packet of Greek and Latin books.
If you accept them, then their worth is great.
BAPTISTA.   Lucentio is your name — of whence I pray?
TRANIO.   Of Pisa, sir, son to Vincentio.   100
BAPTISTA.   A mighty man of Pisa; by report
  I know him well. You are very welcome sir.
  [*To* HORTENSIO] Take you the lute, [*To* LUCENTIO] and you the set
  of books.
  You shall go see your pupils presently.
  Holla, within!

Enter a SERVANT.

  Sirrah, lead these gentlemen   105
To my two daughters, and tell them both
These are their tutors; bid them use them well.

Exit SERVANT, *with* HORTENSIO, LUCENTIO, *and* BIONDELLO.

We will go walk a little in the orchard,
And then to dinner. You are passing welcome,
And so I pray you all to think yourselves.   110
PETRUCHIO.   Signior Baptista, my business asketh haste,
  And every day I cannot come to woo.
  You knew my father well, and in him me,
  Left solely heir to all his lands and goods,
  Which I have bettered rather than decreased.   115
  Then tell me, if I get your daughter's love,
  What dowry shall I have with her to wife?
BAPTISTA.   After my death, the one half of my lands,
  And in possession twenty thousand crowns.
PETRUCHIO.   And for that dowry, I'll assure her of   120
  Her widowhood, be it that she survive me,
  In all my lands and leases whatsoever.
  Let specialties° be therefore drawn between us,
  That covenants may be kept on either hand.
BAPTISTA.   Ay, when the special thing is well obtained,   125
  That is, her love; for that is all in all.
PETRUCHIO.   Why that is nothing; for I tell you father,
  I am as peremptory as she proud-minded.

123. specialties: formal contracts.

And where two raging fires meet together,
They do consume the thing that feeds their fury. 130
Though little fire grows great with little wind,
Yet extreme gusts will blow out fire and all.
So I to her, and so she yields to me,
For I am rough, and woo not like a babe.

BAPTISTA. Well mayst thou woo, and happy be thy speed. 135
But be thou armed for some unhappy words.

PETRUCHIO. Ay, to the proof, as mountains are for winds,
That shake not, though they blow perpetually.

Enter HORTENSIO, *with a wounded head.*

BAPTISTA. How now, my friend, why dost thou look so pale?

HORTENSIO. For fear, I promise you, if I look pale. 140

BAPTISTA. What, will my daughter prove a good musician? .

HORTENSIO. I think she'll sooner prove a soldier.
Iron may hold with her, but never lutes.

BAPTISTA. Why then thou canst not break her to the lute?

HORTENSIO. Why, no, for she hath broke the lute to me. 145
I did but tell her she mistook her frets,
And bowed her hand to teach her fingering;
When, with a most impatient devilish spirit,
Frets call you these? quoth she, I'll fume with them.
And with that word she struck me on the head, 150
And through the instrument my pate made way,
And there I stood amazed for a while,
As on a pillory, looking through the lute;
While she did call me rascal fiddler
And twangling Jack, with twenty such vile terms, 155
As had she studied to misuse me so.

PETRUCHIO. Now, by the world, it is a lusty wench.
I love her ten times more than e'er I did.
O how I long to have some chat with her.

BAPTISTA. Well, go with me, and be not so discomfited. 160
Proceed in practice with my younger daughter;
She's apt to learn, and thankful for good turns.
Signior Petruchio, will you go with us,
Or shall I send my daughter Kate to you?

PETRUCHIO. I pray you do. I will attend her here, 165

And woo her with some spirit when she comes.
Say that she rail, why then I'll tell her plain,
She sings as sweetly as a nightingale.
Say that she frown, I'll say she looks as clear
As morning roses newly washed with dew.   170
Say she be mute, and will not speak a word,
Then I'll commend her volubility,
And say she uttereth piercing eloquence.
If she do bid me pack, I'll give her thanks,
As though she bid me stay by her a week.   175
If she deny to wed, I'll crave the day
When I shall ask the banns, and when be married.
But here she comes; and now, Petruchio, speak.

Enter KATHARINE.

Good morrow, Kate, for that's your name I hear.
KATHARINE. Well have you heard, but something hard of hearing;   180
    They call me Katharine, that do talk of me.
PETRUCHIO. You lie in faith, for you are called plain Kate,
    And bonny Kate, and sometimes Kate the curst.
    But Kate, the prettiest Kate in Christendom,
    Kate of Kate-Hall, my super-dainty Kate,   185
    For dainties are all Kates,° and therefore Kate,
    Take this of me, Kate of my consolation —
    Hearing thy mildness praised in every town,
    Thy virtues spoke of, and thy beauty sounded,
    Yet not so deeply as to thee belongs,   190
    Myself am moved to woo thee for my wife.
KATHARINE. Moved? In good time. Let him that moved you hither
    Remove you hence; I knew you at the first
    You were a moveable.
PETRUCHIO.   Why, what's a moveable?
KATHARINE. A joint-stool.
PETRUCHIO.   Thou hast hit it. Come sit on me.   195
KATHARINE. Asses are made to bear, and so are you.
PETRUCHIO. Women are made to bear, and so are you.
KATHARINE. No such jade as you, if me you mean.

186. For . . . Kates: a pun on *cates* (dainties).

PETRUCHIO. Alas, good Kate, I will not burthen thee.
For knowing thee to be but young and light — 200
KATHARINE. Too light for such a swain as you to catch,
And yet as heavy as my weight should be.
PETRUCHIO. Should be? Should — buzz!
KATHARINE.   Well ta'en, and like a buzzard.
PETRUCHIO. O slow-winged turtle, shall a buzzard take thee?
KATHARINE. Ay, for a turtle, as he takes a buzzard. 205
PETRUCHIO. Come, come, you wasp, i' faith you are too angry.
KATHARINE. If I be waspish, best beware my sting.
PETRUCHIO. My remedy is then to pluck it out.
KATHARINE. Ay, if the fool could find it where it lies.
PETRUCHIO. Who knows not where a wasp does wear his sting? 210
In his tail.
KATHARINE.   In his tongue.
PETRUCHIO.   Whose tongue?
KATHARINE. Yours if you talk of tails, and so farewell.
PETRUCHIO. Nay, come again.
Good Kate, I am a gentleman.
KATHARINE.   That I'll try.

[She strikes him.]

PETRUCHIO. I swear I'll cuff you, if you strike again. 215
KATHARINE. So may you lose your arms.
If you strike me, you are no gentleman;
And if no gentleman, why then no arms.°
PETRUCHIO. A herald, Kate? O put me in thy books.
KATHARINE. What is your crest, a coxcomb? 220
PETRUCHIO. A combless cock, so Kate will be my hen.
KATHARINE. No cock of mine, you crow too like a craven.
PETRUCHIO. Nay, come, Kate, come, you must not look so sour.
KATHARINE. It is my fashion when I see a crab.
PETRUCHIO. Why here's no crab, and therefore look not sour. 225
KATHARINE. There is, there is.
PETRUCHIO. Then show it me.
KATHARINE.   Had I a glass, I would.
PETRUCHIO. What, you mean my face?
KATHARINE.   Well aimed of such a young one.

216–18. So . . . arms: This speech puns on the coat of arms of a gentleman.

PETRUCHIO. Now, by Saint George, I am too young for you.

KATHARINE. Yet you are withered.

PETRUCHIO.   'Tis with cares.

KATHARINE.   I care not. 230

PETRUCHIO. Nay hear you, Kate. In sooth you 'scape not so.

KATHARINE. I chafe you if I tarry. Let me go.

PETRUCHIO. No, not a whit; I find you passing gentle.
    'Twas told me you were rough, and coy, and sullen,
    And now I find report a very liar. 235
    For thou art pleasant, gamesome, passing courteous,
    But slow in speech, yet sweet as spring-time flowers.
    Thou canst not frown, thou canst not look askance,
    Nor bite the lip, as angry wenches will;
    Nor hast thou pleasure to be cross in talk. 240
    But thou with mildness entertain'st thy wooers,
    With gentle conference, soft, and affable.
    Why does the world report that Kate doth limp?
    O slanderous world, Kate like a hazel-twig
    Is straight, and slender, and as brown in hue 245
    As hazel-nuts, and sweeter than the kernels.
    O let me see thee walk. Thou dost not halt.

KATHARINE. Go, fool, and whom thou keep'st command.

PETRUCHIO. Did ever Dian° so become a grove
    As Kate this chamber with her princely gait? 250
    O be thou Dian, and let her be Kate;
    And then let Kate be chaste, and Dian sportful.

KATHARINE. Where did you study all this goodly speech?

PETRUCHIO. It is extempore, from my mother-wit.

KATHARINE. A witty mother, witless else her son. 255

PETRUCHIO. Am I not wise?

KATHARINE.   Yes, keep you warm.

PETRUCHIO. Marry so I mean, sweet Katharine, in thy bed.
    And therefore, setting all this chat aside,
    Thus in plain terms — your father hath consented
    That you shall be my wife; your dowry 'greed on; 260
    And will you, nill you, I will marry you.
    Now Kate, I am a husband for your turn,
    For by this light, whereby I see thy beauty,

---

249. **Dian:** Diana, goddess of chastity and of the chase (hunt).

Thy beauty that doth make me like thee well,
Thou must be married to no man but me.   265
For I am he am born to tame you Kate,
And bring you from a wild Kate to a Kate
Conformable as other household Kates.

Enter BAPTISTA, GREMIO, *and* TRANIO.

Here comes your father. Never make denial;
I must, and will have Katharine to my wife.   270
BAPTISTA.   Now, Signior Petruchio, how speed you with my daughter?
PETRUCHIO.   How but well, sir? How but well?
It were impossible I should speed amiss.
BAPTISTA.   Why how now, daughter Katharine? In your dumps?
KATHARINE.   Call you me daughter? Now I promise you,   275
You have showed a tender fatherly regard,
To wish me wed to one half lunatic,
A mad-cap ruffian, and a swearing Jack,
That thinks with oaths to face the matter out.
PETRUCHIO.   Father, 'tis thus — yourself and all the world   280
That talked of her, have talked amiss of her.
If she be curst, it is for policy,
For she's not froward, but modest as the dove.
She is not hot, but temperate as the morn.
For patience she will prove a second Grissel,°   285
And Roman Lucrece° for her chastity.
And to conclude, we have 'greed so well together,
That upon Sunday is the wedding-day.
KATHARINE.   I'll see thee hanged on Sunday first.
GREMIO.   Hark, Petruchio, she says she'll see thee hanged first. 290
TRANIO.   Is this your speeding? Nay then good night our part.
PETRUCHIO.   Be patient, gentlemen, I choose her for myself.
If she and I be pleased, what's that to you?
'Tis bargained 'twixt us twain, being alone,
That she shall still be curst in company.   295
I tell you 'tis incredible to believe
How much she loves me: O the kindest Kate!

285. **Grissel**: allusion to a popular Italian story of the patient Griselda who endured a great deal from her husband. 286. **Lucrece**: a noble Roman who killed herself when her honor had been forcibly violated.

She hung about my neck, and kiss on kiss
She vied so fast, protesting oath on oath,
That in a twink she won me to her love. 300
O you are novices, 'tis a world to see
How tame when men and women are alone,
A meacock° wretch can make the curstest shrew.
Give me thy hand, Kate, I will unto Venice,
To buy apparel 'gainst the wedding-day. 305
Provide the feast father, and bid the guests.
I will be sure my Katharine shall be fine.
BAPTISTA. I know not what to say — but give me your hands.
God send you joy, Petruchio, 'tis a match.
GREMIO *and* TRANIO. Amen, say we; we will be witnesses. 310
PETRUCHIO. Father, and wife, and gentlemen, adieu.
I will to Venice; Sunday comes apace.
We will have rings, and things, and fine array;
[*Sings*] *And kiss me, Kate, we will be married o' Sunday.*

> *Exeunt* PETRUCHIO *and* KATHARINE *severally.**
GREMIO. Was ever match clapped up so suddenly? 315
BAPTISTA. Faith gentlemen, now I play a merchant's part,
And venture madly on a desperate mart.
TRANIO. 'Twas a commodity lay fretting by you.
'Twill bring you gain, or perish on the seas.
BAPTISTA. The gain I seek is, quiet in the match. 320
GREMIO. No doubt but he hath got a quiet catch.
But now, Baptista, to your younger daughter.
Now is the day we long have looked for.
I am your neighbour, and was suitor first.
TRANIO. And I am one that love Bianca more 325
Than words can witness, or your thoughts can guess.
GREMIO. Youngling, thou canst not love so dear as I.
TRANIO. Greybeard, thy love doth freeze.
GREMIO.   But thine doth fry,
Skipper stand back, 'tis age that nourisheth.
TRANIO. But youth in ladies' eyes that flourisheth. 330
BAPTISTA. Content you, gentlemen, I will compound this strife.
'Tis deeds must win the prize, and he of both
That can assure my daughter greatest dower,

303. meacock: cowardly. * severally: by separate exits.

Shall have my Bianca's love.
Say Signior Gremio, what can you assure her?   335
GREMIO. First, as you know, my house within the city,
Is richly furnished with plate and gold,
Basins and ewers, to lave her dainty hands;
My hangings all of Tyrian tapestry;
In ivory coffers I have stuffed my crowns;   340
In cypress chests my arras counterpoints,
Costly apparel, tents, and canopies,
Fine linen, Turkey cushions bossed with pearl,
Valance of Venice gold in needlework;
Pewter and brass, and all things that belong   345
To house or housekeeping. Then at my farm
I have a hundred milch kine to the pail,
Six score fat oxen standing in my stalls,
And all things answerable to this portion.
Myself am struck in years I must confess;   350
And if I die to-morrow this is hers,
If whilst I live she will be only mine.
TRANIO. That only came well in. Sir, list to me.
I am my father's heir and only son.
If I may have your daughter to my wife,   355
I'll leave her houses three or four as good,
Within rich Pisa walls, as any one
Old Signior Gremio has in Padua;
Besides, two thousand ducats by the year
Of fruitful land, all which shall be her jointure.   360
What, have I pinched you, Signior Gremio?
GREMIO. Two thousand ducats by the year of land!
My land amounts but to so much in all.
That she shall have, besides an argosy°
That now is lying in Marseilles' road.   365
What, have I choked you with an argosy?
TRANIO. Gremio, 'tis known my father hath no less
Than three great argosies, besides two galliasses,°
And twelve tight galleys.° These I will assure her,
And twice as much whate'er thou offer'st next.   370

364. argosy: large, richly laden ship. 368. galliasses: fast merchant vessels.
369. galleys: merchant vessels propelled by oars.

GREMIO. Nay, I have offered all, I have no more,
    And she can have no more than all I have.
    If you like me, she shall have me and mine.
TRANIO. Why, then the maid is mine from all the world
    By your firm promise. Gremio is out-vied.   375
BAPTISTA. I must confess your offer is the best,
    And let your father make her the assurance,
    She is your own, else you must pardon me.
    If you should die before him, where's her dower?
TRANIO. That's but a cavil. He is old, I young.   380
GREMIO. And may not young men die as well as old?
BAPTISTA. Well, gentlemen,
    I am thus resolved. On Sunday next, you know
    My daughter Katharine is to be married.
    Now on the Sunday following, shall Bianca   385
    Be bride to you, if you make this assurance;
    If not, to Signior Gremio.
    And so I take my leave, and thank you both.
GREMIO. Adieu, good neighbour.   *Exit* BAPTISTA.
                      Now I fear thee not.
    Sirrah, young gamester, your father were a fool   390
    To give thee all, and in his waning age
    Set foot under thy table. Tut, a toy;
    An old Italian fox is not so kind, my boy.   *Exit.*
TRANIO. A vengeance on your crafty withered hide.
    Yet I have faced it with a card of ten.   395
    'Tis in my head to do my master good.
    I see no reason but supposed Lucentio
    Must get a father, called supposed Vincentio;
    And that's a wonder. Fathers commonly
    Do get their children; but in this case of wooing,   400
    A child shall get a sire, if I fail not of my cunning.   *Exit.*

ACT III

Enter LUCENTIO *as* CAMBIO, HORTENSIO *as* LICIO, *and* BIANCA.

LUCENTIO. Fiddler, forbear; you grow too forward, sir.
　　Have you so soon forgot the entertainment
　　Her sister Katharine welcomed you withal?
HORTENSIO. But, wrangling pedant, this is
　　The patroness of heavenly harmony.　　　　　　　　　　5
　　Then give me leave to have prerogative,
　　And when in music we have spent an hour,
　　Your lecture shall have leisure for as much.
LUCENTIO. Preposterous ass, that never read so far,
　　To know the cause why music was ordained.　　　　　10
　　Was it not to refresh the mind of man
　　After his studies, or his usual pain?
　　Then give me leave to read philosophy,
　　And while I pause, serve in your harmony.
HORTENSIO. Sirrah, I will not bear these braves° of thine.　15
BIANCA. Why, gentlemen, you do me double wrong,
　　To strive for that which resteth in my choice.
　　I am no breeching scholar° in the schools;
　　I'll not be tied to hours, nor 'pointed times,
　　But learn my lessons as I please myself.　　　　　　20
　　And, to cut off all strife, here sit we down.
　　Take you your instrument, play you the whiles,
　　His lecture will be done ere you have tuned.
HORTENSIO. You'll leave his lecture when I am in tune?
LUCENTIO. That will be never. Tune your instrument.　　25

　　　　　　　　　[HORTENSIO *retires.*]

BIANCA. Where left we last?
LUCENTIO. Here, madam.

　　　　　　　　　[*Reads*]
　　Hic ibat Simois, hic est Sigeia tellus,
　　　Hic steterat Priami regia celsa senis.°

15. braves: insults. 18. breeching scholar: student young enough to be whipped.
28–29. Hic . . . senis: a passage from the Roman poet Ovid: "Here ran the
river Simois; here is the land of Sigeia; here stood the high palace of old Priam."

BIANCA. Conster° them. 30

LUCENTIO. *Hic ibat*, as I told you before — *Simois*, I am Lucentio —
hic est, son unto Vincentio of Pisa — *Sigeia tellus*, disguised thus
to get your love — *Hic steterat*, and that Lucentio that comes
a-wooing — *Priami*, is my man Tranio — *regia*, bearing my port°
— *celsa senis*, that we might beguile the old pantaloon. 35

HORTENSIO. [*Comes forward*] Madam, my instrument's in tune.

BIANCA. Let's hear.

[*He plays.*]

O fie, the treble jars.

LUCENTIO. Spit in the hole man,
And tune again.°

BIANCA. Now let me see if I can conster it.
Hic ibat Simois, I know you not — *hic est Sigeia tellus*, I trust 40
you not — *Hic steterat Priami*, take heed he hear us not — *regia*,
presume not — *celsa senis*, despair not.

HORTENSIO. Madam, 'tis now in tune.

LUCENTIO. All but the base.°

HORTENSIO. The base is right, 'tis the base knave that jars.
[*Aside*] How fiery and forward our pedant is. 45
Now for my life the knave doth court my love.
Pedascule,° I'll watch you better yet.

BIANCA. In time I may believe, yet I mistrust.

LUCENTIO. Mistrust it not, for sure Aeacides
Was Ajax, called so from his grandfather.° 50

BIANCA. I must believe my master, else, I promise you,
I shall be arguing still upon that doubt.
But let it rest. Now, Licio, to you.
Good masters, take it not unkindly pray,
That I have been thus pleasant with you both. 55

HORTENSIO. [*To* LUCENTIO] You may go walk, and give me leave awhile.
My lessons make no music in three parts.

---

30. Conster: construe, that is, translate and interpret. (Lucentio's response is, instead, to interline his own wooing.) **34. bearing my port:** carrying himself as if he
were me. **37–38. Spit . . . again:** insulting remark, implying that Hortensio is
playing a mere pipe or flute and not the more genteel lute, a stringed instrument.
43. base: pun on *bass*. **47. Pedascule:** pedant. **49–50. for . . . grandfather:** This
remark is said aloud to deceive Hortensio into thinking that the Latin lesson is still
in progress. (Several of the Greek heroes were descended from Aeacus.)

LUCENTIO. Are you so formal, sir? Well I must wait —
     [*Aside*] And watch withal, for but I be deceived,
     Our fine musician groweth amorous.   60
HORTENSIO. Madam, before you touch the instrument,
     To learn the order of my fingering,
     I must begin with rudiments of art,
     To teach you gamut° in a briefer sort,
     More pleasant, pithy, and effectual,   65
     Than hath been taught by any of my trade.
     And there it is in writing, fairly drawn.
BIANCA. Why, I am past my gamut long ago.
HORTENSIO. Yet read the gamut of Hortensio.
BIANCA. [*Reads*] Gamut *I am, the ground of all accord.*   70
               A re, *to plead Hortensio's passion;*
               B mi, *Bianca, take him for thy lord,*
               C fa ut, *that loves with all affection.*
               D sol re, *one clef, two notes have I;*
               E la mi, *show pity or I die.*   75
     Call you this gamut? Tut I like it not.
     Old fashions please me best; I am not so nice
     To change true rules for odd inventions.

                    Enter a SERVANT.

SERVANT. Mistress, your father prays you leave your books,
     And help to dress your sister's chamber up.   80
     You know to-morrow is the wedding-day.
BIANCA. Farewell, sweet masters both, I must be gone.
                              Exeunt BIANCA *and* SERVANT.
LUCENTIO. Faith, mistress, then I have no cause to stay.   *Exit.*
HORTENSIO. But I have cause to pry into this pedant;
     Methinks he looks as though he were in love.   85
     Yet if thy thoughts, Bianca, be so humble,
     To cast thy wandering eyes on every stale,°
     Seize thee that list. If once I find thee ranging,°
     Hortensio will be quit with thee by changing.   *Exit.*

---

64. **gamut:** the whole series of recognized musical notes. The eight tones of
the major scale are denoted by these syllables: *do* (sometimes *ut*), *re, mi, fa, sol,
la, ti, do* (sometimes *ut*). 87. **stale:** lure, decoy. 88. **ranging:** wandering, straying.

SCENE II. *The same. The Square, before* BAPTISTA'S *house.*

Enter BAPTISTA, GREMIO, TRANIO *as* LUCENTIO, KATHARINE,
BIANCA, LUCENTIO *as* CAMBIO, *and others, with* ATTENDANTS.

BAPTISTA. [*To* TRANIO] Signior Lucentio, this is the 'pointed day
    That Katharine and Petruchio should be married,
    And yet we hear not of our son-in-law.
    What will be said? What mockery will it be,
    To want the bridegroom when the priest attends   5
    To speak the ceremonial rites of marriage.
    What says Lucentio to this shame of ours?
KATHARINE. No shame but mine. I must forsooth be forced
    To give my hand, opposed against my heart,
    Unto a mad-brain rudesby,° full of spleen,   10
    Who wooed in haste, and means to wed at leisure.
    I told you, I, he was a frantic fool,
    Hiding his bitter jests in blunt behaviour;
    And to be noted for a merry man,
    He'll woo as husband, 'point the day of marriage,   15
    Make feast, invite friends, and proclaim the banns,
    Yet never means to wed where he hath wooed.
    Now must the world point at poor Katharine,
    And say, lo, there is mad Petruchio's wife,
    If it would please him come and marry her.   20
TRANIO. Patience, good Katharine, and Baptista too.
    Upon my life Petruchio means but well,
    Whatever fortune stays him from his word.
    Though he be blunt, I know him passing wise;
    Though he be merry, yet withal he's honest.   25
KATHARINE. Would Katharine had never seen him though.
                      Exit weeping, followed by BIANCA *and others.*
BAPTISTA. Go, girl, I cannot blame thee now to weep,
    For such an injury would vex a saint,
    Much more a shrew of thy impatient humour.

Enter BIONDELLO.

BIONDELLO. Master, master, old news! And such news as you never   30
    heard of!

           10. rudesby: unmannerly person, ruffian.

BAPTISTA. Is it new and old too? How may that be?

BIONDELLO. Why, is it not news to hear of Petruchio's coming?

BAPTISTA. Is he come?

BIONDELLO. Why, no, sir. 35

BAPTISTA. What then?

BIONDELLO. He is coming.

BAPTISTA. When will he be here?

BIONDELLO. When he stands where I am, and sees you there.

TRANIO. But say, what to thine old news? 40

BIONDELLO. Why Petruchio is coming, in a new hat and an old jerkin;
a pair of old breeches thrice turned; a pair of boots that have been
candle-cases, one buckled, another laced; an old rusty sword ta'en
out of the town armoury, with a broken hilt, and chapeless;° with
two broken points; his horse hipped — with an old mothy 45
saddle, and stirrups of no kindred — besides, possessed with the
glanders,° and like to mose in the chine;° troubled with the lampass,° infected with the fashions,° full of windgalls, sped with
spavins, rayed with the yellows, past cure of the fives, stark spoiled
with the staggers, begnawn with the bots; swayed in the back, 50
and shoulder-shotten; near-legged before,° and with a half-cheeked
bit, and a headstall of sheep's leather, which being restrained to
keep him from stumbling, hath been often burst, and new-repaired
with knots; one girth six times pieced, and a woman's crupper of
velure, which hath two letters for her name, fairly set down 55
in studs, and here and there pieced with packthread.

BAPTISTA. Who comes with him?

BIONDELLO. O sir, his lackey, for all the world caparisoned like the horse;
with a linen stock° on one leg, and a kersey boot-hose° on the
other, gartered with a red and blue list;° an old hat, and the 60
humour of forty fancies pricked in't for a feather: a monster, a very
monster in apparel, and not like a Christian footboy or a gentleman's lackey.

TRANIO. 'Tis some odd humour pricks him to this fashion.
Yet oftentimes he goes but mean-apparelled. 65

44. chapeless: lacking a sheath. 47. glanders: a disease of horses; mose in the
chine: run at the nostrils. 47–48. lampass: a swelling behind the teeth. 48. fashions:
a skin disease. 48–51. windgalls . . . before: a series of horse ailments, bespeaking
a totally broken-down nag. 59. stock: stocking; kersey boot-hose: overstockings
made of coarse cloth. 60. list: strip of waste material at the end of a piece of
weaving.

BAPTISTA. I am glad he's come, howsoe'er he comes.

BIONDELLO. Why, sir, he comes not.

BAPTISTA. Didst thou not say he comes?

BIONDELLO. Who? That Petruchio came?

BAPTISTA. Ay, that Petruchio came. 70

BIONDELLO. No, sir, I say his horse comes, with him on his back.

BAPTISTA. Why that's all one.

BIONDELLO. [*Sings*] *Nay by Saint Jamy,*
   I hold you a penny,
   A horse and a man 75
   Is more than one,
   And yet not many.

   Enter PETRUCHIO *and* GRUMIO.

PETRUCHIO. Come, where be these gallants? Who's at home?

BAPTISTA. You're welcome, sir.

PETRUCHIO. And yet I come not well. 80

BAPTISTA. And yet you halt not.

TRANIO. Not so well apparelled as I wish you were.

PETRUCHIO. Were it not better I should rush in thus?
  But where is Kate? Where is my lovely bride?
  How does my father? Gentles, methinks you frown. 85
  And wherefore gaze this goodly company,
  As if they saw some wondrous monument,
  Some comet, or unusual prodigy?

BAPTISTA. Why, sir, you know this is your wedding-day.
  First we were sad, fearing you would not come, 90
  Now sadder that you come so unprovided.
  Fie, doff this habit, shame to your estate,
  An eye-sore to our solemn festival.

TRANIO. And tell us what occasion of import
  Hath all so long detained you from your wife, 95
  And sent you hither so unlike yourself?

PETRUCHIO. Tedious it were to tell, and harsh to hear.
  Sufficeth I am come to keep my word,
  Though in some part enforced to digress,
  Which at more leisure I will so excuse, 100
  As you shall well be satisfied withal.
  But where is Kate? I stay too long from her.

The morning wears, 'tis time we were at church.
TRANIO. See not your bride in these unreverent robes.
　　Go to my chamber, put on clothes of mine.　　　　　　105
PETRUCHIO. Not I, believe me. Thus I'll visit her.
BAPTISTA. But thus I trust you will not marry her.
PETRUCHIO. Good sooth even thus. Therefore ha' done with words;
　　To me she's married, not unto my clothes.
　　Could I repair what she will wear in me,　　　　　　110
　　As I can change these poor accoutrements,
　　'Twere well for Kate, and better for myself.
　　But what a fool am I to chat with you,
　　When I should bid good morrow to my bride,
　　And seal the title with a lovely kiss.　　　　　　115
　　　　　　　　　Exeunt PETRUCHIO *and* GRUMIO.
TRANIO. He hath some meaning in his mad attire.
　　We will persuade him, be it possible,
　　To put on better ere he go to church.
BAPTISTA. I'll after him, and see the event of this.
　　　　　　　Exeunt BAPTISTA, GREMIO, *and* ATTENDANTS.
TRANIO. But sir, to love concerneth us to add　　　　　　120
　　Her father's liking, which to bring to pass,
　　As I before imparted to your worship,
　　I am to get a man — whate'er he be,
　　It skills° not much, we'll fit him to our turn —
　　And he shall be Vincentio of Pisa,　　　　　　125
　　And make assurance here in Padua
　　Of greater sums than I have promised.
　　So shall you quietly enjoy your hope,
　　And marry sweet Bianca with consent.
LUCENTIO. Were it not that my fellow-schoolmaster　　　　　　130
　　Doth watch Bianca's steps so narrowly,
　　'Twere good methinks to steal our marriage,
　　Which once performed, let all the world say no,
　　I'll keep mine own despite of all the world.
TRANIO. That by degrees we mean to look into,　　　　　　135
　　And watch our vantage in this business.
　　We'll over-reach the greybeard Gremio,
　　The narrow-prying father Minola,

　　　　　　124. skills: matters.

The quaint musician, amorous Licio;
All for my master's sake, Lucentio.   140

Enter GREMIO.

Signior Gremio, came you from the church?
GREMIO.   As willingly as e'er I came from school.
TRANIO.   And is the bride and bridegroom coming home?
GREMIO.   A bridegroom say you? 'Tis a groom indeed,
A grumbling groom, and that the girl shall find.   145
TRANIO.   Curster than she? Why 'tis impossible.
GREMIO.   Why he's a devil, a devil, a very fiend.
TRANIO.   Why she's a devil, a devil, the devil's dam.
GREMIO.   Tut, she's a lamb, a dove, a fool to him.
I'll tell you, Sir Lucentio — when the priest   150
Should ask if Katharine should be his wife,
Ay, by gogs-wouns,° quoth he, and swore so loud,
That all amazed the priest let fall the book,
And as he stooped again to take it up,
This mad-brained bridegroom took him such a cuff,   155
That down fell priest and book, and book and priest.
Now take them up quoth he, if any list.°
TRANIO.   What said the wench when he rose again?
GREMIO.   Trembled and shook. For why, he stamped and swore,
As if the vicar meant to cozen° him.   160
But after many ceremonies done,
He calls for wine. A health quoth he, as if
He had been aboard, carousing to his mates
After a storm; quaffed off the muscadel,
And threw the sops all in the sexton's face;   165
Having no other reason,
But that his beard grew thin and hungerly,
And seemed to ask him sops as he was drinking.
This done, he took the bride about the neck,
And kissed her lips with such a clamorous smack,   170
That at the parting all the church did echo.
And I seeing this, came thence for very shame;
And after me I know the rout is coming.

152. gogs-wouns: euphemism for "God's wounds." **157. list:** care. **160. cozen:**
cheat.

Such a mad marriage never was before.
Hark, hark, I hear the minstrels play.   175

Enter minstrels playing, cross the stage, and exeunt. Enter
PETRUCHIO, KATHARINE, BIANCA, BAPTISTA, HORTENSIO, GRUMIO,
and ATTENDANTS.

PETRUCHIO. Gentlemen and friends, I thank you for your pains.
    I know you think to dine with me to-day,
    And have prepared great store of wedding cheer.
    But so it is, my haste doth call me hence,
    And therefore here I mean to take my leave.   180
BAPTISTA. Is't possible you will away to-night?
PETRUCHIO. I must away to-day before night come.
    Make it no wonder. If you knew my business,
    You would entreat me rather go than stay.
    And, honest company, I thank you all,   185
    That have beheld me give away myself
    To this most patient, sweet, and virtuous wife.
    Dine with my father, drink a health to me,
    For I must hence; and farewell to you all.
TRANIO. Let us entreat you stay till after dinner.   190
PETRUCHIO. It may not be.
GREMIO.   Let me entreat you.
PETRUCHIO. It cannot be.
KATHARINE.   Let me entreat you.
PETRUCHIO. I am content.
KATHARINE.   Are you content to stay?
PETRUCHIO. I am content you shall entreat me stay,
    But yet not stay, entreat me how you can.   195
KATHARINE. Now, if you love me, stay.
PETRUCHIO.   Grumio, my horse.
GRUMIO. Ay, sir, they be ready, the oats have eaten the horses.
KATHARINE. Nay, then,
    Do what thou canst, I will not go to-day,
    No, nor to-morrow — not till I please myself.   200
    The door is open sir, there lies your way;
    You may be jogging whiles your boots are green.
    For me, I'll not be gone till I please myself.

       'Tis like you'll prove a jolly surly groom,
       That take it on you at the first so roundly. 205
PETRUCHIO. O Kate, content thee, prithee be not angry.
KATHARINE. I will be angry, what hast thou to do?
       Father, be quiet, he shall stay my leisure.
GREMIO. Ay marry sir, now it begins to work.
KATHARINE. Gentlemen, forward to the bridal dinner. 210
       I see a woman may be made a fool,
       If she had not a spirit to resist.
PETRUCHIO. They shall go forward, Kate, at thy command.
       Obey the bride, you that attend on her.
       Go to the feast, revel and domineer, 215
       Carouse full measure to her maidenhead,
       Be mad and merry, or go hang yourselves.
       But for my bonny Kate, she must with me.
       Nay, look not big, nor stamp, nor stare, nor fret;
       I will be master of what is mine own. 220
       She is my goods, my chattels; she is my house,
       My household stuff, my field, my barn,
       My horse, my ox, my ass, my any thing.
       And here she stands, touch her whoever dare.
       I'll bring mine action on the proudest he 225
       That stops my way in Padua. Grumio,
       Draw forth thy weapon, we are beset with thieves.
       Rescue thy mistress if thou be a man.
       Fear not, sweet wench, they shall not touch thee, Kate.
       I'll buckler thee against a million. 230
                Exeunt PETRUCHIO, KATHARINE, *and* GRUMIO.
BAPTISTA. Nay, let them go, a couple of quiet ones.
GREMIO. Went they not quickly, I should die with laughing.
TRANIO. Of all mad matches never was the like.
LUCENTIO. Mistress, what's your opinion of your sister?
BIANCA. That being mad herself, she's madly mated. 235
GREMIO. I warrant him Petruchio is Kated.
BAPTISTA. Neighbours and friends, though bride and bridegroom wants
       For to supply the places at the table,
       You know there wants no junkets° at the feast.

           239. junkets: delicacies.

Lucentio, you shall supply the bridegroom's place, 240
And let Bianca take her sister's room.

TRANIO. Shall sweet Bianca practise how to bride it?

BAPTISTA. She shall, Lucentio. Come gentlemen, let's go. *Exeunt.*

ACT IV

SCENE I. PETRUCHIO's *country house.*

Enter GRUMIO.

GRUMIO. Fie, fie on all tired jades, on all mad masters, and all foul ways!
Was ever man so beaten? Was ever man so rayed? Was ever man
so weary? I am sent before to make a fire, and they are coming after
to warm them. Now were not I a little pot, and soon hot, my very
lips might freeze to my teeth, my tongue to the roof of my 5
mouth, my heart in my belly, ere I should come by a fire to thaw
me; but I with blowing the fire shall warm myself, for considering
the weather, a taller man than I will take cold. Holla, ho! Curtis!

Enter CURTIS.

CURTIS. Who is that calls so coldly?

GRUMIO. A piece of ice. If thou doubt it, thou mayst slide from my 10
shoulder to my heel, with no greater a run but my head and my
neck. A fire, good Curtis.

CURTIS. Is my master and his wife coming, Grumio?

GRUMIO. O ay, Curtis, ay, and therefore fire, fire; cast on no water.

CURTIS. Is she so hot a shrew as she's reported? 15

GRUMIO. She was, good Curtis, before this frost. But thou know'st winter
tames man, woman and beast; for it hath tamed my old master,
and my new mistress, and myself, fellow Curtis.

CURTIS. I prithee, good Grumio, tell me, how goes the world?

GRUMIO. A cold world Curtis in every office but thine, and therefore 20
fire. Do thy duty, and have thy duty, for my master and mistress
are almost frozen to death.

CURTIS. There's fire ready, and therefore, good Grumio, the news?

GRUMIO. Why [*Sings*] *Jack boy, ho boy* — and as much news as thou
  wilt.   25
CURTIS. Come, you are so full of cony-catching.°
GRUMIO. Why, therefore fire, for I have caught extreme cold. Where's the
  cook? Is supper ready, the house trimmed, rushes strewed, cobwebs
  swept, the serving men in their new fustian, their white stockings,
  and every officer his wedding garment on? Be the Jacks fair   30
  within, the Jills fair without, the carpets laid, and everything in
  order?
CURTIS. All ready; and therefore I pray thee, news.
GRUMIO. First, know my horse is tired, my master and mistress fallen out.
CURTIS. How?   35
GRUMIO. Out of their saddles into the dirt, and thereby hangs a tale.
CURTIS. Let's ha't, good Grumio.
GRUMIO. Lend thine ear.
CURTIS. Here.
GRUMIO. There.   40

[Cuffs him.]

CURTIS. This 'tis to feel a tale, not to hear a tale.
GRUMIO. And therefore 'tis called a sensible tale; and this cuff was but to
  knock at your ear, and beseech listening. Now I begin, imprimis°
  we came down a foul hill, my master riding behind my mistress —
CURTIS. Both of one horse?   45
GRUMIO. What's that to thee?
CURTIS. Why, a horse.
GRUMIO. Tell thou the tale — but hadst thou not crossed me, thou shouldst
  have heard how her horse fell, and she under her horse; thou
  shouldst have heard in how miry a place; how she was be- 50
  moiled, how he left her with the horse upon her, how he beat me
  because her horse stumbled, how she waded through the dirt to
  pluck him off me; how he swore, how she prayed, that never
  prayed before; how I cried, how the horses ran away, how her
  bridle was burst; how I lost my crupper, with many things of 55
  worthy memory, which now shall die in oblivion, and thou return
  unexperienced to thy grave.
CURTIS. By this reck'ning, he is more shrew than she.
GRUMIO. Ay, and that thou and the proudest of you all shall find when

26. cony-catching: cheating. 43. imprimis: firstly.

he comes home. But what talk I of this? Call forth Nathaniel, 60
Joseph, Nicholas, Philip, Walter, Sugarsop and the rest. Let their
heads be slickly combed, their blue coats brushed, and their garters
of an indifferent knit. Let them curtsy with their left legs, and not
presume to touch a hair of my master's horse-tail, till they kiss their
hands. Are they all ready? 65

CURTIS. They are.

GRUMIO. Call them forth.

CURTIS. Do you hear, ho? You must meet my master to countenance my
mistress.

GRUMIO. Why she hath a face of her own. 70

CURTIS. Who knows not that?

GRUMIO. Thou it seems, that calls for company to countenance her.

CURTIS. I call them forth to credit her.

GRUMIO. Why she comes to borrow nothing of them.

Enter SERVANTS.

NATHANIEL. Welcome home, Grumio. 75

PHILIP. How now, Grumio.

JOSEPH. What, Grumio.

NICHOLAS. Fellow Grumio.

NATHANIEL. How now, old lad.

GRUMIO. Welcome you — how now you — what you — fellow you — 80
and thus much for greeting. Now my spruce companions, is all
ready, and all things neat?

NATHANIEL. All things is ready. How near is our master?

GRUMIO. E'en at hand, alighted by this. And therefore be not — Cock's
passion, silence, I hear my master. 85

Enter PETRUCHIO *and* KATHARINE.

PETRUCHIO. Where be these knaves? What, no man at door
  To hold my stirrup, nor to take my horse?
  Where is Nathaniel, Gregory, Philip?

ALL SERVANTS. Here, here sir, here sir.

PETRUCHIO. Here sir, here sir, here sir, here sir! 90
  You logger-headed and unpolished grooms.
  What, no attendance? No regard? No duty?
  Where is the foolish knave I sent before?

GRUMIO. Here sir, as foolish as I was before.

PETRUCHIO. You peasant swain, you whoreson malt-horse drudge!   95
    Did I not bid thee meet me in the park,
    And bring along these rascal knaves with thee?
GRUMIO. Nathaniel's coat, sir, was not fully made,
    And Gabriel's pumps were all unpinked° i' th' heel.
    There was no link to colour Peter's hat,   100
    And Walter's dagger was not come from sheathing.
    There were none fine, but Adam, Rafe, and Gregory;
    The rest were ragged, old, and beggarly,
    Yet as they are, here are they come to meet you.
PETRUCHIO. Go rascals, go, and fetch my supper in.   105

                                    Exeunt SERVANTS.

    [*Sings*] *Where is the life that late I led?*
    Where are those — Sit down, Kate, and welcome.
    Food, food, food, food!

                Enter SERVANTS *with supper.*

    Why, when I say? Nay, good sweet Kate, be merry.
    Off with my boots, you rogues. You villains, when?   110
    [*Sings*] *It was the friar of orders gray,*
        As he forth walked on his way —
    Out you rogue, you pluck my foot awry.
    Take that, and mend the plucking off the other.

                        [*Strikes him.*]

    Be merry, Kate. Some water here. What ho!   115

                Enter SERVANT *with water.*

    Where's my spaniel Troilus? Sirrah, get you hence,
    And bid my cousin Ferdinand come hither.   *Exit another* SERVANT.
    One, Kate, that you must kiss, and be acquainted with.
    Where are my slippers? Shall I have some water?
    Come, Kate, and wash, and welcome heartily.   120
    You whoreson villain, will you let it fall?

                        [*Strikes him.*]

KATHARINE. Patience, I pray you, 'twas a fault unwilling.

        99. unpinked: not pierced by eyelet holes (hence, unready).

PETRUCHIO.   A whoreson beetle-headed, flap-eared knave!
        Come, Kate, sit down, I know you have a stomach.°
        Will you give thanks, sweet Kate, or else shall I?   125
        What's this, mutton?
FIRST SERVANT.   Ay.
PETRUCHIO.   Who brought it?
PETER.   I.
PETRUCHIO.   'Tis burnt, and so is all the meat.
        What dogs are these! Where is the rascal cook?
        How durst you villains bring it from the dresser,
        And serve it thus to me that love it not?   130
        There, take it to you, trenchers, cups, and all.

                    [*Throws the meat, etc., at them.*]

        You heedless joltheads and unmannered slaves!
        What, do you grumble? I'll be with you straight.
                                Exeunt SERVANTS *pursued by* PETRUCHIO.
KATHARINE.   I pray you, husband, be not so disquiet.
        The meat was well, if you were so contented.   135
PETRUCHIO.   I tell thee, Kate, 'twas burnt and dried away,
        And I expressly am forbid to touch it,
        For it engenders choler,° planteth anger;
        And better 'twere that both of us did fast,
        Since of ourselves, ourselves are choleric,   140
        Than feed it with such over-roasted flesh.
        Be patient, to-morrow't shall be mended,
        And for this night we'll fast for company.
        Come I will bring thee to thy bridal chamber.   *Exeunt.*

                    Enter SERVANTS *severally.*

NATHANIEL.   Peter, didst ever see the like?   145
PETER.   He kills her in her own humour.

                    Enter CURTIS.

GRUMIO.   Where is he?

    124. stomach: He makes a pun on *stomach* as indicating pride and anger.
138. choler: hastiness of temper.

CURTIS.   In her chamber,
         Making a sermon of continency to her;
         And rails, and swears, and rates, that she, poor soul,   150
         Knows not which way to stand, to look, to speak,
         And sits as one new risen from a dream.
         Away, away, for he is coming hither.   *Exeunt.*

                         Enter PETRUCHIO.

PETRUCHIO.   Thus have I politicly begun my reign,
         And 'tis my hope to end successfully.   155
         My falcon now is sharp, and passing empty,
         And till she stoop,° she must not be full-gorged,
         For then she never looks upon her lure.°
         Another way I have to man my haggard,°
         To make her come, and know her keeper's call.   160
         That is, to watch her, as we watch these kites,°
         That bate, and beat,° and will not be obedient.
         She eat no meat to-day, nor none shall eat.
         Last night she slept not, nor to-night she shall not.
         As with the meat, some undeserved fault   165
         I'll find about the making of the bed;
         And here I'll fling the pillow, there the bolster,
         This way the coverlet, another way the sheets.
         Ay, and amid this hurly I intend
         That all is done in reverent care of her;   170
         And in conclusion, she shall watch all night,
         And if she chance to nod, I'll rail and brawl,
         And with the clamour keep her still awake.
         This is a way to kill a wife with kindness,
         And thus I'll curb her mad and headstrong humour.   175
         He that knows better how to tame a shrew,
         Now let him speak, 'tis charity to shew.   *Exit.*

   157. **stoop:** swoop down on her prey. 158. **lure:** artificial prey or bait used in
training a hawk. 159. **man my haggard:** tame my haggard. (A haggard is a mature wild hawk, more difficult to tame than one captured while a nestling.)
161. **kites:** a small, inferior kind of hawk. 162. **bate, and beat:** flap and beat (their
wings).

Enter TRANIO *as* LUCENTIO, *and* HORTENSIO *as* LICIO.

TRANIO. Is't possible friend, Licio, that Mistress Bianca
Doth fancy any other but Lucentio?
I tell you sir, she bears me fair in hand.
HORTENSIO. Sir, to satisfy you in what I have said,
Stand by, and mark the manner of his teaching.   5

[They stand aside.]

Enter BIANCA *and* LUCENTIO *as* CAMBIO.

LUCENTIO. Now, mistress, profit you in what you read?
BIANCA. What, master, read you? First resolve me that.
LUCENTIO. I read that I profess, the Art to Love.
BIANCA. And may you prove, sir, master of your art.
LUCENTIO. While you, sweet dear, prove mistress of my heart.   10

[They retire.]

HORTENSIO. Quick proceeders,° marry! Now tell me I pray,
You that durst swear that your mistress Bianca
Loved none in the world so well as Lucentio.
TRANIO. O despiteful love, unconstant womankind!
I tell thee, Licio, this is wonderful.   15
HORTENSIO. Mistake no more, I am not Licio,
Nor a musician, as I seem to be,
But one that scorn to live in this disguise,
For such a one as leaves a gentleman,
And makes a god of such a cullion.°   20
Know, sir, that I am called Hortensio.
TRANIO. Signior Hortensio, I have often heard
Of your entire affection to Bianca,
And since mine eyes are witness of her lightness,
I will with you, if you be so contented,   25
Forswear Bianca and her love for ever.
HORTENSIO. See how they kiss and court. Signior Lucentio,
Here is my hand, and here I firmly vow

11. **proceeders:** students. (In English academic usage they are said to "proceed"
to a degree.) 20. **cullion:** a low wretch.

Never to woo her more, but do forswear her,
As one unworthy all the former favours   30
That I have fondly flattered her withal.
TRANIO.   And here I take the like unfeigned oath,
Never to marry with her, though she would entreat.
Fie on her! See how beastly she doth court him.
HORTENSIO.   Would all the world but he had quite forsworn.   35
For me, that I may surely keep mine oath,
I will be married to a wealthy widow,
Ere three days pass, which hath as long loved me
As I have loved this proud disdainful haggard.
And so farewell, Signior Lucentio.   40
Kindness in women, not their beauteous looks,
Shall win my love — and so, I take my leave,
In resolution as I swore before.   *Exit* HORTENSIO.

LUCENTIO *and* BIANCA *advance.*

TRANIO.   Mistress Bianca, bless you with such grace,
As 'longeth to a lover's blessed case.   45
Nay, I have ta'en you napping gentle love,
And have forsworn you, with Hortensio.
BIANCA.   Tranio, you jest, but have you both forsworn me?
TRANIO.   Mistress, we have.
LUCENTIO.   Then we are rid of Licio.
TRANIO.   I' faith, he'll have a lusty widow now,   50
That shall be wooed and wedded in a day.
BIANCA.   God give him joy.
TRANIO.   Ay, and he'll tame her.
BIANCA.   He says so, Tranio.
TRANIO.   Faith he is gone unto the taming school.
BIANCA.   The taming school? What, is there such a place?   55
TRANIO.   Ay, mistress, and Petruchio is the master,
That teacheth tricks eleven and twenty long,
To tame a shrew, and charm her chattering tongue.

Enter BIONDELLO.

BIONDELLO.   O master, master, I have watched so long,
That I am dog-weary, but at last I spied   60

An ancient angel° coming down the hill,
Will serve the turn.
TRANIO.   What is he Biondello?
BIONDELLO. Master, a mercatant,° or a pedant,
  I know not what, but formal in apparel,
  In gait and countenance surly like a father.   65
LUCENTIO. And what of him, Tranio?
TRANIO. If he be credulous, and trust my tale,
  I'll make him glad to seem Vincentio,
  And give assurance to Baptista Minola,
  As if he were the right Vincentio.   70
  Take in your love, and then let me alone.

                          Exeunt LUCENTIO *and* BIANCA.

                    Enter PEDANT.

PEDANT. God save you, sir.
TRANIO.   And you, sir, you are welcome.
  Travel you far on, or are you at the furthest?
PEDANT. Sir, at the furthest for a week or two,
  But then up further, and as far as Rome,   75
  And so to Tripoli, if God lend me life.
TRANIO. What countryman, I pray?
PEDANT.   Of Mantua.
TRANIO. Of Mantua, sir? Marry, God forbid!
  And come to Padua, careless of your life?
PEDANT. My life, sir? How, I pray? For that goes hard.   80
TRANIO. 'Tis death for any one in Mantua
  To come to Padua — know you not the cause?
  Your ships are stayed at Venice, and the Duke,
  For private quarrel 'twixt your Duke and him,
  Hath published and proclaimed it openly.   85
  'Tis marvel, but that you are but newly come,
  You might have heard it else proclaimed about.
PEDANT. Alas, sir, it is worse for me than so,
  For I have bills for money by exchange
  From Florence, and must here deliver them.   90
TRANIO. Well, sir, to do you courtesy,

  61. angel: that is, messenger from Heaven. **63. mercatant:** merchant.

This will I do, and this I will advise you —
First, tell me, have you ever been at Pisa?
PEDANT.   Ay, sir, in Pisa have I often been,
      Pisa renowned for grave citizens.   95
TRANIO.   Among them know you one Vincentio?
PEDANT.   I know him not, but I have heard of him.
      A merchant of incomparable wealth.
TRANIO.   He is my father, sir, and sooth to say,
      In countenance somewhat doth resemble you.   100
BIONDELLO.   [Aside] As much as an apple doth an oyster, and all one.
TRANIO.   To save your life in this extremity,
      This favour will I do you for his sake,
      And think it not the worst of all your fortunes,
      That you are like to Sir Vincentio.   105
      His name and credit shall you undertake,
      And in my house you shall be friendly lodged.
      Look that you take upon you as you should.
      You understand me, sir — so shall you stay
      Till you have done your business in the city.   110
      If this be courtesy, sir, accept of it.
PEDANT.   O sir, I do, and will repute you ever
      The patron of my life and liberty.
TRANIO.   Then go with me, to make the matter good.
      This by the way I let you understand,   115
      My father is here looked for every day,
      To pass assurance of a dower in marriage
      'Twixt me and one Baptista's daughter here.
      In all these circumstances I'll instruct you.
      Go with me, sir, to clothe you as becomes you.   *Exeunt.*   120

SCENE III. *A room in* PETRUCHIO's *house*.

Enter KATHARINE *and* GRUMIO.

GRUMIO.   No, no, forsooth, I dare not for my life.
KATHARINE.   The more my wrong, the more his spite appears.
      What, did he marry me to famish me?
      Beggars that come unto my father's door,
      Upon entreaty have a present alms;   5

If not, elsewhere they meet with charity.
But I, who never knew how to entreat,
Nor never needed that I should entreat,
Am starved for meat, giddy for lack of sleep;
With oaths kept waking, and with brawling fed;   10
And that which spites me more than all these wants,
He does it under name of perfect love;
As who should say, if I should sleep or eat,
'Twere deadly sickness or else present death.
I prithee go, and get me some repast,   15
I care not what, so it be wholesome food.

GRUMIO. What say you to a neat's foot?°
KATHARINE. 'Tis passing good, I prithee let me have it.
GRUMIO. I fear it is too choleric a meat.
   How say you to a fat tripe finely broiled?   20
KATHARINE. I like it well, good Grumio, fetch it me.
GRUMIO. I cannot tell, I fear 'tis choleric.
   What say you to a piece of beef and mustard?
KATHARINE. A dish that I do love to feed upon.
GRUMIO. Ay, but the mustard is too hot a little.   25
KATHARINE. Why then the beef, and let the mustard rest.
GRUMIO. Nay then I will not, you shall have the mustard,
   Or else you get no beef of Grumio.
KATHARINE. Then both, or one, or any thing thou wilt.
GRUMIO. Why then the mustard without the beef.   30
KATHARINE. Go get thee gone, thou false deluding slave,

                        [*Beats him.*]

   That feed'st me with the very name of meat.
   Sorrow on thee, and all the pack of you
   That triumph thus upon my misery.
   Go get thee gone, I say.   35

          Enter PETRUCHIO *and* HORTENSIO *with meat.*

PETRUCHIO. How fares my Kate? What, sweeting, all amort?°
HORTENSIO. Mistress, what cheer?
KATHARINE.   Faith as cold as can be.

   17. **neat's foot:** calf's foot. 36. **amort:** sick to death, dejected.

PETRUCHIO. Pluck up thy spirits, look cheerfully upon me,
    Here love, thou seest how diligent I am,
    To dress thy meat myself, and bring it thee: 40
    I am sure, sweet Kate, this kindness merits thanks.
    What, not a word? Nay then, thou lov'st it not.
    And all my pains is sorted to no proof.
    Here, take away this dish.
KATHARINE.   I pray you let it stand.
PETRUCHIO. The poorest service is repaid with thanks,   45
    And so shall mine before you touch the meat.
KATHARINE. I thank you, sir.
HORTENSIO. Signior Petruchio, fie, you are to blame.
    Come Mistress Kate, I'll bear you company.
PETRUCHIO. [*Aside to* HORTENSIO] Eat it up all, Hortensio, if thou lov'st me.
    [*To* KATHARINE] Much good do it unto thy gentle heart.   51
    Kate, eat apace. And now my honey love,
    Will we return unto thy father's house,
    And revel it as bravely as the best,
    With silken coats and caps, and golden rings,   55
    With ruffs and cuffs, and farthingales, and things;
    With scarfs, and fans, and double change of bravery,
    With amber bracelets, beads, and all this knavery.
    What, hast thou dined? The tailor stays thy leisure,
    To deck thy body with his ruffling treasure.   60

Enter TAILOR.

Come, tailor, let us see these ornaments.
Lay forth the gown.

Enter HABERDASHER.

             What news with you, sir?
HABERDASHER. Here is the cap your worship did bespeak.
PETRUCHIO. Why, this was moulded on a porringer;
    A velvet dish. Fie, fie, 'tis lewd and filthy,   65
    Why 'tis a cockle or a walnut-shell,
    A knack, a toy, a trick, a baby's cap.
    Away with it, come, let me have a bigger.
KATHARINE. I'll have no bigger. This doth fit the time,
    And gentlewomen wear such caps as these.   70

PETRUCHIO. When you are gentle, you shall have one too,
And not till then.
HORTENSIO. [*Aside*]   That will not be in haste.
KATHARINE. Why, sir, I trust I may have leave to speak,
And speak I will. I am no child, no babe;
Your betters have endured me say my mind,   75
And if you cannot, best you stop your ears.
My tongue will tell the anger of my heart,
Or else my heart, concealing it, will break,
And rather than it shall, I will be free
Even to the uttermost as I please in words.   80
PETRUCHIO. Why, thou sayst true, it is a paltry cap,
A custard-coffin, a bauble, a silken pie.
I love thee well in that thou lik'st it not.
KATHARINE. Love me or love me not, I like the cap,
And it I will have, or I will have none.   85
PETRUCHIO. Thy gown? Why ay — come tailor let us see't.
O mercy God, what masking stuff is here?
What's this? A sleeve? 'Tis like a demi-cannon.
What, up and down carved like an apple tart?
Here's snip, and nip, and cut, and slish and slash,   90
Like to a censer in a barber's shop.
Why what a devil's name, tailor, call'st thou this?
HORTENSIO. [*Aside*] I see she's like to have neither cap nor gown.
TAILOR. You bid me make it orderly and well,
According to the fashion, and the time.   95
PETRUCHIO. Marry, and did. But if you be remembered,
I did not bid you mar it to the time.
Go hop me over every kennel home,
For you shall hop without my custom sir.
I'll none of it. Hence, make your best of it.   100
KATHARINE. I never saw a better-fashioned gown,
More quaint, more pleasing, nor more commendable.
Belike you mean to make a puppet of me.
PETRUCHIO. Why, true, he means to make a puppet of thee.
TAILOR. She says your worship means to make a puppet of her.   105
PETRUCHIO. O monstrous arrogance! Thou liest, thou thread, thou thimble,
Thou yard, three-quarters, half-yard, quarter, nail,

Thou flea, thou nit, thou winter-cricket° thou!
Braved in mine own house with a skein of thread?
Away thou rag, thou quantity, thou remnant,   110
Or I shall so be-mete° thee with thy yard,
As thou shalt think on prating whilst thou livest.
I tell thee I, that thou hast marred her gown.

TAILOR.   Your worship is deceived, the gown is made
Just as my master had direction.   115
Grumio gave order how it should be done.

GRUMIO.   I gave him no order; I gave him the stuff.

TAILOR.   But how did you desire it should be made?

GRUMIO.   Marry, sir with needle and thread.

TAILOR.   But did you not request to have it cut?   120

GRUMIO.   Thou hast faced° many things.

TAILOR.   I have.

GRUMIO.   Face not me. Thou hast braved many men, brave not me; I
will neither be faced nor braved. I say unto thee, I bid thy master
cut out the gown, but I did not bid him cut it to pieces. Ergo,   125
thou liest.

TAILOR.   Why here is the note of the fashion to testify.

PETRUCHIO.   Read it.

GRUMIO.   The note lies in's throat if he say I said so.

TAILOR.   [Reads] Imprimis, a loose-bodied gown —   130

GRUMIO.   Master, if ever I said loose-bodied gown, sew me in the skirts
of it, and beat me to death with a bottom of brown thread. I said
a gown.

PETRUCHIO.   Proceed.

TAILOR.   With a small compassed cape.   135

GRUMIO.   I confess the cape.

TAILOR.   With a trunk sleeve.

GRUMIO.   I confess two sleeves.

TAILOR.   The sleeves curiously cut.

PETRUCHIO.   Ay, there's the villainy.   140

GRUMIO.   Error i' th' bill sir, error i' th' bill. I commanded the sleeves
should be cut out, and sewed up again, and that I'll prove upon
thee, though thy little finger be armed in a thimble.

108. winter-cricket: i.e., starved and shriveled. 111. be-mete: measure; i.e., beat
you with your yardstick. 121. faced: a pun upon the word *face: facing*, a garment
with a lining of decorations, and *facing* or meeting a danger.

TAILOR.   This is true that I say, an I had thee in place where, thou shouldst
　　know it.　　　　　　　　　　　　　　　　　　　　　　　　145

GRUMIO.   I am for thee straight. Take thou the bill, give me thy mete-
　　yard, and spare not me.

HORTENSIO.   God-a-mercy, Grumio, then he shall have no odds.

PETRUCHIO.   Well, sir, in brief, the gown is not for me.

GRUMIO.   You are i' th' right, sir, 'tis for my mistress.　　　　150

PETRUCHIO.   Go take it up unto thy master's use.

GRUMIO.   Villain, not for thy life. Take up my mistress' gown for thy
　　master's use!

PETRUCHIO.   Why, sir, what's your conceit in that?

GRUMIO.   O sir, the conceit is deeper than you think for.　　　155
　　Take up my mistress' gown to his master's use!
　　O fie, fie, fie!

PETRUCHIO.   [*Aside to* HORTENSIO] Hortensio, say thou wilt see the tailor
　　paid.
　　[*To* TAILOR] Go take it hence; be gone, and say no more.

HORTENSIO.   Tailor, I'll pay thee for thy gown to-morrow.　　　160
　　Take no unkindness of his hasty words.
　　Away, I say, commend me to thy master.

　　　　　　　　　　　　　　　　Exeunt TAILOR *and* HABERDASHER.

PETRUCHIO.   Well, come, my Kate, we will unto your father's,
　　Even in these honest mean habiliments.
　　Our purses shall be proud, our garments poor;　　　　165
　　For 'tis the mind that makes the body rich.
　　And as the sun breaks through the darkest clouds,
　　So honour peereth in the meanest habit.
　　What, is the jay more precious than the lark,
　　Because his feathers are more beautiful?　　　　　170
　　Or is the adder better than the eel,
　　Because his painted skin contents the eye?
　　O no, good Kate, neither art thou the worse
　　For this poor furniture and mean array.
　　If thou account'st it shame, lay it on me,　　　　　175
　　And therefore frolic; we will hence forthwith,
　　To feast and sport us at thy father's house.
　　Go call my men, and let us straight to him,
　　And bring our horses unto Long-lane end.
　　There will we mount, and thither walk on foot.　　　180

Let's see, I think 'tis now some seven o'clock,
And well we may come there by dinner-time.
KATHARINE. I dare assure you, sir, 'tis almost two,
And 'twill be supper-time ere you come there.
PETRUCHIO. It shall be seven ere I go to horse.   185
Look what I speak, or do, or think to do,
You are still crossing it, Sirs, let't alone,
I will not go to-day, and ere I do,
It shall be what o'clock I say it is.
HORTENSIO. Why so this gallant will command the sun.   *Exeunt.* 190

SCENE IV. *Padua. The Square, before* BAPTISTA'*s house.*

Enter TRANIO, *and the* PEDANT *dressed like* VINCENTIO.

TRANIO. Sir, this is the house, please it you that I call?
PEDANT. Ay, what else? And but I be deceived,
Signior Baptista may remember me,
Near twenty years ago in Genoa,
Where we were lodgers at the Pegasus.   5
TRANIO. 'Tis well, and hold your own in any case,
With such austerity as 'longeth to a father.

Enter BIONDELLO.

PEDANT. I warrant you. But, sir, here comes your boy,
'Twere good he were schooled.
TRANIO. Fear you not him. Sirrah Biondello,   10
Now do your duty throughly, I advise you.
Imagine 'twere the right Vincentio.
BIONDELLO. Tut, fear not me.
TRANIO. But hast thou done thy errand to Baptista?
BIONDELLO. I told him that your father was at Venice,   15
And that you looked for him this day in Padua.
TRANIO. Thou'rt a tall fellow, hold thee that to drink.

Enter BAPTISTA *and* LUCENTIO *as* CAMBIO.

Here comes Baptista — set your countenance, sir.
Signior Baptista, you are happily met.
[*To the* PEDANT] Sir, this is the gentleman I told you of.   20

I pray you stand good father to me now,
Give me Bianca for my patrimony.
PEDANT. Soft son.
    Sir, by your leave, having come to Padua
    To gather in some debts, my son Lucentio   25
    Made me acquainted with a weighty cause
    Of love between your daughter and himself.
    And, for the good report I hear of you,
    And for the love he beareth to your daughter,
    And she to him, to stay him not too long,   30
    I am content, in a good father's care,
    To have him matched, and if you please to like
    No worse than I, upon some agreement
    Me shall you find ready and willing
    With one consent to have her so bestowed.   35
    For curious I cannot be with you,
    Signior Baptista, of whom I hear so well.
BAPTISTA. Sir, pardon me in what I have to say;
    Your plainness and your shortness please me well.
    Right true it is your son Lucentio here   40
    Doth love my daughter, and she loveth him,
    Or both dissemble deeply their affections.
    And therefore if you say no more than this,
    That like a father you will deal with him,
    And pass my daughter a sufficient dower,   45
    The match is made, and all is done:
    Your son shall have my daughter with consent.
TRANIO. I thank you, sir. Where then do you hold best
    We be affied and such assurance ta'en,
    As shall with either part's agreement stand?   50
BAPTISTA. Not in my house, Lucentio, for you know
    Pitchers have ears, and I have many servants;
    Besides, old Gremio is hearkening still,
    And happily we might be interrupted.
TRANIO. Then at my lodging, an it like you.   55
    There doth my father lie; and there this night
    We'll pass the business privately and well.
    Send for your daughter by your servant here,
    My boy shall fetch the scrivener presently.

The worst is this, that at so slender warning,   60
You are like to have a thin and slender pittance.
BAPTISTA. It likes me well. Cambio, hie you home,
    And bid Bianca make her ready straight;
    And if you will tell what hath happened,
    Lucentio's father is arrived in Padua,   65
    And how she's like to be Lucentio's wife.
BIONDELLO. I pray the gods she may with all my heart.
TRANIO. Dally not with the gods, but get thee gone.   *Exit* BIONDELLO.
    Signior Baptista, shall I lead the way?
    Welcome, one mess is like to be your cheer.   70
    Come, sir, we will better it in Pisa.
BAPTISTA. I follow you.   *Exeunt* TRANIO, PEDANT, *and* BAPTISTA.

Enter BIONDELLO.

BIONDELLO.   Cambio —
LUCENTIO.   What sayst thou, Biondello?
BIONDELLO.   You saw my master wink and laugh upon you?   75
LUCENTIO.   Biondello, what of that?
BIONDELLO.   Faith nothing, but has left me here behind to expound the
    meaning or moral of his signs and tokens.
LUCENTIO.   I pray thee moralize them.
BIONDELLO.   Then thus. Baptista is safe talking with the deceiving   80
    father of a deceitful son.
LUCENTIO.   And what of him?
BIONDELLO.   His daughter is to be brought by you to the supper.
LUCENTIO.   And then?
BIONDELLO.   The old priest at Saint Luke's church is at your com-   85
    mand at all hours.
LUCENTIO.   And what of all this?
BIONDELLO.   I cannot tell, except they are busied about a counterfeit as-
    surance. Take you assurance of her, cum privilegio ad imprimen-
    dum solum,° to th' church — take the priest, clerk, and some   90
    sufficient honest witnesses:
    If this be not that you look for, I have no more to say,
    But bid Bianca farewell for ever and a day.

[*Going.*]

89–90. cum . . . solum: with the sole right to print (the language of a copyright contract).

LUCENTIO. Hear'st thou, Biondello?

BIONDELLO. I cannot tarry. I knew a wench married in an afternoon 95
as she went to the garden for parsley to stuff a rabbit, and so may
you sir. And so adieu sir. My master hath appointed me to go to
Saint Luke's, to bid the priest be ready to come against you come
with your appendix.° *Exit.*

LUCENTIO. I may and will, if she be so contented. 100
She will be pleased, then wherefore should I doubt?
Hap what hap may, I'll roundly go about her.
It shall go hard if Cambio go without her. *Exit.*

99. **appendix:** a pun on *appendage.*

SCENE V. *The highway to Padua.*

Enter PETRUCHIO, KATHARINE, HORTENSIO, *and* SERVANTS.

PETRUCHIO. Come on i' God's name, once more toward our father's.
Good lord how bright and goodly shines the moon!

KATHARINE. The moon? The sun. It is not moonlight now.

PETRUCHIO. I say it is the moon that shines so bright.

KATHARINE. I know it is the sun that shines so bright. 5

PETRUCHIO. Now, by my mother's son, and that's myself,
It shall be moon, or star, or what I list,
Or e'er I journey to your father's house.
Go on, and fetch our horses back again.
Evermore crossed and crossed, nothing but crossed! 10

HORTENSIO. [*Aside to* KATHARINE] Say as he says, or we shall never go.

KATHARINE. Forward, I pray, since we have come so far,
And be it moon, or sun, or what you please.
An if you please to call it a rush-candle,
Henceforth I vow it shall be so for me. 15

PETRUCHIO. I say it is the moon.

KATHARINE.   I know it is the moon.

PETRUCHIO. Nay then you lie. It is the blessed sun.

KATHARINE. Then God be blessed, it is the blessed sun,
But sun it is not, when you say it is not,
And the moon changes even as your mind. 20
What you will have it named, even that it is,
And so it shall be still for Katharine.

HORTENSIO. [*Aside*] Petruchio, go thy ways, the field is won.
PETRUCHIO. Well, forward, forward, thus the bowl should run,
    And not unluckily against the bias.°   25

Enter VINCENTIO.

    But, soft, company is coming here.
    [*To* VINCENTIO] Good morrow, gentle mistress, where away?
    Tell me, sweet Kate, and tell me truly too,
    Hast thou beheld a fresher gentlewoman?
    Such war of white and red within her cheeks!   30
    What stars do spangle heaven with such beauty,
    As those two eyes become that heavenly face?
    Fair lovely maid, once more good day to thee.
    Sweet Kate, embrace her for her beauty's sake.
HORTENSIO. [*Aside*] 'A will make the man mad, to make a woman of him.
KATHARINE. Young budding virgin, fair, and fresh, and sweet,   36
    Whither away, or where is thy abode?
    Happy the parents of so fair a child;
    Happier the man whom favourable stars
    Allots thee for his lovely bedfellow.   40
PETRUCHIO. Why, how now, Kate, I hope thou art not mad.
    This is a man, old, wrinkled, faded, withered,
    And not a maiden, as thou sayst he is.
KATHARINE. Pardon, old father, my mistaking eyes,
    That have been so bedazzled with the sun,   45
    That every thing I look on seemeth green.
    Now I perceive thou art a reverend father.
    Pardon, I pray thee, for my mad mistaking.
PETRUCHIO. Do, good old grandsire, and withal make known
    Which way thou travellest; if along with us,   50
    We shall be joyful of thy company.
VINCENTIO. Fair sir, and you my merry mistress,
    That with your strange encounter much amazed me,
    My name is called Vincentio, my dwelling Pisa,
    And bound I am to Padua, there to visit   55
    A son of mine, which long I have not seen.

    25. bias: In the game of bowls, the bowl was not a perfect sphere, but so made that one side somewhat protruded — this protrusion, called the *bias,* caused the bowl to take a curving, indirect course.

PETRUCHIO. What is his name?

VINCENTIO.   Lucentio, gentle sir.

PETRUCHIO. Happily met, the happier for thy son.
　　And now by law, as well as reverend age,
　　I may entitle thee my loving father.   60
　　The sister to my wife, this gentlewoman,
　　Thy son by this hath married. Wonder not,
　　Nor be not grieved; she is of good esteem,
　　Her dowry wealthy, and of worthy birth;
　　Beside, so qualified, as may beseem   65
　　The spouse of any noble gentleman.
　　Let me embrace with old Vincentio,
　　And wander we to see thy honest son,
　　Who will of thy arrival be full joyous.

VINCENTIO. But is this true, or is it else your pleasure,   70
　　Like pleasant travellers to break a jest
　　Upon the company you overtake?

HORTENSIO. I do assure thee, father, so it is.

PETRUCHIO. Come, go along, and see the truth hereof,
　　For our first merriment hath made thee jealous.°   75

　　　　　　　　Exeunt PETRUCHIO, KATHARINE, VINCENTIO *and* SERVANTS.

HORTENSIO. Well, Petruchio, this has put me in heart.
　　Have to my widow, and if she be froward,
　　Then hast thou taught Hortensio to be untoward.   *Exit.*

　　　　　　75. jealous: suspicious.

ACT V

SCENE I. *Padua. The Square, before* LUCENTIO's *house.*

Enter GREMIO. *Then enter* BIONDELLO, LUCENTIO, *and* BIANCA.

BIONDELLO. Softly and swiftly, sir, for the priest is ready.

LUCENTIO. I fly, Biondello; but they may chance to need thee at home,
　　therefore leave us.

BIONDELLO. Nay, faith, I'll see the church o' your back, and then come back to my master as soon as I can.   5

Exeunt LUCENTIO, BIANCA, *and* BIONDELLO.

GREMIO. I marvel Cambio comes not all this while.

Enter PETRUCHIO, KATHARINE, VINCENTIO, GRUMIO, *and*
SERVANTS.

PETRUCHIO. Sir, here's the door, this is Lucentio's house.
My father's bears more toward the marketplace.
Thither must I, and here I leave you, sir.

VINCENTIO. You shall not choose but drink before you go.   10
I think I shall command your welcome here,
And by all likelihood some cheer is toward.

[*Knocks.*]

GREMIO. They're busy within; you were best knock louder.

Enter PEDANT *above.*

PEDANT. What's he that knocks as he would beat down the gate?

VINCENTIO. Is Signior Lucentio within, sir?   15

PEDANT. He's within sir, but not to be spoken withal.

VINCENTIO. What if a man bring him a hundred pound or two to make
merry withal?

PEDANT. Keep your hundred pounds to yourself, he shall need none so
long as I live.   20

PETRUCHIO. Nay, I told you your son was well beloved in Padua. Do you
hear, sir? To leave frivolous circumstances, I pray you tell Signior
Lucentio that his father is come from Pisa, and is here at the door
to speak with him.

PEDANT. Thou liest. His father is come from Mantua, and here look-   25
ing out at the window.

VINCENTIO. Art thou his father?

PEDANT. Ay, sir, so his mother says, if I may believe her.

PETRUCHIO. [*To* VINCENTIO] Why how now gentleman! Why this is flat
knavery to take upon you another man's name.   30

PEDANT. Lay hands on the villain. I believe 'a means to cozen somebody
in this city under my countenance.

Enter BIONDELLO.

BIONDELLO. I have seen them in the church together. God send 'em good

shipping. But who is here? Mine old master Vincentio! Now we
are undone, and brought to nothing.   35
VINCENTIO. Come hither crack-hemp.°
BIONDELLO. I hope I may choose, sir.
VINCENTIO. Come hither, you rogue. What, have you forgot me?
BIONDELLO. Forgot you? No, sir. I could not forget you, for I never saw
you before in all my life.   40
VINCENTIO. What, you notorious villain, didst thou never see thy master's
father, Vincentio?
BIONDELLO. What, my old worshipful old master? Yes, marry sir, see
where he looks out of the window.
VINCENTIO. Is't so, indeed?   45

[Beats BIONDELLO.]

BIONDELLO. Help, help, help, here's a madman will murder me!   *Exit.*
PEDANT. Help son, help, Signior Baptista!
PETRUCHIO. Prithee Kate, let's stand aside and see the end of this con-
troversy.

[*They retire.*]

Enter PEDANT *below;* BAPTISTA, TRANIO, *and* SERVANTS.

TRANIO. Sir, what are you that offer to beat my servant?   50
VINCENTIO. What am I, sir? Nay, what are you, sir? O immortal gods! O
fine villain! A silken doublet, a velvet hose, a scarlet cloak, and a
copatain hat! O I am undone, I am undone! While I play the good
husband at home, my son and my servant spend all at the university.
TRANIO. How now, what's the matter?   55
BAPTISTA. What, is the man lunatic?
TRANIO. Sir, you seem a sober ancient gentleman by your habit. But your
words show you a madman. Why sir, what 'cerns it you if I wear
pearl and gold? I thank my good father, I am able to maintain it.
VINCENTIO. Thy father? O villain, he is a sail-maker in Bergamo.   60
BAPTISTA. You mistake, sir, you mistake, sir. Pray what do you think is
his name?
VINCENTIO. His name? As if I knew not his name. I have brought him
up ever since he was three years old, and his name is Tranio.
PEDANT. Away, away, mad ass! His name is Lucentio, and he is mine   65
only son, and heir to the lands of me, Signior Vincentio.

36. crack-hemp: one who will stretch a rope (i.e., be hanged).

VINCENTIO. Lucentio? O he hath murdered his master. Lay hold on him,
I charge you, in the Duke's name. O my son, my son! Tell me thou
villain, where is my son Lucentio?

TRANIO. Call forth an officer.   70

Enter SERVANT *with* OFFICER.

Carry this mad knave to the gaol. Father Baptista, I charge you see
that he be forthcoming.

VINCENTIO. Carry me to the gaol?

GREMIO. Stay, officer, he shall not go to prison.

BAPTISTA. Talk not, Signior Gremio. I say he shall go to prison.   75

GREMIO. Take heed, Signior Baptista, lest you be cony-catched in this
business. I dare swear this is the right Vincentio.

PEDANT. Swear if thou darest.

GREMIO. Nay, I dare not swear it.

TRANIO. Then thou wert best say that I am not Lucentio.   80

GREMIO. Yes, I know thee to be Signior Lucentio.

BAPTISTA. Away with the dotard, to the gaol with him!

VINCENTIO. Thus strangers may be haled and abused.
O monstrous villainy!

Enter BIONDELLO, *with* LUCENTIO *and* BIANCA.

BIONDELLO. O we are spoiled, and yonder he is. Deny him, forswear   85
him, or else we are all undone.

LUCENTIO. Pardon, sweet father.

[*Kneels.*]

VINCENTIO.   Lives my sweet son?
                    Exeunt BIONDELLO, TRANIO, *and* PEDANT.

BIANCA. Pardon, dear father.

[*Kneels.*]

BAPTISTA.   How hast thou offended?
Where is Lucentio?

LUCENTIO.   Here's Lucentio,
Right son unto the right Vincentio,   90
That have by marriage made thy daughter mine,
While counterfeit supposes bleared thine eyne.

GREMIO. Here's packing, with a witness, to deceive us all!

VINCENTIO. Where is that damned villain Tranio,
 That faced and braved me in this matter so? 95
BAPTISTA. Why tell me, is not this my Cambio?
BIANCA. Cambio is changed into Lucentio.
LUCENTIO. Love wrought these miracles. Bianca's love
 Made me exchange my state with Tranio,
 While he did bear my countenance in the town, 100
 And happily I have arrived at last
 Unto the wished haven of my bliss.
 What Tranio did, myself enforced him to;
 Then pardon him, sweet father, for my sake.
VINCENTIO. I'll slit the villain's nose that would have sent me to the gaol.
BAPTISTA. [*To* LUCENTIO] But do you hear, sir? Have you married my 106
 daughter without asking my good will?
VINCENTIO. Fear not, Baptista, we will content you, go to.
 But I will in to be revenged for this villainy. *Exit.*
BAPTISTA. And I, to sound the depth of this knavery. *Exit.* 110
LUCENTIO. Look not pale, Bianca, thy father will not frown.

 Exeunt LUCENTIO *and* BIANCA.

GREMIO. My cake is dough, but I'll in among the rest;
 Out of hope of all, but my share of the feast. *Exit.*

[PETRUCHIO *and* KATHARINE *come forward.*]

KATHARINE. Husband, let's follow, to see the end of this ado.
PETRUCHIO. First kiss me, Kate, and we will. 115
KATHARINE. What, in the midst of the street?
PETRUCHIO. What, art thou ashamed of me?
KATHARINE. No, sir, God forbid, but ashamed to kiss.
PETRUCHIO. Why, then let's home again. Come sirrah, let's away.
KATHARINE. Nay, I will give thee a kiss [*Kisses him*]; now pray thee, love,
 stay. 120
PETRUCHIO. Is not this well? Come, my sweet Kate.
 Better once than never, for never too late. *Exeunt.*

SCENE II. *A room in* LUCENTIO'*s house.*

Enter BAPTISTA, VINCENTIO, GREMIO, PEDANT, LUCENTIO, BIANCA,
 PETRUCHIO, KATHARINE, HORTENSIO *and* WIDOW, BIONDELLO *and*
 GRUMIO; TRANIO *with* SERVANTS *bringing in a banquet.*

LUCENTIO.   At last, though long, our jarring notes agree,
        And time it is, when raging war is done,
        To smile at 'scapes and perils overblown.
        My fair Bianca, bid my father welcome,
        While I with selfsame kindness welcome thine.   5
        Brother Petruchio, sister Katharina,
        And thou, Hortensio, with thy loving widow,
        Feast with the best, and welcome to my house.
        My banquet is to close our stomachs up
        After our great good cheer. Pray you sit down,   10
        For now we sit to chat, as well as eat.

                          [*They sit.*]

PETRUCHIO.   Nothing but sit and sit, and eat and eat!
BAPTISTA.   Padua affords this kindness, son Petruchio.
PETRUCHIO.   Padua affords nothing but what is kind.
HORTENSIO.   For both our sakes I would that word were true.   15
PETRUCHIO.   Now for my life, Hortensio fears his widow.
WIDOW.   Then never trust me if I be afeard.
PETRUCHIO.   You are very sensible, and yet you miss my sense;
        I mean Hortensio is afeard of you.
WIDOW.   He that is giddy thinks the world turns round.   20
PETRUCHIO.   Roundly replied.
KATHARINE.   Mistress, how mean you that?
WIDOW.   Thus I conceive by him.
PETRUCHIO.   Conceives by me? How likes Hortensio that?
HORTENSIO.   My widow says, thus she conceives her tale.
PETRUCHIO.   Very well mended. Kiss him for that good widow.   25
KATHARINE.   He that is giddy thinks the world turns round —
        I pray you tell me what you meant by that.
WIDOW.   Your husband, being troubled with a shrew,
        Measures my husband's sorrow by his woe —
        And now you know my meaning.   30
KATHARINE.   A very mean meaning.
WIDOW.   Right, I mean you.
KATHARINE.   And I am mean indeed, respecting you.
PETRUCHIO.   To her, Kate!
HORTENSIO.   To her, widow!
PETRUCHIO.   A hundred marks, my Kate does put her down.   35

HORTENSIO. That's my office.

PETRUCHIO. Spoke like an officer — ha' to thee lad.

[*Drinks to* HORTENSIO.]

BAPTISTA. How likes Gremio these quick-witted folks?

GREMIO. Believe me, sir, they butt together well.

BIANCA. Head and butt — an hasty-witted body   40
    Would say your head and butt were head and horn.

VINCENTIO. Ay, mistress bride, hath that awakened you?

BIANCA. Ay, but not frighted me, therefore I'll sleep again.

PETRUCHIO. Nay that you shall not; since you have begun,
    Have at you for a bitter jest or two.   45

BIANCA. Am I your bird? I mean to shift my bush,
    And then pursue me as you draw your bow.
    You are welcome all.   *Exeunt* BIANCA, KATHARINE, *and* WIDOW.

PETRUCHIO. She hath prevented me. Here, Signior Tranio,
    This bird you aimed at, though you hit her not.   50
    Therefore a health to all that shot and missed.

TRANIO. O sir, Lucentio slipped me like his greyhound,
    Which runs himself, and catches for his master.

PETRUCHIO. A good swift simile, but something currish.

TRANIO. 'Tis well, sir, that you hunted for yourself.   55
    'Tis thought your deer does hold you at a bay.

BAPTISTA. O, o, Petruchio! Tranio hits you now.

LUCENTIO. I thank thee for that gird good Tranio.

HORTENSIO. Confess, confess, hath he not hit you here?

PETRUCHIO. 'A has a little galled me, I confess;   60
    And as the jest did glance away from me,
    'Tis ten to one it maimed you two outright.

BAPTISTA. Now in good sadness, son Petruchio,
    I think thou hast the veriest shrew of all.

PETRUCHIO. Well, I say no. And therefore, for assurance,   65
    Let's each one send unto his wife,
    And he whose wife is most obedient,
    To come at first when he doth send for her,
    Shall win the wager which we will propose.

HORTENSIO. Content — what's the wager?

LUCENTIO.   Twenty crowns.   70

PETRUCHIO. Twenty crowns?

I'll venture so much of my hawk or hound,
But twenty times so much upon my wife.

LUCENTIO. A hundred then.

HORTENSIO. Content.

PETRUCHIO. A match, 'tis done.

HORTENSIO. Who shall begin? 75

LUCENTIO. That will I.

Go, Biondello, bid your mistress come to me.

BIONDELLO. I go. *Exit.*

BAPTISTA. Son, I'll be your half, Bianca comes.

LUCENTIO. I'll have no halves. I'll bear it all myself. 80

Enter BIONDELLO.

How now, what news?

BIONDELLO. Sir, my mistress sends you word
That she is busy, and she cannot come.

PETRUCHIO. How? She's busy, and she cannot come?
Is that an answer?

GREMIO. Ay, and a kind one too.
Pray God, sir, your wife send you not a worse. 85

PETRUCHIO. I hope, better.

HORTENSIO. Sirrah Biondello, go and entreat my wife
To come to me forthwith. *Exit* BIONDELLO.

PETRUCHIO. O ho, entreat her!
Nay then she must needs come.

HORTENSIO. I am afraid, sir,
Do what you can, yours will not be entreated. 90

Enter BIONDELLO.

Now, where's my wife?

BIONDELLO. She says you have some goodly jest in hand,
She will not come. She bids you come to her.

PETRUCHIO. Worse and worse, she will not come! O vile,
Intolerable, not to be endured! 95
Sirrah Grumio, go to your mistress;
Say I command her come to me. *Exit* GRUMIO.

HORTENSIO. I know her answer.

PETRUCHIO. What?

HORTENSIO. She will not.

PETRUCHIO. The fouler fortune mine, and there an end.

BAPTISTA. Now by my holidame here comes Katharina. 100
KATHARINE. What is your will, sir, that you send for me?
PETRUCHIO. Where is your sister, and Hortensio's wife?
KATHARINE. They sit conferring by the parlour fire.
PETRUCHIO. Go fetch them hither. If they deny to come,
 Swinge° me them soundly forth unto their husbands. 105
 Away I say, and bring them hither straight. *Exit* KATHARINE.
LUCENTIO. Here is a wonder, if you talk of a wonder.
HORTENSIO. And so it is. I wonder what it bodes.
PETRUCHIO. Marry peace it bodes, and love, and quiet life,
 An awful rule, and right supremacy; 110
 And to be short, what not that's sweet and happy.
BAPTISTA. Now fair befall thee, good Petruchio.
 The wager thou hast won, and I will add
 Unto their losses twenty thousand crowns;
 Another dowry to another daughter, 115
 For she is changed, as she had never been.
PETRUCHIO. Nay, I will win my wager better yet,
 And show more sign of her obedience,
 Her new-built virtue and obedience.

Enter KATHARINE, *with* BIANCA *and* WIDOW.

See where she comes, and brings your froward wives 120
As prisoners to her womanly persuasion.
Katharine, that cap of yours becomes you not.
Off with that bauble, throw it under foot.

[She obeys.]

WIDOW. Lord, let me never have a cause to sigh,
 Till I be brought to such a silly pass. 125
BIANCA. Fie, what a foolish duty call you this?
LUCENTIO. I would your duty were as foolish too.
 The wisdom of your duty, fair Bianca,
 Hath cost me a hundred crowns since suppertime.
BIANCA. The more fool you for laying° on my duty. 130
PETRUCHIO. Katharine I charge thee, tell these headstrong women,

105. Swinge: beat, like a game-beater. 130. laying: betting.

What duty they do owe their lords and husbands.

WIDOW.   Come, come, you're mocking; we will have no telling.

PETRUCHIO.   Come on, I say, and first begin with her.

WIDOW.   She shall not.   135

PETRUCHIO.   I say she shall — and first begin with her.

KATHARINE.   Fie, fie, unknit that threatening unkind brow,
            And dart not scornful glances from those eyes,
            To wound thy lord, thy king, thy governor.
            It blots thy beauty, as frosts do bite the meads,   140
            Confounds thy fame, as whirlwinds shake fair buds,
            And in no sense is meet or amiable.
            A woman moved, is like a fountain troubled,
            Muddy, ill-seeming, thick, bereft of beauty,
            And while it is so, none so dry or thirsty   145
            Will deign to sip, or touch one drop of it.
            Thy husband is thy lord, thy life, thy keeper,
            Thy head, thy sovereign; one that cares for thee,
            And for thy maintenance; commits his body
            To painful labour both by sea and land;   150
            To watch the night in storms, the day in cold,
            Whilst thou liest warm at home, secure and safe;
            And craves no other tribute at thy hands
            But love, fair looks, and true obedience —
            Too little payment for so great a debt.   155
            Such duty as the subject owes the prince,
            Even such a woman oweth to her husband;
            And when she is froward, peevish, sullen, sour,
            And not obedient to his honest will,
            What is she but a foul contending rebel,   160
            And graceless traitor to her loving lord?
            I am ashamed that women are so simple
            To offer war, where they should kneel for peace;
            Or seek for rule, supremacy, and sway,
            When they are bound to serve, love, and obey.   165
            Why are our bodies soft, and weak, and smooth,
            Unapt to toil and trouble in the world,
            But that our soft conditions, and our hearts,
            Should well agree with our external parts?
            Come, come, you froward and unable worms,   170

My mind hath been as big as one of yours,
My heart as great, my reason haply more,
To bandy word for word, and frown for frown.
But now I see our lances are but straws;
Our strength as weak, our weakness past compare,   175
That seeming to be most, which we indeed least are.
Then vail your stomachs,° for it is no boot,°
And place your hands below your husband's foot.
In token of which duty, if he please,
My hand is ready, may it do him ease.   180

PETRUCHIO.   Why, there's a wench! Come on, and kiss me, Kate.
LUCENTIO.   Well go thy ways, old lad, for thou shalt ha't.
VINCENTIO.   'Tis a good hearing, when children are toward.
LUCENTIO.   But a harsh hearing, when women are froward.
PETRUCHIO.   Come, Kate, we'll to bed.   185
We three are married, but you two are sped.°
[*To* LUCENTIO] 'Twas I won the wager, though you hit the white.°
And being a winner, God give you good night.

Exeunt PETRUCHIO *and* KATHARINE.

HORTENSIO.   Now go thy ways, thou hast tamed a curst shrow.°
LUCENTIO.   'Tis a wonder, by your leave, she will be tamed so.   *Exeunt.*

177. **vail your stomachs:** give up your pride; **boot:** advantage. 186. **sped:** done
for. 187. **hit the white:** the center of the target (also a pun on the name Bianca,
which means "white"). 189. **shrow:** Here the word *shrew* is spelled to rhyme with
the word *so.*

For Study and Writing

INDUCTION, SCENE i

1. By having the play begin with
a practical joke, what tone is established for all that is to follow? How
does the arrival of the players serve to
strengthen this tone?

2. What do the Lord's last three
lines (132–34) suggest to us about
jests in this time and place, and perhaps about the nature of practical
jokes at any time?

INDUCTION, SCENE ii

Lurking behind every play, every
counterfeit of life, every pretense people make of being persons other than
they are, is the mystery of identity.
How does Sly express this mystery?

Do you think an imposture such as was played upon him could be carried out successfully upon you or anyone you know? How does Sly, or anyone, know who he is but by identification with familiar surroundings and associates? What does Sly's case have in common with that of a victim of amnesia?

ACT I, SCENE i

As in most comedies of this type, the plot is a maze of complexities and disguises. To keep all its threads in order later, we must make certain that we understand each of the early complications.

1. Who are the open rivals for Bianca's hand?

2. What is the impediment to their courtship?

3. What is the purpose of the exchange of identities between Lucentio and Tranio?

4. What does Tranio mean when he says (lines 32–33) he hopes that his master, in his studies, will not be "so devote to Aristotle's checks,/As Ovid be an outcast quite abjured"?

ACT III, SCENE ii

1. Why did Petruchio come for the wedding in such ludicrous dress?

2. Why do you think Shakespeare chose to have the wedding described by Gremio rather than to have it take place on stage? Consider all aspects of the matter with regard both to theatrical effect and to preparation for the scenes that follow.

3. When Petruchio takes leave before the feast, what does he mean by saying (lines 183–84): "If you knew my business,/You would entreat me rather go than stay"?

4. What two meanings can be found in Grumio's words (line 197), "the oats have eaten the horses"?

5. Discuss Katharine's brief flare-up of defiance about the wedding feast. What does Gremio mean by saying (line 209) "now it begins to work"? Why does Katharine make this attempt to resist? What do you think would have been the outcome if Petruchio had softened?

ACT IV, SCENE ii

1. What causes Hortensio to forsake his courtship of Bianca?

2. Explain why it was necessary to have the Pedant pose as Lucentio's father.

ACT IV, SCENE iii

Cite and explain lines by Katharine, in her brief scene with Grumio, that offer a key to her character.

ACT V, SCENE i

What words in this scene are the true sign of Katharine's surrender? Why are they a truer indication of her surrender than her capitulation in Act IV, Scene v, when she was willing to call the sun the moon, at Petruchio's command?

Looking Back at the Play as a Whole

1. There are definite assumptions in this play about love and marriage. In what way are these marriage arrangements completely unsentimental? Analyze *all* the expectations that

seem to accompany a betrothal, on both sides. Are these expectations good or bad?

2. In what way do we see represented a romantically sentimental attitude about "falling in love"?

3. Can these two concepts (marriage as a contract and love as an infatuation) exist side by side other than in make-believe?

4. Katharine is outspoken in her relations with Petruchio. What is suggested in the final scene about the attitudes of Bianca and the Widow toward their husbands?

5. Interpret Katharine's character and behavior in such a way as to put her shrewishness in a more sympathetic light — that is, to justify her acting shrewishly. Cover in this justification her attitude and manner not only toward prospective suitors but also toward Bianca (including Katharine's unquestionable meanness to Bianca in Act II, Scene i).

6. What qualities does Petruchio possess that may well be what Katharine has been looking for all along? What qualities does Katharine possess that may well be what Petruchio has been looking for all along?

7. Contrast Petruchio to other men in the play; contrast Katharine to other women in the play.

8. On the question of shrews, consider whether a man can be "henpecked" without essentially deserving such treatment.

AFTERWORD

If we were to view this play as the story of an unpleasant woman who is simply overpowered by a brutal, money-seeking man, we would hardly find it appealing. But only a most literal-minded, imperceptive person could view it thus — a person with little response to comedy and with no awareness that there are distinct kinds of comedy, each with its own way of presenting character. This comedy is farce, or extravaganza.

The Taming of the Shrew, as its places and names show us, is in the mode of the popular Italian comedy of the Renaissance. This type of play dealt in broad, standard *types,* or stock characters. Familiar among these were the scolding woman, or shrew; the swashbuckling, madcap gallant; the wily servant; the wealthy father; the gentle beauty; the pining suitor; the suitor too old for courtship — all these are recognizable in the principal cast of *The Taming of the Shrew.* The little device of the practical joke on Christopher Sly performs two functions: it puts the Italian story in an English frame, and it emphasizes the *formal, conventional* nature of the central comedy.

We are not meant to worry about the fine points of psychology and behavior that would concern us if we were seeing an attempt at realistic character-portrayal from a modern point of view. Even so, once we have grasped the broad assumptions on which the play rests, we see that beneath them lie general truths about human nature that fit the modern world as well as the Renaissance world; for essential human nature has not changed. Stock types are very close to truth, even though, being standardized characters, they are oversimplifications, with little room for the subtleties that go with individuality.

By comparison with most of those around them, Petruchio and Katharine are highly individualistic. At the same time they are remarkably alike, being male and female counterparts of each other's temperaments.

Petruchio undoubtedly does mean to "wive it wealthily" (as does everyone else in the marriage negotiations of the place and age), but we can assume that his attitude of otherwise not caring what he gets is adopted by him simply to pave the way for his boldly taking on a woman no other man can stand up to. We can assume that he likes her on sight — she is acknowledged to be beautiful. The sweet blandness of Bianca is not for a taste such as his. When, in Act II, Scene i, he hears how Kate smashed the lute over Hortensio's head, he cries:

> Now by the world, it is a lusty wench.
> I love her ten times more than e'er I did.

In short, he exults that she is spirited, for so is he.

Katharine is not content with commonplace men whom she can dominate. She is heartily bored with meek people of either sex — her distaste for them is the reason for her bullying of her cloying sister Bianca. She wants a match proper for one of her mettle. She puts everyone to the test. She tests Petruchio at several points, and a knuckling-under by him at any of those times would mean the end of their relationship. Both of them know this. Both understand that they are playing a game, and both know its rules. It is not until Act V, Scene i, after many trials, after submissions to his arbitrary will that might have been simply the results of bullying, that she first kisses him voluntarily and calls him "love."

The Katharine who performs her dutiful obedience when Petruchio makes his wager at the end is no browbeaten, broken-spirited slave. Tongue in cheek, she is asserting her love for this "shrew-tamer" and at the same time mocking the other two women, who as wives are supposedly so much more submissive and desirable than she.

Katharine and Petruchio's rowdy duel throughout this whirlwind courtship and wedding — their testing of each other as to how far each may be pushed — is a mock campaign on an immemorial theme of comedy, a theme used by writers from the time of the ancient Greek, Aristophanes,[1] to that of the late James Thurber,[2] the war between men and women.

In his biography of Shakespeare,[3] the Oxford historian A. L. Rowse remarks:

> Petruchio's taming of the bad-tempered, cross-bit Kate is not brutal — and nothing could be more crude or improper than the old Victorian habit of equipping him with a whip. For, observe, he never once beats her; she once, at the beginning, beats him. Then she receives her lesson, by way of ridicule: his "mad" conduct holds up a mirror to her own bad behavior, and shows her what it looks like from outside. Even so, the taming is conducted in the language of love, for in fact he loves her in spite of herself; in the end, the sense of this transpires to her, and brings her not only to her senses, and civilized conduct, but to love of him. It is, of course, knock-about farce, but with much psychological sense in it. It is hardly likely that Shakespeare was wrong in the matter and those who think themselves more exquisitely sensitive about women right.

[1] **Aristophanes:** Athenian comic poet (c. 448–c. 388 B.C.), widely recognized as the greatest of ancient comedians (eleven of his plays survive). [2] **James Thurber:** American writer and artist (1894–1961), managing editor of the *New Yorker,* to which he contributed humorous essays and drawings. [3] *William Shakespeare* (Harper & Row, 1963).

The poems that follow are various in kind, subject matter, and historical period. They have in common the straightforward assumption that man and his life are valuable. Some, like Shakespeare's "Winter" and Keats's "To Autumn," describe aspects of the natural world that man inhabits and, in doing so, assert the importance of such simple facts of existence as seasons, things, and fellow beings. Others, like Frost's "The Code" and Milton's "To the Lord General Cromwell," assert man's basic dignity and his right to hard-won independence. Some are about death, a subject that may seem strange as an aspect of affirmation unless one reflects that the death of man is important only if his life is too. Some are funny, some extremely serious. All view mortal existence as something at least worth accepting and perhaps worth cherishing.

The Argument of His Book

by Robert Herrick

(1591–1674)

I sing of Brooks, of Blossoms, Birds, and Bowers:
Of April, May, of June, and July-Flowers.
I sing of May-poles, Hock-carts, Wassails, Wakes,
Of Bride-grooms, Brides, and of their Bridal-cakes.
I write of Youth, of Love, and have access   5
By these to sing of cleanly-wantonness.
I sing of Dews, of Rains, and piece by piece
Of Balm, of Oil, of Spice, and Amber-Greece,
I sing of Times trans-shifting; and I write
How Roses first came red and Lilies white.   10
I write of Groves, of Twilights, and I sing
The Court of Mab, and of the Fairy-King.
I write of Hell; I sing (and ever shall)
Of Heaven, and hope to have it after all.

1. Having read the poem carefully, what do you think is the meaning of the term *argument* in the title?

2. What distinction do you see between those things Herrick "writes"

about in this poem and those he "sings" about?

3. In what way or ways should the last two words of the poem be understood?

4. What does the poet particularly like or value in life?

Winter [1]

by William Shakespeare
(1564–1616)

When icicles hang by the wall,
  And Dick the shepherd blows his nail,
And Tom bears logs into the hall,
  And milk comes frozen home in pail,
When blood is nipp'd and ways be foul,   5
  Then nightly sings the staring owl,
        Tu-whit!
Tu-who! — a merry note,
While greasy Joan doth keel the pot.

When all aloud the wind doth blow,   10
  And coughing drowns the parson's saw,
And birds sit brooding in the snow,
  And Marian's nose looks red and raw,
When roasted crabs hiss in the bowl,
  Then nightly sings the staring owl,   15
        Tu-whit!
Tu-who! — a merry note,
While greasy Joan doth keel the pot.

[1] From *Love's Labour's Lost,* Act V, Scene ii.

For Study and Writing

1. This poem is a picture of one part of life in Elizabethan England. With what kind of people is the poem

concerned? Where do they live?

2. People who lived in Shakespeare's England had a good many reasons for hating and fearing winter. It was hard in those times to keep

warm, dry, fed, healthy, or even alive during the cold season. To what extent are hardships and distress associated with winter in this poem?

3. What pleasures or attractive qualities of winter are alluded to?

4. Writers often achieve an effect of reality by presenting carefully selected details of everyday human life as parts of a general impression which is finally not everyday or in the usual sense realistic, but special, emotional, and romantic. Comment on Shakespeare's use of such a device in "Winter." Compare the poem in this respect with Herrick's "The Argument of His Book."

5. What is the effect of the chorus with which each stanza ends? Is it in any sense ironic?

The Parson [1]

by Geoffrey Chaucer

(c. 1340–1400)

A good man was ther of religioun,
And was a poure Persoun of a toun,
But riche he was of holy thoght and werk.
He was also a lerned man, a clerk,°
That Christes gospel trewely wolde preche;   5
His parisshens° devoutly wolde he teche.
Benygne he was, and wonder diligent,
And in adversitee ful pacient,
And swich° he was preved ofte sithes.°
     Ful looth were hym to cursen° for his tithes,°   10
But rather wolde he yeven,° out of doute,
Un-to his poure parisshens aboute
Of his offrynge and eek of his substaunce.°
He koude in litel thyng have suffisaunce.
Wyd was his parisshe, and houses fer asonder,   15
But he ne lafte nat,° for reyn ne thonder,
In siknesse nor in meschief,° to visite

[1] From the General Prologue to *The Canterbury Tales*. **4. clerk:** scholar. **6. parisshens:** parishioners. **9. swich:** such; **preved ofte sithes:** proved oftentimes. **10. Ful . . . cursen:** He was very loath to excommunicate; **tithes:** dues for the Church, consisting of one tenth of the individual's yearly income or production. **11. yeven:** give. **13. eek . . . substaunce:** also of his own food and property. **16. ne lafte nat:** did not neglect. **17. meschief:** trouble.

The ferreste° in his parisshe, muche and lite,°
Up-on his feet, and in his hond a staf.
    This noble ensample to his sheep he yaf,°   20
That first he wroghte, and afterward he taughte.
Out of the gospel he tho wordes caughte,
And this figure he added eek ther-to,
That if gold ruste, what sholde iren do?
For if a preest be foule, on whom we truste,   25
No wonder is a lewed° man to ruste;
And shame it is, if a preest take keep,°
A shiten shepherde and a clene sheep.
Wel oghte a preest ensample for to yive,
By his clennesse, how that his sheep sholde lyve.   30
    He sette nat his benefice to hyre,°
And leet his sheep encombred in the myre,
And ran to Londoun, un-to Seint Poules,
To seken hym a chauntrye for soules,°
Or with a bretherhede° to been withholde;°   35
But dwelte at hoom, and kepte wel his folde,
So that the wolf ne made it nat myscarye;
He was a shepherde and noght a mercenarye.
    And thogh he hooly were and vertuous,
He was noght to synful men despitous,°   40
Ne of his speche daungerous ne digne,°
But in his techyng discreet and benigne.
To drawen folk to hevene by fairnesse,
By good ensample, this was his bisynesse;
But it were° any persone obstinat,   45
What so he were, of heigh or lowe estat,
Hym wolde be snybben° sharply for the nonys.°
    A bettre preest I trowe that nowher noon ys.
He wayted after° no pompe and reverence,
Ne maked hym a spiced° conscience,   50
But Christes loore,° and his apostles twelve,
He taughte, but first he folwed it hym-selve.

---

18. ferreste: farthest; muche and lite: great and small. 20. yaf: gave. 26. lewed: ignorant. 27. keep: heed. 31. sette . . . hyre: did not rent out his parish to a curate. 34. chauntrye for soules: endowment for singing masses for the dead. 35. bretherhede: religious fraternity or guild; to been withholde: to be retained (as chaplain). 40. despitous: spiteful. 41. daungerous ne digne: haughty nor disdainful. 45. But it were: but if there were. 47. snybben: rebuke, reprove; nonys: occasion. 49. wayted after: expected or demanded. 50. spiced: overscrupulous. 51. loore: lore (teaching).

For Study and Writing

1. In what statements about the Parson does the poet offer his own opinion of his subject? How common are such direct statements of the author's opinion in other poetry and prose you have read in this book?

2. How is the strength of the Parson's faith in God and in goodness implied by the circumstances of his daily life as described in the poem?

3. Besides his goodness as a man and a priest, is anything particular described directly or by implication about the Parson's personality? Cite lines.

4. Robert Herrick was an English country parson, and from all reports an exceptionally good one. What significant differences do you find between Herrick's affirmations in "The Argument of His Book" and those of Chaucer's Parson?

The Ballad of the Foxhunter

by *William Butler Yeats*

(1865-1939)

"Lay me in a cushioned chair;
Carry me, ye four,
With cushions here and cushions there
To see the world once more.

"To stable and to kennel go;   5
Bring what is there to bring;
Lead my Lollard to and fro,
Or gently in a ring.

"Put the chair upon the grass:
Bring Rody and his hounds,   10
That I may contented pass
From these earthly bounds."

His eyelids droop, his head falls low,
His old eyes cloud with dreams;
The sun upon all things that grow   15
Falls in sleepy streams.

Brown Lollard treads upon the lawn,
And to the armchair goes,

And now the old man's dreams are gone,
He smooths the long brown nose.   20

And now moves many a pleasant tongue
Upon his wasted hands,
For leading aged hounds and young
The huntsman near him stands.

"Huntsman Rody, blow the horn,   25
Make the hills reply."
The huntsman loosens on the morn
A gay wandering cry.

Fire is in the old man's eyes,
His fingers move and sway,   30
And when the wandering music dies
They hear him feebly say,

"Huntsman Rody, blow the horn,
Make the hills reply."
"I cannot blow upon my horn,   35
I can but weep and sigh."

Servants round his cushioned place
Are with new sorrow wrung;
Hounds are gazing on his face,
Aged hounds and young.   40

One blind hound only lies apart
On the sun-smitten grass;
He holds deep commune with his heart:
The moments pass and pass;

The blind hound with a mournful din   45
Lifts slow his wintry head;
The servants bear the body in;
The hounds wail for the dead.

For Study and Writing

1. What are the various points of
view from which the dying of the
foxhunter is seen in the poem?

2. Who or what must Lollard be?

3. What does the repeated mention
of cushions and cushioned show the
reader?

4. Why do you suppose Rody can

blow the horn the first time he is
asked to do so but not the second?

5. What is different about the old
blind hound, besides his age and
blindness?

6. What simple facts about the foxhunter's active life are shown the
reader?

7. What does the poet assume about
the nature of horses and dogs?

The Code

by Robert Frost
(*1875–1963*)

There were three in the meadow by the brook
Gathering up windrows, piling cocks of hay,
With an eye always lifted toward the west
Where an irregular sun-bordered cloud
Darkly advanced with a perpetual dagger 5
Flickering across its bosom. Suddenly
One helper, thrusting his pitchfork in the ground,
Marched himself off the field and home. One stayed.
The town-bred farmer failed to understand.
"What is there wrong?"

             "Something you just now said." 10

"What did I say?"
         "About our taking pains."

"To cock the hay? — because it's going to shower?
I said that more than half an hour ago.
I said it to myself as much as you."

"You didn't know. But James is one big fool. 15
He thought you meant to find fault with his work.
That's what the average farmer would have meant.
James would take time, of course, to chew it over
Before he acted: he's just got round to act."

"He is a fool if that's the way he takes me." 20

"Don't let it bother you. You've found out something.
The hand that knows his business won't be told

To do work better or faster — those two things.
I'm as particular as anyone:
Most likely I'd have served you just the same. 25
But I know you don't understand our ways.
You were just talking what was in your mind,
What was in all our minds, and you weren't hinting.
Tell you a story of what happened once:
I was up here in Salem at a man's 30
Named Sanders with a gang of four or five
Doing the haying. No one liked the boss.
He was one of the kind sports call a spider,
All wiry arms and legs that spread out wavy
From a humped body nigh as big's a biscuit, 35
But work! that man could work, especially
If by so doing he could get more work
Out of his hired help. I'm not denying
He was hard on himself. I couldn't find
That he kept any hours — not for himself. 40
Daylight and lantern-light were one to him:
I've heard him pounding in the barn all night.
But what he liked was someone to encourage.
Them that he couldn't lead he'd get behind
And drive, the way you can, you know, in mowing — 45
Keep at their heels and threaten to mow their legs off.
I'd seen about enough of his bulling tricks
(We call that bulling). I'd been watching him.
So when he paired off with me in the hayfield
To load the load, thinks I, Look out for trouble. 50
I built the load and topped it off; old Sanders
Combed it down with a rake and says, 'O.K.'
Everything went well till we reached the barn
With a big jag to empty in a bay.
You understand that meant the easy job 55
For the man up on top of throwing *down*
The hay and rolling it off wholesale,
Where on a mow it would have been slow lifting.
You wouldn't think a fellow'd need much urging
Under those circumstances, would you now? 60
But the old fool seizes his fork in both hands,
And looking up bewhiskered out of the pit,
Shouts like an army captain, 'Let her come!'

Thinks I, D'ye mean it? 'What was that you said?'
I asked out loud, so's there'd be no mistake,   65
'Did you say, Let her come?' 'Yes, let her come.'
He said it over, but he said it softer.
Never you say a thing like that to a man,
Not if he values what he is. God, I'd as soon
Murdered him as left out his middle name.   70
I'd built the load and knew right where to find it.
Two or three forkfuls I picked lightly round for
Like meditating, and then I just dug in
And dumped the rackful on him in ten lots.
I looked over the side once in the dust   75
And caught sight of him treading-water-like,
Keeping his head above. 'Damn ye,' I says,
'That gets ye!' He squeaked like a squeezed rat.
That was the last I saw or heard of him.
I cleaned the rack and drove out to cool off.   80
As I sat mopping hayseed from my neck,
And sort of waiting to be asked about it,
One of the boys sings out, 'Where's the old man?'
'I left him in the barn under the hay.
If ye want him, ye can go and dig him out.'   85
They realized from the way I swobbed my neck
More than was needed something must be up.
They headed for the barn; I stayed where I was.
They told me afterward. First they forked hay,
A lot of it, out into the barn floor.   90
Nothing! They listened for him. Not a rustle.
I guess they thought I'd spiked him in the temple
Before I buried him, or I couldn't have managed.
They excavated more. 'Go keep his wife
Out of the barn.' Someone looked in a window,   95
And curse me if he wasn't in the kitchen
Slumped way down in a chair, with both his feet
Against the stove, the hottest day that summer.
He looked so clean disgusted from behind
There was no one that dared to stir him up,   100
Or let him know that he was being looked at.
Apparently I hadn't buried him
(I may have knocked him down); but my just trying
To bury him had hurt his dignity.
He had gone to the house so's not to meet me.   105

He kept way from us all afternoon.
We tended to his hay. We saw him out
After a while picking peas in his garden:
He couldn't keep away from doing something."

"Weren't you relieved to find he wasn't dead?"   110

"No! and yet I don't know — it's hard to say.
I went about to kill him fair enough."

"You took an awkward way. Did he discharge you?"

"Discharge me? No! He knew I did just right."

For Study and Writing

1. There are four main characters in this narrative. Who are they and how does each stand in relation to the "code" of the poem's title?

2. With regard to murder, what is the attitude of the hired man who tells the story to the city-bred farmer?

3. How is it made clear in the poem that the incident which directly precedes the attempted burial of Sanders is not the only cause of that event?

4. What similarities are evident between "The Code" and William Faulkner's story "The Tall Men"?

5. What parts of this poem are comic? How closely involved are these parts with the serious or ominous aspects of the poem?

6. How dependent on the rural setting is the poem's effect? Does the specific work that all the characters are doing have particular importance?

CHORUS FROM **Hellas**

by Percy Bysshe Shelley

(1792–1822)

The world's great age begins anew,
   The golden years return,
The earth doth like a snake renew
   Her winter weeds outworn:
Heaven smiles, and faiths and empires gleam,   5
Like wrecks of a dissolving dream.

A brighter Hellas rears its mountains
  From waves serener far;
A new Peneus rolls his fountains
  Against the morning star.   10
Where the fairer Tempes bloom, there sleep
Young Cyclads on a sunnier deep.

A loftier Argo cleaves the main,
  Fraught with a later prize;
Another Orpheus sings again,   15
  And loves, and weeps, and dies.
A new Ulysses leaves once more
Calypso for his native shore.

Oh, write no more the tale of Troy,
  If earth Death's scroll must be!   20
Nor mix with Laian rage the joy
  Which dawns upon the free:
Although a subtler Sphinx renew
Riddles of death Thebes never knew.

Another Athens shall arise,   25
  And to remoter time
Bequeath, like sunset to the skies,
  The splendour of its prime;
And leave, if nought so bright may live,
All earth can take or Heaven can give.   30

Saturn and Love their long repose
  Shall burst, more bright and good
Than all who fell, than One who rose,
  Than many unsubdued:
Not gold, not blood, their altar dowers,   35
But votive tears and symbol flowers.

Oh, cease! Must hate and death return?
  Cease! Must men kill and die?
Cease! Drain not to its dregs the urn
  Of bitter prophecy.   40
The world is weary of the past,
Oh, might it die, or rest at last!

For Study and Writing

1. *Hellas* means "Greece." In what sense and for what purpose does Shelley use the term in this poem? Is his reference, for example, geographical?

2. With what allusions and images does Shelley glorify "the world's great age," and "the golden years"?

3. What warning is in line 3?

4. How is this implication developed and given form as the poem continues? What reaction to it does the poet express?

To the Lord General Cromwell
On the Proposals of Certain Ministers
At the Committee for Propagation of the Gospel

by John Milton
(1608–1674)

Cromwell, our chief of men, who through a cloud
　Not of war only, but detractions rude,
　Guided by faith and matchless fortitude,
　To peace and truth thy glorious way hast plough'd,
And on the neck of crownèd Fortune proud　　　　　　5
　Hast rear'd God's trophies, and his work pursued,
　While Darwen stream, with blood of Scots imbru'd,
　And Dunbar field resound thy praises loud,
And Worcester's laureate wreath; yet much remains
　To conquer still: peace hath her victories　　　　　10
　No less renown'd than war; new foes arise
Threat'ning to bind our souls with secular chains:
　Help us to save free conscience from the paw
　Of hireling wolves whose gospel is their maw.

For Study and Writing

1. This sonnet is written to the great puritan military leader and Lord Protector of England, Oliver Cromwell. What are the achievements for which the poet praises him? What qualities, according to Milton, have made such achievements possible?

2. It was under the rule of Cromwell that the execution of King Charles I occurred (1649). What attitude toward the event is implied?

3. In what sense is this sonnet addressed to Cromwell as advice or even as a warning?

Do Not Go Gentle into That Good Night

by *Dylan Thomas*

(1914–1953)

Do not go gentle into that good night,
Old age should burn and rave at close of day;
Rage, rage against the dying of the light.

Though wise men at their end know dark is right,
Because their words have forked no lightning they   5
Do not go gentle into that good night.

Good men, the last wave by, crying how bright
Their frail deeds might have danced in a green bay,
Rage, rage against the dying of the light.

Wild men who caught and sang the sun in flight,   10
And learn, too late, they grieved it on its way,
Do not go gentle into that good night.

Grave men, near death, who see with blinding sight
Blind eyes could blaze like meteors and be gay,
Rage, rage against the dying of the light.   15

And you, my father there on the sad height,
Curse, bless, me now with your fierce tears, I pray.
Do not go gentle into that good night.
Rage, rage against the dying of the light.

For Study and Writing

1. What paradox or apparent contradiction may be inferred from the title line of this poem?

2. Various sorts of men are admonished not to "go gentle" and are urged to "rage." What are the varieties of men considered by the poet and what are the different reasons that he presses on them?

3. How is the poet's attitude toward death different from the attitudes of Ransom and Yeats in "Dead Boy" and "The Ballad of the Foxhunter"?

4. How does the poet manage to merge his personal emotion with a general attitude toward human life in this poem?

Dead Boy

by John Crowe Ransom

(1888–)

The little cousin is dead, by foul subtraction,
A green bough from Virginia's aged tree,
And none of the county kin like the transaction,
Nor some of the world of outer dark, like me.

A boy not beautiful, nor good, nor clever,   5
A black cloud full of storms too hot for keeping,
A sword beneath his mother's heart — yet never
Woman bewept her babe as this is weeping.

A pig with a pasty face, so I had said,
Squealing for cookies, kinned by poor pretense   10
With a noble house. But the little man quite dead,
I see the forebears' antique lineaments.

The elder men have strode by the box of death
To the wide flag porch, and muttering low send round
The bruit of the day. O friendly waste of breath!   15
Their hearts are hurt with a deep dynastic wound.

He was pale and little, the foolish neighbors say;
The first-fruits, saith the Preacher, the Lord hath taken;
But this old tree's late branch wrenched away,
Grieving the sapless limbs, the shorn and shaken.   20

For Study and Writing

1. What is the literal meaning of the following words: *subtraction, transaction, pasty, lineaments, flag, bruit, dynastic, shorn?*

2. The aged tree, used as an image in the first stanza and the last, is an old Virginia family. What seems to be the relation of the poet to the place and the family?

3. What was the boy like when he was alive? The poet gives both a personal view and a more general one.

4. Apparently, the poet did not think much of the family's claim to noble blood ("kinned by poor pretense") when the boy was alive. In the third stanza he tells us that he feels differently about it now. What caused the change?

5. Having looked up *bruit,* you

should recognize the paradox in stanza four between that term and "muttering low." Can you resolve it?

6. Why is the grief felt by the elder men called "a deep dynastic wound"?

7. Why are the neighbors "foolish"?

8. How are the event and the state of the family summed up in the final metaphor of the poem?

God's Grandeur

by Gerard Manley Hopkins
(1844-1889)

The world is charged with the grandeur of God.
  It will flame out, like shining from shook foil;
  It gathers to a greatness, like the ooze of oil
Crushed. Why do men then now not reck his rod?
Generations have trod, have trod, have trod;   5
  And all is seared with trade; bleared, smeared with toil;
  And wears man's smudge and shares man's smell: the soil
Is bare now, nor can foot feel, being shod.

And for all this, nature is never spent;
  There lives the dearest freshness deep down things;   10
  And though the last lights off the black West went
    Oh, morning, at the brown brink eastward, springs —
Because the Holy Ghost over the bent
  World broods with warm breast and with ah! bright wings.

For Study and Writing

1. What is the antecedent of *this* in the first line of the second stanza?

2. What does the poet mean in the last line of the first stanza by "nor can foot feel, being shod"?

3. What is the particular relationship which the poet here asserts to be between the visible world of nature and God? What effect does he seem

to feel that this relationship ought to have on human life? To what extent does he indicate that it does affect man?

4. In *Out of the Silent Planet,* C. S. Lewis uses the term "bent" as it is used in line 13 of this poem. Indeed, Hopkins is surely Lewis's source for the usage. Do you think both writers use the term to mean the same thing?

5. Hopkins is known as a poetic

original, a poet who, practicing his art in a rather conservative literary period, shocked his contemporaries with strange images and radical devices. What images and poetic techniques in this poem strike you as particularly unusual? Do you see any similarity between the poetic style of Hopkins and that of John Donne ("The Canonization")?

Brahma

by Ralph Waldo Emerson
(1803–1882)

If the red slayer think he slays,
    Or if the slain think he is slain,
They know not well the subtle ways
    I keep, and pass, and turn again.

Far or forgot to me is near;   5
    Shadow and sunlight are the same;
The vanished gods to me appear;
    And one to me are shame and fame.

They reckon ill who leave me out;
    When me they fly, I am the wings;   10
I am the doubter and the doubt,
    And I the hymn the Brahmin sings.

The strong gods pine for my abode,
    And pine in vain the sacred Seven;
But thou, meek lover of the good!   15
    Find me, and turn thy back on heaven.

For Study and Writing

1. Emerson said to his daughter, who had reported that many readers were puzzled by this poem, "If you tell them to say Jehovah instead of Brahma, they will not feel any perplexity." To what extent does his advice clarify the poem for you?

2. Contrast "Brahma" with "God's Grandeur," another religious interpretation of man and his place in the universe.

3. A basic consideration of every

religious or philosophic system is the problem of evil: the question of how a world created by a good God or on a principle of goodness can contain such evil as is evident in human existence. What is the solution presented by Emerson in "Brahma"?

4. What, in the context of the poem, does its last word mean? Does it, for example, mean that in finding "me" one loses blessedness, goodness, or salvation?

Sonnet XVIII

by *William Shakespeare*
(*1564–1616*)

Shall I compare thee to a summer's day?
Thou art more lovely and more temperate:
Rough winds do shake the darling buds of May,
And summer's lease hath all too short a date;
Sometimes too hot the eye of heaven shines,   5
And often is his gold complexion dimm'd;
And every fair from fair sometime declines,
By chance, or nature's changing course, untrimm'd.
But thy eternal summer shall not fade
Nor lose possession of that fair thou ow'st;   10
Nor shall Death brag thou wander'st in his shade,
When in eternal lines to time thou grow'st —
    So long as men can breathe, or eyes can see,
    So long lives this, and this gives life to thee.

For Study and Writing

1. What reasons does the poet give for answering as he does the rhetorical question in line 1?

2. What idea in this sonnet is similar to the theme of Dylan Thomas's "Do Not Go Gentle into That Good Night"?

3. Contrast the images in this poem with those in "God's Grandeur" and in "The Canonization." How is Shakespeare's Sonnet XVIII otherwise similar to Donne's poem?

4. What challenge does the poet make to death and oblivion in this poem? Do you feel that he can make good his defiance?

The Canonization

by John Donne

(1572–1631)

For God's sake hold your tongue, and let me love;
  Or chide my palsy, or my gout,
My five gray hairs, or ruin'd fortune flout;
  With wealth your state, your mind with arts improve,
    Take you a course, get you a place,   5
    Observe His Honor, or His Grace,
Or the King's real, or his stampèd face
  Contemplate; what you will, approve,
  So you will let me love.

Alas, alas, who's injur'd by my love?   10
  What merchant's ships have my sighs drown'd?
Who says my tears have overflow'd his ground?
  When did my colds a forward spring remove?
    When did the heats which my veins fill
    Add one more to the plaguy bill?   15
Soldiers find wars, and lawyers find out still
  Litigious men, which quarrels move,
  Though she and I do love.

Call us what you will, we are made such by love;
  Call her one, me another fly,   20
We're tapers too, and at our own cost die,
  And we in us find th' Eagle and the Dove.
    The Phoenix riddle hath more wit
    By us; we two being one, are it.
So to one neutral thing both sexes fit,   25
  We die and rise the same, and prove
  Mysterious by this love.

We can die by it, if not live by love,
  And if unfit for tombs and hearse
Our legend be, it will be fit for verse;   30
  And if no piece of chronicle we prove,
    We'll build in sonnets pretty rooms;
    As well a well-wrought urn becomes
The greatest ashes, as half-acre tombs,

And by these hymns, all shall approve 35
Us canoniz'd for love;

And thus invoke us: "You whom reverend love
    Made one another's hermitage;
You, to whom love was peace, that now is rage;
    Who did the whole world's soul contract, and drove 40
        Into the glasses of your eyes
        (So made such mirrors, and such spies,
    That they did all to you epitomize)
        Countries, towns, courts: beg from above
        A pattern of your love!" 45

For Study and Writing

1. What is the tone and rather special effect of the first line of the poem?

2. What do you suppose "the King's real, or his stampèd face" (line 7) to mean?

3. In some of his poems John Donne expresses the emotions and the circumstances of love between the sexes in terms usually associated with religious doctrine or observance. In others, he expresses religious ideas in concrete amorous images. Explain the combination of the amorous and the religious in this poem.

4. "The plaguy bill" (line 15) refers to the list of people who have died of the dread disease that decimated the cities of Europe in Donne's lifetime. In what detail does the poet develop the similarity he imagines between his state and that of a victim of the bubonic plague?

AFTERWORD

Faulkner's "The Tall Men" and Plutarch's comparison of "Demosthenes and Cicero" affirm the worth of man and his life in terms of honor, pride, and discipline that "make a man worth preserving, make him of any value," as the old marshal says at the close of Faulkner's story. Such categories cannot exist without the assumption that life is valuable and meaningful. Its value and meaning find expression in what a man does.

None of Faulkner's characters or Plutarch's subjects are faultless men. To use C. S. Lewis and Gerard Manley Hopkins's term, all are "bent." But if we have an affirmative view of life, even when we say a man is bad, we do not say he is valueless. The refusal to discount any man completely has been explicit in almost everything read thus far in this course.

To understand the placing of knock-about farce such as *The Taming of the Shrew* in the category of affirmative images requires an understanding of the nature of simple comedy. It is boundlessly affirmative because it is gay: gayety cannot exist unless life is held valuable.

Yet a word of caution is needed. The affirmations in this section have not been made by disguising the complexity, hardship, and pain of real life. The strongest affirmation is a response to those hard facts — including death itself.

We must beware what J. B. Priestley [1] in a fine essay [2] calls vulgar optimism: "The men who are for ever slapping one on the back and saying that everything will come out right are bad enough, but more intolerable are those persons who will persist in slapping humanity itself on the back and regarding all life with an unchanging grin of approval." Priestley contrasts such men with "Shakespeare among the poets, Fielding and Thackeray among the novelists, Lamb among the essayists, and Johnson among — shall I say — the literary figures; and when I remember what they have known, drudgery, poverty and disease, mad sisters and young wives dead or insane, and all the smaller ills of life besides; when I remember those things and read their work, noting their humor and pathos, their flashes of indignation, their wise wonder, their lasting kindliness, I understand how life, that is neither rosewater nor bitter aloes, should be approached."

Thus it is that the affirmative images cannot be contemplated in isolation. For fuller dimensions of life we proceed to consider its ironic and tragic images, not as contradictions of its affirmative images but as extensions of them.

[1] English novelist, dramatist, and essayist (1894–).   [2] "On Vulgar Optimism."

A PRACTICE TEST

I. Read the following paragraph carefully.

> Worship of a Hero is transcendent admiration of a Great Man.
> I say great men are still admirable! I say there is, at bottom, noth-
> ing else admirable! No nobler feeling than this of admiration for
> one higher than himself dwells in the breast of man. It is to this
> hour, and at all hours, the vivifying influence in man's life.
>
> THOMAS CARLYLE (1795–1881), *On Heroes,*
> *Hero-Worship, and the Heroic in History.*

Having made sure that you understand completely the assertions
made about man by the author in this passage, write an essay evaluating these assertions and considering them in the light of attitudes expressed or implied by authors you have studied in this course.

II. The following two passages describe the same scene. Contrast their
styles and, using specific examples to support your points, show *how*
one of them expresses the more concrete attitude toward the circumstances depicted.

> The uproar in that small, barn-like structure, built of im-
> ported pine boards, and raised clear of the ground, was simply
> stunning. An instrumental uproar, screaming, grunting, whining,
> sobbing, scraping, squeaking some kind of lively air; while a
> grand piano, operated upon by a bony, red-faced woman with
> bad-tempered nostrils, rained hard notes like hail through the
> tempest of fiddles. The small platform was filled with white mus-
> lin dresses and crimson sashes slanting from shoulders provided
> with bare arms, which sawed away without respite.
>
> JOSEPH CONRAD (1857–1924), *Victory.*

> The little pine-board auditorium was filled with noise. The din
> of badly played string instruments at some lively tune was ter-
> rible. An unpleasant-looking woman banged away at a piano in
> accompaniment. The girls in the orchestra were dressed in short-
> sleeved white dresses; they had red sashes across their chests.
> They plied their violins on and on.

III. Read the following poem before answering the questions that follow.

I taste a liquor never brewed,
From tankards scooped in pearl;
Not all the vats upon the Rhine
Yield such an alcohol!

Inebriate of air am I,
And debauchee of dew,
Reeling, through endless summer days,
From inns of molten blue.

When landlords turn the drunken bee
Out of the foxglove's door,
When butterflies renounce their drams,
I shall but drink the more!

Till seraphs swing their snowy hats,
And saints to windows run,
To see the little tippler
Leaning against the sun!

EMILY DICKINSON (1830–1886)

1. What exactly is the liquor on which the poet intoxicates herself?
2. What specific likenesses does she assert to exist between her kind of drunkenness and the alcoholic kind?
3. What differences does she state or imply exist between the two kinds of intoxication?
4. What idea or attitude is the poet trying to express? What effect does her rather bizarre choice of image have on her attempt?
5. Explain the last four lines of the poem.

The affirmative image of man, as we have viewed it, rests on a direct assertion of life's value. It measures man by his best behavior and accomplishments. Valid and important as such a measurement undoubtedly is, alone it is insufficient as a means for examining so complex a matter as the character of human life.

The observer whose attitude is skeptical is able to find some questionable element in virtually all intentions and actions of man. In the detached perspective of such an observer, the assumptions that underlie affirmative images of man appear to be filled with contradictions and surprises. An attitude of skeptical reserve is the basis of the ironic images of man.

On its simplest level, irony is a way of underlining what is clearly apparent by stating it in contradictory or outrageously incongruous terms. Thus we say in disgust at something clumsily done, "Well, that is certainly a deft piece of work!" Giving the name of Little John to the huge lieutenant of Robin Hood's band was an irony; it emphasized the visible fact of his size by contradicting it.

A somewhat more sophisticated form of irony is implicit in an incident that has an outcome significantly different from what was expected. An example is this old Eastern anecdote told by W. Somerset Maugham: [1]

DEATH SPEAKS

There was a merchant in Bagdad who sent his servant to market to buy provisions and in a little while the servant came back, white and trembling, and said, "Master, just now when I was in the marketplace I was jostled by a woman in the crowd and when I turned, I saw it was Death that jostled me. She looked at me and made a threatening gesture; now, lend me your horse, and I will ride away from this city and avoid my fate. I will go to Samarra and there Death will not find me."

The merchant lent him his horse, and the servant mounted it, and he dug his spurs in its flanks, and as fast as the horse could gallop he went.

Then the merchant went down to the marketplace and he saw

[1] English novelist, playwright, and short-story writer (1874–1965).

me standing in the crowd and he came to me and said, "Why did you make a threatening gesture to my servant when you saw him this morning?"

"That was not a threatening gesture," I said, "it was only a start of surprise. I was astonished to see him in Bagdad, for I had an appointment with him tonight in Samarra."

In literature, irony brings under question all assumptions and expectations, tacitly challenges all assertions, is somewhat pessimistic, regards disappointment or disillusionment as more likely than fulfillment, expects more letdown than triumph. It is a corrective to shallow optimism, to complacency, to oversimplifications of many kinds. It sees life and character in complex patterns. The ironic tone may enter into any literary mood from comedy to tragedy. In comedy it lends an edge to satire and its laughter is mocking; in tragedy it exhibits the often-bitter fruits of pride, ambition, or power. Such an aspect of irony is in the lines from Shelley's well-known sonnet "Ozymandias," in which is quoted the inscription on a shattered monument in the desert:

> "My name is Ozymandias, king of kings;
> Look on my works, ye Mighty, and despair!"

A distinguished English critic, George Saintsbury (1845–1933), in his essay "Irony" says:

To mean something different from, or additional to, what you ostensibly say is perhaps the very simplest, most universal, and most accurate description, if not definition, of what, in the European literature of the last two milleniums and a half or thereabouts, has been meant by Irony.

Saintsbury observes further:

I have known instances where irony seemed to be confused with humor. . . . An ironist without humor is almost inconceivable and if he could exist he would be not human but diabolic — intolerable also, I should think, to his fellow devils. But many humorists manage to exist without being at all obviously ironical.

So varied and universal are the uses of irony that it is present to some extent in most literature. The readings in the following section have been selected to give the ironic attitude a particular emphasis.

Florence Nightingale

by Lytton Strachey (1880–1932)

Lytton Strachey infused vigor and color into the art of biography at a time when, in England, it was drab and lifeless. He broke away from a prevailing pattern of ponderous, multi-volumed, "definitive" lives and returned to the brevity with which Plutarch had launched the art.

In 1918 Strachey published *Eminent Victorians,* a book of four biographical essays on Cardinal Manning, Florence Nightingale, Dr. Arnold of Rugby, and General Gordon of Khartoum. The book created a sensation. Compression and distinction of style had been restored to biography. Later Strachey carried his brilliant, intensely personal method into longer biographies in *Queen Victoria* (1921) and *Elizabeth and Essex* (1928).

In the minds of some people Florence Nightingale is only a name vaguely associated with nursing. In the following pages you will find an extraordinary life brought into sharp focus against the background of Victorian England. Strachey acknowledged indebtedness to "an honorable exception to the current commodity, Sir Edward Cook's excellent *Life of Florence Nightingale,* without which my [his] own study, though composed on a very different scale and from a decidedly different angle, could not have been written." To use his words, "scale" and "angle" are what give individuality to his portrait. The scale is comparable to Plutarch's; the angle is strikingly different.

I

Everyone knows the popular conception of Florence Nightingale. The saintly, self-sacrificing woman, the delicate maiden of high degree who threw aside the pleasures of a life of ease to succour the afflicted, the Lady with the Lamp, gliding through the horrors of the hospital at Scutari, and consecrating with the radiance of her goodness the dying soldier's couch — the vision is familiar to all. But the truth was different. The Miss Nightingale of fact was not as facile fancy painted her. She worked in another fashion, and towards another end; she moved under the stress of an impetus which finds no place in the popular imagination. A Demon possessed her. Now demons, whatever else they may be, are full of interest. And so it happens that in the real Miss Nightingale there was more that was interesting than in the legendary one; there was also less that was agreeable.

Her family was extremely well-to-do, and connected by marriage with a spreading circle of other well-to-do families. There was a large country house in Derbyshire; there was another in the New Forest; there were Mayfair rooms for the London season and all its finest parties; there were tours on the Continent with even more than the usual number of Italian operas and of glimpses at the celebrities of Paris. Brought up among such advantages, it was only natural to suppose that Florence would show a proper appreciation of them by doing her duty in that state of life unto which it had pleased God to call her — in other words, by marrying, after a fitting number of dances and dinner-parties, an eligible gentleman, and living happily ever afterwards. Her sister, her cousins, all the young ladies of her acquaintance, were either getting ready to do this or had already done it. It was inconceivable that Florence should dream of anything else; yet dream she did. Ah! To do her duty in that state of life unto which it had pleased God to call her! Assuredly she would not be behindhand in doing her duty; but unto what state of life *had* it pleased God to call her? That was the question. God's calls are many, and they are strange. Unto what state of life had it pleased Him to call Charlotte

Corday,[1] or Elizabeth of Hungary?[2] What was that secret voice in her ear, if it was not a call? Why had she felt, from her earliest years, those mysterious promptings towards . . . she hardly knew what but certainly towards something very different from anything around her? Why, as a child in the nursery, when her sister had shown a healthy pleasure in tearing her dolls to pieces, had *she* shown an almost morbid one in sewing them up again? Why was she driven now to minister to the poor in their cottages, to watch by sick-beds, to put her dog's wounded paw into elaborate splints as if it was a human being? Why was her head filled with queer imaginations of the country house at Embley turned, by some enchantment, into a hospital, with herself as matron moving about among the beds? Why was even her vision of heaven itself filled with suffering patients to whom she was being useful? So she dreamed and wondered, and, taking out her diary, she poured into it the agitations of her soul. And then the bell rang, and it was time to go and dress for dinner.

As the years passed, a restlessness began to grow upon her. She was unhappy, and at last she knew it. Mrs. Nightingale, too, began to no-

[1] **Charlotte Corday:** assassin of Marat, who was a leader of the French Revolution.
[2] **Elizabeth of Hungary:** a saint (1207–1231). She was Queen of Thuringia.

tice that there was something wrong. It was very odd; what could be the matter with dear Flo? Mr. Nightingale suggested that a husband might be advisable; but the curious thing was that she seemed to take no interest in husbands. And with her attractions, and her accomplishments, too! There was nothing in the world to prevent her making a really brilliant match. But no! She would think of nothing but how to satisfy that singular craving of hers to be *doing* something. As if there was not plenty to do in any case, in the ordinary way, at home. There was the china to look after, and there was her father to be read to after dinner. Mrs. Nightingale could not understand it; and then one day her perplexity was changed to consternation and alarm. Florence announced an extreme desire to go to Salisbury Hospital for several months as a nurse; and she confessed to some visionary plan of eventually setting up in a house of her own in a neighbouring village, and there founding "something like a Protestant Sisterhood, without vows, for women of educated feelings." The whole scheme was summarily brushed aside as preposterous; and Mrs. Nightingale, after the first shock of terror, was able to settle down again more or less comfortably to her embroidery. But Florence, who was now twenty-five and felt that the dream of her life had been shattered, came near to desperation.

And, indeed, the difficulties in her path were great. For not only was it an almost unimaginable thing in those days for a woman of means to make her own way in the world and to live in independence, but the particular profession for which Florence was clearly marked out both by her instincts and her capacities was at that time a peculiarly disreputable one. A "nurse" meant then a coarse old woman, always ignorant, usually dirty, often brutal, a Mrs. Gamp,[1] in bunched-up sordid garments, tippling at the brandy-bottle or indulging in worse irregularities. The nurses in the hospitals were especially notorious for immoral conduct; sobriety almost unknown among them; and they could hardly be trusted to carry out the simplest medical duties. Certainly, things have changed since those days; and that they *have* changed is due, far more than to any other human being, to Miss Nightingale herself. It is not to be wondered at that her parents should have shuddered at the notion of their daughter devoting her life to such an occupation. "It was as if," she herself said afterwards, "I had wanted to be a kitchen-maid." Yet the want, absurd, impracticable as it was, not only remained fixed immovably in her heart, but grew in intensity day by day. Her wretchedness deepened into a morbid melancholy. Everything about her was vile, and she herself, it was clear, to have deserved such misery, was

[1] **Mrs. Gamp:** Sarah Gamp, a character in Dickens's *Martin Chuzzlewit.*

even viler than her surroundings. Yes, she had sinned — "standing before God's judgment seat." "No one," she declared, "has so grieved the Holy Spirit"; of that she was quite certain. It was in vain that she prayed to be delivered from vanity and hypocrisy, and she could not bear to smile or to be gay, "because she hated God to hear her laugh, as if she had not repented of her sin."

A weaker spirit would have been overwhelmed by the load of such distresses — would have yielded or snapped. But this extraordinary young woman held firm, and fought her way to victory. With an amazing persistency, during the eight years that followed her rebuff over Salisbury Hospital, she struggled and worked and planned. While superficially she was carrying on the life of a brilliant girl in high society, while internally she was a prey to the tortures of regret and of remorse, she yet possessed the energy to collect the knowledge and to undergo the experience which alone could enable her to do what she had determined she would do in the end. In secret she devoured the reports of medical commissions, the pamphlets of sanitary authorities, the histories of hospitals and homes. She spent the intervals of the London season in ragged schools and workhouses. When she went abroad with her family, she used her spare time so well that there was hardly a great hospital in Europe with which she

was not acquainted, hardly a great city whose slums she had not passed through. She managed to spend some days in a convent school in Rome, and some weeks as a "Sœur de Charité" [1] in Paris. Then, while her mother and sister were taking the waters at Carlsbad, she succeeded in slipping off to a nursing institution at Kaiserswerth, where she remained for more than three months. This was the critical event of her life. The experience which she gained as a nurse at Kaiserswerth formed the foundation of all her future action and finally fixed her in her career.

But one other trial awaited her. The allurements of the world she had brushed aside with disdain and loathing; she had resisted the subtler temptation which, in her weariness, had sometimes come upon her, of devoting her baffled energies to art or literature; the last ordeal appeared in the shape of a desirable young man. Hitherto, her lovers had been nothing to her but an added burden and a mockery; but now — . For a moment, she wavered. A new feeling swept over her — a feeling which she had never known before, which she was never to know again. The most powerful and the profoundest of all the instincts of humanity laid claim upon her. But it rose before her, that instinct, arrayed — how could it be otherwise? — in the inevitable habiliments of a Victorian marriage;

[1] "Sœur de Charité": (French) Sister of Charity.

and she had the strength to stamp it underfoot.

I have an intellectual nature which requires satisfaction [she noted], and that would find it in him. I have a passional nature which requires satisfaction, and that would find it in him. I have a moral, an active nature which requires satisfaction, and that would not find it in his life. Sometimes I think that I will satisfy my passional nature at all events. . . .

But no, she knew in her heart that it could not be. "To be nailed to a continuation and exaggeration of my present life . . . to put it out of my power ever to be able to seize the chance of forming for myself a true and rich life" — that would be a suicide. She made her choice, and refused what was at least a certain happiness for a visionary good which might never come to her at all. And so she returned to her old life of waiting and bitterness.

The thoughts and feelings that I have now [she wrote] I can remember since I was six years old. A profession, a trade, a necessary occupation, something to fill and employ all my faculties, I have always felt essential to me, I have always longed for. The first thought I can remember, and the last, was nursing work; and in the absence of this, education work, but more the education of the bad than of the young. . . . Everything has been tried, foreign travel, kind friends, everything. My God! What is to become of me?

A desirable young man? Dust and ashes! What was there desirable in such a thing as that? "In my thirty-first year," she noted in her diary, "I see nothing desirable but death."

Three more years passed, and then at last the pressure of time told; her family seemed to realize that she was old enough and strong enough to have her way; and she became the superintendent of a charitable nursing home in Harley Street.[1] She had gained her independence, though it was in a meagre sphere enough; and her mother was still not quite resigned: surely Florence might at least spend the summer in the country. At times, indeed, among her intimates, Mrs. Nightingale almost wept. "We are ducks," she said with tears in her eyes, "who have hatched a wild swan." But the poor lady was wrong; it was not a swan that they had hatched; it was an eagle.

II

Miss Nightingale had been a year in her nursing home in Harley Street, when Fate knocked at the door. The Crimean War[2] broke out; the battle of the Alma was fought; and the terrible condition of our military hospitals at Scutari

[1] Harley Street: London street where many doctors have offices.
[2] Crimean War: fought (1854–56) by Russia against Turkey, which was aided by Great Britain, France, and Sardinia. Military operations were confined mainly to the Crimean peninsula.

began to be known in England. It sometimes happens that the plans of Providence are a little difficult to follow, but on this occasion all was plain; there was a perfect co-ordination of events. For years Miss Nightingale had been getting ready; at last she was prepared — experienced, free, mature, yet still young — she was thirty-four — desirous to serve, accustomed to command: at that precise moment the desperate need of a great nation came, and she was there to satisfy it. If the war had fallen a few years earlier, she would have lacked the knowledge, perhaps even the power, for such a work; a few years later and she would, no doubt, have been fixed in the routine of some absorbing task, and, moreover, she would have been growing old. Nor was it only the coincidence of Time that was remarkable. It so fell out that Sidney Herbert was at the War Office and in the Cabinet; and Sidney Herbert was an intimate friend of Miss Nightingale's, convinced, from personal experience in charitable work, of her supreme capacity. After such premises, it seems hardly more than a matter of course that her letter, in which she offered her services for the East, and Sidney Herbert's letter, in which he asked for them, should actually have crossed in the post. Thus it all happened, without a hitch. The appointment was made, and even Mrs. Nightingale, overawed by the magnitude of the venture, could only approve. A pair of faithful friends offered themselves as personal attendants; thirty-eight nurses were collected; and within a week of the crossing of the letters Miss Nightingale, amid a great burst of popular enthusiasm, left for Constantinople.

Among the numerous letters which she received on her departure was one from Dr. Manning,[1] who at that time was working in comparative obscurity as a Catholic priest in Bayswater. "God will keep you," he wrote, "and my prayer for you will be that your one object of Worship, Pattern of Imitation, and source of consolation and strength may be the Sacred Heart of our Divine Lord."

To what extent Dr. Manning's prayer was answered must remain a matter of doubt; but this much is certain, that, if ever a prayer was needed, it was needed then for Florence Nightingale. For dark as had been the picture of the state of affairs at Scutari, revealed to the English public in the despatches of the *Times* correspondent and in a multitude of private letters, yet the reality turned out to be darker still. What had occurred was, in brief, the complete break-down of our medical arrangements at the seat of war. The origins of this awful failure were complex and manifold; they stretched back through long

[1] **Dr. Manning**: Henry Edward Manning (1808–1892), Anglican minister who in 1851 had joined the Roman Catholic Church (in 1875 he was made a cardinal).

years of peace and carelessness in England; they could be traced through endless ramifications of administrative incapacity — from the inherent faults of confused systems to the petty bunglings of minor officials, from the inevitable ignorance of Cabinet Ministers to the fatal exactitudes of narrow routine. In the inquiries which followed it was clearly shown that the evil was in reality that worst of all evils — one which has been caused by nothing in particular and for which no one in particular is to blame. The whole organisation of the war machine was incompetent and out of date. The old Duke [1] had sat for a generation at the Horse Guards [2] repressing innovations with an iron hand. There was an extraordinary overlapping of authorities, an almost incredible shifting of responsibilities to and fro. As for such a notion as the creation and the maintenance of a really adequate medical service for the army — in that atmosphere of aged chaos, how could it have entered anybody's head? Before the war, the easy-going officials at Westminster were naturally persuaded that all was well — or at least as well as could be expected; when someone, for instance, actu-

ally had the temerity to suggest the formation of a corps of army nurses, he was at once laughed out of court. When the war had begun, the gallant British officers in control of affairs had other things to think about than the petty details of medical organisation. Who had bothered with such trifles in the Peninsula? [3] And surely, on that occasion, we had done pretty well. Thus the most obvious precautions were neglected, the most necessary preparations put off from day to day. The principal medical officer of the army, Dr. Hall, was summoned from India at a moment's notice, and was unable to visit England before taking up his duties at the front. And it was not until after the battle of the Alma, when we had been at war for many months, that we acquired hospital accommodations at Scutari for more than a thousand men. Errors, follies, and vices on the part of individuals there doubtless were; but, in the general reckoning, they were of small account — insignificant symptoms of the deep disease of the body politic — the enormous calamity of administrative collapse.

Miss Nightingale arrived at Scutari — a suburb of Constantinople, on the Asiatic side of the Bosphorus — on November 4th, 1854; it was ten days after the battle of Bala-

---

[1] **The old Duke:** the Duke of Wellington (1769–1852), often called "the Iron Duke," victor over Napoleon at Waterloo in 1815.

[2] **Horse Guards:** government building in London, headquarters of the Horse Guards, cavalry serving as guards of the royal household and personal escort of the sovereign.

[3] **Peninsula:** Iberian Peninsula, where Portugal and Spain, together with Great Britain, waged against Napoleon a series of campaigns known as the Peninsular War (1808–14).

clava,[1] and the day before the battle of Inkerman. The organisation of the hospitals, which had already given way under the stress of the battle of the Alma, was now to be subjected to the further pressure which these two desperate and bloody engagements implied. Great detachments of wounded were already beginning to pour in. The men, after receiving such summary treatment as could be given them at the smaller hospitals in the Crimea itself, were forthwith shipped in batches of two hundred across the Black Sea to Scutari. This voyage was in normal times one of four days and a half; but the times were no longer normal, and now the transit often lasted for a fortnight or three weeks. It received, not without reason, the name of "the middle passage." Between, and sometimes on the decks, the wounded, the sick, and the dying were crowded — men who had just undergone the amputation of limbs, men in the clutches of fever or of frostbite, men in the last stages of dysentery and cholera — without beds, sometimes without blankets, often hardly clothed. The one or two surgeons on board did what they could; but medical stores were lacking, and the only form of nursing available was that provided by a handful of invalid soldiers, who were usually themselves prostrate

by the end of the voyage. There was no other food besides the ordinary salt rations of ship diet; and even the water was sometimes so stored that it was out of reach of the weak. For many months, the average of deaths during these voyages was seventy-four in the thousand; the corpses were shot out into the waters; and who shall say that they were the most unfortunate? At Scutari, the landing-stage, constructed with all the perverseness of Oriental ingenuity, could only be approached with great difficulty, and, in rough weather, not at all. When it was reached, what remained of the men in the ships had first to be disembarked, and then conveyed up a steep slope of a quarter of a mile to the nearest of the hospitals. The most serious cases might be put upon stretchers — for there were far too few for all; the rest were carried or dragged up the hill by such convalescent soldiers as could be got together, who were not too obviously infirm for the work. At last the journey was accomplished; slowly, one by one, living or dying, the wounded were carried up into the hospital. And in the hospital what did they find?

Lasciate ogni speranza voi ch'entrate:[2] the delusive doors bore no such inscription; and yet behind them Hell yawned. Want, neglect,

---

[1] **Balaclava**: At this battle occurred the disastrous cavalry charge that Tennyson made famous in his poem "The Charge of the Light Brigade."

[2] *Lasciate . . . entrate:* (Italian) "Abandon all hope, ye who enter here." In the first book of Dante's *Divine Comedy,* this is part of the inscription over the gate of Hell.

confusion, misery — in every shape and in every degree of intensity — filled the endless corridors and the vast apartments of the gigantic barrack-house, which, without forethought or preparation, had been hurriedly set aside as the chief shelter for the victims of the war. The very building itself was radically defective. Huge sewers underlay it, and cess-pools loaded with filth wafted their poison into the upper rooms. The floors were in so rotten a condition that many of them could not be scrubbed; the walls were thick with dirt; incredible multitudes of vermin swarmed everywhere. And, enormous as the building was, it was yet too small. It contained four miles of beds, crushed together so close that there was but just room to pass between them. Under such conditions, the most elaborate system of ventilation might well have been at fault; but here there was no ventilation. The stench was indescribable. "I have been well acquainted," said Miss Nightingale, "with the dwellings of the worst parts of most of the great cities in Europe, but have never been in any atmosphere which I could compare with that of the Barrack Hospital at night." The structural defects were equalled by the deficiencies in the commonest objects of hospital use. There were not enough bedsteads; the sheets were of canvas, and so coarse that the wounded men recoiled from them, begging to be left in their blankets; there was no bedroom

furniture of any kind, and empty beer-bottles were used for candlesticks. There were no basins, no towels, no soap, no brooms, no mops, no trays, no plates; there were neither slippers nor scissors, neither shoebrushes nor blacking; there were no knives or forks or spoons. The supply of fuel was constantly deficient. The cooking arrangements were preposterously inadequate, and the laundry was a farce. As for purely medical materials, the tale was no better. Stretchers, splints, bandages — all were lacking; and so were the most ordinary drugs.

To replace such wants, to struggle against such difficulties, there was a handful of men overburdened by the strain of ceaseless work, bound down by the traditions of official routine, and enfeebled either by old age or inexperience or sheer incompetence. They had proved utterly unequal to their task. The principal doctor was lost in the imbecilities of a senile optimism. The wretched official whose business it was to provide for the wants of the hospital was tied fast hand and foot by red tape. A few of the younger doctors struggled valiantly, but what could they do? Unprepared, disorganised, with such help only as they could find among the miserable band of convalescent soldiers drafted off to tend their sick comrades, they were faced with disease, mutilation, and death in all their most appalling forms, crowded multitudinously about them in an ever-increasing mass. They were like men in a shipwreck, fighting, not for safety, but for the next moment's bare existence — to gain, by yet another frenzied effort, some brief respite from the waters of destruction.

In these surroundings, those who had been long inured to scenes of human suffering — surgeons with a world-wide knowledge of agonies, soldiers familiar with fields of carnage, missionaries with remembrances of famine and of plague — yet found a depth of horror which they had never known before. There were moments, there were places, in the Barrack Hospital at Scutari, where the strongest hand was struck with trembling, and the boldest eye would turn away its gaze.

Miss Nightingale came, and she, at any rate, in that Inferno, did not abandon hope. For one thing, she brought material succour. Before she left London she had consulted Dr. Andrew Smith, the head of the Army Medical Board, as to whether it would be useful to take out stores of any kind to Scutari; and Dr. Andrew Smith had told her that "nothing was needed." Even Sidney Herbert had given her similar assurances; possibly, owing to an oversight, there might have been some delay in the delivery of the medical stores, which, he said, had been sent out from England "in profusion," but "four days would have remedied this." She preferred to trust her own instincts, and at

Marseilles purchased a large quantity of miscellaneous provisions, which were of the utmost use at Scutari. She came, too, amply provided with money — in all, during her stay in the East, about £7000 reached her from private sources; and, in addition, she was able to avail herself of another valuable means of help. At the same time as herself, Mr. Macdonald, of the *Times,* had arrived at Scutari, charged with the duty of administering the large sums of money collected through the agency of that newspaper in aid of the sick and wounded; and Mr. Macdonald had the sense to see that the best use he could make of the *Times* Fund was to put it at the disposal of Miss Nightingale.

I cannot conceive [wrote an eye-witness], as I now calmly look back on the first three weeks after the arrival of the wounded from Inkerman, how it could have been possible to have avoided a state of things too disastrous to contemplate, had not Miss Nightingale been there, with the means placed at her disposal by Mr. Macdonald.

But the official view was different. What! Was the public service to admit, by accepting outside charity, that it was unable to discharge its own duties without the assistance of private and irregular benevolence? Never! And accordingly when Lord Stratford de Redcliffe, our Ambassador at Constantinople, was asked by Mr. Macdonald to indicate how the *Times* Fund could best be employed, he answered that there was indeed one object to which it might very well be devoted — the building of an English Protestant Church at Pera.

Mr. Macdonald did not waste further time with Lord Stratford, and immediately joined forces with Miss Nightingale. But, with such a frame of mind in the highest quarters, it is easy to imagine the kind of disgust and alarm with which the sudden intrusion of a band of amateurs and females must have filled the minds of the ordinary officers and the ordinary military surgeon. They could not understand it; what had women to do with war? Honest Colonels relieved their spleen by the cracking of heavy jokes about "the Bird"; while poor Dr. Hall, a rough terrier of a man, who had worried his way to the top of his profession, was struck speechless with astonishment, and at last observed that Miss Nightingale's appointment was extremely droll.

Her position was, indeed, an official one, but it was hardly the easier for that. In the hospitals it was her duty to provide the services of herself and her nurses when they were asked for by the doctors, and not until then. At first some of the surgeons would have nothing to say to her, and, though she was welcomed by others, the majority were hostile and suspicious. But gradually she gained ground. Her good will could not be denied, and her capacity

could not be disregarded. With consummate tact, with all the gentleness of supreme strength, she managed at last to impose her personality upon the susceptible, overwrought, discouraged, and helpless group of men in authority who surrounded her. She stood firm; she was a rock in the angry ocean; with her alone was safety, comfort, life. And so it was that hope dawned at Scutari. The reign of chaos and old night began to dwindle; order came upon the scene, and common sense, and forethought, and decision, radiating out from the little room off the great gallery in the Barrack Hospital where, day and night, the Lady Superintendent was at her task. Progress might be slow, but it was sure. The first sign of a great change came with the appearance of some of those necessary objects with which the hospitals had been unprovided for months. The sick men began to enjoy the use of towels and soap, knives and forks, combs and tooth-brushes. Dr. Hall might snort when he heard of it, asking, with a growl, what a soldier wanted with a tooth-brush; but the good work went on. Eventually the whole business of purveying to the hospitals was, in effect, carried out by Miss Nightingale. She alone, it seemed, whatever the contingency, knew where to lay her hands on what was wanted; she alone could dispense her stores with readiness; above all, she alone possessed the art of circumventing the pernicious influences of official etiquette. This was her greatest enemy, and sometimes even she was baffled by it. On one occasion 27,000 shirts, sent out at her instance by the Home Government, arrived, were landed, and were only waiting to be unpacked. But the official "Purveyor" intervened; "he could not unpack them," he said, "without a Board." Miss Nightingale pleaded in vain; the sick and wounded lay half-naked shivering for want of clothing; and three weeks elapsed before the Board released the shirts. A little later, however, on a similar occasion, Miss Nightingale felt that she could assert her own authority. She ordered a Government consignment to be forcibly opened, while the miserable "Purveyor" stood by, wringing his hands in departmental agony.

Vast quantities of valuable stores sent from England lay, she found, engulfed in the bottomless abyss of the Turkish Customs House. Other ship-loads, buried beneath munitions of war destined for Balaclava, passed Scutari without a sign, and thus hospital materials were sometimes carried to and fro three times over the Black Sea, before they reached their destination. The whole system was clearly at fault, and Miss Nightingale suggested to the home authorities that a Government Store House should be instituted at Scutari for the reception and distribution of the consignments. Six months after her arrival this was done.

In the meantime she had reor-ganised the kitchens and the laundries in the hospitals. The ill-cooked hunks of meat, vilely served at irregular intervals, which had hitherto been the only diet for the sick men, were replaced by punctual meals, well-prepared and appetising, while strengthening extra foods — soups and wines, and jellies ("preposterous luxuries," snarled Dr. Hall) — were distributed to those who needed them. One thing, however, she could not effect. The separation of the bones from the meat was no part of official cookery: the rule was that the food must be divided into equal portions, and if some of the portions were all bone — well, every man must take his chance. The rule, perhaps, was not a very good one; but there it was. "It would require a new Regulation of the Service," she was told, "to bone the meat." As for the washing arrangements, they were revolutionised. Up to the time of Miss Nightingale's arrival the number of shirts which the authorities had succeeded in washing was seven. The hospital bedding, she found, was "washed" in cold water. She took a Turkish house, had boilers installed, and employed soldiers' wives to do the laundry work. The expenses were defrayed from her own funds and that of the *Times;* and henceforward the sick and wounded had the comfort of clean linen.

Then she turned her attention to their clothing. Owing to military exigencies the greater number of the men had abandoned their kits; their knapsacks were lost forever; they possessed nothing but what was on their persons, and that was usually only fit for speedy destruction. The "Purveyor," of course, pointed out that, according to the regulations, all soldiers should bring with them into hospital an adequate supply of clothing, and he declared that it was no business of his to make good their deficiencies. Apparently, it was the business of Miss Nightingale. She procured socks, boots, and shirts in enormous quantities; she had trousers made, she rigged up dressing-gowns. "The fact is," she told Sidney Herbert, "I am now clothing the British Army."

All at once, word came from the Crimea that a great new contingent of sick and wounded might shortly be expected. Where were they to go? Every available inch in the wards was occupied; the affair was serious and pressing, and the authorities stood aghast. There were some dilapidated rooms in the Barrack Hospital, unfit for human habitation, but Miss Nightingale believed that if measures were promptly taken they might be made capable of accommodating several hundred beds. One of the doctors agreed with her; the rest of the officials were irresolute: it would be a very expensive job, they said; it would involve building; and who could take the responsibility? The proper course was that a representation should be made to the Direc-tor-General of the Army Medical Department in London; then the Director-General would apply to the Horse Guards, the Horse Guards would move the Ordnance, the Ordnance would lay the matter before the Treasury, and if the Treasury gave its consent, the work might be correctly carried through, several months after the necessity for it had disappeared. Miss Nightingale, however, had made up her mind, and she persuaded Lord Stratford — or thought she had persuaded him — to give his sanction to the required expenditure. A hundred and twenty-five workmen were immediately engaged, and the work was begun. The workmen struck; whereupon Lord Stratford washed his hands of the whole business. Miss Nightingale engaged two hundred other workmen on her own authority, and paid the bill out of her own resources. The wards were ready by the required date; five hundred sick men were received in them; and all the utensils, including knives, forks, spoons, cans and towels, were supplied by Miss Nightingale.

This remarkable woman was in truth performing the function of an administrative chief. How had this come about? Was she not in reality merely a nurse? Was it not her duty simply to tend to the sick? And indeed, was it not as a ministering angel, a gentle "lady with a lamp" that she actually impressed the minds of her contemporaries? No doubt that was so; and yet it is no less certain that, as she herself said, the specific business of nursing was "the least important of the functions into which she had been forced." It was clear that in the state of disorganisation into which the hospitals at Scutari had fallen the most pressing, the really vital, need was for something more than nursing; it was for the necessary elements of civilised life — the commonest material objects, the most ordinary cleanliness, the rudimentary habits of order and authority. "Oh, dear Miss Nightingale," said one of her party as they were approaching Constantinople, "when we land, let there be no delays, let us get straight to nursing the poor fellows!" "The strongest will be wanted at the wash-tub," was Miss Nightingale's answer. And it was upon the wash-tub, and all that the wash-tub stood for, that she expended her greatest energies. Yet to say that is perhaps to say too much. For to those who watched her at work among the sick, moving day and night from bed to bed, with that unflinching courage, with that indefatigable vigilance, it seemed as if the concentrated force of an undivided and unparalleled devotion could hardly suffice for that portion of her task alone. Wherever, in those vast wards, suffering was at its worst and the need for help was greatest, there, as if by magic, was Miss Nightingale. Her superhuman equanimity would, at the moment of some ghastly operation, nerve the victim to endure and almost to

hope. Her sympathy would assuage the pangs of dying and bring back to those still living something of the forgotten charm of life. Over and over again her untiring efforts rescued those whom the surgeons had abandoned as beyond the possibility of cure. Her mere presence brought with it a strange influence. A passionate idolatry spread among the men: they kissed her shadow as it passed. They did more. "Before she came," said a soldier, "there was cussin' and swearin', but after that it was as 'oly as a church." The most cherished privilege of the fighting man was abandoned for the sake of Miss Nightingale. In those "lowest sinks of human misery," as she herself put it, she never heard the use of one expression "which could distress a gentlewoman."

She was heroic; and these were the humble tributes paid by those of grosser mould to that high quality. Certainly, she was heroic. Yet her heroism was not of that simple sort so dear to the readers of novels[1] and the compilers of hagiologies[1] — the romantic sentimental heroism with which mankind loves to invest its chosen darlings: it was made of sterner stuff. To the wounded soldier on his couch of agony she might well appear in the guise of a gracious angel of mercy; but the military surgeons, and the orderlies, and her own nurses, and the "Purveyor," and Dr. Hall, and even Lord Stratford himself could

[1] hagiologies: lives of saints.

tell a different story. It was not by gentle sweetness and womanly self-abnegation that she had brought order out of chaos in the Scutari Hospitals, that, from her own resources, she had clothed the British Army, that she had spread her dominion over the serried and reluctant powers of the official world; it was by strict method, by stern discipline, by rigid attention to detail, by ceaseless labour, by the fixed determination of an indomitable will. Beneath her cool and calm demeanour lurked fierce and passionate fires. As she passed through the wards in her plain dress, so quiet, so unassuming, she struck the casual observer simply as the pattern of a perfect lady; but the keener eye perceived something more than that — the serenity of high deliberation in the scope of the capacious brow, the sign of power in the dominating curve of the thin nose, and the traces of a harsh and dangerous temper — something peevish, something mocking, and yet something precise — in the small and delicate mouth. There was humour in the face; but the curious watcher might wonder whether it was humour of a very pleasant kind; might ask himself, even as he heard the laughter and marked the jokes with which she cheered the spirits of her patients, what sort of sardonic merriment this same lady might not give vent to, in the privacy of her chamber. As for her voice, it was true of it, even more than her countenance, that it "had that in it one must fain call master." Those clear tones were in no need of emphasis: "I never heard her raise her voice," said one of her companions. Only, when she had spoken, it seemed as if nothing could follow but obedience. Once, when she had given some direction, a doctor ventured to remark that the thing could not be done. "But it must be done," said Miss Nightingale. A chance bystander, who heard the words, never forgot through all his life the irresistible authority of them. And they were spoken quietly — very quietly indeed.

Late at night, when the long miles of beds lay wrapped in darkness, Miss Nightingale would sit at work in her little room, over her correspondence. It was one of the most formidable of all her duties. There were hundreds of letters to be written to the friends and relations of soldiers; there was the enormous mass of official documents to be dealt with; there were her own private letters to be answered; and, most important of all, there was the composition of her long and confidential reports to Sidney Herbert. These were by no means official communications. Her soul, pent up all day in the restraint and reserve of a vast responsibility, now at last poured itself out in these letters with all its natural vehemence, like a swollen torrent through an open sluice. Here, at least, she did not mince matters. Here she painted in her darkest colours the hideous scenes which surrounded her; here she tore away remorselessly the last veils still shrouding the abominable truth. Then she would fill pages with recommendations and suggestions, with criticisms of the minutest details of organisation, with elaborate calculations of contingencies, with exhaustive analyses and statistical statements piled up in breathless eagerness one on top of the other. And then her pen, in the virulence of its volubility, would rush on to the discussion of individuals, to the denunciation of an incompetent surgeon or the ridicule of a self-sufficient nurse. Her sarcasm searched the ranks of the officials with the deadly and unsparing precision of a machine-gun. Her nicknames were terrible. She respected no one: Lord Stratford, Lord Raglan, Lady Stratford, Dr. Andrew Smith, Dr. Hall, the Commissary-General, the Purveyor — she fulminated against them all. The intolerable futility of mankind obsessed her like a nightmare, and she gnashed her teeth against it. "I do well to be angry," [1] was the burden of her cry. How many just men were there at Scutari? How many who cared at all for the sick, or had done anything for their relief? Were there ten? Were there five? Was there even one? She could not be sure.

At one time, during several weeks, her vituperations descended upon the head of Sidney Herbert himself. He had misinterpreted her

wishes, he had traversed her positive instructions, and it was not until he had admitted his error and apologised in abject terms that he was allowed again into favour. While this misunderstanding was at its height an aristocratic young gentleman arrived at Scutari with a recommendation from the Minister. He had come out from England filled with a romantic desire to render homage to the angelic heroine of his dreams. He had, he said, cast aside his life of ease and luxury; he would devote his days and nights to the service of that gentle lady; he would perform the most menial offices, he would "fag" [2] for her, he would be her footman — and feel requited by a single smile. A single smile, indeed, he had, but it was of an unexpected kind. Miss Nightingale at first refused to see him, and then, when she consented, believing that he was an emissary sent by Sidney Herbert to put her in the wrong over their dispute, she took notes of her conversation with him, and insisted on his signing them at the end of it. The young gentleman returned to England by the next ship.

This quarrel with Sidney Herbert was, however, an exceptional incident. Alike by him, and by Lord Panmure, his successor at the War

[1] "I . . . angry": quotation from the Bible (Jonah, 4:9).

[2] "fag": a term used in the British public schools (which are what we would call private schools); a schoolboy "fags" when he does menial chores for another schoolboy in a higher form or grade.

Office, she was firmly supported; and the fact that during the whole of her stay at Scutari she had the Home Government at her back, was her trump card in her dealings with the hospital authorities. Nor was it only the Government that was behind her: public opinion in England early recognised the high importance of her mission, and its enthusiastic appreciation of her work soon reached an extraordinary height. The Queen herself was deeply moved. She made repeated inquiries as to the welfare of Miss Nightingale; she asked to see her accounts of the wounded, and made her the intermediary between the throne and the troops.

Let Mrs. Herbert know [she wrote to the War Minister] that I wish Miss Nightingale and the ladies would tell these poor noble, wounded, and sick men that *no one* takes a warmer interest or feels *more* for their sufferings or admires their courage and heroism *more* than their Queen. Day and night she thinks of her beloved troops. So does the Prince.[1] Beg Mrs. Herbert to communicate these last words to those ladies, as I know that *our* sympathy is much valued by these noble fellows.

The letter was read aloud in the wards by the Chaplain. "It is a very feeling letter," said the men.

And so the months passed, and that fell winter which had begun with Inkerman and had dragged it-

[1] Prince: Albert, the Prince Consort, husband of Queen Victoria.

self out through the long agony of the investment of Sebastopol,[2] at last was over. In May, 1855, after six months of labour, Miss Nightingale could look with something like satisfaction at the condition of the Scutari hospitals. Had they done nothing more than survive the terrible strain which had been put upon them, it would have been a matter for congratulation; but they had done much more than that; they had marvellously improved. The confusion and the pressure in the wards had come to an end; order reigned in them, and cleanliness; the supplies were bountiful and prompt; important sanitary works had been carried out. One simple comparison of figures was enough to reveal the extraordinary change: the rate of mortality among the cases treated had fallen from 42 per cent to 22 per thousand. But still the indefatigable lady was not satisfied. The main problem had been solved — the physical needs of the men had been provided for; their mental and spiritual needs remained. She set up and furnished reading-rooms and recreation-rooms. She started classes and lectures. Officers were amazed to see her treating their men as if they were human beings, and assured her that she would only end by

[2] investment of Sebastopol: siege of Sebastopol by British, French, and Turks, 1854–55. The name of the city is the title of a book by Count Leo Tolstoy (1828–1910), who fought in the campaign on the Russian side.

"spoiling the brutes." But that was not Miss Nightingale's opinion, and she was justified. The private soldier began to drink less, and even — though that seemed impossible — to save his pay. Miss Nightingale became a banker for the army, receiving and sending home large sums of money every month. At last, reluctantly, the Government followed suit, and established machinery of its own for the remission of money. Lord Panmure, however, remained sceptical; "It will do no good," he pronounced; "the British soldier is not a remitting animal." But, in fact, during the next six months, £71,000 was sent home.

Amid all these activities, Miss Nightingale took up the further task of inspecting the hospitals in the Crimea itself. The labour was extreme, and the conditions of life were almost intolerable. She spent whole days in the saddle, or was driven over those bleak and rocky heights in a baggage cart. Sometimes she stood for hours in the heavily falling snow, and would only reach her hut at dead of night after walking for miles through perilous ravines. Her powers of resistance seemed incredible, but at last they were exhausted. She was attacked by fever, and for a moment came very near to death. Yet she worked on; if she could not move, she could at least write; and write she did until her mind had left her; and after it had left her, in what seemed the delirious trance of death itself, she still wrote. When, after

many weeks, she was strong enough to travel, she was to return to England, but she utterly refused. She would not go back, she said, before the last of the soldiers had left Scutari.

This happy moment had almost arrived, when suddenly the smouldering hostilities of the medical authorities burst out into a flame. Dr. Hall's labours had been rewarded by a K.C.B.[1] — letters which, as Miss Nightingale told Sidney Herbert, she could only suppose to mean "Knight of the Crimean Burial-grounds" — and the honour had turned his head. He was Sir John, and he would be thwarted no longer. Disputes had lately arisen between Miss Nightingale and some of the nurses in the Crimean hospitals. The situation had been embittered by rumours of religious dissensions, for, while the Crimean nurses were Roman Catholics, many of those at Scutari were suspected of a regrettable propensity towards the tenets of Dr. Pusey.[2] Miss Nightingale was by no means disturbed by these sectarian differences, but any suggestion that her supreme authority over all the nurses with the Army was in doubt was enough to rouse her to fury;

[1] K.C.B.: Knight Commander of the Bath, a British order of high distinction. (Among those upon whom it has been bestowed in our time is Sir Winston Churchill.)

[2] Dr. Pusey: English theologian (1800–1882), leader in the Oxford movement to revitalize the Church of England.

and it appeared that Mrs. Bridgeman, the Reverend Mother in the Crimea, had ventured to call that authority in question. Sir John Hall thought that his opportunity had come, and strongly supported Mrs. Bridgeman — or, as Miss Nightingale preferred to call her, the "Reverend Brickbat." There was a violent struggle; Miss Nightingale's rage was terrible. Dr. Hall, she declared, was doing his best to "root her out of the Crimea." She would bear it no longer; the War Office was playing her false; there was only one thing to be done — Sidney Herbert must move for the production of papers in the House of Commons, so that the public might be able to judge between her and her enemies. Sidney Herbert with great difficulty calmed her down. Orders were immediately dispatched putting her supremacy beyond doubt, and the Reverend Brickbat withdrew from the scene. Sir John, however, was more tenacious. A few weeks later, Miss Nightingale and her nurses visited the Crimea for the last time, and the brilliant idea occurred to him that he could crush her by a very simple expedient — he would starve her into submission; and he actually ordered that no rations of any kind should be supplied to her. He had already tried this plan with great effect upon an unfortunate medical man whose presence in the Crimea he had considered an intrusion; but he was now to learn that such tricks

were thrown away upon Miss Nightingale. With extraordinary foresight, she had brought with her a great supply of food; she succeeded in obtaining more at her own expense and by her own exertions; and thus for ten days, in that inhospitable country, she was able to feed herself and twenty-four nurses. Eventually the military authorities intervened in her favour, and Sir John had to confess that he was beaten.

It was not until July, 1856 — four months after the Declaration of Peace — that Miss Nightingale left Scutari for England. Her reputation was now enormous, and the enthusiasm of the public was unbounded. The Royal approbation was expressed by the gift of a brooch, accompanied by a private letter.

You are, I know, well aware [wrote Her Majesty] of the high sense I entertain of the Christian devotion which you have displayed during this great and bloody war, and I need hardly repeat to you how warm my admiration is for your services, which are fully equal to those of my dear and brave soldiers, whose sufferings you have had the *privilege* of alleviating in so merciful a manner. I am, however, anxious of marking my feelings in a manner which I trust will be agreeable to you, and therefore send you with this letter a brooch, the form and emblems of which commemorate your great and blessed work, and which I hope you will wear as a mark of the high approbation of your Sovereign!

"It will be a very great satisfaction to me," Her Majesty added, "to make the acquaintance of one who has set so bright an example to our sex."

The brooch, which was designed by the Prince Consort, bore a St. George's cross in red enamel, and the Royal cypher surmounted by diamonds. The whole was encircled by the inscription, "Blessed are the Merciful."

III

The name of Florence Nightingale lives in the memory of the world by virtue of the lurid and heroic adventure of the Crimea. Had she died — as she nearly did — upon her return to England, her reputation would hardly have been different; her legend would have come down to us almost as we know it to-day — that gentle vision of female virtue which first took shape before the adoring eyes of the sick soldiers at Scutari. Yet, as a matter of fact, she lived for more than half a century after the Crimean War; and during the greater part of that long period all the energy and all the devotion of her extraordinary nature were working at their highest pitch. What she accomplished in those years of unknown labour could, indeed, hardly

have been more glorious than her Crimean triumphs; but it was certainly more important. The true history was far stranger even than the myth. In Miss Nightingale's own eyes the adventure of the Crimea was a mere incident — scarcely more than a useful stepping-stone in her career. It was the fulcrum with which she hoped to move the world; [1] but it was only the fulcrum. For more than a generation she was to sit in secret, working her lever: and her real life began at the very moment when, in the popular imagination, it had ended.

She arrived in England in a shattered state of health. The hardships and the ceaseless effort of the last two years had undermined her nervous system; her heart was pronounced to be affected; she suffered constantly from fainting-fits and terrible attacks of utter physical prostration. The doctors declared that one thing alone would save her — a complete and prolonged rest. But that was also the one thing with which she would have nothing to do. She had never been in the habit of resting; why should she begin now? Now, when her opportunity had come at last; now, when the iron was hot, and it was time to strike? No; she had work to do;

[1] **move the world:** an allusion to a statement made by Archimedes (287–212 B.C.) about the principle of the lever: "Give me but one firm spot on which to stand, and I will move the earth."

and, come what might, she would do it. The doctors protested in vain; in vain her family lamented and entreated, in vain her friends pointed out to her the madness of such a course. Madness? Mad — possessed — perhaps she was. A demoniac frenzy had seized upon her. As she lay upon her sofa, gasping, she devoured blue-books,[1] dictated letters, and, in the intervals of her palpitations, cracked her febrile jokes. For months at a stretch she never left her bed. For years she was in daily expectation of Death. But she would not rest. At this rate, the doctors assured her, even if she did not die, she would become an invalid for life. She could not help that; there was the work to be done; and, as for rest, very likely she might rest . . . when she had done it.

Wherever she went, in London or in the country, in the hills of Derbyshire, or among the rhododendrons at Embley, she was haunted by a ghost. It was the spectre of Scutari — the hideous vision of the organisation of a military hospital. She would lay that phantom, or she would perish. The whole system of the Army Medical Department, the education of the Medical Officer, the regulations of hospital procedure . . . *rest?* How could she rest while these things were as they were, while, if the like necessity were to arise again, the like results would follow? And,

even in peace and at home, what was the sanitary condition of the Army? The mortality in the barracks was, she found, nearly double the mortality in civil life. "You might as well take 1100 men every year out upon Salisbury Plain and shoot them," she said. After inspecting the hospitals at Chatham, she smiled grimly. "Yes, this is one more symptom of the system which, in the Crimea, put to death 16,000 men." Scutari had given her knowledge; and it had given her power too: her enormous reputation was at her back — an incalculable force. Other works, other duties, might lie before her; but the most urgent, the most obvious of all was to look to the health of the Army.

One of her very first steps was to take advantage of the invitation which Queen Victoria had sent her to the Crimea, together with the commemorative brooch. Within a few weeks of her return, she visited Balmoral,[2] and had several interviews both with the Queen and the Prince Consort. "She put before us," wrote the Prince in his diary, "all the defects of our present military hospital system and the reforms that are needed." She related the whole story of her experiences in the East; and, in addition, she managed to have some long and confidential talks with His Royal Highness on metaphysics and re-

[1] **blue-books:** official government publications, generally dull, ponderous tomes.

[2] **Balmoral:** a royal castle in the Scottish Highlands, built under the direction of Prince Albert as a vacation retreat.

ligion. The impression which she created was excellent. "Sie gefällt uns sehr," noted the Prince, "ist sehr bescheiden." [1] Her Majesty's comment was different — "Such a *head!* I wish we had her at the War Office."

But Miss Nightingale was not at the War Office, and for a very simple reason: she was a woman. Lord Panmure, however, *was* (though indeed the reason for that was not quite so simple); and it was upon Lord Panmure that the issue of Miss Nightingale's efforts for reform must primarily depend. That burly Scottish nobleman had not, in spite of his most earnest endeavours, had a very easy time of it as Secretary of State for War. He had come into office in the middle of the Sebastopol campaign, and had felt himself very well fitted for the position, since he had acquired in former days an inside knowledge of the Army — as a Captain of Hussars.[2] It was this inside knowledge which had enabled him to inform Miss Nightingale with such authority that "the British soldier is not a remitting animal." And perhaps it was this same consciousness of a command of his subject which had impelled him to write a dispatch to Lord Raglan,[3] blandly informing the Commander-in-Chief in the

Field just how he was neglecting his duties, and pointing out to him that if he would only try he really might do a little better next time. Lord Raglan's reply, calculated as it was to make its recipient sink into the earth, did not quite have that effect upon Lord Panmure, who, whatever might have been his faults, had never been accused of being supersensitive. However, he allowed the matter to drop; and a little later Lord Raglan died — worn out, some people said, by work and anxiety. He was succeeded by an excellent red-nosed old gentleman, General Simpson, whom nobody had ever heard of, and who took Sebastopol. But Lord Panmure's relations with him were hardly more satisfactory than his relations with Lord Raglan; for, while Lord Raglan had been too independent, poor General Simpson erred in the opposite direction, perpetually asked advice, suffered from lumbago, doubted, his nose growing daily redder and redder, whether he was fit for his post, and, by alternate mails, sent in and withdrew his resignation. Then, too, both the General and the Minister suffered acutely from that distressingly useful new invention, the electric telegraph. On one occasion General Simpson felt obliged actually to expostulate.

I think, my Lord [he wrote], that some telegraphic messages reach us that cannot be sent under due authority, and are perhaps unknown to you,

[1] "Sie . . . bescheiden": (German) "We like her very much, . . . she is very modest."

[2] Hussars: light cavalry.

[3] Lord Raglan: our word *raglan* comes from clothes worn by this British field marshal.

although under the protection of your Lordship's name. For instance, I was called up last night, a dragoon having come express with a telegraphic message in these words, "Lord Panmure to General Simpson — Captain Jarvis has been bitten by a centipede. How is he now?"

General Simpson might have put up with this, though to be sure it did seem "rather too trifling an affair to call for a dragoon to ride a couple of miles in the dark that he may knock up the Commander of the Army out of the very small allowance of sleep permitted him"; but what was really more than he could bear was to find "upon sending in the morning another mounted dragoon to inquire after Captain Jarvis, four miles off, that he never has been bitten at all, but has had a boil, from which he is fast recovering." But Lord Panmure had troubles of his own. His favourite nephew, Captain Dowbiggan, was at the front, and to one of his telegrams to the Commander-in-Chief the Minister had taken occasion to append the following carefully qualified sentence — "I recommend Dowbiggan to your notice, should you have a vacancy, and if he is fit." Unfortunately, in those early days, it was left to the discretion of the telegraphist to compress the messages which passed through his hands; so that the result was that Lord Panmure's delicate appeal reached its destination in the laconic form of "Look after

Dowb." The Headquarters Staff were at first extremely puzzled; they were at last extremely amused. The story spread; and "Look after Dowb" remained for many years the familiar formula for describing official hints in favour of deserving nephews.

And now that all this was over, now that Sebastopol had been, somehow or another, taken; now that peace was, somehow or another, made; now that the troubles of office might surely be expected to be at an end at last — here was Miss Nightingale breaking in upon the scene, with her talk about the state of the hospitals and the necessity for sanitary reform. It was most irksome; and Lord Panmure almost began to wish that he was engaged upon some more cogenial occupation — discussing, perhaps, the constitution of the Free Church of Scotland — a question in which he was profoundly interested. But no; duty was paramount; and he set himself, with a sigh of resignation, to the task of doing as little of it as he possibly could.

"The Bison" his friends called him; and the name fitted both his physical demeanour and his habit of mind. That large low head seemed to have been created for butting rather than for anything else. There he stood, four-square and menacing, in the doorway of reform; and it remained to be seen whether the bulky mass, upon whose solid hide even the barbed arrows of Lord Raglan's scorn had made no mark, would prove amenable to the pressure of Miss Nightingale. Nor was he alone in the doorway. There loomed behind him the whole phalanx of professional conservatism, the stubborn supporters of the out-of-date, the worshippers and the victims of War Office routine. Among these it was only natural that Dr. Andrew Smith, the head of the Army Medical Department, should have been pre-eminent — Dr. Andrew Smith, who had assured Miss Nightingale before she left England that "nothing was wanted at Scutari." Such were her opponents; but she too was not without allies. She had gained the ear of Royalty — which was something; at any moment that she pleased she could gain the ear of the public — which was a great deal. She had a host of admirers and friends; and — to say nothing of her personal qualities — her knowledge, her tenacity, her tact — she possessed, too, one advantage which then, far more even than now, carried an immense weight — she belonged to the highest circle of society. She moved naturally among Peers[1] and Cabinet Ministers — she was one of their own set; and in those days their set was a very narrow one. What kind of attention would such persons have paid to some middle-class woman with whom they were not acquainted, who possessed great experience of army nursing and had

decided views upon hospital reform? They would have politely ignored her; but it was impossible to ignore Flo Nightingale. When she spoke, they were obliged to listen; and, when they had once begun to do that — what might not follow? She knew her power, and she used it. She supported her weightiest minutes with familiar witty little notes. The Bison began to look grave. It might be difficult — it might be damned difficult — to put down one's head against the white hand of a lady.

Of Miss Nightingale's friends, the most important was Sidney Herbert.[2] He was a man upon whom the good fairies seemed to have showered, as he lay in his cradle, all their most enviable gifts. Well born, handsome, rich, the master of Wilton — one of those great country-houses, clothed with the glamour of a historic past, which are the peculiar glory of England — he possessed, besides all these advantages, so charming, so lively, so gentle a disposition that no one who had once come near him could ever be his enemy. He was, in fact, a man of whom it was difficult not to say that he was a perfect English gentleman. For his virtues were equal even to his good fortune. He was religious — deeply religious: "I am more and more

[1] Peers: nobles (ascending order of rank: baron, viscount, earl, marquess, duke).

[2] Herbert: The Herbert family, headed by the Earl of Pembroke, is one of the proudest families of the English nobility; Sidney Herbert was the younger son of the Earl.

convinced every day," he wrote, when he had been for some years a Cabinet Minister, "that in politics, as in everything else, nothing can be right which is not in accordance with the spirit of the Gospel." No one was more unselfish; he was charitable and benevolent to a remarkable degree; and he devoted the whole of his life with an unwavering conscientiousness to the public service. With such a character, with such opportunities, what high hopes must have danced before him, what radiant visions of accomplished duties, of ever-increasing usefulness, of beneficent power, of the consciousness of disinterested success! Some of those hopes and visions were, indeed, realised; but, in the end, the career of Sidney Herbert seemed to show that, with all their generosity, there was some gift or other — what was it? — some essential gift — which the good fairies had withheld, and that even the qualities of a perfect English gentleman may be no safeguard against anguish, humiliation, and defeat.

That career would certainly have been very different if he had never known Miss Nightingale. The alliance between them, which had begun with her appointment to Scutari, which had grown closer and closer while the war lasted, developed, after her return, into one of the most extraordinary of friendships. It was the friendship of a man and a woman intimately bound together by their devotion to a public cause; mutual affection, of course, played a part in it, but it was an incidental part; the whole soul of the relationship was a community of work. Perhaps out of England such an intimacy could hardly have existed — an intimacy so utterly untinctured not only by passion itself but by the suspicion of it. For years Sidney Herbert saw Miss Nightingale almost daily, for long hours together, corresponding with her incessantly when they were apart; and the tongue of scandal was silent; and one of the most devoted of her admirers was his wife. But what made the connection still more remarkable was the way in which the parts that were played in it were divided between the two. The man who acts, decides, and achieves; the woman who encourages, applauds, and — from a distance — inspires: — the combination is common enough; but Miss Nightingale was neither an Aspasia [1] nor an Egeria.[2] In her case it is almost true to say that the roles were reversed; the qualities of pliancy and sympathy fell to the man, those of command and initiative to the woman. There was one

[1] Aspasia: the mistress of Pericles, ruler of Athens in its greatest period (fifth century B.C.). Aspasia was renowned for learning, wit, and beauty.

[2] Egeria: in Roman religion, a nymph who was the consort and adviser of Numa Pompilius, second legendary king of Rome, in succession to Romulus.

thing only which Miss Nightingale lacked in her equipment for public life; she had not — she never could have — the public power and authority which belong to the successful politician. That power and authority Sidney Herbert possessed; the fact was obvious, and the conclusion no less so: it was through the man that the woman must work her will. She took hold of him, taught him, shaped him, absorbed him, dominated him through and through. He did not resist — he did not wish to resist; his natural inclination lay along the same path as hers; only that terrific personality swept him forward at her own fierce pace and with her own relentless stride. Swept him — where to? Ah! Why had he ever known Miss Nightingale? If Lord Panmure was a bison, Sidney Herbert, no doubt, was a stag — a comely, gallant creature springing through the forest; but the forest is a dangerous place. One has the image of those wide eyes fascinated suddenly by something feline, something strong; there is a pause; and then the tigress has her claws in the quivering haunches; and then ——!

Besides Sidney Herbert, she had other friends who, in a more restricted sphere, were hardly less essential to her. If, in her condition of bodily collapse, she were to accomplish what she was determined that she should accomplish, the attentions and the services of others would be absolutely indispensable.

Helpers and servers she must have; and accordingly there was soon formed about her a little group of devoted disciples upon whose affections and energies she could implicitly rely. Devoted, indeed, these disciples were, in no ordinary sense of the term; for certainly she was no light task-mistress, and he who set out to be of use to Miss Nightingale was apt to find, before he had gone very far, that he was in truth being made use of in good earnest — to the very limit of his endurance and his capacity. Perhaps, even beyond those limits; why not? Was she asking of others more than she was giving herself? Let them look at her lying there pale and breathless on the couch; could it be said that she spared herself? Why, then, should she spare others? And it was not for her own sake that she made these claims. For her own sake, indeed! No! They all knew it! it was for the sake of the work. And so the little band, bound body and soul in that strange servitude, laboured on ungrudgingly. Among the most faithful was her "Aunt Mai," her father's sister, who from the earliest days had stood beside her, who had helped her to escape from the thraldom of family life, who had been with her at Scutari, and who now acted almost the part of mother to her, watching over her with infinite care in all the movements and uncertainties which her state of health involved. Another constant attendant was her brother-in-law, Sir

Harry Verney, whom she found particularly valuable in parliamentary affairs. Arthur Clough,[1] the poet, also a connection by marriage, she used in other ways. Ever since he had lost his faith at the time of the Oxford Movement, Clough had passed his life in a condition of considerable uneasiness, which was increased rather than diminished by the practice of poetry. Unable to decide upon the purpose of an existence whose savour had fled together with his belief in the Resurrection, his spirits lowered still further by ill-health, and his income not all that it should be, he had determined to seek the solution of his difficulties in the United States of America. But, even there, the solution was not forthcoming; and when, a little later, he was offered a post in a government department at home, he accepted it, came to live in London, and immediately fell under the influence of Miss Nightingale. Though the purpose of existence might be still uncertain and its nature still unsavoury, here, at any rate, under the eye of this inspired woman, was something real, something earnest: his only doubt was — could he be of any use? Certainly he could. There were a great number of miscellaneous little jobs which there was nobody handy to do. For instance, when Miss Nightingale was travelling, there were

the railway-tickets to be taken; and there were proof-sheets to be corrected; and then there were parcels to be done up in brown paper, and carried to the post. Certainly he could be useful. And so, upon such occupations as these, Arthur Clough was set to work. "This that I see, is not all," he comforted himself by reflecting, "and this that I do is but little; nevertheless it is good, though there is better than it."

As time went on, her "Cabinet," as she called it, grew larger. Officials with whom her work brought her into touch and who sympathised with her objects, were pressed into her service; and old friends of the Crimean days gathered round her when they returned to England. Among these the most indefatigable was Dr. Sutherland, a sanitary expert, who for more than thirty years acted as her confidential private secretary, and surrendered to her purposes literally the whole of his life. Thus sustained and assisted, thus slaved for and adored, she prepared to beard the Bison.

Two facts soon emerged, and all that followed turned upon them. It became clear, in the first place, that that imposing mass was not immovable, and, in the second, that its movement, when it did move, would be exceedingly slow. The Bison was no match for the lady. It was in vain that he put down his head and planted his feet in the earth; he could not withstand her; the white hand forced him back. But the process was an extraordi-

---

[1] **Arthur Clough**: This is the Arthur Hugh Clough (1819–1861) who published the translations of Plutarch used earlier in this course.

narily gradual one. Dr. Andrew Smith and all his War Office phalanx stood behind, blocking the way; the poor Bison groaned inwardly, and cast a wistful eye towards the happy pastures of the Free Church of Scotland; then slowly, with infinite reluctance, step by step, he retreated, disputing every inch of the ground.

The first great measure, which, supported as it was by the Queen, the Cabinet, and the united opinion of the country, it was impossible to resist, was the appointment of a Royal Commission to report upon the health of the Army. The question of the composition of the Commission then immediately arose; and it was over this matter that the first hand-to-hand encounter between Lord Panmure and Miss Nightingale took place. They met, and Miss Nightingale was victorious; Sidney Herbert was appointed Chairman; and, in the end the only member of the Commission opposed to her views was Dr. Andrew Smith. During the interview, Miss Nightingale made an important discovery: she found that "the Bison was bullyable" — the hide was the hide of a Mexican buffalo, but the spirit was the spirit of an Alderney calf. And there was one thing above all others which the huge creature dreaded — an appeal to public opinion. The faintest hint of such a terrible eventuality made his heart dissolve within him; he would agree to anything — he would cut short his grouse-shooting — he would make a speech in the House of Lords — he would even overrule Dr. Andrew Smith — rather than that. Miss Nightingale held the fearful threat in reserve — she would speak out what she knew; she would publish the truth to the whole world, and let the whole world judge between them. With supreme skill, she kept this sword of Damocles poised above the Bison's head, and more than once she was actually on the point of really dropping it. For his recalcitrancy grew and grew. The *personnel* of the Commission once determined upon, there was a struggle, which lasted for six months, over the nature of its powers. Was it to be an efficient body, armed with the right of full inquiry and wide examination, or was it to be a polite official contrivance for exonerating Dr. Andrew Smith? The War Office phalanx closed its ranks, and fought tooth and nail; but it was defeated: the Bison was bullyable.

Three months from this day [Miss Nightingale had written at last] I publish my experience of the Crimean Campaign, and my suggestions for improvement, unless there has been a fair and tangible pledge by that time for reform.

Who could face that?

And, if the need came, she meant to be as good as her word. For she had now determined, whatever might be the fate of the Commission, to draw up her own report upon the questions at issue. The labour involved was enormous; her health was almost desperate; but she did not flinch, and after six months of incredible industry she had put together and written with her own hand her "Notes affecting the Health, Efficiency, and Hospital Administration of the British Army." This extraordinary composition, filling more than eight hundred closely printed pages, laying down vast principles of far-reaching reform, discussing the minutest details of a multitude of controversial subjects, containing an enormous mass of information of the most varied kinds — military, statistical, sanitary, architectural — was never given to the public, for the need never came; but it formed the basis of the Report of the Royal Commission; and it remains to this day the leading authority on the medical administration of armies.

Before it had been completed the struggle over the powers of the Commission had been brought to a victorious close. Lord Panmure had given way once more; he had immediately hurried to the Queen to obtain her consent; and only then, when her Majesty's initials had been irrevocably affixed to the fatal document, did he dare to tell Dr. Andrew Smith what he had done. The Commission met, and another immense load fell upon Miss Nightingale's shoulders. To-day she would, of course, have been one of the Commission herself; but at that time the idea of a woman appearing in such a capac-

ity was unheard of; and no one even suggested the possibility of Miss Nightingale's doing so. The result was that she was obliged to remain behind the scenes throughout, to coach Sidney Herbert in private at every important juncture, and to convey to him and to her other friends upon the Commission the vast funds of her expert knowledge — so essential in the examination of witnesses — by means of innumerable consultations, letters, and memoranda. It was even doubtful whether the proprieties would admit of her giving evidence; and at last, as a compromise, her modesty only allowed her to do so in the form of written answers to written questions. At length the grand affair was finished. The Commission's Report, embodying almost word for word the suggestions of Miss Nightingale, was drawn up by Sidney Herbert. Only one question remained to be answered — would anything, after all, be done? Or would the Royal Commission, like so many other Royal Commissions before and since, turn out to have achieved nothing but the concoction of a very fat blue-book on a very high shelf?

And so the last and the deadliest struggle with the Bison began. Six months had been spent in coercing him into granting the Commission effective powers; six more months were occupied by the work of the Commission; and now yet another six were to pass in extorting from him the means whereby the recommendations of the Commission might be actually carried out. But, in the end the thing was done. Miss Nightingale seemed indeed, during these months, to be upon the very brink of death. Accompanied by the faithful Aunt Mai, she moved from place to place — to Hampstead, to Highgate, to Derbyshire, to Malvern — in what appeared to be a last desperate effort to find health somewhere; but she carried that with her which made health impossible. Her desire for work could now scarcely be distinguished from mania. At one moment she was writing a "last letter" to Sidney Herbert; at the next she was offering to go out to India to nurse the sufferers in the Mutiny.[1] When Dr. Sutherland wrote, imploring her to take a holiday, she raved. Rest! — I am lying without my head, without my claws, and you all peck at me. It is *de rigueur, d'obligation*,[2] like the saying something to one's hat, when one goes into church, to say to me all that has been said to me 110 times a day during the last three months. It is the *obbligato* on the violin, and the twelve violins all practise it together, like the clocks striking 12 o'clock at night all over London, till I say like Xavier de Maistre,[3] *Assez, je le sais,*

je ne le sais que trop.[4] I am not a penitent; but you are like the R. C. confessor, who says what is *de rigueur. . . .*

Her wits began to turn, and there was no holding her. She worked like a slave in a mine. She began to believe, as she had begun to believe at Scutari, that none of her fellow-workers had their hearts in the business; if they had, why did they not work as she did? She could only see slackness and stupidity around her. Dr. Sutherland, of course, was grotesquely muddle-headed; and Arthur Clough incurably lazy. Even Sidney Herbert . . . oh yes, he had simplicity and candour and quickness of perception, no doubt; but he was an eclectic; and what could one hope for from a man who went away to fish in Ireland just when the Bison most needed bullying? As for the Bison himself he had fled to Scotland, where he remained buried for many months. The fate of the vital recommendation in the Commission's Report — the appointment of four Sub-Commissions charged with the duty of determining upon the details of the proposed reforms and of putting them into execution — still hung in the balance. The Bison consented to everything; and then, on a flying visit to London, withdrew his consent and hastily returned to Scotland. Then for many weeks all business was suspended; he had gout — gout in the

[1] the Mutiny: the Sepoy Rebellion in India (1857–58) against British rule.

[2] *de rigueur, d'obligation:* (French) strictly required by etiquette, obligatory.

[3] Xavier de Maistre: French soldier and writer (1763–1852) who served in the Russian army.

[4] *Assez . . . trop:* (French) Enough, I know it, I know it only too well.

hands, so that he could not write. "His gout was always handy," remarked Miss Nightingale. But eventually it was clear even to the Bison that the game was up, and the inevitable surrender came.

There was, however, one point in which he triumphed over Miss Nightingale. The building of Netley Hospital had been begun, under his orders, before her return to England. Soon after her arrival she examined the plans, and found that they reproduced all the worst faults of an out-of-date and mischievous system of hospital construction. She therefore urged that the matter should be reconsidered, and in the meantime building stopped. But the Bison was obdurate; it would be very expensive, and in any case it was too late. Unable to make any impression on him, and convinced of the extreme importance of the question, she determined to appeal to a higher authority. Lord Palmerston was Prime Minister; she had known him from her childhood; he was a near neighbour of her father's in the New Forest. She went down to the New Forest, armed with the plans of the proposed hospital and all the relevant information, stayed the night at Lord Palmerston's house, and convinced him of the necessity of rebuilding Netley.

It seems to me [Lord Palmerston wrote to Lord Panmure] that at Netley all consideration of what would best tend to the comfort and recovery of the patients has been sacrificed to the vanity of the architect, whose sole object has been to make a building which should cut a dash when looked at from the Southampton river. . . . Pray, therefore, stop all further progress in the work until the matter can be duly considered.

But the Bison was not to be moved by one peremptory letter, even if it was from the Prime Minister. He put forth all his powers of procrastination, Lord Palmerston lost interest in the subject, and so the chief military hospital in England was triumphantly completed on unsanitary principles, with unventilated rooms, and with all the patients' windows facing northeast.

But now the time had come when the Bison was to trouble and to be troubled no more. A vote in the House of Commons brought about the fall of Lord Palmerston's Government, and Lord Panmure found himself at liberty to devote the rest of his life to the Free Church of Scotland. After a brief interval, Sidney Herbert became Secretary of State for War. Great was the jubilation in the Nightingale Cabinet; the day of achievement had dawned at last. The next two and a half years (1859-61) saw the introduction of the whole system of reforms for which Miss Nightingale had been struggling so fiercely — reforms which make Sidney Herbert's tenure of power at the War Office an important epoch in the history of the British Army. The four Sub-Commissions, firmly established under the immediate control of the Minister, and urged forward by the relentless perseverance of Miss Nightingale, set to work with a will. The barracks and the hospitals were remodelled; they were properly ventilated and warmed and lighted for the first time; they were given a water supply which actually supplied water, and kitchens where, strange to say, it was possible to cook. Then the great question of the Purveyor — that portentous functionary whose powers and whose lack of powers had weighed like a nightmare upon Scutari — was taken in hand, and new regulations were laid down, accurately defining his responsibilities and his duties. One Sub-Commission reorganised the medical statistics of the Army. Another established — in spite of the last convulsive efforts of the Department — an Army Medical School. Finally the Army Medical Department itself was completely reorganised; an administrative code was drawn up; and the great and novel principle was established that it was as much a part of the duty of the authorities to look after the soldier's health as to look after his sickness. Besides this, it was at last officially admitted that he had a moral and intellectual side. Coffee-rooms and reading-rooms, gymnasiums and workshops were instituted. A new era did in truth appear to have begun. Already by 1861 the mortality in the Army had decreased by one half since the days of the Crimea. It was no wonder that even vaster possibilities began now to open out before Miss Nightingale. One thing was still needed to complete and to assure her triumphs. The Army Medical Department was indeed reorganised; but the great central machine was still untouched. The War Office itself — ! — If she could remould *that* nearer to her heart's desire — there indeed would be a victory! And until that final act was accomplished, how could she be certain that all the rest of her achievements might not, by some capricious turn of Fortune's wheel — a change of Ministry, perhaps, replacing Sidney Herbert by some puppet of the permanent official gang — be swept to limbo in a moment?

Meanwhile, still ravenous for more and yet more work, her activities had branched out into new directions. The army in India claimed her attention. A Sanitary Commission, appointed at her suggestion, and working under her auspices, did for our troops there what the four Sub-Commissions were doing for those at home. At the same time, these very years which saw her laying the foundations of the whole modern system of medical work in the army, saw her also beginning to bring her knowledge, her influence, and her activity into the service of the country at large. Her *Notes on Hospitals* (1859) revolutionised the theory of hospital construction and hospital management. She was immediately recognised as the leading expert upon all the questions involved; her advice flowed unceasingly and in all directions, so that there is no great hospital today which does not bear upon it the impress of her mind. Nor was this all. With the opening of the Nightingale Training School for Nurses at St. Thomas's Hospital (1860), she became the founder of modern nursing.

But a terrible crisis was now fast approaching. Sidney Herbert had consented to undertake the root and branch reform of the War Office. He had sallied forth into that tropical jungle of festooned obstructiveness, of intertwisted irresponsibilities, of crouching prejudices, of abuses grown stiff and rigid with antiquity, which for so many years to come was destined to lure reforming ministers to their doom.

The War Office [said Miss Nightingale] is a very slow office, an enormously expensive office, and one in which the Minister's intentions can be entirely negatived by all his sub-departments, and those of each of the sub-departments by every other.

It was true; and, of course, at the first rumour of a change, the old phalanx of reaction was bristling with its accustomed spears. At its head stood no longer Dr. Andrew Smith, who, some time since, had followed the Bison into outer darkness, but a yet more formidable figure, the permanent Under-Secretary himself, Sir Benjamin Hawes —

Ben Hawes the Nightingale Cabinet irreverently dubbed him — a man remarkable even among civil servants for adroitness in baffling inconvenient inquiries, resource in raising false issues, and, in short, a consummate command of all the arts of officially sticking in the mud. "Our scheme will probably result in Ben Hawes's resignation," Miss Nightingale said; "and that is another of its advantages." Ben Hawes himself, however, did not quite see it in that light. He set himself to resist the wishes of the Minister by every means in his power. The struggle was long and desperate; and, as it proceeded, it gradually became evident to Miss Nightingale that something was the matter with Sidney Herbert. What was it? His health, never very strong, was, he said, in danger of collapsing under the strain of his work. But, after all, what is illness, when there is a War Office to be reorganised? Then he began to talk of retiring altogether from public life. The doctors were consulted, and declared that, above all things, what was necessary was rest. Rest! She grew seriously alarmed. Was it possible that, at the last moment, the crowning wreath of victory was to be snatched from her grasp? She was not to be put aside by doctors; they were talking nonsense; the necessary thing was not rest but the reform of the War Office; and, besides, she knew very well from her own case what one could do even when one was on the point of death. She expostulated vehemently, passionately: the goal was so near, so very near; he could not turn back now! At any rate, he could not resist Miss Nightingale. A compromise was arranged. Very reluctantly, he exchanged the turmoil of the House of Commons for the dignity of the House of Lords,[1] and he remained at the War Office. She was delighted. "One fight more, the best and the last," she said.

For several more months the fight did indeed go on. But the strain upon him was greater even than she perhaps could realise. Besides the intestine war in his office, he had to face a constant battle in the Cabinet with Mr. Gladstone [2] — a more redoubtable antagonist even than Ben Hawes — over the estimates. His health grew worse and worse. He was attacked by fainting-fits; and there were some days when he could only just keep himself going by gulps of brandy. Miss Nightingale spurred him forward with her encouragements and her admonitions, her zeal and her example. But at last his spirit began to sink as well as his body. He could no longer hope; he could no longer desire; it was useless, all useless; it was utterly impossible. He had failed. The dreadful moment came when the truth was forced upon

him: he would never be able to reform the War Office. But a yet more dreadful moment lay behind; he must go to Miss Nightingale and tell her that he was a failure, a beaten man.

Blessed are the merciful! What strange ironic prescience had led Prince Albert, in the simplicity of his heart, to choose that motto for the Crimean brooch? The words hold a double lesson; and, alas! when she brought herself to realise at length what was indeed the fact and what there was no helping, it was not in mercy that she turned upon her old friend.

Beaten! [she exclaimed] Can't you see that you've simply thrown away the game? And with all the winning cards in your hands! And so noble a game! Sidney Herbert beaten! And beaten by Ben Hawes! It is a worse disgrace. . . . [her full rage burst out at last] a worse disgrace than the hospitals at Scutari.

He dragged himself away from her, dragged himself to Spa, hoping vainly for a return of health, and then, despairing, back again to England, to Wilton, to the majestic house standing there resplendent in the summer sunshine, among the great cedars which had lent their shade to Sir Philip Sidney,[3] and

[1] **exchanged . . . Lords:** Sidney Herbert was made a baron in 1861.
[2] **Mr. Gladstone:** William Ewart Gladstone (1809–1898), British statesman, dominant personality of the Liberal Party (1868–1894). He served four times as prime minister.

[3] **Sir Philip Sidney:** English soldier, statesman, author (1554–1586). He was the last of the mirrors of knighthood; his sister, the wife of the Earl of Pembroke, was one of Sidney Herbert's ancestors.

all those familiar, darling haunts of beauty which he loved, each one of them, "as if they were persons"; and at Wilton he died. After having received the Eucharist he had become perfectly calm; then, almost unconscious, his lips were seen to be moving. Those about him bent down. "Poor Florence! Poor Florence!" they just caught. ". . . Our joint work . . . unfinished . . . tried to do . . ." and they could hear no more.

When the onward rush of a powerful spirit sweeps a weaker one to its destruction, the commonplaces of the moral judgment are better left unmade. If Miss Nightingale had been less ruthless, Sidney Herbert would not have perished; but then, she would not have been Miss Nightingale. The force that created was the force that destroyed. It was her Demon that was responsible. When the fatal news reached her, she was overcome by agony. In the revulsion of her feelings, she made a worship of the dead man's memory; and the facile instrument which had broken in her hand she spoke of for ever after as her "Master." Then, almost at the same moment, another blow fell upon her. Arthur Clough, worn out by labours very different from those of Sidney Herbert, died too: never more would he tie up her parcels. And yet a third disaster followed. The faithful Aunt Mai did not, to be sure, die; no, she did something almost worse: she left Miss Nightingale. She was growing old, and she felt that she had closer and more imperative duties with her own family. Her niece could hardly forgive her. She poured out, in one of her enormous letters, a passionate diatribe upon the faithlessness, the lack of sympathy, the stupidity, the ineptitude of women. Her doctrines had taken no hold among them; she had never known one who had *appris à apprendre;* [1] she could not even get a woman secretary; "they don't know the names of the Cabinet Ministers — they don't know which of the Churches has Bishops and which not." As for the spirit of self-sacrifice, well — Sidney Herbert and Arthur Clough were men, and they indeed had shown their devotion; but women — ! She would mount three widow's caps "for a sign." The first two would be for Clough and for her Master; but the third, "the biggest widow's cap of all" — would be for Aunt Mai. She did well to be angry; she was deserted in her hour of need; and, after all, could she be sure that even the male sex was so impeccable? There was Dr. Sutherland, bungling as usual. Perhaps even he intended to go off, one of these days, too? She gave him a look, and he shivered in his shoes. No! — she grinned sardonically; she would always have Dr. Sutherland. And then she reflected that there was one thing more that she would always have — her work.

[1] *appris à apprendre:* (French) learned [how] to learn.

IV

Sidney Herbert's death finally put an end to Miss Nightingale's dream of a reformed War Office. For a moment, indeed, in the first agony of her disappointment, she had wildly clutched at a straw; she had written to Mr. Gladstone to beg him to take up the burden of Sidney Herbert's work. And Mr. Gladstone had replied with a sympathetic account of the funeral.

Succeeding Secretaries of State managed between them to undo a good deal of what had been accomplished, but they could not undo it all; and for ten years more (1862–72) Miss Nightingale remained a potent influence at the War Office. After that, her direct connection with the army came to an end, and her energies began to turn more and more completely towards more general objects. Her work upon hospital reform assumed enormous proportions; she was able to improve the conditions in infirmaries and workhouses; and one of her most remarkable papers forestalls the recommendations of the Poor Law Commission of 1909. Her training school for nurses, with all that it involved in initiative, control, responsibility, and combat, would have been enough in itself to have absorbed the whole efforts of at least two lives of ordinary vigour. And at the same time her work in connection with India, which had begun with the Sanitary Commission on the Indian Army, spread and ramified in a multitude of directions. Her tentacles reached the India Office and succeeded in establishing a hold even upon those slippery high places. For many years it was *de rigueur* for the newly appointed Viceroy, before he left England, to pay a visit to Miss Nightingale.

After much hesitation, she had settled down in a small house in South Street, where she remained for the rest of her life. That life was a very long one; the dying woman reached her ninety-first year. Her ill-health gradually diminished; the crises of extreme danger became less frequent, and at last, altogether ceased; she remained an invalid, but an invalid of a curious character — an invalid who was too weak to walk downstairs and who worked far harder than most Cabinet Ministers. Her illness, whatever it may have been, was certainly not inconvenient. It involved seclusion; and an extraordinary, an unparalleled seclusion was, it might almost have been said, the mainspring of Miss Nightingale's life. Lying on her sofa in the little upper room in South Street, she combined the intense vitality of a dominating woman of the world with the mysterious and romantic quality of a myth. She was a legend in her lifetime, and she knew it. She tasted the joys of power, like those Eastern Emperors whose autocratic rule was based upon invisibility, with the mingled satisfactions of obscurity and fame. And she found the machinery of illness hardly less effective as a barrier against the eyes of men than the ceremonial of a palace. Great statesmen and renowned generals were obliged to beg for audiences; admiring princesses from foreign countries found that they must see her at her own time, or not at all; and the ordinary mortal had no hope of ever getting beyond the downstairs sitting-room and Dr. Sutherland. For that indefatigable disciple did, indeed, never desert her. He might be impatient, he might be restless, but he remained. His "incurable looseness of thought," for so she termed it, continued at her service to the end. Once, it is true, he had actually ventured to take a holiday; but he was recalled, and he did not repeat the experiment. He was wanted downstairs. There he sat, transacting business, answering correspondence, interviewing callers, and exchanging innumerable notes with the unseen power above. Sometimes word came down that Miss Nightingale was just well enough to see one of her visitors. The fortunate man was led up, was ushered, trembling, into the shaded chamber, and, of course, could never afterwards forget the interview. Very rarely, indeed, once or twice a year, perhaps, but nobody could be quite certain, in deadly secrecy, Miss Nightingale went out for a drive in the Park. Unrecognised, the living legend flitted for a moment before the common gaze. And the precaution was necessary; for there were times when, at some public function, the rumour of her presence was spread abroad; and ladies, mistaken by the crowd for Miss Nightingale, were followed, pressed upon, and vehemently supplicated — "Let me touch your shawl," — "Let me stroke your arm"; such was the strange adoration in the hearts of the people. That vast reserve of force lay there behind her; she could use it, if she would. But she preferred never to use it. On occasions, she might hint or threaten; she might balance the sword of Damocles over the head of the Bison; she might, by a word, by a glance, remind some refractory minister, some unpersuadable viceroy, sitting in audience with her in the little upper room, that she was something more than a mere sick woman, that she had only, so to speak, to go to the window and wave her handkerchief, for . . . dreadful things to follow. But that was enough; they understood; the myth was there — obvious, portentous, impalpable; and so it remained to the last.

With statesmen and governors at her beck and call, with her hands on a hundred strings, with mighty provinces at her feet, with foreign governments agog for her counsel, building hospitals, training nurses — she still felt that she had not enough to do. She sighed for more worlds to conquer — more, and yet more. She looked about her — what was there left? Of course! Philosophy! After the world of action, the world of thought. Having set right the health of the British Army, she would now do the same good service for the religious convictions of mankind. She had long noticed — with regret — the growing tendency towards free-thinking among artisans. With regret, but not altogether with surprise; the current teaching of Christianity was sadly to seek; nay, Christianity itself was not without its defects. She would rectify these errors. She would correct the mistakes of the Churches; she would point out just where Christianity was wrong; and she would explain to the artisans what the facts of the case really were. Before her departure for the Crimea, she had begun this work; and now, in the intervals of her other labours, she completed it. Her "Suggestions for Thought to the Searchers after Truth among the Artisans of England" (1860), unravels, in the course of three portly volumes, the difficulties — hitherto, curiously enough, unsolved — connected with such matters as Belief in God, the Plan of Creation, the Origin of Evil, the Future Life, Necessity and Free Will, Law, and the Nature of Morality. The Origin of Evil, in particular, held no perplexities for Miss Nightingale. "We cannot conceive," she remarks, "that Omnipotent Righteousness would find satisfaction in *solitary existence.*" This being so, the only question remaining to be asked is, "What beings should we then conceive that God would create?" Now, He cannot create perfect beings, "since,

essentially, perfection is one"; if He did so, He would only be adding to Himself. Thus the conclusion is obvious: He *must* create *im*perfect ones. Omnipotent Righteousness, faced by the intolerable *impasse* of a solitary existence, finds itself bound, by the very nature of the case, to create the hospitals at Scutari. Whether this argument would have satisfied the artisans, was never discovered, for only a very few copies of the book were printed for private circulation. One copy was sent to Mr. Mill,[1] who acknowledged it in an extremely polite letter. He felt himself obliged, however, to confess that he had not been altogether convinced by Miss Nightingale's proof of the existence of God. Miss Nightingale was surprised and mortified; she had thought better of Mr. Mill; for surely her proof of the existence of God could hardly be improved upon. "A law," she had pointed out, "implies a lawgiver." Now the Universe is full of laws — the law of gravitation, the law of the excluded middle,[2] and many others; hence it follows that the Universe has a lawgiver — and what would Mr. Mill be satisfied with, if he was not satisfied with that?

Perhaps Mr. Mill might have asked why the argument had not

---

[1] **Mr. Mill:** John Stuart Mill (1806–1873), English philosopher and economist.

[2] **law of the excluded middle:** a principle in logic: if one of two contradictory statements is denied, the other must be affirmed.

been pushed to its logical conclusion. Clearly, if we are to trust the analogy of human institutions, we must remember that laws are, as a matter of fact, not dispensed by lawgivers, but passed by Act of Parliament. Miss Nightingale, however, with all her experience of public life, never stopped to consider the question whether God might not be a Limited Monarchy.

Yet her conception of God was certainly not orthodox. She felt towards Him as she might have felt towards a glorified sanitary engineer; and in some of her speculations she seems hardly to distinguish between the Deity and the Drains. As one turns over these singular pages, one has the impression that Miss Nightingale has got the Almighty too into her clutches, and that, if He is not careful, she will kill Him with overwork.

Then, suddenly, in the very midst of the ramifying generalities of her metaphysical disquisitions there is an unexpected turn, and the reader is plunged all at once into something particular, something personal, something impregnated with intense experience — a virulent invective upon the position of women in the upper ranks of society. Forgetful alike of her high argument and of the artisans, the bitter creature rails through a hundred pages of close print at the falsities of family life, the ineptitudes of marriage, the emptiness of convention, in the spirit of an Ibsen or a Samuel But-

ler.[1] Her fierce pen, shaking with intimate anger, depicts in biting sentences the fearful fate of an unmarried girl in a wealthy household. It is a *cri du cœur;*[2] and then, as suddenly, she returns once more to instruct the artisans upon the nature of Omnipotent Righteousness.

Her mind was, indeed, better qualified to dissect the concrete and distasteful fruits of actual life than to construct a coherent system of abstract philosophy. In spite of her respect for Law, she was never at home with a generalisation. Thus, though the great achievement of her life lay in the immense impetus which she gave to the scientific treatment of sickness, a true comprehension of the scientific method itself was alien to her spirit. Like most great men of action — perhaps like all — she was simply an empiricist. She believed in what she saw, and she acted accordingly; beyond that she would not go. She had found in Scutari that fresh air and light played an effective part in the prevention of the maladies with which she had to deal; and that was enough for her; she would not inquire further; what were the general principles underlying that fact

[1] **Ibsen . . . Butler:** Both Henrik Ibsen (1828–1906), Norwegian dramatist and poet, and Samuel Butler (1835–1902), English author, unveiled truths which the society of their day preferred to keep hidden.

[2] *cri du cœur:* (French) cry from the heart.

— or even whether there were any — she refused to consider. Years after the discoveries of Pasteur and Lister,[1] she laughed at what she called the "germ-fetish." There was no such thing as "infection"; she had never seen it, therefore it did not exist. But she *had* seen the good effects of fresh air; therefore there could be no doubt about them; and therefore it was essential that the bedrooms of patients should be well ventilated. Such was her doctrine; and in those days of hermetically sealed windows it was a very valuable one. But it was a purely empirical doctrine, and thus it led to some unfortunate results. When, for instance, her influence in India was at its height, she issued orders that all hospital windows should be invariably kept open. The authorities, who knew what an open window in the hot weather meant, protested, but in vain; Miss Nightingale was incredulous. She knew nothing of the hot weather, but she did know the value of fresh air — from personal experience; the authorities were talking nonsense and the windows must be kept open all the year round. There was a great

[1] Pasteur and Lister: Louis Pasteur (1822–1895), a French chemist, formulated the theory that bacteria cause infection; Joseph Lister (1827–1912), an English surgeon, brought to surgery the principle of antisepsis, an outgrowth of Pasteur's theory. In 1865 Lister proved the effectiveness of his methods, thus founding modern antiseptic surgery.

outcry from all the doctors in India, but she was firm; and for a moment it seemed possible that her terrible commands would have to be put into execution. Lord Lawrence, however, was Viceroy, and he was able to intimate to Miss Nightingale, with sufficient authority, that he himself had decided upon the question, and that his decision must stand, even against her own. Upon that, she gave way, but reluctantly and quite unconvinced; she was only puzzled by the unexpected weakness of Lord Lawrence. No doubt, if she had lived to-day, and if her experience had lain, not among cholera cases at Scutari but among yellow-fever cases in Panama, she would have declared fresh air a fetish, and would have maintained to her dying day that the only really effective way of dealing with disease was by the destruction of mosquitoes.

Yet her mind, so positive, so realistic, so ultra-practical, had its singular revulsions, its mysterious moods of mysticism and of doubt. At times, lying sleepless in the early hours, she fell into long strange agonized meditations, and then, seizing a pencil, she would commit to paper the confessions of her soul. The morbid longings of her pre-Crimean days came over her once more; she filled page after page with self-examination, self-criticism, self-surrender. "O Father," she wrote, "I submit, I resign myself,

I accept with all my heart this stretching out of Thy hand to save me. . . . O how vain it is, the vanity of vanities, to live in men's thoughts instead of God's! " She was lonely, she was miserable. " Thou knowest that through all these horrible twenty years, I have been supported by the belief that I was working with Thee who wert bringing everyone, even our poor nurses, to perfection,"—and yet, after all, what was the result? Had not even she been an unprofitable servant? One night, waking suddenly, she saw, in the dim light of the night-lamp, tenebrous shapes upon the wall. The past rushed back upon her. "Am I she who once stood on that Crimean height?" she wildly asked — " 'The Lady with a lamp shall stand. . . .' The lamp shows me only my utter shipwreck."

She sought consolation in the writings of the Mystics and in a correspondence with Mr. Jowett.[1] For many years the Master of Balliol acted as her spiritual adviser. He discussed with her in a series of enormous letters the problems of religion and philosophy; he criticised her writings on those subjects with the tactful sympathy of a cleric who was also a man of the world; and he even ventured to

attempt at times to instil into her rebellious nature some of his own peculiar suavity. "I sometimes think," he told her, "that you ought seriously to consider how your work may be carried on, not with less energy, but in a calmer spirit. I am not blaming the past. . . . But I want the peace of God to settle on the future." He recommended her to spend her time no longer in "conflicts with Government offices," and to take up some literary work. He urged her to "work out her notion of Divine Perfection," in a series of essays for *Fraser's Magazine*. She did so; and the result was submitted to Mr. Froude,[2] who pronounced the second essay to be "even more pregnant than the first. I cannot tell," he said, "how sanitary, with disordered intellects, the effects of such papers will be." Mr. Carlyle,[3] indeed, used different language, and some remarks of his about a lost lamb bleating on the mountains having been unfortunately repeated to Miss Nightingale, all Mr. Jowett's suavity was required to keep the peace. In a letter of fourteen sheets, he turned her attention from the painful topic towards a discussion of Quietism.[4] "I don't

[1] **Mr. Jowett:** Benjamin Jowett (1817–1893), classical scholar, clergyman, Master of Balliol College of Oxford University, one of the greatest educators England has had. He is well known largely for his translation of the *Dialogues* of Plato.

[2] **Mr. Froude:** James Anthony Froude (1818–1894), historian and editor of *Fraser's Magazine*.

[3] **Mr. Carlyle:** Thomas Carlyle (1795–1881), Scottish historian and man of letters.

[4] **Quietism:** a form of religious mysticism cultivating an indifference to worldly or outward activities.

see why," said the Master of Balliol, "active life might not become a sort of passive life too." And then, he added, "I sometimes fancy there are possibilities of human character much greater than have been realised." She found such sentiments helpful, underlining them in blue pencil; and, in return, she assisted her friend with a long series of elaborate comments upon the *Dialogues* of Plato, most of which he embodied in the second edition of his translation. Gradually her interest became more personal; she told him never to work again after midnight, and he obeyed her. Then she helped him to draw up a special form of daily service for the College Chapel, with selections from the Psalms, under the heads of "God the Lord, God the Judge, God the Father, and God the Friend," — though, indeed, this project was never realised; for the Bishop of Oxford disallowed the alterations, exercising his legal powers, on the advice of Sir Travers Twiss.

Their relations became intimate. "The spirit of the twenty-third psalm and the spirit of the nineteenth psalm should be united in our lives," Mr. Jowett said. Eventually, she asked him to do her a singular favour. Would he, knowing what he did of her religious views, come to London and administer to her the Holy Sacrament? He did not hesitate, and afterwards declared that he would always regard the occasion as a solemn event in his life. He was devoted to her; though the precise nature of his feelings towards her never quite transpired. Her feelings towards him were more mixed. At first, he was "that great and good man" — "that true saint, Mr. Jowett"; but, as time went on, some gall was mingled with the balm; the acrimony of her nature asserted itself. She felt that she gave more sympathy than she received; she was exhausted, she was annoyed, by his conversation. Her tongue, one day, could not refrain from shooting out at him. "He comes to me, and he talks to me," she said, "as if I were someone else."

V

At one time she had almost decided to end her life in retirement, as a patient at St. Thomas's Hospital. But partly owing to the persuasions of Mr. Jowett, she changed her mind; for forty-five years she remained in South Street; and in South Street she died. As old age approached, though her influence with the official world gradually diminished, her activities seemed to remain as intense and widespread as before. When hospitals were to be built, when schemes of sanitary reform were in agitation, when wars broke out, she was still the adviser of all Europe. Still, with a characteristic self-assurance, she watched from her Mayfair bedroom over the welfare of India. Still, with an indefatigable enthusiasm, she pushed forward the work, which, perhaps, was nearer to her heart, more completely her own, than all the rest — the training of nurses. In her moments of deepest depression, when her greatest achievements seemed to lose their lustre, she thought of her nurses, and was comforted. The ways of God, she found, were strange indeed. "How inefficient I was in the Crimea," she noted. "Yet He has raised up from it trained nursing."

At other times she was better satisfied. Looking back, she was amazed by the enormous change which, since her early days, had come over the whole treatment of illness, the whole conception of public and domestic health — a change in which, she knew, she had played her part. One of her Indian admirers, the Aga Khan,[1] came to visit her. She expatiated on the marvellous advances she had lived to see in the management of hospitals, in drainage, in ventilation, in sanitary work of every kind. There was a pause; and then, "Do you think you are improving?" asked the Aga Khan. She was a little taken aback, and said, "What do you mean by 'improving'?" He replied, "Believing more in God." She saw that he had a view of God which was different from hers. "A most interesting man," she noted after the interview; "but you could never teach him sanitation."

[1] the Aga Khan: hereditary ruler of a Moslem sect.

When old age actually came, something curious happened. Destiny, having waited very patiently, played a queer trick on Miss Nightingale. The benevolence and public spirit of that long life had only been equalled by its acerbity. Her virtue had dwelt in hardness, and she had poured forth her unstinted usefulness with a bitter smile upon her lips. And now the sarcastic years brought the proud woman her punishment. She was not to die as she had lived. The sting was to be taken out of her: she was to be made soft; she was to be reduced to compliance and complacency. The change came gradually, but at last it was unmistakable. The terrible commander who had driven Sidney Herbert to his death, to whom Mr. Jowett had applied the words of Homer, ἄμοτον μεμαῦια — raging insatiably — now accepted small compliments with gratitude, and indulged in sentimental friendships with young girls. The author of *Notes on Nursing* — that classical compendium of the besetting sins of the sisterhood, drawn up with the detailed acrimony, the vindictive relish, of a Swift — now spent long hours in composing sympathetic Addresses to Probationers, whom she petted and wept over in turn. And, at the same time there appeared a corresponding alteration in her physical mould. The thin, angular woman, with her haughty eye and her acrid mouth had vanished; and in her place was the rounded bulky form of a fat old lady, smiling all day long. Then something else became visible. The brain which had been steeled at Scutari was indeed, literally, growing soft. Senility — an ever more and more amiable senility — descended. Towards the end, consciousness itself grew lost in a roseate haze, and melted into nothingness. It was just then, three years before her death, when she was eighty-seven years old (1907), that those in authority bethought them that the opportune moment had come for bestowing a public honour on Florence Nightingale. She was offered the Order of Merit. That Order, whose roll contains, among other distinguished names, those of Sir Laurence Alma-Tadema [1] and Sir Edward Elgar [2] is remarkable chiefly for the fact that, as its title indicates, it is bestowed because its recipient deserves it, and for no other reason. Miss Nightingale's representatives accepted the honour, and her name, after a lapse of many years, once more appeared in the Press. Congratulations from all sides came pouring in. There was a universal burst of enthusiasm — a final revivification of the ancient myth. Among her other admirers, the German Emperor took this opportunity of expressing his feelings towards her. "His Majesty," wrote the German Ambassador, "having just brought to a close a

[1] Sir Laurence Alma-Tadema: painter (1836–1912).
[2] Sir Edward Elgar: composer (1857–1934).

most enjoyable stay in the beautiful neighbourhood of your old home near Romsey, has commanded me to present you with some flowers as a token of his esteem." Then, by Royal command, the Order of Merit was brought to South Street, and there was a little ceremony of presentation. Sir Douglas Dawson, after a short speech, stepped forward, and handed the insignia of the Order to Miss Nightingale. Propped up by pillows, she dimly recognised that some compliment was being paid her. "Too kind — too kind," she murmured; and she was not ironical.

For Study

PART I

1. Strachey says at the outset, "A Demon possessed her." Discuss the meaning of this statement. Identify and describe the nature of her demon. Why does Strachey add that demons "are full of interest"?

2. What do you think Strachey means by "God's calls are many, and they are strange"?

3. Discuss his remark about Florence's sister's "healthy pleasure in tearing her dolls to pieces" and the contrast he makes of Florence's "almost morbid one in sewing them up again."

4. Discuss Mrs. Nightingale's reactions to Florence's "singular craving" to be *doing* something." What was the nature of the "shock of terror" her mother felt?

1. Consider the scene in which Miss Nightingale was battling red tape to get supplies while the "Purveyor" stood by, "wringing his hands in departmental agony." What is the nature of the "agony"? How would you explain the state of mind that depends upon red tape? Consider the problem of dividing the soldiers' meat into equal portions. Of another problem it is later asked, "Who could take the responsibility?" What relationship may this question have to the immemorial problem of red tape?

2. Discuss the difference between "romantic sentimental heroism" and the "sterner stuff" of which Strachey says Florence Nightingale's heroism was made.

PART III

1. Analyze the tone and implications of the passage about Sidney Herbert (pages 399–401), giving special attention to the metaphor of the stag and the tigress.

2. Analyze the tone and implications of the passage about Arthur Clough (page 402).

PART V

1. Explain the irony in the last episode of the biography and in Strachey's closing words: ". . . and she was not ironical."

For Writing

1. Review the series of questions Strachey asks in his second paragraph (page 377), and offer your speculations upon as many as you can.

2. Discuss the connection between the least appealing aspects of Miss Nightingale's character, as Strachey presents it, and her great accomplishments. Is it possible that her faults were related to her virtues and necessary to her achievements?

AFTERWORD

In his Preface to *Eminent Victorians,* Strachey defines his own intentions as a biographer:

> With us, the most delicate and humane of all the branches of the art of writing has been relegated to the journeymen of letters; we do not reflect that it is perhaps as difficult to write a good life as to live one. These two fat volumes with which it is our custom to commemorate the dead — who does not know them, with their ill-digested masses of material, their slipshod style, their tone of tedious panegyric, their lamentable lack of selection, of detachment, of design? They are as familiar as the cortege of the under-

taker, and wear the same air of slow, funereal barbarism. One is tempted to suppose, of some of them, that they were composed by that functionary, as the final item of his job. The studies in this book are indebted, in more ways than one, to such works — works which certainly deserve the name of Standard Biographies. For they have provided me not only with much indispensable information, but with something even more precious — an example. How many lessons are to be learnt from them! But it is hardly necessary to particularize. To preserve, for instance, a becoming brevity — a brevity which excludes everything that is redundant and nothing that is significant — that, surely, is the first duty of the biographer. The second, no less surely, is to maintain his own freedom of spirit. It is not his business to be complimentary; it is his business to lay bare the facts of the case, as he understands them. That is what I have aimed at in this book — to lay bare the facts of some cases, as I understand them, dispassionately, impartially, and without ulterior intentions. To quote the words of a master — *"Je n'impose rien; je ne propose rien: j'expose."* ["I impose nothing; I propose nothing: I expose."]

In the opening paragraph of the biography you have just read, Strachey tells us bluntly that Miss Nightingale was not like the popular image of her. His primary point is the statement that "in the real Miss Nightingale there was more that was interesting than in the legendary one; there was also less that was agreeable." In this direct stroke Strachey exhibits himself as an archetype of the ironist — one who sets things before us in a way that reverses common assumptions. To do this is his nature, and its stamp is set upon all his work.

The driving force that enabled Florence Nightingale to override stubborn military men and entrenched bureaucrats and to become a legendary success also led her to bully and exhaust many of those who most admired and served her. "The acrimony of her nature" was the sting by which she drove people to do her will. Here is the central ironic fact of the case that the ironic biographer exposes to us.

The Gentleman from San Francisco

by Ivan Bunin (1870–1953)

"The Gentleman from San Francisco" is a story with many levels of meaning. It offers a fascinating wealth of detail about an outwardly glamorous world of great luxury liners, wealth, and expensive pleasure resorts. The surface of the story is deceptive — even to the people in it — but if you are observant, you will see that the author offers many clues as to what, in fact, the story is really about, although you will not be able to interpret these clues until you reach the end. Tone is the key to a great deal. Be alert to its subtleties, from the opening line.

Alas, alas that great city Babylon, that mighty city!

— *Revelation of St. John.*

The Gentleman from San Francisco — neither at Naples nor on Capri could any one recall his name — with his wife and daughter, was on his way to Europe, where he intended to stay for two whole years, solely for the pleasure of it.

He was firmly convinced that he had a full right to a rest, enjoyment, a long comfortable trip, and what not. This conviction had a two-fold reason: first, he was rich, and second, despite his fifty-eight years, he was just about to enter the stream of life's pleasures. Until now he had not really lived, but simply existed, to be sure — fairly well, yet putting off his fondest hopes for the future. He toiled unweariedly — the Chinese, whom he imported by thousands for his works, knew full well what it meant, — and finally he saw that he had made much, and that he had nearly come up to the level of those whom he had once taken as a model, and he decided to catch his breath. The class of people to which he belonged was in the habit of beginning its enjoyment of life with a trip to Europe, India, Egypt. He made up his mind to do the same. Of course, it was first of all himself that he desired to reward for the years of toil, but he was also glad for his wife and daughter's sake. His wife was never distinguished by any extraordinary impressionability, but then, all elderly American women are ardent travelers. As for his daughter, a girl of marriageable age, and somewhat sickly — travel was the very thing she needed. Not to speak of the benefit to her health, do not happy meetings occur during travels? Abroad, one may chance to sit at the same table with a prince, or examine frescoes side by side with a multi-millionaire.

The itinerary the Gentleman from San Francisco planned out was an extensive one. In December and January he expected to relish the sun of southern Italy, monuments of antiquity, the tarantella, and serenades of wandering minstrels, and that which at his age is felt most keenly — the love, not entirely disinterested though, of young Neapolitan girls. The Carnival days he planned to spend at Nice and Monte Carlo, which at that time of the year is the meeting-place of the choicest society, the society upon which depend all the blessings of civilization: the cut of dress suits, the stability of thrones, the declaration of wars, the prosperity of hotels. Some of these people passionately give themselves over to automobile and boat races, others to roulette, others, again, busy themselves with what is called flirtation, and others shoot pigeons, which soar so beautifully from the dove-cote, hover a while over the emerald lawn, on the background of the forget-me-not colored sea, and then suddenly hit the ground, like little white lumps. Early March he wanted to devote to Florence, and at Easter, to hear the *Miserere* in Paris. His plans also included Venice, Paris, bull-baiting at Seville, bathing on the British Islands, also Athens, Constantinople, Palestine, Egypt, and even Japan, of course, on the way back. . . . And at first things went very well indeed.

It was the end of November, and all the way to Gibraltar the ship sailed across seas which were either clad by icy darkness or swept by storms carrying wet snow. But there were no accidents, and the vessel did not even roll. The passengers — all people of consequence — were numerous, and the steamer, the famous *Atlantis,* resembled the most expensive European hotel with all improvements: a night refreshment-bar, Oriental baths, even a newspaper of its own. The manner of living was a most aristocratic one; passengers rose early, awakened by the shrill voice of a bugle, filling the corridors at the gloomy hour when the day broke slowly and sulkily over the grayish-green watery desert, which rolled heavily in the fog. After putting on their flannel pajamas, they took coffee, chocolate, cocoa; they seated themselves in marble baths, went through their exercises, whetting their appetites and increasing their sense of well-being, dressed for the day, and had their breakfast. Till eleven o'clock they were supposed to stroll on the deck, breathing in the chill freshness of the ocean, or they played table-tennis, or other games which arouse the appetite. At eleven o'clock a collation was served consisting of sandwiches and bouillon, after which people read their newspapers, quietly waiting for luncheon, which was more nourishing and varied than the breakfast. The next two hours were given to rest; all the decks were crowded then with steamer chairs, on which the passengers, wrapped in plaids, lay stretched, dozing lazily, or watching the cloudy sky and the foamy-fringed water hillocks flashing beyond the sides of the vessel. At five o'clock, refreshed and gay, they drank strong, fragrant tea; at seven the sound of the bugle announced a dinner of nine courses. . . . Then the Gentleman from San Francisco, rubbing his hands in an onrush of vital energy, hastened to his luxurious state-room to dress.

In the evening, all the decks of the *Atlantis* yawned in the darkness, shone with their innumerable fiery eyes, and a multitude of servants worked with increased feverishness in the kitchens, dish-washing compartments, and wine-cellars. The ocean, which heaved about the sides of the ship, was dreadful, but no one thought of it. All had faith in the controlling power of the captain, a red-headed giant, heavy and very sleepy, who, clad in a uniform with broad golden stripes, looked like a huge idol, and but rarely emerged, for the benefit of the public, from his mysterious retreat. On the forecastle, the siren gloomily roared or screeched in a fit of mad rage, but few of the diners heard the siren: its hellish voice was covered by the sounds of an excellent string orchestra, which played ceaselessly and exquisitely in a vast hall, decorated with marble and spread with velvety carpets. The hall was flooded with torrents of light, radiated by crystal lustres and

gilt chandeliers; it was filled with a throng of bejeweled ladies in low-necked dresses, of men in dinner-coats, graceful waiters, and deferential maîtres-d'hôtel. One of these — who accepted wine orders exclusively — wore a chain on his neck like some lord-mayor. The evening dress and the ideal linen made the Gentleman from San Francisco look very young. Dry-skinned, of average height, strongly, though irregularly built, glossy with thorough washing and cleaning, and moderately animated, he sat in the golden splendor of this palace. Near him stood a bottle of amber-colored Johannisberg, and goblets of most delicate glass and of varied sizes, surmounted by a frizzled bunch of fresh hyacinths. There was something Mongolian in his yellowish face with its trimmed silvery moustache; his large teeth glimmered with gold fillings, and his strong, bald head had a dull glow, like old ivory. His wife, a big, broad and placid woman, was dressed richly, but in keeping with her age. Complicated, but light, transparent, and innocently immodest was the dress of his daughter, tall and slender, with magnificent hair gracefully combed; her breath was sweet with violet-scented tablets, and she had a number of tiny and most delicate pink dimples near her lips and between her slightly-powered shoulder blades. . . .

The dinner lasted two whole hours, and was followed by dances in the dancing hall, while the men — the Gentleman from San Francisco among them — made their way to the refreshment-bar. There, with their feet on tables, smoking Havana cigars and drinking themselves purple in the face, they settled the destinies of nations on the basis of the latest political and stock-exchange news. Outside, the ocean tossed up black mountains with a thud; and the snowstorm hissed furiously in the rigging grown heavy with slush; the ship trembled in every limb, struggling with the storm and ploughing with difficulty the shifting and seething mountainous masses that threw far and high their foaming tails; the siren groaned in agony, choked by storm and fog; the watchmen in their towers froze and almost went out of their minds under the superhuman stress of attention. Like the gloomy and sultry mass of the inferno, like its last, ninth circle,[1] was the submersed womb of the steamer, where monstrous furnaces yawned with red-hot open jaws, and emitted deep, hooting sounds, and where the stokers, stripped to the waist, and purple with reflected flames, bathed in their own dirty, acid sweat. And here, in the refreshment-bar, carefree men, with their feet encased in dancing shoes, on the table, sipped cognac and liqueurs, swam in waves of spiced

[1] The reference is to "Inferno" (Hell), Part I of Dante's *Divine Comedy*. In fact, the ninth circle of its divisions was a place of ice.

smoke, and exchanged subtle remarks, while in the dancing-hall everything sparkled and radiated light, warmth and joy. The couples now turned around in a waltz, now swayed in the tango; and the music, sweetly shameless and sad, persisted in its ceaseless entreaties. . . . There were many persons of note in this magnificent crowd; an ambassador, a dry, modest old man; a great millionaire, shaved, tall, of an indefinite age, who, in his old-fashioned dress-coat, looked like a prelate; also a famous Spanish writer, and an international belle, already slightly faded and of dubious morals. There was also among them a loving pair, exquisite and refined, whom everybody watched with curiosity and who did not conceal their bliss; he danced only with her, sang — with great skill — only to her accompaniment, and they were so charming, so graceful. The captain alone knew that they had been hired by the company at a good salary to play at love, and that they had been sailing now on one, now on another steamer, for quite a long time.

In Gibraltar everybody was gladdened by the sun, and by the weather which was like early spring. A new passenger appeared aboard the *Atlantis* and aroused everybody's interest. It was the crown-prince of an Asiatic state, who traveled incognito, a small man, very nimble, though looking as if made of wood, broad-faced, narrow-eyed, in gold-rimmed glasses, somewhat disagreeable because of his long moustache, which was sparse like that of a corpse, but otherwise — charming, plain, modest. In the Mediterranean the breath of winter was again felt. The seas were heavy and motley like a peacock's tail; and the waves, stirred up by the gay gusts of the tramontane, tossed their white crests under a sparkling and perfectly clear sky. Next morning, the sky grew paler and the skyline misty. Land was near. Then Ischia and Capri came in sight, and one could descry, through an opera-glass, Naples, looking like pieces of sugar strewn at the foot of an indistinct dove-colored mass, and above them, a snow-covered chain of distant mountains. The decks were crowded, many ladies and gentlemen put on light fur-coats; Chinese servants, bandy-legged youths — with pitch-black braids down to the heels and with girlish, thick eyelashes — always quiet and speaking in a whisper, were carrying to the foot of the staircases, plaid wraps, canes, and crocodile-leather valises and hand-bags. The daughter of the Gentleman from San Francisco stood near the prince, who, by a happy chance, had been introduced to her the evening before, and feigned to be looking steadily at something far-off, which he was pointing out to her, while he was, at the same time, explaining something, saying something rapidly and quietly. He was so small that he looked like a boy among other men, and he was not hand-some at all. And then there was something strange about him; his glasses, derby, and coat were most commonplace, but there was something horse-like in the hair of his sparse moustache, and the thin, tanned skin of his flat face looked as though it were somewhat stretched and varnished. But the girl listened to him, and so great was her excitement that she could hardly grasp the meaning of his words; her heart palpitated with incomprehensible rapture and with pride that he was standing and speaking with her and nobody else. Everything about him was different: his dry hands, his clean skin, under which flowed ancient kingly blood, even his light shoes and his European dress, plain, but singularly tidy — everything hid an inexplicable fascination and engendered thoughts of love. And the Gentleman from San Francisco, himself, in a silk-hat, gray leggings, patent leather shoes, kept eyeing the famous beauty who was standing near him, a tall, stately blonde, with eyes painted according to the latest Parisian fashion, and a tiny, bent peeled-off pet-dog, to whom she addressed herself. And the daughter, in a kind of vague perplexity, tried not to notice him.

Like all wealthy Americans he was very liberal when traveling, and believed in the complete sincerity and good-will of those who so painstakingly fed him, served him day and night, anticipating his slightest desire, protected him from dirt and disturbance, hauled things for him, hailed carriers, and delivered his luggage to hotels. So it was everywhere, and it had to be so at Naples. Meanwhile, Naples grew and came nearer. The musicians, with their shining brass instruments had already formed a group on the deck, and all of a sudden deafened everybody with the triumphant sounds of a ragtime march. The giant captain, in his full uniform appeared on the bridge and like a gracious pagan idol, waved his hands to the passengers, — and it seemed to the Gentleman from San Francisco — as it did to all the rest — that for him alone thundered the march, so greatly loved by proud America, and that him alone did the captain congratulate on the safe arrival. And when the *Atlantis* had finally entered the port and all its many-decked mass leaned against the quay, and the gangplank began to rattle heavily, — what a crowd of porters, with their assistants, in caps with golden galloons, what a crowd of various boys and husky ragamuffins with pads of colored postal cards attacked the Gentleman from San Francisco, offering their services! With kindly contempt he grinned at these beggars, and, walking towards the automobile of the hotel where the prince might stop, muttered between his teeth, now in English, now in Italian — "Go away! *Via. . . .*"

Immediately, life at Naples began to follow a set routine. Early in the morning breakfast was served in the gloomy dining-room, swept by a wet draught from the open windows looking upon a stony garden, while outside the sky was cloudy and cheerless, and a crowd of guides swarmed at the door of the vestibule. Then came the first smiles of the warm roseate sun, and from the high suspended balcony, a broad vista unfolded itself: Vesuvius, wrapped to its base in radiant morning vapors; and the pearly ripple, touched to silver of the bay, the delicate outline of Capri in the skyline; tiny asses dragging two-wheeled buggies along the soft, sticky embankment, and detachments of little soldiers marching somewhere to the tune of cheerful and defiant music.

Next on the day's program was a slow automobile ride along crowded, narrow, and damp corridors of streets, between high, many-windowed buildings. It was followed by visits to museums, lifelessly clean and lighted evenly and pleasantly, but as though with the dull light cast by snow; then to churches, cold, smelling of wax, always alike: a majestic entrance, closed by a ponderous, leather curtain, and inside — a vast void, silence, quiet flames of seven-branched candlesticks, sending forth a red glow from where they stood at the farther end, on the bedecked altar — a lonely, old woman lost among the dark wooden benches, slippery gravestones under the feet, and somebody's "Descent from the Cross," infallibly famous. At one o'clock — luncheon on the mountain of San-Martius, where at noon the choicest people gathered and where the daughter of the Gentleman from San Francisco once almost fainted with joy, because it seemed to her that she saw the prince in the hall, although she had learned from the newspapers that he had temporarily left for Rome. At five o'clock it was customary to take tea at the hotel, in a smart *salon,* where it was far too warm because of the carpets and the blazing fireplaces; and then came dinnertime — and again did the mighty, commanding voice of the gong resound throughout the building, again did silk rustle and the mirrors reflect files of ladies in low-necked dresses ascending the staircases, and again the splendid palatial dining hall opened with broad hospitality, and again the musicians' jackets formed red patches on the estrade, and the black figures of the waiters swarmed around the maître-d'hôtel, who, with extraordinary skill, poured a thick pink soup into plates. . . . As everywhere, the dinner was the crown of the day. People dressed for it as for a wedding, and so abundant was it in food, wines, mineral waters, sweets and fruits, that about eleven o'clock in the evening chambermaids would carry to all the rooms hot-water bags.

That year, however, December did not happen to be a very propitious one. The doormen were abashed when people spoke to them about the weather, and shrugged their shoulders guiltily, mumbling that they could not recollect such a year, although, to tell the truth, it was not the first year they mumbled those words, usually adding that "things are terrible everywhere"; that unprecedented showers and storms had broken out on the Riviera; that it was snowing in Athens; that Aetna, too, was all blocked up with snow, and glowed brightly at night; and that tourists were fleeing from Palermo to save themselves from the cold spell. . . .

That winter, the morning sun daily deceived Naples; towards noon the sky would invariably grow gray, and a light rain would begin to fall, growing thicker and duller. Then the palms at the hotel-porch glistened disagreeably like wet tin, the town appeared exceptionally dirty and congested, the museums too monotonous, the cigars of the drivers in their rubber raincoats, which flattened in the wind like wings, intolerably stinking, and the energetic flapping of their whips over their thin-necked nags — obviously false. The shoes of the signors who cleaned the street-car tracks were in a frightful state; the women who splashed in the mud, with black hair unprotected from the rain, were ugly and short-legged; and the humidity mingled with the foul smell of rotting fish, that came from the foaming sea, was simply disheartening. And so, early-morning quarrels began to break out between the Gentleman from San Francisco and his wife; and their daughter now grew pale and suffered from headaches, and now became animated, enthusiastic over everything, and at such times was lovely and beautiful. Beautiful were the tender, complex feelings which her meeting with the ungainly man aroused in her — the man in whose veins flowed unusual blood; for, after all, it does not matter what in particular stirs up a maiden's soul: money, or fame, or nobility of birth. . . . Everybody assured the tourists that it was quite different at Sorrento and on Capri, that lemon-trees were blossoming there, that it was warmer and sunnier there, the morals purer, and the wine less adulterated. And the family from San Francisco decided to set out with all their luggage for Capri. They planned to settle down at Sorrento, but first to visit the island, tread the stones where stood Tiberius' palaces, examine the fabulous wonders of the Blue Grotto, and listen to the bagpipes of Abruzzi, who roam about the island during the whole month preceding Christmas and sing the praises of the Madonna.

On the day of departure — a very memorable day for the family from San Francisco — the sun did not appear even in the morning. A heavy winter fog covered Vesuvius down to its very base and hung like a gray curtain low over the leaden surge of the sea, hiding it completely at a distance of half a mile.

Capri was completely out of sight, as though it had never existed on this earth. And the little steamboat which was making for the island tossed and pitched so fiercely that the family lay prostrated on the sofas in the miserable cabin of the little steamer, with their feet wrapped in plaids and their eyes shut because of their nausea. The older lady suffered, as she thought, most; several times she was overcome with sea-sickness, and it seemed to her then she was dying, but the chambermaid, who repeatedly brought her the basin and who for many years, in heat and in cold, had been tossing on these waves, ever on the alert, ever kindly to all — the chambermaid only laughed. The lady's daughter was frightfully pale and kept a slice of lemon between her teeth. Not even the hope of an unexpected meeting with the prince at Sorrento, where he planned to arrive on Christmas, served to cheer her. The Gentleman from San Francisco, who was lying on his back, dressed in a large overcoat and a big cap, did not loosen his jaws throughout the voyage. His face grew dark, his moustache white, and his head ached heavily; for the last few days, because of the bad weather, he had drunk far too much in the evenings.

And the rain kept on beating against the rattling window panes, and water dripped down from them on the sofas; the howling wind attacked the masts, and sometimes, aided by a heavy sea, it laid the little steamer on its side, and then something below rolled about with a rattle.

While the steamer was anchored at Castellamare and Sorrento, the situation was more cheeful; but even here the ship rolled terribly, and the coast with all its precipices, gardens and pines, with its pink and white hotels and hazy mountains clad in curling verdure, flew up and down as if it were on swings. The rowboats hit against the sides of the steamer, the sailors and the deck passengers shouted at the top of their voices, and somewhere a baby screamed as if it were being crushed to pieces. A wet wind blew through the door, and from a wavering barge flying the flag of the Hotel Royal, an urchin kept on unwearyingly shouting "Kgoyal-al! Hotel Kgoyal-al! . . ." inviting tourists. And the Gentleman from San Francisco felt like the old man that he was — and it was with weariness and animosity that he thought of all these "Royals," "Splendids," "Excelsiors," and of all those greedy bugs, reeking with garlic, who are called Italians. Once, during a stop, having opened his eyes and half-risen from the sofa, he noticed in the shadow of the rock beach a heap of stone huts, miserable, mildewed through and through, huddled close by the water, near boats, rags, tin-boxes, and brown fishing nets — and as he remembered that this was the very Italy he had come to enjoy, he felt a great despair. . . . Finally, in twi-

light, the black mass of the island began to grow nearer, as though burrowed through at the base by red fires; the wind grew softer, warmer, more fragrant; from the dock-lanterns huge golden serpents flowed down the tame waves which undulated like black oil. . . . Then, suddenly, the anchor rumbled and fell with a splash into the water, the fierce yells of the boatman filled the air — and at once everyone's heart grew easy. The electric lights in the cabin grew more brilliant, and there came a desire to eat, drink, smoke, move. . . . Ten minutes later the family from San Francisco found themselves in a large ferry-boat; fifteen minutes later they trod the stones of the quay, and then seated themselves in a small lighted car which, with a buzz, started to ascend the slope, while vineyard stakes, half-ruined stone fences, and wet, crooked lemon-trees, in spots shielded by straw sheds, with their glimmering orange-colored fruit and thick glossy foliage, were sliding down past the open car windows. . . . After rain, the earth smells sweetly in Italy, and each of her islands has a fragrance of its own.

The Island of Capri was dark and damp on that evening. But for a while it grew animated and lit up, in spots, as always in the hour of the steamer's arrival. On the top of the hill, at the station of the *funiculaire,* there stood already the crowd of those whose duty it was to receive properly the Gentleman from

San Francisco. The rest of the tourists hardly deserved any attention. There were a few Russians, who had settled on Capri, untidy, absent-minded people, absorbed in their bookish thoughts, spectacled, bearded, with the collars of their cloth overcoats raised. There was also a company of long-legged, long-necked, round-headed German youths in Tyrolean costume and with linen bags on their backs, who need no one's services, are everywhere at home, and are by no means liberal in their expenses. The Gentleman from San Francisco, who kept quietly aloof from both the Russians and Germans, was noticed at once. He and his ladies were hurriedly helped from the car, a man ran before them to show them the way, and they were again surrounded by boys and those thickset Caprean peasant women, who carry on their heads the trunks and valises of wealthy travelers. Their tiny, wooden foot-stools rapped against the pavement of the small square, which looked almost like an opera square and over which an electric lantern swung in the damp wind; the gang of urchins whistled like birds and turned somersaults, and as the Gentleman from San Francisco passed among them, it all looked like a stage scene; he went first under some kind of mediaeval archway, beneath houses huddled close together, and then along a steep echoing lane which led to the hotel entrance, flooded with light. At the left, a palm tree raised its

tuft above the flat roofs, and higher up, blue stars burned in the black sky. And again things looked as though it was in honor of the guests from San Francisco that the stony damp little town had awakened on its rocky island in the Mediterranean, that it was they who had made the owner of the hotel so happy and beaming, and that the Chinese gong, which had sounded the call to dinner through all the floors as soon as they entered the lobby, had been waiting only for them.

The owner, an elegant young man who met the guests with a polite and exquisite bow, for a moment startled the Gentleman from San Francisco. Having caught sight of him, the Gentleman from San Francisco suddenly recollected that on the previous night, among other confused images which disturbed his sleep, he had seen this very man. His vision resembled the hotel keeper to a dot, had the same head, the same hair, shining and scrupulously combed, and wore the same frock-coat with rounded skirts. Amazed, he almost stopped for a while. But as there was not a mustard-seed of what is called mysticism in his heart, his surprise subsided at once; in passing the corridor of the hotel he jestingly told his wife and daughter about this strange coincidence of dream and reality. His daughter alone glanced at him with alarm, longing suddenly compressed her heart, and such a strong feeling of solitude on this strange, dark island seized her that she almost began to cry. But, as usual, she said nothing about her feeling to her father.

A person of high dignity, Rex XVII, who had spent three entire weeks on Capri, had just left the island, and the guests from San Francisco were given the apartments he had occupied. At their disposal was put the most handsome and skillful chambermaid, a Belgian, with a figure rendered slim and firm by her corset, and with a starched cap, shaped like a small, indented crown; and they had the privilege of being served by the most well-appearing and portly footman, a black, fiery-eyed Sicilian, and by the quickest waiter, the small, stout Luigi, who was a fiend at cracking jokes and had changed many places in his life. Then the maître-d'hôtel, a Frenchman, gently rapped at the door of the American gentleman's room. He came to ask whether the gentleman and the ladies would dine, and in case they would, which he did not doubt, to report that there was to be had that day lobsters, roast beef, asparagus, pheasants, etc., etc.

The floor was still rocking under the Gentleman from San Francisco — so sea-sick had the wretched Italian steamer made him — yet he slowly, though awkwardly, shut the window which had banged when the maître-d'hôtel entered and which let in the smell of the distant kitchen and wet flowers in the garden, and answered with slow

distinctiveness, that they would dine, that their table must be placed farther away from the door, in the depth of the hall, that they would have local wine and champagne, moderately dry and but slightly cooled. The maître-d'hôtel approved the words of the guest in various intonations, which all meant, however, only one thing: there is and can be no doubt that the desires of the Gentleman from San Francisco are right and that everything would be carried out, in exact conformity with his words. At last he inclined his head and asked delicately:

"Is that all, sir?"

And having received in reply a slow "Yes," he added that to-day they were going to have the tarantella danced in the vestibule by Carmella and Giuseppe, known to all Italy and to "the entire world of tourists."

"I saw her on post-card pictures," said the Gentleman from San Francisco in a tone of voice which expressed nothing. "And this Giuseppe, is he her husband?"

"Her cousin, sir," answered the maître-d'hôtel.

The Gentleman from San Francisco tarried a little, evidently musing on something, but said nothing, then dismissed him with a nod of his head.

Then he started making preparations, as though for a wedding: he turned on all the electric lamps, and filled the mirrors with reflections of light and the sheen of furniture, and opened trunks; he began to shave and to wash himself, and the sound of his bell was heard every minute in the corridor, crossing with other impatient calls which came from the rooms of his wife and daughter. Luigi, in his red apron, with the ease characteristic of stout people, made funny faces at the chambermaids, who were dashing by with tile buckets in their hands, making them laugh until the tears came. He rolled head over heels to the door and, tapping with his knuckles, asked with feigned timidity and with an obsequiousness which he knew how to render idiotic:

"Ha sonata, Signore?" (Did you ring, sir?)

And from behind the door a slow, grating, insultingly polite voice, answered:

"Yes, come in."

What did the Gentleman from San Francisco think and feel on that evening forever memorable to him? It must be said frankly: absolutely nothing exceptional. The trouble is that everything on this earth appears too simple. Even had he felt anything deep in his heart, a premonition that something was going to happen, he would have imagined that it was not going to happen so soon, at least not at once. Besides, as is usually the case just after sea-sickness is over, he was very hungry, and he anticipated with real delight the first spoonful of soup and the first gulp of wine; therefore, he was performing the habitual process of dressing, in a state of excitement which left no time for reflection.

Having shaved and washed himself, and dexterously put in place a few false teeth, he then, standing before the mirror, moistened and vigorously plastered what was left of his thick pearly-colored hair, close to his tawny-yellow skull. Then he put on, with some effort, a tight-fitting undershirt of cream-colored silk, fitted tight to his strong, aged body with its waist swelling out because of an abundant diet; and he pulled black silk socks and patent-leather dancing shoes on his dry feet with their fallen arches. Squatting down, he set right his black trousers, drawn high by means of silk suspenders, adjusted his snow-white shirt with its bulging front, put the buttons into the shining cuffs, and began the painful process of hunting up the front button under the hard collar. The floor was still swaying under him, the tips of his fingers hurt terribly, the button at times painfully pinched the flabby skin in the depression under his Adam's apple, but he persevered, and finally, with his eyes shining from the effort, his face blue because of the narrow collar which squeezed his neck, he triumphed over the difficulties — and all exhausted, he sat down before the pier-glass, his reflected image repeating itself in all the mirrors.

"It's terrible!" he muttered, lowering his strong, bald head and making no effort to understand what was terrible; then, with a careful and habitual gesture, he examined his short fingers with gouty callosities in the joints, and their large, convex, almond-colored nails, and repeated with conviction, "It's terrible!"

But here the stentorian voice of the second gong sounded throughout the house, as in a heathen temple. And having risen hurriedly, the Gentleman from San Francisco drew his tie more taut and firm around his collar, and pulled together his abdomen by means of a tight waistcoat, put on a dinner-coat, set to rights the cuffs, and for the last time he examined himself in the mirror. . . . This Carmella, tawny as a mulatto, with fiery eyes, in a dazzling dress in which orange-color predominated, must be an extraordinary dancer — it occurred to him. And cheerfully leaving his room, he walked on the carpet to his wife's chamber and asked in a loud tone of voice if they would be long.

"In five minutes, papa!" answered cheerfully and gaily a girlish voice. "I am combing my hair."

"Very well," said the Gentleman from San Francisco.

And thinking of her wonderful hair streaming on her shoulders, he slowly walked down along corridors and staircases spread with red velvet carpets — looking for the library. The servants he met hugged the walls, and he walked by as if not noticing them. An old lady, late for dinner, already bowed with

years, with milk-white hair, yet bare-necked, in a light-gray silk dress, hurried at top speed, but she walked in a mincing, funny, hen-like manner, and he easily overtook her. At the glass door of the dining hall, where the guests had already gathered and started eating, he stopped before the table crowded with boxes of matches and Egyptian cigarettes, took a great Manilla cigar, and threw three liras on the table. On the winter veranda he glanced into the open window; a stream of soft air came to him from the darkness, the top of the old palm loomed up before him afar-off, with its boughs spread among the stars and looking gigantic, and the distant even noise of the sea reached his ear. In the library-room, snug, quiet, a German in round silver-bowed glasses and with crazy, wondering eyes stood turning the rustling pages of a newspaper. Having coldly eyed him, the Gentleman from San Francisco seated himself in a deep leather armchair near a lamp under a green hood, put on his pince-nez and, twitching his head because of the collar which choked him, hid himself from view behind a newspaper. He glanced at a few headlines, read a few lines about the interminable Balkan war, and turned over the page with a habitual gesture. Suddenly, the lines blazed up with a glassy sheen, the veins of his neck swelled, his eyes bulged out, the pince-nez fell from his nose. . . . He dashed forward, wanted to swallow air — and made a wild, rattling noise; his lower jaw dropped, dropped on his shoulder and began to shake, the shirt-front bulged out — and the whole body, writhing, the heels catching in the carpet, slowly fell to the floor in a desperate struggle with an invisible foe. . . .

Had not the German been in the library, this frightful accident would have been quickly and adroitly hushed up. The body of the Gentleman from San Francisco would have been rushed away to some far corner — and none of the guests would have known of the occurrence. But the German dashed out of the library with outcries and spread the alarm all over the house. And many rose from their meal, upsetting chairs, others growing pale, ran along the corridors to the library, and the question, asked in many languages, was heard: "What is it? What has happened?" And no one was able to answer it clearly, no one understood anything, for until this very day men still wonder most at death and most absolutely refuse to believe in it. The owner rushed from one guest to another, trying to keep back those who were running and soothe them with hasty assurances that this was nothing, a mere trifle, a little fainting-spell by which a Gentleman from San Francisco had been overcome. But no one listened to him; many saw how the footmen and waiters tore from the gentleman his tie, collar, waistcoat, the rumpled evening coat, and even — for no visible reason — the dancing shoes from his black silk-covered feet. And he kept on writhing. He obstinately struggled with death; he did not want to yield to the foe that attacked him so unexpectedly and grossly. He shook his head, emitted rattling sounds like one throttled, and turned up his eye-balls like one drunk with wine. When he was hastily brought into Number Forty-three — the smallest, worst, dampest, and coldest room at the end of the lower corridor — and stretched on the bed — his daughter came running, her hair falling over her shoulders. Then came his wife, big, heavy, almost completely dressed for dinner, her mouth round with terror.

In a quarter of an hour all was again in good trim at the hotel. But the evening was irreparably spoiled. Some tourists returned to the dining-hall and finished their dinner; but they kept silent, and it was obvious that they took the accident as a personal insult, while the owner went from one guest to another shrugging his shoulders in impotent and appropriate irritation, feeling like one innocently victimized, assuring everyone that he understood perfectly well "how disagreeable this is," and giving his word that he would take all "the measures that are within his power" to do away with the trouble. Yet it was found necessary to cancel the tarantella. The unnecessary electric lamps were put out; most of the guests left for the beer-hall; and it grew so quiet in the hotel that one could distinctly hear the tick-tock of the clock in the lobby, where a lonely parrot babbled something in its expressionless manner, stirring in its cage, and trying to fall asleep with its paw clutching the upper perch in a most absurd manner. The Gentleman from San Francisco lay stretched in a cheap iron bed, under coarse woolen blankets, dimly lighted by a single gas-burner fastened in the ceiling. An icebag slid down on his wet, cold forehead. His blue, already lifeless face grew gradually cold; the hoarse, rattling noise which came from his mouth, lighted by the glimmer of the golden fillings, gradually weakened. It was not the Gentleman from San Francisco that was emitting those weird sounds; he was no more — someone else did it. His wife and daughter, the doctor, the servants were standing and watching him apathetically. Suddenly, that which they expected and feared happened. The rattling sound ceased. And slowly, slowly, in everybody's sight a pallor stole over the face of the dead man, and his features began to grow thinner and more luminous, beautiful with the beauty that he had long shunned and that became him well. . . .

The proprietor entered. *"Gia e morto,"* whispered the doctor to him. The proprietor shrugged his shoulders indifferently. The older lady, with tears slowly running down her cheeks, approached him and said timidly that now the deceased must be taken to his room.

"O, no, madam," answered the proprietor politely, but without any amiability and not in English, but in French. He was no longer interested in the trifle which the guests from San Francisco could now leave at his cash-office. "This is absolutely impossible," he said, and added in the form of an explanation that he valued this apartment highly, and if he satisfied her desire, this would become known over Capri and the tourists would begin to avoid it.

The girl, who had looked at him strangely, sat down, and with her handkerchief to her mouth began to cry. Her mother's tears dried up at once, and her face flared up. She raised her tone, began to demand, using her own language and still unable to realize that the respect for her was absolutely gone. The proprietor, with polite dignity, cut her short: "If madam does not like the ways of this hotel, he dare not detain her." And he firmly announced that the corpse must leave the hotel that very day, at dawn, that the police had been informed, that an agent would call immediately and attend to all the necessary formalities. . . . "Is it possible to get on Capri at least a plain coffin?" madam asks. . . . Unfortunately not; by no means, and as for making one, there will be no time. It will be necessary to arrange things some other way. . . . For instance, he gets English soda-water in big, oblong boxes. . . . The partitions could be taken out from such a box. . . .

By night, the whole hotel was asleep. A waiter opened the window in Number Forty-three — it faced a corner of the garden where a consumptive banana-tree grew in the shadow of a high stone wall set with broken glass on the top — turned out the electric light, locked the door, and went away. The deceased remained alone in the darkness. Blue stars looked down at him from the black sky; the cricket in the wall started his melancholy, carefree song. In the dimly lighted corridor two chambermaids were sitting on the window-sill, mending something. Then Luigi came in, in slippered feet, with a heap of clothes on his arm.

"*Pronto?*" — he asked in a stage whisper, as if greatly concerned, directing his eyes toward the terrible door at the end of the corridor. And waving his free hand in that direction, "*Partenza!*" he cried out in a whisper, as if seeing off a train — and the chambermaids, choking with noiseless laughter, put their heads on each other's shoulders.

Then, stepping softly, he ran to the door, slightly rapped at it, and inclining his ear, asked most obsequiously in a subdued tone of voice:

"*Ha sonata, Signore?*"

And, squeezing his throat and thrusting his lower jaw forward, he answered himself in a drawling, grating, sad voice, as if from behind the door:

"Yes, come in. . . ."

At dawn, when the window panes in Number Forty-three grew white and a damp wind rustled in the leaves of the banana-tree, when the pale-blue morning sky rose and stretched over Capri, and the sun, rising from behind the distant mountains of Italy, touched into gold the pure, clearly outlined summit of Monte Solaro, when the masons, who mended the paths for the tourists on the island, went out to their work — an oblong box was brought to room Number Forty-three. Soon it grew very heavy and painfully pressed against the knees of the assistant doorman who was conveying it in a one-horse carriage along the white highroad which wound on the slopes, among stone fences and vineyards, all the way down to the seacoast. The driver, a sickly man, with red eyes, in an old short-sleeved coat and in worn-out shoes, had a drunken headache; all night long he had played dice at the eatinghouse — and he kept on flogging his vigorous little horse. According to Sicilian custom, the animal was heavily burdened with decoration: all sorts of bells tinkled on the bridle, which was ornamented with colored woolen fringes; there were bells also on the edge of the high saddle; and a bird's feather, two feet long, stuck in the trimmed crest of the horse, nodded up and down. The driver kept silence: he was depressed by his wrongheadedness and vices, by the fact that last night he had lost in gambling all the copper coins with which his pockets had been full — neither more nor less than four liras and forty centesimi. But on such a morning, when the air is so fresh and the sea stretches nearby and the sky is serene with a morning serenity — a headache passes rapidly and one becomes carefree again. Besides, the driver was also somewhat cheered by the unexpected earnings which the Gentleman from San Francisco, who bumped his dead head against the walls of the box behind his back, had brought him. The little steamer, shaped like a great bug, which lay far down, on the tender and brilliant blue filling to the brim the Neapolitan bay, was blowing the signal of departure — and the sounds swiftly resounded all over Capri. Every bend of the island, every ridge and stone were seen as distinctly as if there were no air between heaven and earth. Near the quay the driver was overtaken by the head doorman, who conducted in an auto the wife and daughter of the Gentleman from San Francisco. Their faces were pale and their eyes sunken with tears and a sleepless night. And in ten minutes the little steamer was again stirring up the water and picking its way towards Sorrento and Castellamare, carrying the American family away from Capri forever. . . . Meanwhile, peace and rest were restored on the island.

Two thousand years ago there had lived on that island a man [1] who became utterly entangled in his own brutal and filthy actions. For some unknown reason he usurped the rule over millions of men and found himself bewildered by the absurdity of this power, while the fear that someone might kill him unawares made him commit deeds inhuman beyond all measure. And mankind has forever retained his memory; and those who, taken together, now rule the world, as incomprehensibly and, essentially, as cruelly as he did, come from all the corners of the earth to look at the remnants of the stone house he inhabited, which stands on one of the steepest cliffs of the island. On that wonderful morning the tourists, who had come to Capri for precisely that purpose, were still asleep in the various hotels; but tiny long-eared asses under red saddles were already being led to the hotel entrances. Americans and Germans, men and women, old and young, after having arisen and breakfasted heartily, were to scramble on them; and the old beggarwomen of Capri, with sticks in their sinewy hands, were again to run after them along stony, mountainous paths, all the way up to the summit of Monte Tiberia. The dead old man from San Francisco, who had planned to keep the tourists company but who had, instead, only scared them by reminding

[1] The Roman Emperor Tiberius, during whose reign Jesus Christ was crucified.

them of death, was already shipped to Naples; and soothed by this, the travellers slept soundly, and silence reigned over the island. The stores in the little town were still closed, with the exception of the fish and greens market on the tiny square. Among the plain people who filled it, going about their business, stood idly by, as usual, Lorenzo, a tall old boatman, a carefree reveller and once a handsome man famous all over Italy, who had many times served as a model for painters. He had brought and already sold — for a song — two big sea-crawfish, which he had caught at night and which were rustling in the apron of Don Cataldo, the cook of the hotel where the family from San Francisco had been lodged — and now Lorenzo could stand calmly until nightfall, wearing princely airs, showing off his rags, his clay pipe with its long reed mouth-piece, and his red woolen cap, tilted on one ear. Meanwhile, among the precipices of Monte Solare, down the ancient Phoenician road, cut in the rocks in the form of a gigantic staircase, two Abruzzi mountaineers were coming from Anacapri. One carried under his leather mantle a bagpipe, a large goat's skin with two pipes; the other, something in the nature of a wooden flute. They walked, and the entire country, joyous, beautiful, sunny, stretched below them: the rocky shoulders of the island, which lay at their feet, the fabulous blue in which it swam, the shining

morning vapors over the sea westward, beneath the dazzling sun, and the wavering masses of Italy's mountains, both near and distant, whose beauty human word is powerless to render. . . . Midway they slowed up. Overshadowing the road stood, in a grotto of the rock wall of Monte Solare, the Holy Virgin, all radiant, bathed in the warmth and the splendor of the sun. The rust of her snow-white plaster-of-Paris vestures and queenly crown was touched into gold, and there were meekness and mercy in her eyes raised towards the heavens, towards the eternal and beatific abode of her thrice-blessed Son. They bared their heads, applied the pipes to their lips, and praises flowed on, candid and humbly joyous, praises to the sun and the morning, to Her, the Immaculate Intercessor for all who suffer in this evil and beautiful world, and to Him who had been born of her womb in the cavern of Bethlehem, in a hut of lowly shepherds in distant Judea.

As for the body of the dead Gentleman from San Francisco, it was on its way home, to the shores of the New World, where a grave awaited it. Having undergone many humiliations and suffered much human neglect, having wandered about a week from one port warehouse to another, it finally got on that same famous ship which had brought the family, such a short while ago and with such a pomp, to the Old World. But now he was concealed from the living: in a tar-coated coffin he was lowered deep into the black hold of the steamer. And again did the ship set out on its far sea-journey. At night it sailed by the island of Capri; and, for those who watched it from the island, its lights slowly disappearing in the dark sea, it seemed infinitely sad. But there, on the vast steamer, in its lighted halls shining with brilliance and marble, a noisy dancing party was going on, as usual.

On the second and third night there was again a ball — this time in mid-ocean, during the furious storm sweeping over the ocean, which roared like a funeral mass and rolled up mountainous seas fringed with mourning silvery foam. The Devil, who from the rocks of Gibraltar, the stony gateway of two worlds, watched the ship vanish into night and storm, could hardly distinguish from behind the snow the innumerable fiery eyes of the ship. The Devil was as huge as a cliff, but the ship was even bigger, a many-storied, many-stacked giant, created by the arrogance of the New Man with the old heart. The blizzard battered the ship's rigging and its broad-necked stacks whitened with snow, but it remained firm, majestic — and terrible. On its uppermost deck, amidst a snowy whirlwind there loomed up in loneliness the cozy, dimly lighted cabin where, only half awake, the vessel's ponderous pilot reigned over

its entire mass, bearing the semblance of a pagan idol. He heard the wailing moans and the furious screeching of the siren, choked by the storm; but the nearness of that which was behind the wall and which in the last account was incomprehensible to him, removed his fears. He was reassured by the thought of the large, armored cabin, which now and then was filled with mysterious rumbling sounds and with the dry creaking of blue fires, flaring up and exploding around a man with a metallic headpiece, who was eagerly catching the indistinct voices of the vessels that hailed him, hundreds of miles away. At the very bottom, in the under-water womb of the *Atlantis,* the huge masses of tanks and various other machines, their steel parts shining dully, wheezed with steam and oozed hot water and oil; here was the gigantic kitchen, heated by hellish furnaces, where the motion of the vessel was being generated; here seethed those forces terrible in their concentration which were transmitted to the keel of the vessel, and into that endless round tunnel, which was lighted by electricity and looked like a gigantic cannon barrel, where slowly, with a punctuality and certainty that crushes the human soul, a colossal shaft was revolving in its oily nest, like a living monster stretching in its lair. As for the middle part of the *Atlantis,* its warm luxurious cabins, dining-rooms, and halls, they radiated light and joy, were astir with a chattering smartly-dressed crowd, were filled with the fragrance of fresh flowers, and resounded with a string orchestra. And again did the slender supple pair of hired lovers painfully turn and twist and at times clash convulsively amid the splendor of lights, silks, diamonds, and bare feminine shoulders: she — a sinfully modest pretty girl, with lowered eyelashes and an innocent hair-dressing; he — a tall, young man, with black hair, looking as if it were pasted, pale with powder, in most exquisite patent-leather shoes, in a narrow long-skirted dresscoat — a beautiful man resembling a leech. And no one knew that this couple had long since been weary of torturing themselves with a feigned beatific torture under the sounds of shamefully melancholy music; nor did any one know what lay deep, deep, beneath them, on the very bottom of the hold, in the neighborhood of the gloomy and sultry maw of the ship, that heavily struggled with the ocean, the darkness, and the storm. . . .

For Study and Writing

1. Why is the Gentleman left nameless? Why at the very beginning does the author mention that no one in Naples or Capri remembers his name?

2. What was the Gentleman seeking on his trip?

3. What subtle implication is there in calling the evening of the Gentle-

man's arrival on Capri "that evening forever memorable to him"?

4. When describing how the Gentleman dressed himself and observing that he thought of nothing exceptional, why does the author add: "The trouble is that everything on this earth appears too simple"?

5. What is the change in the attitude of people toward the Gentleman after his stroke and death? Would this change occur in every context or only in such a special one as this? Explore this question, for it is the heart of the story. Notice that the Gentleman has now become "the dead old man from San Francisco."

6. Do you consider the story to be chiefly about one person in particular or about people and things in general? The answer is a matter of opinion, so state yours clearly and defend it.

7. What is the attitude of the author toward the life being led by this rich American and those among whom he is moving? Support your answer by specific references to the text.

8. Do you feel some kind of sympathy, if not for the Gentleman, for his wife and daughter? Explain this sympathy, or lack of it, and show what the author has done in the story to develop or suppress it.

9. The description of the apoplectic stroke is vivid. Reread it carefully (pages 434–35). How does it harmonize with the comic or satiric aspects of the story? What function may a scene of such stark reality have in a story about a delusion?

10. Bunin remarks about the im-

mediate public reaction to the Gentleman's fall in the reading room: ". . . no one understood anything, for until this very day men still wonder most at death and most absolutely refuse to believe in it." This is a paradoxical statement. Can you explain or resolve the paradox? (A novel which deals interestingly with this idea is Nevil Shute's *On the Beach,* Morrow, 1957.)

11. Why will not the proprietor allow the Gentleman's body to be taken back to the best suite?

12. Comment on some of the specific ironic elements in the story:

> the large, long soda-water box room Number Forty-three
> the Gentleman's preparations, "as if for a wedding ceremony"
> the "exquisitely" romantic shipboard couple
> the return trip
> the prince
> the actions of the sea
> the Gentleman's attitude toward servants

13. Explain the relevance of the Biblical text set at the head of the story: "Alas, alas that great city Babylon, that mighty city!"

14. Study the details of the Gentleman's final dressing for dinner. Retrospectively, what foreshadowings do you see for what is so soon to happen? How does his manner of dress and dressing contribute to his stroke, which is a consequence of high blood pressure?

15. What does the change in the manner of the hotel owner and the staff, after the stroke, tell you about the worth of bought courtesies?

16. After the body has been shipped off to Naples, why does Bunin turn back to a reflection about the Emperor Tiberius? What association of ideas is there between Capri in the Emperor's day and Capri in this story?

17. What significance do you see in the author's statement that the Devil was watching the ship from Gibraltar? Take into consideration the images used in describing the depths of the ship at both the beginning and the end. In terms of these images, what might be said to have become of the Gentleman?

18. At the end we are told, for the second time, that no one knew the truth about the romantic couple dancing and that no one knew about the coffin in the hold. How do you relate this "no one knew" of the story to the actual world in which we live?

AFTERWORD

This is a satirical story. Satire commonly uses comic methods to expose and attack folly or vice. No one is likely to laugh happily or heartily at this tale; yet one might, upon finishing it, reconsider the comic implications of its very first words:

> The Gentleman from San Francisco — neither at Naples nor on Capri could any one recall his name — with his wife and daughter, was on his way to Europe, where he intended to stay for two whole years, solely for the pleasure of it.

There are, of course, obvious ironies involved in the statement of the Gentleman's intentions, once we know what actually happens. Think particularly how this passage relates to Bunin's description of the welcome given the American family at the hotel on Capri. They are immediately distinguished from other tourists, put in the choicest apartments, treated with the utmost affability, and given the best service. It seems as though the Chinese gong in the dining room sounded only for them. Yet afterward — no one remembered his name.

If his comic sense is reasonably alert, the reader will have observed the contrast between the apparent interest and the actual indifference of the hotel people and will have seen that in a number of ways things were not as they ought to be. When the doctor pronounces the Gentleman dead, "The proprietor shrugged his shoulders indifferently." If we think that the dead should be treated with respect, we see it is not so here. If we think that people should be sincerely interested in each other's welfare, we see that it is not so here. If we think that men should be respected for what they are rather than for what they have, we find that here it is not the case. If the Gentleman thinks that his wealth should provide him security and dignity, the facts of the matter contradict him.

Up to the moment of the Gentleman's stroke, the world has seemed to him to be as it ought to be. One absurdly simple, inevitable change has exposed the error: he is no longer able to spend money, and he is a potential damper upon the carefree spending of others. The life of the Gentleman has been based, Bunin tells us, on a foolish and ugly assumption. Yet we are not asked to pity the dead man or to admire the tenacity with which he goes to his doom. Rather we are invited to laugh, or at least to regard with detached, satirical eye the ridiculousness and folly of it all.

The death of the Gentleman — so graphically presented — shows us something about his life. To make clear this point is chiefly why he dies: so that we may discover what poor, ineffectual creatures he and his family really are behind the luxury and power of their daily lives, as well as what misleading and temporary qualities such luxury and power are.

"What fools these mortals be!" Puck says in Shakespeare's *A Midsummer Night's Dream* — surely one of the basic statements of all that is comic in the world. But since we are all mortal, and foolish, it may also seem to us at times one of the basically important statements about all that is sad in the world, as well.

Bunin's story is so detached in its view of the Gentleman that we are able to keep our distance and observe his foolishness and death without painful personal involvement or identification. After all, *we* don't assume that *our* enormous wealth gives *us* princely rights over all peoples and all facilities for ever and ever. *We* don't ignore all faces and all interests except those that serve our own appetites and profit. *We* don't exploit thousands of coolies. *We* didn't die of an apoplectic stroke in the reading room of a hotel on Capri. No, this Gentleman from San Francisco is apart from us, we feel.

In two ways the Gentleman is a man apart, a soul separate from others. At first he sets himself apart through the callousness and self-centeredness of wealth and power that turn most people into things or objects for him. He appears remote even from his wife and daughter, who seem reduced to mere satellites in orbit around him as he makes his stately progress through what he regards as his universe. After his stroke — even before the swiftly following death — he is set apart again by the shrinking of the pleasure-seekers from what has happened to him and by the cold determination of the hotel owner to pack him out of sight and dispose of him. At once he is reduced from a royal suite to a soda-water packing case. His very coffin, at first, is a makeshift.

Yet the story does stir a certain disquiet in us, because this man is not in every sense apart from us. We share with him our common mortality. We witness the exploding of a foolish and selfish man's presumptions — having seen all along that they must explode. But we are not allowed to watch the fireworks in utter complacency. The satirical spectacle of a deluded being who pompously ignores the facts and is suddenly struck by the truth when he is least expecting it is refined and made more thought-provoking by the fact that this deluded being, like ourselves, is part of the fabric of mankind.

We should not forget, either, that the ship has been an ancient and persistent metaphor for society, indeed for the whole world. The great liner on which the Gentleman goes and returns has more than a touch of this symbolism. Because of it, the author lavishes much attention upon the ship and its many levels, and the complex relationships of the people aboard, who are not always what they seem. Its name was not idly chosen: *Atlantis* is the label of a legendary lost continent and civilization. The ship even has its own Hell, its nether regions; and Bunin describes the Devil watching its passage from Gibraltar.

Bartleby the Scrivener

A Story of Wall Street [1]

by Herman Melville (1819–1891)

"Bartleby the Scrivener" is a relatively little-known short story by one of the greatest, most famous American authors. As sometimes happens to artists of the first rank, Herman Melville was not recognized at his real worth during his own lifetime by any but a discerning few. Even *Moby Dick,* the novel on which his popular renown now justly rests, sold poorly and was poorly reviewed in the years immediately following its publication (1851); and what success as a literary man Melville did have before his death rested mainly on his exotic novels of south-sea adventure. This state of affairs must have been particularly galling to Melville; for, although as a young sailor he had traveled and enjoyed the far places of the watery world, his real and abiding interest as man and writer was analysis of the problems of the individual as a feeling, thinking creature.

The story which follows is one of the group that Melville published as *The Piazza Tales* in the years after writing *Moby Dick*. Disappointed by his great novel's reception, Melville at this point was desperately trying both to preserve his identity as a professional literary man and to produce the kind of art that he felt was his necessary mission and vocation.

The Bartleby of the title, you will see, is a man who, like his creator, is out of step with the society around him. Melville preferred not to write romantic travel books; Bartleby prefers not to perform the duties assigned him by his superior and approved by his peers. Perhaps Melville's contemporaries found the author's insistence on writing in his own way, in spite of the economic and public failure that inevitably followed, as baffling and irritating as the other characters in "Bartleby" find the scrivener's obdurateness. However this may be, Bartleby's behavior is surely hard to explain. Perhaps you will find it as irritating as do Turkey, Nippers, and the narrator. Melville does not explain it; indeed the only positive thing about Bartleby that we are left with is the man's resolute consistency. But is there anything in the social contract which requires that a man's choice of action be understood by anyone else?

---

[1] First published anonymously in *Putnam's Monthly Magazine*, November, 1853. Reprinted in *The Piazza Tales*, 1856.

I am a rather elderly man. The nature of my avocations for the last thirty years has brought me into more than ordinary contact with what would seem an interesting and somewhat singular set of men, of whom as yet nothing that I know of has ever been written: — I mean the law-copyists, or scriveners. I have known very many of them, professionally and privately, and if I pleased, could relate divers histories, at which good-natured gentlemen might smile, and sentimental souls might weep. But I waive the biographies of all other scriveners for a few passages in the life of Bartleby, who was a scrivener the strangest I ever saw or heard of. While of other law-copyists I might write the complete life, of Bartleby nothing of that sort can be done. I believe that no materials exist for a full and satisfactory biography of this man. It is an irreparable loss to literature. Bartleby was one of those beings of whom nothing is ascertainable, except from the original sources, and in his case those are very small. What my own astonished eyes saw of Bartleby, *that* is all I know of him, except, indeed, one vague report which will appear in the sequel.

Ere introducing the scrivener, as he first appeared to me, it is fit I make some mention of myself, my *employés,* my business, my chambers, and general surroundings; because some such description is indispensable to an adequate understanding of the chief character about to be presented.

Imprimis: I am a man who, from his youth upward, has been filled with a profound conviction that the easiest way of life is the best. Hence, though I belong to a profession proverbially energetic and nervous, even to turbulence, at times, yet nothing of that sort have I ever suffered to invade my peace. I am one of those unambitious lawyers who never addresses a jury, or in any way draws down public applause; but in the cool tranquillity of a snug retreat, do a snug business among rich men's bonds and mortgages and title-deeds. All who know me, consider me an eminently *safe* man. The late John Jacob Astor, a personage little given to poetic enthusiasm, had no hesitation in pronouncing my first grand point to be prudence; my next, method. I do not speak it in vanity, but simply record the fact, that I was not unemployed in my profession by the late John Jacob Astor; a name which, I admit, I love to repeat, for it hath a rounded and orbicular sound to it, and rings like unto bullion. I will freely add, that I was not insensible to the late John Jacob Astor's good opinion.

Some time prior to the period at which this little history begins, my avocations had been largely increased. The good old office, now extinct in the State of New York, of a Master in Chancery, had been conferred upon me. It was not a very arduous office, but very pleasantly remunerative. I seldom lose my temper; much more seldom indulge in dangerous indignation at wrongs and outrages; but I must be permitted to be rash here and declare, that I consider the sudden and violent abrogation of the office of Master in Chancery, by the new Constitution, as a —— premature act; inasmuch as I had counted upon a life-lease of the profits, whereas I only received those of a few short years. But this is by the way.

My chambers were upstairs at No. —— Wall Street. At one end they looked upon the white wall of the interior of a spacious sky-light shaft, penetrating the building from top to bottom. This view might have been considered rather tame than otherwise, deficient in what landscape painters call "life." But if so, the view from the other end of my chambers offered, at least, a contrast, if nothing more. In that direction my windows commanded an unobstructed view of a lofty brick wall, black by age and everlasting shade; which wall required no spy-glass to bring out its lurking beauties, but for the benefit of all near-sighted spectators, was pushed up to within ten feet of my window panes. Owing to the great height of the surrounding buildings, and my chambers being on the second floor, the interval between this wall and mine not a little resembled a huge square cistern.

At the period just preceding the advent of Bartleby, I had two persons as copyists in my employment, and a promising lad as an office-boy.

First, Turkey; second, Nippers; third, Ginger Nut. These may seem names, the like of which are not usually found in the Directory. In truth they were nicknames, mutually conferred upon each other by my three clerks, and were deemed expressive of their respective persons or characters. Turkey was a short, pursy Englishman of about my own age, that is, somewhere not far from sixty. In the morning, one might say, his face was of a fine florid hue, but after twelve o'clock, meridian — his dinner hour — it blazed like a grate full of Christmas coals; and continued blazing — but, as it were, with a gradual wane — till 6 o'clock P.M. or thereabouts, after which I saw no more of the proprietor of the face, which, gaining its meridian with the sun, seemed to set with it, to rise, culminate, and decline the following day, with the like regularity and undiminished glory. There are many singular coincidences I have known in the course of my life, not the least among which was the fact, that exactly when Turkey displayed his fullest beams from his red and radiant countenance, just then, too, at that critical moment, began the daily period when I considered his business capacities as seriously disturbed for the remainder of the twenty-four hours. Not that he was absolutely idle, or averse to business then; far from it. The difficulty was, he was apt to be altogether too energetic. There was a strange, inflamed, flurried, flighty recklessness of activity about him. He would be incautious in dipping his pen into his inkstand. All his blots upon my documents, were dropped there after twelve o'clock, meridian. Indeed, not only would he be reckless and sadly given to making blots in the afternoon, but some days he went further, and was rather noisy. At such times, too, his face flamed with augmented blazonry, as if cannel coal had been heaped on anthracite. He made an unpleasant racket with his chair; spilled his sand-box; in mending his pens, impatiently split them all to pieces, and threw them on the floor in a sudden passion; stood up and leaned over his table, boxing his papers about in a most indecorous manner, very sad to behold in an elderly man like him. Nevertheless, as he was in many ways a most valuable person to me, and all the time before twelve o'clock, meridian, was the quickest, steadiest creature, too, accomplishing a great deal of work in a style not easy to be matched — for these reasons, I was willing to overlook his eccentricities, though indeed, occasionally, I remonstrated with him. I did this very gently, however, because, though the civilest, nay, the blandest and most reverential of men in the morning, yet in the afternoon he was disposed, upon provocation, to be slightly rash with his tongue, in fact, insolent. Now, valuing his morning services as I did, and resolving not to lose them — yet, at the same time, made uncomfortable by his inflamed ways after twelve o'clock; and being a man of peace, unwilling by my admonitions to call forth unseemly retorts from him — I took upon me, one Saturday noon (he was always worse on Saturdays), to hint to him, very kindly, that perhaps now that he was growing old, it might be well to abridge his labours; in short, he need not come to my chambers after twelve o'clock, but, dinner over, had best go home to his lodgings and rest himself till tea-time. But no; he insisted upon his afternoon devotions. His countenance became intolerably fervid, as he oratorically assured me — gesticulating, with a long ruler, at the other side of the room — that if his services in the morning were useful, how indispensable, then, in the afternoon?

"With submission, sir," said Turkey on this occasion, "I consider myself your right-hand man. In the morning I but marshal and deploy my columns; but in the afternoon I put myself at their head, and gallantly charge the foe, thus!" — and he made a violent thrust with the ruler.

"But the blots, Turkey," intimated I.

"True, — but, with submission, sir, behold these hairs! I am getting old. Surely, sir, a blot or two of a warm afternoon is not to be severely urged against grey hairs. Old age — even if it blot the page — is honourable. With submission, sir, we *both* are getting old."

This appeal to my fellow-feeling was hardly to be resisted. At all events, I saw that go he would not. So I made up my mind to let him stay, resolving, nevertheless, to see to it, that during the afternoon he had to do with my less important papers.

Nippers, the second on my list, was a whiskered, sallow, and, upon the whole, rather piratical-looking young man of about five and twenty. I always deemed him the victim of two evil powers — ambition and indigestion. The ambition was evinced by a certain impatience of the duties of a mere copyist — an unwarrantable usurpation of strictly professional affairs, such as the original drawing up of legal documents. The indigestion seemed betokened in an occasional nervous testiness and grinning irritability, causing the teeth to audibly grind together over mistakes committed in copying; unnecessary maledictions, hissed, rather than spoken, in the heat of business; and especially by a continual discontent with the height of the table where he worked. Though of a very ingenious mechanical turn, Nippers could never get this table to suit him. He put chips under it, blocks of various sorts, bits of pasteboard, and at last went so far as to attempt an exquisite adjustment by final pieces of folded blotting-paper. But no invention would answer. If, for the sake of easing his back, he brought the table lid at a sharp angle well up towards his chin, and wrote there

like a man using the steep roof of a Dutch house for his desk — then he declared that it stopped the circulation in his arms. If now he lowered the table to his waistbands, and stooped over it in writing, then there was a sore aching in his back. In short, the truth of the matter was, Nippers knew not what he wanted. Or, if he wanted anything, it was to be rid of a scrivener's table altogether. Among the manifestations of his diseased ambition was a fondness he had for receiving visits from certain ambiguous-looking fellows in seedy coats, whom he called his clients. Indeed I was aware that not only was he, at times, considerable of a ward-politician, but he occasionally did a little business at the Justices' courts, and was not unknown on the steps of the Tombs.[1] I have good reason to believe, however, that one individual who called upon him at my chambers, and who, with a grand air, he insisted was his client, was no other than a dun, and the alleged title-deed, a bill. But with all his failings, and the annoyances he caused me, Nippers, like his compatriot Turkey, was a very useful man to me; wrote a neat, swift hand; and, when he chose, was not deficient in a gentlemanly sort of deportment. Added to this, he always dressed in a gentlemanly sort of way; and so, incidentally, reflected credit upon my chambers. Whereas with respect to Turkey, I had much ado to keep him from

[1] **Tombs:** a prison.

being a reproach to me. His clothes were apt to look oily and smell of eating-houses. He wore his pantaloons very loose and baggy in summer. His coats were execrable; his hat not to be handled. But while the hat was a thing of indifference to me, inasmuch as his natural civility and deference, as a dependent Englishman, always led him to doff it the moment he entered the room, yet his coat was another matter. Concerning his coats, I reasoned with him; but with no effect. The truth was, I suppose, that a man with so small an income, could not afford to sport such a lustrous face and a lustrous coat at one and the same time. As Nippers once observed, Turkey's money went chiefly for red ink. One winter day I presented Turkey with a highly-respectable looking coat of my own, a padded grey coat, of a most comfortable warmth, and which buttoned straight up from the knee to the neck. I thought Turkey would appreciate the favour, and abate his rashness and obstreperousness of afternoons. But no. I verily believe that buttoning himself up in so downy and blanket-like a coat had a pernicious effect upon him; upon the same principle that too much oats are bad for horses. In fact, precisely as a rash, restive horse is said to feel his oats, so Turkey felt his coat. It made him insolent. He was a man whom prosperity harmed.

Though concerning the self-indulgent habits of Turkey I had my own private surmises, yet touching Nippers I was well persuaded that whatever might be his faults in other respects, he was, at least, a temperate young man. But, indeed, nature herself seemed to have been his vintner, and at his birth charged him so thoroughly with an irritable, brandy-like disposition, that all subsequent potations were needless. When I consider how, amid the stillness of my chambers, Nippers would sometimes impatiently rise from his seat, and stooping over his table, spread his arms wide apart, seize the whole desk, and move it, and jerk it, with a grim, grinding motion on the floor, as if the table were a perverse voluntary agent, intent on thwarting and vexing him; I plainly perceive that for Nippers, brandy and water were altogether superfluous.

It was fortunate for me that, owing to its peculiar cause — indigestion — the irritability and consequent nervousness of Nippers, were mainly observable in the morning, while in the afternoon he was comparatively mild. So that Turkey's paroxysms only coming on about twelve o'clock, I never had to do with their eccentricities at one time. Their fits relieved each other like guards. When Nippers's was on, Turkey's was off; and *vice versa*. This was a good natural arrangement under the circumstances.

Ginger Nut, the third on my list, was a lad some twelve years old. His father was a carman, ambitious of seeing his son on the bench instead of a cart, before he died. So he sent him to my office as student at law, errand boy, and cleaner and sweeper, at the rate of one dollar a week. He had a little desk to himself, but he did not use it much. Upon inspection, the drawer exhibited a great array of the shells of various sorts of nuts. Indeed, to this quick-witted youth the whole noble science of the law was contained in a nut-shell. Not the least among the employments of Ginger Nut, as well as one which he discharged with the most alacrity, was his duty as cake and apple purveyor for Turkey and Nippers. Copying law papers being proverbially a dry, husky sort of business, my two scriveners were fain to moisten their mouths very often with Spitzenbergs to be had at the numerous stalls nigh the Custom House and Post Office. Also, they sent Ginger Nut very frequently for that peculiar cake — small, flat, round, and very spicy — after which he had been named by them. Of a cold morning, when business was but dull, Turkey would gobble up scores of these cakes, as if they were mere wafers — indeed they sell them at the rate of six or eight for a penny — the scrape of his pen blending with the crunching of the crisp particles in his mouth. Of all the fiery afternoon blunders and flurried rashnesses of Turkey, was his once moistening a ginger-cake between his lips, and clapping it on to a mortgage for a seal. I came within an ace of dismissing him then. But he mollified me by making an oriental bow and saying — "With submission, sir, it was generous of me to find you in stationery on my own account."

Now my original business — that of a conveyancer and title hunter, and drawer-up of recondite documents of all sorts — was considerably increased by receiving the master's office. There was now great work for scriveners. Not only must I push the clerks already with me, but I must have additional help. In answer to my advertisement, a motionless young man one morning stood upon my office threshold, the door being open, for it was summer. I can see that figure now — pallidly neat, pitiably respectable, incurably forlorn! It was Bartleby.

After a few words touching his qualifications, I engaged him, glad to have among my corps of copyists a man of so singularly sedate an aspect, which I thought might operate beneficially upon the flighty temper of Turkey, and the fiery one of Nippers.

I should have stated before that ground glass folding-doors divided my premises into two parts, one of which was occupied by my scriveners, the other by myself. According to my humour I threw open these doors, or closed them. I resolved to assign Bartleby a corner by the folding-doors, but on my side of them, so as to have this quiet man within easy call, in case any trifling thing was to be done. I placed his desk close up to a small side-window in that part of the room, a window which originally had afforded a lateral view of certain grimy backyards and bricks, but which, owing to subsequent erections, commanded at present no view at all, though it gave some light. Within three feet of the panes was a wall, and the light came down from far above, between two lofty buildings, as from a very small opening in a dome. Still further to a satisfactory arrangement, I procured a high green folding screen, which might entirely isolate Bartleby from my sight, though not remove him from my voice. And thus, in a manner, privacy and society were conjoined.

At first Bartleby did an extraordinary quantity of writing. As if long famishing for something to copy, he seemed to gorge himself on my documents. There was no pause for digestion. He ran a day and night line, copying by sun-light and by candle-light. I should have been quite delighted with his application, had he been cheerfully industrious. But he wrote on silently, palely, mechanically.

It is, of course, an indispensable part of a scrivener's business to verify the accuracy of his copy, word by word. Where there are two or more scriveners in an office, they assist each other in this examination, one reading from the copy, the other holding the original. It is a very dull, wearisome, and lethargic affair. I can readily imagine that to some sanguine temperaments it would be altogether intolerable. For example, I cannot credit that the mettlesome poet Byron would have contentedly sat down with Bartleby to examine a law document of, say five hundred pages, closely written in a crimpy hand.

Now and then, in the haste of business, it had been my habit to assist in comparing some brief document myself, calling Turkey or Nippers for this purpose. One object I had in placing Bartleby so handy to me behind the screen, was to avail myself of his services on such trivial occasions. It was on the third day, I think, of his being with me, and before any necessity had arisen for having his own writing examined, that, being much hurried to complete a small affair I had in hand, I abruptly called to Bartleby. In my haste and natural expectancy of instant compliance, I sat with my head bent over the original on my desk, and my right hand sideways, and somewhat nervously extended with the copy, so that immediately upon emerging from his retreat, Bartleby might snatch it and proceed to business without the least delay.

In this very attitude did I sit when I called to him, rapidly stating what it was I wanted him to do — namely, to examine a small paper with me. Imagine my surprise, nay, my consternation, when without moving from his privacy, Bartleby in a singularly mild, firm voice, replied, "I would prefer not to."

I sat awhile in perfect silence, rallying my stunned faculties. Immediately it occurred to me that my ears had deceived me, or Bartleby had entirely misunderstood my meaning. I repeated my request in the clearest tone I could assume. But in quite as clear a one came the previous reply, "I would prefer not to."

"Prefer not to," echoed I, rising in high excitement, and crossing the room with a stride. "What do you mean? Are you moon-struck? I want you to help me compare this sheet here — take it," and I thrust it towards him.

"I would prefer not to," said he.

I looked at him steadfastly. His face was leanly composed; his grey eye dimly calm. Not a wrinkle of agitation rippled him. Had there been the least uneasiness, anger, impatience or impertinence in his manner; in other words, had there been anything ordinarily human about him; doubtless I should have violently dismissed him from the premises. But as it was, I should have as soon thought of turning my pale plaster-of-Paris bust of Cicero out of doors. I stood gazing at him awhile, as he went on with his own writing, and then reseated myself at my desk. This is very strange, thought I. What had one best do? But my business hurried me. I concluded to forget the matter for the present, preserving it for my future leisure. So calling Nippers from the other room, the paper was speedily examined.

A few days after this, Bartleby concluded four lengthy documents, being quadruplicates of a week's testimony taken before me in my High Court of Chancery. It became necessary to examine them. It was an important suit, and great accuracy was imperative. Having all things arranged, I called Turkey, Nippers and Ginger Nut from the next room, meaning to place the four copies in the hands of my four clerks, while I should read from the original. Accordingly Turkey, Nippers and Ginger Nut had taken their seats in a row, each with his document in hand, when I called to Bartleby to join this interesting group.

"Bartleby! quick, I am waiting."

I heard a slow scrape of his chair legs on the uncarpeted floor, and soon he appeared standing at the entrance of his hermitage.

"What is wanted?" said he mildly.

"The copies, the copies," said I hurriedly. "We are going to examine them. There" — and I held towards him the fourth quadruplicate.

"I would prefer not to," he said, and gently disappeared behind the screen.

For a few moments I was turned into a pillar of salt, standing at the head of my seated column of clerks. Recovering myself, I advanced towards the screen, and demanded the reason for such extraordinary conduct.

"*Why* do you refuse?"

"I would prefer not to."

With any other man I should have flown outright into a dreadful passion, scorned all further words, and thrust him ignominiously from my presence. But there was something about Bartleby that not only strangely disarmed me, but in a wonderful manner touched and disconcerted me. I began to reason with him.

"These are your own copies we are about to examine. It is labour saving to you, because one examination will answer for your four papers. It is common usage. Every copyist is bound to help examine his copy. Is it not so? Will you not speak? Answer!"

"I prefer not to," he replied in a flute-like tone. It seemed to me that while I had been addressing him, he carefully revolved every statement that I made; fully comprehended the meaning; could not gainsay the irresistible conclusion; but, at the same time, some paramount consideration prevailed with him to reply as he did.

"You are decided, then, not to comply with my request — a request made according to common usage and common sense?"

He briefly gave me to understand that on that point my judgment was sound. Yes: his decision was irreversible.

It is not seldom the case that when a man is browbeaten in some unprecedented and violently unreasonable way, he begins to stagger in his own plainest faith. He begins, as it were, vaguely to surmise that, wonderful as it may be, all the justice and all the reason are on the other side. Accordingly, if any disinterested persons are present, he turns to them for some reinforcement for his own faltering mind.

"Turkey," said I, "what do you think of this? Am I not right?"

"With submission, sir," said Turkey, with his blandest tone, "I think that you are."

"Nippers," said I, "what do *you* think of it?"

"I think I should kick him out of the office."

(The reader of nice perceptions will perceive that, it being morning, Turkey's answer is couched in polite and tranquil terms but Nippers's reply in ill-tempered ones. Or, to repeat a previous sentence, Nippers's ugly mood was on duty, and Turkey's off.)

"Ginger Nut," said I, willing to enlist the smallest suffrage in my behalf, "what do *you* think of it?"

"I think, sir, he's a little *luny*," replied Ginger Nut, with a grin.

"You hear what they say," said I, turning towards the screen, "come forth and do your duty."

But he vouchsafed no reply. I pondered a moment in sore perplexity. But once more business hurried me. I determined again to postpone the consideration of this dilemma to my future leisure. With a little trouble we made out to examine the papers without Bartleby, though at every page or two, Turkey deferentially dropped his opinion that this proceeding was quite out of the common; while Nippers, twitching in his chair with a dyspeptic nervousness, ground out between his set teeth occasional hissing maledictions against the stubborn oaf behind the screen. And for his (Nippers's) part, this was the first and the last time he would do another man's business without pay.

Meanwhile Bartleby sat in his hermitage, oblivious to everything but his own peculiar business there.

Some days passed, the scrivener being employed upon another lengthy work. His late remarkable conduct led me to regard his ways narrowly. I observed that he never went to dinner; indeed that he never went anywhere. As yet I had never of my personal knowledge known him to be outside of my office. He was a perpetual sentry in the corner. At about eleven o'clock though, in the morning, I noticed that Ginger Nut would advance towards the opening in Bartleby's screen, as if silently beckoned thither by a gesture invisible to me where I sat. The boy would then leave the office jingling a few pence, and reappear with a handful of ginger-nuts which he delivered in the hermitage, receiving two of the cakes for his trouble.

He lives, then, on ginger-nuts, thought I; never eats a dinner, properly speaking; he must be a vegetarian then; but no; he never eats even vegetables, he eats nothing but ginger-nuts. My mind then ran on in reveries concerning the probable effects upon the human constitution of living entirely on ginger-nuts. Ginger-nuts are so called because they contain ginger as one of their peculiar constituents, and the final flavouring one. Now what was ginger? A hot, spicy thing. Was Bartleby hot and spicy? Not at all. Ginger, then, had no effect upon Bartleby. Probably he preferred it should have none.

Nothing so aggravates an earnest person as a passive resistance. If the individual so resisted be of a not inhumane temper, and the resisting one perfectly harmless in his passivity; then, in the better moods of the former, he will endeavour charitably to construe to his imagination what proves impossible to be solved by his judgment. Even so, for the most part, I regarded Bartleby and his ways. Poor fellow! thought I, he means no mischief; it is plain he intends no insolence; his aspect sufficiently evinces that his eccentricities are involuntary. He is useful to me. I can get along with him. If I turn him away, the chances are he will fall in with some less indulgent employer, and then he will be rudely treated, and perhaps driven forth miserably to starve. Yes. Here I can cheaply purchase a delicious self-approval. To befriend Bartleby; to humour him in his strange willfulness, will cost me little or nothing, while I lay up in my soul what will eventually prove a sweet morsel for my conscience. But this mood was not invariable with me. The passiveness of Bartleby sometimes irritated me. I felt strangely goaded on to encounter him in new opposition, to elicit some angry spark from him answerable to my own. But indeed I might as well have essayed to strike fire with my knuckles against a bit of Windsor soap. But one afternoon the evil impulse in me mastered me, and the following little scene ensued:

"Bartleby," said I, "when those papers are all copied, I will compare them with you."

"I would prefer not to."

"How? Surely you do not mean to persist in that mulish vagary?"

No answer.

I threw open the folding-doors near by, and turning upon Turkey and Nippers, exclaimed in an excited manner:

"He says, a second time, he won't examine his papers. What do you think of it, Turkey?"

It was afternoon, be it remembered. Turkey sat glowing like a brass boiler, his bald head steaming, his hands reeling among his blotted papers.

"Think of it?" roared Turkey; "I think I'll just step behind his screen, and black his eyes for him!"

So saying, Turkey rose to his feet and threw his arms into a pugilistic position. He was hurrying away to make good his promise, when I detained him, alarmed at the effect of incautiously rousing Turkey's combativeness after dinner.

"Sit down, Turkey," said I, "and hear what Nippers has to say. What do you think of it, Nippers? Would I not be justified in immediately dismissing Bartleby?"

"Excuse me, that is for you to decide, sir. I think his conduct quite unusual, and indeed unjust, as regards Turkey and myself. But it may only be a passing whim."

"Ah," exclaimed I, "you have strangely changed your mind then — you speak very gently of him now."

"All beer," cried Turkey; "gentleness is effects of beer — Nippers and I dined together to-day. You see how gentle *I* am, sir. Shall I go and black his eyes?"

"You refer to Bartleby, I suppose. No, not to-day, Turkey," I replied; "pray, put up your fists."

I closed the doors, and again advanced towards Bartleby. I felt additional incentives tempting me to my fate. I burned to be rebelled against again. I remembered that Bartleby never left the office.

"Bartleby," said I, "Ginger Nut is away; just step round to the Post Office, won't you? (it was but a three minutes' walk), and see if there is anything for me."

"I would prefer not to."

"You *will* not?"

"I *prefer* not."

I staggered to my desk, and sat there in a deep study. My blind inveteracy returned. Was there any other thing in which I could procure myself to be ignominiously repulsed by this lean, penniless wight? — my hired clerk? What added thing is there, perfectly reasonable, that he will be sure to refuse to do?

"Bartleby!"

No answer.

"Bartleby," in a louder tone.

No answer.

"Bartleby," I roared.

Like a very ghost, agreeably to the laws of magical invocation, at the third summons, he appeared at the entrance of his hermitage.

"Go to the next room, and tell Nippers to come to me."

"I prefer not to," he respectfully and slowly said, and mildly disappeared.

"Very good, Bartleby," said I, in a quiet sort of serenely severe self-possessed tone, intimating the unalterable purpose of some terrible retribution very close at hand. At the moment I half intended something of the kind. But upon the whole, as it was drawing towards my dinner-hour, I thought it best to put on my hat and walk home for the day, suffering much from perplexity and distress of mind.

Shall I acknowledge it? The conclusion of this whole business was, that it soon became a fixed fact of my chambers, that a pale young scrivener, by the name of Bartleby, had a desk there; that he copied for me at the usual rate of four cents a folio (one hundred words); but he was permanently exempt from examining the work done by him, that duty being transferred to Turkey and Nippers, out of compliment doubtless to their superior acuteness; moreover, said Bartleby was never on any account to be despatched on the most trivial errand of any sort; and that even if entreated to take upon him such a matter, it was generally understood that he would prefer not to — in other words, that he would refuse point-blank.

As days passed on, I became considerably reconciled to Bartleby. His steadiness, his freedom from all dissipation, his incessant industry (except when he chose to throw himself into a standing revery behind his screen), his great stillness, his unalterableness of demeanour under all circumstances, made him a valuable acquisition. One prime thing was this — *he was always there;* — first in the morning, continually through the day, and the last at night. I had a singular confidence in his honesty. I felt my most precious papers perfectly safe in his hands. Sometimes to be sure I could not, for the very soul of me, avoid falling into sudden spasmodic passions with him. For it was exceeding difficult to bear in mind all the time those strange peculiarities, privileges, and unheard of exemptions, forming the tacit stipulations on Bartleby's part under which he remained in my office. Now and then, in the eagerness of despatching pressing business, I would inadvertently summon Bartleby, in a short, rapid tone, to put his finger, say, on the incipient tie of a bit of red tape with which I was about compressing some papers. Of course, from behind the screen the usual answer, "I prefer not to," was sure to come; and then, how could a human creature with the common infirmities of our nature, refrain from bitterly exclaiming upon such perverseness — such unreasonableness. However, every added repulse of this sort which I received only tended to lessen the probability of my repeating the inadvertence.

Here it must be said, that according to the custom of most legal gentlemen occupying chambers in densely-populated law buildings, there were several keys to my door. One was kept by a woman residing in the attic, which person weekly scrubbed and daily swept and dusted my apartments. Another was kept by Turkey for convenience' sake. The third I sometimes carried in my own pocket. The fourth I knew not who had.

Now, one Sunday morning I happened to go to Trinity Church, to hear a celebrated preacher, and finding myself rather early on the ground, I thought I would walk round to my chambers for awhile. Luckily I had my key with me; but upon applying it to the lock, I found it resisted by something inserted from the inside. Quite surprised, I called out; when to my consternation a key was turned from within; and thrusting his lean visage at me, and holding the door ajar, the apparition of Bartleby appeared, in his shirt sleeves, and otherwise in a strangely tattered dishabille, saying quietly that he was sorry, but he was deeply engaged just then, and — preferred not admitting me at present. In a brief word or two, he moreover added, that perhaps I had better walk round the block two or three times, and by that time he would probably have concluded his affairs.

Now, the utterly unsurmised appearance of Bartleby, tenanting my law-chambers of a Sunday morning, with his cadaverously gentlemanly *nonchalance,* yet withal firm and self-possessed, had such a strange effect upon me, that incontinently I slunk away from my own door, and did as desired. But not without sundry twinges of impotent rebellion against the mild effrontery of this unaccountable scrivener. Indeed, it was his wonderful mildness chiefly, which not only disarmed me, but unmanned me, as it were. For I consider that one, for the time, is in a way unmanned when he tranquilly permits his hired clerk to dictate to him, and order him away from his own premises. Furthermore, I was full of uneasiness as to what Bartleby could possibly be doing in my office in his shirt sleeves, and in an otherwise dismantled condition of a Sunday morning. Was anything amiss going on? Nay, that was out of the question. It was not to be thought of for a moment that Bartleby was an immoral person. But what could he be doing there — copying? Nay again, whatever might be his eccentricities, Bartleby was an eminently decorous person. He would be the last man to sit down to his desk in any state approaching to nudity. Besides, it was Sunday; and there was something about Bartleby that forbade the supposition that he would by any secular occupation violate the proprieties of the day.

Nevertheless, my mind was not pacified; and full of a restless curiosity, at last I returned to the door. Without hindrance I inserted my key, opened it, and entered. Bartleby was not to be seen. I looked round anxiously, peeped behind his screen; but it was very plain that he was gone. Upon more closely examining the place, I surmised that for an indefinite period Bartleby must have ate, dressed, and slept in my office, and that too without plate, mirror, or bed. The cushioned seat of a rickety old sofa in one corner bore the faint impress of a lean, reclining form. Rolled away under his desk, I found a blanket; under the empty grate, a blacking box and brush; on a chair, a tin basin, with soap and a ragged towel; in a newspaper a few crumbs of ginger-nuts and a morsel of cheese. Yes, thought I, it is evident enough that Bartleby has been making his home here, keeping bachelor's hall all by himself. Immediately then the thought came sweeping across me, What miserable friendlessness and loneliness are here revealed! His poverty is great; but his solitude, how horrible! Think of it. Of a Sunday, Wall Street is deserted as Petra;[1]

and every night of every day it is an emptiness. This building too, which of week-days hums with industry and life, at nightfall echoes with sheer vacancy, and all through Sunday is forlorn. And here Bartleby makes his home; sole spectator of a solitude which he has seen all populous — a sort of innocent and transformed Marius brooding among the ruins of Carthage![2]

For the first time in my life a feeling of overpowering stinging melancholy seized me. Before, I had never experienced aught but a not-unpleasing sadness. The bond of a common humanity now drew me irresistibly to gloom. A fraternal melancholy! For both I and Bartleby were sons of Adam. I remembered the bright silks and sparkling faces I had seen that day, in gala trim, swan-like sailing down the Mississippi of Broadway; and I contrasted them with the pallid copyist, and thought to myself, Ah, happiness courts the light, so we deem the world is gay; but misery hides aloof, so we deem that misery there is none. These sad fancyings — chimeras, doubtless, of a sick and silly brain — led on to other and more special thoughts, concerning the eccentricities of Bartleby. Presentiments of strange discoveries hovered round me. The scrivener's pale form appeared to me laid out, among uncaring strangers, in its

[1] **Petra:** Ancient rock city of Trans-Jordan. Although it had for many centuries been a wealthy and celebrated city with a vast caravan trade, it dropped from history for more than a thousand years, its famous ruins being discovered by the Swiss traveler-author Burckhardt in 1812.

[2] **Marius . . . Carthage:** Marius (c. 155–86 B.C.), a dangerously ambitious Roman general, fled to Africa after his defeat in a civil war.

shivering winding sheet.

Suddenly I was attracted by Bartleby's closed desk, the key in open sight left in the lock.

I mean no mischief, seek the gratification of no heartless curiosity, thought I; besides, the desk is mine, and its contents, too, so I will make bold to look within. Everything was methodically arranged, the papers smoothly placed. The pigeon holes were deep, and, removing the files of documents, I groped into their recesses. Presently I felt something there, and dragged it out. It was an old bandana handkerchief, heavy and knotted. I opened it, and saw it was a savings bank. I now recalled all the quiet mysteries which I had noted in the man. I remembered that he never spoke but to answer; that though at intervals he had considerable time to himself, yet I had never seen him reading — no, not even a newspaper; that for long periods he would stand looking out, at his pale window behind the screen, upon the dead brick wall; I was quite sure he never visited any refectory or eating-house; while his pale face clearly indicated that he never drank beer like Turkey, or tea and coffee even, like other men; that he never went anywhere in particular that I could learn; never went out for a walk, unless indeed that was the case at present; that he had declined telling who he was, or whence he came or whether he had any relatives in the world; that though so thin and pale, he never complained of ill health. And more than all, I remembered a certain unconscious air of pallid — how shall I call it? — of pallid haughtiness, say, or rather an austere reserve about him, which had positively awed me into my tame compliance with his eccentricities, when I had feared to ask him to do the slightest incidental thing for me, even though I might know, from his long-continued motionlessness, that behind his screen he must be standing in one of those dead-wall reveries of his.

Revolving all these things, and coupling them with the recently discovered fact that he made my office his constant abiding place and home, and not forgetful of his morbid moodiness; revolving all these things, a prudential feeling began to steal over me. My first emotions had been those of pure melancholy and sincerest pity; but just in proportion as the forlornness of Bartleby grew and grew to my imagination, did that same melancholy merge into fear, that pity into repulsion. So true it is, and so terrible, too, that up to a certain point the thought or sight of misery enlists our best affections; but, in certain special cases, beyond that point it does not. They err who would assert that invariably this is owing to the inherent selfishness of the human heart. It rather proceeds from a certain hopelessness of remedying excessive and organic ill. To a sensitive being, pity is not seldom pain. And when at last it is perceived that such pity cannot lead to effectual succour, common sense bids the soul be rid of it. What I saw that morning persuaded me that the scrivener was the victim of innate and incurable disorder. I might give alms to his body; but his body did not pain him; it was his soul that suffered, and his soul I could not reach.

I did not accomplish the purpose of going to Trinity Church that morning. Somehow, the things I had seen disqualified me for the time from church-going. I walked homeward, thinking what I would do with Bartleby. Finally, I resolved upon this: — I would put certain calm questions to him the next morning, touching his history, etc., and if he declined to answer them openly and unreservedly (and I suppose he would prefer not), then to give him a twenty dollar bill over and above whatever I might owe him, and tell him his services were no longer required; but that if in any other way I could assist him, I would be happy to do so, especially if he desired to return to his native place, wherever that might be, I would willingly help to defray the expenses. Moreover, if, after reaching home, he found himself at any time in want of aid, a letter from him would be sure of a reply.

The next morning came.

"Bartleby," said I, gently calling to him behind his screen.

No reply.

"Bartleby," said I, in a still gentler tone, "come here; I am not going to ask you to do anything you would prefer not to do — I simply wish to speak to you."

Upon this he noiselessly slid into view.

"Will you tell me, Bartleby, where you were born?"

"I would prefer not to."

"Will you tell me *anything* about yourself?"

"I would prefer not to."

"But what reasonable objection can you have to speak to me? I feel friendly towards you."

He did not look at me while I spoke, but kept his glance fixed upon my bust of Cicero, which, as I then sat, was directly behind me, some six inches above my head.

"What is your answer, Bartleby?" said I, after waiting a considerable time for a reply, during which his countenance remained immovable, only there was the faintest conceivable tremor of the white, attenuated mouth.

"At present I prefer to give no answer," he said, and retired into his hermitage.

It was rather weak in me I confess, but his manner on this occasion nettled me. Not only did there seem to lurk in it a certain calm disdain, but his perverseness seemed ungrateful, considering the undeniable good usage and indulgence he had received from me.

Again I sat ruminating what I should do. Mortified as I was at his behaviour, and resolved as I had been to dismiss him when I entered my office, nevertheless I strangely felt something superstitious knocking at my heart, and forbidding me to carry out my purpose, and denouncing me for a villain if I dared to breathe one bitter word against this forlornest of mankind. At last, familiarly drawing my chair behind his screen, I sat down and said: "Bartleby, never mind then about revealing your history; but let me entreat you, as a friend, to comply as far as may be with the usages of this office. Say now you will help to examine papers to-morrow or next day: in short, say now that in a day or two you will begin to be a little reasonable:— say so, Bartleby."

"At present I would prefer not to be a little reasonable," was his mildly cadaverous reply.

Just then the folding-doors opened, and Nippers approached. He seemed suffering from an unusually bad night's rest, induced by severer indigestion than common. He overheard those final words of Bartleby.

"*Prefer not,* eh?" gritted Nippers — "I'd *prefer* him, if I were you, sir," addressing me — "I'd *prefer* him; I'd give him preferences, the stubborn mule! What is it, sir, pray, that he prefers not to do now?"

Bartleby moved not a limb.

"Mr. Nippers," said I, "I'd prefer that you would withdraw for the present."

Somehow, of late I had got into the way of involuntarily using this word *prefer* upon all sorts of not exactly suitable occasions. And I trembled to think that my contact with the scrivener had already and seriously affected me in a mental way. And what further and deeper aberration might it not yet produce? This apprehension had not been without efficacy in determining me to summary means.

As Nippers, looking very sour and sulky, was departing, Turkey blandly and deferentially approached.

"With submission, sir," said he, "yesterday I was thinking about Bartleby here, and I think that if he would but prefer to take a quart of good ale every day, it would do much towards mending him, and enabling him to assist in examining his papers."

"So you have got the word, too," said I, slightly excited.

"With submission, what word, sir?" asked Turkey, respectfully crowding himself into the contracted space behind the screen, and by so doing, making me jostle the scrivener. "What word, sir?"

"I would prefer to be left alone here," said Bartleby, as if offended at being mobbed in his privacy.

"*That's* the word, Turkey," said I — "*that's* it."

"Oh, *prefer?* oh, yes — queer word. I never use it myself. But, sir, as I was saying, if he would but prefer — "

"Turkey," interrupted I, "you will please withdraw."

"Oh, certainly, sir, if you prefer that I should."

As he opened the folding-door to

retire, Nippers at his desk caught a glimpse of me, and asked whether I would prefer to have a certain paper copied on blue paper or white. He did not in the least roguishly accent the word *prefer*. It was plain that it involuntarily rolled from his tongue. I thought to myself, surely I must get rid of a demented man, who already has in some degree turned the tongues, if not the heads, of myself and clerks. But I thought it prudent not to break the dismission at once.

The next day I noticed that Bartleby did nothing but stand at his window in his dead-wall revery. Upon asking him why he did not write, he said that he had decided upon doing no more writing.

"Why, how now? what next?" exclaimed I, "do no more writing?"

"No more."

"And what is the reason?"

"Do you not see the reason for yourself?" he indifferently replied.

I looked steadfastly at him, and perceived that his eyes looked dull and glazed. Instantly it occurred to me, that his unexampled diligence in copying by his dim window for the first few weeks of his stay with me might have temporarily impaired his vision.

I was touched. I said something in condolence with him. I hinted that, of course, he did wisely in abstaining from writing for a while, and urged him to embrace that opportunity of taking wholesome exercise in the open air. This, however, he did not do. A few days after

this, my other clerks being absent, and being in a great hurry to despatch certain letters by the mail, I thought that, having nothing else earthly to do, Bartleby would surely be less inflexible than usual, and carry these letters to the Post Office. But he blankly declined. So, much to my inconvenience, I went myself.

Still added days went by. Whether Bartleby's eyes improved or not, I could not say. To all appearance, I thought they did. But when I asked him if they did, he vouchsafed no answer. At all events, he would do no copying. At last, in reply to my urgings, he informed me that he had permanently given up copying.

"What!" exclaimed I; "suppose your eyes should get entirely well — better than ever before — would you not copy then?"

"I have given up copying," he answered and slid aside.

He remained, as ever, a fixture in my chamber. Nay — if that were possible — he became still more of a fixture than before. What was to be done? He would do nothing in the office: why should he stay there? In plain fact, he had now become a millstone to me, not only useless as a necklace, but afflictive to bear. Yet I was sorry for him. I speak less than truth when I say that, on his own account, he occasioned me uneasiness. If he would but have named a single relative or friend, I would instantly have written, and urged their taking the poor fellow away to some convenient retreat.

But he seemed alone, absolutely alone in the universe. A bit of wreckage in the mid-Atlantic. At length, necessities connected with my business tyrannized over all other considerations. Decently as I could, I told Bartleby that in six days' time he must unconditionally leave the office. I warned him to take measures, in the interval, for procuring some other abode. I offered to assist him in this endeavour, if he himself would but take the first step towards a removal. "And when you finally quit me, Bartleby," added I, "I shall see that you go away not entirely unprovided. Six days from this hour, remember."

At the expiration of that period, I peeped behind the screen, and lo! Bartleby was there.

I buttoned up my coat, balanced myself; advanced slowly towards him, touched his shoulder, and said, "The time has come; you must quit this place; I am sorry for you; here is money; but you must go."

"I would prefer not," he replied, with his back still towards me.

"You *must*."

He remained silent.

Now I had an unbounded confidence in this man's common honesty. He had frequently restored to me sixpences and shillings carelessly dropped upon the floor, for I am apt to be very reckless in such shirt-button affairs. The proceeding then which followed will not be deemed extraordinary.

"Bartleby," said I, "I owe you twelve dollars on account; here are thirty-two; the odd twenty are yours. — Will you take it?" and I handed the bills towards him.

But he made no motion.

"I will leave them here then," putting them under a weight on the table. Then taking my hat and cane and going to the door, I tranquilly turned and added — "After you have removed your things from these offices, Bartleby, you will of course lock the door — since every one is now gone for the day but you — and if you please, slip your key underneath the mat, so that I may have it in the morning. I shall not see you again; so good-bye to you. If hereafter, in your new place of abode I can be of any service to you, do not fail to advise me by letter. Good-bye, Bartleby, and fare you well."

But he answered not a word; like the last column of some ruined temple, he remained standing mute and solitary in the middle of the otherwise deserted room.

As I walked home in a pensive mood, my vanity got the better of my pity. I could not but highly plume myself on my masterly management in getting rid of Bartleby. Masterly I call it, and such it must appear to any dispassionate thinker. The beauty of my procedure seemed to consist in its perfect quietness. There was no vulgar bullying, no bravado of any sort, no choleric hectoring, no striding to and fro across the apartment, jerking out vehement commands for Bartleby to bundle himself off with his beggarly traps. Nothing of the kind. Without loudly bidding Bartleby depart — as an inferior genius might have done — I assumed the ground that depart he must; and upon that assumption built all I had to say. The more I thought over my procedure, the more I was charmed with it. Nevertheless, next morning, upon awakening, I had my doubts, — I had somehow slept off the fumes of vanity. One of the coolest and wisest hours a man has, is just after he awakes in the morning. My procedure seemed as sagacious as ever — but only in theory. How it would prove in practice — there was the rub. It was truly a beautiful thought to have assumed Bartleby's departure; but, after all, that assumption was simply my own, and none of Bartleby's. The great point was, not whether I had assumed that he would quit me, but whether he would prefer so to do. He was more a man of preferences than assumptions.

After breakfast, I walked down town, arguing the probabilities *pro* and *con*. One moment I thought it would prove a miserable failure, and Bartleby would be found all alive at my office as usual; the next moment it seemed certain that I should see his chair empty. And so I kept veering about. At the corner of Broadway and Canal Street, I saw quite an excited group of people standing in earnest conversation.

"I'll take odds he doesn't," said a voice as I passed.

"Doesn't go? — done!" said **I**, "put up your money."

I was instinctively putting my hand in my pocket to produce my own, when I remembered that this was an election day. The words I had overheard bore no reference to Bartleby, but to the success or non-success of some candidate for the mayoralty. In my intent frame of mind, I had, as it were, imagined that all Broadway shared in my excitement, and were debating the same question with me. I passed on, very thankful that the uproar of the street screened my momentary absent-mindedness.

As I had intended, I was earlier than usual at my office door. I stood listening for a moment. All was still. He must be gone. I tried the knob. The door was locked. Yes, my procedure had worked to a charm; he indeed must be vanished. Yet a certain melancholy mixed with this: I was almost sorry for my brilliant success. I was fumbling under the door mat for the key, which Bartleby was to have left there for me, when accidently my knee knocked against a panel, producing a summoning sound, and in response a voice came to me from within — "Not yet; I am occupied."

It was Bartleby.

I was thunderstruck. For an instant I stood like the man who, pipe in mouth, was killed one cloudless afternoon long ago in Virginia, by summer lightning; at his own warm open window he was killed, and remained leaning out there upon the dreamy afternoon, till some one touched him, and he fell.

"Not gone!" I murmured at last. But again obeying that wondrous ascendency which the inscrutable scrivener had over me — and from which ascendency, for all my chafing, I could not completely escape — I slowly went down stairs and out into the street, and while walking round the block, considered what I should next do in this unheard-of perplexity. Turn the man out by an actual thrusting I could not; to drive him away by calling him hard names would not do; calling in the police was an unpleasant idea; and yet, permit him to enjoy his cadaverous triumph over me — this too I could not think of. What was to be done? Or, if nothing could be done, was there anything further that I could *assume* in the matter? Yes, as before I had prospectively assumed that Bartleby would depart, so now I might retrospectively assume that departed he was. In the legitimate carrying out of this assumption, I might enter my office in a great hurry, and pretending not to see Bartleby at all, walk straight against him as if he were air. Such a proceeding would in a singular degree have the appearance of a homethrust. It was hardly possible that Bartleby would withstand such an application of the doctrine of assumptions. But, upon second thought, the success of the plan

seemed rather dubious. I resolved to argue the matter over with him again.

"Bartleby," said I, entering the office, with a quietly severe expression, "I am seriously displeased. I am pained, Bartleby. I had thought better of you. I had imagined you of such a gentlemanly organization, that in any delicate dilemma a slight hint would suffice — in short, an assumption; but it appears I am deceived. Why," I added, unaffectedly starting, "you have not even touched that money yet," pointing to it, just where I had left it the evening previous.

He answered nothing.

"Will you, or will you not, quit me?" I now demanded in a sudden passion, advancing close to him.

"I would prefer *not* to quit you," he replied, gently emphasizing the *not.*

"What earthly right have you to stay here? Do you pay any rent? Do you pay my taxes? Or is this property yours?"

He answered nothing.

"Are you ready to go on and write now? Are your eyes recovered? Could you copy a small paper for me this morning? or help examine a few lines? or step round to the Post Office? In a word, will you do any thing at all, to give a colouring to your refusal to depart the premises?"

He silently retired into his hermitage.

I was now in such a state of nervous resentment that I thought it but prudent to check myself, at present, from further demonstrations. Bartleby and I were alone. I remembered the tragedy of the unfortunate Adams and the still more unfortunate Colt in the solitary office of the latter; and how poor Colt, being dreadfully incensed by Adams, and imprudently permitting himself to get wildly excited, was at unawares hurried into his fatal act — an act which certainly no man could possibly deplore more than the actor himself. Often it had occurred to me in my ponderings upon the subject, that had that altercation taken place in the public street, or at a private residence, it would not have terminated as it did. It was the circumstance of being alone in a solitary office, upstairs, of a building entirely unhallowed by humanizing domestic associations — an uncarpeted office, doubtless, of a dusty, haggard sort of appearance; — this it must have been, which greatly helped to enhance the irritable desperation of the hapless Colt.

But when this old Adam of resentment rose in me and tempted me concerning Bartleby, I grappled him and threw him. How? Why, simply by recalling the divine injunction: "A new commandment give I unto you, that ye love one another." Yes, this it was that saved me. Aside from higher considerations, charity often operates as a vastly wise and prudent principle — a great safeguard to its possessor. Men have committed murder for jealousy's sake, and anger's sake, and hatred's sake, and selfishness' sake, and spiritual pride's sake; but no man that ever I heard of, ever committed a diabolical murder for sweet charity's sake. Mere self-interest, then, if no better motive can be enlisted, should, especially with high-tempered men, prompt all beings to charity and philanthropy. At any rate, upon the occasion in question, I strove to drown my exasperated feelings towards the scrivener by benevolently construing his conduct. Poor fellow, poor fellow! thought I, he doesn't mean any thing; and besides, he has seen hard times, and ought to be indulged.

I endeavoured also immediately to occupy myself, and at the same time to comfort my despondency. I tried to fancy that in the course of the morning, at such time as might prove agreeable to him, Bartleby, of his own free accord, would emerge from his hermitage, and take up some decided line of march in the direction of the door. But no. Half-past twelve o'clock came; Turkey began to glow in the face, overturn his inkstand, and become generally obstreperous; Nippers abated down into quietude and courtesy; Ginger Nut munched his noon apple; and Bartleby remained standing at his window in one of his profoundest dead-wall reveries. Will it be credited? Ought I to acknowledge it? That afternoon I left the office without saying one further word to him.

Some days now passed, during which at leisure intervals I looked a little into "Edwards on the Will," and "Priestley on Necessity." Under the circumstances, those books induced a salutary feeling. Gradually I slid into the persuasion that these troubles of mine, touching the scrivener, had been all predestinated from eternity, and Bartleby was billeted upon me for some mysterious purpose of an all-wise Providence, which it was not for a mere mortal like me to fathom. Yes, Bartleby, stay there behind your screen, thought I; I shall persecute you no more; you are harmless and noiseless as any of these old chairs; in short, I never feel so private as when I know you are here. At least I see it, I feel it; I penetrate to the predestinated purpose of my life. I am content. Others may have loftier parts to enact; but my mission in this world, Bartleby, is to furnish you with office room for such period as you may see fit to remain.

I believe that this wise and blessed frame of mind would have continued with me had it not been for the unsolicited and uncharitable remarks obtruded upon me by my professional friends who visited the rooms. But thus it often is, that the constant friction of illiberal minds wears out at last the best resolves of the more generous. Though to be sure, when I reflected upon it, it was not strange that people entering my office should be struck by the peculiar aspect of the unaccountable Bartleby, and so be tempted to throw out some sinister observations concerning him. Sometimes an attorney having business with me, and calling at my office, and finding no one but the scrivener there, would undertake to obtain some sort of precise information from him touching my whereabouts; but without heeding his idle talk, Bartleby would remain standing immovable in the middle of the room. So, after contemplating him in that position for a time, the attorney would depart, no wiser than he came.

Also, when a reference was going on, and the room full of lawyers and witnesses, and business was driving fast, some deeply occupied legal gentleman present, seeing Bartleby wholly unemployed, would request him to run round to his (the legal gentleman's) office and fetch some papers for him. Thereupon, Bartleby would tranquilly decline, and yet remain idle as before. Then the lawyer would give a great stare, and turn to me. And what could I say? At last I was made aware that all through the circle of my professional acquaintance, a whisper of wonder was running round, having reference to the strange creature I kept at my office. This worried me very much. And as the idea came upon me of his possibly turning out a long-lived man, and keep occupying my chambers, and denying my authority; and perplexing my visitors; and scandalizing my professional reputation; and casting a general gloom over the premises; keeping soul and body together to the last upon his savings (for doubtless he spent but half a dime a day), and in the end perhaps outlive me, and claim possession of my office by right of his perpetual occupancy: as all these dark anticipations crowded upon me more and more, and my friends continually intruded their relentless remarks upon the apparition in my room, a great change was wrought in me. I resolved to gather all my faculties together, and for ever rid me of this intolerable incubus. Ere revolving any complicated project, however, adapted to this end, I first simply suggested to Bartleby the propriety of his permanent departure. In a calm and serious tone, I commended the idea to his careful and mature consideration. But having taken three days to meditate upon it, he apprised me that his original determination remained the same; in short, that he still preferred to abide with me.

What shall I do? I now said to myself, buttoning up my coat to the last button. What shall I do? what ought I to do? what does conscience say I *should* do with this man, or, rather, ghost? Rid myself of him, I must; go, he shall. But how? You will not thrust him, the poor, pale, passive mortal — you will not thrust such a helpless creature out of your door? you will not dishonour yourself by such cruelty? No, I will not, I cannot do that. Rather would I let him live and die here, and then mason up his remains in the wall. What then will you do? For all your coaxing, he will not budge. Bribes he leaves under your own paper-weight on your table; in short, it is quite plain that he prefers to cling to you.

Then something severe, something unusual must be done. What! surely you will not have him collared by a constable, and commit his innocent pallor to the common jail? And upon what ground could you procure such a thing to be done? — a vagrant, is he? What! he a vagrant, a wanderer, who refuses to budge? It is because he will *not* be a vagrant, then, that you seek to count him *as* a vagrant. That is too absurd. No visible means of support: there I have him. Wrong again: for indubitably he *does* support himself, and that is the only unanswerable proof that any man can show of his possessing the means so to do. No more then. Since he will not quit me, I must quit him. I will change my offices; I will move elsewhere; and give him fair notice, that if I find him on my new premises I will then proceed against him as a common trespasser.

Acting accordingly, next day I thus addressed him: "I find these chambers too far from the City Hall; the air is unwholesome. In a word, I propose to remove my offices next week, and shall no longer require your services. I tell you this now, in order that you may seek another place."

He made no reply, and nothing more was said.

On the appointed day I engaged carts and men, proceeded to my chambers, and having but little furniture, everything was removed in a few hours. Throughout all, the scrivener remained standing behind the screen, which I directed to be removed the last thing. It was withdrawn; and being folded up like a huge folio, left him the motionless occupant of a naked room. I stood in the entry watching him a moment, while something from within me upbraided me.

I re-entered, with my hand in my pocket — and — and my heart in my mouth.

"Good-bye, Bartleby; I am going — good-bye, and God some way bless you; and take that," slipping something in his hand. But it dropped upon the floor and then — strange to say — I tore myself from him whom I had so longed to be rid of.

Established in my new quarters, for a day or two I kept the door locked, and started at every footfall in the passages. When I returned to my rooms after any little absence, I would pause at the threshold for an instant, and attentively listen, ere applying my key. But these fears were needless. Bartleby never came nigh me.

I thought all was going well, when a perturbed looking stranger visited me, inquiring whether I was the person who had recently occupied rooms at No. —— Wall Street.

Full of forebodings, I replied that I was.

"Then sir," said the stranger, who proved a lawyer, "you are responsible for the man you left there. He refuses to do any copying, he refuses to do anything; and he says he prefers not to; and he refuses to quit the premises."

"I am very sorry, sir," said I, with assumed tranquillity, but an inward tremor, "but, really, the man you allude to is nothing to me — he is no relation or apprentice of mine, that you should hold me responsible for him."

"In mercy's name, who is he?"

"I certainly cannot inform you. I know nothing about him. Formerly I employed him as a copyist; but he has done nothing for me now for some time past."

"I shall settle him then — good morning, sir."

Several days passed, and I heard nothing more; and though I often felt a charitable prompting to call at the place and see poor Bartleby, yet a certain squeamishness of I know not what withheld me.

All is over with him, by this time, thought I at last, when through another week no further intelligence reached me. But coming to my room the day after, I found several persons waiting at my door in a high state of nervous excitement.

"That's the man — here he comes," cried the foremost one,

whom I recognized as the lawyer who had previously called upon me alone.

"You must take him away, sir, at once," cried a portly person among them, advancing upon me, and whom I knew to be the landlord of No. —— Wall Street. "These gentlemen, my tenants, cannot stand it any longer; Mr. B——," pointing to the lawyer, "has turned him out of his room, and he now persists in haunting the building generally, sitting upon the banisters of the stairs by day, and sleeping in the entry by night. Everybody here is concerned; clients are leaving the offices; some fears are entertained of a mob; something you must do, and that without delay."

Aghast at this torrent, I fell back before it, and would fain have locked myself in my new quarters. In vain I persisted that Bartleby was nothing to me — no more than to any one else there. In vain: — I was the last person known to have anything to do with him, and they held me to the terrible account. Fearful then of being exposed in the papers (as one person present obscurely threatened) I considered the matter, and at length said, that if the lawyer would give me a confidential interview with the scrivener, in his (the lawyer's) own room, I would that afternoon strive my best to rid them of the nuisance they complained of.

Going up stairs to my old haunt, there was Bartleby silently sitting upon the banister at the landing.

"What are you doing here, Bartleby?" said I.

"Sitting upon the banister," he mildly replied.

I motioned him into the lawyer's room, who then left us.

"Bartleby," said I, "are you aware that you are the cause of great tribulation to me, by persisting in occupying the entry after being dismissed from the office?"

No answer.

"Now one of two things must take place. Either you must do something, or something must be done to you. Now what sort of business would you like to engage in? Would you like to re-engage in copying for some one?"

"No; I would prefer not to make any change."

"Would you like a clerkship in a dry-goods store?"

"There is too much confinement about that. No, I would not like a clerkship; but I am not particular."

"Too much confinement," I cried, "why, you keep yourself confined all the time!"

"I would prefer not to take a clerkship," he rejoined, as if to settle that little item at once.

"How would a bartender's business suit you? There is no trying of the eyesight in that."

"I would not like it at all; though, as I said before, I am not particular."

His unwonted wordiness inspirited me. I returned to the charge.

"Well then, would you like to

travel through the country collecting bills for the merchants? That would improve your health."

"No, I would prefer to be doing something else."

"How then would going as a companion to Europe to entertain some young gentleman with your conversation — how would that suit you?"

"Not at all. It does not strike me that there is anything definite about that. I like to be stationary. But I am not particular."

"Stationary you shall be then," I cried, now losing all patience, and for the first time in all my exasperating connection with him fairly flying into a passion. "If you do not go away from these premises before night, I shall feel bound — indeed I *am* bound — to — to — to quit the premises myself!" I rather absurdly concluded, knowing not with what possible threat to try to frighten his immobility into compliance. Despairing of all further efforts, I was precipitately leaving him, when a final thought occurred to me — one which had not been wholly unindulged before.

"Bartleby," said I, in the kindest tone I could assume under such exciting circumstances, "will you go home with me now — not to my office, but my dwelling — and remain there till we can conclude upon some convenient arrangement for you at our leisure? Come, let us start now, right away."

"No: at present I would prefer not to make any change at all."

I answered nothing; but effectually dodging every one by the suddenness and rapidity of my flight, rushed from the building, ran up Wall Street towards Broadway, and then jumping into the first omnibus, was soon removed from pursuit. As soon as tranquillity returned I distinctly perceived that I had now done all that I possibly could, both in respect to the demands of the landlord and his tenants, and with regard to my own desire and sense of duty, to benefit Bartleby, and shield him from rude persecution. I now strove to be entirely carefree and quiescent; and my conscience justified me in the attempt; though indeed it was not so successful as I could have wished. So fearful was I of being again hunted out by the incensed landlord and his exasperated tenants, that, surrendering my business to Nippers, for a few days I drove about the upper part of the town and through the suburbs, in my rockaway; crossed over to Jersey City and Hoboken, and paid fugitive visits to Manhattanville and Astoria. In fact I almost lived in my rockaway for the time.

When again I entered my office, lo, a note from the landlord lay upon the desk. I opened it with trembling hands. It informed me that the writer had sent to the police, and had Bartleby removed to the Tombs as a vagrant. Moreover, since I knew more about him than any one else, he wished me to appear at that place, and make a suitable statement of the facts. These tidings had a conflicting effect upon me. At first I was indignant; but at last almost approved. The landlord's energetic, summary disposition had led him to adopt a procedure which I do not think I would have decided upon myself; and yet as a last resort, under such peculiar circumstances, it seemed the only plan.

As I afterwards learned, the poor scrivener, when told that he must be conducted to the Tombs, offered not the slightest obstacle, but in his own pale, unmoving way silently acquiesced.

Some of the compassionate and curious bystanders joined the party; and headed by one of the constables, arm-in-arm with Bartleby, the silent procession filed its way through all the noise, and heat, and joy of the roaring thoroughfares at noon. The same day I received the note I went to the Tombs, or, to speak more properly, the Halls of Justice. Seeking the right officer, I stated the purpose of my call, and was informed that the individual I described was indeed within. I then assured the functionary that Bartleby was a perfectly honest man, and greatly to be compassionated, however unaccountably eccentric. I narrated all I knew, and closed by suggesting the idea of letting him remain in as indulgent confinement as possible till something less harsh might be done — though indeed I hardly knew what. At all events, if nothing else

could be decided upon, the almshouse must receive him. I then begged to have an interview.

Being under no disgraceful charge, and quite serene and harmless in all his ways, they had permitted him freely to wander about the prison, and especially in the inclosed grass-platted yards thereof. And so I found him there, standing all alone in the quietest of the yards, his face towards a high wall — while all around, from the narrow slits of the jail windows, I thought I saw peering out upon him the eyes of murderers and thieves.

"Bartleby!"

"I know you," he said, without looking round — "and I want nothing to say to you."

"It was not I that brought you here, Bartleby," said I, keenly pained at his implied suspicion. "And to you, this should not be so vile a place. Nothing reproachful attaches to you by being here. And see, it is not so sad a place as one might think. Look, there is the sky and here is the grass."

"I know where I am," he replied, but would say nothing more, and so I left him.

As I entered the corridor again a broad, meat-like man in an apron accosted me, and jerking his thumb over his shoulder said — "Is that your friend?"

"Yes."

"Does he want to starve? If he does, let him live on the prison fare, that's all."

"Who are you?" asked I, not

knowing what to make of such an unofficially speaking person in such a place.

"I am the grub-man. Such gentlemen as have friends here, hire me to provide them with something good to eat."

"Is this so?" said I, turning to the turnkey.

He said it was. "Well then," said I, slipping some silver into the grub-man's hands (for so they called him), "I want you to give particular attention to my friend there; let him have the best dinner you can get. And you must be as polite to him as possible."

"Introduce me, will you?" said the grub-man, looking at me with an expression which seemed to say he was all impatience for an opportunity to give a specimen of his breeding.

Thinking it would prove of benefit to the scrivener, I acquiesced; and asking the grub-man his name, went up with him to Bartleby.

"Bartleby, this is Mr. Cutlets; you will find him very useful to you."

"Your sarvant, sir, your sarvant," said the grub-man, making a low salutation behind his apron. "Hope you find it pleasant here, sir; — spacious grounds — cool apartments, sir — hope you'll stay with us some time — try to make it agreeable. May Mrs. Cutlets and I have the pleasure of your company to dinner, sir, in Mrs. Cutlets's private room?"

"I prefer not to dine to-day," said Bartleby, turning away. "It would disagree with me; I am unused to dinners." So saying, he slowly moved to the other side of the inclosure and took up a position fronting the dead-wall.

"How's this?" said the grub-man, addressing me with a stare of astonishment. "He's odd, ain't he?"

"I think he is a little deranged," said I, sadly.

"Deranged? deranged is it? Well now, upon my word, I thought that friend of yourn was a gentleman forger; they are always pale and genteel-like, them forgers. I can't help pity 'em — can't help it, sir. Did you know Monroe Edwards?" he added touchingly, and paused. Then, laying his hand pityingly on my shoulder, sighed, "He died of the consumption at Sing-Sing. So you weren't acquainted with Monroe?"

"No, I was never socially acquainted with any forgers. But I cannot stop longer. Look to my friend yonder. You will not lose by it. I will see you again."

Some few days after this, I again obtained admission to the Tombs, and went through the corridors in quest of Bartleby; but without finding him.

"I saw him coming from his cell not long ago," said a turnkey, "maybe he's gone to loiter in the yards."

So I went in that direction.

"Are you looking for the silent man?" said another turnkey passing me. "Yonder he lies — sleeping in the yard there. 'Tis not twenty minutes since I saw him lie down."

The yard was entirely quiet. It was not accessible to the common prisoners. The surrounding walls, of amazing thickness, kept off all sounds behind them. The Egyptian character of the masonry weighed upon me with its gloom. But a soft imprisoned turf grew under foot. The heart of the eternal pyramids, it seemed, wherein by some strange magic, through the clefts grass-seed, dropped by birds, had sprung.

Strangely huddled at the base of the wall — his knees drawn up, and lying on his side, his head touching the cold stones — I saw the wasted Bartleby. But nothing stirred. I paused; then went close up to him; stooped over, and saw that his dim eyes were open; otherwise he seemed profoundly sleeping. Something prompted me to touch him. I felt his hand, when a tingling shiver ran up my arm and down my spine to my feet.

The round face of the grub-man peered upon me now. "His dinner is ready. Won't he dine to-day, either? Or does he live without dining?"

"Lives without dining," said I, and closed the eyes.

"Eh! — He's asleep, ain't he?"

"With kings and counsellors," murmured I.

There would seem little need for proceeding further in this history. Imagination will readily supply the meagre recital of poor Bartleby's interment. But ere parting with the reader, let me say, that if this little narrative has sufficiently interested him, to awaken curiosity as to who Bartleby was, and what manner of life he led prior to the present narrator's making his acquaintance, I can only reply, that in such curiosity I fully share — but am wholly unable to gratify it. Yet here I hardly know whether I should divulge one little item of rumour, which came to my ear a few months after the scrivener's decease. Upon what basis it rested, I could never ascertain; and hence, how true it is I cannot now tell. But inasmuch as this vague report has not been without a certain strange suggestive interest to me, however sad, it may prove the same with some others; and so I will briefly mention it. The report was this: that Bartleby had been a subordinate clerk in the Dead Letter Office at Washington, from which he had been suddenly removed by a change in the administration. When I think over this rumour I cannot adequately express the emotions which seize me. Dead letters! does it not sound like dead men? Conceive a man by nature and misfortune prone to a pallid hopelessness: can any business seem more fitted to heighten it than that of continually handling these dead letters, and assorting them for the flames? For by the cartload they are annually burned. Sometimes from out the folded paper the pale clerk takes a ring: — the finger it was meant for, perhaps, moulders in the grave; a bank-note sent in swiftest charity: — he whom it would relieve, nor eats nor hungers any more; pardon for those who died despairing; hope for those who died unhoping; good tidings for those who died stifled by unrelieved calamities. On errands of life, these letters speed to death. Ah Bartleby! Ah humanity!

For Study and Writing

1. How does the narrator of "Bartleby the Scrivener" describe himself? What does he claim as his own outstanding quality? What other qualities does he ascribe to himself by implication?

2. What does the narrator know about Turkey, Nippers, and Ginger Nut? What does he apparently *not* know about them?

3. Discuss the relationship which the narrator wants to maintain with his employees. How does the arrival of Bartleby threaten to disturb this relationship?

4. Why does the narrator ask Turkey, Nippers, and Ginger Nut about the Bartleby problem? What are the immediate and general results of his inquiries?

5. When the narrator first mentions Bartleby's name, he says that the scrivener was the strangest he ever saw or heard of. What is so strange about Bartleby? Is it arguable that the narrator and his other employees are strange and Bartleby is reasonable?

6. Why does the narrator want to give Bartleby extra money when he tries to get the scrivener to leave?

7. What do the narrator's visits to the Tombs indicate about his attitude toward Bartleby? Do you have any reason to assume that personal affection is involved?

8. What is significant about Bartleby's "I would prefer not to" as opposed to a more definite refusal to comply?

9. When the narrator approaches Bartleby in the prison yard, the latter says, "I know you . . . and I want nothing to say to you." A few lines later he replies to the narrator's cheery exposition of the situation by saying "I know where I am." How much is implied by Bartleby or by the author in these two affirmations of knowledge?

10. Which of these is the story principally about: Bartleby or the narrator?

The Blue Hotel

by Stephen Crane (1871–1900)

"The Blue Hotel" is a subtle, complex, eventful story. It unfolds absorbingly, but its elements of action, scene, and character are so skillfully planned and fitted that you cannot see the meaning of many parts until you have read all. As in the case of every great story, its particular events support generalizations about life at large. Crane's novel *The Red Badge of Courage* must stand as his masterwork, yet this remarkable short story may well be the finest single gem of his craft. Crane was also a fine poet; and you will see throughout this tale the poetic images that are the hallmark of his wonderfully simple yet intensely individual style.

I

The Palace Hotel at Fort Romper was painted a light blue, a shade that is on the legs of a kind of heron, causing the bird to declare its position against any background. The Palace Hotel, then, was always screaming and howling in a way that made the dazzling winter landscape of Nebraska seem only a grey swampish hush. It stood alone on the prairie, and when the snow was falling the town two hundred yards away was not visible. But when the traveller alighted at the railway station he was obliged to pass the Palace Hotel before he could come upon the company of low clapboard houses which composed Fort Romper, and it was not to be thought that any traveller could pass the Palace Hotel without looking at it. Pat Scully, the proprietor, had proved himself a master of strategy when he chose his paints. It is true that on clear days, when the great transcontinental expresses, long lines of swaying Pullmans, swept through Fort Romper, passengers were overcome at the sight, and the cult that knows the brown-reds and the subdivisions of the dark greens of the East expressed shame, pity, horror, in a laugh. But to the citizens of this prairie town and to the people who would naturally stop there, Pat Scully had performed a feat. With this opulence and splendour, these creeds, classes, egotisms, that streamed through Romper on the rails day after day, they had no colour in common.

As if the displayed delights of such a blue hotel were not sufficiently enticing, it was Scully's habit to go every morning and evening to meet the leisurely trains that stopped at Romper and work his seductions upon any man that he might see wavering, gripsack in hand.

One morning, when a snow-crusted engine dragged its long string of freight cars and its one passenger coach to the station, Scully performed the marvel of catching three men. One was a shaky and quick-eyed Swede, with a great shining cheap valise; one was a tall bronzed cowboy, who was on his way to a ranch near the Dakota line; one was a little silent man from the East, who didn't look it, and didn't announce it. Scully practically made them prisoners. He was so nimble and merry and kindly that each probably felt it would be the height of brutality to try to escape. They trudged off over the creaking board sidewalks in the wake of the eager little Irishman. He wore a heavy fur cap squeezed tightly down on his head. It caused his two red ears to stick out stiffly, as if they were made of tin.

At last, Scully, elaborately, with boisterous hospitality, conducted them through the portals of the blue hotel. The room which they entered was small. It seemed to be merely a proper temple for an enormous stove, which, in the centre, was humming with godlike violence. At various points on its surface the iron had become luminous and glowed yellow from the heat. Beside the stove Scully's son Johnnie was playing High-Five with an old farmer who had whiskers both grey and sandy. They were quarrelling. Frequently the old farmer turned his face toward a box of sawdust — coloured brown from tobacco juice — that was behind the stove, and spat with an air of great impatience and irritation. With a loud flourish of words Scully destroyed the game of cards, and bustled his son upstairs with part of the baggage of the new guests. He himself conducted them to three basins of the coldest water in the world. The cowboy and the Easterner burnished themselves fiery red with this water, until it seemed to be some kind of metal-polish. The Swede, however, merely dipped his fingers gingerly and with trepidation. It was notable that throughout this series of small ceremonies the three travellers were made to feel that Scully was very benevolent. He was conferring great favours upon them. He handed the towel from one to another with an air of philanthropic impulse.

Afterward they went to the first room, and, sitting about the stove, listened to Scully's officious clamour at his daughters, who were preparing the midday meal. They reflected in the silence of experienced men who tread carefully amid new people. Nevertheless, the old farmer, stationary, invincible in his chair near the warmest part of the stove, turned his face from the sawdust-box frequently and addressed a glowing commonplace to the strangers. Usually he was answered in short but adequate sentences by either the cowboy or the Easterner. The Swede said nothing. He seemed to be occupied in making furtive estimates of each man in the room. One might have thought that he had the sense of silly suspicion which comes to guilt. He resembled a badly frightened man.

Later, at dinner, he spoke a little, addressing his conversation entirely to Scully. He volunteered that he had come from New York, where for ten years he had worked as a tailor. These facts seemed to strike Scully as fascinating, and afterward he volunteered that he had lived at Romper for fourteen years. The Swede asked about the crops and the price of labour. He seemed barely to listen to Scully's extended replies. His eyes continued to rove from man to man.

Finally, with a laugh and a wink, he said that some of these Western communities were very dangerous; and after his statement he straightened his legs under the table, tilted his head, and laughed again, loudly. It was plain that the demonstration had no meaning to the others. They looked at him wondering and in silence.

II

As the men trooped heavily back into the front room, the two little windows presented views of a turmoiling sea of snow. The huge arms of the wind were making attempts — mighty, circular, futile — to embrace the flakes as they sped. A gate-post like a still man with a blanched face stood aghast amid this profligate fury. In a hearty voice Scully announced the presence of a blizzard. The guests of the blue hotel, lighting their pipes, assented with grunts of lazy masculine contentment. No island of the sea could be exempt in the degree of this little room with its humming stove. Johnnie, son of Scully, in a tone which defined his opinion of his ability as a card-player, challenged the old farmer of both grey and sandy whiskers to a game of High-Five. The farmer agreed with a contemptuous and bitter scoff. They sat close to the stove, and squared their knees under a wide board. The cowboy and the Easterner watched the game with interest. The Swede remained near the window, aloof, but with a countenance that showed signs of an inexplicable excitement.

The play of Johnnie and the greybeard was suddenly ended by another quarrel. The old man arose while casting a look of heated scorn at his adversary. He slowly buttoned his coat, and then stalked with fabulous dignity from the room. In the discreet silence of all the other men the Swede laughed. His laughter rang somehow childish. Men by this time had begun to look at him askance, as if they wished to inquire what ailed him.

A new game was formed jocosely. The cowboy volunteered to become a partner of Johnnie, and they all then turned to ask the Swede to throw in his lot with the little Easterner. He asked some questions about the game, and, learning that it wore many names, and that he had played it when it was under an alias, he accepted the invitation. He strode toward the men nervously, as if he expected to be assaulted. Finally, seated, he gazed from face to face and laughed shrilly. This laugh was so strange that the Easterner looked up quickly, the cowboy sat intent and with his mouth open, and Johnnie paused, holding the cards with still fingers.

Afterward there was a short silence. Then Johnnie said, "Well, let's get at it. Come on now!" They pulled their chairs forward until their knees were bunched under the board. They began to play, and their interest in the game caused the others to forget the manner of the Swede.

The cowboy was a board-whacker. Each time that he held superior cards he whanged them, one by one, with exceeding force, down upon the improvised table, and took the tricks with a glowing air of prowess and pride that sent thrills of indignation into the hearts of his opponents. A game with a board-whacker in it is sure to become intense. The countenances of the Easterner and the Swede were miserable whenever the cowboy thundered down his aces and kings, while Johnnie, his eyes gleaming with joy, chuckled and chuckled.

Because of the absorbing play none considered the strange ways of the Swede. They paid strict heed to the game. Finally, during a lull caused by a new deal, the Swede suddenly addressed Johnnie: "I suppose there have been a good many men killed in this room." The jaws of the others dropped and they looked at him.

"What in hell are you talking about?" said Johnnie.

The Swede laughed again his blatant laugh, full of a kind of false courage and defiance. "Oh, you know what I mean all right," he answered.

"I'm a liar if I do!" Johnnie protested. The card was halted, and the men stared at the Swede. Johnnie evidently felt that as the son of the proprietor he should make a direct inquiry. "Now, what might you be drivin' at, mister?" he asked. The Swede winked at him. It was a wink full of cunning. His fingers shook on the edge of the board. "Oh, maybe you think I have been to nowheres. Maybe you think I'm a tenderfoot?"

"I don't know nothin' about you," answered Johnnie, "and I don't give a damn where you've been. All I got to say is that I don't know what you're driving at. There hain't never been nobody killed in this room."

The cowboy, who had been steadily gazing at the Swede, then spoke: "What's wrong with you, mister?"

Apparently it seemed to the Swede that he was formidably menaced. He shivered and turned white near the corners of his mouth. He sent an appealing glance in the direction of the little Easterner. During these moments he did not forget to wear his air of advanced pot-valour.[1] "They say they don't know what I mean," he remarked mockingly to the Easterner.

The latter answered after prolonged and cautious reflection. "I don't understand you," he said, impassively.

The Swede made a movement then which announced that he thought he had encountered treachery from the only quarter where he had expected sympathy, if not help. "Oh, I see you are all against me. I see — "

The cowboy was in a state of deep stupefaction. "Say," he cried, as he tumbled the deck violently down upon the board, "say, what are you gittin' at, hey?"

The Swede sprang up with the celerity of a man escaping from a snake on the floor. "I don't want to fight!" he shouted. "I don't want to fight!"

The cowboy stretched his long legs indolently and deliberately. His hands were in his pockets. He spat into the sawdust-box. "Well, who the hell thought you did?" he inquired.

The Swede backed rapidly toward a corner of the room. His hands were out protectingly in front of his chest, but he was mak-

ing an obvious struggle to control his fright. "Gentlemen," he quavered, "I suppose I am going to be killed before I can leave this house! I suppose I am going to be killed before I can leave this house!" In his eyes was the dying-swan look.[2] Through the windows could be seen the snow turning blue in the shadow of dusk. The wind tore at the house, and some loose thing beat regularly against the clapboards like a spirit tapping.

A door opened, and Scully himself entered. He paused in surprise as he noted the tragic attitude of the Swede. Then he said, "What's the matter here?"

The Swede answered him swiftly and eagerly: "These men are going to kill me."

"Kill you!" ejaculated Scully. "Kill you! What are you talkin'?"

The Swede made the gesture of a martyr.

Scully wheeled sternly upon his son. "What is this, Johnnie?"

The lad had grown sullen. "Damned if I know," he answered. "I can't make no sense to it." He began to shuffle the cards, fluttering them together with an angry snap. "He says a good many men have been killed in this room, or something like that. And he says he's goin' to be killed here too. I don't know what ails him. He's crazy, I shouldn't wonder."

Scully then looked for explana-

---

[1] pot-valour: courage bolstered by drink.

[2] dying-swan look: Traditionally the swan is said to know in advance of its impending death.

tion to the cowboy, but the cowboy simply shrugged his shoulders.

"Kill you?" said Scully again to the Swede. "Kill you? Man, you're off your nut."

"Oh, I know," burst out the Swede. "I know what will happen. Yes, I'm crazy — yes. Yes, of course, I'm crazy — yes. But I know one thing — " There was a sort of sweat of misery and terror upon his face. "I know I won't get out of here alive."

The cowboy drew a deep breath, as if his mind was passing into the last stages of dissolution. "Well, I'm doggoned," he whispered to himself.

Scully wheeled suddenly and faced his son. "You've been troublin' this man!"

Johnnie's voice was loud with its burden of grievance. "Why, good Gawd, I ain't done nothin' to 'im."

The Swede broke in. "Gentlemen, do not disturb yourselves, I will leave this house. I will go away, because" — he accused them dramatically with his glance — "because I do not want to be killed."

Scully was furious with his son. "Will you tell me what is the matter, you young divil? What's the matter, anyhow? Speak out!"

"Blame it!" cried Johnnie in despair, "don't I tell you I don't know? He — he says we want to kill him, and that's all I know. I can't tell what ails him."

The Swede continued to repeat: "Never mind, Mr. Scully; never mind. I will leave this house. I will

go away, because I do not wish to be killed. Yes, of course, I am crazy — yes. But I know one thing! I will go away. I will leave this house. Never mind, Mr. Scully; never mind. I will go away."

"You will not go 'way," said Scully. "You will not go 'way until I hear the reason of this business. If anybody has troubled you I will take care of him. This is my house. You are under my roof, and I will not allow any peaceable man to be troubled here." He cast a terrible eye upon Johnnie, the cowboy, and the Easterner.

"Never mind, Mr. Scully; never mind. I will go away. I do not wish to be killed." The Swede moved toward the door which opened upon the stairs. It was evidently his intention to go at once for his baggage.

"No, no," shouted Scully peremptorily; but the white-faced man slid by him and disappeared. "Now," said Scully severely, "what does this mane?"

Johnnie and the cowboy cried together: "Why, we didn't do nothin' to 'im!"

Scully's eyes were cold. "No," he said, "you didn't?"

Johnnie swore a deep oath. "Why, this is the wildest loon I ever see. We didn't do nothin' at all. We were jest sittin' here playin' cards, and he — "

The father suddenly spoke to the Easterner. "Mr. Blanc," he asked, "what has these boys been doin'?"

The Easterner reflected again. "I

didn't see anything wrong at all," he said at last, slowly.

Scully began to howl. "But what does it mane?" He stared ferociously at his son. "I have a mind to lather you for this, me boy."

Johnnie was frantic. "Well, what have I done?" he bawled at his father.

III

"I think you are tongue-tied," said Scully finally to his son, the cowboy, and the Easterner; and at the end of this scornful sentence he left the room.

Upstairs the Swede was swiftly fastening the straps of his great valise. Once his back happened to be half turned toward the door, and, hearing a noise there, he wheeled and sprang up, uttering a loud cry. Scully's wrinkled visage showed grimly in the light of the small lamp he carried. This yellow effulgence, streaming upward, coloured only his prominent features, and left his eyes, for instance, in mysterious shadow. He resembled a murderer.

"Man! man!" he exclaimed, "have you gone daffy?"

"Oh, no! Oh, no!" rejoined the other. "There are people in this world who know pretty nearly as much as you do — understand?"

For a moment they stood gazing at each other. Upon the Swede's deathly pale cheeks were two spots brightly crimson and sharply edged, as if they had been carefully painted. Scully placed the light on the table and sat himself on the edge of the bed. He spoke ruminatively. "By cracky, I never heard of such a thing in my life. It's a complete muddle. I can't, for the soul of me, think how you ever got this idea into your head." Presently he lifted his eyes and asked: "And did you sure think they were going to kill you?"

The Swede scanned the old man as if he wished to see into his mind. "I did," he said at last. He obviously suspected that this answer might precipitate an outbreak. As he pulled on a strap his whole arm shook, the elbow wavering like a bit of paper.

Scully banged his hand impressively on the footboard of the bed. "Why, man, we're goin' to have a line of ilictric street-cars in this town next spring."

"'A line of electric street-cars,'" repeated the Swede, stupidly.

"And," said Scully, "there's a new railroad goin' to be built down from Broken Arm to here. Not to mintion the four churches and the smashin' big brick school-house. Then there's the big factory, too. Why, in two years Romper'll be a met-tro-*pol*-is."

Having finished the preparation of his baggage, the Swede straightened himself. "Mr. Scully," he said, with sudden hardihood, "how much do I owe you?"

"You don't owe me anythin'," said the old man, angrily.

"Yes, I do," retorted the Swede. He took seventy-five cents from his pocket and tendered it to Scully; but the latter snapped his fingers in disdainful refusal. However, it happened that they both stood gazing in a strange fashion at three silver pieces on the Swede's open palm.

"I'll not take your money," said Scully at last. "Not after what's been goin' on here." Then a plan seemed to strike him. "Here," he cried, picking up his lamp and moving toward the door. "Here! Come with me a minute."

"No," said the Swede, in overwhelming alarm.

"Yes," urged the old man. "Come on! I want you to come and see a picter — just across the hall — in my room."

The Swede must have concluded that his hour was come. His jaw dropped and his teeth showed like a dead man's. He ultimately followed Scully across the corridor, but he had the step of one hung in chains.

Scully flashed the light high on the wall of his own chamber. There was revealed a ridiculous photograph of a little girl. She was leaning against a balustrade of gorgeous decoration, and the formidable bang to her hair was prominent. The figure was as graceful as an upright sled-stake, and, withal, it was of the hue of lead. "There," said Scully, tenderly, "that's the picter of my little girl that died. Her name was Carrie. She had the purtiest hair you ever saw! I was that fond of her, she — "

Turning then, he saw that the Swede was not contemplating the picture at all, but, instead, was keeping keen watch on the gloom in the rear.

"Look, man!" cried Scully, heartily. "That's the picter of my little gal that died. Her name was Carrie. And then here's the picter of my oldest boy, Michael. He's a lawyer in Lincoln, an' doin' well. I gave that boy a grand eddication, and I'm glad for it now. He's a fine boy. Look at 'im now. Ain't he bold as blazes, him there in Lincoln, an honoured an' respicted gintleman! An honoured and respicted gintleman," concluded Scully with a flourish. And, so saying, he smote the Swede jovially on the back.

The Swede faintly smiled.

"Now," said the old man, "there's only one more thing." He dropped suddenly to the floor and thrust his head beneath the bed. The Swede could hear his muffled voice. "I'd keep it under me piller if it wasn't for that boy Johnnie. Then there's the old woman — Where is it now? I never put it twice in the same place. Ah, now come out with you!"

Presently he backed clumsily from under the bed, dragging with him an old coat rolled into a bundle. "I've fetched him," he muttered. Kneeling on the floor, he unrolled the coat and extracted from its heart a large yellow-brown whisky-bottle.

His first manœuvre was to hold

the bottle up to the light. Reassured, apparently, that nobody had been tampering with it, he thrust it with a generous movement toward the Swede.

The weak-kneed Swede was about to eagerly clutch this element of strength, but he suddenly jerked his hand away and cast a look of horror upon Scully.

"Drink," said the old man affectionately. He had risen to his feet, and now stood facing the Swede.

There was a silence. Then again Scully said: "Drink!"

The Swede laughed wildly. He grabbed the bottle, put it to his mouth; and as his lips curled absurdly around the opening and his throat worked, he kept his glance, burning with hatred, upon the old man's face.

IV

After the departure of Scully the three men, with the cardboard still upon their knees, preserved for a long time an astounded silence. Then Johnnie said: "That's the doddangedest Swede I ever see."

"He ain't no Swede," said the cowboy, scornfully.

"Well, what is he then?" cried Johnnie. "What is he then?"

"It's my opinion," replied the cowboy deliberately, "he's some kind of a Dutchman." It was a venerable custom of the country to entitle as Swedes all light-haired men who spoke with a heavy tongue. In consequence the idea of the cowboy was not without its

daring. "Yes, sir," he repeated. "It's my opinion this feller is some kind of a Dutchman."

"Well, he says he's a Swede, anyhow," muttered Johnnie, sulkily. He turned to the Easterner: "What do you think, Mr. Blanc?"

"Oh, I don't know," replied the Easterner.

"Well, what do you think makes him act that way?" asked the cowboy.

"Why, he's frightened." The Easterner knocked his pipe against a rim of the stove. "He's clear frightened out of his boots."

"What at?" cried Johnnie and the cowboy together.

The Easterner reflected over his answer.

"What at?" cried the others again.

"Oh, I don't know, but it seems to me this man has been reading dime novels, and he thinks he's right out in the middle of it — the shootin' and stabbin' and all."

"But," said the cowboy, deeply scandalized, "this ain't Wyoming, ner none of them places. This is Nebrasker."

"Yes," added Johnnie, "an' why don't he wait till he gits *out West?*"

The travelled Easterner laughed. "It isn't different there even — not in these days. But he thinks he's right in the middle of hell."

Johnnie and the cowboy mused long.

"It's awful funny," remarked Johnnie at last.

"Yes," said the cowboy. "This is a queer game. I hope we don't git snowed in, because then we'd have to stand this here man bein' around with us all the time. That wouldn't be no good."

"I wish pop would throw him out," said Johnnie.

Presently they heard a loud stamping on the stairs, accompanied by ringing jokes in the voice of old Scully, and laughter, evidently from the Swede. The men around the stove stared vacantly at each other. "Gosh!" said the cowboy. The door flew open, and old Scully, flushed and anecdotal, came into the room. He was jabbering at the Swede, who followed him, laughing bravely. It was the entry of two roisterers from a banquet hall.

"Come now," said Scully sharply to the three seated men, "move up and give us a chance at the stove." The cowboy and the Easterner obediently sidled their chairs to make room for the new-comers. Johnnie, however, simply arranged himself in a more indolent attitude, and then remained motionless.

"Come! Git over, there," said Scully.

"Plenty of room on the other side of the stove," said Johnnie.

"Do you think we want to sit in the draught?" roared the father.

But the Swede here interposed with a grandeur of confidence. "No, no. Let the boy sit where he likes," he cried in a bullying voice to the father.

"All right! All right!" said Scully, deferentially. The cowboy and the Easterner exchanged glances of wonder.

The five chairs were formed in a crescent about one side of the stove. The Swede began to talk; he talked arrogantly, profanely, angrily. Johnnie, the cowboy, and the Easterner maintained a morose silence, while old Scully appeared to be receptive and eager, breaking in constantly with sympathetic ejaculations.

Finally the Swede announced that he was thirsty. He moved in his chair, and said that he would go for a drink of water.

"I'll git it for you," cried Scully at once.

"No," said the Swede, contemptuously. "I'll get it for myself." He arose and stalked with the air of an owner off into the executive parts of the hotel.

As soon as the Swede was out of hearing Scully sprang to his feet and whispered intensely to the others: "Upstairs he thought I was tryin' to poison 'im."

"Say," said Johnnie, "this makes me sick. Why don't you throw 'im out in the snow?"

"Why, he's all right now," declared Scully. "It was only that he was from the East, and he thought this was a tough place. That's all. He's all right now."

The cowboy looked with admiration upon the Easterner. "You were straight," he said. "You were on to that there Dutchman."

"Well," said Johnnie to his father, "he may be all right now, but I don't see it. Other time he was scared, but now he's too fresh."

Scully's speech was always a combination of Irish brogue and idiom, Western twang and idiom, and scraps of curiously formal diction taken from the story-books and newspapers. He now hurled a strange mass of language at the head of his son. "What do I keep? What do I keep? What do I keep?" he demanded, in a voice of thunder. He slapped his knee impressively, to indicate that he himself was going to make reply, and that all should heed. "I keep a hotel," he shouted. "A hotel, do you mind? A guest under my roof has sacred privileges. He is to be intimidated by none. Not one word shall he hear that would prijudice him in favour of goin' away. I'll not have it. There's no place in this here town where they can say they iver took in a guest of mine because he was afraid to stay here." He wheeled suddenly upon the cowboy and the Easterner. "Am I right?"

"Yes, Mr. Scully," said the cowboy, "I think you're right."

"Yes, Mr. Scully," said the Easterner, "I think you're right."

V

At six-o'clock supper, the Swede fizzed like a fire-wheel. He sometimes seemed on the point of bursting into riotous song, and in all his madness he was encouraged by old Scully. The Easterner was encased in reserve; the cowboy sat in wide-mouthed amazement, forgetting to eat, while Johnnie wrathily demolished great plates of food. The daughters of the house, when they were obliged to replenish the biscuits, approached as warily as Indians, and, having succeeded in their purpose, fled with ill-concealed trepidation. The Swede domineered the whole feast, and he gave it the appearance of a cruel bacchanal. He seemed to have grown suddenly taller; he gazed, brutally disdainful, into every face. His voice rang through the room. Once when he jabbed out harpoon-fashion with his fork to pinion a biscuit, the weapon nearly impaled the hand of the Easterner, which had been stretched quietly out for the same biscuit.

After supper, as the men filed toward the other room, the Swede smote Scully ruthlessly on the shoulder. "Well, old boy, that was a good, square meal." Johnnie looked hopefully at his father; he knew that shoulder was tender from an old fall; and, indeed, it appeared for a moment as if Scully was going to flame out over the matter, but in the end he smiled a sickly smile and remained silent. The others understood from his manner that he was admitting his responsibility for the Swede's new view-point.

Johnnie, however, addressed his parent in an aside. "Why don't you license somebody to kick you downstairs?" Scully scowled darkly by way of reply.

When they were gathered about the stove, the Swede insisted on another game of High-Five. Scully gently deprecated the plan at first, but the Swede turned a wolfish glare upon him. The old man subsided, and the Swede canvassed the others. In his tone there was always a great threat. The cowboy and the Easterner both remarked indifferently that they would play. Scully said that he would presently have to go to meet the 6:58 train, and so the Swede turned menacingly upon Johnnie. For a moment their glances crossed like blades, and then Johnnie smiled and said, "Yes, I'll play."

They formed a square, with the little board on their knees. The Easterner and the Swede were again partners. As the play went on, it was noticeable that the cowboy was not board-whacking as usual. Meanwhile, Scully, near the lamp, had put on his spectacles and, with an appearance curiously like an old priest, was reading a newspaper. In time he went out to meet the 6:58 train, and, despite his precautions, a gust of polar wind whirled into the room as he opened the door. Besides scattering the cards, it chilled the players to the marrow. The Swede cursed frightfully. When Scully returned, his entrance disturbed a cosy and friendly scene. The Swede again cursed. But presently they were once more intent, their heads bent forward and their hands moving swiftly. The Swede had adopted the fashion of board-whacking.

Scully took up his paper and for a long time remained immersed in matters which were extraordinarily remote from him. The lamp burned badly, and once he stopped to adjust the wick. The newspaper, as he turned from page to page, rustled with a slow and comfortable sound. Then suddenly he heard three terrible words: "You are cheatin'!"

Such scenes often prove that there can be little of dramatic import in environment. Any room can present a tragic front; any room can be comic. This little den was now hideous as a torture-chamber. The new faces of the men themselves had changed it upon the instant. The Swede held a huge fist in front of Johnnie's face, while the latter looked steadily over it into the blazing orbs of his accuser. The Easterner had grown pallid; the cowboy's jaw had dropped in that expression of bovine amazement which was one of his important mannerisms. After the three words, the first sound in the room was made by Scully's paper as it floated forgotten to his feet. His spectacles had also fallen from his nose, but by a clutch he had saved them in air. His hand, grasping the spectacles, now remained poised awkwardly and near his shoulder. He stared at the card-players.

Probably the silence was while a second elapsed. Then, if the floor had been suddenly twitched out from under the men they could not have moved quicker. The five had projected themselves headlong toward a common point. It happened that Johnnie, in rising to hurl himself upon the Swede, had stumbled slightly because of his curiously instinctive care for the cards and the board. The loss of the moment allowed time for the arrival of Scully, and also allowed the cowboy time to give the Swede a great push which sent him staggering back. The men found tongue together, and hoarse shouts of rage, appeal, or fear burst from every throat. The cowboy pushed and jostled feverishly at the Swede, and the Easterner and Scully clung wildly to Johnnie; but through the smoky air, above the swaying bodies of the peace-compellers, the eyes of the two warriors ever sought each other in glances of challenge that were at once hot and steely.

Of course the board had been overturned, and now the whole company of cards was scattered over the floor, where the boots of the men trampled the fat and painted kings and queens as they gazed with their silly eyes at the war that was waging above them.

Scully's voice was dominating the yells. "Stop now! Stop, I say! Stop, now — "

Johnnie, as he struggled to burst through the rank formed by Scully and the Easterner, was crying, "Well, he says I cheated! He says I cheated! I won't allow no man to say I cheated! If he says I cheated, he's a —— ——!"

The cowboy was telling the Swede, "Quit, now! Quit, d'ye hear — "

The screams of the Swede never ceased: "He did cheat! I saw him! I saw him — "

As for the Easterner, he was importuning in a voice that was not heeded: "Wait a moment, can't you? Oh, wait a moment. What's the good of a fight over a game of cards? Wait a moment — "

In this tumult no complete sentences were clear. "Cheat" — "Quit" — "He says" — these fragments pierced the uproar and rang out sharply. It was remarkable that, whereas Scully undoubtedly made the most noise, he was the least heard of any of the riotous band.

Then suddenly there was a great cessation. It was as if each man had paused for breath; and although the room was still lighted with the anger of men, it could be seen that there was no danger of immediate conflict, and at once Johnnie, shouldering his way forward, almost succeeded in confronting the Swede. "What did you say I cheated for? What did you say I cheated for? I don't cheat, and I won't let no man say I do!"

The Swede said, "I saw you! I saw you!"

"Well," cried Johnnie, "I'll fight

any man what says I cheat!"

"No, you won't," said the cowboy. "Not here."

"Ah, be still, can't you?" said Scully, coming between them.

The quiet was sufficient to allow the Easterner's voice to be heard. He was repeating, "Oh, wait a moment, can't you? What's the good of a fight over a game of cards? Wait a moment!"

Johnnie, his red face appearing above his father's shoulder, hailed the Swede again. "Did you say I cheated?"

The Swede showed his teeth. "Yes."

"Then," said Johnnie, "we must fight."

"Yes, fight," roared the Swede. He was like a demoniac. "Yes, fight! I'll show you what kind of a man I am! I'll show you who you want to fight! Maybe you think I can't fight! Maybe you think I can't! I'll show you, you skin, you card-sharp! Yes, you cheated! You cheated! You cheated!"

"Well, let's go at it, then, mister," said Johnnie, coolly.

The cowboy's brow was beaded with sweat from his efforts in intercepting all sorts of raids. He turned in despair to Scully. "What are you goin' to do now?"

A change had come over the Celtic visage of the old man. He now seemed all eagerness; his eyes glowed.

"We'll let them fight," he answered, stalwartly. "I can't put up

with it any longer. I've stood this damned Swede till I'm sick. We'll let them fight."

VI

The men prepared to go out of doors. The Easterner was so nervous that he had great difficulty in getting his arms into the sleeves of his new leather coat. As the cowboy drew his fur cap down over his ears his hands trembled. In fact, Johnnie and old Scully were the only ones who displayed no agitation. These preliminaries were conducted without words.

Scully threw open the door. "Well, come on," he said. Instantly a terrific wind caused the flame of the lamp to struggle at its wick, while a puff of black smoke sprang from the chimney-top. The stove was in mid-current of the blast, and its voice swelled to equal the roar of the storm. Some of the scarred and bedabbled cards were caught up from the floor and dashed helplessly against the farther wall. The men lowered their heads and plunged into the tempest as into a sea.

No snow was falling, but great whirls and clouds of flakes, swept up from the ground by the frantic winds, were streaming southward with the speed of bullets. The covered land was blue with the sheen of an unearthly satin, and there was no other hue save where, at the low, black railway station — which seemed incredibly distant — one light gleamed like a tiny jewel. As the men floundered into a thigh-deep drift, it was known that the Swede was bawling out something. Scully went to him, put a hand on his shoulder, and projected an ear. "What's that you say?" he shouted.

"I say," bawled the Swede again, "I won't stand much show against this gang. I know you'll all pitch on me."

Scully smote him reproachfully on the arm. "Tut, man!" he yelled. The wind tore the words from Scully's lips and scattered them far alee.[1]

"You are all a gang of — " boomed the Swede, but the storm also seized the remainder of this sentence.

Immediately turning their backs upon the wind, the men had swung around a corner to the sheltered side of the hotel. It was the function of the little house to preserve here, amid this great devastation of snow, an irregular V-shape of heavily encrusted grass, which crackled beneath the feet. One could imagine the great drifts piled against the windward side. When the party reached the comparative peace of this spot it was found that the Swede was still bellowing.

"Oh, I know what kind of a thing this is! I know you'll all pitch on me. I can't lick you all!"

Scully turned upon him panther-fashion. "You'll not have to whip all of us. You'll have to whip my son Johnnie. An' the man what troubles

[1] alee: downwind.

you durin' that time will have me to dale with."

The arrangements were swiftly made. The two men faced each other, obedient to the harsh commands of Scully, whose face, in the subtly luminous gloom, could be seen set in the austere impersonal lines that are pictured on the countenances of the Roman veterans. The Easterner's teeth were chattering, and he was hopping up and down like a mechanical toy. The cowboy stood rock-like.

The contestants had not stripped off any clothing. Each was in his ordinary attire. Their fists were up, and they eyed each other in a calm that had the elements of leonine cruelty in it.

During this pause, the Easterner's mind, like a film, took lasting impressions of three men — the iron-nerved master of the ceremony; the Swede, pale, motionless, terrible; and Johnnie, serene yet ferocious, brutish yet heroic. The entire prelude had in it a tragedy greater than the tragedy of action, and this aspect was accentuated by the long, mellow cry of the blizzard, as it sped the tumbling and wailing flakes into the black abyss of the south.

"Now!" said Scully.

The two combatants leaped forward and crashed together like bullocks. There was heard the cushioned sound of blows, and of a curse squeezing out from between the tight teeth of one.

As for the spectators, the Easterner's pent-up breath exploded from him with a pop of relief, absolute relief from the tension of the preliminaries. The cowboy bounded into the air with a yowl. Scully was immovable as from supreme amazement and fear at the fury of the fight which he himself had permitted and arranged.

For a time the encounter in the darkness was such a perplexity of flying arms that it presented no more detail than would a swiftly revolving wheel. Occasionally a face, as if illumined by a flash of light, would shine out, ghastly and marked with pink spots. A moment later, the men might have been known as shadows, if it were not for the involuntary utterance of oaths that came from them in whispers.

Suddenly a holocaust of warlike desire caught the cowboy, and he bolted forward with the speed of a broncho. "Go it, Johnnie! go it! Kill him! Kill him!"

Scully confronted him. "Kape back," he said; and by his glance the cowboy could tell that this man was Johnnie's father.

To the Easterner there was a monotony of unchangeable fighting that was an abomination. This confused mingling was eternal to his sense, which was concentrated in a longing for the end, the priceless end. Once the fighters lurched near him, and as he scrambled hastily backward he heard them breathe like men on the rack.

"Kill him, Johnnie! Kill him! Kill him! Kill him!" The cowboy's face was contorted like one of those agony masks in museums.

"Keep still," said Scully, icily.

Then there was a sudden loud grunt, incomplete, cut short, and Johnnie's body swung away from the Swede and fell with sickening heaviness to the grass. The cowboy was barely in time to prevent the mad Swede from flinging himself upon his prone adversary. "No, you don't," said the cowboy, interposing an arm. "Wait a second."

Scully was at his son's side. "Johnnie! Johnnie, me boy!" His voice had a quality of melancholy tenderness. "Johnnie! Can you go on with it?" He looked anxiously down into the bloody, pulpy face of his son.

There was a moment of silence, and then Johnnie answered in his ordinary voice, "Yes, I — it — yes."

Assisted by his father he struggled to his feet. "Wait a bit now till you git your wind," said the old man.

A few paces away the cowboy was lecturing the Swede. "No, you don't! Wait a second!"

The Easterner was plucking at Scully's sleeve. "Oh, this is enough," he pleaded. "This is enough! Let it go as it stands. This is enough!"

"Bill," said Scully, "git out of the road." The cowboy stepped aside. "Now." The combatants were actuated by a new caution as they advanced toward collision. They glared at each other, and then the Swede aimed a lightning blow that carried with it his entire weight. Johnnie was evidently half stupid from weakness, but he miraculously dodged, and his fist sent the overbalanced Swede sprawling.

The cowboy, Scully, and the Easterner burst into a cheer that was like a chorus of triumphant soldiery, but before its conclusion the Swede had scuffled agilely to his feet and come in berserk abandon at his foe. There was another perplexity of flying arms, and Johnnie's body again swung away and fell, even as a bundle might fall from a roof. The Swede instantly staggered to a little wind-waved tree and leaned upon it, breathing like an engine, while his savage and flame-lit eyes roamed from face to face as the men bent over Johnnie. There was a splendour of isolation in his situation at this time which the Easterner felt once when, lifting his eyes from the man on the ground, he beheld that mysterious and lonely figure, waiting.

"Are you any good yet, Johnnie?" asked Scully in a broken voice.

The son gasped and opened his eyes languidly. After a moment he answered, "No — I ain't — any good — any — more." Then, from shame and bodily ill, he began to weep, the tears furrowing down through the blood-stains on his face. "He was too — too — too heavy for me."

Scully straightened and addressed the waiting figure. "Stranger," he said, evenly, "it's all up with our side." Then his voice changed into that vibrant huskiness which is commonly the tone of the most simple and deadly announcements. "Johnnie is whipped."

Without replying, the victor moved off on the route to the front door of the hotel.

The cowboy was formulating new and unspellable blasphemies. The Easterner was startled to find that they were out in a wind that seemed to come direct from the shadowed arctic floes. He heard again the wail of the snow as it was flung to its grave in the south. He knew now that all this time the cold had been sinking into him deeper and deeper, and he wondered that he had not perished. He felt indifferent to the condition of the vanquished man.

"Johnnie, can you walk?" asked Scully.

"Did I hurt — hurt him any?" asked the son.

"Can you walk, boy? Can you walk?"

Johnnie's voice was suddenly strong. There was a robust impatience in it. "I asked you whether I hurt him any!"

"Yes, yes, Johnnie," answered the cowboy, consolingly; "he's hurt a good deal."

They raised him from the ground, and as soon as he was on his feet he went tottering off, rebuffing all attempts at assistance. When the party rounded the corner they were fairly blinded by the pelting of the snow. It burned their faces like fire. The cowboy carried Johnnie through the drift to the door. As they entered, some cards again rose from the floor and beat against the wall.

The Easterner rushed to the stove. He was so profoundly chilled that he almost dared to embrace the glowing iron. The Swede was not in the room. Johnnie sank into a chair and, folding his arms on his knees, buried his face in them. Scully, warming one foot and then the other at a rim of the stove, muttered to himself with Celtic mournfulness. The cowboy had removed his fur cap, and with a dazed and rueful air he was running one hand through his tousled locks. From overhead they could hear the creaking of boards, as the Swede tramped here and there in his room.

The sad quiet was broken by the sudden flinging open of a door that led toward the kitchen. It was instantly followed by an inrush of women. They precipitated themselves upon Johnnie amid a chorus of lamentation. Before they carried their prey off to the kitchen, there to be bathed and harangued with that mixture of sympathy and abuse which is a feat of their sex, the mother straightened herself and fixed old Scully with an eye of stern reproach. "Shame be upon you, Patrick Scully!" she cried. "Your own son, too. Shame be upon you!"

"There, now! Be quiet, now!" said the old man, weakly.

"Shame be upon you, Patrick Scully!" The girls, rallying to this slogan, sniffed disdainfully in the direction of those trembling accomplices, the cowboy and the Easterner. Presently they bore Johnnie away, and left the three men to dismal reflection.

VII

"I'd like to fight this here Dutchman myself," said the cowboy, breaking a long silence.

Scully wagged his head sadly. "No, that wouldn't do. It wouldn't be right. It wouldn't be right."

"Well, why wouldn't it?" argued the cowboy. "I don't see no harm in it."

"No," answered Scully, with mournful heroism. "It wouldn't be right. It was Johnnie's fight, and now we mustn't whip the man just because he whipped Johnnie."

"Yes, that's true enough," said the cowboy; "but — he better not get fresh with me, because I couldn't stand no more of it."

"You'll not say a word to him," commanded Scully, and even then they heard the tread of the Swede on the stairs. His entrance was made theatric. He swept the door back with a bang and swaggered to the middle of the room. No one looked at him. "Well," he cried, insolently, at Scully, "I s'pose you'll tell me now how much I owe you?"

The old man remained stolid. "You don't owe me nothin'."

"Huh!" said the Swede, "huh! Don't owe 'im nothin'."

The cowboy addressed the Swede.

"Stranger, I don't see how you come to be so gay around here."

Old Scully was instantly alert. "Stop!" he shouted, holding his hand forth, fingers upward. "Bill, you shut up!"

The cowboy spat carelessly into the sawdust-box. "I didn't say a word, did I?" he asked.

"Mr. Scully," called the Swede, "how much do I owe you?" It was seen that he was attired for departure, and that he had his valise in his hand.

"You don't owe me nothin'," repeated Scully in the same imperturbable way.

"Huh!" said the Swede. "I guess you're right. I guess if it was any way at all, you'd owe me somethin'. That's what I guess." He turned to the cowboy. "'Kill him! Kill him! Kill him!'" he mimicked, and then guffawed victoriously. "'Kill him!'" He was convulsed with ironical humour.

But he might have been jeering the dead. The three men were immovable and silent, staring with glassy eyes at the stove.

The Swede opened the door and passed into the storm, giving one derisive glance backward at the still group.

As soon as the door was closed, Scully and the cowboy leaped to their feet and began to curse. They trampled to and fro, waving their arms and smashing into the air with their fists. "Oh, but that was a hard minute!" wailed Scully. "That was a hard minute! Him there leerin'

and scoffin'! One bang at his nose was worth forty dollars to me that minute! How did you stand it, Bill?"

"How did I stand it?" cried the cowboy in a quivering voice. "How did I stand it? Oh!"

The old man burst into sudden brogue. "I'd loike to take that Swade," he wailed, "and hould 'im down on a shtone flure and bate 'im to a jelly wid a shtick!"

The cowboy groaned in sympathy. "I'd like to git him by the neck and ha-ammer him" — he brought his hand down on a chair with a noise like a pistol-shot — "hammer that there Dutchman until he couldn't tell himself from a dead coyote!"

"I'd bate 'im until he — "

"I'd show *him* some things — "

And then together they raised a yearning, fanatic cry — "Oh-o-oh! if we only could — "

"Yes!"

"Yes!"

"And then I'd — "

"O-o-oh!"

VIII

The Swede, tightly gripping his valise, tacked across the face of the storm as if he carried sails. He was following a line of little naked, grasping trees which, he knew, must mark the way of the road. His face, fresh from the pounding of Johnnie's fists, felt more pleasure than pain in the wind and the driving snow. A number of square shapes loomed upon him finally, and he knew them as the houses of the main body of the town. He found a street and made travel along it, leaning heavily upon the wind whenever, at a corner, a terrific blast caught him.

He might have been in a deserted village. We picture the world as thick with conquering and elate humanity, but here, with the bugles of the tempest pealing, it was hard to imagine a peopled earth. One viewed the existence of man then as a marvel, and conceded a glamour of wonder to these lice which were caused to cling to a whirling, fire-smitten, ice-locked, disease-stricken, space-lost bulb. The conceit of man was explained by this storm to be the very engine of life. One was a coxcomb [1] not to die in it. However, the Swede found a saloon.

In front of it an indomitable red light was burning, and the snowflakes were made blood-colour as they flew through the circumscribed territory of the lamp's shining. The Swede pushed open the door of the saloon and entered. A sanded expanse was before him, and at the end of it four men sat about a table drinking. Down one side of the room extended a radiant bar, and its guardian was leaning upon his elbows listening to the talk of the men at the table. The Swede dropped his valise upon the floor and, smiling fraternally upon the barkeeper, said, "Gimme some

[1] coxcomb: conceited fellow.

whisky, will you?" The man placed a bottle, a whisky-glass, and a glass of ice-thick water upon the bar. The Swede poured himself an abnormal portion of whisky and drank it in three gulps. "Pretty bad night," remarked the bartender, indifferently. He was making the pretension of blindness which is usually a distinction of his class; but it could have been seen that he was furtively studying the half-erased blood-stains on the face of the Swede. "Bad night," he said again.

"Oh, it's good enough for me," replied the Swede, hardily, as he poured himself some more whisky. The barkeeper took his coin and manœuvred it through its reception by the highly nickelled cash-machine. A bell rang; a card labelled "20 cts." had appeared.

"No," continued the Swede, "this isn't too bad weather. It's good enough for me."

"So?" murmured the barkeeper, languidly.

The copious drams made the Swede's eyes swim, and he breathed a trifle heavier. "Yes, I like this weather. I like it. It suits me." It was apparently his design to impart a deep significance to these words.

"So?" murmured the bartender again. He turned to gaze dreamily at the scroll-like birds and bird-like scrolls which had been drawn with soap upon the mirrors in back of the bar.

"Well, I guess I'll take another drink," said the Swede, presently. "Have something?"

"No, thanks; I'm not drinkin'," answered the bartender. Afterward he asked, "How did you hurt your face?"

The Swede immediately began to boast loudly. "Why, in a fight. I thumped the soul out of a man down here at Scully's hotel."

The interest of the four men at the table was at last aroused.

"Who was it?" said one.

"Johnnie Scully," blustered the Swede. "Son of the man what runs it. He will be pretty near dead for some weeks, I can tell you. I made a nice thing of him, I did. He couldn't get up. They carried him in the house. Have a drink?"

Instantly the men in some subtle way encased themselves in reserve. "No, thanks," said one. The group was of curious formation. Two were prominent local business men; one was the district attorney; and one was a professional gambler of the kind known as "square." But a scrutiny of the group would not have enabled an observer to pick the gambler from the men of more reputable pursuits. He was, in fact, a man so delicate in manner, when among people of fair class, and so judicious in his choice of victims, that in the strictly masculine part of the town's life he had come to be explicitly trusted and admired. People called him a thoroughbred. The fear and contempt with which his craft was regarded were undoubtedly the reason why his quiet dignity shone conspicuous above the quiet dignity of men who might be merely hatters, billiard-markers, or grocery clerks. Beyond an occasional unwary traveller who came by rail, this gambler was supposed to prey solely upon reckless and senile farmers, who, when flush with good crops, drove into town in all the pride and confidence of an absolutely invulnerable stupidity. Hearing at times in circuitous fashion of the despoilment of such a farmer, the important men of Romper invariably laughed in contempt of the victim, and if they thought of the wolf at all, it was with a kind of pride at the knowledge that he would never dare think of attacking their wisdom and courage. Besides, it was popular that this gambler had a real wife and two real children in a neat cottage in a suburb, where he led an exemplary home life; and when any one even suggested a discrepancy in his character, the crowd immediately vociferated descriptions of this virtuous family circle. Then men who led exemplary home lives, and men who did not lead exemplary home lives, all subsided in a bunch, remarking that there was nothing more to be said.

However, when a restriction was placed upon him — as, for instance, when a strong clique of members of the new Pollywog Club refused to permit him, even as a spectator, to appear in the rooms of the organization — the candour and gentleness with which he accepted the judgment disarmed many of his foes and made his friends more desperately partisan. He invariably distinguished between himself and a respectable Romper man so quickly and frankly that his manner actually appeared to be a continual broadcast compliment.

And one must not forget to declare the fundamental fact of his entire position in Romper. It is irrefutable that in all affairs outside his business, in all matters that occur eternally and commonly between man and man, this thieving card-player was so generous, so just, so moral, that, in a contest, he could have put to flight the consciences of nine tenths of the citizens of Romper.

And so it happened that he was seated in this saloon with the two prominent local merchants and the district attorney.

The Swede continued to drink raw whisky, meanwhile babbling at the barkeeper and trying to induce him to indulge in potations. "Come on. Have a drink. Come on. What — no? Well, have a little one, then. By gawd, I've whipped a man to-night, and I want to celebrate. I whipped him good, too. Gentlemen," the Swede cried to the men at the table, "have a drink?"

"Ssh!" said the barkeeper.

The group at the table, although furtively attentive, had been pretending to be deep in talk, but now a man lifted his eyes toward the Swede and said, shortly, "Thanks. We don't want any more."

At this reply the Swede ruffled out his chest like a rooster. "Well," he exploded, "it seems I can't get anybody to drink with me in this town. Seems so, don't it? Well!"

"Ssh!" said the barkeeper.

"Say," snarled the Swede, "don't you try to shut me up. I won't have it. I'm a gentleman, and I want people to drink with me. And I want 'em to drink with me now. *Now* — do you understand?" He rapped the bar with his knuckles.

Years of experience had calloused the bartender. He merely grew sulky. "I hear you," he answered.

"Well," cried the Swede, "listen hard then. See those men over there? Well, they're going to drink with me, and don't you forget it. Now you watch."

"Hi!" yelled the barkeeper, "this won't do!"

"Why won't it?" demanded the Swede. He stalked over to the table, and by chance laid his hand upon the shoulder of the gambler. "How about this?" he asked wrathfully. "I asked you to drink with me."

The gambler simply twisted his head and spoke over his shoulder. "My friend, I don't know you."

"Oh, hell!" answered the Swede, "come and have a drink."

"Now, my boy," advised the gambler, kindly, "take your hand off my shoulder and go 'way and mind your own business." He was a little, slim man, and it seemed strange to hear him use this tone of heroic patronage to the burly Swede. The other men at the table said nothing.

"What! You won't drink with me, you little dude? I'll make you, then! I'll make you!" The Swede had grasped the gambler frenziedly at the throat, and was dragging him from his chair. The other men sprang up. The barkeeper dashed around the corner of his bar. There was a great tumult, and then was seen a long blade in the hand of the gambler. It shot forward, and a human body, this citadel of virtue, wisdom, power, was pierced as easily as if it had been a melon. The Swede fell with a cry of supreme astonishment.

The prominent merchants and the district attorney must have at once tumbled out of the place backward. The bartender found himself hanging limply to the arm of a chair and gazing into the eyes of a murderer.

"Henry," said the latter, as he wiped his knife on one of the towels that hung beneath the bar rail, "you tell 'em where to find me. I'll be home, waiting for 'em." Then he vanished. A moment afterward the barkeeper was in the street dinning [1] through the storm for help and, moreover, companionship.

The corpse of the Swede, alone in the saloon, had its eyes fixed upon a dreadful legend that dwelt atop of the cash-machine: "This registers the amount of your purchase."

IX

Months later, the cowboy was frying pork over the stove of a little

[1] **dinning:** making a continuous cry.

ranch near the Dakota line, when there was a quick thud of hoofs outside, and presently the Easterner entered with the letters and the papers.

"Well," said the Easterner at once, "the chap that killed the Swede has got three years. Wasn't much, was it?"

"He has? Three years?" The cowboy poised his pan of pork, while he ruminated upon the news. "Three years. That ain't much."

"No. It was a light sentence," replied the Easterner as he unbuckled his spurs. "Seems there was a good deal of sympathy for him in Romper."

"If the bartender had been any good," observed the cowboy, thoughtfully, "he would have gone in and cracked that there Dutchman on the head with a bottle in the beginnin' of it and stopped all this here murderin'."

"Yes, a thousand things might have happened," said the Easterner, tartly.

The cowboy returned his pan of pork to the fire, but his philosophy continued. "It's funny, ain't it? If he hadn't said Johnnie was cheatin' he'd be alive this minute. He was an awful fool. Game played for fun, too. Not for money. I believe he was crazy."

"I feel sorry for that gambler," said the Easterner.

"Oh, so do I," said the cowboy. "He don't deserve none of it for killin' who he did."

"The Swede might not have been

killed if everything had been square."

"Might not have been killed?" exclaimed the cowboy. "Everythin' square? Why, when he said that Johnnie was cheatin' and acted like such a jackass? And then in the saloon he fairly walked up to git hurt?" With these arguments the cowboy browbeat the Easterner and reduced him to rage.

"You're a fool!" cried the Easterner, viciously. "You're a bigger jackass than the Swede by a million majority. Now let me tell you one thing. Let me tell you something. Listen! Johnnie *was* cheating!"

" 'Johnnie,' " said the cowboy, blankly. There was a minute of silence, and then he said, robustly, "Why, no. The game was only for fun."

"Fun or not," said the Easterner, "Johnnie was cheating. I saw him. I know it. I saw him. And I refused to stand up and be a man. I let the Swede fight it out alone. And you — you were simply puffing around the place and wanting to fight. And then old Scully himself! We are all in it! This poor gambler isn't even a noun. He is kind of an adverb. Every sin is the result of a collaboration. We, five of us, have collaborated in the murder of this Swede. Usually there are from a dozen to forty women really involved in every murder, but in this case it seems to be only five men — you, I, Johnnie, old Scully; and that fool of an unfortunate gambler came merely as a culmination, the apex of a hu-

man movement, and gets all the punishment."

The cowboy, injured and rebellious, cried out blindly into this fog of mysterious theory: "Well, I didn't do anythin', did I?"

For Study

The large number of questions that follow is a tribute to the story's complexity. You may find the questions persistent to the point of cross-examination, yet an honest grappling with them will increase enormously your appreciation of the story and of Crane's gifts as an artist. You will have to reread the story closely in order to cope with the questions. Read them through first, however, both to see how far you can answer them from your first reading and also to benefit by having them sharpen and direct your attention to details in your rereading.

1. What is the formal name of the blue hotel?

2. Why do you think Crane did not call the hotel by its formal name in the title of the story? We might say the color of the hotel is "garish," a word which means too bright and gaudy, causing people to stare. That is what he means when he says it "was always screaming and howling." How does this color, which clashes with its surroundings, harmonize with the setting, tone, and even events of the story?

3. Read carefully the last three sentences of paragraph one, page 478,

beginning "It is true that . . ." They tell us something about differences of social background, environment, class, and taste. Who is meant by "the cult that knows the brown-reds and the subdivisions of the dark greens. . . ."? Why do they express "shame, pity, horror, in a laugh"? What is meant by the statement that the people of Romper and the "creeds, classes, egotisms" passing through on trains "had no color in common"? Do you think Crane is taking sides with one or the other or simply objectively noting a fact?

4. Why was the Swede so frightened and suspicious from the beginning? What was the source of the fearful expectations he had?

5. When, after much persuasion and evidence, the Swede is convinced that he is *not* in a dangerous place, what change comes over him? What is ironic about this? Just before the Swede meets his abrupt fate, what role is he himself playing in terms of the impression of this place that he had had at first? State your own feeling about the Swede — sympathy or lack of sympathy — and explain it.

6. When the Swede accused Johnnie of cheating, did you believe the charge at the time? There are subtle clues about this matter early in the story. Can you find them?

7. Why does the Swede laugh so much? What is the character of this laughter? Observe that it changes somewhat with the Swede's changes of mood. Consider these changes. How does his occasional winking fit the pattern?

8. What is your appraisal of the Swede's courage? This question should not be treated as a simple one. Consider not only his fearfulness but also his belligerence and his fight with Johnnie. Explain your over-all conclusion in terms of the factors that influence you.

9. Why does the Swede watch the beginning of the card game between Johnnie and the grey-beard farmer with "an inexplicable excitement"? (Crane does not mean the excitement to be inexplicable to us. What, then, does he mean?)

10. Why did Johnnie chuckle as the board-whacking cowboy "thundered down his aces and kings" in the first game the four play? How is it that the Swede becomes the board-whacker the next time?

11. As you look back from later in the story, what implications now seem buried in the dialogue with Johnnie (page 481) after the Swede has said: "I suppose there have been a good many men killed in this room"?

12. What does the Swede mean when he says to Scully, "There are people in this world who know pretty nearly as much as you do — understand?"

13. What does Scully mean when he says, "Why, man, we're goin' to have a line of ilictric street-cars in this town next spring"? Consider also the lines that follow (page 484).

14. Why does Scully show the picture of little Carrie, deceased, and the other details of his family life? What signs are there in this scene that John-

nie is Scully's particular problem, in more ways than one?

15. Why does the Swede hesitate to drink when Scully proffers the bottle? Why does he overdrink when at last he accepts? Do you think the liquor is responsible for his ensuing change of mood? What other factors may contribute to it?

16. As the men speculate about the Swede while he is with Scully, what impression do we get of the cowboy's breadth of understanding about foreigners? Explain.

17. Do you think there is any significance in the Easterner's being called Mr. Blanc? How much do we know about him? What do you make of the statement, when we first see him, that he was from the East but "didn't look it, and didn't announce it"? What is he doing when last we see him?

18. Discuss the peculiar "relativity" in the cowboy's scandalized assertion, "This is Nebrasker" and Johnnie's question, "Why don't he wait till he gits *out West?*"

19. Why do the cowboy and the Easterner exchange glances of wonder when Scully and the Swede reenter the room? Why is the cowboy then filled with admiration for the Easterner?

20. Consider Scully's big speech at the end of Part IV (page 488). What can you read into it concerning father and son? Do you think any past history is reflected here? If so, what might it be?

21. As the men are leaving the supper table, we are told about Scully that "The others understood from his manner that he was admitting his responsibility for the Swede's new viewpoint." What does this statement mean?

22. When Scully is reading the paper as the card game goes on, why does Crane say he is "immersed in matters which were extraordinarily remote from him"?

23. Discuss the immediate situation and the first scramble of events that follow the "three terrible words" (page 489). Why "terrible"? Discuss the line, "Such scenes often prove that there can be little of dramatic import in environment." Wherein is this statement ironic in relation to the Swede's original imagined fears? How do these persistent fears show themselves again as the men go outside for the fight? Since, as we are told in the aftermath of the story, no money was at stake in this game, what was the importance of the accusation? Why was there a fight, as the Easterner kept protesting, just "over a game of cards"?

24. What significance is there in Johnnie's "curiously instinctive care for the cards and the board"?

25. Why does Crane make a point of the image of "the whole company of cards . . . scattered over the floor, where the boots of the men trampled the fat and painted kings and queens as they gazed with their silly eyes at the war that was waging above them"?

26. As all prepare to go out for the fight, why do you think Johnnie and Scully are "the only ones who dis-

played no agitation"? May their lack of agitation relate to the question about previous history in number 20, above?

27. In the tableau just before the fight begins (page 489), can you justify the words about Johnnie, "brutish yet heroic"? Why does Crane say the prelude to the fight has in it "a tragedy greater than the tragedy of action"?

28. On page 493 explain: "by his glance the cowboy could tell that this man was Johnnie's father." Discuss the "melancholy tenderness" in the voice of Scully when questioning the fallen Johnnie.

29. What implication for the story as a whole may lie in that "splendour of isolation" the Easterner sees in the victorious Swede?

30. Is there any significance in the fact that the cowboy, not Scully, answers Johnnie's repeated question, "Did I hurt him any?"

31. Why do you think Crane emphasizes, as they go indoors, that "some cards again rose from the floor and beat against the wall"?

32. What factor or force in society, both present and past, is represented by the brief appearance of the women and by what they say and do?

33. What kind of victor does the Swede prove to be?

34. Discuss the outburst of Scully and the cowboy when the Swede has left. Why does Scully lapse into the Irish brogue? What is the meaning of this scene?

35. In the scene in the saloon (pages 497–500), we see the Swede, finally, as

a man unconsciously but nontheless determinedly bent upon self-destruction. He has the misfortune not to know when he really is menaced and when he is not. Analyze the scene to demonstrate this ignorance. Explain his "supreme astonishment" when he falls.

36. What is the significance of the word *merely,* so unobtrusively dropped into the sentence (page 498) comparing the professional gambler with the reputable businessmen of the town?

37. What is meant by "an absolutely invulnerable stupidity" in speaking of farmers whom the gambler fleeces?

38. Discuss what Crane says of the way the gambler is regarded by citizens of the town and the status he has in its society. What kind of image do the townspeople have of the gambler, and why does this view of him have value for them?

39. Comment on these words used as the Swede is stabbed: "a human body, this citadel of virtue, wisdom, power, was pierced as easily as if it had been a melon." What is the tone and viewpoint of this statement?

40. Two short paragraphs (page 500) explain the attitudes of the other men present at the stabbing toward that event. Discuss these specifically. Wherein does the cowboy, in the postscript to the story, feel that the barkeeper has failed to play his proper role? When the barkeeper runs out shouting for help, why does Crane add that he was also calling for "companionship"?

41. What irony may lurk in the mention of the Swede's corpse in connection with the legend atop the cash register?

42. The story is over at this point and, by classical principles, what follows violates its dramatic unity and is an anticlimax. Crane, the skilled craftsman, knew these principles perfectly well. What function and values does the postscript have that persuaded him to include it?

43. Explain the interesting grammatical metaphor: "This poor gambler isn't even a noun. He is kind of an adverb."

44. Apropos to the Easterner's final speech, who is more responsible for the Swede's death — the five men or the Swede himself? If the question cannot be answered definitively, nevertheless it can be discussed profitably. That we should discuss it is one of Crane's aims in writing the story.

45. Answer the cowboy's final question (page 501).

46. This story is chiefly about whom? Support your opinion.

For Discussion or Writing

1. Give a careful summary of the character of Scully or Johnnie; or give a joint study of father and son.

2. Interpret these lines: "We picture the world as thick with conquering and elate humanity, but here, with the bugles of the tempest pealing, it was hard to imagine a peopled earth. One viewed the existence of man then as a marvel, and conceded a glamour of wonder to these lice which were caused to cling to a whirling, fire-smitten, ice-locked, disease-stricken, space-lost bulb. The conceit of man was explained by this storm to be the very engine of life. One was a coxcomb not to die in it." What light do these lines cast on the story as a whole? Relate them to the works in Part I of this book, "The Idea of Man."

3. Sum up the character of the cowboy; of the Easterner.

4. Discuss both in general and in its specific context the statement, "Every sin is the result of a collaboration."

The Bottle Imp

by Robert Louis Stevenson (1850–1894)

This deftly humorous, laconic story is one of Robert Louis Stevenson's freshest, most unusual short tales. It is haunted by danger of the most fearful fate that a man may dread: eternal damnation. The bottle is a distant, sinister cousin of Aladdin's lamp. The lamp's magic was neutral magic in a very different moral vision; the bottle's magic is black magic. This story is not, like the many versions of the Faust legend, a case of selling one's soul to the devil; it is rather a case of gambling with him in desperate chance, with a soul at stake.

There was a man of the island of Hawaii, whom I shall call Keawe; for the truth is, he still lives, and his name must be kept secret; but the place of his birth was not far from Honaunau, where the bones of Keawe the Great lie hidden in a cave. This man was poor, brave, and active; he could read and write like a schoolmaster; he was a first-rate mariner besides, sailed for some time in the island steamers, and steered a whale-boat on the Hamakua coast. At length it came in Keawe's mind to have a sight of the great world and foreign cities, and he shipped on a vessel bound to San Francisco.

This is a fine town, with a fine harbour, and rich people uncountable; and, in particular, there is one hill which is covered with palaces. Upon this hill Keawe was one day taking a walk, with his pocket full of money, viewing the great houses upon either hand with pleasure. "What fine houses these are!" he was thinking, "and how happy must these people be who dwell in them, and take no care for the morrow!" The thought was in his mind when he came abreast of a house that was smaller than some others, but all finished and beautiful like a toy; the steps of that house shone like silver, and the borders of the garden bloomed like garlands, and the windows were bright like diamonds; and Keawe stopped and wondered at the excellence of all he saw. So stopping, he was aware of a man that looked forth upon him through a window, so clear, that Keawe could see him as you see a fish in a pool upon the reef. The man was elderly, with a bald head and a black beard; and his face was heavy with sorrow, and he bitterly sighed. And the truth of it is, that as Keawe looked in upon the man, and the man looked out upon Keawe, each envied the other.

All of a sudden the man smiled and nodded, and beckoned Keawe to enter, and met him at the door of the house.

"This is a fine house of mine," said the man, and bitterly sighed. "Would you not care to view the chambers?"

So he led Keawe all over it, from the cellar to the roof, and there was nothing there that was not perfect of its kind, and Keawe was astonished.

"Truly," said Keawe, "this is a beautiful house; if I lived in the like of it, I should be laughing all day long. How comes it, then, that you should be sighing?"

"There is no reason," said the man, "why you should not have a house in all points similar to this, and finer, if you wish. You have some money, I suppose?"

"I have fifty dollars," said Keawe; "but a house like this will cost more than fifty dollars."

The man made a computation. "I am sorry you have no more," said he, "for it may raise you trouble in the future; but it shall be yours at fifty dollars."

"The house?" asked Keawe.

"No, not the house," replied the man; "but the bottle. For, I must tell you, although I appear to you so rich and fortunate, all my fortune, and this house itself and its garden, came out of a bottle not much bigger than a pint. This is it."

And he opened a lockfast place, and took out a round-bellied bottle with a long neck; the glass of it was white like milk, with changing rainbow colours in the grain. Within-insides something obscurely moved, like a shadow and a fire.

"This is the bottle," said the man; and, when Keawe laughed, "You do not believe me?" he added. "Try, then, for yourself. See if you can break it."

So Keawe took the bottle up and dashed it on the floor till he was weary; but it jumped on the floor like a child's ball, and was not injured.

"This is a strange thing," said Keawe. "For by the touch of it, as well as by the look, the bottle should be of glass."

"Of glass it is," replied the man, sighing more heavily than ever; "but the glass of it was tempered in the flames of hell. An imp lives in it, and that is the shadow we behold there moving; or, so I suppose. If any man buy this bottle the imp is at his command; all that he desires — love, fame, money, houses like this house, ay, or a city like this city — all are his at the word uttered. Napoleon had this bottle, and by it he grew to be the king of the world; but he sold it at the last and fell. Captain Cook had this bottle, and by it he found his way to so many islands; but he, too, sold it, and was slain upon Hawaii. For, once it is sold, the power goes and the protection; and unless a man remain content with what he has, ill will befall him."

"And yet you talk of selling it yourself?" Keawe said.

"I have all I wish, and I am growing elderly," replied the man. "There is one thing the imp cannot do — he cannot prolong life;

and it would not be fair to conceal from you there is a drawback to the bottle; for if a man die before he sells it, he must burn in hell for ever."

"To be sure, that is a drawback and no mistake," cried Keawe. "I would not meddle with the thing. I can do without a house, thank God; but there is one thing I could not be doing with one particle, and that is to be damned."

"Dear me, you must not run away with things," returned the man. "All you have to do is to use the power of the imp in moderation, and then sell it to some one else, as I do to you, and finish your life in comfort."

"Well, I observe two things," said Keawe. "All the time you keep sighing like a maid in love, that is one; and, for the other, you sell this bottle very cheap."

"I have told you already why I sigh," said the man. "It is because I fear my health is breaking up; and, as you said yourself, to die and go to the devil is a pity for any one. As for why I sell so cheap, I must explain to you there is a peculiarity about the bottle. Long ago, when the devil brought it first upon earth, it was extremely expensive, and was sold first of all to Prester John [1] for many millions of dollars;

---

[1] **Prester John:** (Priest John) a powerful priest-king of medieval legend, earliest associated with the Far East, but later with Ethiopia. He is the subject of a romantic adventure novel by John Buchan, *Prester John,* 1910.

but it cannot be sold at all, unless sold at a loss. If you sell it for as much as you paid for it, back it comes to you again like a homing pigeon. It follows that the price has kept falling in these centuries, and the bottle is now remarkably cheap. I bought it myself from one of my great neighbours on this hill, and the price I paid was only ninety dollars. I could sell it for as high as eighty-nine dollars and ninety-nine cents, but not a penny dearer, or back the thing must come to me. Now, about this there are two bothers. First, when you offer a bottle so singular for eighty-odd dollars, people suppose you to be jesting. And second — but there is no hurry about that — and I need not go into it. Only remember it must be coined money that you sell it for."

"How am I to know that this is all true?" asked Keawe.

"Some of it you can try at once," replied the man. "Give me your fifty dollars, take the bottle, and wish your fifty dollars back into your pocket. If that does not happen, I pledge you my honour I will cry off the bargain and restore your money."

"You are not deceiving me?" said Keawe.

The man bound himself with a great oath.

"Well, I will risk that much," said Keawe, "for that can do no harm," and he paid over his money to the man, and the man handed him the bottle.

"Imp of the bottle," said Keawe,

"I want my fifty dollars back." And sure enough, he had scarce said the word before his pocket was as heavy as ever.

"To be sure this is a wonderful bottle," said Keawe.

"And now good-morning to you, my fine fellow, and the devil go with you for me," said the man.

"Hold on," said Keawe, "I don't want any more of this fun. Here, take your bottle back."

"You have bought it for less than I paid for it," replied the man, rubbing his hands. "It is yours now; and, for my part, I am only concerned to see the back of you." And with that he rang for his Chinese servant, and had Keawe shown out of the house.

Now, when Keawe was in the street, with the bottle under his arm, he began to think. "If all is true about this bottle, I may have made a losing bargain," thinks he. "But, perhaps the man was only fooling me." The first thing he did was to count his money; the sum was exact — forty-nine dollars American money, and one Chili piece. "That looks like the truth," said Keawe. "Now I will try another part."

The streets in that part of the city were as clean as a ship's decks, and though it was noon, there were no passengers. Keawe set the bottle in the gutter and walked away. Twice he looked back, and there was the milky, round-bellied bottle where he left it. A third time he looked back, and turned a corner; but he had scarce done so, when something knocked upon his elbow, and behold! it was the long neck sticking up; and, as for the round belly, it was jammed into the pocket of his pilot-coat.

"And that looks like the truth," said Keawe.

The next thing he did was to buy a corkscrew in a shop, and go apart into a secret place in the fields. And there he tried to draw the cork, but as often as he put the screw in, out it came again, and the cork as whole as ever.

"This is some new sort of cork," said Keawe, and all at once he began to shake and sweat, for he was afraid of that bottle.

On his way back to the port-side he saw a shop where a man sold shells and clubs from the wild islands, old heathen deities, old coined money, pictures from China and Japan, and all manner of things that sailors bring in their sea-chests. And here he had an idea. So he went in and offered the bottle for a hundred dollars. The man of the shop laughed at him at first, and offered him five; but, indeed, it was a curious bottle, such glass was never blown in any human glassworks, so prettily the colours shone under the milky white, and so strangely the shadow hovered in the midst; so after he had disputed awhile after the manner of his kind, the shopman gave Keawe sixty silver dollars for the thing and set it on a shelf in the midst of his window.

"Now," said Keawe, "I have sold

that for sixty which I bought for fifty — or, to say truth, a little less, because one of my dollars was from Chili. Now I shall know the truth upon another point."

So he went back on board his ship, and when he opened his chest, there was the bottle, and had come more quickly than himself. Now Keawe had a mate on board whose name was Lopaka.

"What ails you," said Lopaka, "that you stare in your chest?"

They were alone in the ship's forecastle, and Keawe bound him to secrecy, and told all.

"This is a very strange affair," said Lopaka; "and I fear you will be in trouble about this bottle. But there is one point very clear — that you are sure of the trouble, and you had better have the profit in the bargain. Make up your mind what you want with it; give the order, and if it is done as you desire, I will buy the bottle myself; for I have an idea of my own to get a schooner, and go trading through the islands."

"That is not my idea," said Keawe; "but to have a beautiful house and garden on the Kona Coast, where I was born, the sun shining in at the door, flowers in the garden, glass in the windows, pictures on the walls, and toys and fine carpets on the tables, for all the world like the house I was in this day — only a story higher, and with balconies all about like the King's palace; and to live there without care and make merry with my friends and relatives."

"Well," said Lopaka, "let us carry it back with us to Hawaii; and if all comes true, as you suppose, I will buy the bottle, as I said, and ask a schooner."

Upon that they were agreed, and it was not long before the ship returned to Honolulu, carrying Keawe and Lopaka, and the bottle. They were scarce come ashore when they met a friend upon the beach, who began at once to condole with Keawe.

"I do not know what I am to be condoled about," said Keawe.

"Is it possible you have not heard," said the friend, "your uncle — that good old man — is dead, and your cousin — that beautiful boy — was drowned at sea?"

Keawe was filled with sorrow, and, beginning to weep and to lament, he forgot about the bottle. But Lopaka was thinking to himself, and presently, when Keawe's grief was a little abated, "I have been thinking," said Lopaka, "had not your uncle lands in Hawaii, in the district of Kau?"

"No," said Keawe, "not in Kau: they are on the mountain-side — a little by south Hookena."

"These lands will now be yours?" asked Lopaka.

"And so they will," says Keawe, and began again to lament for his relatives.

"No," said Lopaka, "do not lament at present. I have a thought in my mind. How if this should be the doing of the bottle? For here is the place ready for your house."

"If this be so," cried Keawe, "it is a very ill way to serve me by killing my relatives. But it may be, indeed; for it was in just such a station that I saw the house with my mind's eye."

"The house, however, is not yet built," said Lopaka.

"No, nor like to be!" said Keawe; "for though my uncle has some coffee and ava[1] and bananas, it will not be more than will keep me in comfort; and the rest of that land is the black lava."

"Let us go to the lawyer," said Lopaka; "I have still this idea in my mind."

Now, when they came to the lawyer's, it appeared Keawe's uncle had grown monstrous rich in the last days, and there was a fund of money.

"And here is the money for the house!" cried Lopaka.

"If you are thinking of a new house," said the lawyer, "here is the card of a new architect, of whom they tell me great things."

"Better and better!" cried Lopaka. "Here is all made plain for us. Let us continue to obey orders."

So they went to the architect, and he had drawings of houses on his table.

"You want something out of the way," said the architect. "How do you like this?" and he handed a drawing to Keawe.

Now, when Keawe set eyes on the drawing, he cried out aloud, for

it was the picture of his thought exactly drawn.

"I am in for this house," thought he. "Little as I like the way it comes to me, I am in for it now, and I may as well take the good along with the evil."

So he told the architect all that he wished, and how he would have that house furnished, and about the pictures on the walls and the knick-knacks on the tables; and he asked the man plainly for how much he would undertake the whole affair.

The architect put many questions, and took his pen and made a computation; and when he had done he named the very sum that Keawe had inherited.

Lopaka and Keawe looked at one another and nodded.

"It is quite clear," thought Keawe, "that I am to have this house, whether or no. It comes from the devil, and I fear I will get little good by that; and of one thing I am sure, I will make no more wishes as long as I have this bottle. But with the house I am saddled; and I may as well take the good along with the evil."

So he made his terms with the architect, and they signed a paper; and Keawe and Lopaka took ship again and sailed to Australia; for it was concluded between them they should not interfere at all, but leave the architect and the bottle imp to build and to adorn that house at their own pleasure.

The voyage was a good voyage, only all the time Keawe was hold-

---

[1] ava: a palmlike plant from which an intoxicating liquor can be made.

ing in his breath, for he had sworn he would utter no more wishes, and take no more favours, from the devil. The time was up when they got back. The architect told them that the house was ready, and Keawe and Lopaka took a passage in the *Hall,* and went down Kona way to view the house, and see if all had been done fitly according to the thought that was in Keawe's mind.

Now, the house stood on the mountain-side, visible to ships. Above, the forest ran up into the clouds of rain; below, the black lava fell in cliffs, where the kings of old lay buried. A garden bloomed about that house with every hue of flowers; and there was an orchard of papaia on the one hand and an orchard of herdprint on the other, and right in front, toward the sea, a ship's mast had been rigged up and bore a flag. As for the house, it was three stories high, with great chambers and broad balconies on each. The windows were of glass, so excellent that it was as clear as water and as bright as day. All manner of furniture adorned the chambers. Pictures hung upon the walls in golden frames — pictures of ships, and men fighting, and of the most beautiful women, and of singular places; nowhere in the world are there pictures of so bright a colour as those Keawe found hanging in his house. As for the knick-knacks they were extraordinarily fine: chiming clocks and musical boxes, little men with nod-

ding heads, books filled with pictures, weapons of price from all quarters of the world, and the most elegant puzzles to entertain the leisure of a solitary man. And as no one would care to live in such chambers, only to walk through and view them, the balconies were made so broad that a whole town might have lived upon them in delight; and Keawe knew not which to prefer, whether the back porch, where you got the land-breeze, and looked upon the orchards and the flowers, or the front balcony, where you could drink the wind of the sea, and look down the steep wall of the mountain and see the *Hall* going by once a week or so between Hookena and the hills of Pele, or the schooners plying up the coast for wood and ava and bananas.

When they had viewed all, Keawe and Lopaka sat on the porch.

"Well," asked Lopaka, "is it all as you designed?"

"Words cannot utter it," said Keawe. "It is better than I dreamed, and I am sick with satisfaction."

"There is but one thing to consider," said Lopaka, "all this may be quite natural, and the bottle imp have nothing whatever to say to it. If I were to buy the bottle, and got no schooner after all, I should have put my hand in the fire for nothing. I gave you my word, I know; but yet I think you would not grudge me one more proof."

"I have sworn I would take no

more favours," said Keawe. "I have gone already deep enough."

"This is no favour I am thinking of," replied Lopaka. "It is only to see the imp himself. There is nothing to be gained by that, and so nothing to be ashamed of, and yet, if I once saw him, I should be sure of the whole matter. So indulge me so far, and let me see the imp; and, after that, here is the money in my hand, and I will buy it."

"There is only one thing I am afraid of," said Keawe. "The imp may be very ugly to view, and if you once set eyes upon him you might be very undesirous of the bottle."

"I am a man of my word," said Lopaka. "And here is the money betwixt us."

"Very well," replied Keawe, "I have a curiosity myself. So come, let us have one look at you, Mr. Imp."

Now as soon as that was said, the imp looked out of the bottle, and in again, swift as a lizard; and there sat Keawe and Lopaka turned to stone. The night had quite come, before either found a thought to say or voice to say it with; and then Lopaka pushed the money over and took the bottle.

"I am a man of my word," said he, "and had need to be so, or I would not touch this bottle with my foot. Well, I shall get my schooner and a dollar or two for my pocket; and then I will be rid of this devil as fast as I can. For to tell you the plain truth, the look of him has cast me down."

"Lopaka," said Keawe, "do not you think any worse of me than you can help; I know it is night, and the roads bad, and the pass by the tombs an ill place to go by so late, but I declare since I have seen that little face, I cannot eat or sleep or pray till it is gone from me. I will give you a lantern, and a basket to put the bottle in, and any picture or fine thing in all my house that takes your fancy; and be gone at once, and go sleep at Hookena with Nahinu."

"Keawe," said Lopaka, "many a man would take this ill; above all, when I am doing you a turn so friendly, as to keep my word and buy the bottle; and for that matter, the night and the dark, and the way by the tombs, must be all tenfold more dangerous to a man with such a sin upon his conscience, and such a bottle under his arm. But for my part, I am so extremely terrified myself, I have not the heart to blame you. Here I go, then; and I pray God you may be happy in your house, and I fortunate with my schooner, and both get to heaven in the end in spite of the devil and his bottle."

So Lopaka went down the mountain; and Keawe stood in his front balcony, and listened to the clink of the horse's shoes, and watched the lantern go shining down the path, and along the cliff of caves where the old dead are buried; and all the time he trembled and clasped his hands, and prayed for his friend, and gave glory to God that he himself was escaped out of that trouble.

But the next day came very brightly, and that new house of his was so delightful to behold that he forgot his terrors. One day followed another, and Keawe dwelt there in perpetual joy. He had his place on the back porch; it was there he ate and lived, and read the stories in the Honolulu newspapers; but when any one came by they would go in and view the chambers and the pictures. And the fame of the house went far and wide; it was called *Ka-Hale Nui* — the Great House — in all Kona; and sometimes the Bright House, for Keawe kept a Chinaman, who was all day dusting and furbishing; and the glass, and the gilt, and the fine stuffs, and the pictures, shone as bright as the morning. As for Keawe himself, he could not walk in the chambers without singing, his heart was so enlarged; and when ships sailed by upon the sea, he would fly his colours on the mast.

So time went by, until one day Keawe went upon a visit as far as Kailua to certain of his friends. There he was well feasted; and left as soon as he could the next morning, and rode hard, for he was impatient to behold his beautiful house; and, besides, the night then coming on was the night in which the dead of old days go abroad in the sides of Kona; and having already meddled with the devil, he was the more chary of meeting with the dead. A little beyond Honaunau, looking far ahead, he was aware of a woman bathing in the edge of the sea; and she seemed a well-grown girl, but he thought no more of it. Then he saw her white shift flutter as she put it on, and then her red holoku; and by the time he came abreast of her she was done with her toilet, and had come up from the sea, and stood by the trackside in her red holoku, and she was all freshened with the bath, and her eyes shone and were kind. Now Keawe no sooner beheld her than he drew rein.

"I thought I knew every one in this country," said he. "How comes it that I do not know you?"

"I am Kokua, daughter of Kiano," said the girl, "and I have just returned from Oahu. Who are you?"

"I will tell you who I am in a little," said Keawe, dismounting from his horse, "but not now. For I have a thought in my mind, and if you knew who I was, you might have heard of me, and would not give me a true answer. But tell me, first of all, one thing: are you married?"

At this Kokua laughed out aloud. "It is you who ask questions," she said. "Are you married yourself?"

"Indeed, Kokua, I am not," replied Keawe, "and never thought to be until this hour. But here is the plain truth. I have met you here at the roadside, and I saw your eyes, which are like the stars, and my heart went to you as swift as a bird. And so now, if you want none of me, say so, and I will go on to my own place; but if you think me no worse than any other young man, say so, too, and I will turn aside to your father's for the night, and to-morrow I will talk with the good man."

Kokua said never a word, but she looked at the sea and laughed.

"Kokua," said Keawe, "if you say nothing, I will take that for the good answer; so let us be stepping to your father's door."

She went on ahead of him, still without speech; only sometimes she glanced back and glanced away again, and she kept the strings of her hat in her mouth.

Now, when they had come to the door, Kiano came out on his veranda, and cried out and wel-comed Keawe by name. At that the girl looked over, for the fame of the great house had come to her ears; and, to be sure, it was a great temp-tation. All that evening they were very merry together; and the girl was as bold as brass under the eyes of her parents, and made a mark of Keawe, for she had a quick wit. The next day he had a word with Kiano, and found the girl alone.

"Kokua," said he, "you made a mark of me all the evening; and it is still time to bid me go. I would not tell you who I was, because I have so fine a house, and I feared you would think too much of that house and too little of the man that

loves you. Now you know all, and if you wish to have seen the last of me, say so at once."

"No," said Kokua, but this time she did not laugh, nor did Keawe ask for more.

This was the wooing of Keawe; things had gone quickly; but so an arrow goes, and the ball of a rifle swifter still, and yet both may strike the target. Things had gone fast, but they had gone far also, and the thought of Keawe rang in the maiden's head; she heard his voice in the breach of the surf upon the lava, and for this young man that she had seen but twice she would have left father and mother and her native islands. As for Keawe himself, his horse flew up the path of the mountain under the cliff of tombs, and the sound of the hoofs, and the sound of Keawe singing to himself for pleasure, echoed in the caverns of the dead. He came to the Bright House, and still he was singing. He sat and ate in the broad balcony, and the Chinaman wondered at his master, to hear how he sang between the mouth-fuls. The sun went down into the sea, and the night came; and Keawe walked the balconies by lamplight, high on the mountain, and the voice of his singing startled men on ships.

"Here am I now upon my high place," he said to himself. "Life may be no better; this is the moun-tain-top; and all shelves about me toward the worse. For the first time I will light up the chambers, and bathe in my fine bath with the hot water and the cold, and sleep above in the bed of my bridal chamber."

So the Chinaman had word, and he must rise from sleep and light the furnaces; and as he walked below, beside the boilers, he heard his master singing and rejoicing above him in the lighted chambers. When the water began to be hot the Chinaman cried to his master: and Keawe went into the bath-room; and the Chinaman heard him sing as he filled the marble basin; and heard him sing, and the singing broken, as he undressed; until of a sudden, the song ceased. The Chinaman listened, and listened; he called up the house to Keawe to ask if all were well, and Keawe answered him "Yes," and bade him go to bed; but there was no more singing in the Bright House; and all night long the Chinaman heard his master's feet go round and round the balconies without repose.

Now, the truth of it was this: as Keawe undressed for his bath, he spied upon his flesh a patch like a patch of lichen on a rock, and it was then that he stopped singing. For he knew the likeness of that patch, and knew that he was fallen in the Chinese Evil.[1]

Now, it is a sad thing for any man to fall into this sickness. And it would be a sad thing for any one to leave a house so beautiful and so commodious, and depart from all his friends to the north coast of

[1] Chinese Evil: leprosy.

Molokai,[2] between the mighty cliff and the sea-breakers. But what was that to the case of the man Keawe, he who had met his love but yesterday, and won her but that morning, and now saw all his hopes break, in a moment, like a piece of glass?

Awhile he sat upon the edge of the bath, then sprang, with a cry, and ran outside; and to and fro, to and fro, along the balcony, like one despairing.

"Very willingly could I leave Hawaii, the home of my fathers," Keawe was thinking. "Very lightly could I leave my house, the high-placed, the many-windowed, here upon the mountains. Very bravely could I go to Molokai, to Kalaupapa by the cliffs, to live with the smitten and to sleep there, far from my fathers. But what wrong have I done, what sin lies upon my soul, that I should have encountered Kokua coming cool from the sea-water in the evening? Kokua, the soul ensnarer! Kokua, the light of my life! Her may I never wed, her may I look upon no longer, her may I no more handle with my loving hand; and it is for this, it is for you, O Kokua! that I pour my lamentations!"

Now you are to observe what sort of a man Keawe was, for he might have dwelt there in the Bright House for years, and no one been the wiser of his sickness; but he reckoned nothing of that, if he must

[2] Molokai: an island, site of a great leper colony.

lose Kokua. And again he might have wed Kokua even as he was; and so many would have done, because they have the souls of pigs; but Keawe loved the maid manfully, and he would do her no hurt and bring her in no danger.

A little beyond the midst of the night, there came in his mind the recollection of that bottle. He went round to the back porch, and called to memory the day when the devil had looked forth; and at the thought ice ran in his veins.

"A dreadful thing is the bottle," thought Keawe, "and dreadful is the imp, and it is a dreadful thing to risk the flames of hell. But what other hope have I to cure my sickness or to wed Kokua? What!" he thought, "would I beard the devil once, only to get me a house, and not face him again to win Kokua?"

Thereupon he called to mind it was the next day the *Hall* went by on her return to Honolulu. "There must I go first," he thought, "and see Lopaka. For the best hope that I have now is to find that same bottle I was so pleased to be rid of."

Never a wink could he sleep; the food stuck in his throat; but he sent a letter to Kiano, and about the time when the steamer would be coming, rode down beside the cliff of the tombs. It rained; his horse went heavily; he looked up at the black mouths of the caves, and he envied the dead that slept there and were done with trouble; and called to mind how he had galloped by the day before, and was astonished. So he came down to Hookena, and there was all the country gathered for the steamer as usual. In the shed before the store they sat and jested and passed the news; but there was no matter of speech in Keawe's bosom, and he sat in their midst and looked without on the rain falling on the houses, and the surf beating among the rocks, and the sighs arose in his throat.

"Keawe of the Bright House is out of spirits," said one to another. Indeed, and so he was, and little wonder.

Then the *Hall* came, and the whale-boat carried him on board. The after-part of the ship was full of Haoles — whites — who had been to visit the volcano,[1] as their custom is; and the midst was crowded with Kanakas,[2] and the fore-part with wild bulls from Hilo and horses from Kau; but Keawe sat apart from all in his sorrow, and watched for the house of Kiano. There it sat low upon the shore in the black rocks, and shaded by the coron palms, and there by the door was a red holoku, no greater than a

[1] the volcano: Kilauea, a great active volcano on the island of Hawaii, much visited then and now by tourists. In Chapters 28 and 32–34 of Mark Twain's *Roughing It* (1872), you will find a vivid description of a visit to the volcano, also impressions of cruising on the inter-island schooners and of the sights of Kona and Honaunau at approximately the time of Stevenson's story.

[2] Kanakas: natives of the islands.

fly, and going to and fro with a fly's busyness. "Ah, queen of my heart," he cried, "I'll venture my dear soul to win you!"

Soon after darkness fell and the cabins were lit up, and the Haoles sat and played at the cards and drank whiskey as their custom is; but Keawe walked the deck all night; and all the next day, as they steamed under the lee of Maui or of Molokai, he was still pacing to and fro like a wild animal in a menagerie.

Toward evening they passed Diamond Head, and came to the pier of Honolulu. Keawe stepped out among the crowd and began to ask for Lopaka. It seemed he had become the owner of a schooner — none better in the islands — and was gone upon an adventure as far as Pola-Pola or Kahiki; so there was no help to be looked for from Lopaka. Keawe called to mind a friend of his, a lawyer in the town (I must not tell his name), and inquired of him. They said he was grown suddenly rich, and had a fine new house upon Waikiki shore; and this put a thought in Keawe's head, and he called a hack and drove to the lawyer's house.

The house was all brand new, and the trees in the garden no greater than walking-sticks, and the lawyer, when he came, had the air of a man well pleased.

"What can I do to serve you?" said the lawyer.

"You are a friend of Lopaka's," replied Keawe, "and Lopaka purchased from me a certain piece of goods that I thought you might enable me to trace."

The lawyer's face became very dark. "I do not profess to misunderstand you, Mr. Keawe," said he, "though this is an ugly business to be stirring in. You may be sure I know nothing, but yet I have a guess, and if you would apply in a certain quarter I think you might have news."

And he named the name of a man, which, again, I had better not repeat. So it was for days, and Keawe went from one to another, finding everywhere new clothes and carriages, and fine new houses and men everywhere in great contentment, although, to be sure, when he hinted at his business their faces would cloud over.

"No doubt I am upon the track," thought Keawe. "These new clothes and carriages are all the gifts of the little imp, and these glad faces are the faces of men who have taken their profit and got rid of the accursed thing in safety. When I see pale cheeks and hear sighing, I shall know that I am near the bottle."

So it befell at last that he was recommended to a Haole in Beritania Street. When he came to the door, about the hour of the evening meal, there were the usual marks of the new house, and the young garden, and the electric light shining in the windows; but when the owner came, a shock of hope and fear ran through Keawe; for here was a young man, white as a corpse, and black about the eyes, the hair shedding from his head, and such a look in his countenance as a man may have when he is waiting for the gallows.

"Here it is, to be sure," thought Keawe, and so with this man he noways veiled his errand. "I am come to buy the bottle," said he.

At the word, the young Haole of Beritania Street reeled against the wall.

"The bottle!" he gasped. "To buy the bottle!" Then he seemed to choke, and seizing Keawe by the arm, carried him into a room and poured out wine in two glasses.

"Here is my respects," said Keawe, who had been much about with Haoles in his time. "Yes," he added, "I am come to buy the bottle. What is the price by now?"

At that word the young man let his glass slip through his fingers, and looked upon Keawe like a ghost.

"The price," says he; "the price! You do not know the price?"

"It is for that I am asking you," returned Keawe. "But why are you so much concerned? Is there anything wrong about the price?"

"It has dropped a great deal in value since your time, Mr. Keawe," said the young man, stammering.

"Well, well, I shall have the less to pay for it," says Keawe. "How much did it cost you?"

The young man was as white as a sheet. "Two cents," said he.

"What?" cried Keawe, "two cents? Why, then, you can only sell it for one. And he who buys it —— " The words died upon Keawe's tongue; he who bought it could never sell it again, the bottle and the bottle imp must abide with him until he died, and when he died must carry him to the red end of hell.

The young man of Beritania Street fell upon his knees. "For God's sake, buy it!" he cried. "You can have all my fortune in the bargain. I was mad when I bought it at that price. I had embezzled money at my store; I was lost else; I must have gone to jail."

"Poor creature," said Keawe, "you would risk your soul upon so desperate an adventure, and to avoid the proper punishment of your own disgrace; and you think I could hesitate with love in front of me. Give me the bottle, and the change which I make sure you have all ready. Here is a five-cent piece."

It was as Keawe supposed; the young man had the change ready in a drawer; the bottle changed hands, and Keawe's fingers were no sooner clasped upon the stalk than he had breathed his wish to be a clean man. And, sure enough, when he got home to his room, and stripped himself before a glass, his flesh was whole like an infant's. And here was the strange thing: he had no sooner seen this miracle than his mind was changed within him, and he cared naught for the Chinese Evil, and little enough for Kokua; and had but the one thought, that here he was bound to the bottle imp for time and for eternity, and had no better hope but to be a cinder for ever in the flames of hell. Away ahead of him he saw them blaze with his mind's eye, and his soul shrank, and darkness fell upon the light.

When Keawe came to himself a little, he was aware it was the night when the band played at the hotel. Thither he went, because he feared to be alone; and there, among happy faces, walked to and fro, and heard the tunes go up and down, and saw Berger beat the measure, and all the while he heard the flames crackle, and saw the red fire burning in the bottomless pit. Of a sudden the band played *Hiki-ao-ao;* that was a song that he had sung with Kokua, and at the strain courage returned to him.

"It is done now," he thought, "and once more let me take the good along with the evil."

So it befell that he returned to Hawaii by the first steamer, and as soon as it could be managed he was wedded to Kokua, and carried her up the mountain-side to the Bright House.

Now it was so with these two, that when they were together Keawe's heart was stilled; but as soon as he was alone he fell into a brooding horror, and heard the flames crackle, and saw the red fire burn in the bottomless pit. The girl, indeed, had come to him wholly; her heart leaped in her side at sight of him, her hand clung to his; and she was so fashioned, from the hair

upon her head to the nails upon her toes, that none could see her without joy. She was pleasant in her nature. She had the good word always. Full of song she was, and went to and fro in the Bright House, the brightest thing in its three stories, carolling like the birds. And Keawe beheld and heard her with delight, and then must shrink upon one side, and weep and groan to think upon the price that he had paid for her; and then he must dry his eyes, and wash his face, and go and sit with her on the broad balconies, joining in her songs, and, with a sick spirit, answering her smiles.

There came a day when her feet began to be heavy and her songs more rare; and now it was not Keawe only that would weep apart, but each would sunder from the other and sit in opposite balconies with the whole width of the Bright House betwixt. Keawe was so sunk in his despair, he scarce observed the change, and was only glad he had more hours to sit alone and brood upon his destiny, and was not so frequently condemned to pull a smiling face on a sick heart. But one day, coming softly through the house, he heard the sound of a child sobbing, and there was Kokua rolling her face upon the balcony floor, and weeping like the lost.

"You do well to weep in this house, Kokua," he said. "And yet I would give the head off my body that you (at least) might have been happy."

"Happy!" she cried. "Keawe,

when you lived alone in your Bright House you were the word of the island for a happy man; laughter and song were in your mouth, and your face was as bright as the sunrise. Then you wedded poor Kokua; and the good God knows what is amiss in her — but from that day you have not smiled. Oh!" she cried, "what ails me? I thought I was pretty, and I knew I loved him. What ails me, that I throw this cloud upon my husband?"

"Poor Kokua," said Keawe. He sat down by her side, and sought to take her hand; but that she plucked away. "Poor Kokua," he said, again. "My poor child — my pretty. And I had thought all this while to spare you! Well, you shall know all. Then, at least, you will pity poor Keawe; then you will understand how much he loved you in the past — that he dared hell for your possession — and how much he loves you still (the poor condemned one), that he can yet call up a smile when he beholds you."

With that, he told her all, even from the beginning.

"You have done this for me?" she cried. "Ah, well, then what do I care!" and she clasped and wept upon him.

"Ah, child!" said Keawe, "and yet, when I consider of the fire of hell, I care a good deal!"

"Never tell me," said she, "any man can be lost because he loved Kokua, and no other fault. I tell you, Keawe, I shall save you with these hands, or perish in your company. What! you loved me and gave your soul, and you think I will not die to save you in return?"

"Ah, my dear, you might die a hundred times, and what difference would that make?" he cried, "except to leave me lonely till the time comes of my damnation?"

"You know nothing," said she. "I was educated in a school in Honolulu; I am no common girl. And I tell you I shall save my lover. What is this you say about a cent? But all the world is not American. In England they have a piece they call a farthing, which is about half a cent. Ah! sorrow!" she cried, "that makes it scarcely better, for the buyer must be lost, and we shall find none so brave as my Keawe! But, then, there is France; they have a small coin there which they call a centime, and these go five to the cent or thereabout. We could not do better. Come, Keawe, let us go to the French islands; let us go to Tahiti, as fast as ships can bear us. There we have four centimes, three centimes, two centimes, one centime; four possible sales to come and go on; and two of us to push the bargain. Come, my Keawe! Kiss me, and banish care. Kokua will defend you."

"Gift of God!" he cried. "I cannot think that God will punish me for desiring aught so good! Be it as you will, then, take me where you please: I put my life and my salvation in your hands."

Early the next day Kokua was about her preparations. She took

Keawe's chest that he went with sailoring; and first she put the bottle in a corner, and then packed it with the richest of their clothes and the bravest of the knick-knacks in the house. "For," said she, "we must seem to be rich folks, or who will believe in the bottle?" All the time of her preparation she was as gay as a bird; only when she looked upon Keawe the tears would spring in her eyes, and she must run and kiss him. As for Keawe, a weight was off his soul; now that he had his secret shared, and some hope in front of him, he seemed like a new man, his feet went lightly on the earth, and his breath was good to him again. Yet was terror still at his elbow; and ever and again, as the wind blows out a taper, hope died in him, and he saw the flames toss and the red fire burn in hell.

It was given out in the country they were gone pleasuring to the States, which was thought a strange thing, and yet not so strange as the truth, if any could have guessed it. So they went to Honolulu in the *Hall,* and thence in the *Umatilla* to San Francisco with a crowd of Haoles, and at San Francisco took their passage by the mail brigantine, the *Tropic Bird,* for Papeete, the chief place of the French in the south islands. Thither they came, after a pleasant voyage, on a fair day of the trade wind, and saw the reef with the surf breaking and Motuiti with its palms, and the schooner riding withinside, and the white houses of the town low down along the shore among green trees, and overhead the mountains and the clouds of Tahiti, the wise island.

It was judged the most wise to hire a house, which they did accordingly, opposite the British Consul's to make a great parade of money, and themselves conspicuous with carriages and horses. This it was very easy to do, so long as they had the bottle in their possession; for Kokua was more bold than Keawe, and, whenever she had a mind, called on the imp for twenty or a hundred dollars. At this rate they soon grew to be remarked in the town; and the strangers from Hawaii, their riding and their driving, the fine holokus, and the rich lace of Kokua, became the matter of much talk.

They got on well after the first with the Tahitian language, which is indeed like to the Hawaiian, with a change of certain letters; and as soon as they had any freedom of speech, began to push the bottle. You are to consider it was not an easy subject to introduce; it is not easy to persuade people you are in earnest, when you offer to sell them for four centimes the spring of health and riches inexhaustible. It was necessary besides to explain the dangers of the bottle; and either people disbelieved the whole thing and laughed, or they thought the more of the darker part, became overcast with gravity, and drew away from Keawe and Kokua, as from persons who had dealings with the devil. So far from gaining ground, these two began to find they were avoided in the town; the children ran away from them screaming, a thing intolerable to Kokua; Catholics crossed themselves as they went by; and all persons began with one accord to disengage themselves from their advances.

Depression fell upon their spirits. They would sit at night in their new house, after a day's weariness, and not exchange one word, or the silence would be broken by Kokua bursting suddenly into sobs. Sometimes they would pray together; sometimes they would have the bottle out upon the floor, and sit all evening watching how the shadow hovered in the midst. At such times they would be afraid to go to rest. It was long ere slumber came to them, and, if either dozed off, it would be to wake and find the other silently weeping in the dark, or perhaps, to wake alone, the other having fled from the house and the neighbourhood of that bottle, to pace under the bananas in the little garden, or to wander on the beach by moonlight.

One night it was so when Kokua awoke. Keawe was gone. She felt in the bed and his place was cold. Then fear fell upon her, and she sat up in bed. A little moonshine filtered through the shutters. The room was bright, and she could spy the bottle on the floor. Outside it blew high, the great trees of the avenue cried aloud, and the fallen leaves rattled in the veranda. In the midst of this Kokua was aware of another sound; whether of a beast or of a man she could scarce tell, but it was as sad as death, and cut her to the soul. Softly she arose, set the door ajar, and looked forth into the moonlit yard. There, under the bananas, lay Keawe, his mouth in the dust, and as he lay he moaned.

It was Kokua's first thought to run forward and console him; her second potently withheld her. Keawe had borne himself before his wife like a brave man; it became her little in the hour of weakness to intrude upon his shame. With the thought she drew back into the house.

"Heaven," she thought, "how careless have I been — how weak! It is he, not I, that stands in this eternal peril; it was he, not I, that took the curse upon his soul. It is for my sake, and for the love of a creature of so little worth and such poor help, that he now beholds so close to him the flames of hell — ay, and smells the smoke of it, lying without there in the wind and moonlight. Am I so dull of spirit that never till now I have surmised my duty, or have I seen it before and turned aside? But now, at least, I take up my soul in both the hands of my affection; now I say farewell to the white steps of heaven and the waiting faces of my friends. A love for a love, and let mine be equalled with Keawe's! A soul for a soul, and be it mine to perish!"

She was a deft woman with her hands, and was soon apparelled. She took in her hands the change — the precious centimes they kept ever at their side; for this coin is little used, and they had made provision at a government office. When she was forth in the avenue, clouds came on the wind, and the moon was blackened. The town slept, and she knew not whither to turn till she heard one coughing in the shadow of the trees.

"Old man," said Kokua, "what do you here abroad in the cold night?"

The old man could scarce express himself for coughing, but she made out that he was old and poor, and a stranger in the island.

"Will you do me a service?" said Kokua. "As one stranger to another, and as an old man to a young woman, will you help a daughter of Hawaii?"

"Ah," said the old man. "So you are the witch from the eight islands, and even my old soul you seek to entangle. But I have heard of you, and defy your wickedness."

"Sit down here," said Kokua, "and let me tell you a tale." And she told him the story of Keawe from the beginning to the end.

"And now," said she, "I am his wife, whom he bought with his soul's welfare. And what should I do? If I went to him myself and offered to buy it, he would refuse. But if you go, he will sell it eagerly; I will await you here; you will buy it for four centimes, and I will buy it again for three. And the Lord strengthen a poor girl!"

"If you meant falsely," said the old man, "I think God would strike you dead."

"He would!" cried Kokua. "Be sure He would. I could not be so treacherous, God would not suffer it."

"Give me the four centimes and await me here," said the old man.

Now, when Kokua stood alone in the street, her spirit died. The wind roared in the trees, and it seemed to her the rushing of the flames of hell; the shadows towered in the light of the street lamp, and they seemed to her the snatching hands of evil ones. If she had had the strength, she must have run away, and if she had had the breath she must have screamed aloud; but, in truth, she could do neither, and stood and trembled in the avenue, like an affrighted child.

Then she saw the old man returning, and he had the bottle in his hand.

"I have done your bidding," said he. "I left your husband weeping like a child; to-night he will sleep easy." And he held the bottle forth.

"Before you give it me," Kokua panted, "take the good with the evil — ask to be delivered from your cough."

"I am an old man," replied the other, "and too near the gate of the grave to take a favour from the devil. But what is this? Why do you not take the bottle? Do you hesitate?"

"Not hesitate!" cried Kokua. "I am only weak. Give me a moment.

It is my hand resists, my flesh shrinks back from the accursed thing. One moment only!"

The old man looked upon Kokua kindly. "Poor child!" said he, "you fear: your soul misgives you. Well, let me keep it. I am old, and can never more be happy in this world, and as for the next —— "

"Give it me!" gasped Kokua. "There is your money. Do you think I am so base as that? Give me the bottle."

"God bless you, child," said the old man.

Kokua concealed the bottle under her holoku, said farewell to the old man, and walked off along the avenue, she cared not whither. For all roads were now the same to her, and led equally to hell. Sometimes she walked, and sometimes ran; sometimes she screamed out loud in the night, and sometimes lay by the wayside in the dust and wept. All that she had heard of hell came back to her; she saw the flames blaze, and she smelled the smoke, and her flesh withered on the coals.

Near day she came to her mind again, and returned to the house. It was even as the old man said — Keawe slumbered like a child. Kokua stood and gazed upon his face.

"Now, my husband," said she, "it is your turn to sleep. When you wake it will be your turn to sing and laugh. But for poor Kokua, alas! that meant no evil — for poor Kokua no more sleep, no more singing, no more delight, whether in earth or Heaven."

With that she lay down in the bed by his side, and her misery was so extreme that she fell in a deep slumber instantly.

Late in the morning her husband woke her and gave her the good news. It seemed he was silly with delight, for he paid no heed to her distress, ill though she dissembled it. The words stuck in her mouth, it mattered not; Keawe did the speaking. She ate not a bite, but who was to observe it? For Keawe cleared the dish. Kokua saw and heard him, like some strange thing in a dream; there were times when she forgot or doubted, and put her hands to her brow; to know herself doomed and hear her husband babble, seemed so monstrous.

All the while Keawe was eating and talking, and planning the time of their return, and thanking her for saving him, and fondling her, and calling her the true helper after all. He laughed at the old man that was fool enough to buy that bottle.

"A worthy old man he seemed," Keawe said. "But no one can judge by appearances. For why did the old reprobate require the bottle?"

"My husband," said Kokua, humbly, "his purpose may have been good."

Keawe laughed like an angry man.

"Fiddle-de-dee!" cried Keawe. "An old rogue, I tell you; and an old ass to boot. For the bottle was hard enough to sell at four centimes; and at three it will be quite impossible. The margin is not broad enough, the thing begins to smell of scorching — brrr!" said he, and shuddered. "It is true I bought it myself at a cent, when I knew not there were smaller coins. I was a fool for my pains; there will never be found another, and whoever has that bottle now will carry it to the pit."

"O my husband!" said Kokua. "Is it not a terrible thing to save oneself by the eternal ruin of another? It seems to me I could not laugh. I would be humbled. I would be filled with melancholy. I would pray for the poor holder."

Then Keawe, because he felt the truth of what she said, grew the more angry. "Heighty-teighty!" cried he. "You may be filled with melancholy if you please. It is not the mind of a good wife. If you thought at all of me, you would sit shamed."

Thereupon he went out, and Kokua was alone.

What chance had she to sell that bottle at two centimes? None, she perceived. And if she had any, here was her husband hurrying her away to a country where there was nothing lower than a cent. And here — on the morrow of her sacrifice — was her husband leaving her and blaming her.

She would not even try to profit by what time she had, but sat in the house, and now had the bottle out and viewed it with unutterable fear, and now, with loathing, hid it out of sight.

By and by, Keawe came back, and would have her take a drive.

"My husband, I am ill," she said. "I am out of heart. Excuse me, I can take no pleasure."

Then was Keawe more wroth than ever. With her, because he thought she was brooding over the case of the old man; and with himself because he thought she was right, and was ashamed to be so happy.

"This is your truth," cried he, "and this your affection! Your husband is just saved from eternal ruin, which he encountered for the love of you — and you can take no pleasure! Kokua, you have a disloyal heart."

He went forth again furious, and wandered in the town all day. He met friends, and drank with them; they hired a carriage and drove into the country, and there drank again. All the time Keawe was ill at ease, because he was taking this pastime while his wife was sad, and because he knew in his heart that she was more right than he; and the knowledge made him drink the deeper.

Now, there was an old brutal Haole drinking with him, one that had been a boatswain of a whaler — a runaway, a digger in gold mines, and convict in prisons. He had a low mind and a foul mouth; he loved to drink and to see others drunken; and he pressed the glass upon Keawe. Soon there was no more money in the company.

"Here, you!" says the boatswain, "you are rich, you have been always saying. You have a bottle or some foolishness."

"Yes," says Keawe, "I am rich! I will go back and get some money from my wife, who keeps it."

"That's a bad idea, mate," said the boatswain. "Never you trust a petticoat with dollars. They're all as false as water; you keep an eye on her."

Now, this word struck in Keawe's mind; for he was muddled with what he had been drinking.

"I should not wonder but she was false indeed," thought he. "Why else should she be so cast down at my release? But I will show her I am not the man to be fooled. I will catch her in the act."

Accordingly, when they were back in town, Keawe bade the boatswain wait for him at the corner, by the old calaboose, and went forward up the avenue alone to the door of his house. The night had come again; there was a light within, but never a sound; and Keawe crept about the corner, opened the back door softly, and looked in.

There was Kokua on the floor, the lamp at her side; before her was a milk-white bottle, with a round belly and a long neck; and as she viewed it, Kokua wrung her hands.

A long time Keawe stood and looked in the doorway. At first he was struck stupid; and then fear fell upon him that the bargain had been made amiss, and the bottle had come back to him as it came at San Francisco; and at that his knees were loosened, and the fumes of the wine departed from his head like mists off a river in the morning. And then he had another thought; and it was a strange one, that made his cheeks to burn.

"I must make sure of this," thought he.

So he closed the door, and went softly round the corner again, and then came noisily in, as though he were but now returned. And, lo! by the time he opened the front door no bottle was to be seen; and Kokua sat in a chair and started up like one awakened out of sleep.

"I have been drinking all day and making merry," said Keawe. "I have been with good companions, and now I only come back for money, and return to drink and carouse with them again."

Both his face and voice were as stern as judgment, but Kokua was too troubled to observe.

"You do well to use your own, my husband," said she, and her words trembled.

"Oh, I do well in all things," said Keawe, and he went straight to the chest and took out money. But he looked besides in the corner where they kept the bottle, and there was no bottle there.

At that the chest heaved upon the floor like a sea-billow, and the house span about him like a wreath of smoke, for he saw she was lost now, and there was no escape. "It is what I feared," he thought. "It is she who has bought it."

And then he came to himself a little and rose up; but the sweat streamed on his face as thick as the rain and as cold as the well-water.

"Kokua," said he, "I said to you to-day what ill became me. Now I return to house with my jolly companions," and at that he laughed a little quietly. "I will take more pleasure in the cup if you forgive me."

She clasped his knees in a moment; she kissed his knees with flowing tears.

"Oh," she cried, "I asked but a kind word!"

"Let us never one think hardly of the other," said Keawe, and was gone out of the house.

Now, the money that Keawe had taken was only some of that store of centime pieces they had laid in at their arrival. It was very sure he had no mind to be drinking. His wife had given her soul for him, now he must give his for hers; no other thought was in the world with him.

At the corner, by the old calaboose, there was the boatswain waiting.

"My wife has the bottle," said Keawe, "and, unless you help me to recover it, there can be no more money and no more liquor to-night."

"You do not mean to say you are serious about that bottle?" cried the boatswain.

"There is the lamp," said Keawe. "Do I look as if I was jesting?"

"That is so," said the boatswain. "You look as serious as a ghost."

"Well, then," said Keawe, "here are two centimes; you must go to my wife in the house, and offer her these for the bottle, which (if I am not much mistaken) she will give you instantly. Bring it to me here, and I will buy it back from you for one; for that is the law with this bottle, that it still must be sold for a less sum. But whatever you do, never breathe a word to her that you have come from me."

"Mate, I wonder are you making a fool of me?" asked the boatswain.

"It will do you no harm if I am," returned Keawe.

"That is so, mate," said the boatswain.

"And if you doubt me," added Keawe, "you can try. As soon as you are clear of the house, wish to have your pocket full of money, or a bottle of the best rum, or what you please, and you will see the virtue of the thing."

"Very well, Kanaka," says the boatswain. "I will try; but if you are having your fun out of me, I will take my fun out of you with a belaying-pin."

So the whaler-man went off up the avenue; and Keawe stood and waited. It was near the same spot where Kokua had waited the night before; but Keawe was more resolved, and never faltered in his purpose; only his soul was bitter with despair.

It seemed a long time he had to wait before he heard a voice singing in the darkness of the avenue. He knew the voice to be the boatswain's; but it was strange how drunken it appeared upon a sudden.

Next the man himself came stumbling into the light of the lamp. He had the devil's bottle buttoned in his coat; another bottle was in his hand; and even as he came in view he raised it to his mouth and drank.

"You have it," said Keawe. "I see that."

"Hands off!" cried the boatswain jumping back. "Take a step near me, and I'll smash your mouth. You thought you could make a cat's paw of me, did you?"

"What do you mean?" cried Keawe.

"Mean?" cried the boatswain. "This is a pretty good bottle, this is; that's what I mean. How I got it for two centimes I can't make out; but I am sure you sha'n't have it for one."

"You mean you won't sell?" gasped Keawe.

"No, sir," cried the boatswain. "But I'll give you a drink of the rum, if you like."

"I tell you," said Keawe, "the man who has that bottle goes to hell."

"I reckon I'm going anyway," returned the sailor; "and this bottle's the best thing to go with I've struck yet. No, sir!" he cried again, "this is my bottle now, and you can go and fish for another."

"Can this be true?" Keawe cried. "For your own sake, I beseech you, sell it me!"

"I don't value any of your talk," replied the boatswain. "You thought I was a flat, now you see I'm not; and there's an end. If you won't have a swallow of the rum, I'll have one myself. Here's your health, and good-night to you!"

So off he went down the avenue toward town, and there goes the bottle out of the story.

But Keawe ran to Kokua [1] light as the wind; and great was their joy that night; and great, since then, has been the peace of all their days in the Bright House.

[1] **Kokua:** This name has a special significance: it is the Hawaiian word for someone who surrenders his own life to help another; its most specific application was to those men or women who voluntarily accompanied lepers to their dreadful banishment at Molokai to tend them and finally perish with them.

For Study and Writing

1. At the beginning of the story, when Keawe and the bearded man in San Francisco look at each other through the window, why does each envy the other? What ironic generalization can you observe here about the mutual envy of strangers?

2. Who were among the previous owners of the bottle? Who was the first?

3. Explain the difficulty in the fact that the bottle must be sold for less than the price paid for it. Why would an increasing price not have the same dangers — or the same interest? What kind of money must be used in the transaction? What do you think may be the significance of the latter re-

quirement? Can you link this with lines 690–92 in Book I of *Paradise Lost:* "Let none admire/That riches grow in Hell; that soil may best/Deserve the precious bane"?

4. What is sinister about the way in which Keawe's first major wish is fulfilled? What is not quite certain about it, as Lopaka observes? Do these circumstances suggest any general quality about the devil's favors?

5. What do you think is the origin of Keawe's leprosy? Discuss possible views of the matter.

6. If, in the treachery of all demon favors, there is apt to be some nasty aftereffect from even brief ownership of the bottle, what factor may protect both Keawe and Kokua in their last transaction with it?

7. Why will not the old man whom Kokua sends to buy the bottle from Keawe use it to rid himself of his racking cough?

8. Each owner of the bottle is some-how set apart from his fellow men while he has it. Explain why this isolation occurs. How is it demonstrated especially between Keawe and Kokua?

9. This story is essentially light-hearted in tone, though an ominous threat hovers over it. The special quality of the story is derived from this mixture of tonal elements. A happy ending requires that both Keawe and Kokua be delivered from the bottle. Yet the author has the difficult problem of getting the bottle out of their hands without spoiling the tone of the story and marring our satisfaction with its ending. Discuss the nature of this problem. Why cannot the bottle be sold to just anyone, so long as Keawe and Kokua are rid of it? Analyze Stevenson's solution. Do you find it acceptable? Explain your answer.

10. Give a brief character study of Keawe, being sure to state and prove his chief characteristics.

AFTERWORD

Few stories of men trafficking with the devil have happy endings. Stephen Vincent Benét's "The Devil and Daniel Webster" is possibly the best-known other example. No explanation is needed as to why such stories might end disastrously. Into "The Bottle Imp," as in the case of any other tale of its kind, numerous meanings can be read. One of these certainly is that none of us can avoid evil altogether, especially in the transactions of power and wealth. Whatever we do is almost always fraught with some moral hazard. The bottle may represent all the moral compromises by which a man may gain profit or otherwise advance himself.

Caveat emptor, "let the buyer beware," a phrase reflecting the antiquity of man's swindling propensities, means that he should watch out lest something be put over on him. Stevenson is original in the concept that with this dangerous bottle the seller himself must caution the buyer to beware. The peril of the bottle is not only that the one who dies in possession of it will be damned. Even for those who have escaped that fate and have seen, with a cry of joy at their reprieve, the bottle pass into other hands, there remains the fact — enigmatic, unprovable, yet intuitively felt as a certainty — that in the treachery of the devil's bargains, each wish granted by the bottle comes at a concealed high cost — the death of Keawe's uncle, the taint of leprosy.

By metaphor, this story poses questions concerning our awareness of peril to our souls, our recognition that the best of us sometimes court and accept the devil's favors, and our realization that in time we must make sure to cleanse ourselves. It is significant that the conditions of the bottle require that in every sale full warning be given about its dangers.

Someone might argue that the story is immoral because the gains acquired by the devil's favors are kept after the bottle is disposed of. In pure, abstract morality this point is a good one. But we do not live by pure, abstract morality; and Stevenson is saying, in part, that in an imperfect world all our gains are compromised and that we must do what we can to recognize the elements of evil and put them away from us. As the story makes quite clear, to do this isn't easy.

Base Details

by Siegfried Sassoon

(*1886–*)

If I were fierce and bald and short of breath,
    I'd live with scarlet Majors at the Base,
And speed glum heroes up the line to death.
    You'd see me with my puffy petulant face,
Guzzling and gulping in the best hotel,   5
    Reading the Roll of Honor. "Poor young chap,"
I'd say — "I used to know his father well.
    Yes, we've lost heavily in this last scrap."
And when the war is done and youth stone dead,
    I'd toddle safely home and die — in bed.   10

For Study and Writing

1. Explain the words *Base, scarlet,* and *scrap* as used here.

2. Exactly how is shocking indifference expressed?

3. On what ironies does the satirical quality of this poem depend?

4. Comment on the suitability of the rhyme scheme.

5. Suppose yourself in the position of "the scarlet Majors" who might read this poem. What reactions or retorts might you have to the poem?

Batter My Heart

by John Donne

(*1572?–1631*)

Batter my heart, three-personed God, for you
As yet but knock, breathe, shine, and seek to mend;
That I may rise and stand, o'erthrow me and bend
Your force to break, blow, burn, and make me new.
I, like an usurped town, to another due,   5

Labour to admit you, but oh, to no end;
Reason, your viceroy in me, me should defend,
But is captived, and proves weak or untrue.
Yet dearly I love you, and would be lovèd fain,
But am betrothed unto your enemy: 10
Divorce me, untie or break that knot again,
Take me to you, imprison me, for I,
Except you enthrall me, never shall be free,
Nor ever chaste, except you ravish me.

For Study and Writing

1. Explain the paradox set forth in the first two lines of this sonnet.

2. In what two specific images (a simile and a metaphor) does John Donne express his own state in relation to God?

3. In what ways is this poem constructed on a conventional or formal pattern? What seems unconventional or informal?

4. John Donne was the most popular preacher of his time in England. To what extent does this poem show his ability to combine the material and the spiritual in understandable terms?

Aunt Helen

by T. S. Eliot
(*1888–1965*)

Miss Helen Slingsby was my maiden aunt,
And lived in a small house near a fashionable square
Cared for by servants to the number of four.
Now when she died there was silence in heaven
And silence at her end of the street.   5
The shutters were drawn and the undertaker wiped his feet —
He was aware that this sort of thing had occurred before.
The dogs were handsomely provided for,
But shortly afterwards the parrot died too.
The Dresden clock continued ticking on the mantelpiece,   10
And the footman sat upon the dining-table
Holding the second housemaid on his knees —
Who had always been so careful while her mistress lived.

For Study and Writing

1. What specific things, animals, and people were included in Miss Helen Slingsby's household?

2. How does each detail of the answer to the preceding question show us Aunt Helen's life and personality?

3. What effect is the poet attempting to achieve when he tells us that there was silence in heaven and also "at her end of the street"?

4. How might the undertaker's awareness exemplify ironical understatement?

5. What is significant about *where* the footman is sitting?

6. Why does the poet mention that the Dresden clock "continued ticking"?

7. In what detail is Aunt Helen's actual death described to us?

8. At the end of line 9, what is the point of *too*? Does it refer only to the previous death of Aunt Helen?

9. About what had the second housemaid been "so careful" while Aunt Helen was alive?

10. Is the poet grieved at the passing of his Aunt Helen?

Sonnet LXXXVII

by William Shakespeare

(1564–1616)

Farewell! thou art too dear for my possessing,
And like enough thou know'st thy estimate:°
The charter of thy worth° gives thee releasing,
My bonds in thee are all determinate.
For how do I hold thee but by thy granting?   5
And for that riches where is my deserving?
The cause of this fair gift in me is wanting,
And so my patent back again is swerving.°
Thyself thou gav'st, thy own worth then not knowing,
Or me, to whom thou gav'st it, else mistaking;   10
So thy great gift, upon misprision growing,°
Comes home again, on better judgment making.°
    Thus have I had thee, as a dream doth flatter,
    In sleep a king, but, waking, no such matter.

2. estimate: worth. 3. The . . . worth: the privilege your dignity gave you. 8. my . . . swerving: i.e., the love granted to me is reverting to its original possessor (the phrase suggests a royal patent for a monopoly). 11. upon misprision growing: arising out of an erroneous estimate. 12. on . . . making: as a result of a review of the case in a higher court.

1. Such words as *estimate* (line 2), *charter* (line 3), *determinate* (line 4), and *patent* (line 8) are common technical terms in the language of law and finance. What other "business" terms do you find in the poem?

2. *Dear,* of course, means expensive. What else does it mean? What is the ironic effect of the use of the word *dear* in line 1?

3. Consider the emotional intensity of the final couplet. What is its part in the ironic tone of the poem as a whole?

The Maldive Shark

by Herman Melville

(1819–1891)

About the Shark, phlegmatical one,
Pale sot of the Maldive sea,
The sleek little pilot-fish, azure and slim,
How alert in attendance be.
From his saw-pit of mouth, from his charnel of maw   5
They have nothing of harm to dread,
But liquidly glide on his ghastly flank
Or before his Gorgonian head;
Or lurk in the port of serrated teeth
In white triple tiers of glittering gates,   10
And there find a haven when peril's abroad,
An asylum in jaws of the Fates!
They are friends; and friendly they guide him to prey,
Eyes and brains to the dotard lethargic and dull,
Pale ravener of horrible meat.   15

For Study and Writing

1. Explain in detail Melville's use of the following terms: *phlegmatical* (line 1), *sot* (line 2), *dotard* (line 14).

2. What words in the poem express the terrifying aspects of the Shark? Explain.

3. What ironies are implicit in the relationship between the pilot fish and the Shark? (See particularly line 13.)

4. What part does color play in the imagery of this poem?

5. How does Melville manage to make the pilot fish quite as nasty, in their own way, as the Shark himself?

Dust Is the Only Secret

by Emily Dickinson

(1830–1886)

Dust is the only secret,
Death the only one
You cannot find out all about
In his native town:
Nobody knew his father,   5
Never was a boy,
Hadn't any playmates
Or early history.

Industrious, laconic,
Punctual, sedate,   10
Bolder than a Brigand,
Swifter than a Fleet,
Builds like a bird too,
Christ robs the nest . . .
Robin after robin   15
Smuggled to rest!

For Study and Writing

1. The great American poet Emily Dickinson never married and lived most of her life seeing almost no one but her immediate family and a very few friends in her home in Amherst, Massachusetts. Yet from this timid, retiring life poured some of the most vigorous and daring images in the language. Consider, for example, line 14: "Christ robs the nest." In context, it is very far indeed from being irreverent, but it produces the kind of shock that we experience in John Donne's poetry ("Batter My Heart," for example). Compare the two poets in this respect.

2. This poem is not about the death of any specific person. Do you regard it, consequently, with more detachment than you do, for example, "Aunt Helen"?

3. Although the poem is not about any particular person's death, there is, through the device of personification, an individual in it who is described in some detail. Why may Death be said to be "Industrious, laconic,/Punctual, sedate"?

4. The personification of Death is a fairly common occurrence in literature and in less formal human utterance. Shakespeare has Hamlet speak of "this fell sergeant, Death," who is "strict in his arrest." When the Gen-

tleman from San Francisco falls in the
reading room, he struggles with death
as with a person. What sort of person
is Death in the first stanza of Emily

Dickinson's poem? Do you find an
element of the comic in her choice?
What happens to the personification
by the end of the poem?

The World Is Too Much with Us

by William Wordsworth

(1770–1850)

The world is too much with us; late and soon,
Getting and spending, we lay waste our powers;
Little we see in Nature that is ours;
We have given our hearts away, a sordid boon!
This Sea that bares her bosom to the moon,   5
The winds that will be howling at all hours,
And are upgathered now like sleeping flowers;
For this, for everything, we are out of tune;
It moves us not. Great God! I'd rather be
A Pagan suckled in a creed outworn;   10
So might I, standing on this pleasant lea,
Have glimpses that would make me less forlorn;
Have sight of Proteus rising from the sea;
Or hear old Triton blow his wreathèd horn.

For Study and Writing

1. Although humor and satire are
frequently (perhaps in some degree
always) ironic, irony may also appear
in the expression of other quite different moods and attitudes. Compare
"The World Is Too Much with Us"
to other poems in this section with this
fact in mind.

2. Proteus and Triton (lines 13 and

14) are sea gods in Greek mythology.
To what ends does the poet employ
this classical allusion?

3. What precisely does the poet
mean and not mean by the word
world in line 1?

4. What exactly does he mean by
"we are out of tune" (line 8)?

5. Do you consider "Great God!"
(line 9) an oath? a prayer? an exclamation? Explain.

Ode on the Death of a Favourite Cat
Drowned in a Tub of Goldfishes

by *Thomas Gray*

(*1716–1771*)

'Twas on a lofty vase's side,
Where China's gayest art had dy'd
   The azure flowers that blow;
Demurest of the tabby kind,
The pensive Selima reclined,   5
   Gazed on the lake below.

Her conscious tail her joy declared;
The fair round face, the snowy beard,
   The velvet of her paws,
Her coat, that with the tortoise vies,   10
Her ears of jet, and emerald eyes,
   She saw; and purred applause.

Still had she gaz'd; but 'midst the tide
Two angel forms were seen to glide,
   The genii of the stream: 15
Their scaly armour's Tyrian° hue
Thro' richest purple to the view
   Betray'd a golden gleam.

The hapless nymph with wonder saw:
A whisker first and then a claw,   20
   With many an ardent wish,
She stretch'd in vain to reach the prize.
What female heart can gold despise?
   What cat's averse to fish?

Presumptuous maid! with looks intent   25
Again she stretch'd, again she bent,
   Nor knew the gulf between.
(Malignant Fate sat by, and smil'd)
The slipp'ry verge her feet beguil'd
   She tumbled headlong in.   30

---

16. **Tyrian:** purple. In ancient times purple dye was made from shellfish at the port of Tyre in Phoenicia.

Eight times emerging from the flood
She mew'd to ev'ry watery god,
    Some speedy aid to send.
No dolphin° came, no nereid° stirr'd:
Nor cruel Tom, nor Susan heard.   35
    A fav'rite has no friend!

From hence, ye beauties, undeceiv'd,
Know, one false step is ne'er retriev'd,
    And be with caution bold.
Not all that tempts your wand'ring eyes   40
And heedless hearts, is lawful prize;
    Nor all that glisters, gold.

34. dolphin: In Greek legend the poet Arion, who had been cast adrift by pirates, was brought safely to shore by a dolphin; **nereid:** sea nymph.

For Study and Writing

1. What object or objects does the verb *saw* in line 12 have?

2. Discuss the mock-heroic tone of this poem. What part does Gray's use of classical allusion play in establishing this tone?

3. What is the exact meaning in context of *undeceiv'd* (line 37)?

4. To whom, besides the late Selima, is the moral admonition of this poem addressed? What exactly is this moral admonition?

5. On what ironical quality in human life is the poem based?

Captain Carpenter
by *John Crowe Ransom*
(*1888–*)

Captain Carpenter rose up in his prime
Put on his pistols and went riding out
But had got wellnigh nowhere at that time
Till he fell in with ladies in a rout.°

It was a pretty lady and all her train   5
That played with him so sweetly but before
An hour she'd taken a sword with all her main
And twined° him of his nose for evermore.

4. rout: band, retinue. **8. twined:** parted.

Captain Carpenter mounted up one day
And rode straightway into a stranger rogue   10
That looked unchristian but be that as may
The Captain did not wait upon prologue.

But drew upon him out of his great heart
The other swung against him with a club
And cracked his two legs at the shinny part   15
And let him roll and stick like any tub.

Captain Carpenter rode many a time
From male and female took he sundry harms
He met the wife of Satan crying "I'm
The she-wolf bids you shall bear no more arms."   20

Their strokes and counters whistled in the wind
I wish he had delivered half his blows
But where she should have made off like a hind
The bitch bit off his arms at the elbows.

And Captain Carpenter parted with his ears   25
To a black devil that used him in this wise
O Jesus ere his threescore and ten years
Another had plucked out his sweet blue eyes.

Captain Carpenter got up on his roan
And sallied from the gate in hell's despite   30
I heard him asking in the grimmest tone
If any enemy yet there was to fight?

"To any adversary it is fame
If he risk to be wounded by my tongue
Or burnt in two beneath my red heart's flame   35
Such are the perils he is cast among.

"But if he can he has a pretty choice
From an anatomy with little to lose
Whether he cut my tongue and take my voice
Or whether it be my round red heart he choose."   40

It was the neatest knave that ever was seen
Stepping in perfume from his lady's bower

Who at this word put in his merry mien
And fell on Captain Carpenter like a tower.

I would not knock old fellows in the dust   45
But there lay Captain Carpenter on his back
His weapons were the old heart in his bust
And a blade shook between rotten teeth alack.

The rogue in scarlet and grey soon knew his mind
He wished to get his trophy and depart   50
With gentle apology and touch refined
He pierced him and produced the Captain's heart.

God's mercy rest on Captain Carpenter now
I thought him Sirs an honest gentleman
Citizen husband soldier and scholar enow   55
Let jangling kites eat of him if they can.

But God's deep curses follow after those
That shore him of his goodly nose and ears
His legs and strong arms at the two elbows
And eyes that had not watered seventy years.   60

The curse of hell upon the sleek upstart
That got the Captain finally on his back
And took the red red vitals of his heart
And made the kites to whet their beaks clack clack.

For Study and Writing

1. What is the sequence of events narrated in "Captain Carpenter"?

2. What sort of man is Captain Carpenter? What various methods does the poet use to describe him?

3. What details in the poem assure us that its action does not take place in the everyday world of reality, but in a world of romantic allegory and symbol?

4. In the seventh stanza (line 27) appears a reference to the Captain's "threescore and ten years." His age is again alluded to in stanza fifteen (line 60). What meaning do you think these references contribute to the poem?

5. Notice Ransom's apparently whimsical use of archaic terms and situations in this poem. Note too his use of rather shocking images and epithets. Perhaps there is even a suggestion of the comic or absurd when such devices are applied to the story of the defeat and death of a noble old man. Is the poem meant to be funny?

A PRACTICE TEST

I. The following passage describes a moonlight stroll taken by a gallant young army officer and a charming young girl.

> "Oh, those stars, those stars!" Miss Rebecca would say, turning her twinkling green eyes up towards them. "I feel myself almost a spirit when I gaze upon them."
>
> "Oh . . . ah . . . yes, so do I exactly, Miss Sharp," the other enthusiast replied. "You don't mind my cigar, do you, Miss Sharp?" Miss Sharp loved the smell of a cigar out of doors beyond anything in the world . . . and she just tasted one too, in the prettiest way possible, and gave a little puff, and a little scream, and a little giggle, and restored the delicacy to the captain; who twirled his moustache, and straightway puffed it into a blaze that glowed quite red in the dark plantation and swore . . . "Jove . . . aw . . . Gad . . . aw . . . it's the finest segaw I ever smoked in the world . . . aw," . . . for his intellect and conversation were alike brilliant and becoming to a heavy young dragoon.

1. Suppose that Miss Sharp had kept her lovely face raised as they strolled and had said, "I really feel more than human when I look at such stars." In such a case how might the reader's impressions of Miss Sharp differ from those evoked by the opening lines of the passage quoted above?

2. Why does the author use the term "the other enthusiast" (lines 4–5) to denote the captain? What is meant by "the dark plantation" in line 11?

3. The adjective *little* is repeated three times in lines 8–9. What effect does this usage have on the description of Miss Sharp's actions?

4. What fairly common circumstance is expressed through a fairly common image in lines 10 and 11? In what detail is the image presented here unusually?

5. How is Miss Sharp's success expressed in this paragraph?

6. What, apparently, does the author assume about dragoon (cavalry) officers?

II. Answer the following questions after a careful reading of the poem.

Provide, Provide

by *Robert Frost*

(1874–1963)

The witch that came (the withered hag)
To wash the steps with pail and rag
Was once the beauty Abishag,°

The picture pride of Hollywood.
Too many fall from great and good   5
For you to doubt the likelihood.

Die early and avoid the fate.
Or if predestined to die late,
Make up your mind to die in state.

Make the whole stock exchange your own!   10
If need be occupy a throne,
Where nobody can call *you* crone.

Some have relied on what they knew;
Others on being simply true.
What worked for them might work for you.   15

No memory of having starred
Atones for later disregard,
Or keeps the end from being hard.

Better to go down dignified
With boughten friendship at your side   20
Than none at all. Provide, provide!

3. Abishag: King David's beautiful young attendant in his old age (I Kings 1:1–4).

1. What is the image in the first two lines of this poem?
2. The sentence in the first stanza runs on to the end of the first line of the second stanza. Explain the effect of this device.
3. What is the relation of the fifth stanza to the poem as a whole?
4. How does the poet establish a sort of universality in time in this poem?

5. What irony is implicit in the word *dignified* as it is used in the context of the final stanza?

III. Write a well-organized essay evaluating the following statement through a discussion of three literary works you have encountered in this section ("Ironic images") of this course. Do not hesitate to use for references and comparisons other pertinent parts of your reading.

> What, however, distinguishes the satirist from most other creative writers is the extent to which he is dependent on the agreement or approval of his readers.
>
> JAMES SUTHERLAND, *English Satire* (Cambridge, 1962).

The essence of tragedy is that although life is in itself a positive good, an inexplicable, terrible shadow falls across it. The tragic image of man is that of a thwarted god, a creature who is endowed with the priceless attributes of reason and soul but who must, for reasons intensely felt but only partly understood, suffer disaster because of the very nature of the universe. Note that it is not disaster alone that evokes the tragic sense — it is the combination, or rather the collision, of man at his best with the inexorable enmity of things as they are.

Perhaps the tragic is best exemplified in terms of death, which is the customary (though not the inevitable) catastrophe in formal tragedy. From the tragic point of view, death appears as a kind of intolerable injustice that a being such as man should be able to overcome. Man, after all, is the only creature who can, strictly speaking, be afraid to die — the only creature who is capable of grasping the concept of death. However unpleasant the reactions of a calf led to slaughter may be, they are purely physical. Man alone cries out, "I cannot die. I should be immortal!" And man alone knows, "I must die." The tension resulting from this knowledge and signaled by this cry characterizes the tragic. Passion and knowledge, presented as awe-inspiring, almost godlike qualities, produce that moving spectacle, exclusively the property of humanity at its greatest: tragic suffering.

In the tragic view of life, *fall* is a key word. It implies both height and depth, both ascent and descent. One cannot, after all, fall from the bottom. The Greeks understood tragedy to be the fall of a great and able man, because of some flaw in his nature, some inevitable fault in his actions, from a place of prominence and power to the depth of utter ruin, often (though not always) given form as death. Such a classic tragic figure must *suffer* ruin, and to do so he must understand his fall and his own part in bringing it about. He must also be capable of valuing what he has lost, the place from which he has fallen. A great change occurs in everyone and everything involved in such a fall. People and events are seen and understood in a new light. As W. B. Yeats says in his poem "Easter 1916" (page 802):

All changed, changed utterly:
A terrible beauty is born.

This "terrible beauty" is the effect of tragedy as a literary form; it renders appealing the tragic as it appears in the events of actual human life, even in those that may not be tragedies in the strict classical sense. It results from a double vision — a vision at one and the same time of both the grandeur and the doom of man. It comes from an almost unbearable look at human greatness in the context of mortality.

Artistically speaking, if disaster smites an ordinary person through no fault of his own or through events to which he is oblivious (if, for example, he is struck down by an air-conditioner falling from a thirtieth-floor window), we do not call the event tragic. It is in essence pathetic. Indeed it may even be comic. The death of the Gentleman from San Francisco is not tragic. He has no idea that he is going to die; he is operating on the bland, unthinking assumption that his life will continue indefinitely. The tragic figure must be uncommon, extraordinary; and he must be aware of what is happening to himself.

Tragic figures of a high order have complex characters. Although they may do great evil, we do not think of them as being primarily villains or wicked men. What attracts our attention is their greatness as they battle with their destinies. A story that merely confronts good heroes with bad villains is melodrama, an art form that rarely contains even the slightest trace of true tragedy.

Most of the tragedies of Shakespeare and his contemporaries conform to the ancient Greek convention that the subject of tragedy must be a person of great eminence — a king, a prince, an acknowledged hero. This convention is suitable for audiences drawn from societies in which greatness is closely linked to political and social status and in which such status is usually conferred by birth rather than achieved by luck or effort. Yet a society that does not have kings or princes or heroes of the traditional kind is not without the possibility of tragic characters. The criteria of tragic greatness are stature, dignity, strength of character, and comprehension — the profound comprehension that brings most intense suffering. As the world of man changes, these criteria may appear in quite different forms. In the works now to be studied, you will observe the differences among two kings, Oedipus and Lear, and a man named Kurtz.

Oedipus the King

by Sophocles (496?–406 B.C.)

TRANSLATED BY DUDLEY FITTS AND ROBERT FITZGERALD

It is seldom that the greatest accomplishments in an art form come in one of the earliest periods in the development of that form, but such is the case of tragic drama: the ancient Greeks, who invented it, carried it to unsurpassed heights. Though imitated for many centuries, Greek tragedy has never been equalled in its classic form. Later writers who attained equal heights in tragedy used a different approach and form, such as romantic tragedy, of which Shakespeare is the foremost master.

Among the splendors of Greek tragedy, the single play that looms above the rest in stark, menacing grandeur is Sophocles's *Oedipus the King* (in Greek, *Oedipus Tyrannus;* in Latin, *Oedipus Rex*).

Most Greek tragedies were written as parts of trilogies, to be performed together in sequence in open-air theaters. The later parts of Sophocles's dramatization of the doom of the royal house of Thebes are *Oedipus at Colonus* and *Antigone*. Unlike the parts of many earlier Greek tragedies, each of the parts of this trilogy is a drama that can stand alone.

In contrast to later theater, that of the Greeks deals largely with events that have occurred before the beginning of the play and with actions that happen offstage. What happens onstage is the tying together of threads of cause and effect and motive. In the Oedipus story, all violent actions except the final self-punishments have taken place long ago. The dramatic fascination — increased, not lessened, by the fact that the audience knows the story well — lies in seeing a proud man's pursuit of truth draw him relentlessly, step by step, to frightful self-knowledge.

Some years before the play begins, Thebes had been terrorized by a monster called the Sphinx, which had the head and the breast of a woman on the body of a lioness. She stopped all who passed and demanded the answer to a riddle, on pain of death. None had been able to solve the riddle, and countless victims had died. Then young Oedipus, coming to the city as a venturesome and ambitious stranger, gave the correct answer [1] and slew the Sphinx. He was welcomed as liberator and King, and he married the widowed Queen of Thebes.

---

[1] The riddle: What creature walks on four legs in the morning, on two in midday, and on three in the evening? The answer: Man, who crawls on all fours as an infant, then walks on two legs, then uses the third leg of a cane in old age.

OEDIPUS, *King of Thebes, supposed son of Polybos and Meropê, King and Queen of Corinth*

IOKASTÊ, *wife of Oedipus and widow of the late King Laïos*

KREON, *brother of Iokastê, a prince of Thebes*

TEIRESIAS, *a blind seer who serves Apollo*

PRIEST

MESSENGER, *from Corinth*

SHEPHERD, *former servant of Laïos*

SECOND MESSENGER, *from the palace*

CHORUS OF THEBAN ELDERS

CHORAGOS, *leader of the Chorus*

ANTIGONE and ISMENE, *young daughters of Oedipus and Iokastê (They appear in the Éxodos but do not speak.)*

SUPPLIANTS, GUARDS, SERVANTS

THE SCENE. *Before the palace of* OEDIPUS, *King of Thebes. A central door and two lateral doors open onto a platform which runs the length of the façade. On the platform, right and left, are altars; and three steps lead down into the orchêstra, or chorus-ground. At the beginning of the action, these steps are crowded by suppliants who have brought branches and chaplets of olive leaves and who sit in various attitudes of despair.*

PROLOGUE

OEDIPUS *enters.*

OEDIPUS. My children, generations of the living
In the line of Kadmos,° nursed at his ancient hearth:
Why have you strewn yourselves before these altars
In supplication, with your boughs and garlands?
The breath of incense rises from the city   5
With a sound of prayer and lamentation.
                                      Children,

2. **Kadmos:** the founder of Thebes and great-grandfather of Laïos. See Scene I, lines 254–55. The "line of Kadmos" would be all the citizens of Thebes, just as Thebes itself is called the "house of Kadmos." See Prologue, line 32.

I would not have you speak through messengers,
And therefore I have come myself to hear you —
I, Oedipus, who bear the famous name.

[*To a* PRIEST] You, there, since you are eldest in the company,   10
Speak for them all, tell me what preys upon you,
Whether you come in dread, or crave some blessing:
Tell me, and never doubt that I will help you
In every way I can; I should be heartless
Were I not moved to find you suppliant here.   15

PRIEST.   Great Oedipus, O powerful king of Thebes!
You see how all the ages of our people
Cling to your altar steps: here are boys
Who can barely stand alone, and here are priests
By weight of age, as I am a priest of God,   20
And young men chosen from those yet unmarried;
As for the others, all that multitude,
They wait with olive chaplets in the squares,
At the two shrines of Pallas,° and where Apollo°
Speaks in the glowing embers.

                            Your own eyes   25
Must tell you: Thebes is tossed on a murdering sea
And can not lift her head from the death surge.
A rust consumes the buds and fruits of the earth;
The herds are sick; children die unborn,
And labor is vain. The god of plague and pyre   30
Raids like detestable lightning through the city,
And all the house of Kadmos is laid waste,
All emptied, and all darkened: Death alone
Battens upon the misery of Thebes.

You are not one of the immortal gods, we know;   35
Yet we have come to you to make our prayer
As to the man surest in mortal ways
And wisest in the ways of God. You saved us
From the Sphinx, that flinty singer, and the tribute
We paid to her so long; yet you were never   40

---

24. Pallas: Athenê, the goddess regarded as the preserver of the state and the patroness of the fine and useful arts, particularly agriculture; **Apollo:** the god of punishment, and also the god of healing, of music, and of prophecy. He is the patron of Teiresias and of the oracle at Delphi.

Better informed than we, nor could we teach you:
A god's touch, it seems, enabled you to help us.

Therefore, O mighty power, we turn to you:
Find us our safety, find us a remedy,
Whether by counsel of the gods or of men. 45
A king of wisdom tested in the past
Can act in a time of troubles, and act well.
Noblest of men, restore
Life to your city! Think how all men call you
Liberator for your boldness long ago; 50
Ah, when your years of kingship are remembered,
Let them not say *We rose, but later fell* —
Keep the State from going down in the storm!
Once, years ago, with happy augury,
You brought us fortune; be the same again! 55
No man questions your power to rule the land:
But rule over men, not over a dead city!
Ships are only hulls, high walls are nothing,
When no life moves in the empty passageways.

OEDIPUS.   Poor children! You may be sure I know 60
All that you longed for in your coming here.
I know that you are deathly sick; and yet,
Sick as you are, not one is as sick as I.
Each of you suffers in himself alone
His anguish, not another's; but my spirit 65
Groans for the city, for myself, for you.

I was not sleeping, you are not waking me.
No, I have been in tears for a long while
And in my restless thought walked many ways.
In all my search I found one remedy, 70
And I have adopted it: I have sent Kreon,
Son of Menoikeus, brother of the Queen,
To Delphi, Apollo's place of revelation,
To learn there, if he can,
What act or pledge of mine may save the city. 75
I have counted the days, and now, this very day,
I am troubled, for he has overstayed his time.
What is he doing? He has been gone too long.

Yet whenever he comes back, I should do ill   80
Not to take any action the god orders.
PRIEST. It is a timely promise. At this instant
    They tell me Kreon is here.
OEDIPUS.   O Lord Apollo!
May his news be fair as his face is radiant!
PRIEST. Good news, I gather! he is crowned with bay,°
    The chaplet is thick with berries.
OEDIPUS.   We shall soon know;   85
He is near enough to hear us now.

Enter KREON.

                    O prince:
Brother: son of Menoikeus:
What answer do you bring us from the god?
KREON. A strong one. I can tell you, great afflictions
    Will turn out well, if they are taken well.   90
OEDIPUS. What was the oracle? These vague words
    Leave me still hanging between hope and fear.
KREON. Is it your pleasure to hear me with all these
    Gathered around us? I am prepared to speak,
    But should we not go in?
OEDIPUS.   Speak to them all,   95
It is for them I suffer, more than for myself.
KREON. Then I will tell you what I heard at Delphi.

In plain words
The god commands us to expel from the land of Thebes
An old defilement we are sheltering.   100
It is a deathly thing, beyond cure;
We must not let it feed upon us longer.
OEDIPUS. What defilement? How shall we rid ourselves of it?
KREON. By exile or death, blood for blood. It was
    Murder that brought the plague-wind on the city.   105
OEDIPUS. Murder of whom? Surely the god has named him?
KREON. My lord: Laïos once ruled this land,
    Before you came to govern us.
OEDIPUS.   I know;

84. bay: the laurel, sacred to Apollo, worn in a chaplet or wreath around the
head as a symbol of victory.

I learned of him from others; I never saw him.

KREON. He was murdered; and Apollo commands us now   110
To take revenge upon whoever killed him.

OEDIPUS. Upon whom? Where are they? Where shall we find a clue
To solve that crime, after so many years?

KREON. Here in this land, he said. Search reveals
Things that escape an inattentive man.   115

OEDIPUS. Tell me: Was Laïos murdered in his house,
Or in the fields, or in some foreign country?

KREON. He said he planned to make a pilgrimage.
He did not come home again.

OEDIPUS.   And was there no one,
No witness, no companion, to tell what happened?   120

KREON. They were all killed but one, and he got away
So frightened that he could remember one thing only.

OEDIPUS. What was that one thing? One may be the key
To everything, if we resolve to use it.

KREON. He said that a band of highwaymen attacked them,   125
Outnumbered them, and overwhelmed the king.

OEDIPUS. Strange, that a highwayman should be so daring —
Unless some faction here bribed him to do it.

KREON. We thought of that. But after Laïos' death
New troubles arose and we had no avenger.   130

OEDIPUS. What troubles could prevent your hunting down the killers?

KREON. The riddling Sphinx's song
Made us deaf to all mysteries but her own.

OEDIPUS. Then once more I must bring what is dark to light.
It is most fitting that Apollo shows,   135
As you do, this compunction for the dead.
You shall see how I stand by you, as I should,
Avenging this country and the god as well,
And not as though it were for some distant friend,
But for my own sake, to be rid of evil.   140
Whoever killed King Laïos might — who knows? —
Lay violent hands even on me — and soon.
I act for the murdered king in my own interest.

Come, then, my children: leave the altar steps,
Lift up your olive boughs!

And summon the people of Kadmos to gather here.
I will do all that I can; you may tell them that. *Exit a* PAGE.
So, with the help of God,
We shall be saved — or else indeed we are lost.

PRIEST. Let us rise, children. It was for this we came, 150
And now the king has promised it.
Phoibos° has sent us an oracle; may he descend
Himself to save us and drive out the plague.

[*Exeunt* OEDIPUS *and* KREON *into the palace by the central
door. The* PRIEST *and the* SUPPLIANTS *disperse R and L. After
a short pause the* CHORUS *enters the orchêstra.*]

152. Phoibos: Apollo; the name means "light" or "pure."

PÁRODOS *

CHORUS. [STROPHE I

What is God° singing in his profound
Delphi of gold and shadow? 155
What oracle for Thebes, the sunwhipped city?
Fear unjoints me, the roots of my heart tremble.
Now I remember, O Healer, your power, and wonder:
Will you send doom like a sudden cloud, or weave it
Like nightfall of the past? 160
Speak to me, tell me, O
Child of golden Hope, immortal Voice.

[ANTISTROPHE I

Let me pray to Athenê, the immortal daughter of Zeus,
And to Artemis° her sister
Who keeps her famous throne in the market ring, 165

* Párodos: the "parade" or entrance of the Chorus. *Strophe* and *antistrophe* are
alternating stanzas of choral song. When singing the strophe, the Chorus turned
in one direction. The antistrophe, which followed, was constructed symmetrically
to the strophe, and as it was sung, the Chorus turned in the opposite direction.
154. God: Apollo, whose oracle is at Delphi. Four lines below he is named by
another of his attributes: the Healer. 164. Artemis: twin sister of Apollo, who has
many of his attributes and is regarded especially as the goddess of flocks and of
hunting.

And to Apollo, archer° from distant heaven —
O gods, descend! Like three streams leap against
The fires of our grief, the fires of darkness;
Be swift to bring us rest!
As in the old time from the brilliant house   170
Of air you stepped to save us, come again!

Now our afflictions have no end,   [STROPHE 2
Now all our stricken host lies down
And no man fights off death with his mind;
The noble plowland bears no grain,   175
And groaning mothers can not bear —
See, how our lives like birds take wing,
Like sparks that fly when a fire soars,
To the shore of the god of evening.

The plague burns on, it is pitiless,   [ANTISTROPHE 2
Though pallid children laden with death   181
Lie unwept in the stony ways,
And old gray women by every path
Flock to the strand about the altars
There to strike their breasts and cry   185
Worship of Phoibos in wailing prayers:
Be kind, God's golden child!

There are no swords in this attack by fire,   [STROPHE 3
No shields, but we are ringed with cries.
Send the besieger plunging from our homes   190
Into the vast sea-room of the Atlantic
Or into the waves that foam eastward of Thrace —
For the day ravages what the night spares —
Destroy our enemy, lord of the thunder!
Let him be riven by lightning from heaven!   195

Phoibos Apollo, stretch the sun's bowstring,   [ANTISTROPHE 3
That golden cord, until it sing for us,
Flashing arrows in heaven!
                    Artemis, Huntress,
Race with flaring lights upon our mountains!
O scarlet god, O golden-banded brow,   200

166. archer: Apollo is also the god of archery. See Párodos, lines 196–98.

O Theban Bacchos in a storm of Maenads,°

Enter OEDIPUS.

Whirl upon Death, that all the Undying hate!
Come with blinding torches, come in joy!

201. **Theban . . . Maenads:** Bacchos (or Dionysos), the son of Zeus and Semele, who was the daughter of Kadmos, was born in Thebes and regarded as its patron. He is the god of wine and fertility, and is called "scarlet" here because he is flushed from drinking. The Maenads (or Bacchae) are his priestesses, who worked themselves into a kind of frenzy (hence "storm" and "whirl") at the Dionysiac festivals, out of which the Greek drama is believed to have evolved (see Aristotle's *Poetics,* Chapter 4).

SCENE I

OEDIPUS. Is this your prayer? It may be answered. Come,
  Listen to me, act as the crisis demands,   205
  And you shall have relief from all these evils.

  Until now I was a stranger to this tale,
  As I had been a stranger to the crime.
  Could I track down the murderer without a clue?
  But now, friends,   210
  As one who became a citizen after the murder,
  I make this proclamation to all Thebans:

  If any man knows by whose hand Laïos, son of Labdakos,°
  Met his death, I direct that man to tell me everything,
  No matter what he fears for having so long withheld it. 215
  Let it stand as promised that no further trouble
  Will come to him, but he may leave the land in safety.

  Moreover: If anyone knows the murderer to be foreign,
  Let him not keep silent: he shall have his reward from me.
  However, if he does conceal it; if any man   220
  Fearing for his friend or for himself disobeys this edict,
  Hear what I propose to do:

  I solemnly forbid the people of this country,
  Where power and throne are mine, ever to receive that man
  Or speak to him, no matter who he is, or let him 225

213. **Labdakos:** See Scene I, lines 254–55.

Join in sacrifice, lustration, or in prayer.
I decree that he be driven from every house,
Being, as he is, corruption itself to us: the Delphic
Voice of Apollo has pronounced this revelation.
Thus I associate myself with the oracle   230
And take the side of the murdered king.

As for the criminal, I pray to God —
Whether it be a lurking thief, or one of a number —
I pray that that man's life be consumed in evil and wretchedness.
And as for me, this curse applies no less   235
If it should turn out that the culprit is my guest here,
Sharing my hearth.

                    You have heard the penalty.

I lay it on you now to attend to this
For my sake, for Apollo's, for the sick
Sterile city that heaven has abandoned.   240
Suppose the oracle had given you no command:
Should this defilement go uncleansed for ever?
You should have found the murderer: your king,
A noble king, had been destroyed!

                     Now I,
Having the power that he held before me,   245
Having his bed, begetting children there
Upon his wife, as he would have, had he lived —
Their son would have been my children's brother,
If Laïos had had luck in fatherhood!
(And now his bad fortune has struck him down)   250
I say I take the son's part, just as though
I were his son, to press the fight for him
And see it won! I'll find the hand that brought
Death to Labdakos' and Polydoros' child,
Heir of Kadmos' and Agenor's line.°   255
And as for those who fail me,
May the gods deny them the fruit of the earth,
Fruit of the womb, and may they rot utterly!

254–55. Labdakos' . . . line: The child is Laïos, whose father was Labdakos.
Labdakos' father was Polydoros, the son of Kadmos, and Kadmos' father was
Agenor.

Let them be wretched as we are wretched, and worse!

For you, for loyal Thebans, and for all 260
Who find my actions right, I pray the favor
Of justice, and of all the immortal gods.

CHORAGOS. Since I am under oath, my lord, I swear
I did not do the murder, I can not name
The murderer. Phoibos ordained the search; 265
Why did he not say who the culprit was?

OEDIPUS. An honest question. But no man in the world
Can make the gods do more than the gods will.

CHORAGOS. There is an alternative, I think —

OEDIPUS.   Tell me.
Any or all, you must not fail to tell me. 270

CHORAGOS. A lord clairvoyant to the lord Apollo,
As we all know, is the skilled Teiresias.
One might learn much about this from him, Oedipus.

OEDIPUS. I am not wasting time:
Kreon spoke of this, and I have sent for him — 275
Twice, in fact; it is strange that he is not here.

CHORAGOS. The other matter — that old report — seems useless.

OEDIPUS. What was that? I am interested in all reports.

CHORAGOS. The king was said to have been killed by highwaymen.

OEDIPUS. I know. But we have no witnesses to that. 280

CHORAGOS. If the killer can feel a particle of dread,
Your curse will bring him out of hiding!

OEDIPUS.   No.
The man who dared that act will fear no curse.

Enter the blind seer TEIRESIAS, *led by a* PAGE.

CHORAGOS. But there is one man who may detect the criminal.
This is Teiresias, this is the holy prophet 285
In whom, alone of all men, truth was born.

OEDIPUS. Teiresias: seer: student of mysteries,
Of all that's taught and all that no man tells,
Secrets of Heaven and secrets of the earth:
Blind though you are, you know the city lies 290
Sick with plague; and from this plague, my lord,
We find that you alone can guard or save us.

Possibly you did not hear the messengers? Apollo, when we sent to him,
Sent us back word that this great pestilence   295
Would lift, but only if we established clearly
The identity of those who murdered Laïos.
They must be killed or exiled.

                              Can you use
Birdflight° or any art of divination
To purify yourself, and Thebes, and me   300
From this contagion? We are in your hands.
There is no fairer duty
Than that of helping others in distress.

TEIRESIAS. How dreadful knowledge of the truth can be
    When there's no help in truth! I knew this well,   305
    But did not act on it: else I should not have come.

OEDIPUS. What is troubling you? Why are your eyes so cold?

TEIRESIAS. Let me go home. Bear your own fate, and I'll
    Bear mine. It is better so: trust what I say.

OEDIPUS. What you say is ungracious and unhelpful   310
    To your native country. Do not refuse to speak.

TEIRESIAS. When it comes to speech, your own is neither temperate
    Nor opportune. I wish to be more prudent.

OEDIPUS. In God's name, we all beg you —

TEIRESIAS.   You are all ignorant.
    No; I will never tell you what I know.   315
    Now it is my misery; then, it would be yours.

OEDIPUS. What! You do know something, and will not tell us?
    You would betray us all and wreck the State?

TEIRESIAS. I do not intend to torture myself, or you.
    Why persist in asking? You will not persuade me.   320

OEDIPUS. What a wicked old man you are! You'd try a stone's
    Patience! Out with it! Have you no feeling at all?

TEIRESIAS. You call me unfeeling. If you could only see
    The nature of your own feelings . . .

OEDIPUS.   Why,
    Who would not feel as I do? Who could endure   325
    Your arrogance toward the city?

299. Birdflight: Seers such as Teiresias could prophesy from the flight of birds. See Scene I, lines 380–84; Ode I, line 469; Scene III, line 920.

TEIRESIAS. What does it matter?
Whether I speak or not, it is bound to come.
OEDIPUS. Then, if "it" is bound to come, you are bound to tell me.
TEIRESIAS. No, I will not go on. Rage as you please.
OEDIPUS. Rage? Why not!

And I'll tell you what I think: 330
You planned it, you had it done, you all but
Killed him with your own hands: if you had eyes,
I'd say the crime was yours, and yours alone.
TEIRESIAS. So? I charge you, then,
Abide by the proclamation you have made: 335
From this day forth
Never speak again to these men or to me;
You yourself are the pollution of this country.
OEDIPUS. You dare say that! Can you possibly think you have
Some way of going free, after such insolence? 340
TEIRESIAS. I have gone free. It is the truth sustains me.
OEDIPUS. Who taught you shamelessness? It was not your craft.
TEIRESIAS. You did. You made me speak. I did not want to.
OEDIPUS. Speak what? Let me hear it again more clearly.
TEIRESIAS. Was it not clear before? Are you tempting me? 345
OEDIPUS. I did not understand it. Say it again.
TEIRESIAS. I say that you are the murderer whom you seek.
OEDIPUS. Now twice you have spat out infamy. You'll pay for it!
TEIRESIAS. Would you care for more? Do you wish to be really angry?
OEDIPUS. Say what you will. Whatever you say is worthless. 350
TEIRESIAS. I say you live in hideous shame with those
Most dear to you. You can not see the evil.
OEDIPUS. Can you go on babbling like this for ever?
TEIRESIAS. I can, if there is power in truth.
OEDIPUS. There is:
But not for you, not for you, 355
You sightless, witless, senseless, mad old man!
TEIRESIAS. You are the madman. There is no one here
Who will not curse you soon, as you curse me.
OEDIPUS. You child of total night! I would not touch you;
Neither would any man who sees the sun. 360
TEIRESIAS. True: it is not from you my fate will come.
That lies within Apollo's competence,

As it is his concern.

OEDIPUS.   Tell me, who made
These fine discoveries? Kreon? or someone else?

TEIRESIAS. Kreon is no threat. You weave your own doom.   365

OEDIPUS. Wealth, power, craft of statesmanship!
Kingly position, everywhere admired!
What savage envy is stored up against these,
If Kreon, whom I trusted, Kreon my friend,
For this great office which the city once   370
Put in my hands unsought — if for this power
Kreon desires in secret to destroy me!

He has bought this decrepit fortune-teller, this
Collector of dirty pennies, this prophet fraud —
Why, he is no more clairvoyant than I am!

                                     Tell us: 375
Has your mystic mummery ever approached the truth?
When that hellcat the Sphinx was performing here,
What help were you to these people?
Her magic was not for the first man who came along:
It demanded a real exorcist. Your birds —   380
What good were they? or the gods, for the matter of that?
But I came by,
Oedipus, the simple man, who knows nothing —
I thought it out for myself, no birds helped me!
And this is the man you think you can destroy,   385
That you may be close to Kreon when he's king!
Well, you and your friend Kreon, it seems to me,
Will suffer most. If you were not an old man,
You would have paid already for your plot.

CHORAGOS. We can not see that his words or yours   390
Have been spoken except in anger, Oedipus,
And of anger we have no need. How to accomplish
The god's will best: that is what most concerns us.

TEIRESIAS. You are a king. But where argument's concerned
I am your man, as much a king as you.   395
I am not your servant, but Apollo's.
I have no need of Kreon or Kreon's name.

Listen to me. You mock my blindness, do you?

But I say that you, with both your eyes, are blind:
You can not see the wretchedness of your life,   400
Nor in whose house you live, no, nor with whom.
Who are your father and mother? Can you tell me?
You do not even know the blind wrongs
That you have done them, on earth and in the world below.
But the double lash of your parents' curse will whip you   405
Out of this land some day, with only night
Upon your precious eyes.
Your cries then — where will they not be heard?
What fastness of Kithairon° will not echo them?
And that bridal-descant of yours — you'll know it then,   410
The song they sang when you came here to Thebes
And found your misguided berthing.
All this, and more, that you can not guess at now,
Will bring you to yourself among your children.

Be angry, then. Curse Kreon. Curse my words.   415
I tell you, no man that walks upon the earth
Shall be rooted out more horribly than you.
OEDIPUS. Am I to bear this from him? — Damnation
Take you! Out of this place! Out of my sight!
TEIRESIAS. I would not have come at all if you had not asked me.   420
OEDIPUS. Could I have told that you'd talk nonsense, that
You'd come here to make a fool of yourself, and of me?
TEIRESIAS. A fool? Your parents thought me sane enough.
OEDIPUS. My parents again! — Wait: who were my parents?
TEIRESIAS. This day will give you a father, and break your heart.   425
OEDIPUS. Your infantile riddles! Your damned abracadabra!
TEIRESIAS. You were a great man once at solving riddles.
OEDIPUS. Mock me with that if you like; you will find it true.
TEIRESIAS. It was true enough. It brought about your ruin.
OEDIPUS. But if it saved this town?
                                                               430
TEIRESIAS. [To the PAGE] Boy, give me your hand.
OEDIPUS. Yes, boy; lead him away.
                                    — While you are here
We can do nothing. Go; leave us in peace.

409. Kithairon: a mountain near Thebes which assumes greater importance
later in the play.

TEIRESIAS. I will go when I have said what I have to say.
How can you hurt me? And I tell you again: 435
The man you have been looking for all this time,
The damned man, the murderer of Laïos,
That man is in Thebes. To your mind he is foreign-born,
But it will soon be shown that he is a Theban,
A revelation that will fail to please.
                            A blind man,   440
Who has his eyes now; a penniless man, who is rich now;
And he will go tapping the strange earth with his staff.
To the children with whom he lives now he will be
Brother and father — the very same; to her
Who bore him, son and husband — the very same   445
Who came to his father's bed, wet with his father's blood.

Enough. Go think that over.
If later you find error in what I have said,
You may say that I have no skill in prophecy.
                Exit TEIRESIAS, *led by his* PAGE. OEDIPUS *goes into the palace.*

ODE I

CHORUS.   [STROPHE I
The Delphic stone of prophecies   450
Remembers ancient regicide
And a still bloody hand.
That killer's hour of flight has come.
He must be stronger than riderless
Coursers of untiring wind,   455
For the son of Zeus° armed with his father's thunder
Leaps in lightning after him;
And the Furies° hold his track, the sad Furies.

Holy Parnassos'° peak of snow   [ANTISTROPHE I
Flashes and blinds that secret man,   460
That all shall hunt him down:

456. son of Zeus: Apollo. 458. Furies: deities of retribution. 459. Parnassos:
mountain in Phokis, sacred to Apollo, near the Delphic oracle.

Though he may roam the forest shade
Like a bull gone wild from pasture
To rage through glooms of stone.
Doom comes down on him; flight will not avail him;   465
For the world's heart calls him desolate,
And the immortal voices follow, for ever follow.

But now a wilder thing is heard   [STROPHE 2
From the old man skilled at hearing Fate in the wing-beat of a bird.
Bewildered as a blown bird, my soul hovers and can not find   470
Foothold in this debate, or any reason or rest of mind.
But no man ever brought — none can bring
Proof of strife between Thebes' royal house,
Labdakos' line, and the son of Polybos;°
And never until now has any man brought word   475
Of Laïos' dark death staining Oedipus the King.

Divine Zeus and Apollo hold   [ANTISTROPHE 2
Perfect intelligence alone of all tales ever told;
And well though this diviner works, he works in his own night;
No man can judge that rough unknown or trust in second sight,
For wisdom changes hands among the wise.   481
Shall I believe my great lord criminal
At a raging word that a blind old man let fall?
I saw him, when the carrion woman° faced him of old,
Prove his heroic mind. These evil words are lies.   485

474. son of Polybos: Oedipus. Polybos, the King of Corinth, raised Oedipus as
his son after shepherds had brought the infant Oedipus to him. 484. carrion
woman: the Sphinx.

SCENE II

KREON. Men of Thebes:
I am told that heavy accusations
Have been brought against me by King Oedipus.

I am not the kind of man to bear this tamely.

If in these present difficulties   490
He holds me accountable for any harm to him

Through anything I have said or done — why, then,
I do not value life in this dishonor.

It is not as though this rumor touched upon
Some private indiscretion. The matter is grave.   495
The fact is that I am being called disloyal
To the State, to my fellow citizens, to my friends.
CHORAGOS.   He may have spoken in anger, not from his mind.
KREON.   But did you not hear him say I was the one
Who seduced the old prophet into lying?   500
CHORAGOS.   The thing was said; I do not know how seriously.
KREON.   But you were watching him! Were his eyes steady?
Did he look like a man in his right mind?
CHORAGOS.   I do not know.
I can not judge the behavior of great men.
But here is the king himself.

Enter OEDIPUS.

OEDIPUS.   So you dared come back.   505
Why? How brazen of you to come to my house,
You murderer!
                 Do you think I do not know
That you plotted to kill me, plotted to steal my throne?
Tell me, in God's name: am I coward, a fool,
That you should dream you could accomplish this?   510
A fool who could not see your slippery game?
A coward, not to fight back when I saw it?
You are the fool, Kreon, are you not? hoping
Without support or friends to get a throne?
Thrones may be won or bought: you could do neither.   515
KREON.   Now listen to me. You have talked; let me talk, too.
You can not judge unless you know the facts.
OEDIPUS.   You speak well: there is one fact; but I find it hard
To learn from the deadliest enemy I have.
KREON.   That above all I must dispute with you.   520
OEDIPUS.   That above all I will not hear you deny.
KREON.   If you think there is anything good in being stubborn
Against all reason, then I say you are wrong.
OEDIPUS.   If you think a man can sin against his own kind

And not be punished for it, I say you are mad. 525
KREON. I agree. But tell me: what have I done to you?
OEDIPUS. You advised me to send for that wizard, did you not?
KREON. I did. I should do it again.
OEDIPUS.   Very well. Now tell me:
How long has it been since Laïos —
KREON.   What of Laïos?
OEDIPUS. Since he vanished in that onset by the road? 530
KREON. It was long ago, a long time.
OEDIPUS.   And this prophet,
Was he practicing here then?
KREON.   He was; and with honor, as now.
OEDIPUS. Did he speak of me at that time?
KREON.   He never did;
At least, not when I was present.
OEDIPUS.   But . . . the enquiry?
I suppose you held one?
KREON.   We did, but we learned nothing. 535
OEDIPUS. Why did the prophet not speak against me then?
KREON. I do not know; and I am the kind of man
Who holds his tongue when he has no facts to go on.
OEDIPUS. There's one fact that you know, and you could tell it.
KREON. What fact is that? If I know it, you shall have it. 540
OEDIPUS. If he were not involved with you, he could not say
That it was I who murdered Laïos.
KREON. If he says that, you are the one that knows it! —
But now it is my turn to question you.
OEDIPUS. Put your questions. I am no murderer. 545
KREON. First, then: You married my sister?
OEDIPUS.   I married your sister.
KREON. And you rule the kingdom equally with her?
OEDIPUS. Everything that she wants she has from me.
KREON. And I am the third, equal to both of you?
OEDIPUS. That is why I call you a bad friend. 550
KREON. No. Reason it out, as I have done.
Think of this first: Would any sane man prefer
Power, with all a king's anxieties,
To that same power and the grace of sleep?
Certainly not I. 555

I have never longed for the king's power — only his rights.
Would any wise man differ from me in this?
As matters stand, I have my way in everything
With your consent, and no responsibilities.
If I were king, I should be a slave to policy.   560

How could I desire a scepter more
Than what is now mine — untroubled influence?
No, I have not gone mad; I need no honors,
Except those with the perquisites I have now.
I am welcome everywhere; every man salutes me,   565
And those who want your favor seek my ear,
Since I know how to manage what they ask.
Should I exchange this ease for that anxiety?
Besides, no sober mind is treasonable.
I hate anarchy   570
And never would deal with any man who likes it.

Test what I have said. Go to the priestess
At Delphi, ask if I quoted her correctly.
And as for this other thing: if I am found
Guilty of treason with Teiresias,   575
Then sentence me to death. You have my word
It is a sentence I should cast my vote for —
But not without evidence!
                    You do wrong
When you take good men for bad, bad men for good.
A true friend thrown aside — why, life itself   580
Is not more precious!
                    In time you will know this well:
For time, and time alone, will show the just man,
Though scoundrels are discovered in a day.
CHORAGOS.   This is well said, and a prudent man would ponder it.
Judgments too quickly formed are dangerous.   585
OEDIPUS.   But is he not quick in his duplicity?
And shall I not be quick to parry him?
Would you have me stand still, hold my peace, and let
This man win everything, through my inaction?
KREON.   And you want — what is it, then? To banish me?   590
OEDIPUS.   No, not exile. It is your death I want,

So that all the world may see what treason means.

KREON.   You will persist, then? You will not believe me?

OEDIPUS.   How can I believe you?

KREON.   Then you are a fool.

OEDIPUS.   To save myself?

KREON.   In justice, think of me.   595

OEDIPUS.   You are evil incarnate.

KREON.   But suppose that you are wrong?

OEDIPUS.   Still I must rule.

KREON.   But not if you rule badly.

OEDIPUS.   O city, city!

KREON.   It is my city, too!

CHORAGOS.   Now, my lords, be still. I see the queen,
     Iokastê, coming from her palace chambers;   600
     And it is time she came, for the sake of you both.
     This dreadful quarrel can be resolved through her.

                    Enter IOKASTÊ.

IOKASTÊ.   Poor foolish men, what wicked din is this?
     With Thebes sick to death, is it not shameful
     That you should rake some private quarrel up?   605
     [*To* OEDIPUS] Come into the house.

                              —And you Kreon, go now:
     Let us have no more of this tumult over nothing.

KREON.   Nothing? No, sister: what your husband plans for me
     Is one of two great evils: exile or death.

OEDIPUS.   He is right.

                         Why, woman I have caught him squarely   610
     Plotting against my life.

KREON.   No! Let me die
     Accurst if ever I have wished you harm!

IOKASTÊ.   Ah, believe it, Oedipus!
     In the name of the gods, respect this oath of his
     For my sake, for the sake of these people here!   615

CHORAGOS.   [STROPHE 1 *
     Open your mind to her, my lord. Be ruled by her, I beg you!

---

* **Strophe 1**: This apparently begins a Commos (see Aristotle's *Poetics*, Chapter 12), a lament sung by the chief actor and the Chorus, with the strophe and antistrophe functioning as alternating stanzas of the responsive song or chant.

OEDIPUS.   What would you have me do?

CHORAGOS.   Respect Kreon's word. He has never spoken like a fool,
    And now he has sworn an oath.

OEDIPUS.   You know what you ask?

CHORAGOS.   I do.

OEDIPUS.   Speak on, then.

CHORAGOS.   A friend so sworn should not be baited so,   620
    In blind malice, and without final proof.

OEDIPUS.   You are aware, I hope, that what you say
    Means death for me, or exile at the least.

CHORAGOS.   [STROPHE 2
        No, I swear by Helios,° first in Heaven!
        May I die friendless and accurst,   625
        The worst of deaths, if ever I meant that!
            It is the withering fields
                That hurt my sick heart:
                Must we bear all these ills,
                    And now your bad blood as well?   630

OEDIPUS.   Then let him go. And let me die, if I must,
    Or be driven by him in shame from the land of Thebes.
    It is your unhappiness, and not his talk,
    That touches me.
                        As for him —
    Wherever he goes, hatred will follow him.   635

KREON.   Ugly in yielding, as you were ugly in rage!
    Natures like yours chiefly torment themselves.

OEDIPUS.   Can you not go? Can you not leave me?

KREON.   I can.
    You do not know me; but the city knows me,
    And in its eyes I am just, if not in yours.   *Exit* KREON.   640

CHORAGOS.   [ANTISTROPHE 1
        Lady Iokastê, did you not ask the King to go to his chambers?

IOKASTÊ.   First tell me what has happened.

CHORAGOS.   There was suspicion without evidence; yet it rankled
    As even false charges will.

IOKASTÊ.   On both sides?

CHORAGOS.   On both.

624. Helios: the sun-god.

IOKASTÊ. But what was said?

CHORAGOS. Oh let it rest, let it be done with! 645
 Have we not suffered enough?

OEDIPUS. You see to what your decency has brought you:
 You have made difficulties where my heart saw none.

CHORAGOS. [ANTISTROPHE 2
 Oedipus, it is not once only I have told you —
 You must know I should count myself unwise 650
 To the point of madness, should I now forsake you —
   You, under whose hand,
    In the storm of another time,
   Our dear land sailed out free.
   But now stand fast at the helm! 655

IOKASTÊ. In God's name, Oedipus, inform your wife as well:
 Why are you so set in this hard anger?

OEDIPUS. I will tell you, for none of these men deserves
 My confidence as you do. It is Kreon's work,
 His treachery, his plotting against me. 660

IOKASTÊ. Go on, if you can make this clear to me.

OEDIPUS. He charges me with the murder of Laïos.

IOKASTÊ. Has he some knowledge? Or does he speak from hearsay?

OEDIPUS. He would not commit himself to such a charge,
 But he has brought in that damnable soothsayer 665
 To tell his story.

IOKASTÊ. Set your mind at rest.
 If it is a question of soothsayers, I tell you
 That you will find no man whose craft gives knowledge
 Of the unknowable.

     Here is my proof:

An oracle was reported to Laïos once 670
(I will not say from Phoibos himself, but from
His appointed ministers, at any rate)
That his doom would be death at the hands of his own son —
His son, born of his flesh and of mine!

Now, you remember the story: Laïos was killed 675
By marauding strangers where three highways meet;

But his child had not been three days in this world
Before the king had pierced the baby's ankles
And left him to die on a lonely mountainside.

Thus, Apollo never caused that child 680
To kill his father, and it was not Laïos' fate
To die at the hands of his son, as he had feared.
This is what prophets and prophecies are worth!
Have no dread of them.

It is God himself
Who can show us what he wills, in his own way. 685

OEDIPUS. How strange a shadowy memory crossed my mind,
Just now while you were speaking; it chilled my heart.

IOKASTÊ. What do you mean? What memory do you speak of?

OEDIPUS. If I understand you, Laïos was killed
At a place where three roads meet.

So it was said; 690
We have no later story.

OEDIPUS. Where did it happen?

IOKASTÊ. Phokis, it is called: at a place where the Theban Way
Divides into the roads toward Delphi and Daulia.

OEDIPUS. When?

IOKASTÊ. We had the news not long before you came 695
And proved the right to your succession here.

OEDIPUS. Ah, what net has God been weaving for me?

IOKASTÊ. Oedipus! Why does this trouble you?

Do not ask me yet.
First, tell me how Laïos looked, and tell me
How old he was.

IOKASTÊ. He was tall, his hair just touched 700
With white; his form was not unlike your own.

OEDIPUS. I think that I myself may be accurst
By my own ignorant edict.

IOKASTÊ. You speak strangely.
It makes me tremble to look at you, my king.

OEDIPUS. I am not sure that the blind man can not see. 705
But I should know better if you were to tell me —

IOKASTÊ. Anything — though I dread to hear you ask it.

OEDIPUS. Was the king lightly escorted, or did he ride

With a large company, as a ruler should?

IOKASTÊ. There were five men with him in all: one was a herald; 710
And a single chariot, which he was driving.

OEDIPUS. Alas, that makes it plain enough!

But who—
Who told you how it happened?

IOKASTÊ.   A household servant,
The only one to escape.

OEDIPUS.   And is he still
A servant of ours?

IOKASTÊ.   No; for when he came back at last 715
And found you enthroned in the place of the dead king,
He came to me, touched my hand with his, and begged
That I would send him away to the frontier district
Where only the shepherds go—
As far away from the city as I could send him. 720
I granted his prayer; for although the man was a slave,
He had earned more than this favor at my hands.

OEDIPUS. Can he be called back quickly?

IOKASTÊ.   Easily.
But why?

OEDIPUS. I have taken too much upon myself 725
Without enquiry; therefore I wish to consult him.

IOKASTÊ. Then he shall come.

But am I not one also
To whom you might confide these fears of yours?

OEDIPUS. That is your right; it will not be denied you,
Now least of all; for I have reached a pitch 730
Of wild foreboding. Is there anyone
To whom I should sooner speak?

Polybos of Corinth is my father.
My mother is a Dorian: Meropê.
I grew up chief among the men of Corinth 735
Until a strange thing happened—
Not worth my passion, it may be, but strange.

At a feast, a drunken man maundering in his cups
Cries out that I am not my father's son!

I contained myself that night, though I felt anger   740
And a sinking heart. The next day I visited
My father and mother, and questioned them. They stormed,
Calling it all the slanderous rant of a fool;
And this relieved me. Yet the suspicion
Remained always aching in my mind;   745
I knew there was talk; I could not rest;
And finally, saying nothing to my parents,
I went to the shrine at Delphi.

The god dismissed my question without reply;
He spoke of other things.
                          Some were clear,   750
Full of wretchedness, dreadful, unbearable:
As, that I should lie with my own mother, breed
Children from whom all men would turn their eyes;
And that I should be my father's murderer.

I heard all this, and fled. And from that day   755
Corinth to me was only in the stars
Descending in that quarter of the sky,
As I wandered farther and farther on my way
To a land where I should never see the evil
Sung by the oracle. And I came to this country   760
Where, so you say, King Laïos was killed.

I will tell you all that happened there, my lady.

There were three highways
Coming together at a place I passed;
And there a herald came towards me, and a chariot   765
Drawn by horses, with a man such as you describe
Seated in it. The groom leading the horses
Forced me off the road at his lord's command;
But as this charioteer lurched over towards me
I struck him in my rage. The old man saw me   770
And brought his double goad down upon my head
As I came abreast.
                   He was paid back, and more!
Swinging my club in this right hand I knocked him

Out of his car, and he rolled on the ground.

I killed him.

I killed them all.   775
Now if that stranger and Laïos were — kin,
Where is a man more miserable than I?
More hated by the gods? Citizen and alien alike
Must never shelter me or speak to me —
I must be shunned by all.

And I myself   780
Pronounced this malediction upon myself!

Think of it: I have touched you with these hands,
These hands that killed your husband. What defilement!

Am I all evil, then? It must be so,
Since I must flee from Thebes, yet never again   785
See my own countrymen, my own country,
For fear of joining my mother in marriage
And killing Polybos, my father.

Ah,

If I was created so, born to this fate,
Who could deny the savagery of God?   790

O holy majesty of heavenly powers!
May I never see that day! Never!
Rather let me vanish from the race of men
Than know the abomination destined me!

CHORAGOS.   We too, my lord, have felt dismay at this.   795
        But there is hope: you have yet to hear the shepherd.
OEDIPUS.   Indeed, I fear no other hope is left me.
IOKASTÊ.   What do you hope from him when he comes?
OEDIPUS.   This much:
        If his account of the murder tallies with yours,
        Then I am cleared.
IOKASTÊ.   What was it that I said   800
        Of such importance?
OEDIPUS.   Why, "marauders," you said,
        Killed the king, according to this man's story.
        If he maintains that still, if there were several,
        Clearly the guilt is not mine: I was alone.

But if he says one man, singlehanded, did it, 805
Then the evidence all points to me.

IOKASTÊ. You may be sure that he said there were several;
And can he call back that story now? He can not.
The whole city heard it as plainly as I.
But suppose he alters some detail of it: 810
He can not ever show that Laïos' death
Fulfilled the oracle: for Apollo said
My child was doomed to kill him; and my child—
Poor baby!— it was my child that died first.

No. From now on, where oracles are concerned, 815
I would not waste a second thought on any.

OEDIPUS. You may be right.

But come: let someone go
For the shepherd at once. This matter must be settled.

IOKASTÊ. I will send for him.
I would not wish to cross you in anything, 820
And surely not in this.— Let us go in.   *Exeunt into the palace.*

ODE II

CHORUS.   [STROPHE I

Let me be reverent in the ways of right,
Lowly the paths I journey on;
Let all my words and actions keep
The laws of the pure universe 825
From highest Heaven handed down.
For Heaven is their bright nurse,
Those generations of the realms of light;
Ah, never of mortal kind were they begot,
Nor are they slaves of memory, lost in sleep: 830
Their Father is greater than Time, and ages not.

The tyrant is a child of Pride   [ANTISTROPHE I
Who drinks from his great sickening cup
Recklessness and vanity,
Until from his high crest headlong 835
He plummets to the dust of hope.
That strong man is not strong.

But let no fair ambition be denied;
May God protect the wrestler for the State
In government, in comely policy,   840
Who will fear God, and on His ordinance wait.

Haughtiness and the high hand of disdain   [STROPHE 2
Tempt and outrage God's holy law;
And any mortal who dares hold
No immortal Power in awe   845
Will be caught up in a net of pain:
The price for which his levity is sold.
Let each man take due earnings, then,
And keep his hands from holy things,
And from blasphemy stand apart —   850
Else the crackling blast of heaven
Blows on his head, and on his desperate heart.
Though fools will honor impious men,
In their cities no tragic poet sings.

Shall we lose faith in Delphi's obscurities,   [ANTISTROPHE 2
We who have heard the world's core   856
Discredited, and the sacred wood
Of Zeus at Elis praised no more?
The deeds and the strange prophecies
Must make a pattern yet to be understood.   860
Zeus, if indeed you are lord of all,
Throned in light over night and day,
Mirror this in your endless mind:
Our masters call the oracle
Words on the wind, and the Delphic vision blind!   865
Their hearts no longer know Apollo,
And reverence for the gods has died away.

SCENE III

Enter IOKASTÊ.

IOKASTÊ. Princes of Thebes, it has occurred to me
   To visit the altars of the gods, bearing
   These branches as a suppliant, and this incense.   870

Our King is not himself: his noble soul
Is overwrought with fantasies of dread,
Else he would consider
The new prophecies in the light of the old.
He will listen to any voice that speaks disaster,   875
And my advice goes for nothing.

[*She approaches the altar.*]

To you, then, Apollo,
Lycéan° lord, since you are nearest, I turn in prayer.
Receive these offerings, and grant us deliverance
From defilement. Our hearts are heavy with fear
When we see our leader distracted, as helpless sailors   880
Are terrified by the confusion of their helmsman.

Enter MESSENGER.

MESSENGER. Friends, no doubt you can direct me:
Where shall I find the house of Oedipus,
Or, better still, where is the King himself?
CHORAGOS. It is this very place, stranger; he is inside.   885
This is his wife and mother of his children.
MESSENGER. I wish her happiness in a happy house,
Blest in all the fulfillment of her marriage.
IOKASTÊ. I wish as much for you: your courtesy
Deserves a like good fortune. But now, tell me: 890
Why have you come? What have you to say to us?
MESSENGER. Good news, my lady, for your house and your husband.
IOKASTÊ. What news? Who sent you here?
MESSENGER.   I am from Corinth.
The news I bring ought to mean joy for you,
Though it may be you will find some grief in it.   895
IOKASTÊ. What is it? How can it touch us in both ways?
MESSENGER. The word is that the people of the Isthmus
Intend to call Oedipus to be their king.
IOKASTÊ. But old King Polybos — is he not reigning still?
MESSENGER. No. Death holds him in his sepulchre.   900
IOKASTÊ. What are you saying? Polybos is dead?
MESSENGER. If I am not telling the truth, may I die myself.

877. Lycéan: another name for Apollo, meaning "god of light."

IOKASTÊ. [*To a* MAIDSERVANT] Go in, go quickly; tell this to your master.

O riddlers of God's will, where are you now!
This was the man whom Oedipus, long ago,   905
Feared so, fled so, in dread of destroying him —
But it was another fate by which he died.

Enter OEDIPUS.

OEDIPUS. Dearest Iokastê, why have you sent for me?
IOKASTÊ. Listen to what this man says, and then tell me
What has become of the solemn prophecies.   910
OEDIPUS. Who is this man? What is his news for me?
IOKASTÊ. He has come from Corinth to announce your father's death!
OEDIPUS. Is it true, stranger? Tell me in your own words.
MESSENGER. I can not say it more clearly: the king is dead.
OEDIPUS. Was it by treason? Or by an attack of illness?   915
MESSENGER. A little thing brings old men to their rest.
OEDIPUS. It was sickness, then?
MESSENGER.   Yes, and his many years.
OEDIPUS. Ah!
Why should a man respect the Pythian hearth,° or
Give heed to the birds that jangle above his head?   920
They prophesied that I should kill Polybos,
Kill my own father; but he is dead and buried,
And I am here — I never touched him, never,
Unless he died of grief for my departure,
And thus, in a sense, through me. No. Polybos   925
Has packed the oracles off with him underground.
They are empty words.
IOKASTÊ.   Had I not told you so?
OEDIPUS. You had; it was my faint heart that betrayed me.
IOKASTÊ. From now on never think of those things again.
OEDIPUS. And yet — must I not fear my mother's bed?   930
IOKASTÊ. Why should anyone in this world be afraid,
Since Fate rules us and nothing can be foreseen?
A man should live only for the present day.

Have no more fear of sleeping with your mother:

919. **Pythian hearth:** the Delphic oracle, so called because Apollo killed the
serpent Python on the spot where he established the oracle.

How many men, in dreams, have lain with their mothers! 935
No reasonable man is troubled by such things.
OEDIPUS. That is true; only —
If only my mother were not still alive!
But she is alive. I can not help my dread.
IOKASTÊ. Yet this news of your father's death is wonderful. 940
OEDIPUS. Wonderful. But I fear the living woman.
MESSENGER. Tell me, who is this woman that you fear?
OEDIPUS. It is Meropê, man; the wife of King Polybos.
MESSENGER. Meropê? Why should you be afraid of her?
OEDIPUS. An oracle of the gods, a dreadful saying. 945
MESSENGER. Can you tell me about it or are you sworn to silence?
OEDIPUS. I can tell you, and I will.
Apollo said through his prophet that I was the man
Who should marry his own mother, shed his father's blood
With his own hands. And so, for all these years 950
I have kept clear of Corinth, and no harm has come —
Though it would have been sweet to see my parents again.
MESSENGER. And is this the fear that drove you out of Corinth?
OEDIPUS. Would you have me kill my father?
MESSENGER.   As for that
You must be reassured by the news I gave you. 955
OEDIPUS. If you could reassure me, I would reward you.
MESSENGER. I had that in mind, I will confess: I thought
I could count on you when you returned to Corinth.
OEDIPUS. No: I will never go near my parents again.
MESSENGER. Ah, son, you still do not know what you are doing — 960
OEDIPUS. What do you mean? In the name of God tell me!
MESSENGER. —If these are your reasons for not going home.
OEDIPUS. I tell you, I fear the oracle may come true.
MESSENGER. And guilt may come upon you through your parents?
OEDIPUS. That is the dread that is always in my heart. 965
MESSENGER. Can you not see that all your fears are groundless?
OEDIPUS. Groundless? Am I not my parents' son?
MESSENGER. Polybos was not your father.
OEDIPUS.   Not my father?
MESSENGER. No more your father than the man speaking to you.
OEDIPUS. But you are nothing to me!
MESSENGER.   Neither was he. 970

OEDIPUS. Then why did he call me son?

MESSENGER.   I will tell you:
   Long ago he had you from my hands, as a gift.

OEDIPUS. Then how could he love me so, if I was not his?

MESSENGER. He had no children, and his heart turned to you.

OEDIPUS. What of you? Did you buy me? Did you find me by chance?

MESSENGER. I came upon you in the woody vales of Kithairon.°   976

OEDIPUS. And what were you doing there?

MESSENGER.   Tending my flocks.

OEDIPUS. A wandering shepherd?

MESSENGER.   But your savior, son, that day.

OEDIPUS. From what did you save me?

MESSENGER.   Your ankles should tell you that.

OEDIPUS. Ah, stranger, why do you speak of that childhood pain?   980

MESSENGER. I pulled the skewer that pinned your feet together.

OEDIPUS. I have had the mark as long as I can remember.

MESSENGER. That was why you were given the name you bear.°

OEDIPUS. God! Was it my father or my mother who did it?
   Tell me!   985

MESSENGER. I do not know. The man who gave you to me
   Can tell you better than I.

OEDIPUS. It was not you that found me, but another?

MESSENGER. It was another shepherd gave you to me.

OEDIPUS. Who was he? Can you tell me who he was?   990

MESSENGER. I think he was said to be one of Laïos' people.

OEDIPUS. You mean the Laïos who was king here years ago?

MESSENGER. Yes; King Laïos; and the man was one of his herdsmen.

OEDIPUS. Is he still alive? Can I see him?

MESSENGER.   These men here
   Know best about such things.

OEDIPUS.   Does anyone here   995
   Know this shepherd that he is talking about?
   Have you seen him in the fields, or in the town?
   If you have, tell me. It is time things were made plain.

CHORAGOS. I think the man he means is that same shepherd
   You have already asked to see. Iokastê perhaps   1000
   Could tell you something.

   976. **Kithairon**: See Scene I, line 409. 983. **name you bear**: Oedipus means
"swollen foot."

OEDIPUS.   Do you know anything
About him, Lady? Is he the man we have summoned?
Is that the man this shepherd means?

IOKASTÊ.   Why think of him?
Forget this herdsman. Forget it all.
This talk is a waste of time.

OEDIPUS.   How can you say that,   1005
When the clues to my true birth are in my hands?

IOKASTÊ.   For God's love, let us have no more questioning!
Is your life nothing to you?
My own is pain enough for me to bear.

OEDIPUS.   You need not worry. Suppose my mother a slave,   1010
And born of slaves: no baseness can touch you.

IOKASTÊ.   Listen to me, I beg you: do not do this thing!

OEDIPUS.   I will not listen; the truth must be made known.

IOKASTÊ.   Everything that I say is for your own good!

OEDIPUS.   My own good
Snaps my patience, then; I want none of it.   1015

IOKASTÊ.   You are fatally wrong! May you never learn who you are!

OEDIPUS.   Go, one of you, and bring the shepherd here.
Let us leave this woman to brag of her royal name.

IOKASTÊ.   Ah, miserable!
That is the only word I have for you now.   1020
That is the only word I can ever have.   *Exit into the palace.*

CHORAGOS.   Why has she left us, Oedipus? Why has she gone
In such a passion of sorrow? I fear this silence:
Something dreadful may come of it.

OEDIPUS.   Let it come!
However base my birth, I must know about it.   1025
The Queen, like a woman, is perhaps ashamed
To think of my low origin. But I
Am a child of Luck; I can not be dishonored.
Luck is my mother; the passing months, my brothers,
Have seen me rich and poor.
                                        If this is so,   1030
How could I wish that I were someone else?
How could I not be glad to know my birth?

ODE III

CHORUS.   [STROPHE
    If ever the coming time were known
    To my heart's pondering,
    Kithairon, now by Heaven I see the torches   1035
    At the festival of the next full moon,
    And see the dance, and hear the choir sing
    A grace to your gentle shade:
    Mountain where Oedipus was found,
    O mountain guard of a noble race!   1040
    May the god° who heals us lend his aid,
    And let that glory come to pass
    For our king's cradling-ground.

    Of the nymphs that flower beyond the years,   [ANTISTROPHE
    Who bore you, royal child,   1045
    To Pan of the hills or the timberline Apollo,
    Cold in delight where the upland clears,
    Or Hermês for whom Kyllenê's° heights are piled?
    Or flushed° as evening cloud,
    Great Dionysos, roamer of mountains,   1050
    He — was it he who found you there,
    And caught you up in his own proud
    Arms from the sweet god-ravisher°
    Who laughed by the Muses' fountains?°

1041. god: Apollo, the healer. **1048. Kyllenê:** mountain sacred to Hermês, god of eloquence and prudence, and herald of Zeus. **1049. flushed:** Dionysos (Bacchos) again is flushed with wine. See Párodos, line 200. **1053. god-ravisher:** the nymph, whom the Chorus suggests was Oedipus's mother. **1054. Muses' fountains:** springs of Helicon, a mountain range sacred to Apollo and the Muses.

SCENE IV

OEDIPUS. Sirs: though I do not know the man,   1055
    I think I see him coming, this shepherd we want:
    He is old, like our friend here, and the men

Bringing him seem to be servants of my house.
But you can tell, if you have ever seen him.

Enter SHEPHERD *escorted by* SERVANTS.

CHORAGOS.   I know him, he was Laïos' man. You can trust him.   1060

OEDIPUS.   Tell me first, you from Corinth: is this the shepherd
    We were discussing?

MESSENGER.   This is the very man.

OEDIPUS.   [*To* SHEPHERD] Come here. No, look at me. You must answer
    Everything I ask. — You belonged to Laïos?

SHEPHERD.   Yes: born his slave, brought up in his house.   1065

OEDIPUS.   Tell me: what kind of work did you do for him?

SHEPHERD.   I was a shepherd of his, most of my life.

OEDIPUS.   Where mainly did you go for pasturage?

SHEPHERD.   Sometimes Kithairon, sometimes the hills near-by.

OEDIPUS.   Do you remember ever seeing this man out there?   1070

SHEPHERD.   What would he be doing there? This man?

OEDIPUS.   This man standing here. Have you ever seen him before?

SHEPHERD.   No. At least, not to my recollection.

MESSENGER.   And that is not strange, my lord. But I'll refresh
    His memory: he must remember when we two   1075
    Spent three whole seasons together, March to September,
    On Kithairon or thereabouts. He had two flocks;
    I had one. Each autumn I'd drive mine home
    And he would go back with his to Laïos' sheepfold. —
    Is this not true, just as I have described it?   1080

SHEPHERD.   True, yes; but it was all so long ago.

MESSENGER.   Well, then: do you remember, back in those days,
    That you gave me a baby boy to bring up as my own?

SHEPHERD.   What if I did? What are you trying to say?

MESSENGER.   King Oedipus was once that little child.   1085

SHEPHERD.   Damn you, hold your tongue!

OEDIPUS.   No more of that!
    It is your tongue needs watching, not this man's.

SHEPHERD.   My king, my master, what is it I have done wrong?

OEDIPUS.   You have not answered his question about the boy.

SHEPHERD.   He does not know . . . He is only making trouble . . .   1090

OEDIPUS.   Come, speak plainly, or it will go hard with you.

SHEPHERD.   In God's name, do not torture an old man!

OEDIPUS. Come here, one of you; bind his arms behind him.

SHEPHERD. Unhappy king! What more do you wish to learn?

OEDIPUS. Did you give this man the child he speaks of?

SHEPHERD.   I did.   1095

        And I would to God I had died that very day.

OEDIPUS. You will die now unless you speak the truth.

SHEPHERD. Yet if I speak the truth, I am worse than dead.

OEDIPUS. [*To* ATTENDANT] He intends to draw it out, apparently —

SHEPHERD. No! I have told you already that I gave him the boy.   1100

OEDIPUS. Where did you get him? From your house? From somewhere
        else?

SHEPHERD. Not from mine, no. A man gave him to me.

OEDIPUS. Is that man here? Whose house did he belong to?

SHEPHERD. For God's love, my King, do not ask me any more!

OEDIPUS. You are a dead man if I have to ask you again.   1105

SHEPHERD. Then . . . Then the child was from the palace of Laïos.

OEDIPUS. A slave child? or a child of his own line?

SHEPHERD. Ah, I am on the brink of dreadful speech!

OEDIPUS. And I of dreadful hearing. Yet I must hear.

SHEPHERD. If you must be told, then . . .

                 They said it was Laïos' child;   1110

        But it is your wife who can tell you about that.

OEDIPUS. My wife! — Did she give it to you?

SHEPHERD.   My lord, she did.

OEDIPUS. Do you know why?

SHEPHERD.   I was told to get rid of it.

OEDIPUS. Oh heartless mother!

SHEPHERD.   But in dread of prophecies . . .

OEDIPUS. Tell me.

SHEPHERD.   It was said that the boy would kill his own father.

OEDIPUS. Then why did you give him over to this old man?   1116

SHEPHERD. I pitied the baby, my king,

        And I thought that this man would take him far away
        To his own country.

               He saved him — but for what a fate!

        For if you are what this man says you are,   1120

        No man living is more wretched than Oedipus.

OEDIPUS. Ah God!

        It was true!

All the prophecies!
                              —Now,
O Light, may I look on you for the last time!
I, Oedipus,   1125
Oedipus, damned in his birth, in his marriage damned,
Damned in the blood he shed with his own hand!

[*He rushes into the palace.*]

ODE IV

    Alas for the seed of men.
    What measure shall I give these generations
    That breathe on the void and are void   1130
    And exist and do not exist?
    Who bears more weight of joy
    Than mass of sunlight shifting in images,
    Or who shall make his thought stay on
    That down time drifts away?   1135
    Your splendor is all fallen.
    O naked brow of wrath and tears,
    O change of Oedipus!
    I who saw your days call no man blest —
    Your great days like ghósts góne.   1140

    That mind was a strong bow.   [ANTISTROPHE I
    Deep, how deep you drew it then, hard archer,
    At a dim fearful range,
    And brought dear glory down!
    You overcame the stranger° —   1145
    The virgin with her hooking lion claws —
    And though death sang, stood like a tower
    To make pale Thebes take heart.
    Fortress against our sorrow!
    True king, giver of laws,   1150
    Majestic Oedipus!

        1145. stranger: the Sphinx.

No prince in Thebes had ever such renown,
No prince won such grace of power.

And now of all men ever known   [STROPHE 2
Most pitiful is this man's story: 1155
His fortunes are most changed, his state
Fallen to a low slave's
Ground under bitter fate.
O Oedipus, most royal one!
The great door that expelled you to the light   1160
Gave at night — ah, gave night to your glory:
As to the father, to the fathering son.
All understood too late.
How could that queen whom Laïos won,
The garden that he harrowed at his height,   1165
Be silent when that act was done?

But all eyes fail before time's eye,   [ANTISTROPHE 2
All actions come to justice there.
Though never willed, though far down the deep past,
Your bed, your dread sirings,   1170
Are brought to book at last.
Child by Laïos doomed to die,
Then doomed to lose that fortunate little death,
Would God you never took breath in this air
That with my wailing lips I take to cry: 1175
For I weep the world's outcast.
I was blind, and now I can tell why:
Asleep, for you had given ease of breath
To Thebes, while the false years went by.

ÉXODOS *

Enter, from the palace, SECOND MESSENGER.

SECOND MESSENGER. Elders of Thebes, most honored in this land,   1180
    What horrors are yours to see and hear, what weight
    Of sorrow to be endured, if, true to your birth,

---

* Éxodos: the final, or exit, song of the Chorus.

You venerate the line of Labdakos!
I think neither Istros nor Phasis, those great rivers,
Could purify this place of all the evil   1185
It shelters now, or soon must bring to light —
Evil not done unconsciously, but willed.

The greatest griefs are those we cause ourselves.
CHORAGOS.   Surely, friend, we have grief enough already;
What new sorrow do you mean?
SECOND MESSENGER.   The Queen is dead.   1190
CHORAGOS.   O miserable Queen! But at whose hand?
SECOND MESSENGER.   Her own.
The full horror of what happened you can not know,
For you did not see it; but I, who did, will tell you
As clearly as I can how she met her death.

When she had left us,   1195
In passionate silence, passing through the court,
She ran to her apartment in the house,
Her hair clutched by the fingers of both hands.
She closed the doors behind her; then, by that bed
Where long ago the fatal son was conceived —   1200
That son who should bring about his father's death —
We heard her call upon Laïos, dead so many years,
And heard her wail for the double fruit of her marriage,
A husband by her husband, children by her child.

Exactly how she died I do not know: 1205
For Oedipus burst in moaning and would not let us
Keep vigil to the end: it was by him
As he stormed about the room that our eyes were caught.
From one to another of us he went, begging a sword,
Hunting the wife who was not his wife, the mother   1210
Whose womb had carried his own children and himself.
I do not know: it was none of us aided him,
But surely one of the gods was in control!
For with a dreadful cry
He hurled his weight, as though wrenched out of himself, 1215
At the twin doors: the bolts gave, and he rushed in.
And there we saw her hanging, her body swaying

From the cruel cord she had noosed about her neck.
A great sob broke from him, heartbreaking to hear,
As he loosed the rope and lowered her to the ground. 1220

I would blot out from my mind what happened next!
For the king ripped from her gown the golden brooches
That were her ornament, and raised them, and plunged them down
Straight into his own eyeballs, crying, 'No more,
No more shall you look on the misery about me, 1225
The horrors of my own doing! Too long you have known
The faces of those whom I should never have seen,
Too long been blind to those for whom I was searching!
From this hour, go in darkness!' And as he spoke,
He struck at his eyes — not once, but many times; 1230
And the blood spattered his beard,
Bursting from his ruined sockets like red hail.

So from the unhappiness of two this evil has sprung,
A curse on the man and woman alike. The old
Happiness of the house of Labdakos 1235
Was happiness enough: where is it today?
It is all wailing and ruin, disgrace, death — all
The misery of mankind that has a name —
And it is wholly and for ever theirs.

CHORAGOS. Is he in agony still? Is there no rest for him? 1240
SECOND MESSENGER. He is calling for someone to open the doors wide
So that all the children of Kadmos may look upon
His father's murderer, his mother's — no,
I can not say it!
                                And then he will leave Thebes,
Self-exiled, in order that the curse 1245
Which he himself pronounced may depart from the house.
He is weak, and there is none to lead him,
So terrible is his suffering.
                                But you will see:
Look, the doors are opening; in a moment
You will see a thing that would crush a heart of stone. 1250

[*The central door is opened;* OEDIPUS, *blinded, is led in.*]

CHORAGOS. Dreadful indeed for men to see.

Never have my own eyes
Looked on a sight so full of fear.

Oedipus!
What madness came upon you, what daemon   1255
Leaped on your life with heavier
Punishment than a mortal man can bear?
No: I can not even
Look at you, poor ruined one.
And I would speak, question, ponder,   1260
If I were able. No.
You make me shudder.

OEDIPUS. God.   God.
Is there a sorrow greater?
Where shall I find harbor in this world?   1265
My voice is hurled far on a dark wind.
What has God done to me?

CHORAGOS.   Too terrible to think of, or to see.

OEDIPUS.   [STROPHE 1°
O cloud of night,
Never to be turned away: night coming on,   1270
I can not tell how: night like a shroud!
My fair winds brought me here.
                              O God. Again
The pain of the spikes where I had sight,
The flooding pain
Of memory, never to be gouged out.   1275

CHORAGOS.   This is not strange.
You suffer it all twice over, remorse in pain,
Pain in remorse.

OEDIPUS.   Ah dear friend   [ANTISTROPHE 1
Are you faithful even yet, you alone?   1280
Are you still standing near me, will you stay here,
Patient, to care for the blind?
                              The blind man!
Yet even blind I know who it is attends me,

    1269. Strophe 1. another Commos. See Scene II, line 616.

By the voice's tone —
Though my new darkness hide the comforter.   1285
CHORAGOS. Oh fearful act!
What god was it drove you to rake black
Night across your eyes?

OEDIPUS. Apollo. Apollo. Dear   [STROPHE 2
Children, the god was Apollo.   1290
He brought my sick, sick fate upon me.
But the blinding hand was my own!
How could I bear to see
When all my sight was horror everywhere?
CHORAGOS. Everywhere; that is true.   1295
OEDIPUS. And now what is left?
Images? Love? A greeting even,
Sweet to the senses? Is there anything?
Ah, no, friends: lead me away.
Lead me away from Thebes.
                               Lead the great wreck   1300
And hell of Oedipus, whom the gods hate.
CHORAGOS. Your misery, you are not blind to that.
Would God you had never found it out!

OEDIPUS.   [ANTISTROPHE 2
Death take the man who unbound
My feet on that hillside   1305
And delivered me from death to life! What life?
If only I had died,
This weight of monstrous doom
Could not have dragged me and my darlings down.
CHORAGOS. I would have wished the same.   1310
OEDIPUS. Oh never to have come here
With my father's blood upon me! Never
To have been the man they call his mother's husband!
Oh accurst! Oh child of evil,
To have entered that wretched bed —
                               the selfsame one!   1315
More primal than sin itself, this fell to me.
CHORAGOS. I do not know what words to offer you.

You were better dead than alive and blind.

OEDIPUS. Do not counsel me any more. This punishment
That I have laid upon myself is just.   1320
If I had eyes,
I do not know how I could bear the sight
Of my father, when I came to the house of Death,
Or my mother: for I have sinned against them both
So vilely that I could not make my peace   1325
By strangling my own life.

                  Or do you think my children,
Born as they were born, would be sweet to my eyes?
Ah never, never! Nor this town with its high walls,
Nor the holy images of the gods.
                For I,
Thrice miserable! — Oedipus, noblest of all the line   1330
Of Kadmos, have condemned myself to enjoy
These things no more, by my own malediction
Expelling that man whom the gods declared
To be a defilement in the house of Laïos.
After exposing the rankness of my own guilt,   1335
How could I look men frankly in the eyes?
No, I swear it,
If I could have stifled my hearing at its source,
I would have done it and made all this body
A tight cell of misery, blank to light and sound: 1340
So I should have been safe in my dark mind
Beyond external evil.
            Ah Kithairon!
Why did you shelter me? When I was cast upon you,
Why did I not die? Then I should never
Have shown the world my execrable birth.   1345

Ah Polybos! Corinth, city that I believed
The ancient seat of my ancestors: how fair
I seemed, your child! And all the while this evil
Was cancerous within me!
            For I am sick
In my own being, sick in my origin.   1350

O three roads, dark ravine, woodland and way

Where three roads met: you, drinking my father's blood,
My own blood, spilled by my own hand: can you remember
The unspeakable things I did there, and the things
I went on from there to do?

O marriage, marriage!   1355
The act that engendered me, and again the act
Performed by the son in the same bed —

Ah, the net
Of incest, mingling fathers, brothers, sons,
With brides, wives, mothers: the last evil
That can be known by men: no tongue can say   1360
How evil!

No. For the love of God, conceal me
Somewhere far from Thebes; or kill me; or hurl me
Into the sea, away from men's eyes for ever.

Come, lead me. You need not fear to touch me.
Of all men, I alone can bear this guilt.   1365

Enter KREON.

CHORAGOS. Kreon is here now. As to what you ask,
        He may decide the course to take. He only
        Is left to protect the city in your place.
OEDIPUS. Alas, how can I speak to him? What right have I
        To beg his courtesy whom I have deeply wronged?   1370
KREON. I have not come to mock you, Oedipus,
        Or to reproach you, either.

[*To* ATTENDANTS]   — You, standing there:
        If you have lost all respect for man's dignity,
        At least respect the flame of Lord Helios:
        Do not allow this pollution to show itself   1375
        Openly here, an affront to the earth
        And Heaven's rain and the light of day. No, take him
        Into the house as quickly as you can.
        For it is proper
        That only the close kindred see his grief.   1380
OEDIPUS. I pray you in God's name, since your courtesy
        Ignores my dark expectation, visiting

With mercy this man of all men most execrable:
Give me what I ask — for your good, not for mine.

KREON. And what is it that you turn to me begging for?   1385

OEDIPUS. Drive me out of this country as quickly as may be
  To a place where no human voice can ever greet me.

KREON. I should have done that before now — only,
  God's will had not been wholly revealed to me.

OEDIPUS. But his command is plain: the parricide   1390
  Must be destroyed. I am that evil man.

KREON. That is the sense of it, yes; but as things are,
  We had best discover clearly what is to be done.°

OEDIPUS. You would learn more about a man like me?

KREON. You are ready now to listen to the god.   1395

OEDIPUS. I will listen. But it is to you
  That I must turn for help. I beg you, hear me.

The woman in there —
Give her whatever funeral you think proper:
She is your sister.
    — But let me go, Kreon!   1400
Let me purge my father's Thebes of the pollution
Of my living here, and go out to the wild hills,
To Kithairon, that has won such fame with me,
The tomb my mother and father appointed for me,
And let me die there, as they willed I should.   1405
And yet I know
Death will not ever come to me through sickness
Or in any natural way: I have been preserved
For some unthinkable fate. But let that be.

As for my sons, you need not care for them.   1410
They are men, they will find some way to live.
But my poor daughters, who have shared my table,
Who never before have been parted from their father —
Take care of them, Kreon; do this for me.

And will you let me touch them with my hands   1415
A last time, and let us weep together?

  1393. We . . . done: Apparently Kreon will consult the Delphic oracle once
more.

Be kind, my lord,
Great prince, be kind!

Could I but touch them,
They would be mine again, as when I had my eyes.

Enter ANTIGONE *and* ISMENE, *attended.*

Ah, God!   1420
Is it my dearest children I hear weeping?
Has Kreon pitied me and sent my daughters?
KREON. Yes, Oedipus: I knew that they were dear to you
In the old days, and know you must love them still.
OEDIPUS. May God bless you for this — and be a friendlier   1425
Guardian to you than he has been to me!

Children, where are you?
Come quickly to my hands: they are your brother's —
Hands that have brought your father's once clear eyes
To this way of seeing —

Ah dearest ones,   1430
I had neither sight nor knowledge then, your father
By the woman who was the source of his own life!
And I weep for you — having no strength to see you —
I weep for you when I think of the bitterness
That men will visit upon you all your lives.   1435
What homes, what festivals can you attend
Without being forced to depart again in tears?
And when you come to marriageable age,
Where is the man, my daughters, who would dare
Risk the bane that lies on all my children?   1440
Is there any evil wanting? Your father killed
His father; sowed the womb of her who bore him;
Engendered you at the fount of his own existence!
That is what they will say of you.

Then, whom
Can you ever marry? There are no bridegrooms for you,   1445
And your lives must wither away in sterile dreaming.

O Kreon, son of Menoikeus!
You are the only father my daughters have,

Since we, their parents, are both of us gone for ever.
They are your own blood: you will not let them   1450
Fall into beggary and loneliness;
You will keep them from the miseries that are mine!
Take pity on them; see, they are only children,
Friendless except for you. Promise me this,
Great prince, and give me your hand in token of it.   1455

[KREON *clasps his right hand.*]

Children:
I could say much, if you could understand me,
But as it is, I have only this prayer for you:
Live where you can, be as happy as you can—
Happier, please God, than God has made your father.   1460

KREON. Enough. You have wept enough. Now go within.

OEDIPUS. I must; but it is hard.

KREON.   Time eases all things.

OEDIPUS. You know my mind, then?

KREON.   Say what you desire.

OEDIPUS. Send me from Thebes!

KREON.   God grant that I may!

OEDIPUS. But since God hates me . . .

KREON.   No, he will grant your wish.   1465

OEDIPUS. You promise?

KREON.   I can not speak beyond my knowledge.

OEDIPUS. Then lead me in.

KREON. Come now, and leave your children.

OEDIPUS. No! Do not take them from me!

KREON.   Think no longer
That you are in command here, but rather think   1470
How, when you were, you served your own destruction.

Exeunt into the house all but the CHORUS;
the CHORAGOS *chants directly to the audience.*

CHORAGOS. Men of Thebes: look upon Oedipus.

This is the king who solved the famous riddle
And towered up, most powerful of men.

No mortal eyes but looked on him with envy,   1475
Yet in the end ruin swept over him.

Let every man in mankind's frailty
Consider his last day; and let none
Presume on his good fortune until he find
Life, at his death, a memory without pain.   1480

For Study and Writing

1. Consider the opening speech of Oedipus, and then his second speech, beginning with line 60. From what he says in his second speech, what do we perceive about the nature of his opening address?

2. What subtle signs of Oedipus's character are visible in the Prologue? Consider his final speech and also the tone of his remarks in the dialogue with Kreon (pages 551–52).

3. In the speech of the Priest, how are Oedipus's earlier great deeds for Thebes said to have been made possible?

SCENE I

1. When the chorus leader (Choragos) asks why Phoibos did not "say who the culprit was" (line 266), Oedipus replies that "no man in the world/Can make the gods do more than the gods will." With this observation in mind, consider why Teiresias had not long ago told what he knew. In this connection consider Scene II, lines 536 and 683–85.

2. Discuss the irony in Oedipus's statement (line 283): "The man who dared that act will fear no curse."

3. Consider the meaning of the word *seer* in connection with Teiresias, who is blind. Trace and discuss all the play on the words *eyes, sight,* and *blindness* in the bitter charges and countercharges of this scene.

4. Explain Teiresias's use of the words *temperate* and *opportune* in lines 312–13.

5. Discuss Teiresias's words (line 341), "I have gone free."

6. In his anger with Teiresias, what expression of *hubris,* the overweening pride that offends the gods, does Oedipus utter? Compare his words with the Priest's statement in the Prologue.

7. Consider and discuss the unanswered question in the exchange about riddles (lines 426–30).

ODE I

Read closely and interpret Antistrophe 2 (lines 477–85), considering especially "For wisdom changes hands among the wise."

SCENE II

1. Interpret the speech of the Choragos (line 504), "I can not judge the behavior of great men."

2. In this scene we discover that

authority in Thebes legally rests in a triumvirate. How does this information add to our knowledge of Oedipus's character? How does it illuminate his speech and behavior in the Prologue and Scene I?

3. Discuss what Kreon says in lines 551–62, and show what it reveals about his character.

4. Consider line 591 in the light of Teiresias's comment about temperate words. How may this aspect of Oedipus's character bear upon the death of Laïos and upon the question of Oedipus's responsibility for his own fate? What does Kreon say later in this same scene that bears further on this question and seems to refer to a well-known trait in Oedipus?

5. Explain the significance of the servant's request, lines 715–20.

6. In Oedipus's description of his fatal encounter with Laïos, what is revealed of each man's character?

ODE II

Read closely and weigh carefully this magnificent Ode, a superb poem in itself.

1. Why is it introduced at precisely this point in the play?

2. How does the Chorus specifically rebuke the rulers of Thebes? Should the Chorus also rebuke themselves for Antistrophe 2 of Ode I (lines 477–85)?

SCENE III

1. Interpret Iokastê's opening speech in the light of Ode II.

2. Explain how and why Iokastê and Oedipus were speaking at cross-purposes at the close of this scene (lines 1001–21).

3. In what way do lines 1027–32 contribute final touches to Oedipus's folly?

ODE IV

Discuss this Ode, with special attention to lines 1139 and 1173.

Looking Back at the Play as a Whole

1. Give an appraisal of Oedipus's character. Be mindful of strengths and weaknesses, virtues and shortcomings, and the ways in which such seemingly contradictory qualities can overlap. Be specific and support your views with allusions and quotations.

2. It is the nature of great tragedy to raise unanswered — indeed perhaps unanswerable — questions, for the deep dilemmas of life give it the tragic dimension. No one has ever resolved neatly and satisfactorily the degree to which Oedipus is a helpless victim of a predetermined fate or is responsible for the catastrophes that overwhelm him. Give your views of the problem, supported by evidence and argument. In this connection, weigh lines 789–90.

3. Did Laïos incur guilt in attempting to slay his own child to protect himself? Did he deserve a better fate than he got? Consider the case of Iokastê, too, in the light of line 1114: "Oh heartless mother!"

4. If (or when) you have read *King Lear,* compare its concluding view of life with that of this play.

AFTERWORD

In drama the Greeks prized unity of time, place, and action. It was not always achieved, but *Oedipus the King* is perfect in this respect. In its single setting before the palace of the Theban kings, the play flows in unbroken continuity, with no interruptions or lapses of time. Dramatic intensity is always heightened by such unity.

Since the Greek audience knew the story of Oedipus, they were not waiting to see what would happen. They knew the terrible discoveries the proud king would make. They wanted to watch *how* these discoveries were made, identifying themselves with Oedipus in the painful anticipation of what awaited him. The resulting suspense, which we too should feel, is the high suspense of involvement, of caring, of feeling that something in what is happening is related to our lives, however different we and our circumstances may be.

The Greek audience was interested also to see what illumination Sophocles would cast upon the bare, familiar outlines of the story. Each teller, or dramatizer, colors and interprets a story by what he puts in the mouths of its characters. Thus the audience looked to Sophocles not just for an account of what happened but also for light as to what it meant.

One of the puzzles of Greek drama involves prophecies and fate, on the one hand, and the question of responsibility, on the other. Did the foretelling that Oedipus would slay his father and marry his mother mean that these events were inevitable, that he was the victim of a pre-determined fate, that he was *compelled* to do these things?

Probably most Greeks, like most people since then, took this to be the case. If we accept such a view, it would seem to acquit Oedipus of any guilt or responsibility: he acted without either choice or knowledge.

This is the crucial question of the play. Oedipus states it in an anguished cry:

> Ah,
> If I was created so, born to this fate,
> Who could deny the savagery of God?

Yet he *feels* guilty, and so does Iokastê. Both punish themselves. The oracle says Oedipus is a "pollution." This is a hard line; it says evil is evil and guilt is guilt whether you intended it or knew it or not. And this may be so.

But another view is possible. Foreknowledge (prophecy) does not necessarily imply predestination. It may simply mean that some see more clearly than others the end toward which events are leading — as when we prophesy of a notorious spendthrift that he will go broke, or of a delinquent that he will have trouble with the law.

Then what about supernatural prophecy, with explicit details about happenings yet to come? The prophecies about the fate of Oedipus were made by the gods, or at least by one of them, Apollo.

Even here speculations are possible both about the prescience of the gods and about the nature of time. As a man in an airplane may see two cars headed for collision at the crest of a hill, neither car being yet able to see the other, so by analogy we can suppose the god to have foreseen the "collision" of Oedipus and Laïos and its chain of consequences. As for seeing the future, this may be thought of as a relative matter. Man is *in* time as he understands it by his own life and death. Immortal gods are outside or above such time. They may see a finished action and "foretell" it without necessarily compelling it. Its inevitability then would simply be that it *has happened* in an immortal vision of time before we have got to the event in the thin running thread of the present, which is our own experience of time.

Foretold or not, *why* did it happen? Like events not foretold, it is the result of certain human actions and traits of character. Both the shepherds, who as messengers bring such awful news, had been actors in the story, motivated solely and ironically by unselfish pity for a victimized baby.

Why do the gods reveal a part of the pattern to one person and other parts to others? For what reason other than to force people into moral choices and to observe their decisions?

Laïos was a man who, out of fear for his own life, wished to murder his son. We know of men who would give their lives to save a son. He demonstrates what many fables show: the futility of a man's trying to evade the fate in which he believes. Laïos's effort to do so is craven. He fails to save himself and makes himself guilty of an attempt to commit child-murder. Did Laïos deserve better than he got?

Iokastê consented to the deed — "Oh heartless mother!" the anguished Oedipus cries even in the shock of discovery. Did she not earn her fate? At the end of Scene III, badly shaken but still misunderstanding what is happening, Oedipus says, "I am a child of Luck. . . . Luck is my mother. . . ." But this metaphoric mother has delivered him to destruction just as his natural mother had done.

How are we to judge Oedipus? Ironically, mistaken about his parents' identities, he tried to avoid his destiny by removing himself from his supposed mother and father. Yet might he not earlier have found out more? Had he never questioned the history of those swollen feet from which he got his name? If he feared that he was to kill his father, why did he not take the one sure precaution: that of not killing *anyone?* The haughty, intemperate natures of father and son produced the slaying at the crossroads. Perhaps Oedipus could not have avoided the rest. Yet he heightens the impact of his fall by the excessive pride of his bearing and by his confidence that he will not be involved in the truths he is determined to bring to light.

But even his faults do not obscure the fact that he is a nobler man than his father had been. When the first partial disclosure — that of his slaying of Laïos — has emerged, he does not shrink from pressing on. He does not comfort himself by an evasion. And whereas Iokastê for a time repudiates oracles as false, he never questions the truth of the prophecy about himself. Nor does he fall into base self-pity. Instead of claiming that he is not to blame for his deeds, he insists upon his guilt; he will not accept the diminishment of manhood that absence of responsibility would imply. He punishes himself for "the horrors of my own doing!" and calls for exile. He is keenly aware of the ironies that have accompanied his seemingly triumphant career. He laments "the flooding pain/Of memory, never to be gouged out," but only after having acknowledged "My fair winds brought me here." It is these qualities that maintain the greatness of the fallen king, putting him far above decent but mediocre Kreon, who is happy to have high position without responsibility.

Oedipus speaks of "the great wreck/And hell of Oedipus, whom the gods hate," but later it will be proved that they do not hate him, however savagely life may have dealt with him. In *Oedipus at Colonus,* the next play of Sophocles's Theban trilogy, Theseus, the hero-king of Athens, gives aid and shelter to the blind exile. That the gods have indeed reserved a special destiny for Oedipus is shown in an extraordinary scene in which he is taken to a nobly mysterious death, somehow hallowed in a manner not common to men. Even in the present play, in spite of his bitter words about the hatred of the gods, he has a premonition of a special end, without comprehending what it means (lines 1407–09):

> Death will not ever come to me through sickness
> Or in any natural way: I have been preserved
> For some unthinkable fate.

In *Oedipus at Colonus* the blind exile is carried into a dimension beyond tragedy. Illumination is cast into the terrible darkness in which the present play closes. It is reported of his death:

> No fiery thunderbolt of the god removed him in that hour, nor any rising of storm from the sea; but either a messenger from the gods, or the world of the dead, the nether adamant, riven for him in love, without pain; for the passing of the man was not with lamentation, or in sickness and suffering, but, above mortal's, wonderful.

No matter how the speculative questions about fate and responsibility are answered — and no one can answer them except for himself — the somber comment of the play about life in general is unequivocal. In Ode IV the chorus says of Oedipus:

> I who saw your days call no man blest —

At the very end, the Choragos says directly, admonishingly, to the audience:

> Let every man in mankind's frailty
> Consider his last day; and let none
> Presume on his good fortune until he find
> Life, at his death, a memory without pain.

A classical parallel occurs in Plutarch's life of Solon the lawgiver. Solon visited the court of Croesus, King of Lydia, reputed to be the wealthiest man in the world. Croesus displayed all his wealth and waited complacently for Solon to hail him as a fortunate man. Solon would not do so, even when pressed by the angry king, saying in effect, "You aren't dead yet." Some years later, Lydia was conquered and Croesus was taken prisoner by Cyrus, King of Persia. Croesus was about to be beheaded at the feet of Cyrus when, on his knees, he cried out, "O, Solon!" Puzzled, Cyrus inquired what was meant. He was so chastened when he heard the story that he spared Croesus's life and kept him in dignity in the court for the rest of his life.

In Ode II, the Chorus rises to a peak of dignity and beauty. The poem is truly reverential, a noble hymn to God (note its unmistakable tone of monotheism despite its being nominally within the Olympian tradition) and a meditation upon life. The cautionary words at the play's end should be weighed in the spirit of this great Ode.

The Tragedy of King Lear

by William Shakespeare (1564–1616)

Many people say that *King Lear* is the greatest of Shakespeare's works. These people can, if they like, find passionate and formidable opponents in the ranks of those who make the same assertion for *Hamlet,* or *Macbeth,* or *Othello.* Ensuing debates may provide intellectual exercise, recreation, and knowledge, but rarely do they change the positions of the contestants. Opinion may be changed by argument, but not real love, and it is love which inspires such an assertion as, *"King Lear* is Shakespeare's greatest work." When we respond to a work of art so intensely that we demand from others an admission of its supremacy, we are not being reasonable; we are in love. In a sense we have no more right to make such a demand than we have to expect other people to agree with us on the superiority of our wife, husband, son, or daughter.

When we encounter a work of art (or a person, for that matter) that evokes frequently this kind of strong, apparently unreasonable love, we can be fairly certain that we are in the presence of something special. And we can, whether in the end we fall in love ourselves or not, find out what it is that makes up that specialness.

As a well-established playwright, actor, and producer, William Shakespeare wrote *King Lear* at the height of his powers, probably in 1605. Official records specify that the work was "played before the Kinges maiestie at Whitehall upon St. Stephens night" (December 26) in 1606. Perhaps you will think *King Lear* rather grim for a Christmas revel; but James I, besides being the "Kinges maiestie," was an ardent, perceptive connoisseur of the theater and had to have the very best of it available for his special occasions. There could have been little doubt that year that the work of the author of the recent *Hamlet* and *Othello* and of so many earlier successes was the very best.

Most of those in the audiences of the time, certainly including King James, were familiar with the general story of King Lear before seeing Shakespeare's play. The prehistoric king of Britain had been a shadowy figure of legend for centuries. Geoffrey of Monmouth had in the twelfth century recorded a melodramatic chronicle of the ancient monarch and his three daughters; the popular sixteenth-century historian, Holinshed, enlarged on Geoffrey's tale; and a play about King Lear, crude and of unknown authorship, had been on and off the London stages since 1594.

But even if you have never encountered the story before, you will note as others have that this play contains hauntingly familiar events, people, and themes. It presents some of the oldest and most universal circumstances of life; its stuff is the stuff of myth and legend.

DRAMATIS PERSONAE

LEAR, *King of Britain*
KING OF FRANCE
DUKE OF BURGUNDY
DUKE OF CORNWALL
DUKE OF ALBANY
EARL OF KENT
EARL OF GLOUCESTER
EDGAR, *son of Gloucester*
EDMUND, *bastard son of Gloucester*
CURAN, *a courtier*
OSWALD, *steward to Goneril*
OLD MAN, *tenant of Gloucester*
DOCTOR

FOOL *to Lear*
A CAPTAIN, *under Edmund*
GENTLEMAN, *attendant on Cordelia*
HERALD
SERVANTS *to Cornwall*
GONERIL
REGAN   } *daughters of Lear*
CORDELIA
KNIGHTS *attending on Lear,* GENTLE-
MEN, MESSENGERS, SOLDIERS, *and* AT-
TENDANTS

SCENE: *Britain*

ACT I

SCENE I. KING LEAR'*s palace.*

Enter KENT, GLOUCESTER, *and* EDMUND.

KENT. I thought the King had more affected° the Duke of Albany than Cornwall.

GLOUCESTER. It did always seem so to us. But now in the division of the kingdom it appears not which of the dukes he values most, for equalities are so weighed, that curiosity in neither can make 5 choice of either's moiety.°

KENT.° Is not this your son, my lord?

1. **affected:** favored. 6. **moiety:** share, portion. 7. Kent and Gloucester have apparently just left the royal council. What has been the subject of that meeting? How definite are their impressions of the King's plans?

GLOUCESTER. His breeding, sir, hath been at my charge. I have so often blushed to acknowledge him, that now I am brazed to't.

KENT. I cannot conceive° you. 10

GLOUCESTER. Sir, this young fellow's mother could; whereupon she grew round-wombed, and had indeed, sir, a son for her cradle, ere she had a husband for her bed. Do you smell a fault?

KENT. I cannot wish the fault undone, the issue of it being so proper.

GLOUCESTER. But I have a son, sir, by order of law, some year elder 15 than this, who yet is no dearer in my account, though this knave came something saucily to the world before he was sent for. Yet was his mother fair; there was good sport at his making, and the whoreson must be acknowledged. Do you know this noble gentleman, Edmund? 20

EDMUND. No, my lord.

GLOUCESTER. My Lord of Kent. Remember him hereafter as my honourable friend.

EDMUND. My services to your lordship.

KENT. I must love you, and sue to know you better. 25

EDMUND. Sir, I shall study deserving.

GLOUCESTER. He hath been out nine years, and away he shall again. The King is coming.

Sennet.* Enter one bearing a coronet, LEAR, CORNWALL, AL-
BANY, GONERIL, REGAN, CORDELIA, *and* ATTENDANTS.

LEAR. Attend the Lords of France and Burgundy,° Gloucester.

GLOUCESTER. I shall, my lord.   *Exeunt* GLOUCESTER *and* EDMUND. 30

LEAR. Meantime we shall express our darker purpose.
  Give me the map there. Know that we have divided
  In three our kingdom; and 'tis our fast intent
  To shake all cares and business from our age,
  Conferring them on younger strengths, while we 35
  Unburdened crawl toward death. Our son of Cornwall,
  And you, our no less loving son of Albany,
  We have this hour a constant will to publish
  Our daughters' several dowers, that future strife

10. conceive: understand. * Sennet: trumpet call to announce the approach of a procession. 29. the Lords . . . Burgundy: the King of France and the Duke of Burgundy. (During much of the Middle Ages, Burgundy, which is now known chiefly as a wine-producing region in eastern France, was a more or less independent dukedom, as powerful and important as the kingdom of France.)

May be prevented now. The princes, France and Burgundy, 40
Great rivals in our youngest daughter's love,
Long in our Court have made their amorous sojourn,
And here are to be answered. Tell me, my daughters —
Since now we will divest us both of rule,
Interest of territory, cares of state — 45
Which of you shall we say doth love us most,
That we our largest bounty may extend
Where nature doth with merit challenge.° Goneril,
Our eldest born, speak first.

GONERIL.   Sir, I love you more than word can wield the matter, 50
Dearer than eyesight, space, and liberty,
Beyond what can be valued, rich or rare,
No less than life, with grace, health, beauty, honour,
As much as child e'er loved, or father found;
A love that makes breath poor, and speech unable — 55
Beyond all manner of so much I love you.

CORDELIA.   [Aside] What shall Cordelia speak? Love, and be silent.

LEAR.   Of all these bounds, even from this line to this,
With shadowy forests and with champains° riched,
With plenteous rivers, and wide-skirted meads, 60
We make thee lady. To thine and Albany's issue
Be this perpetual.° What says our second daughter?
Our dearest Regan, wife of Cornwall? Speak.

REGAN.   I am made of that self metal as my sister,
And prize me at her worth. In my true heart, 65
I find she names my very deed of love.
Only she comes too short, that I profess
Myself an enemy to all other joys,
Which the most precious square of sense possesses,
And find I am alone felicitate° 70
In your dear Highness' love.

CORDELIA.   [Aside]   Then poor Cordelia —
And yet not so, since I am sure my love's
More ponderous than my tongue.

LEAR.   To thee, and thine hereditary ever,

48. What does Lear apparently mean by the words *nature* and *merit*?
59. champains: arable fields. 62. What does this word tell about Lear's attitude
toward his own pronouncements? 70. felicitate: made happy.

Remain this ample third of our fair kingdom,
No less in space, validity, and pleasure,
Than that conferred on Goneril. Now our joy,
Although our last and least, to whose young love
The vines of France and milk of Burgundy
Strive to be interest. What can you say, to draw
A third more opulent than your sisters? Speak.

CORDELIA. Nothing, my lord.

LEAR. Nothing?

CORDELIA. Nothing.

LEAR. Nothing will come of nothing. Speak again.

CORDELIA. Unhappy that I am, I cannot heave
My heart into my mouth.° I love your Majesty
According to my bond, no more nor less.

LEAR. How, how, Cordelia? Mend your speech a little,
Lest you may mar your fortunes.

CORDELIA.   Good my lord,
You have begot me, bred me, loved me. I
Return those duties back as are right fit,
Obey you, love you, and most honour you.
Why have my sisters husbands, if they say
They love you all? Haply when I shall wed,
That lord whose hand must take my plight shall carry
Half my love with him, half my care, and duty.
Sure I shall never marry like my sisters,
To love my father all.

LEAR. But goes thy heart with this?

CORDELIA.   Ay, my good lord.

LEAR. So young, and so untender?°

CORDELIA. So young my lord, and true.

LEAR. Let it be so, thy truth then be thy dower.
For by the sacred radiance of the sun,
The mysteries of Hecate° and the night,
By all the operation of the orbs
From whom we do exist, and cease to be,
Here I disclaim all my paternal care,

87. How does this figure of speech compare in *tone* with what Goneril and
Regan have been saying? 101. Why does Lear call Cordelia's heart "untender"?
105. Hecate: goddess of the moon and of magic.

Propinquity and property of blood,°
And as a stranger to my heart and me   110
Hold thee from this for ever. The barbarous Scythian,°
Or he that makes his generation messes
To gorge his appetite,° shall to my bosom
Be as well neighboured, pitied, and relieved,
As thou my sometime daughter.

KENT.   Good my liege —   115

LEAR.   Peace Kent,
Come not between the dragon and his wrath.
I loved her most, and thought to set my rest
On her kind nursery. — Hence, and avoid my sight. —
So be my grave my peace, as here I give   120
Her father's heart from her. Call France. Who stirs?
Call Burgundy. Cornwall and Albany,
With my two daughters' dowers digest the third.
Let pride, which she calls plainness, marry her.
I do invest you jointly with my power,   125
Pre-eminence, and all the large effects
That troop with majesty. Ourself by monthly course,
With reservation of an hundred knights,
By you to be sustained, shall our abode
Make with you by due turn. Only we shall retain   130
The name, and all th' addition to a King.
The sway, revenue, execution of the rest,
Beloved sons, be yours, which to confirm,
This coronet part between you.°

KENT.   Royal Lear,
Whom I have ever honoured as my King,   135
Loved as my father, as my master followed,
As my great patron thought on in my prayers —

LEAR.   The bow is bent and drawn, make from the shaft.

KENT.   Let it fall rather, though the fork° invade

109. Lear disclaims any physical relationship with Cordelia. Is he overlooking
certain limitations to the power of even a king? 111. Scythian: Scythians, a no-
madic people of the Black Sea area who, for Elizabethans, were standard examples of primitive ferocity. 112–13. he . . . appetite: i.e., he that feeds glutton-
ously on his own children. 134. Lear wants to be called by the kingly title and to
have the attentions due the person of a king. What exactly *is* he giving up?
139. fork: point of a forked arrow.

The region of my heart. Be Kent unmannerly, 140
When Lear is mad. What wouldst thou do, old man?
Think'st thou that duty shall have dread to speak,
When power to flattery bows? To plainness honour's bound,
When majesty falls to folly. Reserve thy state,
And in thy best consideration check 145
This hideous rashness. Answer my life my judgement;,
Thy youngest daughter does not love thee least,
Nor are those empty-hearted whose low sounds
Reverb° no hollowness.

LEAR.   Kent, on thy life no more.
KENT. My life I never held but as a pawn° 150
Το wage against thine enemies; ne'er feared to lose it,
Thy safety being motive.
LEAR.   Out of my sight!
KENT. See better, Lear, and let me still remain
The true blank° of thine eye.
LEAR. Now by Apollo —
KENT.   Now by Apollo, King, 155
Thou swear'st thy gods in vain.
LEAR.   O vassal! Miscreant!°
ALBANY *and* CORNWALL. Dear sir, forbear.
KENT. Kill thy physician, and the fee bestow
Upon the foul disease. Revoke thy gift,
Or whilst I can vent clamour from my throat, 160
I'll tell thee thou dost evil.
LEAR.   Hear me, recreant!°
On thine allegiance,° hear me!
That thou hast sought to make us break our vow,
Which we durst never yet, and with strained pride
To come between our sentence and our power, 165
Which nor our nature nor our place can bear,

---

149. **Reverb.** reverberate, re-echo. **150.** Kent's metaphor is from the ancient game of chess. Pawns are the least valuable pieces on the board, and they are sacrificed readily in order to protect more important pieces. Against which of Lear's enemies is Kent ready to sacrifice his pawn now? **154. blank:** center of target, bull's eye (hence, the thing aimed at). **156. Miscreant:** literally, misbeliever. **161. recreant:** one who breaks his oath of fealty, a traitor. **162.** Why do you suppose that Lear calls on Kent's allegiance when he has called him "recreant"?

Our potency made good,° take thy reward.
Five days we do allot thee for provision
To shield thee from disasters of the world,
And on the sixth to turn thy hated back   170
Upon our kingdom. If on the tenth day following
Thy banished trunk° be found in our dominions,
The moment is thy death. Away! By Jupiter,
This shall not be revoked.

KENT.   Fare thee well, King; sith thus thou wilt appear,   175
Freedom lives hence, and banishment is here.
[*To* CORDELIA] The gods to their dear shelter take thee, maid,
That justly think'st, and hast most rightly said.
[*To* REGAN *and* GONERIL] And your large speeches may your deeds
    approve,
That good effects may spring from words of love.   180
Thus Kent, o princes, bids you all adieu;
He'll shape his old course in a country new.   *Exit.*

Flourish.* *Enter* GLOUCESTER, *with* KING OF FRANCE, BURGUNDY,
    and ATTENDANTS.

GLOUCESTER.   Here's France and Burgundy, my noble lord.
LEAR.   My Lord of Burgundy,
We first address toward you, who with this King   185
Hath rivalled for our daughter. What in the least
Will you require in present dower with her,
Or cease your quest of love?
BURGUNDY.   Most royal Majesty,
I crave no more than hath your Highness offered,
Nor will you tender less.
LEAR.   Right noble Burgundy,   190
When she was dear to us, we did hold her so,
But now her price is fallen. Sir, there she stands.
If aught within that little-seeming substance,
Or all of it, with our displeasure pieced,°
And nothing more, may fitly like° your Grace,   195
She's there, and she is yours.
BURGUNDY.   I know no answer.

167. **Our . . . good:** our (my) power being now asserted. 172. **trunk:** body.
* **Flourish:** trumpet fanfare. 194. **pieced:** added to it. 195. **fitly like:** suitably please.

LEAR.   Will you, with those infirmities she owes,°
         Unfriended, new adopted to our hate,
         Dowered with our curse, and strangered with our oath,
         Take her, or leave her?

BURGUNDY.   Pardon me, royal sir;   200
         Election makes not up in such conditions.°

LEAR.   Then leave her, sir; for, by the power that made me,
         I tell you all her wealth [To FRANCE] For you, great King,
         I would not from your love make such a stray,°
         To match you where I hate, therefore beseech you   205
         T' avert your liking a more worthier way
         Than on a wretch whom nature is ashamed
         Almost t' acknowledge hers.°

KING OF FRANCE.   This is most strange,
         That she whom even but now was your best object,
         The argument° of your praise, balm of your age,   210
         The best, the dearest, should in this trice of time
         Commit a thing so monstrous, to dismantle
         So many folds of favour. Sure her offence
         Must be of such unnatural degree,
         That monsters it;° or your fore-vouched affection   215
         Fall into taint, which to believe of her,
         Must be a faith that reason without miracle
         Should never plant in me.°

CORDELIA.   I yet beseech your Majesty —
         If for I want that glib and oily art,
         To speak and purpose not;° since what I well intend,   220
         I'll do't before I speak — that you make known
         It is no vicious blot, murder, or foulness,
         No unchaste action, or dishonoured step,
         That hath deprived me of your grace and favour;
         But even for want of that for which I am richer,   225
         A still-soliciting eye,° and such a tongue

197. owes: owns, possesses. 201. Election . . . conditions: an impersonal way
of saying, "You leave me no choice." 204. from . . . stray: remove myself so far
from showing love to you. 208. Again, what assumptions does Lear seem to have
about nature? 210. argument: theme, topic. 215. monsters it: makes it a monster.
216–18. which . . . me: that is so contrary to reason that only a miracle could
make me believe it. 220. purpose not: not mean it. 226. still-soliciting eye: a look
that forever implies its owner's interest in getting something for himself.

That I am glad I have not, though not to have it
Hath lost me in your liking.
LEAR.   Better thou
Hadst not been born, than not t' have pleased me better.°
KING OF FRANCE. Is it but this? A tardiness in nature°   230
Which often leaves the history unspoke
That it intends to do? My Lord of Burgundy,
What say you to the lady? Love's not love
When it is mingled with regards that stand
Aloof from the entire point. Will you have her?   235
She is herself a dowry.
BURGUNDY.   Royal King,
Give but that portion which yourself proposed,
And here I take Cordelia by the hand,
Duchess of Burgundy.
LEAR. Nothing. I have sworn, I am firm.   240
BURGUNDY. I am sorry then you have so lost a father,
That you must lose a husband.
CORDELIA.   Peace be with Burgundy.
Since that respects of fortune are his love,
I shall not be his wife.
KING OF FRANCE. Fairest Cordelia, that art most rich being poor,   245
Most choice forsaken, and most loved despised,
Thee and thy virtues here I seize upon.
Be it lawful I take up what's cast away.
Gods, gods! 'Tis strange that from their cold'st neglect
My love should kindle to inflamed respect.   250
Thy dowerless daughter, King, thrown to my chance,
Is Queen of us, of ours, and our fair France.
Not all the dukes of wat'rish° Burgundy
Can buy this unprized precious maid of me.
Bid them farewell, Cordelia, though unkind;   255
Thou losest here, a better where to find.
LEAR. Thou hast her, France; let her be thine, for we
Have no such daughter, nor shall ever see
That face of hers again. Therefore be gone,

229. What does Lear's retort to Cordelia's request reveal about his attitude
toward what has happened in this scene? 230. tardiness in nature: natural reticence.
253. wat'rish: with the double meaning of "having many rivers" and "fable."

Without our grace, our love, our benison.°   260
Come, noble Burgundy.°

      Flourish. Exeunt LEAR, BURGUNDY, CORNWALL,
        ALBANY, GLOUCESTER, *and* ATTENDANTS.

KING OF FRANCE. Bid farewell to your sisters.

CORDELIA. The jewels of our father,° with washed eyes
 Cordelia leaves you. I know you what you are,
 And like a sister am most loth to call   265
 Your faults as they are named. Love well our father.
 To your professed bosoms I commit him,
 But yet, alas, stood I within his grace,
 I would prefer him to a better place.
 So farewell to you both.   270

REGAN. Prescribe not us our duty.

GONERIL.   Let your study
 Be to content your lord, who hath received you
 At fortune's alms. You have obedience scanted,
 And well are worth the want that you have wanted.°

CORDELIA. Time shall unfold what plighted° cunning hides,   275
 Who covers faults, at last with shame derides.
 Well may you prosper.

KING OF FRANCE.   Come, my fair Cordelia.

      Exeunt KING OF FRANCE *and* CORDELIA.

GONERIL. Sister, it is not little I have to say of what most nearly apper-
 tains to us both. I think our father will hence to-night.

REGAN. That's most certain, and with you; next month with us.   280

GONERIL. You see how full of changes his age is; the observation we have
 made of it hath not been little. He always loved our sister most,
 and with what poor judgement he hath now cast her off appears
 too grossly.

REGAN. 'Tis the infirmity of his age; yet he hath ever but slenderly   285
 known himself.°

GONERIL. The best and soundest of his time hath been but rash, then
 must we look from his age to receive not alone the imperfections

---

260. **benison:** blessing. 261. **Come, noble Burgundy:** In the context, what is
Lear saying to the king of France with these words? 263. How apt is this metaphor? 274. In this punning clause, *want* is used in its meaning of "lack" and
"desire." 275. **plighted:** plaited, i.e., folded, hidden. 286. What do Goneril and
Regan think of Lear's treatment of Cordelia? What do they give us to understand
about his nature prior to this scene of old age?

of long-ingrafted condition,° but therewithal the unruly wayward-
ness that infirm and choleric years bring with them.   290

REGAN.   Such unconstant starts are we like to have from him, as this of
   Kent's banishment.

GONERIL.   There is further compliment° of leave-taking between France
   and him. Pray you let us hit° together; if our father carry authority
   with such disposition as he bears, this last surrender° of his   295
   will but offend us.

REGAN.   We shall further think of it.

GONERIL.   We must do something, and i' th' heat.°   *Exeunt.*

289. **long-ingrafted condition:** temper which has long been part of his nature.
293. **compliment:** ceremony. What is the nature of further *compliment* between
Lear and France likely to be? 294. **hit:** hit it off, agree. 295. **this last surrender:**
Lear's surrender of his power to Goneril and Regan and their husbands. 298. **i' th'
heat:** quickly.

SCENE II. GLOUCESTER's castle.

Enter EDMUND, *with a letter*.

EDMUND.   Thou, Nature, art my goddess, to thy law
   My services are bound. Wherefore should I
   Stand in the plague of custom, and permit
   The curiosity of nations to deprive me,°
   For that I am some twelve or fourteen moonshines   5
   Lag of° a brother? Why bastard? Wherefore base,
   When my dimensions are as well compact,
   My mind as generous,° and my shape as true,
   As honest madam's issue? Why brand they us
   With base? With baseness? Bastardy? Base, base!°   10
   Who in the lusty stealth of nature take
   More composition, and fierce quality,
   Than doth within a dull, stale, tired bed
   Go to th' creating a whole tribe of fops,°

2–4. **Wherefore . . . me:** Edmund speaks of the laws of society (which deprive him of full inheritance because he is illegitimate and the younger son) as
a curse or sickness of unreasoned habit springing from the meddlesomeness of
governments. 6. **Lag of:** behind. Edmund is a year or so younger than Edgar.
8. **generous:** large, strong. Edmund's usage of the word does not bear the modern connotation of unselfishness. 10. **base:** Edmund assumes, probably mistakenly,
that the word *bastard* is formed on the adjective *base*. 14. **fops:** effeminate fools.

Got° 'tween asleep and wake? Well then,   15
Legitimate Edgar, I must have your land.
Our father's love is to the bastard Edmund
As to th' legitimate. Fine word — legitimate!
Well, my legitimate, if this letter speed,
And my invention thrive, Edmund the base   20
Shall to th' legitimate. I grow, I prosper.
Now gods, stand up for bastards.

Enter GLOUCESTER.

GLOUCESTER. Kent banished thus! And France in choler parted!
And the King gone to-night! Prescribed his power,
Confined to exhibition!° All this done   25
Upon the gad.° Edmund, how now! What news?

EDMUND. So please your lordship, none.

GLOUCESTER. Why so earnestly seek you to put up that letter?

EDMUND. I know no news, my lord.

GLOUCESTER. What paper were you reading?   30

EDMUND. Nothing, my lord.°

GLOUCESTER. No? What needed then that terrible dispatch of it into your
pocket? The quality of nothing hath not such need to hide itself.
Let's see. Come, if it be nothing, I shall not need spectacles.

EDMUND. I beseech you sir, pardon me; it is a letter from my brother,   35
that I have not all o'er-read; and for so much as I have perused,
I find it not fit for your o'er-looking.

GLOUCESTER. Give me the letter, sir.

EDMUND. I shall offend either to detain or give it. The contents, as in
part I understand them, are to blame.   40

GLOUCESTER. Let's see, let's see.

EDMUND. I hope, for my brother's justification, he wrote this but as an
essay or taste° of my virtue.

GLOUCESTER. [Reads] *This policy, and reverence of age, makes the world*
bitter to the best of our times; keeps our fortunes from us, till   45
our oldness cannot relish° them. I begin to find an idle and fond

---

15. Got: begotten. 25. The King is now King ceremonially only. 26. Upon the
gad: on the spur of the moment. 31. Nothing, my lord: Remember that these are
Cordelia's very words to *her* father's demand. See what comes of these "nothings,"
which recur often in the play. 43. essay or taste: trial or test. Notice that Edmund's
vocabulary changes with his audience. His private diction is brutally direct.
46. relish: enjoy.

bondage in the oppression of aged tyranny, who sways not as it hath power, but as it is suffered. Come to me, that of this I may speak more. If our father would sleep till I waked him, you should enjoy half his revenue for ever, and live the beloved of your 50 *brother. Edgar.*

Hum! Conspiracy! — *Sleep till I waked him, you should enjoy half his revenue* — My son Edgar! Had he a hand to write this? A heart and brain to breed it in? When came this to you? Who brought it?

EDMUND. It was not brought me, my lord; there's the cunning of it. 55 I found it thrown in at the casement of my closet.

GLOUCESTER. You know the character to be your brother's?

EDMUND. If the matter were good, my lord, I durst swear it were his; but in respect of that, I would fain think it were not.

GLOUCESTER. It is his.° 60

EDMUND. It is his hand, my lord. But I hope his heart is not in the contents.

GLOUCESTER. Has he never before sounded you in this business?

EDMUND. Never, my lord. But I have heard him oft maintain it to be fit, that sons at perfect age, and fathers declined, the father should 65 be as ward to the son, and the son manage his revenue.

GLOUCESTER. O villain, villain — his very opinion in the letter. Abhorred villain, unnatural, detested, brutish villain; worse than brutish! Go, sirrah, seek him: I'll apprehend him. Abominable villain, where is he? 70

EDMUND. I do not well know, my lord. If it shall please you to suspend your indignation against my brother, till you can derive from him better testimony of his intent, you should run a certain course; where, if you violently proceed against him, mistaking his purpose, it would make a great gap in your own honour and shake in 75 pieces the heart of his obedience. I dare pawn down my life for him, that he hath writ this to feel my affection to your honour, and to no other pretence of danger.

GLOUCESTER. Think you so?

EDMUND. If your honour judge it meet, I will place you where you 80 shall hear us confer of this, and by an auricular assurance° have

60. **It is his:** Thinking about unpleasant things is hard and unpleasant work, at least when one thinks toward some conclusion or decision. How does Gloucester's easy acceptance of Edmund's conclusions fit in with what we know about him?
81. **auricular assurance:** proof heard by your own ears.

your satisfaction, and that without any further delay than this very
evening.

GLOUCESTER. He cannot be such a monster.

EDMUND. Nor is not, sure.   85

GLOUCESTER. To his father, that so tenderly and entirely loves him —
heaven and earth! Edmund, seek him out; wind me into him,° I
pray you. Frame the business after your own wisdom. I would un-
state myself, to be in a due resolution.°

EDMUND. I will seek him sir, presently; convey the business as I shall 90
find means, and acquaint you withal.

GLOUCESTER. These late eclipses in the sun and moon portend no good to
us;° though the wisdom of nature can reason° it thus, and thus, yet
nature finds itself scourged by the sequent° effects. Love cools,
friendship falls off, brothers divide. In cities, mutinies; in coun- 95
tries, discord; in palaces, treason; and the bond cracked 'twixt son
and father. This villain of mine comes under the prediction, there's
son against father; the King falls from bias of nature, there's father
against child. We have seen the best of our time. Machinations,
hollowness, treachery, and all ruinous disorders, follow us dis- 100
quietly to our graves. Find out this villain, Edmund; it shall lose
thee nothing, do it carefully. And the noble and true-hearted Kent
banished; his offence, honesty. 'Tis strange.   *Exit.*

EDMUND. This is the excellent foppery° of the world, that when we are
sick in fortune, often the surfeits of our own behaviour, we 105
make guilty of our disasters the sun, the moon, and stars, as if we
were villains on necessity, fools by heavenly compulsion, knaves,
thieves, and treachers° by spherical predominance; drunkards, liars,
and adulterers by an enforced obedience of planetary influence; and
all that we are evil in, by a divine thrusting on. An admirable 110
evasion of whoremaster man, to lay his goatish disposition on the
charge of a star. My father compounded with my mother under the
dragon's tail, and my nativity was under ursa major,° so that it
follows, I am rough and lecherous. Fut, I should have been that I

87. **wind . . . him:** worm yourself into his confidence for me. 88–89. **I . . .
resolution:** I would give up my estate (earldom) to learn the truth. 93. How
does Gloucester's assumption that future disaster is foretold by eclipses and other
disturbances in unhuman nature, rather than by the good or evil actions of himself and others, help to characterize him? **reason:** explain. 94. **sequent:** following, subsequent. 104. **foppery:** weak foolishness. 108. **treachers:** traitors. 113. **ursa
major:** the constellation of the Great Bear.

am, had the maidenliest star in the firmament twinkled on my   115
bastardizing.

Enter EDGAR.

Edgar! Pat. He comes like the catastrophe° of the old comedy.°
My cue is villainous melancholy, with a sigh like Tom o' Bedlam.°
—O these eclipses do portend these divisions. Fa, sol, la, mi.

EDGAR. How now, brother Edmund, what serious contemplation are   120
you in?

EDMUND. I am thinking, brother, of a prediction I read this other day,
what should follow these eclipses.

EDGAR. Do you busy yourself with that?

EDMUND. I promise you, the effects he writes of succeed unhappily;   125
as of unnaturalness between the child and the parent; death, dearth,
dissolutions of ancient amities, divisions in state, menaces and maledictions against king and nobles; needless diffidences, banishment of
friends, dissipation of cohorts, nuptial breaches, and I know not
what.   130

EDGAR. How long have you been a sectary astronomical?°

EDMUND. Come, come, when saw you my father last?

EDGAR. The night gone by.

EDMUND. Spake you with him?

EDGAR. Ay, two hours together.   135

EDMUND. Parted you in good terms? Found you no displeasure in him,
by word, nor countenance?

EDGAR. None at all.

EDMUND. Bethink yourself wherein you may have offended him; and at
my entreaty forbear his presence until some little time hath   140
qualified the heat of his displeasure, which at this instant so rageth
in him, that with the mischief of your person it would scarcely
allay.°

EDGAR. Some villain hath done me wrong.

EDMUND. That's my fear. I pray you, have a continent forbearance   145
till the speed of his rage goes slower; and as I say, retire with me to

---

117. **catastrophe:** final episode; **old comedy:** Edmund, pleased at the way things
are going in accordance with his purposes, likens Edgar's approach to the convenient and contrived appearance of excitement in a conventional melodrama.
118. **Tom o' Bedlam:** a lunatic from the hospital for the insane (Bethlehem or
Bedlam). 131. **sectary astronomical:** follower of the sect of astrologers.
142–43. **with . . . allay:** It would scarcely be lessened even if he injured you.

my lodging, from whence I will fitly bring you to hear my lord speak. Pray ye go, there's my key. If you do stir abroad, go armed.

EDGAR. Armed, brother?

EDMUND. Brother, I advise you to the best; I am no honest man if 150
there be any good meaning toward you. I have told you what I
have seen, and heard — but faintly — nothing like the image and
horror of it. Pray you away.

EDGAR. Shall I hear from you anon?

EDMUND. I do serve you in this business.°   *Exit* EDGAR. 155
A credulous father, and a brother noble,
Whose nature is so far from doing harms,
That he suspects none; on whose foolish honesty
My practices ride easy. I see the business.
Let me, if not by birth, have lands by wit;   160
All with me's meet, that I can fashion fit.   *Exit.*

155. **I do serve you in this business**: How does this line help characterize Edmund? Note also in this scene "That's my fear" and "I am no honest man if there be any good meaning toward you."

SCENE III. ALBANY's *palace.*

Enter GONERIL *and* OSWALD.

GONERIL. Did my father strike my gentleman for chiding of his fool?

OSWALD. Ay, madam.

GONERIL. By day and night, he wrongs me; every hour
He flashes into one gross crime or other,
That sets us all at odds. I'll not endure it.   5
His knights grow riotous, and himself upbraids us
On every trifle. When he returns from hunting,
I will not speak with him, say I am sick;
If you come slack of former services,
You shall do well; the fault of it I'll answer.   10

[Horns within]

OSWALD. He's coming madam, I hear him.

GONERIL. Put on what weary negligence you please,
You and your fellows — I'd have it come to question.
If he distaste it, let him to my sister,

Whose mind and mine I know in that are one: 15
Not to be over-ruled. Idle old man,
That still would manage those authorities
That he hath given away. Now, by my life,
Old fools are babes again, and must be used
With checks as flatteries, when they are seen abused.   20
Remember what I have said.

OSWALD.   Well, madam.

GONERIL. And let his knights have colder looks among you.
What grows of it no matter, advise your fellows so.
I would breed from hence occasions, and I shall,
That I may speak. I'll write straight to my sister   25
To hold my very course.° Prepare for dinner.   *Exeunt.*

26. To . . . course: to do exactly as I am doing.

SCENE IV. *The same.*

Enter KENT, *disguised.*

KENT. If but as well I other accents borrow,
That can my speech defuse,° my good intent
May carry through itself to that full issue
For which I razed° my likeness. Now, banished Kent,
If thou canst serve where thou dost stand condemned,   5
So may it come, thy master whom thou lov'st
Shall find thee full of labours.

Horns within. Enter LEAR, KNIGHTS, *and* ATTENDANTS.

LEAR. Let me not stay a jot for dinner, go get it ready.
                                    Exit an ATTENDANT.
How now, what art thou?

KENT. A man, sir.   10

LEAR. What dost thou profess? What wouldst thou with us?

KENT. I do profess to be no less than I seem; to serve him truly that will
put me in trust, to love him that is honest, to converse with him

2. defuse: diffuse, i.e., disguise. 4. razed: erased, obliterated. A likely assumption here would be that Kent has simply shaved off his beard, but such is not necessarily the case. He states that he has obliterated what he used to look like.

that is wise and says little, to fear judgement, to fight when I cannot choose, and to eat no fish.° 15

LEAR. What art thou?

KENT. A very honest-hearted fellow, and as poor as the King.

LEAR. If thou beest as poor for a subject as he's for a King, thou art poor enough. What wouldst thou?

KENT. Service. 20

LEAR. Who wouldst thou serve?

KENT. You.

LEAR. Dost thou know me, fellow?

KENT. No sir, but you have that in your countenance which I would fain call master. 25

LEAR. What's that?

KENT. Authority.

LEAR. What services canst thou do?

KENT. I can keep honest counsel, ride, run, mar a curious tale in telling it, and deliver a plain message bluntly. That which ordinary men 30 are fit for, I am qualified in, and the best of me, is diligence.

LEAR. How old art thou?

KENT. Not so young sir, to love a woman for singing, nor so old to dote on her for any thing. I have years on my back forty-eight.

LEAR. Follow me, thou shalt serve me; if I like thee no worse after 35 dinner, I will not part from thee yet. Dinner, ho, dinner! Where's my knave? My fool? Go you and call my fool hither.

Exit an ATTENDANT.

Enter OSWALD.

You, you, sirrah, where's my daughter?

OSWALD. So please you — *Exit.*°

LEAR. What says the fellow there? Call the clotpoll° back. [*Exit a* 40 KNIGHT.] Where's my fool, ho? I think the world's asleep.

Enter KNIGHT.

How now? Where's that mongrel?

KNIGHT. He says, my lord, your daughter is not well.

15. eat no fish: not observe the days of fasting (i.e., I am not a Roman Catholic). 39. What specific instruction is Oswald here obeying? 40. clotpoll: clodpole, blockhead. This is one of the nicer (and least accurate) things that Lear calls Oswald.

LEAR. Why came not the slave back to me when I called him?

KNIGHT. Sir, he answered me in the roundest manner, he would not. 45

LEAR. He would not?

KNIGHT. My lord, I know not what the matter is, but to my judgement
your Highness is not entertained with that ceremonious affection
as you were wont; there's a great abatement of kindness appears
as well in the general dependants, as in the duke himself also, 50
and your daughter.

LEAR. Ha! Sayest thou so?

KNIGHT. I beseech you pardon me my lord, if I be mistaken, for my duty
cannot be silent, when I think your Highness wronged.

LEAR. Thou but rememberest me of mine own conception. I have 55
perceived a most faint neglect of late, which I have rather blamed
as mine own jealous curiosity than as a very pretence and purpose
of unkindness; I will look further into't.° But where's my fool? I
have not seen him this two days.

KNIGHT. Since my young lady's going into France sir, the fool hath 60
much pined away.

LEAR. No more of that, I have noted it well. Go you and tell my daughter
I would speak with her. [*Exit an* ATTENDANT.] Go you, call hither
my fool.   *Exit another* ATTENDANT.

Enter OSWALD.

O you sir, you, come you hither, sir. Who am I, sir?   65

OSWALD. My lady's father.

LEAR. My lady's father? My lord's knave! You whoreson dog, you slave,
you cur!

OSWALD. I am none of these, my lord; I beseech your pardon.

LEAR. Do you bandy looks with me, you rascal?   70

[*Strikes him.*]

OSWALD. I'll not be strucken, my lord.

KENT. Nor tripped neither, you base football player.°

[*Trips up his heels.*]

58. What assumption about his own place in the world does Lear reveal in
these words? 72. **base football player:** Times have changed: in Elizabethan England, football was not a socially acceptable sport. This insult would reach Oswald,
since he is trying to seem a gentleman of high position.

LEAR. I thank thee, fellow. Thou serv'st me, and I'll love thee.

KENT. Come sir, arise, away, I'll teach you differences.° Away, away! If you will measure your lubber's° length again, tarry. But away! 75 Go to, have you wisdom? So.

[*Pushes* OSWALD *out.*]

LEAR. Now, my friendly knave, I thank thee, there's earnest of thy service.°

[*Gives* KENT *money.*]

Enter FOOL.

FOOL. Let me hire him too, here's my coxcomb.°

[*Offers* KENT *his cap.*]

LEAR. How now, my pretty knave, how dost thou?   80

FOOL. Sirrah, you were best take my coxcomb.

KENT. Why, fool?

FOOL. Why, for taking one's part that's out of favour. Nay, an thou canst not smile as the wind sits, thou'lt catch cold shortly; there, take my coxcomb. Why this fellow has banished two on's daughters, 85 and did the third a blessing against his will; if thou follow him, thou must needs wear my coxcomb. How now, nuncle?° Would I had two coxcombs, and two daughters.

LEAR. Why, my boy?

FOOL. If I gave them all my living, I'd keep my coxcombs myself. 90 There's mine, beg another of thy daughters.°

LEAR. Take heed sirrah — the whip.

FOOL. Truth's a dog must to kennel; he must be whipped out, when the Lady Brach° may stand by th' fire and stink.

LEAR. A pestilent gall to me.°   95

74. **differences:** differences of rank. 75. **lubber:** big, clumsy fellow. 77–78. **earnest of thy service:** money given on account of services to be rendered, i.e., proof that you are hired. Note that Lear hires the disguised Kent because the latter beats up Goneril's confidential secretary. Compare these grounds with his grounds for exiling Kent in Scene i. 79. **coxcomb:** fool's cap (shaped like a cock's comb or crest), the conventional badge of the official fool. 87. **nuncle:** uncle. It was a conventional joke at medieval courts for the fool, or jester, to pretend a close blood relationship with his royal patron. 91. What is the fool calling Kent and Lear? What are his grounds for doing so in each case? 93–94. **the Lady Brach:** the pet bitch. 95. **A . . . me:** This pestilent fool rubs me on a sore spot.

FOOL. Sirrah, I'll teach thee a speech.

LEAR. Do.

FOOL. Mark it, nuncle.

Have more than thou showest,

Speak less than thou knowest, 100

Lend less than thou owest,°

Ride more than thou goest,°

Learn more than thou trowest,°

Set less than thou throwest;°

Leave thy drink and thy whore, 105

And keep in-a-door,

And thou shalt have more

Than two tens to a score.

KENT. This is nothing, fool.

FOOL. Then 'tis like the breath of an unfeed lawyer, you gave me 110
nothing for't. Can you make no use of nothing, nuncle?

LEAR. Why, no, boy; nothing can be made out of nothing.°

FOOL. [To KENT] Prithee tell him, so much the rent of his land comes to;
he will not believe a fool.

LEAR. A bitter fool. 115

FOOL. Dost thou know the difference my boy, between a bitter fool, and
a sweet one?

LEAR. No lad, teach me.

FOOL.

That lord that counselled thee

To give away thy land, 120

Come place him here by me,

Do thou for him stand.

The sweet and bitter fool

Will presently appear;

The one in motley° here, 125

The other found out there.

LEAR. Dost thou call me fool, boy?

FOOL. All thy other titles thou hast given away, that thou wast born with.

KENT. This is not altogether fool, my lord.

FOOL. No, faith, lords and great men will not let me;° if I had a 130

---

101. owest: own, possess. 102. goest: walk. 103. trowest: know. 104. Set . . .
throwest: Bet less than you can afford to risk at a throw of the dice. 111–12. nothing . . . nothing: Note this echo from earlier scenes. 125. motley: particolored
clothes of a fool. 130. will . . . me: will not let me keep all my folly to myself.

monopoly° out, they would have part an't; and ladies, too, they will not let me have all the fool to myself; they'll be snatching. Nuncle, give me an egg, and I'll give thee two crowns.

LEAR. What two crowns shall they be?

FOOL. Why, after I have cut the egg i' th' middle and eat up the 135 meat, the two crowns of the egg. When thou clovest thy crown i' th' middle, and gav'st way both parts, thou bor'st thine ass on thy back o'er the dirt.° Thou hadst little wit in thy bald crown, when thou gav'st thy golden one away. If I speak like myself in this, let him be whipped that first finds it so. 140

> Fools had ne'er less grace in a year,
> For wise men are grown foppish,
> And know not how their wits to wear,
> Their manners are so apish.°

LEAR. When were you wont to be so full of songs sirrah? 145

FOOL. I have used it, nuncle, ever since thou mad'st thy daughters thy mothers, for when thou gav'st them the rod, and put'st down thine own breeches —

> Then they for sudden joy did weep,
> And I for sorrow sung, 150
> That such a king should play bo-peep,
> And go the fools among.

Prithee, nuncle, keep a schoolmaster that can teach thy fool to lie — I would fain learn to lie.

LEAR. An° you lie, sirrah, we'll have you whipped. 155

FOOL. I marvel what kin thou and thy daughters are, they'll have me whipped for speaking true, thou'lt have me whipped for lying, and sometimes I am whipped for holding my peace. I had rather be any kind o' thing than a fool, and yet I would not be thee, nuncle; thou hast pared thy wit o' both sides, and left nothing i' th' 160 middle —

Enter GONERIL.

here comes one o' the parings.

---

131. **monopoly:** royal patent giving the holder the sole right to deal in some commodity. (The granting of monopolies to courtiers was one of the scandals of the period.) 137–38. **thou . . . dirt:** allusion to an old tale of the typical simpleminded countryman. 141–44. **Fools . . . apish:** There's no job left for fools nowadays, because the wise men are so like them. 155. **An:** if.

LEAR. How now daughter, what makes that frontlet° on?
You are too much of late i' th' frown.

FOOL. Thou wast a pretty fellow when thou hadst no need to care   165
for her frowning; now thou art an O without a figure.° I am better
than thou art now; I am a fool, thou art nothing. [To GONERIL]
Yes, forsooth, I will hold my tongue; so your face bids me, though
you say nothing.
                    Mum, mum.   170
              He that keeps nor crust nor crumb,
              Weary of all, shall want some.
That's a shealed peascod.°

GONERIL. Not only, sir, this your all-licensed° fool,
But other of your insolent retinue   175
Do hourly carp and quarrel, breaking forth
In rank and not-to-be-endured riots. Sir,
I had thought by making this well known unto you,
To have found a safe redress, but now grow fearful,
By what yourself too late have spoke and done,   180
That you protect this course, and put it on
By your allowance; which if you should, the fault
Would not 'scape censure, nor the redresses sleep,
Which in the tender of a wholesome weal,
Might in their working do you that offence,   185
Which else were shame, that then necessity
Will call discreet proceeding.°

FOOL. For you know, nuncle,
              The hedge-sparrow fed the cuckoo so long,
              That it had it head bit off by it young.   190
So out went the candle, and we were left darkling.

LEAR. Are you our daughter?

GONERIL. I would you would make use of your good wisdom,
Whereof I know you are fraught, and put away

---

163. **frontlet:** frown (literally, a band worn on the forehead). 166. **O . . .
figure:** cipher. 173. **shealed peascod:** an empty pea pod. (The fool is pointing to
Lear.) 174. **all-licensed:** allowed to take any liberty. We have seen that the fool
can get away with more than anyone else in talking to Lear. What must his effect
be on humorless people who don't like him? 186–87. **Which . . . proceeding:**
The import is this: if you continue to be a nuisance, I shall be forced to keep my
state peaceful by taking measures that will annoy you and would at other times
be shameful toward a father but would be justified by necessity.

These dispositions, which of late transport you   195
From what you rightly are.

FOOL. May not an ass know when the cart draws the horse? Whoop, Jug,
I love thee.

LEAR. Does any here know me? This is not Lear.
Does Lear walk thus? Speak thus? Where are his eyes?   200
Either his notion weakens, his discernings
Are lethargied. Ha,° waking? 'Tis not so.
Who is it that can tell me who I am?°

FOOL. Lear's shadow.

LEAR. I would learn that, for by the marks of sovereignty, knowl-   205
edge, and reason, I should be false persuaded I had daughters.

FOOL. Which they will make an obedient father.

LEAR. Your name, fair gentlewoman?

GONERIL. This admiration,° sir, is much o' th' savour
Of other your new pranks. I do beseech you   210
To understand my purposes aright,
As you are old, and reverend, should be wise.
Here do you keep a hundred knights and squires,
Men so disordered, so deboshed,° and bold,
That this our court infected with their manners,   215
Shows like a riotous inn; epicurism° and lust
Makes it more like a tavern, or a brothel,
Than a graced palace. The shame itself doth speak
For instant remedy. Be then desired
By her, that else will take the thing she begs,   220
A little to disquantity your train;°
And the remainders that shall still depend,
To be such men as may besort your age,
Which know themselves and you.

LEAR.   Darkness and devils!
Saddle my horses; call my train together.   225
Degenerate bastard, I'll not trouble thee.
Yet have I left a daughter.

---

202. Does Lear pinch himself at this point? 203. This is a central question of
the play. Is it a central question of all tragedies? 209. admiration: astonishment,
wonder. Does Goneril grasp the sense in which Lear's ironic remarks are made?
214. deboshed: debauched. 216. epicurism: in Goneril's mouth, a euphemism for
living for pleasure. 221. disquantity your train: Lessen the number of your followers.

GONERIL. You strike my people, and your disordered rabble
      Make servants of their betters.
LEAR.   Woe, that too late repents.

                        Enter ALBANY.

O sir, are you come?   230
Is it your will? Speak sir. Prepare my horses.
Ingratitude, thou marble-hearted fiend,
More hideous when thou show'st thee in a child,
Than the sea-monster.
ALBANY.   Pray, sir, be patient.
LEAR. [*To* GONERIL] Detested kite,° thou liest.   235
My train are men of choice and rarest parts,
That all particulars of duty know,
And in the most exact regard support
The worships of their name. O most small fault,
How ugly didst thou in Cordelia show,   240
Which like an engine° wrenched my frame of nature
From the fixed place; drew from my heart all love,
And added to the gall. O Lear, Lear, Lear!
Beat at this gate that let thy folly in,

                    [*Strikes his head.*]

And thy dear judgement out. Go, go, my people.   245
ALBANY. My lord, I am guiltless, as I am ignorant
      Of what hath moved you.
LEAR.   It may be so, my lord.
Hear, Nature, hear, dear goddess hear.
Suspend thy purpose, if thou didst intend
To make this creature fruitful.   250
Into her womb convey sterility,
Dry up in her the organs of increase,
And from her derogate° body never spring
A babe to honour her. If she must teem,
Create her child of spleen,° that it may live   255
And be a thwart disnatured torment to her.
Let it stamp wrinkles in her brow of youth,

      235. kite: a carrion bird, a small variety of buzzard. 241. engine: a lever, for
instance. 253. derogate: debased. 255. spleen: malice.

With cadent° tears fret channels in her cheeks,
Turn all her mother's pains and benefits
To laughter, and contempt, that she may feel   260
How sharper than a serpent's tooth it is
To have a thankless child. Away, away!   *Exit.*

ALBANY. Now gods that we adore, whereof comes this?

GONERIL. Never afflict yourself to know more of it;
But let his disposition have that scope   265
As dotage gives it.

Enter LEAR.

LEAR. What, fifty of my followers at a clap?°
Within a fortnight?°

ALBANY.   What's the matter sir?

LEAR. I'll tell thee. [*To* GONERIL] Life and death, I am ashamed
That thou hast power to shake my manhood thus,   270
That these hot tears, which break from me perforce,
Should make thee worth them. Blasts and fogs upon thee!
Th' untented woundings° of a father's curse
Pierce every sense about thee. Old fond eyes,
Beweep this cause again, I'll pluck ye out,   275
And cast you with the waters that you loose
To temper clay. Ha, is't come to this?
Let it be so. I have another daughter,
Who I am sure is kind and comfortable.
When she shall hear this of thee, with her nails   280
She'll flay thy wolvish visage. Thou shalt find,
That I'll resume the shape° which thou dost think
I have cast off for ever.   *Exeunt* LEAR, KENT, *and* ATTENDANTS.

GONERIL.   Do you mark that?

ALBANY. I cannot be so partial, Goneril,
To the great love I bear you — °   285

GONERIL. Pray you, content. What, Oswald, ho!
[*To* FOOL] You, sir, more knave than fool, after your master.

258. cadent: falling. 267. at a clap: at one blow. 267–68. What . . . fortnight?: Lear has discovered that Goneril has ordered fifty of his followers to
depart within a fortnight. 273. untented woundings: raw wounds. 282. What is
this shape? 284–85. I . . . you: i.e., even though my great love makes me partial
to you. (Albany is about to protest his wife's treatment of her father.)

FOOL. Nuncle Lear, nuncle Lear, tarry, take the fool with thee.

               A fox, when one has caught her,
               And such a daughter,   290
               Should sure to the slaughter,
               If my cap would buy a halter:
               So the fool follows after.   *Exit.*

GONERIL. This man hath had good counsel. A hundred knights!
    'Tis politic,° and safe, to let him keep   295
    At point° a hundred knights — yes, that on every dream,
    Each buzz,° each fancy, each complaint, dislike,
    He may enguard his dotage with their powers,
    And hold our lives in mercy. Oswald, I say!

ALBANY. Well, you may fear too far.

GONERIL.   Safer than trust too far.   300
    Let me still take away the harms I fear,
    Not fear still to be taken. I know his heart.
    What he hath uttered I have writ my sister.
    If she sustain him, and his hundred knights,
    When I have showed th' unfitness —

                 Enter OSWALD.

                          How now, Oswald!   305
    What, have you writ that letter to my sister?

OSWALD. Ay, madam.

GONERIL. Take you some company, and away to horse.
    Inform her full of my particular fear,
    And thereto add such reasons of your own,   310
    As may compact it more. Get you gone,
    And hasten your return. [*Exit* OSWALD.] No, no, my lord,
    This milky gentleness and course of yours,
    Though I condemn not, yet under pardon,
    You are much more ataxed° for want of wisdom,   315
    Than praised for harmful mildness.

ALBANY. How far your eyes may pierce I cannot tell;
    Striving to better, oft we mar what's well.

GONERIL. Nay then —

ALBANY. Well, well, th' event.°   *Exeunt.*   320

    295. **politic:** practical, good policy. 296. **At point:** fully armed. 297. **buzz:** rumor. 315. **ataxed:** blamed. 320. **th' event:** i.e., we must see what will happen.

Enter LEAR, KENT, *and* FOOL.

LEAR. Go you before to Gloucester with these letters. Acquaint my daughter no further with any thing you know than comes from her demand out of the letter. If your diligence be not speedy, I shall be there afore you.

KENT. I will not sleep my lord, till I have delivered your letter. *Exit.* 5

FOOL. If a man's brains were in's heels, were't not in danger of kibes?°

LEAR. Ay, boy.

FOOL. Then, I prithee, be merry; thy wit shall not go slipshod.

LEAR. Ha, ha, ha!

FOOL. Shalt see thy other daughter will use thee kindly,° for though 10 she's as like this, as a crab's° like an apple, yet I can tell what I can tell.

LEAR. What canst tell, boy?

FOOL. She will taste as like this as a crab does to a crab. Thou canst tell why one's nose stands i' th' middle on's face? 15

LEAR. No.

FOOL. Why to keep one's eyes of either side's nose, that what a man cannot smell out, he may spy into.

LEAR. I did her wrong.

FOOL. Canst tell how an oyster makes his shell? 20

LEAR. No.

FOOL. Nor I neither; but I can tell why a snail has a house.

LEAR. Why?

FOOL. Why to put's head in; not to give it away to his daughters, and leave his horns without a case. 25

LEAR. I will forget my nature. So kind a father! Be my horses ready?

FOOL. Thy asses are gone about 'em. The reason why the seven stars are no more than seven, is a pretty reason.

LEAR. Because they are not eight?

FOOL. Yes, indeed, thou wouldst make a good fool. 30

LEAR. To take't again perforce.° Monster ingratitude!

FOOL. If thou wert my fool, nuncle, I'd have thee beaten for being old before thy time.

6. kibes: chilblains. 10. kindly: after her kind, according to her nature. 11. crab: crab apple. 31. To . . . perforce: to take it (my kingdom) back by force.

LEAR. How's that?

FOOL. Thou shouldst not have been old, till thou hadst been wise.   35

LEAR. O let me not be mad, not mad, sweet heaven.
Keep me in temper, I would not be mad.

Enter GENTLEMAN.

How now, are the horses ready?

GENTLEMAN. Ready, my lord.

LEAR. Come, boy.   *Exeunt* LEAR *and* GENTLEMAN.   40

FOOL. She that's a maid now, and laughs at my departure,
Shall not be a maid long, unless things be cut shorter.   *Exit.*

ACT II

SCENE I. *Before* GLOUCESTER'*s castle.*

Enter EDMUND *and* CURAN, *at several doors.*

EDMUND. Save thee,° Curan.

CURAN. And you, sir. I have been with your father, and given him notice
that the Duke of Cornwall, and Regan his duchess, will be here
with him this night.

EDMUND. How comes that?   5

CURAN. Nay, I know not. You have heard of the news abroad, I mean
the whispered ones, for they are yet but ear-kissing arguments?°

EDMUND. Not I. Pray you what are they?

CURAN. Have you heard of no likely wars toward, 'twixt the Dukes of
Cornwall and Albany?°   10

EDMUND. Not a word.

CURAN. You may do, then, in time. Fare you well, sir.   *Exit.*

EDMUND. The duke be here to-night? The better. Best.
This weaves itself perforce into my business.°
My father hath set guard to take my brother,   15
And I have one thing of a queasy question°

1. **Save thee:** God save thee (a greeting). 7. **ear-kissing arguments:** whispered rumors. 10. Does the idea of strife between Goneril and Regan's husbands seem improbable? 14. Here Edmund seems to grant, contrary to his earlier assertions, that outside forces *may* have a part in his fortune. What is the extent of his respect for such forces? 16. **queasy question:** question requiring delicate handling. *Queasy* means "on the point of vomiting."

Which I must act. Briefness and fortune work.
Brother, a word; descend.° Brother, I say!

Enter EDGAR.

My father watches. O sir, fly this place,
Intelligence is given where you are hid;   20
You have now the good advantage of the night.
Have you not spoken 'gainst the Duke of Cornwall?
He's coming hither, now i' th' night, i' th' haste,
And Regan with him; have you nothing said
Upon his party 'gainst the Duke of Albany?   25
Advise yourself.

EDGAR.   I am sure on't, not a word.
EDMUND. I hear my father coming. Pardon me,
In cunning,° I must draw my sword upon you.
Draw, seem to defend yourself; now, quit you well —
Yield, come before my father. Light ho, here! —   30
Fly brother — Torches, torches! — So farewell.   *Exit* EDGAR.
Some blood drawn on me would beget opinion°
Of my more fierce endeavour.

[*Stabs his arm.*]

                                  I have seen drunkards
Do more than this in sport. Father, father!
Stop, stop! No help?

Enter GLOUCESTER, *and* SERVANTS *with torches.*

GLOUCESTER.   Now Edmund, where's the villain?   35
EDMUND. Here stood he in the dark, his sharp sword out,
Mumbling of wicked charms, conjuring the moon°
To stand's auspicious mistress.
GLOUCESTER.   But where is he?
EDMUND. Look, sir, I bleed.°
GLOUCESTER.   Where is the villain, Edmund?
EDMUND. Fled this way, sir. When by no means he could —   40

18. **descend:** i.e., from the chamber where you are hiding. 28. **In cunning:** as
a pretense. 32. **beget opinion:** produce the impression. 37. **conjuring the moon:**
calling on Hecate, goddess of witchcraft. 39. Edmund distracts his father from the
pursuit of Edgar by pointing out his wound. Why?

GLOUCESTER. Pursue him, ho! Go after.   *Exeunt* SERVANTS
                                By no means what?

EDMUND.   Persuade me to the murder of your lordship;
          But that I told him the revenging gods
          'Gainst parricides did all their thunders bend,
          Spoke with how manifold and strong a bond   45
          The child was bound to th' father; sir, in fine,
          Seeing how loathly opposite I stood
          To his unnatural purpose, in fell° motion,
          With his prepared sword, he charges home
          My unprovided body, lanced mine arm;   50
          And when he saw my best alarumed spirits
          Bold in the quarrel's right, roused to th' encounter,
          Or whether gasted° by the noise I made,
          Full suddenly he fled.

GLOUCESTER.   **Let him fly far.**
          Not in this land shall he remain uncaught;   55
          And found — dispatch. The noble duke my master,
          My worthy arch° and patron, comes to-night.
          By his authority I will proclaim it,
          That he which finds him shall deserve our thanks,
          Bringing the murderous coward to the stake;   60
          He that conceals him, death.

EDMUND.   When I dissuaded him from his intent,
          And found him pight° to do it, with curst° speech
          I threatened to discover him; he replied,
          Thou unpossessing bastard, dost thou think,   65
          If I would stand against thee, would the reposal
          Of any trust, virtue, or worth in thee,
          Make thy words faithed?° No, what I should deny —
          As this I would, ay though thou didst produce
          My very character° — I'd turn it all   70
          To thy suggestion, plot, and damned practice.
          And thou must make a dullard of the world,
          If they not thought the profits of my death
          Were very pregnant and potential spirits

48. fell: fearful. 53. gasted: aghast, terrified. 57. arch: chief, feudal overlord.
63. pight: determined; curst: bitter. 68. faithed: believed. 70. character: hand-
writing. Why does Edmund bring up this matter of penmanship at this time?

To make thee seek it.°

GLOUCESTER.   O strong and fastened villain,   75
Would he deny his letter? — I never got° him.

[Tucket* within]

Hark, the duke's trumpets; I know not why he comes.
All ports I'll bar;° the villain shall not 'scape,
The duke must grant me that. Besides, his picture
I will send far and near, that all the kingdom   80
May have due note of him; and of my land,
Loyal and natural boy, I'll work the means
To make thee capable.°

Enter CORNWALL, REGAN and ATTENDANTS.

CORNWALL.   How now, my noble friend. Since I came hither,
Which I can call but now — I have heard strange news.   85
REGAN.   If it be true, all vengeance comes too short
Which can pursue th' offender. How dost, my lord?
GLOUCESTER.   O madam, my old heart is cracked, it's cracked.
REGAN.   What, did my father's godson seek your life?
He whom my father named, your Edgar?°   90
GLOUCESTER.   O lady, lady, shame would have it hid.
REGAN.   Was he not companion with the riotous knights
That tend upon my father?
GLOUCESTER.   I know not, madam; 'tis too bad, too bad.
EDMUND.   Yes madam, he was of that consort.   95
REGAN.   No marvel then, though° he were ill affected.
'Tis they have put him on the old man's death,°
To have th' expense and waste of his revenues.
I have this present evening from my sister

75. Note that Edmund, in misquoting his brother, blandly gives his own true motives. 76. got: begot. Gloucester is so misled that ironically he asserts that he is not the father of his legitimate son and assumes that his illegitimate offspring is his "loyal and natural boy." Compare Lear's disavowal of paternity of Cordelia. * Tucket: trumpet call. 78. All . . . bar: I'll have the seaports watched to prevent his escape. 83. capable: capable of succeeding as my heir (i.e., I'll cause you to be legitimatized). 90. Here and in the lines that follow Regan is trying to establish a guilt by association in the mind of Gloucester. As a matter of fact, she is not successful. How does the *attempt* help to characterize her? 96. though: that. 97. put . . . death: persuaded him to bring about the old man's (Gloucester's) death. Regan is pretending to address this remark to her husband.

Been well informed of them, and with such cautions,　　　
That if they come to sojourn at my house,
I'll not be there.
CORNWALL.　　　　　　Nor I, assure thee Regan.
Edmund, I hear that you have shown your father
A child-like office.°
EDMUND.　　　　　　It was my duty, sir.
GLOUCESTER.　He did bewray° his practice, and received　　105
This hurt you see, striving to apprehend him.
CORNWALL.　Is he pursued?
GLOUCESTER.　　　　　　Ay, my good lord.
CORNWALL.　If he be taken, he shall never more
Be feared of doing harm. Make your own purpose,
How in my strength you please.° For you, Edmund,　　110
Whose virtue and obedience doth this instant
So much commend itself,° you shall be ours.
Natures of such deep trust we shall much need.
You we first seize on.
EDMUND.　　　　　　I shall serve you, sir,
Truly, however else.
GLOUCESTER.　　　　　　For him I thank your Grace.　　115
CORNWALL.　You know not why we came to visit you?
REGAN.　Thus out of season, threading dark-eyed night.
Occasions, noble Gloucester, of some poise,°
Wherein we must have use of your advice.
Our father he hath writ, so hath our sister,　　120
Of differences,° which I best thought it fit
To answer from° our home; the several messengers
From hence attend dispatch.° Our good old friend,
Lay comforts to your bosom, and bestow
Your needful counsel to our businesses,　　125
Which craves the instant use.
GLOUCESTER.　　　　　　I serve you, madam.
Your Graces are right welcome.　　　　*Exeunt.*

104. child-like office: filial service. 105. bewray: reveal. 109–10. Make . . .
please: i.e., use my authority for any action you care to take. 111–12. What
sort of virtue and obedience commend themselves to Cornwall? 118. poise:
weight. 121. differences: quarrels. 122. from: away from. 123. attend dispatch:
are waiting to be sent back.

Enter KENT *and* OSWALD, *at several doors.*

OSWALD. Good dawning to thee, friend, art of this house?

KENT. Ay.°

OSWALD. Where may we set our horses?

KENT. I' th' mire.

OSWALD. Prithee, if thou lov'st me, tell me.   5

KENT. I love thee not.

OSWALD. Why, then, I care not for thee.

KENT. If I had thee in Lipsbury pinfold,° I would make thee care for me.

OSWALD. Why dost thou use me thus? I know thee not.

KENT. Fellow, I know thee.   10

OSWALD. What dost thou know me for?

KENT. A knave, a rascal, an eater of broken meats, a base, proud, shallow, beggarly, three-suited, hundred pound, filthy worsted-stocking
knave, a lily-livered,° action-taking, whoreson glass-gazing super-
serviceable finical rogue, one trunk-inheriting slave, one that   15
wouldst be a bawd in way of good service, and art nothing but the
composition of a knave, beggar, coward, pander, and the son and
heir of a mongrel bitch; one whom I will beat into clamorous
whining, if thou deny'st the least syllable of thy addition.°

OSWALD. Why, what a monstrous fellow art thou, thus to rail on one   20
that is neither known of thee, nor knows thee.

KENT. What a brazen-faced varlet art thou, to deny thou knowest me.
Is it two days since I tripped up thy heels, and beat thee before
the King? Draw you rogue, for though it be night, yet the moon
shines; I'll make a sop o' th' moonshine of you, you whoreson   25
cullionly barbermonger.° Draw.

2. Kent is not directly part of Gloucester's household. Why do you think he
answers thus? 8. **Lipsbury pinfold:** There is considerable difference of opinion about
this term. Kent is so angry in this scene that he coins terms very freely and color-
fully. One possibility: "If I had you where you couldn't avoid a punch in the
mouth. . . ." 14. **lily-livered:** cowardly. (The liver was regarded as the seat of
courage.) 19. A classic bit of cussing-out. Note that Kent despises Oswald as a
presumptuous heel who will do absolutely anything to others or to his own self-
respect in order to get ahead. The worst thing Oswald has done of this sort, as
Kent sees it, is to mistreat the King. 26. Note that Kent, the aristocrat in disguise,
makes a good deal of what he conceives to be the lower-class qualities of the
would-be gentleman, Oswald.

[Draws his sword.]

OSWALD. Away, I have nothing to do with thee.

KENT. Draw you rascal, you come with letters against the King, and take
Vanity the puppet's part against the royalty of her father. Draw
you rogue, or I'll so carbonado° your shanks — draw you 30
rascal, come your ways.

OSWALD. Help, ho, murder, help!

KENT. Strike, you slave; stand rogue, stand you neat slave, strike.

[Beats him.]

OSWALD. Help ho! murder, murder!

Enter EDMUND, *with his rapier drawn,* GLOUCESTER, CORNWALL,
REGAN *and* SERVANTS.

EDMUND. How now, what's the matter?° Part! 35

KENT. With you, goodman boy,° if you please; come,
I'll flesh ye;° come on young master.

GLOUCESTER. Weapons? Arms? What's the matter here?

CORNWALL. Keep peace upon your lives;
He dies that strikes again. What is the matter? 40

REGAN. The messengers from our sister, and the King.

CORNWALL. What is your difference,° speak.

OSWALD. I am scarce in breath, my lord.

KENT. No marvel, you have so bestirred your valour. You cowardly rascal, nature disclaims in thee. A tailor made thee. 45

CORNWALL. Thou art a strange fellow. A tailor make a man?°

KENT. A tailor, sir; a stone-cutter, or a painter, could not have made him
so ill, though they had been but two years o' th' trade.

CORNWALL. Speak yet, how grew your quarrel?

OSWALD. This ancient ruffian, sir, whose life I have spared at suit of 50
his gray beard —

KENT. Thou whoreson zed,° thou unnecessary letter° — my lord, if you

30. carbonado: to pierce or slash, as one tenderizes meat for cooking. 35. matter: trouble; also (in Elizabethan usage) quarrel. Edmund uses the term in the
first sense; Kent accepts it in the second. 36. boy: Kent is insulting Edmund by
calling him "boy." 37. flesh ye: give you your first fight. 42. difference: disagree-
ment. 46. The brutish Cornwall has a literal mind. What does Kent mean when
he asserts that a tailor made Oswald? 25. zed: (British) The letter z in reciting
the alphabet; unnecessary letter: The letter z does not exist in Latin and is not
necessary in English since the letter s can take its place.

will give me leave, I will tread this unbolted villain into mortar,
and daub the wall of a jakes° with him. Spare my gray beard, you
wagtail?   55

CORNWALL.   Peace, sirrah!
You beastly knave, know you no reverence?

KENT.   Yes sir, but anger hath a privilege.

CORNWALL.   Why art thou angry?

KENT.   That such a slave as this should wear a sword,   60
Who wears no honesty. Such smiling rogues as these
Like rats oft bite the holy cords° atwain
Which are too intrinse° t' unloose; smooth every passion
That in the natures of their lords rebel,
Bring oil to fire, snow to their colder moods;   65
Renege, affirm,° and turn their halcyon beaks
With every gale and vary of their masters,°
Knowing naught, like dogs, but following.
A plague upon your epileptic visage,
Smile you my speeches, as I were a fool?   70
Goose, if I had you upon Sarum plain,
I'd drive ye cackling home to Camelot.°

CORNWALL.   What, art thou mad old fellow?

GLOUCESTER.   How fell you out, say that.

KENT.   No contraries hold more antipathy   75
Than I and such a knave.

CORNWALL.   Why dost thou call him knave? What is his fault?

KENT.   His countenance likes me not.°

CORNWALL.   No more perchance does mine, nor his, nor hers.

KENT.   Sir, 'tis my occupation to be plain;   80
I have seen better faces in my time
Than stands on any shoulder that I see
Before me, at this instant.

CORNWALL.   This is some fellow,

54. jakes: outhouse, privy. 62. What holy cords does Kent have in mind?
63. intrinse: intrinsic, essential. 66. Renege, affirm: deny, agree (i.e., serve as a
"yes man"). 66–67. turn . . . masters: A kingfisher (halcyon) hung up by the
neck was supposed to be a good weathervane, turning its bill into the prevailing
wind. 71–72. Goose . . . Camelot: Scholars have not agreed on the meaning
of these two lines. Kent is sputtering angry. 78. His . . . not: I don't like his
face. Kent has given up trying to make Cornwall understand his real reasons for
antipathy. Why is Cornwall so dense about them?

Who having been praised for bluntness, doth affect
A saucy roughness, and constrains·the garb   85
Quite from his nature.° He cannot flatter, he;
An honest mind and plain; he must speak truth;
An they will take it, so; if not, he's plain.
These kind of knaves I know, which in this plainness
Harbour more craft, and more corrupter ends,   90
Than twenty silly ducking observants
That stretch their duties nicely.°

KENT.   Sir, in good faith, in sincere verity,
Under th' allowance of your great aspect,
Whose influence like the wreath of radiant fire   95
On flickering Phœbus'° front — °

CORNWALL.   What mean'st by this?

KENT.   To go out of my dialect, which you discommend so much. I know
sir, I am no flatterer; he that beguiled you in a plain accent was a
plain knave, which for my part I will not be, though I should win
your displeasure to entreat me to't.   100

CORNWALL.   What was th' offence you gave him?

OSWALD.   I never gave him any.
It pleased the King his master very late
To strike at me, upon his misconstruction;°
When he, compact,° and flattering his displeasure,   105
Tripped me behind; being down, insulted, railed,
And put upon him such a deal of man,
That worthied him,° got praises of the King
For him attempting° who was self-subdued,°
And in the fleshment° of this dread exploit,   110
Drew on me here again.

KENT.   None of these rogues and cowards
But Ajax is their fool.°

85–86. constrains . . . nature: affects a manner that is quite unnatural. **92.** This
speech must be particularly irritating to Kent. What similarities are there between
Kent's view of Oswald and Cornwall's view of Kent? **96. Phœbus:** Apollo, the sun
god. **93–96.** What sort of man does Kent parody in these lines? What is significant
and characteristic in Cornwall's reaction? **104. upon his misconstruction:** upon
his misinterpreting my words. **105. compact:** acting in concert with the King.
108. worthied him: got him favor. **109. attempting:** attacking; **self-subdued:** not
resisting. **110. fleshment:** excitement. **112.** Kent *may* mean that clever talkers like
Odysseus (and Oswald) are forever defeating better fighters like Ajax (and himself). Cornwall seems to think that he is being identified with the stupid Ajax.

CORNWALL.   Fetch forth the stocks.
    You stubborn ancient knave, you reverend braggart,
    We'll teach you.
KENT.   Sir, I am too old to learn.
    Call not your stocks for me; I serve the King,   115
    On whose employment I was sent to you.
    You shall do small respect, show too bold malice
    Against the grace and person of my master,
    Stocking his messenger.°
CORNWALL. Fetch forth the stocks. As I have life and honour,   120
    There shall he sit till noon.
REGAN. Till noon? Till night my lord, and all night too.
KENT. Why madam, if I were your father's dog,
    You should not use me so.
REGAN.   Sir, being his knave, I will.
CORNWALL. This is a fellow of the self-same colour°   125
    Our sister speaks of. Come, bring away the stocks.

        [*Stocks discovered in the inner stage.*]

GLOUCESTER. Let me beseech your Grace not to do so.
    His fault is much, and the good King his master
    Will check him for't; your purposed low correction
    Is such as basest and contemned'st wretches   130
    For pilferings and most common trespasses
    Are punished with. The King must take it ill,
    That he, so slightly valued in his messenger,
    Should have him thus restrained.
CORNWALL.   I'll answer that.
REGAN. My sister may receive it much more worse,   135
    To have her gentleman abused, assaulted,
    For following her affairs. Put in his legs.°
    Come my good lord, away.   *Exeunt all but* GLOUCESTER *and* KENT.
GLOUCESTER. I am sorry for thee friend, 'tis the duke's pleasure,
    Whose disposition, all the world well knows,   140
    Will not be rubbed nor stopped. I'll entreat for thee.°

    119. A royal messenger of any rank customarily had the status and diplomatic
immunity from punishment that modern governments accord ambassadors. To
put him in the stocks is to offer an intolerable insult to his master. 125. colour:
kind, personality. 137. Note Regan's interest in the details of physical punishment.
141. What is Gloucester's attitude toward the situation?

KENT.   Pray do not sir. I have watched, and travelled hard;
         Some time I shall sleep out, the rest I'll whistle.
         A good man's fortune may grow out at heels.°
         Give you good morrow.°   145
GLOUCESTER.   The duke's to blame in this, 'twill be ill taken.   *Exit.*
KENT.   Good King, that must approve° the common saw,°
         Thou out of heaven's benediction com'st
         To the warm sun.°
         Approach thou beacon to this under globe,°   150
         That by thy comfortable beams I may
         Peruse this letter. Nothing almost sees miracles
         But misery.° I know 'tis from Cordelia,
         Who hath most fortunately been informed
         Of my obscured course° — [*Reads*] *and shall find time*   155
         From this enormous state,° seeking to give
         Losses their remedies.° — All weary and o'erwatched,
         Take vantage heavy eyes, not to behold
         This shameful lodging.
         Fortune good night; smile once more, turn thy wheel.   160

                  [*Sleeps. Curtains drawn.*]

144. A . . . heels: i.e., Even a good man may suffer a shabby fate. What
does the quoting of this proverb suggest about Kent's expectations of rewards and
punishments for good and evil? **145. Give . . . morrow:** Good day to you (good-
bye for today). **147. approve:** confirm; **the common saw:** The well-known saying,
"A good man's fortune may grow out at heels." **148–49. Thou . . . sun:** You
are coming out of the shade into the heat. **150. beacon . . . under globe:** rising
sun. **152–53. Nothing . . . misery:** The miserable are almost the only ones who
appreciate miracles. **155. obscured course:** my actions in disguise. **156. this
enormous state:** these wicked times. **157. Losses their remedies:** Lear's losses or
Kent's?

                  SCENE III. *The open country.*

                       Enter EDGAR.

EDGAR.   I heard myself proclaimed,°
          And by the happy hollow of a tree
          Escaped the hunt. No port is free, no place,
          That guard, and most unusual vigilance,

1. proclaimed: proclaimed as a traitor and fugitive. See Act II, Scene i, lines
79–82.

Does not attend my taking. Whiles I may 'scape,   5
I will preserve myself; and am bethought°
To take the basest and most poorest shape
That ever penury in contempt of man
Brought near to beast; my face I'll grime with filth,
Blanket my loins, elf° all my hairs in knots,   10
And with presented nakedness outface
The winds and persecutions of the sky.
The country gives me proof and precedent
Of Bedlam beggars,° who with roaring voices,
Strike in their numbed and mortified bare arms   15
Pins, wooden pricks, nails, sprigs of rosemary;
And with this horrible object, from low farms,
Poor pelting° villages, sheep cotes, and mills,
Sometime with lunatic bans,° sometime with prayers,
Enforce their charity. Poor Turlygod, poor Tom!°   20
That's something yet. Edgar I nothing am.°   *Exit.*

6. **am bethought:** have decided. 10. **elf:** mat. 14. **Bedlam beggars:** lunatics discharged from Bedlam (or Bethlehem) Hospital, the London madhouse. These beggars were the terror of the countryside. See Act I, Scene ii, line 118. 18. **pelting:** paltry. 19. **bans:** curses. 20. **Poor . . . Tom:** Edgar is rehearsing the names which a bedlam calls himself. 21. **That's . . . am:** As Poor Tom 'a Bedlam, there's still a chance for me; as Edgar, I am a dead man.

SCENE IV. *Before* GLOUCESTER's *castle;* KENT *discovered in the stocks.*

Enter LEAR, FOOL, *and* GENTLEMAN.

LEAR. 'Tis strange that they should so depart from home,
And not send back my messenger.
GENTLEMAN.   As I learned,
The night before there was no purpose° in them
Of this remove.
KENT.   Hail to thee, noble master.
LEAR. Ha!   5
Mak'st thou this shame thy pastime?
KENT.   No, my lord.

3. **purpose:** intention.

FOOL. Ha, ha, he wears cruel garters. Horses are tied by the heads, dogs
and bears by th' neck, monkeys by th' loins, and men by th' legs.
When a man's over-lusty at legs,° then he wears wooden nether-
stocks.°   10

LEAR. What's he that hath so much thy place mistook
To set thee here?°

KENT.   It is both he and she,
Your son and daughter.

LEAR. No.

KENT. Yes.   15

LEAR. No, I say.

KENT. I say, yea.

LEAR. By Jupiter I swear, no.

KENT. By Juno I swear, ay.°

LEAR.   They durst not do't;
They could not, would not do't; 'tis worse than murder,   20
To do upon respect such violent outrage.
Resolve° me with all modest haste, which way
Thou mightst deserve, or they impose this usage,
Coming from us.°

KENT.   My lord, when at their home
I did commend your Highness' letters to them,   25
Ere I was risen from the place that showed
My duty kneeling, came there a reeking post,°
Stewed in his haste, half breathless, panting forth
From Goneril his mistress salutations;
Delivered letters, spite of intermission,°   30
Which presently° they read; on whose contents
They summoned up their meiny,° straight took horse,
Commanded me to follow, and attend
The leisure of their answer, gave me cold looks;
And meeting here the other messenger,   35

9. over-lusty at legs: i.e., a vagabond. 9–10. netherstocks: stockings. 12. What
is the only explanation that Lear can imagine for Kent's being in the stocks?
19. Note that this is not the first head-on clash that Lear and Kent have had. In
both confrontations Kent has been right. What is the significant difference between
the present situation and the previous? 22. Resolve: inform. 24. Coming from us:
Kent had acted as Lear's messenger. 27. reeking post: sweating messenger.
30. spite of intermission: in spite of the delay in reading the letter I brought.
31. presently: immediately. 32. meiny: household, ménage.

Whose welcome I perceived had poisoned mine,
Being the very fellow which of late
Displayed so saucily against your Highness,
Having more man than wit about me, drew.
He raised the house, with loud and coward cries;   40
Your son and daughter found this trespass worth
The shame which here it suffers.
FOOL.   Winter's not gone yet, if the wild geese fly that way.°
               Fathers that wear rags
               Do make their children blind,   45
               But fathers that bear bags
               Shall see their children kind.
               Fortune, that arrant whore,
               Ne'er turns the key to th' poor.
But for all this thou shalt have as many dolours° for thy   50
daughters as thou canst tell° in a year.
LEAR.   O how this mother° swells up toward my heart!
Hysterica passio,° down, thou climbing sorrow,
Thy element's below. Where is this daughter?
KENT.   With the earl, sir, here within.
LEAR.   Follow me not;   55
Stay here.   *Exit.*
GENTLEMAN.   Made you no more offence but what you speak of?
KENT.   None.
How chance the King comes with so small a number?
FOOL.   An thou hadst been set i' th' stocks for that question, thou'dst   60
well deserved it.
KENT.   Why fool?
FOOL.   We'll set thee to school to an ant, to teach thee there's no labouring
i' th' winter. All that follow their noses° are led by their eyes but
blind men, and there's not a nose among twenty but can smell   65
him that's stinking. Let go thy hold when a great wheel runs down
a hill, lest it break thy neck with following. But the great one that
goes upward, let him draw thee after. When a wise man gives thee

43. What sign does the Fool liken to the sight of wild geese flying south on a
deceptively mild winter's day? 50. dolours: griefs and (pun) dollars. 51. tell:
count. 52. mother: called also *hysterica passio* (see next footnote). 53. Hysterica
passio: hysteria, which, as the symptoms sometimes suggest, was thought in
Elizabethan times to rise from the lower organs into the heart and throat. 64. follow their noses: go straight ahead.

better counsel, give me mine again; I would have none but knaves
follow it, since a fool gives it.°   70

        That sir, which serves and seeks for gain,
           And follows but for form,
        Will pack when it begins to rain,
           And leave thee in the storm.
        But I will tarry, the fool will stay,   75
           And let the wise man fly.
        The knave turns fool that runs away;
           The fool no knave perdy.°

KENT. Where learned you this, fool?
FOOL. Not i' th' stocks, fool.   80

Enter LEAR *with* GLOUCESTER.

LEAR. Deny to speak with me? They are sick, they weary,
They have travelled all the night! Mere fetches,°
The images° of revolt and flying off.
Fetch me a better answer.
GLOUCESTER.   My dear lord,
You know the fiery quality of the duke,   85
How unremovable and fixed he is
In his own course.
LEAR. Vengeance, plague, death, confusion!
Fiery? What quality? Why, Gloucester, Gloucester,
I'd speak with the Duke of Cornwall, and his wife.   90
GLOUCESTER. Well, my good lord, I have informed them so.
LEAR. Informed them? Dost thou understand me, man?°
GLOUCESTER. Ay, my good lord.
LEAR. The King would speak with Cornwall; the dear father
Would with his daughter speak, commands — tends — service. 95
Are they informed of this? My breath and blood!
Fiery? The fiery duke? Tell the hot duke that —
No, but not yet, may be he is not well;
Infirmity doth still neglect all office
Whereto our health is bound;° we are not ourselves,   100

70. What wry lesson about common human loyalty is the Fool preaching to the
uncommonly loyal Kent? 78. perdy: by God. 82. fetches: tricks, deceits. 83. images:
exact likenesses. 92. Why does Lear pounce upon Gloucester's use of the word
informed? 99–100. Infirmity . . . bound: i.e., a sick man neglects his duty.

When nature, being oppressed, commands the mind
To suffer with the body; I'll forbear,
And am fallen out with my more headier will,°
To take the indisposed and sickly fit
For the sound man.° Death on my state! Wherefore   105
Should he sit here? This act persuades me,
That this remotion° of the duke and her
Is practice° only. Give me my servant forth.
Go tell the duke and's wife I'd speak with them.
Now, presently.° Bid them come forth and hear me,   110
Or at their chamber door I'll beat the drum,
Till it cry sleep to death.°

GLOUCESTER. I would have all well betwixt you.   *Exit.*

LEAR. O me my heart! My rising heart! But down.

FOOL. Cry to it nuncle, as the cockney did to the eels, when she put   115
'em i' th' paste° alive; she knapped° 'em o' th' coxcombs with a
stick, and cried, down wantons, down. 'Twas her brother, that in
pure kindness to his horse buttered his hay.

Enter CORNWALL, REGAN, GLOUCESTER, *and* SERVANTS.

LEAR. Good morrow to you both.

CORNWALL.   Hail to your Grace.

[KENT *is set at liberty.*]

REGAN. I am glad to see your Highness.   120

LEAR. Regan, I think you are. I know what reason
I have to think so. If thou shouldst not be glad,
I would divorce me from thy mother's tomb,
Sepulchring an adulteress. [*To* KENT] O are you free?
Some other time for that.— Beloved Regan,   125
Thy sister's naught.° O Regan, she hath tied
Sharp-toothed unkindness, like a vulture, here.

[*Points to his heart.*]

I can scarce speak to thee; thou'lt not believe

---

103. **am . . . will:** regret my impulsiveness. 105. Note the change following
this point in the speech. What stage direction might be inserted to make clear
the immediate reason for the change? 107. **remotion:** removal. 108. **practice:** pretense. 110. **presently:** immediately. 112. **cry . . . death:** kill sleep by its noise.
116. **paste:** pastry, pie; **knapped:** cracked. 126. **naught:** wicked.

Of how depraved a quality — O Regan.

REGAN. I pray you sir, take patience; I have hope   130
You less know how to value her desert
Than she to scant her duty.

LEAR.   Say — how is that?

REGAN. I cannot think my sister in the least
Would fail her obligation. If sir perchance
She have restrained the riots of your followers,   135
'Tis on such ground, and to such wholesome end,
As clears her from all blame.

LEAR. My curses on her.

REGAN.   O sir, you are old;
Nature in you stands on the very verge
Of his confine. You should be ruled, and led   140
By some discretion that discerns your state
Better than you yourself. Therefore, I pray you,
That to our sister you do make return;
Say you have wronged her.

LEAR.   Ask her forgiveness?
Do you but mark how this becomes the house° —   145
Dear daughter, I confess that I am old;
Age is unnecessary, on my knees I beg
That you'll vouchsafe me raiment, bed, and food.

[*Kneels*]

REGAN. Good sir, no more; these are unsightly tricks.
Return you to my sister.

LEAR. [*Rises*]   Never, Regan.   150
She hath abated me of half my train;
Looked black upon me, struck me with her tongue
Most serpent-like, upon the very heart.
All the stored vengeances of heaven fall
On her ingrateful top.° Strike her young bones,   155
You taking airs, with lameness.

CORNWALL.   Fie, sir, fie!

LEAR. You nimble lightnings, dart your blinding flames
Into her scornful eyes. Infect her beauty,
You fen-sucked fogs, drawn by the powerful sun,

145. **becomes the house:** i.e., suits my dignity. 155. **top:** head.

       To fall and blister her.°
REGAN.   O the blessed gods,   160
       So will you wish on me when the rash mood —
LEAR. No Regan, thou shalt never have my curse.
       Thy tender-hefted° nature shall not give
       Thee o'er to harshness. Her eyes are fierce, but thine
       Do comfort, and not burn. 'Tis not in thee   165
       To grudge my pleasures, to cut off my train,
       To bandy hasty words, to scant my sizes,°
       And in conclusion, to oppose the bolt
       Against my coming in. Thou better know'st
       The offices of nature, bond of childhood,   170
       Effects of courtesy, dues of gratitude.
       Thy half o' th' kingdom hast thou not forgot,
       Wherein I thee endowed.
REGAN.   Good sir, to th' purpose.°
LEAR. Who put my man i' th' stocks?

                 [Tucket within]

CORNWALL.   What trumpet's that?

                Enter OSWALD.

REGAN. I know't — my sister's. This approves° her letter,   175
       That she would soon be here. — Is your lady come?
LEAR. This is a slave, whose easy-borrowed pride
       Dwells in the fickle grace of her he follows.
       Out varlet,° from my sight.
CORNWALL.   What means your Grace?
LEAR. Who stocked my servant? Regan, I have good hope   180
       Thou didst not know on't.

                Enter GONERIL.

               Who comes here? O heavens,
       If you do love old men, if your sweet sway

---

160. What assumptions are implicit in Lear's appeal to nature (or is it an appeal?) for justice against his oppressor? 163. **tender-hefted:** gently framed. Why does Lear know so much less about his own daughter than do we? 167. **scant my sizes:** reduce my allowances. 173. Why does Regan not consider what Lear has just said "to th' purpose"? 175. **approves:** confirms. 179. **varlet:** knave.

Allow° obedience, if you yourselves are old,
Make it your cause. Send down, and take my part.
[*To* GONERIL] Art not ashamed to look upon this beard?   185
O Regan, will you take her by the hand?

GONERIL.   Why not by th' hand, sir? How have I offended?
All's not offence that indiscretion finds,
And dotage° terms so.

LEAR.   O sides, you are too tough.
Will you yet hold? How came my man i' th' stocks?   190

CORNWALL.   I set him there, sir. But his own disorders
Deserved much less advancement.

LEAR.   You? Did you?

REGAN.   I pray you father, being weak, seem so.°
If till the expiration of your month,
You will return and sojourn with my sister,   195
Dismissing half your train, come then to me.
I am now from home, and out of that provision
Which shall be needful for your entertainment.

LEAR.   Return to her? And fifty men dismissed?
No, rather I abjure all roofs, and choose   200
To wage against the enmity o' th' air,
To be a comrade with the wolf and owl,
Necessity's sharp pinch. Return with her?
Why the hot-blooded France, that dowerless took
Our youngest born, I could as well be brought   205
To knee his throne, and squire-like° pension beg
To keep base life afoot. Return with her?
Persuade me rather to be slave and sumpter°
To this detested groom.°

GONERIL.   At your choice, sir.

LEAR.   I prithee daughter do not make me mad.   210
I will not trouble thee, my child; farewell.
We'll no more meet, no more see one another.

---

183. Allow: approve of. 189. dotage: a contemptuous term for helpless senility.
This may be an ironic answer to Lear's appeal to heaven in behalf of old age.
193. seem so: i.e., act suitably. What is the ruling principle of life for people like
Regan? 206. squire-like: like a servant. A squire was a male attendant, especially
of a great personage. 208. sumpter: pack horse, beast of burden. 209. this detested
groom: Oswald.

But yet thou art my flesh, my blood, my daughter;°
Or rather a disease that's in my flesh,
Which I must needs call mine. Thou art a boil,   215
A plague-sore, or embossed carbuncle°
In my corrupted blood. But I'll not chide thee;
Let shame come when it will, I do not call it;
I do not bid the thunder-bearer° shoot,
Nor tell tales of thee to high-judging Jove.   220
Mend when thou canst, be better at thy leisure;
I can be patient, I can stay with Regan,
I and my hundred knights.

REGAN.   Not altogether so;
    I looked not for you yet, nor am provided
    For your fit welcome. Give ear sir to my sister,   225
    For those that mingle reason with your passion
    Must be content to think you old,° and so —
    But she knows what she does.

LEAR.   Is this well spoken?

REGAN.   I dare avouch it sir. What, fifty followers?
    Is it not well? What should you need of more?   230
    Yea or so many, sith° that both charge and danger°
    Speak 'gainst so great a number? How in one house
    Should many people, under two commands,
    Hold amity? 'Tis hard, almost impossible.°

GONERIL.   Why might not you my lord, receive attendance   235
    From those that she calls servants, or from mine?

REGAN.   Why not my lord? If then they chanced to slack° ye,
    We could control them. If you will come to me —
    For now I spy a danger — I entreat you
    To bring but five and twenty; to no more   240
    Will I give place or notice.

LEAR.   I gave you all.

REGAN.   And in good time you gave it.

LEAR.   Made you my guardians, my depositaries,°

---

213. What change has occurred in Lear since he banished Cordelia? 216. embossed carbuncle: swollen boil. 219. thunder-bearer: Jove (Jupiter), ruler of the
Olympian gods. 226–27. those . . . old: Those who consider your passion with
reason realize that you are old — and should be wise. Note the overt contempt.
231. sith: since; charge and danger: expense and risk of maintaining them.
234. Is this simple common sense? 237. slack: neglect. 243. depositaries: trustees.

But kept a reservation to be followed
With such a number. What, must I come to you   245
With five and twenty? Regan, said you so?
REGAN.   And speak't again, my lord; no more with me.
LEAR.   Those wicked creatures yet do look well-favoured,
When others are more wicked; not being the worst
Stands in some rank of praise. [*To* GONERIL] I'll go with thee;   250
Thy fifty yet doth double five and twenty,
And thou art twice her love.°
GONERIL.   Hear me my lord;
What need you five and twenty? Ten? Or five?
To follow in a house where twice so many
Have a command to tend you?
REGAN.   What need one?   255
LEAR.   O reason not the need. Our basest beggars
Are in the poorest thing superfluous.°
Allow not nature more than nature needs;
Man's life is cheap as beast's. Thou art a lady;
If only to go warm were gorgeous,   260
Why, nature needs not what thou gorgeous wear'st,
Which scarcely keeps thee warm. But for true need —
You heavens, give me that patience, patience I need.
You see me here, you gods, a poor old man,
As full of grief as age, wretched in both.   265
If it be you that stirs these daughters' hearts
Against their father, fool me not so much
To bear it tamely;° touch me with noble anger,
And let not women's weapons, water-drops,
Stain my man's cheeks. No, you unnatural hags,   270
I will have such revenges on you both,
That all the world shall — I will do such things;
What they are, yet I know not, but they shall be
The terrors of the earth. You think I'll weep.
No, I'll not weep.   275

[Storm and tempest]

252. How does Lear measure love here? Is his attitude what it was in Act I,
Scene i? 256–57. Our . . . superfluous: i.e., even the few possessions of a beggar
are not absolutely necessary. 267–68. fool . . . tamely: i.e., do not degrade me to
such a point that I just tamely endure it.

I have full cause of weeping; but this heart
Shall break into a hundred thousand flaws°
Or e'er I'll weep. O fool, I shall go mad.

Exeunt LEAR, GLOUCESTER, KENT, *and* FOOL.

CORNWALL. Let us withdraw, 'twill be a storm.

REGAN. This house is little; the old man and's people   280
Cannot be well bestowed.

GONERIL. 'Tis his own blame; hath put himself from rest,
And must needs taste his folly.

REGAN. For his particular,° I'll receive him gladly,
But not one follower.

GONERIL.   So am I purposed.   285
Where is my Lord of Gloucester?

CORNWALL. Followed the old man forth —

Enter GLOUCESTER.

                    He is returned.

GLOUCESTER. The King is in high rage.

CORNWALL.   Whither is he going?

GLOUCESTER. He calls to horse, but will I know not whither.

CORNWALL. 'Tis best to give him way, he leads himself.   290

GONERIL. My lord, entreat him by no means to stay.

GLOUCESTER. Alack, the night comes on, and the high winds
Do sorely ruffle; for many miles about
There's scarce a bush.

REGAN.   O sir, to wilful men
The injuries that they themselves procure   295
Must be their schoolmasters.° Shut up your doors,
He is attended with a desperate train,
And what they may incense° him to, being apt°
To have his ear abused,° wisdom bids fear.

CORNWALL. Shut up your doors my lord, 'tis a wild night.   300
My Regan counsels well. Come out o' th' storm.   *Exeunt.*

277. flaws: broken pieces. 284. **For his particular:** as for him in particular, i.e., him alone. 296. Is there evident a truth in this line far beyond what Regan means? 298. incense: incite; apt: ready. 299. abused: deceived. Again, what ironic significance is there here beyond Regan's meaning?

ACT III

SCENE I. *A heath. Storm still.**

Enter KENT *and* GENTLEMAN, *at several doors.*

KENT. Who's there, besides foul weather?

GENTLEMAN. One minded like the weather, most unquietly.

KENT. I know you. Where's the King?

GENTLEMAN. Contending with the fretful elements;
    Bids the wind blow the earth into the sea, 5
    Or swell the curled waters 'bove the main,°
    That things° might change or cease; tears his white hair,
    Which the impetuous blasts with eyeless° rage
    Catch in their fury, and make nothing of;
    Strives in his little world of man to outstorm 10
    The to-and-fro conflicting wind and rain.
    This night, wherein the cub-drawn bear° would couch,
    The lion, and the belly-pinched wolf
    Keep their fur dry, unbonneted he runs,
    And bids what will take all.

KENT.   But who is with him? 15

GENTLEMAN. None but the fool, who labours to outjest
    His heart-struck injuries.

KENT.   Sir, I do know you,
    And dare upon the warrant of my note°
    Commend a dear thing° to you. There is division,
    Although as yet the face of it is covered 20
    With mutual cunning, 'twixt Albany and Cornwall;
    Who have — as who have not, that their great stars
    Throned and set high° — servants, who seem no less,
    Which are to France the spies and speculations°

---

* still: continuing. 6. main: mainland. 7. things: everything; the whole order
of nature. 8. eyeless: blind. The elements do not apparently see differences between the good and the evil, the deserving and the undeserving. 12. cub-drawn
bear: she-bear sucked dry (and therefore famished). 18. warrant of my note:
guarantee of my observation (of you). 19. a dear thing: a precious thing, i.e., an
important matter. 22–23. that . . . high: whom Fate has set in exalted positions. 24. speculations: speculators. (In a sense now obsolete, this word meant
"secret observers.")

Intelligent of our state. What hath been seen,   25
Either in snuffs and packings° of the dukes,
Or the hard rein which both of them hath borne
Against the old kind King, or something deeper,
Whereof perchance these are but furnishings° —
But true it is, from France there comes a power°   30
Into this scattered kingdom, who already,
Wise in our negligence, have secret feet
In some of our best ports, and are at point
To show their open banner. Now to you.
If on my credit° you dare build so far   35
To make your speed to Dover, you shall find
Some that will thank you, making just report
Of how unnatural and bemadding sorrow
The King hath cause to plain.°
I am a gentleman of blood and breeding,   40
And from some knowledge and assurance, offer
This office° to you.
GENTLEMAN.   I will talk further with you.
KENT.   No, do not.
For confirmation that I am much more
Than my out-wall,° open this purse, and take   45
What it contains. If you shall see Cordelia,
As fear not but you shall, show her this ring,
And she will tell you who that fellow is
That yet you do not know. Fie on this storm!
I will go seek the King.   50
GENTLEMAN.   Give me your hand. Have you no more to say?
KENT.   Few words, but to effect more than all yet,
That when we have found the King — in which your pain
That way, I'll this° — he that first lights on him
Holla the other.   *Exeunt at several doors.*   55

26. **snuffs and packings:** resentments and plottings. 29. **furnishings:** outward trappings, i.e., pretexts. (The sentence is not finished.) 30. **power:** army. 35. **credit:** trustworthiness. 39. **plain:** complain of. 42. **office:** undertaking, job. 45. **my out-wall:** my appearance as a mere servingman. 53–54. **in . . . this:** in doing which, take pains in that direction, and I'll do the same in this.

Enter LEAR *and* FOOL.

LEAR.   Blow, winds, and crack your cheeks. Rage, blow,
       You cataracts, and hurricanoes,° spout
       Till you have drenched our steeples, drowned the cocks.°
       You sulphurous and thought-executing° fires,
       Vaunt-couriers° of oak-cleaving thunderbolts,   5
       Singe my white head. And thou all-shaking thunder,
       Strike flat the thick rotundity o' th' world,
       Crack nature's moulds,° all germens° spill at once,
       That makes ingrateful man.
FOOL.   O nuncle, Court holy water° in a dry house is better than this 10
       rain-water out o' door. Good nuncle in, ask thy daughters' blessing;
       here's a night pities neither wise men, nor fools.
LEAR.   Rumble thy bellyful. Spit fire, spout rain.
       Nor rain, wind, thunder, fire, are my daughters;
       I tax° not you, you elements, with unkindness.   15
       I never gave you kingdom, called you children;
       You owe me no subscription.° Then let fall
       Your horrible pleasure. Here I stand your slave,
       A poor, infirm, weak, and despised old man.
       But yet I call you servile ministers,°   20
       That will with two pernicious daughters join
       Your high-engendered battles° 'gainst a head
       So old and white as this. O, oho, 'tis foul.°
FOOL.   He that has a house to put's head in has a good head-piece.
              The codpiece that will house,   25
                Before the head has any,
              The head and he shall louse;
                So beggars marry many.
              The man that makes his toe,

---

2. **hurricanoes:** waterspouts. 3. **cocks:** weathervanes. 4. **thought-executing:** killing as quick as thought. 5. **Vaunt-couriers:** forerunners. 8. **nature's moulds:** the moulds in which man is formed; **germens:** seeds. 10. **Court holy water:** flattery. 15. **tax:** accuse. 17. **subscription:** submission. 20. **servile ministers:** slavish agents. 22. **high-engendered battles:** armies created cosmically, on high. 23. Lear has apparently recognized that the heavens do *not* "love old men." With what alternative idea is he now concerned?

What he his heart should make,   30
    Shall of a corn cry woe,
    And turn his sleep to wake.
For there was never yet fair woman, but she made mouths in a glass.
LEAR. No, I will be the pattern of all patience,
    I will say nothing.   35

Enter KENT.

KENT. Who's there?

FOOL. Marry° here's grace, and a codpiece; that's a wise man, and a fool.

KENT. Alas sir are you here? Things that love night
    Love not such nights as these. The wrathful skies
    Gallow° the very wanderers of the dark,   40
    And make them keep their caves. Since I was man,
    Such sheets of fire, such bursts of horrid thunder,
    Such groans of roaring wind, and rain, I never
    Remember to have heard. Man's nature cannot carry
    Th' affliction, nor the fear.

LEAR.   Let the great gods   45
    That keep this dreadful pudder° o'er our heads
    Find out their enemies now. Tremble, thou wretch,
    That hast within thee undivulged crimes,
    Unwhipped of justice. Hide thee, thou bloody hand;
    Thou perjured, and thou simular of virtue°   50
    That art incestuous. Caitiff,° to pieces shake,
    That under covert and convenient seeming
    Has practised on man's life. Close pent-up guilts,
    Rive your concealing continents,° and cry
    These dreadful summoners grace.° I am a man   55
    More sinned against, than sinning.

KENT.   Alack, bare-headed!
    Gracious my lord, hard by here is a hovel,
    Some friendship will it lend you 'gainst the tempest.
    Repose you there, while I to this hard house —

37. **Marry:** Mary (i.e., by the Virgin Mary). 40. **Gallow:** a strong word for
terrify. 46. **pudder:** pother, i.e., turmoil. 50. **simular of virtue:** one who simulates
virtue, a hypocrite. 51. **Caitiff:** wicked wretch. 54. **Rive . . . continents:** Split
open that which covers and conceals you. 54–55. **cry . . . grace:** Ask for mercy
from these dreadful summoners. A summoner was the officer of the ecclesiastical
court who summoned persons to appear to answer charges of immorality.

More harder than the stones whereof 'tis raised,
Which even but now, demanding after you,
Denied me to come in — return, and force
Their scanted courtesy.

LEAR.   My wits begin to turn.°
Come on, my boy. How dost, my boy? Art cold?
I am cold myself. Where is this straw, my fellow?   65
The art of our necessities is strange
That can make vile things precious. Come, your hovel.
Poor fool and knave, I have one part in my heart
That's sorry yet for thee.

FOOL.   [*Sings*] *He that has and a little tiny wit,*   70
                        With hey, ho, the wind and the rain,
                Must make content with his fortunes fit,°
                Though the rain it raineth every day.

LEAR.   True, boy. Come bring us to this hovel.   *Exeunt* LEAR *and* KENT.
FOOL.   This is a brave night to cool a courtezan. I'll speak a prophecy   75
ere I go:

                When priests are more in word than matter;
                When brewers mar their malt with water;
                When nobles are their tailors' tutors;
                No heretics burned, but wenches' suitors;   80
                When every case in law is right;
                No squire in debt, nor no poor knight;
                When slanders do not live in tongues;
                Nor cutpurses come not to throngs;
                When usurers tell their gold i' th' field,   85
                And bawds and whores do churches build,
                Then shall the realm of Albion°
                Come to great confusion.
                Then comes the time, who lives to see't,
                That going shall be used with feet.   90

    This prophecy Merlin shall make, for I live before his time.   *Exit.*

---

    63. This is almost a formal announcement. But see what follows as the first
symptom of turned wits. **72. Must . . . fit:** i.e., must be content with a fortune
as slim as his wit. **87. Albion:** an old name for England.

Enter GLOUCESTER *and* EDMUND.

GLOUCESTER. Alack, alack, Edmund, I like not this unnatural dealing.
When I desired their leave that I might pity him, they took from
me the use of mine own house, charged me on pain of perpetual
displeasure neither to speak of him, entreat for him, nor any way
sustain him.°   5

EDMUND. Most savage and unnatural.

GLOUCESTER. Go to; say you nothing. There is division between the dukes,
and a worse matter than that. I have received a letter this night —
'tis dangerous to be spoken — I have locked the letter in my closet;
these injuries the King now bears will be revenged home.°   10
There is part of a power already footed;° we must incline to the
King. I will look him, and privily° relieve him; go you and maintain talk with the duke, that my charity be not of him perceived.
If he ask for me, I am ill, and gone to bed. If I die for it, as no
less is threatened me, the King my old master must be relieved.   15
There is strange things toward, Edmund, pray you be careful.° *Exit.*

EDMUND. This courtesy,° forbid thee,° shall the duke
Instantly know, and of that letter too.
This seems a fair deserving, and must draw me
That which my father loses — no less than all.   20
The younger rises when the old doth fall.   *Exit.*

5. Gloucester is a sensual man, eager for comfort and specious peace. What
assumptions does he have about right and wrong? 10. home: to the utmost.
11. footed: landed. 12. privily: secretly. 16. What does Gloucester mean by this
admonition? What further meaning does the sentence have for us, who know
Edmund and his plans? 17. This courtesy: the courtesy of relieving the King; forbid thee: forbidden thee.

SCENE IV. *The heath, before a hovel.*

Enter LEAR, KENT, *and* FOOL.

KENT. Here is the place, my lord; good my lord, enter.
The tyranny of the open night's too rough
For nature to endure.

[*Storm still*]

LEAR.   Let me alone.
KENT.   Good my lord, enter here.
LEAR.   Wilt break my heart?
KENT.   I had rather break mine own. Good my lord, enter.   5
LEAR.   Thou think'st 'tis much that this contentious storm
        Invades us to the skin; so 'tis to thee,
        But where the greater malady is fixed,
        The lesser is scarce felt. Thou'dst shun a bear,
        But if thy flight lay toward the roaring sea,   10
        Thou'dst meet the bear i' th' mouth. When the mind's free,°
        The body's delicate; this tempest in my mind
        Doth from my senses take all feeling else
        Save what beats there. Filial ingratitude,
        Is it not as this mouth should tear this hand   15
        For lifting food to't? But I will punish home.
        No, I will weep no more. In such a night
        To shut me out! Pour on, I will endure.
        In such a night as this! O Regan, Goneril —
        Your old kind father, whose frank heart gave all —   20
        O that way madness lies,° let me shun that.
        No more of that.
KENT.   Good my lord, enter here.
LEAR.   Prithee go in thyself, seek thine own ease.°
        This tempest will not give me leave to ponder
        On things would hurt me more. But I'll go in.   25
        In boy, go first. — You houseless poverty —
        Nay get thee in. I'll pray, and then I'll sleep.

                                   Exit FOOL *into the hovel.*

        Poor naked wretches, wheresoe'er you are,
        That bide° the pelting of this pitiless storm,
        How shall your houseless heads, and unfed sides,   30
        Your looped and windowed° raggedness, defend you
        From seasons such as these? O I have ta'en
        Too little care of this! Take physic, pomp;°

    11. **free:** free from cares, untroubled. 21. *What,* exactly, is the way madness
lies? 23. Up to this point Lear has considered other people almost exclusively as
they relate to his own state and welfare. (Recall the nature of his concern for Kent
in the stocks.) 29. **bide:** endure. 31. **looped and windowed:** full of holes and gaps.
33. **Take . . . pomp:** Take medicine, you rich ones. What medicine does he mean?

Expose thyself to feel what wretches feel,
That thou mayst shake the superflux° to them,   35
And show the heavens more just.

EDGAR. [*Within*] Fathom and half, fathom and half!
  Poor Tom!

Enter FOOL *from the hovel.*

FOOL. Come not in here, nuncle, here's a spirit. Help me, help me.
KENT. Give me thy hand. Who's there?   40
FOOL. A spirit, a spirit, he says his name's poor Tom.
KENT. What art thou that dost grumble there i' th' straw? Come forth.

Enter EDGAR *from the hovel, disguised as a madman.**

EDGAR. Away, the foul fiend follows me. Through the sharp hawthorn
  blow the winds. Hum, go to thy cold bed and warm thee.°
LEAR. Didst thou give all to thy daughters? And art thou come   45
  to this?°
EDGAR. Who gives any thing to poor Tom, whom the foul fiend hath led
  through fire, and through flame, through ford and whirlpool, o'er
  bog and quagmire, that hath laid knives under his pillow, and
  halters in his pew,° set ratsbane° by his porridge, made him   50
  proud of heart to ride on a bay trotting-horse over four-inched
  bridges, to course° his own shadow for a traitor. Bless thy five wits,
  Tom's a-cold. O do, de, do, de, do, de. Bless thee from whirlwinds,
  star-blasting, and taking, do poor Tom some charity, whom the
  foul fiend vexes. There could I have him now — and there —   55
  and there again, and there.°

[*Storm still*]

LEAR. What, have his daughters brought him to this pass?
  Couldst thou save nothing? Wouldst thou give 'em all?

35. **superflux:** superfluity, what you do not need. The Christmas carol "Good King Wenceslas" shows a monarch doing precisely what Lear here says should be done. * Recall Edgar's description of his disguise in Act II, Scene iii. Note that he ended that scene with the statement, "Edgar I nothing am." 44. Note how evil, desolation, and death soak through these mad gibberings. 46. What has finally happened? Note how we have been prepared for it. 49–50. **knives . . . pew:** Edgar, as Poor Tom, is claiming that the foul fiend has tempted him to commit suicide. 50. **ratsbane:** rat poison. 52. **course:** to chase after. 56. Here Poor Tom is leaping about, striking at the foul fiend.

FOOL. Nay, he reserved a blanket,° else we had been all shamed.

LEAR. Now all the plagues that in the pendulous° air   60
　　　　Hang fated o'er men's faults light on thy daughters.

KENT. He hath no daughters, sir.

LEAR. Death, traitor; nothing could have subdued nature
　　　　To such a lowness but his unkind daughters.
　　　　Is it the fashion, that discarded fathers   65
　　　　Should have thus little mercy on their flesh?
　　　　Judicious punishment; 'twas this flesh begot
　　　　Those pelican° daughters.

EDGAR. Pillicock sat on Pillicock-hill. Alow; alow, loo, loo!

FOOL. This cold night will turn us all to fools, and madmen.   70

EDGAR. Take heed o' th' foul fiend, obey thy parents, keep thy words
　　　　justly, swear not, commit not with man's sworn spouse; set not thy
　　　　sweet heart on proud array. Tom's a-cold.

LEAR. What hast thou been?

EDGAR. A servingman, proud in heart and mind; that curled my hair,   75
　　　　wore gloves in my cap; served the lust of my mistress' heart, and
　　　　did the act of darkness with her; swore as many oaths as I spake
　　　　words, and broke them in the sweet face of heaven; one that slept
　　　　in the contriving of lust, and waked to do it. Wine loved I deeply,
　　　　dice dearly; and in woman out-paramoured the Turk.° False   80
　　　　of heart, light of ear, bloody of hand; hog in sloth, fox in stealth,
　　　　wolf in greediness, dog in madness, lion in prey. Let not the creak-
　　　　ing of shoes, nor the rustling of silks, betray thy poor heart to
　　　　woman; keep thy foot out of brothels, thy hand out of plackets, thy
　　　　pen from lenders' books, and defy the foul fiend. Still through   85
　　　　the hawthorn blows the cold wind; says suum, mun, nonny. Dol-
　　　　phin my boy, boy sessa, let him trot by.

[Storm still]

LEAR. Thou wert better in a grave, than to answer with thy uncovered
　　　　body this extremity of the skies. Is man no more than this? Con-
　　　　sider him well. Thou ow'st the worm° no silk, the beast no   90

---

59. blanket: Poor Tom's only covering. 60. pendulous: overhanging. 68. pelican:
The pelican was considered the pattern of devoted parenthood because it supposedly fed its young on its own blood. When the young pelicans grew strong,
they turned on their parents, according to tradition. 80. out-paramoured the Turk:
had more mistresses than the Turkish Sultan. 90. worm: silkworm.

hide, the sheep no wool, the cat no perfume. Ha? Here's three on's
are sophisticated.° Thou art the thing itself; unaccommodated
man° is no more but such a poor, bare, forked animal as thou art.
Off, off, you lendings! Come, unbutton here.

[*Pulls at his clothes.*]

FOOL. Prithee, nuncle, be contented, 'tis a naughty night to swim in. 95
Now a little fire in a wild field were like an old lecher's heart, a
small spark, all the rest on's body cold.

Enter GLOUCESTER, *with a torch.*

Look, here comes a walking fire.
EDGAR. This is the foul fiend Flibbertigibbet; he begins at curfew, and
walks till the first cock; he gives the web and the pin,° squints 100
the eye, and makes the hare-lip; mildews the white wheat, and
hurts the poor creature of earth.
      Swithold° footed thrice the 'old;°
      He met the night-mare,° and her nine-fold;°
          Bid her alight, 105
          And her troth plight,
     And, aroint thee,° witch, aroint thee!
GLOUCESTER. How fares your Grace?
LEAR. What's he?
KENT. Who's there? What is't you seek? 110
GLOUCESTER. What are you there? Your names?
EDGAR. Poor Tom, that eats the swimming frog, the toad, the tadpole,
the wall-newt° and the water; that in the fury of his heart, when
the foul fiend rages, eats cow-dung for sallets;° swallows the old
rat and the ditch-dog;° drinks the green mantle° of the stand- 115
ing pool; who is whipped from tithing° to tithing, and stock-
punished, and imprisoned; who hath had three suits to his back,
six shirts to his body,

91–92. Here's . . . sophisticated: Lear is pointing out that he, Kent, and the
Fool are wearing clothes. 92–93. unaccommodated man: man pure and simple.
100. web . . . pin: eye disease and cataract. 103. Swithold: Saint Withold. Thus
begins a five-line charm to keep horses from suffering from nightmare; 'old: wold,
uncultivated downland. 104. night-mare: the fiend that was believed to cause nightmare; nine-fold: nine young. 107. aroint thee: Be gone. 113. wall-newt: lizard.
114. sallets: salads. 115. ditch-dog: dog drowned in a ditch; mantle: scum. 116. tithing: parish.

Horse to ride, and weapon to wear;
But mice, and rats, and such small deer,°   120
Have been Tom's food, for seven long year.
Beware my follower. Peace, Smulkin; peace, thou fiend.°

GLOUCESTER. What, hath your Grace no better company?

EDGAR. The prince of darkness is a gentleman.° Modo he's called, and
Mahu.   125

GLOUCESTER. Our flesh and blood, my lord, is grown so vile,
That it doth hate what gets° it.

EDGAR. Poor Tom's a-cold.

GLOUCESTER. Go in with me; my duty cannot suffer
T' obey in all your daughters' hard commands.   130
Though their injunction be to bar my doors,
And let this tyrannous night take hold upon you,
Yet have I ventured to come seek you out,
And bring you where both fire and food is ready.

LEAR. First let me talk with this philosopher.   135
What is the cause of thunder?

KENT. Good my lord take his offer, go into the house.

LEAR. I'll talk a word with this same learned Theban.°
What is your study?°

EDGAR. How to prevent the fiend, and to kill vermin.   140

LEAR. Let me ask you one word in private.

KENT. Importune him once more to go, my lord,
His wits begin t' unsettle.

[Storm still]

GLOUCESTER.   Canst thou blame him?
His daughters seek his death. Ah, that good Kent,
He said it would be thus — poor banished man.   145
Thou sayst the King grows mad; I'll tell thee friend,
I am almost mad myself. I had a son,
Now outlawed from my blood; he sought my life
But lately, very late. I loved him, friend,
No father his son dearer. True to tell thee,   150

120. deer: game. 122. Recognizing his father, who has had him proclaimed,
Edgar has intensified his mad act. 124. After all, the foul fiend is of an old and
powerful family. 127. gets: begets. 138. Lear, in his mad obsession with the notion
that Poor Tom is a philosopher, refers to him as an ancient Greek of Thebes.
139. study: particular interest or, in modern academic jargon, "special field."

The grief hath crazed my wits. What a night's this!
I do beseech your Grace —

LEAR.   O cry you mercy, sir.°
Noble philosopher, your company.

EDGAR.   Tom's a-cold.

GLOUCESTER.   In fellow, there, into the hovel; keep thee warm.   155

LEAR.   Come, let's in all.

KENT.   This way, my lord.

LEAR.   With him;
I will keep still with my philosopher.

KENT.   Good my lord, soothe him; let him take the fellow.

GLOUCESTER.   Take him you on.

KENT.   Sirrah, come on; go along with us.   160

LEAR.   Come, good Athenian.°

GLOUCESTER.   No words, no words, hush.

EDGAR.   Child Rowland to the dark tower came,
His word was still, fie, foh, and fum,
I smell the blood of a British man.   *Exeunt.* 165

152. O cry you mercy, sir: in effect, "Excuse me, but you are interrupting."
161. Athenian: like "Theban," line 138.

SCENE V. GLOUCESTER'*s castle.*

Enter CORNWALL *and* EDMUND.

CORNWALL.   I will have my revenge ere I depart his house.°

EDMUND.   How, my lord, I may be censured,° that nature thus gives way
to loyalty, something fears me to think of.°

CORNWALL.   I now perceive, it was not altogether your brother's evil disposition made him seek his death; but a provoking merit set 5
awork by a reproveable badness in himself.°

EDMUND.   How malicious is my fortune, that I must repent to be just.°
This is the letter he spoke of, which approves° him an intelligent
party° to the advantages of France. O heavens, that this treason
were not, or not I the detector!   10

1. For what is Cornwall determined to have revenge? 2. censured: judged.
3. something . . . of: alarms me somewhat. Note how Edmund's diction main-
tains his timid, respectful, somewhat pedantic role. 6. How does this speech demonstrate Cornwall's conceptions of good and evil? 7. repent . . . just: be sorry
because I have acted rightly (in betraying my father). 8. approves: proves, confirms. 8–9. intelligent party: spy.

CORNWALL. Go with me to the duchess.

EDMUND. If the matter of this paper be certain, you have mighty business in hand.

CORNWALL. True or false, it hath made thee Earl of Gloucester. Seek out where thy father is, that he may be ready for our apprehension.° 15

EDMUND. [*Aside*] If I find him comforting the King, it will stuff his suspicion more fully. — I will persevere in my course of loyalty, though the conflict be sore between that and my blood.°

CORNWALL. I will lay trust upon thee; and thou shalt find a dearer father in my love.° *Exeunt.* 20

15. apprehension: arrest. 17–18. I . . . blood: Note two possible readings of this sentence. Either Edmund is no longer speaking aside but is talking in his characteristic mealy-mouthed way to Cornwall, or he is still speaking aside and is being ironical. 20. What particular qualifications does Cornwall show in this scene for being a dear and loving foster-father?

SCENE VI. *An outbuilding of the castle.*

Enter KENT *and* GLOUCESTER.

GLOUCESTER. Here is better than the open air, take it thankfully. I will piece out the comfort with what addition I can. I will not be long from you.

KENT. All the power of his wits have given way to his impatience.° The gods reward your kindness. *Exit* GLOUCESTER. 5

Enter LEAR, EDGAR, *and* FOOL.

EDGAR. Frateretto° calls me, and tells me Nero is an angler in the lake of darkness. Pray, innocent, and beware the foul fiend.

FOOL. Prithee, nuncle, tell me, whether a madman be a gentleman or a yeoman?°

LEAR. A king, a king. 10

FOOL. No, he's a yeoman that has a gentleman to his son; for he's a mad yeoman that sees his son a gentleman before him.

LEAR. To have a thousand with red burning spits
Come hissing in upon 'em —

EDGAR. The foul fiend bites my back. 15

FOOL. He's mad that trusts in the tameness of a wolf, a horse's health, a boy's love, or a whore's oath.

4. impatience: strain. 6. Frateretto: a devil's name. Recall the names Modo and Mahu in Scene iv, lines 124–25. 9. yeoman: a freeholder who has not the rank of gentleman.

LEAR. It shall be done; I will arraign them straight.°

[*To* EDGAR] Come sit thou here, most learned Justice.

[*To the* FOOL] Thou, sapient° sir, sit here. — Now, you she-foxes!

EDGAR. Look where he stands and glares. — Want'st thou eyes at   21
trial, madam?

            Come o'er the bourn Bessy to me.

FOOL.   Her boat hath a leak,

            And she must not speak,   25

          Why she dares not come over to thee.

EDGAR. The foul fiend haunts poor Tom in the voice of a nightingale.
Hopdance° cries in Tom's belly for two white herring. Croak not
black angel, I have no food for thee.

KENT. How do you sir? Stand you not so amazed.°   30
Will you lie down and rest upon the cushions?

LEAR. I'll see their trial first. Bring in their evidence.
Thou robed° man of justice, take thy place;
And thou his yoke-fellow of equity,
Bench by his side. [*To* KENT] You are o' th' commission,   35
Sit you too.

EDGAR. Let us deal justly.

       Sleepest or wakest thou, jolly shepherd?

         Thy sheep be in the corn,

       And for one blast of thy minikin° mouth   40

        Thy sheep shall take no harm.

Purr. The cat is gray.

LEAR. Arraign her first; 'tis Goneril. I here take my oath before this honourable assembly, she kicked the poor King her father.°

FOOL. Come hither, mistress. Is your name Goneril?   45

LEAR. She cannot deny it.

FOOL. Cry you mercy,° I took you for a joint-stool.

LEAR. And here's another° whose warped looks proclaim
What store her heart is made on. Stop her there!
Arms, arms, sword, fire! Corruption in the place!   50
False justicer, why hast thou let her 'scape?

18. **arraign them straight:** Bring them immediately to the bar to answer the
charges against them. 20. **sapient:** wise. 28. **Hopdance:** another fiend's name. Poor
Tom associates him with the rumbling of his hungry belly. 30. **so amazed:** in such
a state of confusion. 33. **robed:** another reference to Edgar's blanket. 40. **minikin:**
dainty little. 44. Why does Lear say this? Did she? 48. **another:** Regan.

EDGAR. Bless thy five wits.

KENT. O pity! Sir, where is the patience now
That you so oft have boasted to retain?

EDGAR. [*Aside*] My tears begin to take his part so much,   55
They mar my counterfeiting.°

LEAR. The little dogs and all,
Tray, Blanch, and Sweetheart, see, they bark at me.

EDGAR. Tom will throw his head at them. Avaunt you curs!

          Be thy mouth or black or white,   60
          Tooth that poisons if it bite;
          Mastiff, greyhound, mongrel grim,
          Hound or spaniel, brach or lym,°
          Or bobtail tike or trundle-tail,°
          Tom will make him weep and wail;   65
          For with throwing thus my head,
          Dogs leap the hatch, and all are fled.

Do de, de, de. Sessa! Come, march to wakes and fairs and market
towns. Poor Tom, thy horn° is dry.

LEAR. Then let them anatomize° Regan. See what breeds about her   70
heart. Is there any cause in nature that makes these hard hearts?
[*To* EDGAR] You sir, I entertain° for one of my hundred; only I do
not like the fashion of your garments. You will say they are Persian;
but let them be changed.

KENT. Now good my lord, lie here, and rest awhile.   75

LEAR. Make no noise, make no noise, draw the curtains.
So, so, we'll go to supper i' th' morning.°

FOOL. And I'll go to bed at noon.°

Enter GLOUCESTER.

GLOUCESTER. Come hither, friend. Where is the King my master?

KENT. Here, sir, but trouble him not, his wits are gone.   80

GLOUCESTER. Good friend, I prithee take him in thy arms;
I have o'erheard a plot of death upon him.
There is a litter ready, lay him in't,
And drive toward Dover, friend, where thou shalt meet

56. **counterfeiting:** pretending. 63. **brach or lym:** bitch or bloodhound.
64. **trundle-tail:** curly tail. 69. **horn:** horn bottle carried by beggars to store drink
given them. 70. **anatomize:** dissect. 72. **entertain:** engage. 77. How does this
pathetic, crazy statement reflect what has happened to the world around Lear?
78. This is the Fool's last line. We do not see him after this scene.

Both welcome and protection. Take up thy master. 85
If thou shouldst dally half an hour, his life,
With thine and all that offer to defend him,
Stand in assured loss. Take up, take up;
And follow me, that will to some provision
Give thee quick conduct.

KENT.   Oppressed nature sleeps. 90
This rest might yet have balmed thy broken sinews,°
Which, if convenience will not allow,
Stand in hard cure.° [*To the* FOOL] Come, help to bear thy master;
Thou must not stay behind.

GLOUCESTER.   Come, come, away.

          Exeunt KENT, GLOUCESTER, *and the* FOOL, *bearing off* LEAR.

EDGAR. When we our betters see bearing our woes, 95
We scarcely think our miseries our foes.
Who alone suffers, suffers most i' th' mind,
Leaving free things and happy shows behind;
But then the mind much sufferance doth o'erskip,
When grief hath mates, and bearing fellowship. 100
How light and portable my pain seems now,
When that which makes me bend, makes the King bow —
He childed as I fathered. Tom, away!
Mark the high noises;° and thyself bewray,
When false opinion, whose wrong thoughts defile thee, 105
In thy just proof repeals and reconciles thee.°
What will hap more to-night, safe 'scape the King.
Lurk,° lurk.   *Exit.*

91. sinews: here, nerves. 93. Stand . . . cure: will be difficult to cure. 104. high
noises: the "hue and cry" raised by the pursuers of someone suspected of com-
mitting a crime. 104–06. thyself . . . thee: i.e., do not reveal yourself until the
belief in your guilt is proved wrong and you are called back. 108 Lurk: Be hidden.

SCENE VII. GLOUCESTER'*s castle.*

Enter CORNWALL, REGAN, GONERIL, EDMUND, *and* SERVANTS.

CORNWALL. Post speedily to my lord your husband;° show him this letter
    — the army of France is landed — seek out the traitor Gloucester.
REGAN. Hang him instantly.

    1. your husband: Albany. (These words are addressed to Goneril.)

GONERIL. Pluck out his eyes.

CORNWALL. Leave him to my displeasure. Edmund, keep you our 5
   sister company; the revenges we are bound to take upon your
   traitorous father are not fit for your beholding.° Advise the duke
   where you are going, to a most festinate° preparation; we are
   bound to the like. Our posts° shall be swift and intelligent betwixt
   us. Farewell dear sister; farewell my Lord of Gloucester.°   10

Enter OSWALD.

   How now? Where's the King?

OSWALD. My Lord of Gloucester hath conveyed him hence.
   Some five or six and thirty of his knights,
   Hot questrists° after him, met him at gate,
   Who with some other of the lords dependants,°   15
   Are gone with him toward Dover; where they boast
   To have well armed friends.

CORNWALL.   Get horses for your mistress.

GONERIL. Farewell, sweet lord, and sister.

CORNWALL. Edmund, farewell.   *Exeunt* GONERIL, EDMUND, *and* OSWALD.
                    Go seek the traitor, Gloucester,
   Pinion him like a thief, bring him before us.   *Exeunt* SERVANTS. 20
   Though well° we may not pass upon his life
   Without the form of justice; yet our power
   Shall do a court'sy to our wrath,° which men
   May blame, but not control.

Enter GLOUCESTER, *brought in by* SERVANTS.

                    Who's there? The traitor?

REGAN. Ingrateful fox, 'tis he.   25

CORNWALL. Bind fast his corky° arms.

GLOUCESTER. What means your Graces? Good my friends, consider
   You are my guests. Do me no foul play, friends.

CORNWALL. Bind him, I say.

REGAN.   Hard, hard.

---

7. Note that what Cornwall and Regan do to Gloucester later in this scene is
generally premeditated. 8. festinate: speedy, hasty. 9. posts: messengers. 10. Lord
of Gloucester: Cornwall addresses Edmund thus. 14. questrists: seekers. 15. lords
dependants: nobles of his party. 21. well: This word should be emphasized. There
is precious little form of justice in what follows. 22–23. yet . . . wrath: Yet because of our power we can give vent to our wrath. 26. corky: dry and withered.

[She helps bind him.]

O filthy traitor!

GLOUCESTER. Unmerciful lady as you are, I'm none.   30

CORNWALL. To this chair bind him. Villain, thou shalt find —

[REGAN plucks his beard.]

GLOUCESTER. By the kind gods, 'tis most ignobly done
   To pluck me by the beard.

REGAN. So white, and such a traitor!

GLOUCESTER.   Naughty lady,
   These hairs which thou dost ravish from my chin   35
   Will quicken,° and accuse thee. I am your host;
   With robbers' hands my hospitable favours
   You should not ruffle thus. What will you do?

CORNWALL. Come sir, what letters had you late from France?

REGAN. Be simple-answered, for we know the truth.   40

CORNWALL. And what confederacy have you with the traitors
   Late footed° in the kingdom?

REGAN. To whose hands you have sent the lunatic King?
   Speak.

GLOUCESTER. I have a letter guessingly set down,   45
   Which came from one that's of a neutral heart,
   And not from one opposed.

CORNWALL.   Cunning.

REGAN.   And false.

CORNWALL. Where hast thou sent the King?

GLOUCESTER.   To Dover.

REGAN. Wherefore to Dover? Wast thou not charged at peril —

CORNWALL. Wherefore to Dover? Let him answer that.   50

GLOUCESTER. I am tied to th' stake, and I must stand the course.°

REGAN. Wherefore to Dover?

GLOUCESTER. Because I would not see thy cruel nails
   Pluck out his poor old eyes; nor thy fierce sister
   In his anointed° flesh stick boarish fangs.   55

---

36. **quicken:** come to life. 42. **Late footed:** recently landed. 51. Gloucester's metaphor is drawn from bear-baiting, a popular spectator sport in Elizabethan England. A bear was chained to a stake, and in formal attacks or "courses," teams of fierce mastiffs were set to attack him. 55. **anointed:** Part of the consecration of royalty involves anointing with holy oil. The term here emphasizes the serious sacrilege of an attack on the King.

The sea, with such a storm as his bare head
In hell-black night endured, would have buoyed up°
And quenched the stelled fires;°
Yet, poor old heart, he holp° the heavens to rain.
If wolves had at thy gate howled that stern time,   60
Thou shouldst have said, good porter turn the key.°
All cruels else subscribe° — but I shall see
The winged vengeance° overtake such children.
CORNWALL. See't shalt thou never. Fellows hold the chair.
Upon these eyes of thine I'll set my foot.   65
GLOUCESTER. He that will think to live till he be old,
Give me some help! — O cruel! — O you gods!
REGAN. One side will mock another — th' other too.°
CORNWALL. If you see vengeance —
FIRST SERVANT.   Hold your hand, my lord.
I have served you ever since I was a child;   70
But better service have I never done you
Than now to bid you hold.
REGAN.   How now, you dog!
FIRST SERVANT. If you did wear a beard upon your chin,°
I'd shake it on this quarrel. What do you mean?
CORNWALL. My villain!°   75

[Draws.]

FIRST SERVANT. Nay then come on, and take the chance of anger.

[Draws. CORNWALL *is wounded.]*

REGAN. Give me thy sword. A peasant stand up thus?

[Takes a sword from another SERVANT *and stabs* FIRST SERVANT.*]*

FIRST SERVANT. O I am slain! My lord, you have one eye left
To see some mischief on him. O!

[Dies.]

57. buoyed up: swelled up. 58. stelled fires: light of the stars. 59. holp: helped.
61. turn the key: i.e., open the gate. 62. All . . . subscribe: All other cruel
creatures (but you) agree. 63. The winged vengeance: the vengeance of the gods.
68. Who is doing this deed? 73. did . . . chin: were a man. 75. villain: a serf.
Note that this is not a servant of Gloucester, but one of Cornwall's own who
thus revolts.

CORNWALL. Lest it see more, prevent it — out vile jelly! 80
    Where is thy lustre now?
GLOUCESTER. All dark and comfortless. Where's my son Edmund?
    Edmund, enkindle all the sparks of nature
    To quit° this horrid act.
REGAN.   Out treacherous villain!
    Thou call'st on him that hates thee. It was he 85
    That made the overture° of thy treasons to us;
    Who is too good to pity thee.
GLOUCESTER.   O my follies!
    Then Edgar was abused.
    Kind gods, forgive me that, and prosper him.
REGAN. Go thrust him out at gates, and let him smell 90
    His way to Dover.   *Exit* SERVANT *with* GLOUCESTER.
           How is't, my lord? How look you?
CORNWALL. I have received a hurt. Follow me, lady.
    Turn out that eyeless villain. Throw this slave
    Upon the dunghill. Regan, I bleed apace.
    Untimely comes this hurt. Give me your arm. 95
              Exit CORNWALL, *led by* REGAN.
SECOND SERVANT. I'll never care what wickedness I do,
    If this man come to good.
THIRD SERVANT.   If she live long,
    And in the end meet the old course of death,
    Women will all turn monsters.°
SECOND SERVANT. Let's follow the old earl, and get the bedlam° 100
    To lead him where he would; his roguish madness
    Allows itself to any thing.
THIRD SERVANT. Go thou. I'll fetch some flax and whites of eggs
    To apply to his bleeding face. Now heaven help him!
                  Exeunt severally.

    84. quit: requite, avenge. 86. overture: opening, revelation. 99. The second and third servants have commented on the philosophical implications of what they witnessed. What are these implications? 100. bedlam: Poor Tom.

ACT IV

SCENE I. *The heath.*

Enter EDGAR.

EDGAR. Yet better thus,° and known to be contemned,
    Than still contemned and flattered. To be worst,
    The lowest and most dejected thing of fortune,
    Stands still in esperance,° lives not in fear.
    The lamentable change is from the best;   5
    The worst returns to laughter. Welcome then,
    Thou unsubstantial air that I embrace.
    The wretch that thou hast blown unto the worst
    Owes nothing to thy blasts.

Enter GLOUCESTER, *led by* OLD MAN.

                           But who comes here?
    My father, poorly led? World, world, o world!   10
    But that thy strange mutations make us hate thee,
    Life would not yield to age.
OLD MAN.   O my good lord,
    I have been your tenant, and your father's tenant,
    These fourscore years.
GLOUCESTER. Away, get thee away; good friend, be gone.   15
    Thy comforts can do me no good at all;
    Thee they may hurt.
OLD MAN.   You cannot see your way.
GLOUCESTER. I have no way, and therefore want no eyes.
    I stumbled when I saw. Full oft 'tis seen,
    Our means secure us, and our mere defects   20
    Prove our commodities.° O dear son Edgar,
    The food of thy abused father's wrath;
    Might I but live to see thee in my touch,
    I'd say I had eyes again.
OLD MAN.   How now? Who's there?

    1. thus: in this beggarly condition. **4. esperance:** hope. **20–21. Our . . . com-
modities:** Our propriety makes us secure (hence, careless), and then our defects
(misfortunes) turn out to be benefits (blessings or advantages). What has Gloucester gained from his suffering? How is his case like that of the King?

EDGAR. [*Aside*] O gods! Who is't can say, I am at the worst?   25
    I am worse than e'er I was.

OLD MAN.   'Tis poor mad Tom.

EDGAR. [*Aside*] And worse I may be yet. The worst is not
    So long as we can say, this is the worst.°

OLD MAN. Fellow, where goest?

GLOUCESTER.   Is it a beggar-man?

OLD MAN. Madman and beggar too.   30

GLOUCESTER. He has some reason, else he could not beg.
    I' th' last night's storm, I such a fellow saw;
    Which made me think a man a worm. My son
    Came then into my mind, and yet my mind
    Was then scarce friends with him. I have heard more since.   35
    As flies to wanton boys, are we to the gods;
    They kill us for their sport.°

EDGAR. [*Aside*]   How should this be?
    Bad is the trade that must play fool to sorrow,
    Ang'ring itself and others.° — Bless thee master.

GLOUCESTER. Is that the naked fellow?

OLD MAN.   Ay, my lord.   40

GLOUCESTER. Then prithee get thee away; if for my sake
    Thou wilt o'ertake us hence a mile or twain
    I' th' way toward Dover, do it for ancient love,
    And bring some covering for this naked soul,
    Which I'll entreat to lead me.

OLD MAN.   Alack sir, he is mad.   45

GLOUCESTER. 'Tis the times' plague, when madmen lead the blind.
    Do as I bid thee, or rather do thy pleasure.
    Above the rest, be gone.

OLD MAN. I'll bring him the best 'parel that I have,
    Come on't what will.   *Exit.* 50

GLOUCESTER. Sirrah, naked fellow.

EDGAR. Poor Tom's a-cold. [*Aside*] I cannot daub it° further.

GLOUCESTER. Come hither fellow.

---

28. What is the commonplace idea that Edgar entertained at the beginning of this scene and that he now sees refuted? 37. Compare these two lines to "but I shall see/The winged vengeance overtake such children" (page 671, lines 62–63). 38–39. Bad . . . others: i.e., this business of pretending to be mad and fooling a man in such great distress is dreadful. 52. daub it: plaster it over, i.e., pretend.

EDGAR. [*Aside*] And yet I must. Bless thy sweet eyes, they bleed.

GLOUCESTER. Know'st thou the way to Dover? 55

EDGAR. Both stile, and gate; horse-way, and footpath. Poor Tom hath
been scared out of his good wits. Bless thee good man's son from
the foul fiend. Five fiends have been in poor Tom at once; of lust,
as Obidicut; Hobbididence, prince of dumbness; Mahu, of stealing;
Modo, of murder; and Flibbertigibbet, of mopping and mow- 60
ing,° who since possesses chambermaids and waiting-women. So,
bless thee master.

GLOUCESTER. Here, take this purse, thou whom the heavens' plagues
Have humbled to all strokes. That I am wretched
Makes thee the happier. Heavens, deal so still.° 65
Let the superfluous and lust-dieted man,
That slaves your ordinance,° that will not see
Because he does not feel, feel your power quickly;
So distribution should undo excess,
And each man have enough. Dost thou know Dover? 70

EDGAR. Ay, master.

GLOUCESTER. There is a cliff, whose high and bending head
Looks fearfully in the confined deep.
Bring me but to the very brim of it,
And I'll repair the misery thou dost bear 75
With something rich about me. From that place
I shall no leading need.

EDGAR.   Give me thy arm;
Poor Tom shall lead thee.   *Exeunt.*

60–61. mopping and mowing: making faces and grimaces. 65. Heavens . . .
still: i.e., you gods, deal with others as you have with me. 67. slaves your ordinance: regards your commands as contemptuously as he regards his slaves.

SCENE II. *Before Albany's palace.*

Enter GONERIL *and* EDMUND.

GONERIL. Welcome my lord, I marvel our mild husband
Not met us on the way.

Enter OSWALD.

Now, where's your master?

OSWALD. Madam, within; but never man so changed.
I told him of the army that was landed;
He smiled at it. I told him you were coming;   5
His answer was, the worse. Of Gloucester's treachery,
And of the loyal service of his son,
When I informed him, then he called me sot,
And told me I had turned the wrong side out.
What most he should dislike, seems pleasant to him;   10
What like, offensive.
GONERIL. [*To* EDMUND]   Then shall you go no further.
It is the cowish° terror of his spirit,
That dares not undertake. He'll not feel wrongs,
Which tie° him to an answer. Our wishes on the way
May prove effects.° Back, Edmund, to my brother,°   15
Hasten his musters,° and conduct his powers,°
I must change names at home,° and give the distaff°
Into my husband's hands. This trusty servant°
Shall pass between us; ere long you are like to hear,
If you dare venture in your own behalf,   20
A mistress's° command. Wear this; spare speech,

[Gives a favour.]

Decline your head. This kiss, if it durst speak,
Would stretch thy spirits up into the air.
Conceive,° and fare thee well.
EDMUND. Yours, in the ranks of death.
GONERIL.   My most dear Gloucester.   25

Exit EDMUND.

O, the difference of man and man! To thee
A woman's services are due; my fool°
Usurps my body.
OSWALD.   Madam, here comes my lord.   *Exit.*

Enter ALBANY.

12. **cowish:** cowardly. 14. **tie:** force. 15. **May prove effects:** may come true.
What do you suppose these wishes are? **brother:** brother-in-law, Cornwall.
16. **musters:** assemblings of troops; **powers:** forces. 17. **I . . . home:** I must become the soldier of the house; **distaff:** staff used in spinning; a symbol of house-
wifery. 18. **This trusty servant:** Oswald. Note how accurate was Kent's character-
ization of him. 21. **mistress's:** here, not only female superior but lady-love. 24. **Conceive:** Use your imagination. 27. **my fool:** Albany, Goneril's husband.

GONERIL. I have been worth the whistle.°

ALBANY.   O Goneril,
    You are not worth the dust which the rude wind   30
    Blows in your face. I fear your disposition.
    That nature which contemns its origin°
    Cannot be bordered certain in itself;°
    She that herself will sliver and disbranch
    From her material sap,° perforce must wither,   35
    And come to deadly use.

GONERIL. No more; the text is foolish.°

ALBANY. Wisdom and goodness to the vile seem vile,
    Filths savour but themselves. What have you done?
    Tigers, not daughters, what have you performed?   40
    A father, and a gracious aged man,
    Whose reverence even the head-lugged bear° would lick,
    Most barbarous, most degenerate, have you madded.
    Could my good brother° suffer you to do it?
    A man, a Prince, by him so benefited.   45
    If that the heavens do not their visible spirits
    Send quickly down to tame these vile offences,
    It will come.
    Humanity must perforce prey on itself,
    Like monsters of the deep.

GONERIL.   Milk-livered man,   50
    That bear'st a cheek for blows, a head for wrongs,
    Who hast not in thy brows an eye discerning
    Thine honour from thy suffering, that not know'st
    Fools do those villains pity who are punished
    Ere they have done their mischief.° Where's thy drum?   55
    France spreads his banners in our noiseless land
    With plumed helm. Thy state begins to threat,
    Whilst thou a moral fool sits still and cries,

29. I . . . whistle: There is a proverb: " 'Tis a poor dog that's not worth the whistle." Goneril means that there was once a time when I was attractive enough (to you) to be greeted promptly. 32. origin: Goneril's origin is her father. 33. Cannot . . . itself: cannot be kept within bounds. 35. material sap: sap that is part of herself. 37. the . . . foolish: i.e., your sermon is a silly one. What is the text that Goneril finds foolish? 42. head-lugged bear: bear with its head torn by hounds. 44. my good brother: Cornwall. 55. To call those who have moral scruples cowards and fools is a common practice of those who do not have such scruples.

Alack why does he so?°
ALBANY.   See thyself, devil.
Proper deformity° shows not in the fiend   60
So horrid as in woman.
GONERIL.   O vain° fool.
ALBANY.   Thou changed and self-covered° thing, for shame
Be-monster not thy feature.° Were't my fitness
To let these hands obey my blood,
They are apt enough to dislocate and tear   65
Thy flesh and bones. Howe'er thou art a fiend,
A woman's shape doth shield thee.
GONERIL.   Marry, your manhood — mew!

Enter MESSENGER.

ALBANY.   What news?
MESSENGER.   O my good lord, the Duke of Cornwall's dead,   70
Slain by his servant, going to put out
The other eye of Gloucester.
ALBANY.   Gloucester's eyes!
MESSENGER.   A servant that he bred, thrilled with remorse,
Opposed against the act; bending his sword
To his great master, who thereat enraged,   75
Flew on him, and amongst them felled him dead,
But not without that harmful stroke which since
Hath plucked him after.
ALBANY.   This shows you are above,
You justicers, that these our nether crimes°
So speedily can venge. But, o poor Gloucester,   80
Lost he his other eye?
MESSENGER.   Both, both, my lord.
This letter, madam, craves a speedy answer;
'Tis from your sister.
GONERIL.   [*Aside*]   One way I like this well.
But being widow, and my Gloucester° with her,

59. Goneril, of course, is trying to distract Albany from his horror at her behavior. 60. **Proper deformity**: deformity natural for a fiend. 61. **vain**: futile.
62. **self-covered**: hiding your true self (i.e., devil) under the guise of a woman.
63. **Be-monster . . . feature**: Do not change your appearance into that of a fiend.
(Goneril is scowling her hatred.) 79. **nether crimes**: offenses committed on earth
below. 84. **my Gloucester**: Edmund.

May all the building in my fancy pluck   85
Upon my hateful life.° Another way,
The news is not so tart.° —I'll read, and answer.
ALBANY.   Where was his son, when they did take his eyes?
MESSENGER.   Come with my lady hither.
ALBANY.   He is not here.
MESSENGER.   No, my good lord, I met him back again.°   90
ALBANY.   Knows he the wickedness?
MESSENGER.   Ay, my good lord; 'twas he informed against him,
And quit the house on purpose, that their punishment
Might have the freer course.
ALBANY.   Gloucester, I live
To thank thee for the love thou show'dst the King,   95
And to revenge thine eyes. Come hither friend,
Tell me what more thou know'st.   *Exeunt.*

85–86. May . . . life: Since Regan has Edmund, she may pull down my castle
in the air, making life hateful to me. 87. tart: unpleasant. 90. back again: on his
way back.

SCENE III. *The French camp, near Dover.*

Enter KENT *and* GENTLEMAN.

KENT.   Why the King of France is so suddenly gone back, know you no
reason?
GENTLEMAN.   Something he left imperfect in the state, which since his
coming forth is thought of; which imports to the kingdom so much
fear and danger, that his personal return was most required   5
and necessary.
KENT.   Who hath he left behind him general?
GENTLEMAN.   The Marshal of France, Monsieur La Far.
KENT.   Did your letters pierce the Queen to any demonstration of grief?
GENTLEMAN.   Ay, sir, she took them, read them in my presence,   10
And now and then an ample tear trilled down
Her delicate cheek; it seemed she was a queen
Over her passion,° who most rebel-like,
Sought to be king o'er her.
KENT.   O then it moved her.
GENTLEMAN.   Not to a rage; patience and sorrow strove   15

13. passion: emotion.

Who should express her goodliest. You have seen
Sunshine and rain at once; her smiles and tears
Were like a better way; those happy smilets
That played on her ripe lip seemed not to know
What guests were in her eyes, which parted thence   20
As pearls from diamonds dropped. In brief,
Sorrow would be a rarity most beloved,
If all could so become it.

KENT.   Made she no verbal question?

GENTLEMAN. Faith once or twice she heaved the name of father
Pantingly forth, as if it pressed her heart;   25
Cried, sisters, sisters, shame of ladies, sisters!
Kent! Father! Sisters! What, i' th' storm? I' th' night?
Let pity not be believed. There she shook
The holy water from her heavenly eyes,
And clamour-moistened;° then away she started   30
To deal with grief alone.°

KENT.   It is the stars,
The stars above us govern our conditions,°
Else one self° mate and make could not beget
Such different issues.° You spoke not with her since?

GENTLEMAN. No.   35

KENT. Was this before the King returned?

GENTLEMAN.   No, since.

KENT. Well sir, the poor distressed Lear's i' th' town,°
Who sometime in his better tune° remembers
What we are come about, and by no means
Will yield to see his daughter.

GENTLEMAN.   Why, good sir?   40

KENT. A sovereign shame so elbows him;° his own unkindness
That stripped her from his benediction,° turned her
To foreign casualties,° gave her dear rights

30. clamour-moistened: dampened her sorrowful cries with tears. 31. In what
ways does the Gentleman's account of Cordelia specify her goodness? 32. conditions: characters. Kent, for all his goodness of character, sees life less realistically
than the base Edmund. 33. self: same. 34. issues: children. 37. i' th' town: in the
vicinity. 38. in . . . tune: in his more lucid moments. 41. elbows him: plucks
him by the elbow, reminding him of the past. 42. Recall Lear's words (Act I,
Scene i, lines 259-60): "Therefore be gone/Without our grace, our love, our
benison." 43. casualties: chances, accidents of chance.

To his dog-hearted daughters, these things sting
His mind so venomously that burning shame   45
Detains him from Cordelia.
GENTLEMAN.   Alack, poor gentleman!
KENT. Of Albany's and Cornwall's powers you heard not?
GENTLEMAN. 'Tis so, they are afoot.
KENT. Well sir, I'll bring you to our master Lear,
And leave you to attend him. Some dear cause°   50
Will in concealment wrap me up awhile;
When I am known aright you shall not grieve,
Lending me this acquaintance. I pray you go
Along with me.   *Exeunt.*

50. dear cause: important reason.

SCENE IV. *The same.*

Enter, with drum and colours, CORDELIA, DOCTOR, *and* SOLDIERS.

CORDELIA. Alack, 'tis he; why he was met even now
As mad as the vexed sea, singing aloud,
Crowned with rank fumiter and furrow-weeds,
With hardocks, hemlock, nettles, cuckoo-flowers,
Darnel,° and all the idle weeds that grow   5
In our sustaining corn.° A century° send forth;
Search every acre in the high-grown field,
And bring him to our eye.   *Exit* OFFICER.
                        What can man's wisdom
In the restoring his bereaved sense?
He that helps him take all my outward worth.   10
DOCTOR. There is means, madam.
Our foster-nurse of nature is repose,
The which he lacks; that to provoke in him
Are many simples° operative, whose power
Will close the eye of anguish.

3–5. fumiter . . . Darnel: These are all English wildflowers and weeds. 6. Note
that Lear is distinguished by the conventional trappings of madness: garlands of
weeds and wildflowers. How much relief from the pangs of reality is his madness
apparently allowing him at this point? century: hundred soldiers. 14. simples:
medicinal herbs.

CORDELIA.   All blessed secrets,
All you unpublished virtues of the earth,
Spring with my tears, be aidant and remediate°
In the good man's distress. Seek, seek for him,
Lest his ungoverned rage dissolve the life
That wants the means° to lead it.

Enter MESSENGER.

MESSENGER.   News, madam;   20
The British powers are marching hitherward.
CORDELIA. 'Tis known before. Our preparation stands
In expectation of them. O dear father,
It is thy business that I go about;
Therefore great France   25
My mourning and importuned tears hath pitied.
No blown ambition doth our arms incite,
But love, dear love, and our aged father's right.
Soon may I hear, and see him.   *Exeunt.*

17. **aidant and remediate:** helpful and remedial. 20. **means:** in this case, reason.

SCENE V. *Gloucester's castle.*

Enter REGAN *and* OSWALD.

REGAN. But are my brother's powers set forth?
OSWALD.   Ay, madam.
REGAN. Himself in person there?
OSWALD.   Madam, with much ado.
Your sister is the better soldier.
REGAN. Lord Edmund spake not with your lord at home?
OSWALD. No, madam.   5
REGAN. What might import my sister's letter to him?
OSWALD. I know not, lady.
REGAN. Faith, he is posted hence on serious matter.
It was great ignorance, Gloucester's eyes being out,
To let him live. Where he arrives, he moves   10
All hearts against us. Edmund, I think, is gone,
In pity of his misery, to dispatch

His nighted life; moreover to descry
The strength o' th' enemy.

OSWALD. I must needs after him, madam, with my letter.   15

REGAN. Our troops set forth to-morrow, stay with us.
The ways are dangerous.

OSWALD.   I may not, madam.
My lady charged my duty in this business.

REGAN. Why should she write to Edmund? Might not you
Transport her purposes by word? Belike,   20
Something, I know not what — I'll love thee much,
Let me unseal the letter.

OSWALD.   Madam, I had rather —

REGAN. I know your lady does not love her husband,
I am sure of that; and at her late being here
She gave strange œillades° and most speaking looks   25
To noble Edmund. I know you are of her bosom.°

OSWALD. I, madam?

REGAN. I speak in understanding; y'are, I know't,
Therefore I do advise you take this note.°
My lord is dead; Edmund and I have talked,   30
And more convenient is he for my hand
Than for your lady's. You may gather more.
If you do find him, pray you give him this;°
And when your mistress hears thus much from you,
I pray, desire her call her wisdom to her.°   35
So fare you well.
If you do chance to hear of that blind traitor,
Preferment° falls on him that cuts him off.

OSWALD. Would I could meet him madam, I should show
What party I do follow.

REGAN.   Fare thee well.   *Exeunt.*   40

---

25. œillades: (French) languishing glances. 26. of her bosom: in her confidence. 29. take this note: Take note of this. 33. this: probably this reminder of Regan's widowed, available status — a love-token, like that Goneril gave Edmund — almost certainly not a letter, since no such letter will be found on Oswald's person when later searched by Edgar. 35. Neither duchess is exactly subtle in expressing her appetite, and each knows the other's position. 38. Preferment: promotion.

Enter GLOUCESTER, *and* EDGAR *dressed like a peasant.*

GLOUCESTER. When shall I come to th' top of that same hill?

EDGAR. You do climb up it now. Look how we labour.

GLOUCESTER. Methinks the ground is even.

EDGAR.   Horrible steep.
    Hark, do you hear the sea?

GLOUCESTER.   No, truly.

EDGAR. Why then your other senses grow imperfect   5
    By your eyes' anguish.

GLOUCESTER.   So may it be indeed.
    Methinks thy voice is altered, and thou speak'st
    In better phrase and matter than thou didst.

EDGAR. Y'are much deceived. In nothing am I changed
    But in my garments.

GLOUCESTER.   Methinks y'are better spoken.   10

EDGAR. Come on sir, here's the place; stand still. How fearful
    And dizzy 'tis, to cast one's eyes so low.
    The crows and choughs° that wing the midway air
    Show scarce so gross as beetles. Half way down
    Hangs one that gathers samphire° — dreadful trade.   15
    Methinks he seems no bigger than his head.
    The fishermen, that walk upon the beach,
    Appear like mice; and yond tall anchoring bark,
    Diminished to her cock;° her cock, a buoy
    Almost too small for sight. The murmuring surge,   20
    That on th' unnumbered idle pebbles chafes,
    Cannot be heard so high. I'll look no more,
    Lest my brain turn, and the deficient sight
    Topple down headlong.°

GLOUCESTER.   Set me where you stand.

EDGAR. Give me your hand. You are now within a foot   25
    Of th' extreme verge. For all beneath the moon
    Would I not leap upright.

GLOUCESTER.   Let go my hand.

13. choughs: jackdaws. 15. samphire: a savory herb that grows on the chalk cliffs of Dover. 19. cock: cockboat, the small ship's boat, usually towed behind. 23–24. the . . . headlong: my sight failing, cause me to topple down headlong.

Here friend's another purse; in it a jewel
Well worth a poor man's taking. Fairies and gods°
Prosper it with thee. Go thou further off,   30
Bid me farewell, and let me hear thee going.
EDGAR.   Now fare ye well, good sir.
GLOUCESTER.   With all my heart.
EDGAR.   [*Aside*] Why I do trifle thus with his despair,
Is done to cure it.
GLOUCESTER.   [*Kneels*] O you mighty gods!
This world I do renounce, and in your sights   35
Shake patiently my great affliction off.
If I could bear it longer, and not fall
To quarrel with your great opposeless wills,
My snuff and loathed part of nature° should
Burn itself out. If Edgar live, o bless him.   40
Now fellow, fare thee well.
EDGAR.   Gone sir — farewell.

[GLOUCESTER *falls forward.*]

[*Aside*] And yet I know not how conceit° may rob
The treasury of life, when life itself
Yields to the theft.° Had he been where he thought,
By this had thought been past. Alive or dead? —   45
Ho, you sir! Friend! Hear you, sir! speak!
[*Aside*] Thus might he pass indeed; yet he revives. —
What are you, sir?
GLOUCESTER.   Away, and let me die.
EDGAR.   Hadst thou been aught but gossamer,° feathers, air,
So many fathom down precipitating,   50
Thou'dst shivered like an egg; but thou dost breathe,
Hast heavy substance, bleed'st not, speak'st, art sound.
Ten masts at each° make not the altitude
Which thou hast perpendicularly fell.
Thy life's miracle. Speak yet again.   55

29. As this story is pre-Christian, it is natural for the characters to call on the
gods of the "elder world." 39. My . . . nature: the burnt-out and hateful remnant of my life. The noun *snuff* means the smoking end of a dying candle. 42.
conceit: imagination. 44. Yields . . . theft: i.e., is willing to die. 49. gossamer:
a floating thread of spiderweb. 53. Ten . . . each: ten masts, each on top of
the other.

GLOUCESTER. But have I fall'n or no?

EDGAR. From the dread summit of this chalky bourn.°
      Look up a-height, the shrill-gorged lark° so far
      Cannot be seen or heard; do but look up.°

GLOUCESTER. Alack, I have no eyes.   60
      Is wretchedness deprived that benefit
      To end itself by death? 'Twas yet some comfort,
      When misery could beguile° the tyrant's rage,
      And frustrate his proud will.

EDGAR.   Give me your arm.
      Up. So. How is't? Feel you your legs? You stand.   65

GLOUCESTER. Too well, too well.

EDGAR.   This is above all strangeness.
      Upon the crown o' th' cliff, what thing was that
      Which parted from you?

GLOUCESTER.   A poor unfortunate beggar.

EDGAR. As I stood here below, methought his eyes
      Were two full moons; he had a thousand noses,   70
      Horns whelked° and waved like the enridged sea.
      It was some fiend. Therefore, thou happy father,
      Think that the clearest gods, who make them honours
      Of men's impossibilities,° have preserved thee.

GLOUCESTER. I do remember now; henceforth I'll bear   75
      Affliction, till it do cry out itself,
      Enough, enough, and die.° That thing you speak of,
      I took it for a man; often 'twould say,
      The fiend, the fiend; he led me to that place.

EDGAR. Bear free and patient thoughts.

Enter LEAR, *his hat bedecked with weeds and flowers.*

               But who comes here?°   80

---

57. **bourn:** limit or boundary (of England). 58. **shrill-gorged lark:** shrill-throated lark. The lark flies to a great height to sing. 59. Edgar knows that his father is blind. Why does he ask him to look up? 63. **beguile:** cheat (by suicide). 71. **whelked:** twisted spirally. 73–74. **who . . . impossibilities:** who cause themselves to be honored by performing miracles impossible to men. 77. What lesson has Edgar's trick taught Gloucester? What significance do you find in the fact that the lesson was taught *by a trick?* 80. Perhaps it is part of Edgar's disguise not to recognize Lear. Perhaps Lear is so festooned with foliage that his identity is not immediately distinguishable.

The safer sense will ne'er accommodate
His master thus.°

LEAR. No, they cannot touch me for coining;° I am the King himself.

EDGAR. [*Aside*] O thou side-piercing sight!

LEAR. Nature's above art in that respect.° There's your press-money.° 85
That fellow handles his bow like a crow-keeper;° draw me a
clothier's yard.° Look, look, a mouse! Peace, peace, this piece of
toasted cheese will do't. There's my gauntlet,° I'll prove it on a
giant. Bring up the brown bills.° O well flown, bird;° i' th' clout°
i' th' clout. Hewgh!° Give the word.° 90

EDGAR. Sweet marjoram.°

LEAR. Pass.

GLOUCESTER. I know that voice.

LEAR. Ha! Goneril with a white beard! They flattered me like a dog,
and told me I had white hairs in my beard, ere the black ones 95
were there. To say ay, and no, to everything that I said! Ay, and
no too, was no good divinity.° When the rain came to wet me
once, and the wind to make me chatter; when the thunder would
not peace at my bidding; there I found 'em, there I smelt 'em out.
Go to, they are not men o' their words; they told me I was 100
every thing. 'Tis a lie, I am not ague-proof.°

GLOUCESTER. The trick° of that voice I do well remember;
Is't not the King?

LEAR.   Ay, every inch a King:
When I do stare, see how the subject quakes.

81–82. The . . . thus: i.e., a man in his right senses would never adorn himself thus. 83. coining: making counterfeit money. 85. Nature's . . . respect: i.e.,
the King's authority comes not from his skill or craft but from his nature; press-
money: small sum given to soldiers when they were pressed (drafted) into service.
Lear imagines that he is making a royal inspection of a muster of troops.
86. crow-keeper: boy hired to keep crows from the corn. 87. clothier's yard: The
standard English arrow was a cloth yard in length. Lear wants his imaginary
archer to draw his arrow back a full yard's length. 88. gauntlet: warrior's glove,
thrown down to signify a challenge. 89. brown bills: infantry armed with brown
bills. A bill was a long staff terminating in a hook-shaped blade, which was
varnished to prevent rusting; well flown, bird: Lear likens the flight of an arrow
that he thinks he is watching to the flight of a bird; clout: white cloth target
(archery). 90. Hewgh!: sound of the whizz of the arrow; word: password. 91. Sweet
marjoram: a savory herb. Lear's floral decorations have doubtless suggested this
password to Edgar. 97. no good divinity: not good moral theology. Do these reflections on Lear's long life as King tend to extenuate the pride and blindness he
has been guilty of? 101. ague-proof: fever-proof. 102. trick: distinctive sound.

I pardon that man's life. What was thy cause?° 105
Adultery?
Thou shalt not die. Die for adultery? No,
The wren goes to't, and the small gilded fly
Does lecher in my sight.
Let copulation thrive; for Gloucester's bastard son 110
Was kinder to his father than my daughters
Got 'tween the lawful sheets.
To't luxury° pell-mell, for I lack soldiers.
Behold yond simpering dame,°
Whose face between her forks presages snow, 115
That minces virtue,° and does shake the head
To hear of pleasure's name —
The fitchew° nor the soiled° horse goes to't
With a more riotous appetite.
Down from the waist they are centaurs, 120
Though women all above;
But to the girdle do the gods inherit,
Beneath is all the fiends';
There's hell, there's darkness, there is the sulphurous pit,
Burning, scalding, stench, consumption. Fie, fie, fie; pah, pah! 125
Give me an ounce of civet;° good apothecary sweeten my imagina-
tion. There's money for thee.

GLOUCESTER. O let me kiss that hand.

LEAR. Let me wipe it first, it smells of mortality.

GLOUCESTER. O ruined piece of nature; this great world 130
Shall so wear out to naught. Dost thou know me?

LEAR. I remember thine eyes well enough. Dost thou squiny° at me? No,
do thy worst blind Cupid, I'll not love. Read thou this challenge;
mark but the penning of it.

GLOUCESTER. Were all thy letters suns, I could not see one. 135

EDGAR. [*Aside*] I would not take this from report — it is,
And my heart breaks at it.

105. **cause:** case (at law). Now Lear imagines that he is seated as royal judge
in court. 113. **luxury:** lust. 114. **dame:** Goneril? She has been most sanctimonious
about the rowdy behavior of Lear's hundred knights. We know, although Lear
does not, with what open lust she is now chasing Edmund. 116. **minces virtue:**
walks (minces) with an air of virtue. 118. **fitchew:** polecat; **soiled:** full-fed on
spring grass. 126. **civet:** perfume. A secretion of the civet cat is the basic in-
gredient of many perfumes. 132. **squiny:** look sideways.

LEAR. Read.

GLOUCESTER. What, with the case of eyes?

LEAR. O ho, are you there with me?° No eyes in your head, nor no 140
money in your purse? Your eyes are in a heavy case, your purse in a
light, yet you see how this world goes.

GLOUCESTER. I see it feelingly.

LEAR. What, art mad? A man may see how this world goes, with no
eyes. Look with thine ears. See how yond justice rails upon 145
yond simple thief. Hark in thine ear. Change places; and handy-
dandy,° which is the justice, which is the thief? Thou hast seen a
farmer's dog bark at a beggar?

GLOUCESTER. Ay sir.

LEAR. An the creature run from the cur, there thou mightst behold 150
the great image of authority — a dog's obeyed in office.
Thou, rascal beadle,° hold thy bloody hand;
Why dost thou lash that whore? Strip thine own back;
Thou hotly lusts to use her in that kind
For which thou whipst her. The usurer° hangs the cozener.° 155
Through tattered clothes small vices do appear;
Robes and furred gowns hide all. Plate sin with gold,
And the strong lance of justice hurtless breaks.
Arm it in rags, a pigmy's straw does pierce it.
None does offend, none — I say, none;° I'll able° 'em. 160
Take that of me, my friend, who have the power
To seal the accuser's lips. Get thee glass eyes,
And like a scurvy politician, seem
To see the things thou dost not. — Now, now, now, now.
Pull off my boots; harder, harder; so. 165

EDGAR. [Aside] O matter and impertinency° mixed;
Reason in madness.

LEAR. If thou wilt weep my fortunes, take my eyes.
I know thee well enough, thy name is Gloucester.

140. are . . . me?: Do you agree with me? 146–47. handy-dandy: an allusion
to the nursery game which goes, "Handy-dandy, sugar candy, which hand will
you have?" 152. beadle: parish officer. 155. usurer: lender charging excessive interest. Here the term means one who is respected, such as a rich banker; cozener:
small-time cheat. 160. None . . . none: What is the state of reality, as Lear
now sees it, that makes these words relevant? Note that Lear has not yet seen
Cordelia; able: give royal authorization to. 166. matter and impertinency: i.e.,
sense and nonsense.

Thou must be patient; we came crying hither.   170
Thou know'st, the first time that we smell the air,
We wawl, and cry. I will preach to thee. Mark.

[Takes off his hat.]

GLOUCESTER.   Alack, alack the day!
LEAR.   When we are born, we cry that we are come
    To this great stage of fools. — This' a good block;°   175
    It were a delicate stratagem to shoe
    A troop of horse with felt. I'll put't in proof,°
    And when I have stol'n upon these son-in-laws,
    Then, kill, kill, kill, kill, kill, kill!

Enter GENTLEMAN, *with* ATTENDANTS.

GENTLEMAN.   O here he is; lay hand upon him. Sir,   180
    Your most dear daughter —
LEAR.   No rescue? What, a prisoner? I am even
    The natural fool of fortune.° Use me well,
    You shall have ransom. Let me have surgeons,
    I am cut to th' brains.
GENTLEMAN.   You shall have any thing.   185
LEAR.   No seconds? All myself?
    Why, this would make a man a man of salt,°
    To use his eyes for garden water-pots,
    Ay and laying autumn's dust.
GENTLEMAN.   Good sir —   190
LEAR.   I will die bravely, like a smug bridegroom. What!
    I will be jovial. Come, come, I am a King,
    My masters; know you that.
GENTLEMAN.   You are a royal one, and we obey you.
LEAR.   Then there's life in't. Come, an you get it, you shall get it by   195
    running. Sa, sa, sa, sa.   *Exit running.** ATTENDANTS *follow*.
GENTLEMAN.   A sight most pitiful in the meanest wretch,
    Past speaking of in a King. Thou hast a daughter,

175. This' . . . block: This is a well-blocked hat. Lear has, after his lucid
moment, wandered crazily off the subject he has undertaken so earnestly.
177. I'll . . . proof: I'll try it out. 183. The . . . fortune: born to be fooled by
fortune. 187. man of salt: because tears are salt (see following line). * Compare
the indignity of this exit with the dignity of Lear's first entrance in the play.

Who redeems nature from the general curse
Which twain have brought her to.   200
EDGAR.   Hail, gentle sir.
GENTLEMAN.   Sir, speed you. What's your will?
EDGAR.   Do you hear aught, sir, of a battle toward?°
GENTLEMAN.   Most sure, and vulgar.° Every one hears that,
     Which can distinguish sound.
EDGAR.   But by your favour;
     How near's the other army?   205
GENTLEMAN.   Near, and on speedy foot; the main descry
     Stands on the hourly thought.°
EDGAR.   I thank you, sir; that's all.
GENTLEMAN.   Though that the Queen on special cause is here,
     Her army is moved on.
EDGAR.   I thank you, sir.   *Exit* GENTLEMAN.
GLOUCESTER.   You ever gentle gods, take my breath from me;   210
     Let not my worser spirit tempt me again
     To die before you please.
EDGAR.   Well pray you, father.
GLOUCESTER.   Now good sir, what are you?
EDGAR.   A most poor man, made tame to fortune's blows;
     Who, by the art of known and feeling sorrows,   215
     Am pregnant to° good pity. Give me your hand,
     I'll lead you to some biding.
GLOUCESTER.   Hearty thanks.
     The bounty and the benison of heaven
     To boot, and boot.°

                        Enter OSWALD.

OSWALD.   A proclaimed prize;° most happy!
     That eyeless head of thine was first framed flesh   220
     To raise my fortunes. Thou old unhappy traitor,
     Briefly thyself remember° — the sword is out
     That must destroy thee.

---

   202. **toward:** about to occur. 203. **vulgar:** common (knowledge). 206–07. **the
   . . . thought:** The main body may be expected to come into sight at any hour
   now. 216. **pregnant to:** able to conceive. 219. **To . . . boot:** besides, again and
   again; **A proclaimed prize:** Gloucester, on whose head a price has been put.
   222. **Briefly thyself remember:** i.e., prepare for death by confessing your sins.

GLOUCESTER.   Now let thy friendly hand
    Put strength enough to't.

[EDGAR *interposes*.]

OSWALD.   Wherefore, bold peasant,
    Dar'st thou support a published traitor? Hence,   225
    Lest that th' infection of his fortune take
    Like hold on thee. Let go his arm.
EDGAR. Chill° not let go, zir, without vurther 'casion.
OSWALD. Let go slave, or thou diest.
EDGAR. Good gentleman, go your gait, and let poor volk pass. An   230
    chud ha' bin zwaggered out of my life, 'twould not ha' bin zo long
    as 'tis, by a vortnight.° Nay, come not near th' old man; keep out
    che vor ye, or ise° try whether your costard° or my ballow° be the
    harder; chill be plain with you.
OSWALD. Out, dunghill!   235

[*Thrusts at him*.]

EDGAR. Chill pick your teeth, zir; come, no matter vor your foins.°

[*They fight*. OSWALD *falls*.]

OSWALD. Slave thou hast slain me. Villain,° take my purse;
    If ever thou wilt thrive, bury my body,
    And give the letters which thou find'st about me
    To Edmund earl of Gloucester; seek him out   240
    Upon the English party. O untimely death!
    Death!

[*Dies*.]

EDGAR. I know thee well. A serviceable villain,
    As duteous to the vices of thy mistress
    As badness would desire.
GLOUCESTER.   What, is he dead?   245
EDGAR. Sit you down father; rest you.

228. **Chill:** I'll. Why does Edgar take on this new disguise of rustic dialect?
230–32. **An . . . vortnight:** i.e., if swaggering could kill me, I would have died
a fortnight before now. 233. **che . . . ise:** I warn you, or else; **costard:** slang for
head (literally, apple); **ballow:** staff, cudgel. 236. **foins:** thrusts. 237. **Slave . . .
Villain:** By addressing his conqueror thus, the social-climbing Oswald, even while
dying, expresses his snobbishness.

Let's see these pockets; the letters that he speaks of
May be my friends. He's dead; I am only sorry
He had no other deathsman.° Let us see.
Leave, gentle wax; and manners, blame us not.   250
To know our enemies' minds, we'd rip their hearts;
Their papers is more lawful.

[*Reads*]

Let our reciprocal vows be remembered. You have many oppor-
tunities to cut him off:° if your will want not, time and place will
be fruitfully offered. There is nothing done, if he return the 255
conqueror: then am I the prisoner and his bed my gaol; from the
loathed warmth whereof deliver me, and supply the place for your
labour.

Your — wife, so I would say —
                            Affectionate servant,   260
                                    Goneril.

O indistinguished° space of woman's will!
A plot upon her virtuous husband's life,
And the exchange my brother. Here in the sands,
Thee I'll rake up,° the post unsanctified°   265
Of murderous lechers; and in the mature time,°
With this ungracious paper strike the sight
Of the death-practised duke.° For him 'tis well,
That of thy death and business I can tell.
GLOUCESTER. The King is mad: how stiff° is my vile sense,°   270
That I stand up, and have ingenious feeling°
Of my huge sorrows! Better I were distract;°
So should my thoughts be severed from my griefs,
And woes, by wrong imaginations, lose
The knowledge of themselves.

[*Drum afar off*]

248–49. I . . . deathsman: Edgar is a gentleman and regrets soiling his hands
on Oswald. 254. cut him off: kill him (Albany). 262. indistinguished: extending
beyond the range of sight; limitless. 265. rake up: cover by raking (sand or dust);
post unsanctified: unholy messenger (Oswald). 266. in . . . time: i.e., when the
time is ripe. 268. the death-practised duke: the duke whose death is plotted.
270. stiff: unbending, strong; sense: sanity. 271. ingenious feeling: clear consciousness. 272. distract: mad.

Far off methinks I hear the beaten drum.
Come father, I'll bestow you with a friend.   *Exeunt.*

SCENE VII. *Before a tent in the French camp.*

Enter CORDELIA *and* KENT. DOCTOR *and* GENTLEMAN *follow.*

CORDELIA. O thou good Kent, how shall I live and work,
To match thy goodness? My life will be too short,
And every measure fail me.
KENT. To be acknowledged madam, is o'erpaid.
All my reports go with the modest truth;   5
Nor more, nor clipped, but so.
CORDELIA.   Be better suited;°
These weeds° are memories of those worser hours.
I prithee put them off.
KENT.   Pardon, dear madam,
Yet to be known shortens my made intent.°
My boon I make it, that you know me not   10
Till time and I think meet.
CORDELIA. Then be't so my good lord. [*To* DOCTOR] How does the King?
DOCTOR. Madam, sleeps still.
CORDELIA. O you kind gods,
Cure this great breach in his abused nature.   15
Th' untuned and jarring senses, o wind up°
Of this child-changed father.
DOCTOR.   So please your Majesty
That we may wake the King? He hath slept long.
CORDELIA. Be governed by your knowledge, and proceed
I' th' sway of your own will. Is he arrayed?   20
GENTLEMAN. Ay madam, in the heaviness of sleep
We put fresh garments on him.
DOCTOR. Be by, good madam, when we do awake him.
I doubt not of his temperance.
CORDELIA.   Very well.

6. **suited:** dressed. (Kent is still in disguise.) 7. **weeds:** clothes (i.e., livery worn by Kent as Lear's servant). 9. **shortens . . . intent:** frustrates my formed plan. 16. **wind up:** i.e., as the loose string of a musical instrument is tightened.

DOCTOR. Please you draw near.—Louder the music° there.   25

[*Music.* DOCTOR *draws curtains.* LEAR *discovered on a couch.*]

CORDELIA. O my dear father! Restoration hang
 Thy medicine on my lips, and let this kiss
 Repair those violent harms that my two sisters
 Have in thy reverence made.
KENT.   Kind and dear Princess.
CORDELIA. Had you not been their father, these white flakes   30
 Did challenge pity of them. Was this a face
 To be opposed against the warring winds,
 To stand against the deep dread-bolted thunder,
 In the most terrible and nimble stroke
 Of quick, cross lightning, to watch — poor perdu° —   35
 With this thin helm? Mine enemy's dog,
 Though he had bit me, should have stood that night
 Against my fire; and wast thou fain, poor father,
 To hovel thee with swine and rogues forlorn,
 In short and musty straw? Alack, alack,   40
 'Tis wonder that thy life and wits at once
 Had not concluded all. He wakes, speak to him.
DOCTOR. Madam do you, 'tis fittest.
CORDELIA. How does my royal lord? How fares your Majesty?
LEAR. You do me wrong to take me out o' th' grave.   45
 Thou art a soul in bliss, but I am bound
 Upon a wheel of fire, that mine own tears
 Do scald like molten lead.
CORDELIA.   Sir, do you know me?
LEAR. You are a spirit, I know; where did you die?
CORDELIA. Still, still, far wide.°   50
DOCTOR. He's scarce awake, let him alone awhile.
LEAR. Where have I been? Where am I? Fair daylight?
 I am mightily abused; I should e'en die with pity,
 To see another thus. I know not what to say.
 I will not swear these are my hands; let's see —   55
 I feel this pin prick. Would I were assured

 25. music: thought to be important in the cure of mental derangement.
35. perdu: (French) lone sentry in an exposed and dangerous position (literally,
lost one). **50. wide:** wide from reason.

Of my condition.

CORDELIA.   O look upon me sir,
And hold your hands in benediction o'er me —
No, sir, you must not kneel.

LEAR.   Pray do not mock me.
I am a very foolish fond old man,   60
Fourscore and upward, not an hour more nor less;
And to deal plainly,
I fear I am not in my perfect mind.
Methinks I should know you, and know this man,
Yet I am doubtful. For I am mainly ignorant   65
What place this is; and all the skill I have
Remembers not these garments; nor I know not
Where I did lodge last night. Do not laugh at me,
For as I am a man, I think this lady
To be my child Cordelia.

CORDELIA.   And so I am — I am.   70

LEAR.   Be your tears wet? Yes, faith. I pray weep not.
If you have poison for me, I will drink it.
I know you do not love me, for your sisters
Have, as I do remember, done me wrong.
You have some cause, they have not.

CORDELIA.   No cause, no cause.   75

LEAR.   Am I in France?

KENT.   In your own kingdom, sir.

LEAR.   Do not abuse me.

DOCTOR.   Be comforted good madam, the great rage,
You see, is killed in him: and yet it is danger
To make him even o'er° the time he has lost.   80
Desire him to go in, trouble him no more
Till further settling.

CORDELIA.   Will't please your Highness walk?

LEAR.   You must bear with me.
Pray you now forget, and forgive; I am old and foolish.

                  Exeunt all but KENT *and* GENTLEMAN.

GENTLEMAN.   Holds it true sir, that the Duke of Cornwall was so slain?

KENT.   Most certain sir.   86

80. even o'er: go over.

GENTLEMAN. Who is conductor of his people?

KENT. As 'tis said, the bastard son of Gloucester.

GENTLEMAN. They say Edgar his banished son is with the Earl of Kent
in Germany.   90

KENT. Report is changeable.° 'Tis time to look about, the powers of the
kingdom approach apace.

GENTLEMAN. The arbitrement° is like to be bloody. Fare you well sir.
Exit.

KENT. My point and period° will be thoroughly wrought,
Or well, or ill, as this day's battle's fought.   *Exit.* 95

91. Report is changeable: i.e., rumors are not reliable. 93. arbitrement: decision. 94. point and period: conclusion, ending.

ACT V

SCENE I. *The British camp, near Dover.*

Enter, with drum and colours, EDMUND, REGAN, GENTLEMEN,
and SOLDIERS.

EDMUND. Know° of the duke if his last purpose hold,
Or whether since he is advised by aught
To change the course. He's full of alteration,
And self-reproving. Bring his constant pleasure.° *Exit* GENTLEMAN.

REGAN. Our sister's man is certainly miscarried.   5

EDMUND. 'Tis to be doubted,° madam.

REGAN.   Now sweet lord,
You know the goodness I intend upon you:
Tell me — but truly — but then speak the truth —
Do you not love my sister?

EDMUND.   In honoured love.

REGAN. But have you never found my brother's way,   10
To the forfended° place?

EDMUND.   That thought abuses you.°

1. Know: learn. 4. his constant pleasure: his finally determined plan. Edmund
appears swollen with confidence here. 6. doubted: feared. 11. forfended: forbidden; abuses you: wrongs you, i.e., it is beneath you to have such a thought.

REGAN. I am doubtful that you have been conjunct
    And bosomed with her, as far as we call hers.°
EDMUND. No, by mine honour, madam.
REGAN. I never shall endure her. Dear my lord,   15
    Be not familiar with her.
EDMUND.   Fear me not,
    She and the duke her husband —

Enter, with drum and colours, ALBANY, GONERIL, *and* SOLDIERS.

GONERIL. [*Aside*] I had rather lose the battle, than that sister
    Should loosen him and me.°
ALBANY. Our very loving sister, well be-met.   20
    Sir, this I heard, the King is come to his daughter,
    With others whom the rigour of our state°
    Forced to cry out.° Where I could not be honest,
    I never yet was valiant. For this business,
    It touches us, as France invades our land,   25
    Not bolds the King, with others whom I fear
    Most just and heavy causes make oppose.°
EDMUND. Sir you speak nobly.°
REGAN.   Why is this reasoned?°
GONERIL. Combine together 'gainst the enemy;
    For these domestic and particular broils°   30
    Are not the question here.
ALBANY.   Let's then determine
    With th' ancient of war° on our proceeding.
EDMUND. I shall attend you presently at your tent.
REGAN. Sister, you'll go with us?
GONERIL. No.   35
REGAN. 'Tis most convenient, pray you go with us.°
GONERIL. [*Aside*] O ho, I know the riddle. — I will go.

12–13. I . . . hers: I am afraid that you have been united in intimacy with
her in every way. 19. Note that upon entering, Goneril has found Regan and
Edmund in private conversation. 22. rigour . . . state: harshness of our government. 23. cry out: protest. 24–27. For . . . oppose: For this business concerns us,
not because France is encouraging (emboldening) Lear and others who have
just and weighty reasons to oppose us, but because France is invading our
country. 28. Sir . . . nobly: Is this overt insolence? reasoned: argued. 30. broils:
quarrels. 32. th' ancient of war: those old (experienced) in war. 36. Why is Regan
so anxious that Goneril come along?

As they are going out, enter EDGAR *disguised.*

EDGAR. If e'er your Grace had speech with man so poor,
  Hear me one word.

ALBANY.   I'll overtake you.° — Speak.

       Exeunt all but ALBANY *and* EDGAR.

EDGAR. Before you fight the battle, ope this letter.   40
  If you have victory, let the trumpet sound
  For him that brought it. Wretched though I seem,
  I can produce a champion that will prove
  What is avouched° there. If you miscarry,
  Your business of the world hath so an end,   45
  And machination° ceases. Fortune love you.

ALBANY. Stay till I have read the letter

EDGAR.   I was forbid it.
  When time shall serve, let but the herald cry,
  And I'll appear again.

ALBANY. Why fare thee well, I will o'erlook thy paper. *Exit* EDGAR. 50

Enter EDMUND.

EDMUND. The enemy's in view, draw up your powers.
  Here is the guess of their true strength and forces,
  By diligent discovery, but your haste
  Is now urged on you.

ALBANY.   We will greet the time.°   *Exit.*

EDMUND. To both these sisters have I sworn my love;   55
  Each jealous of the other, as the stung
  Are of the adder. Which of them shall I take?
  Both? One? Or neither? Neither can be enjoyed,
  If both remain alive. To take the widow
  Exasperates, makes mad her sister Goneril,   60
  And hardly shall I carry out my side,°
  Her husband being alive. Now then, we'll use
  His countenance° for the battle, which being done,
  Let her who would be rid of him devise
  His speedy taking off. As for the mercy   65

39. **I'll overtake you:** Albany says these words to those about to leave.
44. **avouched:** declared. 46. **machination:** plotting. 54. **greet the time:** i.e., be
ready when the time comes (to meet the enemy). 61. **carry . . . side:** get my
share. 63. **countenance:** authority, support.

Which he intends to Lear and to Cordelia,
The battle done, and they within our power,
Shall never see his pardon; for my state
Stands on me to defend, not to debate.°   *Exit.*

69. Why is he determined that Lear and Cordelia shall not see Albany's pardon?

SCENE II. *A field between the two camps. Alarum within.*

Enter, with drum and colours, LEAR, CORDELIA, *and* SOLDIERS
over the stage and exeunt. Enter EDGAR *and* GLOUCESTER.

EDGAR. Here, father, take the shadow of this tree
For your good host; pray that the right may thrive.
If ever I return to you again,
I'll bring you comfort.
GLOUCESTER.   Grace go with you sir.   *Exit* EDGAR.

Alarum and retreat within. Enter EDGAR.

EDGAR. Away old man, give me thy hand, away!   5
King Lear hath lost, he and his daughter ta'en.
Give me thy hand. Come on.
GLOUCESTER. No further sir, a man may rot even here.
EDGAR. What, in ill thoughts again? Men must endure
Their going hence, even as their coming hither;   10
Ripeness° is all. Come on.
GLOUCESTER.   And that's true too.   *Exeunt.*

11. Ripeness: perfect readiness.

SCENE III. *The British camp, near Dover.*

Enter, in conquest,* with drum and colours, EDMUND; LEAR
and CORDELIA *as prisoners;* GENTLEMAN, CAPTAIN, *and* SOLDIERS.

EDMUND. Some officers take them away; good guard,
Until their greater pleasures° first be known
That are to censure them.

* Note the complexity of the international situation here. Shakespeare could
hardly have the French win a battle on English soil and expect an Elizabethan
audience to accept it. 2. their greater pleasures: the will of my superiors.

CORDELIA. We are not the first
Who with best meaning have incurred the worst.
For thee, oppressed King, am I cast down, 5
Myself could else out-frown false fortune's frown.
Shall we not see these daughters, and these sisters?

LEAR. No, no, no, no; come let's away to prison:
We two alone will sing like birds i' th' cage.
When thou dost ask me blessing, I'll kneel down, 10
And ask of thee forgiveness. So we'll live,
And pray, and sing, and tell old tales, and laugh
At gilded butterflies;° and hear poor rogues
Talk of court news, and we'll talk with them too,
Who loses, and who wins, who's in, who's out; 15
And take upon's the mystery of things,
As if we were God's spies. And we'll wear out
In a walled prison, packs and sects° of great ones,
That ebb and flow by th' moon.

EDMUND. Take them away.

LEAR. Upon such sacrifices, my Cordelia, 20
The gods themselves throw incense. Have I caught thee?°
He that parts us shall bring a brand from heaven,
And fire us hence° like foxes. Wipe thine eyes;
The good-years shall devour them, flesh and fell,°
Ere they shall make us weep. We'll see 'em starved first. 25
Come. *Exeunt* LEAR *and* CORDELIA, *guarded*.

EDMUND. Come hither, captain, hark.
Take thou this note, go follow them to prison.
One step I have advanced thee, if thou dost
As this instructs thee, thou dost make thy way 30
To noble fortunes. Know thou this, that men
Are as the time is;° to be tender-minded
Does not become a sword. Thy great employment
Will not bear question; either say thou'lt do't,
Or thrive by other means.

CAPTAIN. I'll do't my lord. 35

EDMUND. About it, and write happy when th'hast done.

13. gilded butterflies: i.e., court folk. **18. packs and sects:** parties and factions.
21. Has Lear, in any sense, been *seeking* Cordelia? **23. fire us hence:** drive us out
by fire. **24. fell:** skin. **31–32. men . . . is:** i.e., in brutal times men must be brutes.

Mark, I say instantly, and carry it so
As I have set it down.

CAPTAIN. I cannot draw a cart, nor eat dried oats.
If it be man's work, I'll do't.   *Exit.* 40

    Flourish. Enter ALBANY, GONERIL, REGAN, GENTLEMEN, *and*
                      SOLDIERS.

ALBANY. Sir, you have showed to-day your valiant strain,°
   And fortune led you well; you have the captives
   Who were the opposites° of this day's strife.
   We do require them of you, so to use them
   As we shall find their merits and our safety   45
   May equally determine.

EDMUND.   Sir, I thought it fit
   To send the old and miserable King
   To some retention and appointed guard;
   Whose age has charms in it, whose title more,
   To pluck the common bosom on his side,   50
   And turn our impressed lances° in our eyes
   Which do command them. With him I sent the Queen;
   My reason all the same; and they are ready
   To-morrow, or at further space, t' appear
   Where you shall hold your session.° At this time   55
   We sweat and bleed; the friend hath lost his friend,
   And the best quarrels in the heat are cursed
   By those that feel their sharpness.
   The question of Cordelia and her father
   Requires a fitter place.

ALBANY.   Sir, by your patience,   60
   I hold you but a subject° of this war,
   Not as a brother.

REGAN.   That's as we list° to grace him.
   Methinks our pleasure might have been demanded,

---

    41. valiant strain: noble lineage. Albany refers to Gloucester's half in Edmund's
parentage. **43. opposites:** opponents. **51. impressed lances:** conscripted soldiers.
Edmund reasons logically that the old King may gain sympathy and support from
such soldiers. **55. session:** trial. Why does Edmund tell Albany a lie that a short
time is sure to uncover? **61. but a subject:** i.e., not one who gives orders. **62. That's
. . . list:** That's a matter of how we are inclined. Note Regan's use of "we." She
is assuming the royal prerogative.

Ere you had spoke so far. He led our powers,
Bore the commission of my place and person   65
The which immediacy may well stand up
And call itself your brother.

GONERIL.   Not so hot.
In his own grace he doth exalt himself,
More than in your addition.°

REGAN.   In my rights
By me invested, he compeers° the best.   70

GONERIL. That were the most, if he should husband you.

REGAN. Jesters do oft prove prophets.

GONERIL.   Holla, holla!
That eye that told you so looked but a-squint.°

REGAN. Lady, I am not well, else I should answer
From a full-flowing stomach.° General,   75
Take thou my soldiers, prisoners, patrimony;
Dispose of them, of me, the walls are thine:
Witness the world, that I create thee here
My lord and master.

GONERIL.   Mean you to enjoy him?°

ALBANY. The let-alone° lies not in your good will.   80

EDMUND. Nor in thine, lord.

ALBANY.   Half-blooded fellow, yes.

REGAN. [*To* EDMUND] Let the drum strike, and prove my title thine.

ALBANY. Stay yet, hear reason. Edmund, I arrest thee
On capital treason; and in thy attaint,°
This gilded serpent. [*Points to* GONERIL.] For your claim, fair sister,
I bar it in the interest of my wife;   86
'Tis she is sub-contracted° to this lord,
And I her husband contradict your banns.
If you will marry, make your loves to me —
My lady is bespoke.

GONERIL.   An interlude.°   90

---

69. **your addition:** the title you have given him. 70. **compeers:** equals. 73. **looked but a-squint:** did not see aright. 75. **From . . . stomach:** in full wrath. 79. The significance of this remark and of Regan's complaint that she is not well appears shortly. 80. **let-alone:** power to prevent. 84. **in thy attaint:** i.e., as an accomplice in your crime. 87. **sub-contracted:** betrothed. 90. **An interlude:** i.e., this is mere play-acting. Perhaps Goneril refers contemptuously to Albany's irony in particular.

ALBANY. Thou art armed, Gloucester. Let the trumpet sound.
If none appear to prove upon thy person
Thy heinous, manifest, and many treasons,
There is my pledge. [*Throws down a glove.*] I'll make it on thy heart,
Ere I taste bread, thou art in nothing less   95
Than I have here proclaimed thee.

REGAN.   Sick, o sick!

GONERIL.   [*Aside*] If not, I'll ne'er trust medicine.°

EDMUND.   There's my exchange. [*Throws down a glove.*] What in the
world he is
That names me traitor, villain-like he lies.
Call by thy trumpet; he that dares approach,   100
On him, on you, who not, I will maintain
My truth and honour firmly.

ALBANY.   A herald, ho!

EDMUND.   A herald, ho, a herald!

ALBANY.   Trust to thy single° virtue, for thy soldiers,
All levied in my name, have in my name   105
Took their discharge.

REGAN.   My sickness grows upon me.

ALBANY.   She is not well, convey her to my tent.   *Exit* REGAN.

Enter HERALD.

Come hither, herald. Let the trumpet sound,
And read out this.

[*A trumpet sounds.*]

HERALD.   [*Reads*] *If any man of quality or degree, within the lists of* 110
the army, will maintain upon Edmund, supposed Earl of Gloucester,
that he is a manifold traitor, let him appear by the third sound of
the trumpet: he is bold in his defence.

[*First trumpet*]

HERALD.   Again! [*Second trumpet*]
Again! [*Third trumpet*]   115

[*Trumpet answers within.*]

97. medicine: in this case, poison. 104. single: solitary, unaided.

Enter EDGAR, *armed,* a trumpet before him.*

ALBANY. Ask him his purposes, why he appears
　　Upon this call o' th' trumpet.

HERALD.　　　　　　　　　　　What are you?
　　Your name, your quality, and why you answer
　　This present summons?

EDGAR.　　　　　　　　　Know, my name is lost
　　By treason's tooth bare-gnawn and canker-bit,°　　　　　120
　　Yet am I noble as the adversary
　　I come to cope.

ALBANY.　　　　　　　Which is that adversary?

EDGAR. What's he that speaks for Edmund, Earl of Gloucester?

EDMUND. Himself — what sayest thou to him?

EDGAR.　　　　　　　　　　　Draw thy sword,
　　That if my speech offend a noble heart,　　　　　　125
　　Thy arm may do thee justice; here is mine.
　　Behold, it is the privilege of mine honours,
　　My oath, and my profession.° I protest —
　　Maugre° thy strength, youth, place, and eminence,
　　Despite thy victor sword and fire-new fortune,　　　130
　　Thy valour and thy heart — thou art a traitor;
　　False to thy gods, thy brother, and thy father,
　　Conspirant 'gainst this high illustrious prince.
　　And from th' extremest upward of thy head,
　　To the descent and dust below thy foot,　　　　　135
　　A most toad-spotted traitor. Say thou no,
　　This sword, this arm, and my best spirits are bent
　　To prove upon thy heart, whereto I speak,
　　Thou liest.

EDMUND.　　　　　In wisdom I should ask thy name,
　　But since thy outside looks so fair and warlike,　　140
　　And that thy tongue some say of breeding° breathes,
　　What safe and nicely° I might well delay,
　　By rule of knighthood, I disdain and spurn.

* **armed:** Edgar is wearing full armor, his face being concealed by his closed helmet. **120. canker-bit:** eaten away as though by a cankerworm (a kind of caterpillar). **128. profession:** profession as a knight. **129. Maugre:** in spite of. **141. say of breeding:** suggestion of your having been well-bred. **142. nicely:** according to fine distinctions, i.e., strictly speaking.

Back do I toss these treasons to thy head;
With the hell-hated lie o'erwhelm thy heart;   145
Which — for they yet glance by, and scarcely bruise —
This sword of mine shall give them instant way,
Where they shall rest for ever. Trumpets speak!

[Alarums. They fight. EDMUND *falls.]*

ALBANY. Save him, save him.
GONERIL.   This is practice,° Gloucester.
By the law of war, thou wast not bound to answer   150
An unknown opposite; thou art not vanquished,
But cozened,° and beguiled.
ALBANY.   Shut your mouth, dame,
Or with this paper shall I stop it. Hold sir,
Thou worse than any name, read thine own evil.
No tearing, lady, I perceive you know it.   155

[Gives the letter to EDMUND.]

GONERIL. Say if I do, the laws are mine, not thine.
Who can arraign me for't?°
ALBANY.   Most monstrous! O!
Know'st thou this paper?
GONERIL.   Ask me not what I know.   *Exit.*
ALBANY. Go after her, she's desperate, govern her.   *Exit* GENTLEMAN.
EDMUND. What you have charged me with, that have I done,   160
And more, much more; the time will bring it out.
'Tis past, and so am I. But what art thou
That hast this fortune on me? If thou'rt noble,
I do forgive thee.
EDGAR.   Let's exchange charity.
I am no less in blood than thou art, Edmund;   165
If more, the more th'hast wronged me.
My name is Edgar, and thy father's son.
The gods are just, and of our pleasant vices
Make instruments to plague us.°

149. practice: trickery, treachery. 152. cozened: cheated. 157. Goneril's attitude
toward life is consistent at least. 169. Compare these two lines with Gloucester's
(Act IV, Scene i, lines 36–37): "As flies to wanton boys are we to the gods,/They
kill us for their sport."

The dark and vicious place where thee he got°   170
Cost him his eyes.
EDMUND.   Th'hast spoken right, 'tis true.
The wheel is come full circle;° I am here.
ALBANY.   Methought thy° very gait did prophesy
A royal nobleness. I must embrace thee.
Let sorrow split my heart, if ever I   175
Did hate thee, or thy father.
EDGAR.   Worthy prince,
I know't.
ALBANY.   Where have you hid yourself?
How have you known the miseries of your father?
EDGAR.   By nursing them, my lord. List a brief tale;
And when 'tis told, o that my heart would burst.   180
The bloody proclamation to escape,
That followed me so near — o our lives' sweetness,
That we the pain of death would hourly die
Rather than die at once — taught me to shift
Into a madman's rags, t' assume a semblance   185
That very dogs disdained, and in this habit
Met I my father with his bleeding rings,
Their precious stones new lost; became his guide,
Led him, begged for him, saved him from despair.
Never — o fault — revealed myself unto him,   190
Until some half hour past, when I was armed;
Not sure, though hoping of this good success,
I asked his blessing, and from first to last
Told him my pilgrimage. But his flawed heart,
Alack too weak the conflict to support,   195
'Twixt two extremes of passion, joy and grief,
Burst smilingly.
EDMUND.   This speech of yours hath moved me,
And shall perchance do good, but speak you on;
You look as you had something more to say.
ALBANY.   If there be more, more woeful, hold it in,   200
For I am almost ready to dissolve,
Hearing of this.

170. got: begot. 172. The . . . circle: i.e., I end as I began — an outcast
of fortune. 173. thy: Edgar's.

EDGAR. This would have seemed a period°
To such as love not sorrow; but another,
To amplify too much, would make much more,
And top extremity.° 205
Whilst I was big in clamour,° came there in a man,
Who having seen me in my worst estate,°
Shunned my abhorred society, but then finding
Who 'twas that so endured, with his strong arms
He fastened on my neck, and bellowed out 210
As he'd burst heaven, threw him on my father,
Told the most piteous tale of Lear and him
That ever ear received: which in recounting
His grief grew puissant,° and the strings of life
Began to crack. Twice then the trumpets sounded, 215
And there I left him tranced.°

ALBANY. But who was this?

EDGAR. Kent sir, the banished Kent, who in disguise
Followed his enemy King° and did him service
Improper for a slave.

Enter GENTLEMAN with a bloody knife.

GENTLEMAN. Help, help; o help!

EDGAR. What kind of help?

ALBANY. Speak man. 220

EDGAR. What means this bloody knife?

GENTLEMAN. 'Tis hot, it smokes,
It came even from the heart of — o she's dead!

ALBANY. Who dead? speak man.

GENTLEMAN. Your lady sir, your lady; and her sister
By her is poisoned; she confesses it. 225

EDMUND. I was contracted to them both. All three
Now marry in an instant.°

Enter KENT.

---

202. **period:** proper ending point. 205. **top extremity:** exceed the extreme limit of what could be endured. 206. **big in clamour:** loud in my grieving. 207. **worst estate:** poorest condition (as Poor Tom). 214. **puissant:** powerful, overmastering. 216. **tranced:** in a faint. 218. **his enemy King:** the King who had declared him an enemy. 227. Remember Edmund's response to Goneril's love-making in Act IV, Scene ii, line 25: "Yours, in the ranks of death."

EDGAR. Here comes Kent.

ALBANY. Produce the bodies, be they alive or dead. *Exit* GENTLEMAN.
This judgement of the heavens, that makes us tremble,
Touches us not with pity.° — O is this he? 230
The time will not allow the compliment
Which very manners urges.

KENT. I am come
To bid my King and master aye good night.
Is he not here?

ALBANY. Great thing of us forgot.
Speak Edmund, where's the King? And where's Cordelia? 235

[*The bodies of* GONERIL *and* REGAN *are brought in.*]

Seest thou this object, Kent?

KENT. Alack, why thus?

EDMUND. Yet Edmund was beloved.
The one the other poisoned for my sake,
And after slew herself.°

ALBANY. Even so. Cover their faces. 240

EDMUND. I pant for life. Some good I mean to do,
Despite of mine own nature. Quickly send —
Be brief in it — to the castle, for my writ
Is on the life of Lear, and on Cordelia.
Nay, send in time.°

ALBANY. Run, run, o run. 245

EDGAR. To who my lord? Who has the office? Send
Thy token of reprieve.°

EDMUND. Well thought on, take my sword;
Give it the captain.

ALBANY. Haste thee for thy life. *Exit* EDGAR.

EDMUND. He hath commission from thy wife and me 250
To hang Cordelia in the prison, and
To lay the blame upon her own despair,
That she fordid herself.

230. How does Albany regard the fate of his wife and his sister-in-law? What view of life does his assumption about their fate support? 239. Is Edmund turning soft? Or is he struggling still for power in the feeble form of attention? 245. If Edmund has been moved earlier, why has he put off the rescue of Lear and Cordelia until it is too late? If he knows it is too late, why does he do it at all? 247. token of reprieve: sign that Lear and Cordelia are reprieved.

ALBANY. The gods defend her. Bear him hence awhile.

[EDMUND *is borne off*.]

Enter LEAR, *with* CORDELIA *dead in his arms;* EDGAR, GENTLE-
MAN, *and others.*

LEAR. Howl, howl, howl! O you are men of stones.   255
          Had I your tongues and eyes, I'd use them so
          That heaven's vault should crack. She's gone forever.
          I know when one is dead, and when one lives;
          She's dead as earth. Lend me a looking-glass;
          If that her breath will mist or stain the stone,°   260
          Why then she lives.
KENT.   Is this the promised end?°
EDGAR. Or image of that horror?
ALBANY.   Fall, and cease.°
LEAR. This feather stirs, she lives; if it be so,
          It is a chance which does redeem all sorrows
          That ever I have felt.
KENT.   O my good master.   265
LEAR. Prithee away.
EDGAR.   'Tis noble Kent your friend.
LEAR. A plague upon you, murderers, traitors all.
          I might have saved her; now she's gone for ever.
          Cordelia, Cordelia, stay a little. Ha!
          What is't thou sayst? — Her voice was ever soft,   270
          Gentle, and low, an excellent thing in woman.
          I killed the slave that was a-hanging thee.
GENTLEMAN. 'Tis true my lords, he did.
LEAR.   Did I not fellow?
          I have seen the day, with my good biting falchion°
          I would have made them skip. I am old now,   275
          And these same crosses° spoil me. Who are you?
          Mine eyes are not o' th' best, I'll tell you straight.

260. stone: glass. 261. One of the central themes and questions of the play: Is
this the justice we can expect from nature, life, the gods? 262. Fall, and cease:
i.e., let Doomsday come and the world end. Contrast Albany's sentiment here
with his grim, righteous satisfaction with the judgment of the heavens on Goneril
and Regan. 274. falchion: short curved sword. As we have cause to know already,
Lear's physical power is remarkable for a man of his age. 276. crosses: sorrows,
troubles.

KENT. If fortune brag of two she loved and hated,
    One of them we behold.

LEAR. This is a dull sight. Are you not Kent?

KENT.   The same.   280
    Your servant Kent. Where is your servant Caius?°

LEAR. He's a good fellow, I can tell you that.
    He'll strike, and quickly too — he's dead and rotten.

KENT. No my good lord, I am the very man —

LEAR. I'll see that straight.   285

KENT. That from your first of difference° and decay,
    Have followed your sad steps.

LEAR.   You are welcome hither.°

KENT. Nor no man else. All's cheerless, dark, and deadly.
    Your eldest daughters have fordone themselves,
    And desperately are dead.

LEAR.   Ay, so I think.   290

ALBANY. He knows not what he says, and vain is it
    That we present us to him.

EDGAR.   Very bootless.

Enter GENTLEMAN.

GENTLEMAN. Edmund is dead, my lord.

ALBANY.   That's but a trifle here.°
    You lords and noble friends, know our intent.
    What comfort to this great decay may come   295
    Shall be applied. For us, we will resign,
    During the life of this old Majesty,
    To him our absolute power — [*To* EDGAR *and* KENT] you to your
        rights,
    With boot,° and such addition as your honours
    Have more than merited. All friends shall taste   300
    The wages of their virtue, and all foes
    The cup of their deservings.° O see, see!°

LEAR. And my poor fool° is hanged. No, no, no life?

281. **Caius:** evidently the name assumed by Kent in his disguise. 286. **difference:** changed state. 287. Note the heartbreaking irony of this courtesy in this context. 293. How suitable an epitaph do you think this is for Edmund? 299. **boot:** advantage. 302. What is Albany trying, despite fate, to establish as best he can? **O see, see!:** These words are caused by a sudden change in Lear. 303. **my poor fool:** Cordelia. (*Fool* is often used as a term of affection.)

Why should a dog, a horse, a rat, have life,
And thou no breath at all? Thou'lt come no more, 305
Never, never, never, never, never.
Pray you undo this button. Thank you sir.
Do you see this? Look on her, look her lips —
Look there, look there —

[*Dies.*]

EDGAR.   He faints. My lord, my lord!
KENT.   Break heart, I prithee break.
EDGAR.   Look up my lord.   310
KENT.   Vex not his ghost. O let him pass. He hates him,
That would upon the rack° of this tough world
Stretch him out longer.
EDGAR.   He is gone indeed.
KENT.   The wonder is, he hath endured so long;
He but usurped° his life.   315
ALBANY.   Bear them from hence. Our present business
Is general woe. [*To* KENT *and* EDGAR] Friends of my soul, you twain
Rule in this realm, and the gored state sustain.
KENT.   I have a journey sir, shortly to go.
My master calls me, I must not say no.°   320
EDGAR.   The weight of this sad time we must obey,
Speak what we feel, not what we ought to say.
The oldest hath borne most; we that are young
Shall never see so much, nor live so long.

Exeunt, with a dead march.

312. rack: a machine for torture in Elizabethan times. The victim was
stretched gradually until his bones were drawn from their sockets. 315. usurped:
maintained it without proper title. 320. This is a statement of Kent's feelings, not
necessarily a literal prophecy of his death. We recall, however, that earlier Edgar
believed Kent near death from a broken heart.

For Study and Writing

1. Following is a list of some of the
situations that make up the plot of
King Lear. How are these situations
made specific, given "local habitations

and names" in the play? Have you encountered any of these situations in
your previous reading?

   a. A father trusts the wrong chil-
     dren.

   b. A man must choose between

what he knows is right and what would be more comfortable.

c. Loyalty is rejected, but is loyalty still.

d. A clever man is caught in his own cleverness.

e. A man who is innocent and righteous in his own eyes cannot understand why he is visited with appalling catastrophe.

f. A person sees the truth but is kept by force from acting on it.

g. The patient, wronged, and good lose.

h. The patient, wronged, and good win.

i. Fools speak the truth; the wise speak foolishly.

j. Authority loses force and ceases to exist.

2. *King Lear* is a work that examines and tests a great many kinds of personal relationships. What are the bonds that bind Kent to Lear, Oswald to Goneril, Edgar to Gloucester, Goneril to Albany, Gloucester to Edmund, Regan to Edmund?

3. What is the basis for enmity in each of the following cases: Edmund against Edgar, Goneril against Lear, Kent against Oswald, Lear against Cordelia, Albany against Goneril, the first servant against Cornwall and Regan, Goneril against Regan?

4. Misunderstanding is one of the oldest, most familiar, most troublesome facts of human relationship. As such, it is a frequent tool of the literary artist. In Act I of *King Lear,* the old King's failure to see things as they are is central to the action. He is by no means the only character in the play who misunderstands. What other characters in the play are found with the same failing? What results from their cases?

5. In what details do Gloucester's character and life parallel Lear's? In what ways is it made clear that Gloucester is the lesser of the two?

6. "Tigers, not daughters," says Albany of Goneril and Regan (Act IV, Scene ii, line 40). What other examples of animal imagery are applied directly to these sisters in the course of the play? Going beyond the simple fact of their basic savagery, how can you argue for the applicability of such imagery?

AFTERWORD

One of the most striking qualities of *King Lear* is toughness. It is tough in the sense that its strength and urgency have not been weakened by the passage of time. This kind of toughness in a story owes a good deal to the universality of its situations and is the common quality of all great writing of the past that we read and study today. *King Lear* is tough also in the sense that it is difficult for its audiences, intellectually and emotionally. But the most significant toughness of *King Lear* is the result of its author's refusal to step back or turn away from the grimmest, most terrible facts of human existence. Here is a story without sentimentality and, in some respects, almost without mercy. Here is a view of life in which second chances are not to be expected or, should they appear, to be trusted. In the world of this play, the consequences of folly, weakness, and vice are not canceled or softened; the rain falls steadily on the just and the unjust. The cold of heart are free to follow their devices, and consequently the good, the gentle, the loving must die. Powerful and savage beasts in human forms are set loose; and they predictably rend and tear, not sparing their parents, their mates, or each other.

This kind of toughness is not as common a quality as one might imagine. For many people such a picture of life is so depressing, so terrible that they turn away from it, averting their eyes. As a matter of fact, Nahum Tate, a late-seventeenth-century playwright and producer, actually changed *King Lear* for popular production on the stage. He gave it a happy ending, with Cordelia alive and Lear restored. Tate evidently felt that by altering the play so that it expressed how life ought to be, he was improving it greatly and doing Shakespeare a favor. Many people in the ensuing years agreed with him, and the happy-ending version was standard on the stage for a century and a half.

This circumstance underlines questions on which the very nature of art may be said to depend. Is it the artist's task to try to improve the world by showing how things ought to be? Most adults (probably including Nahum Tate) would agree that mankind behaves in a self-centered, uncouth way and that justice is — outwardly, at least — a frighteningly uncertain factor in real life. Can the artist, by presenting good and evil, so tangled in real life, as being sharply distinct and as being specifically and appropriately rewarded or punished, show the way to a better state of human affairs?

The Shakespeare who wrote *King Lear* evidently did not think so; but this does not mean that either he or his play, in all its toughness, is morally neutral. The world of *King Lear* is a world where savagery is very near the surface of manners, where the gods are far away, where cruelty and injustice appear to be part of the very nature of things. It is certainly a mirror-image of the world Shakespeare sensed around himself, and it is probably a fairly accurate representation of the world a sensitive and intelligent person observes in real life today. But it is not a morally worthless world; it is not a world without significant goodness.

Toughness of the *King Lear* sort is a kind of honesty; but it is not, as many writers in our century have imagined, to be achieved simply by asserting that nothing is worth anything and that degradation, violence, and faithlessness are the sole components of life. Artists who have taken this superficial turn toward toughness are in a way closer to Nahum Tate than to Shakespeare. In asserting that utter moral cynicism is the proof of artistic truth, they have often tended to set up an unconscious creative ideal: the representation of life as it ought *not* to be. And they have often become so absorbed in this ideal that they have come to enjoy a perverse satisfaction in emphasizing each new evidence of universal degradation. In doing this, such writers are in fact being not tough but sentimental in a particularly unpleasant way.

What Shakespeare recognized — this is something such writers do not grasp — is that a tough view of life is not compatible with the view that life is utterly worthless. If goodness and order do not exist, if they are not to be treasured, the rejection of such values in favor of evil and degradation is without meaning. Without such positive affirmations of good as are presented by Cordelia, Kent, the Fool, Edgar, and the servant who stands up against the bestial Cornwall in the eye-gouging scene, *King Lear* would not be tough in the sense suggested, but merely sensationally slimy and blood-curdling.

One of the facts of real life to which Shakespeare holds up the mirror in *King Lear* is the conflict between youth and age. This is a touchy subject, for we are all personally involved in it and are likely to become increasingly involved in it until we die. We don't like to believe that there is a conflict of interests between ourselves and those to whom we are closely bound by blood, custom, or affection. We don't like to face the fact that young people and older people are different. But it is true, and fathers-and-sons nights ("Dads are Pals"), identical mother-and-daughter costumes, and unctuous mouthings about "senior citizens" cannot obliterate this difference. The toughness of *King Lear* in this regard stands in stark contrast to the weak silliness of a society that tries to pretend that all its members are the same age. Much of this play is concerned with the hard truth that the old and the young see life differently and pursue different goals, and consequently are very likely to find themselves in each other's way. There is, from Shakespeare's point of view, only one thing that can completely bridge the gap of difference. It is love — love like that which Edgar and Cordelia have for their parents, love like that which

Gloucester and Lear learn in the end. Anyone who reads *King Lear* with understanding sees that this kind of love is not a mere matter of habit or personal attraction. It is, in the tough words of St. Paul, a love that "suffereth long, and is kind . . . envieth not . . . vaunteth not itself, is not puffed up . . . seeketh not her own, is not easily provoked . . . believeth all things, hopeth all things, endureth all things." [1] Such love is essentially sacrificial.

Much less demanding and far more common than love as a means of maintaining orderly relationships between different sorts of people are certain practical compromises, based for the most part on force and authority. You may remember how, in Rudyard Kipling's *The First Jungle Book,* the wolf pack is accustomed to kill its leader when he gets too old to hunt or fight. Up to this point, his authority is wisely unchallenged. Just so are Goneril and Regan wisely bound to their father so long as he has genuine power over them, something to give or withhold. As is the custom in such cases, the sisters pretend that their practical attachment is love. In Act I, Scene i, lines 50–52, Goneril says:

> Sir, I love you more than word can wield the matter,
> Dearer than eyesight, space, and liberty,
> Beyond what can be valued, rich or rare. . . .

But when the old man in his vanity has accepted such cosmetics of love for the real complexion of her attachment and has given up his power, Goneril growls honestly (Act I, Scene iii, lines 16–20):

> Idle old man,
> That still would manage those authorities
> That he hath given away. Now by my life,
> Old fools are babes again, and must be used
> With checks as flatteries, when they are seen abused.

We miss most of the point of all this if we fail to see the tough and complex way in which Shakespeare develops the theme of difference in age. Lear is a very old man, and his attitudes, plans, and whims are outrageous from the point of view of everyone else in the play and of most of the audience. In the first act he is an old fool behaving like an infant. He wants to have all play and no work. He wants to be petted and flattered, and he wants to believe that love consists of such carryings-on (after all, such love would seem to be pure delight). He does not know

---

[1] I Corinthians 13:14–7.

his friends from his enemies — he is like a small child who "hates" his parents when they discipline him and "loves" strangers when they offer him indigestible candy or dangerous toys. Those who really do love Lear — Cordelia, Kent, and the Fool — try to correct these follies, only to be mistreated for their pains, while Goneril, Regan, and Cornwall encourage his childishness as long as it is of practical value for them to do so.

When Lear has given up the power to enforce attachment, his behavior, of course, becomes inconvenient to those who have encouraged it. There can be no question but that a houseguest like Lear, surrounded by a hundred fun-loving knights, is a trying addition to Goneril's ménage. The king's favorites — the disguised and violent Kent and the "all-licensed fool" — make a tense situation worse. The practical sisters are equal to the occasion. They systematically strip Lear of the feeble power he has retained, which amounts to little more than the power to make a nuisance of himself, and willingly let him go out on the heath to die.

Thus would the matter end except for the fact that Lear is a good deal more than merely an old man who by frittering away his authority has lost at a primitive level the conflict between generations. He is an extraordinary man. He is concerned not only with what has happened to himself but with what it all means. And in addition, of course, there are a few people who really love Lear and for whom his faults and follies, with their consequences, are not reasons to eliminate him but causes for help and pity.

Lear's first reaction as he realizes what Goneril and Regan are up to is that the circumstance is *unnatural*. "Is it not as this mouth should tear this hand/For lifting food to 't?" he asks (Act III, Scene iv, lines 15-16). As he wanders through the revelations of the storm and his insanity, he exchanges this attitude for one closer to despair, realizing that for children to devour parents too feeble to defend themselves is indeed natural and that what has happened to him is representative of the way things are. When, after being rescued by Cordelia, he awakens to find her at his bedside, he significantly does not include her in nature but says Act V, Scene vii, lines 45-47, 49):

> You do me wrong to take me out o' th' grave.
> Thou art a soul in bliss, but I am bound
> Upon a wheel of fire. . . .
> You are a spirit, I know; where did you die?

Surely it is evident that in this play Shakespeare takes a long, tough look at the question: what is the nature of nature? The great nineteenth-century critic, A. C. Bradley, notes that in *King Lear* "we see a world which generates terrible evil in profusion." How much of this profusion is the result of "natural" behavior? Edmund, the self-appointed disciple and interpreter of nature, assures us that, beneath the thin veneer of "the curiosity of nations" and "the plague of custom," natural man is a predatory beast who is simply and contemptibly incompetent if he does not grab everything for himself that circumstances allow. (You will see that this speculation is a central idea in Conrad's *Heart of Darkness,* which is our next selection.) Is it natural to sacrifice oneself for others? Is it natural to be kind? Is it natural to be virtuous? Is it natural to be nice?

If to be natural is to behave on the same principles as do the lower animals so frequently used as images in *King Lear,* the answer to each of these questions is of course no. Lear himself arrives at a point where he claims to see no difference between the behavior of "the small gilded fly" and that of man. The force of this conclusion leaves a permanent scar, in spite of the healing powers of Cordelia. When father and daughter are led away to prison in the last act, Lear likens himself and Cordelia to singing birds in a cage. When she is dead in his arms, he cries, "Why should a dog, a horse, a rat, have life,/And thou no breath at all?"

But does the play finally support the supposition that man's natural behavior is what Edmund reasons it to be and what Goneril, Regan, and Cornwall exemplify? Are Cordelia, Kent, and Edgar unnatural — or impossibly supernatural? Are events such as Gloucester's decision to help the old King at his own extreme peril *unnatural* occurrences?

In the story of Edgar we may find an answer. Edgar lacks Cordelia's luminous force much as Gloucester lacks Lear's greatness. Although the virtuous qualities of Edgar and Cordelia are in kind the same, we are able to consider him more dispassionately than her. Edgar's manner of speech, his fairly commonplace ideas,[1] his ultimate success — in short, the secondary position in which the author has put him in the emotional pattern of the play — all this makes him ordinary by contrast with the princess. Yet within the limits of personality and circumstance assigned him by the playwright, Edgar's active love and piety, like Cordelia's, redeem nature from the general curse.

When Edgar, who not only is good but believes that goodness is intrinsic to nature, assumes the role of Poor Tom on the heath, we see a

[1] "The lamentable change is from the best;
The worst returns to laughter. . . ." (Act IV, Scene i, lines 5–6)

situation that reflects clearly the world as Shakespeare presents it in this play. For the mad Lear, Poor Tom is strong evidence that man is a worm. But we do not forget what Lear does not know: Poor Tom is Edgar in disguise. That Edgar should be the voice of despair and the mad tabulator of what is so truly terrible in life is one of the tough and tragic paradoxes of the play. The hopeful man seems without hope; what is good seems to be the most helpless evil. But hope and goodness are undeniably there — they are, in fact, the reality behind the disguise. Or, to look at it in another way, the mad beggar whom Lear accepts as his "philosopher" is two people at once: degraded, bestialized man and ideal man. Circumstances have forced the ideal man to take cover; but he is there, behind the filth and rags and apparent moral degradation. Edgar's acts and decisions, furthermore, are his own, not Poor Tom's. And this, in spite of suffering and death, is the case in the play as a whole: goodness must go underground while evil rends and tears humanity and itself, but evil cannot destroy goodness or keep it hidden indefinitely.

Your attention should be directed to two other areas. One is the matter of language and poetry. Even critics who have objected to *King Lear* as too huge for the stage have agreed that the work is one of the world's great poems. Whether for most modern readers the poetry of *King Lear* can be appreciated separately from the work as drama is dubious, but this is certain: you will never find word mastery, imagery, and rhythm in English to surpass those you find here. Finally, note what a wealth of situations is in this play. Here is a partial list: escapes in disguise, conversations with mad people, war, torture, sexual misbehavior, suicide, brawls, murder, legal injustice, misuse of royal power, conspiracy, a duel, social protest, a mighty storm. All these and more are made vividly real in five acts. Think about that.

Heart of Darkness

by Joseph Conrad (1857–1924)

Josef Theodor Konrad Nalecz Korzeniowski left his native Poland at seventeen and for many years had virtually no home but the sea. After voyages as seaman and officer on ships of various nations, he became firmly attached to the British merchant marine. Adopting the country with the service, he anglicized his name to Joseph Conrad. When he retired from the sea in 1894, he did so, amazingly enough, to spend the rest of his life as an English novelist. In fact this man, who learned English after he was grown, who spoke it all his life with a pronounced accent, and who did not start to write seriously in the language of his adoption until his mid-thirties, is recognized as one of the greatest prose stylists and creative artists in English fiction.

Many of the situations encountered in Conrad's tales are developments of things that he himself did or heard in his years as a seafarer. The setting and general circumstances of *Heart of Darkness* emerge from a tour Conrad made as a steamboat captain on the Congo in 1890. Marlow's descriptions and attitudes reflect Conrad's own observations of Belgian colonialism. But do not approach *Heart of Darkness* simply as a romantic reminiscence thinly disguised as fiction. He took his task as an artist seriously: "And art itself may be defined as a single-minded attempt to render the highest kind of justice to the visible universe, by bringing to light the truth, manifold and one, underlying its every aspect."

A most important aspect of the visible universe is the nature of men — their weaknesses, strengths, illusions, and values. Conrad deals with a number of types of men; but, like most tellers of tales, he is principally concerned with those men who are in some way extraordinary. Indeed, his careful, often contemptuous treatment of ordinary characters may seem to you a device to set off the extraordinary ones. The story that follows is chiefly about *two* extraordinary men (note their similarities and differences): Marlow, the narrator, and Kurtz, the "universal genius."

I

The *Nellie,* a cruising yawl, swung to her anchor without a flutter of the sails, and was at rest. The flood had made, the wind nearly calm, and being bound down the river, the only thing for it was to come to and wait for the turn of the tide.

The sea-reach of the Thames stretched before us like the beginning of an interminable waterway. In the offing the sea and the sky were welded together without a joint, and in the luminous space the tanned sails of the barges drifting up with the tide seemed to stand still in red clusters of canvas sharply peaked, with gleams of varnished sprits. A haze rested on the low shores that ran out to sea in vanishing flatness. The air was dark above Gravesend, and farther back still seemed condensed into a mournful gloom, brooding motionless over the biggest, and the greatest, town on earth.

The Director of Companies was our captain and our host. We four affectionately watched his back as he stood in the bows looking to seaward. On the whole river there was nothing that looked half so nautical. He resembled a pilot, which to a seaman is trustworthiness personified. It was difficult to realise his work was not out there in the luminous estuary, but behind him, within the brooding gloom.

Between us there was, as I have already said somewhere, the bond of the sea. Besides holding our hearts together through long periods of separation, it had the effect of making us tolerant of each other's yarns — and even convictions. The Lawyer — the best of old fellows — had, because of his many years and many virtues, the only cushion on deck, and was lying on the only rug. The Accountant had brought out already a box of dominoes, and was toying architecturally with the bones. Marlow sat cross-legged right aft, leaning against the mizzenmast. He had sunken cheeks, a yellow complexion, a straight back, an ascetic aspect, and with his arms dropped, the palms of hands outwards, resembled an idol. The Director, satisfied the anchor had good hold, made his way aft and sat down amongst us. We exchanged a few words lazily. Afterwards there was silence on board the yacht. For some reason or other we did not begin that game of dominoes. We felt meditative, and fit for nothing but placid staring. The day was ending in a serenity of still and exquisite brilliance. The water shone pacifically; the sky, without a speck, was a benign immensity of unstained light; the very mist on the Essex marshes was like a gauzy and radiant fabric, hung from the wooded rises inland, and draping the low shores in diaphanous folds. Only the gloom to the west, brooding over the upper reaches, became more sombre every minute, as if angered by the approach of the sun.

And at last, in its curved and imperceptible fall, the sun sank low, and from glowing white changed to a dull red without rays and without heat, as if about to go out suddenly, stricken to death by the touch of that gloom brooding over a crowd of men.

Forthwith a change came over the waters, and the serenity became less brilliant but more profound. The old river in its broad reach rested unruffled at the decline of day, after ages of good service done to the race that peopled its banks, spread out in the tranquil dignity of a waterway leading to the uttermost ends of the earth. We looked at the venerable stream not in the vivid flush of a short day that comes and departs for ever, but in the august light of abiding memories. And indeed nothing is easier for a man who has, as the phrase goes, "followed the sea" with reverence and affection, than to evoke the great spirit of the past upon the lower reaches of the Thames. The tidal current runs to and fro in its unceasing service, crowded with memories of men and ships it has borne to the rest of home or to the battles of the sea. It had known and served all the men of whom the nation is proud, from Sir Francis Drake to Sir John Franklin,[1] knights all, titled and untitled — the great knights-errant of the sea. It had borne all the ships whose names are like jewels flashing in the night of time, from the *Golden Hind* returning with her round flanks full of treasure, to be visited by the Queen's Highness and thus pass out of the gigantic tale, to the *Erebus* and *Terror,* bound on other conquests — and that never returned. It had known the ships and the men. They had sailed from Deptford, from Greenwich, from Erith

[1] **Sir John Franklin:** (1786–1847) naval officer and Arctic explorer.

— the adventurers and the settlers; kings' ships and the ships of men on 'Change; captains, admirals, the dark "interlopers" of the Eastern trade, and the commissioned "generals" of East India fleets. Hunters for gold or pursuers of fame, they all had gone out on that stream, bearing the sword, and often the torch, messengers of the might within the land, bearers of a spark from the sacred fire. What greatness had not floated on the ebb of that river into the mystery of an unknown earth! . . . The dreams of men, the seed of commonwealths, the germs of empires.

The sun set; the dusk fell on the stream, and lights began to appear along the shore. The Chapman lighthouse, a three-legged thing erect on a mud-flat, shone strongly. Lights of ships moved in the fairway — a great stir of lights going up and going down. And farther west on the upper reaches the place of the monstrous town was still marked ominously on the sky, a brooding gloom in sunshine, a lurid glare under the stars.

"And this also," said Marlow suddenly, "has been one of the dark places of the earth."

He was the only man of us who still "followed the sea." The worst that could be said of him was that he did not represent his class. He was a seaman, but he was a wanderer too, while most seamen lead, if one may so express it, a sedentary life. Their minds are of the stay-at-home order, and their home is always with them — the ship; and so is their country — the sea. One ship is very much like another, and the sea is always the same. In the immutability of their surroundings the foreign shores, the foreign faces, the changing immensity of life, glide past, veiled not by a sense of mystery but by a slightly disdainful ignorance; for there is nothing mysterious to a seaman unless it be the sea itself, which is the mistress of his existence and as inscrutable as Destiny. For the rest, after his hours of work, a casual stroll or a casual spree on shore suffices to unfold for him the secret of a whole continent, and generally he finds the secret not worth knowing. The yarns of seamen have a direct simplicity, the whole meaning of which lies within the shell of a cracked nut. But Marlow was not typical (if his propensity to spin yarns be excepted), and to him the meaning of an episode was not inside like a kernel but outside, enveloping the tale which brought it out only as a glow brings out a haze, in the likeness of one of these misty halos that sometimes are made visible by the spectral illumination of moonshine.[1]

His remark did not seem at all surprising. It was just like Marlow. It was accepted in silence. No one took the trouble to grunt even; and presently he said, very slow:

"I was thinking of very old times, when the Romans first came here, nineteen hundred years ago — the other day. . . . Light came out of this river since — you say Knights? Yes; but it is like a running blaze on a plain, like a flash of lightning in the clouds. We live in the flicker — may it last as long as the old earth keeps rolling! But darkness was here yesterday. Imagine the feelings of a commander of a fine — what d'ye call 'em — trireme [2] in the Mediterranean, ordered suddenly to the north; run overland across the Gauls in a hurry; put in charge of one of these craft the legionaries — a wonderful lot of handy men they must have been too — used to build, apparently by the hundred, in a month or two, if we may believe what we read. Imagine him here — the very end of the world, a sea the colour of lead, a sky the colour of smoke, a kind of ship about as rigid as a concertina — and going up this river with stores, or orders, or what you like. Sandbanks, marshes, forests, savages — precious little to eat fit for a civilised man, nothing but Thames water to drink. No Falernian wine here, no going ashore. Here and there a military camp lost in a wilderness, like a needle in a bundle of hay — cold, fog, tempests, disease, exile, and death — death skulking in the air, in the water, in the bush. They must have been dying like flies here. Oh yes — he did it. Did it very well, too, no doubt, and without thinking much

[1] Note this critical statement. Marlow is to be narrator of this tale.

[2] **trireme:** an ancient galley having three rowers seated on each bench.

about it either, except afterwards to brag of what he had gone through in his time, perhaps. They were men enough to face the darkness. And perhaps he was cheered by keeping his eye on a chance of promotion to the fleet at Ravenna by and by, if he had good friends in Rome and survived the awful climate. Or think of a decent young citizen in a toga — perhaps too much dice, you know — coming out here in the train of some prefect, or tax-gatherer, or trader, even, to mend his fortunes. Land in a swamp, march through the woods, and in some inland post feel the savagery, the utter savagery, had closed round him — all that mysterious life of the wilderness that stirs in the forest, in the jungles, in the hearts of wild men. There's no initiation either into such mysteries. He has to live in the midst of the incomprehensible, which is also detestable. And it has a fascination, too, that goes to work upon him. The fascination of the abomination — you know. Imagine the growing regrets, the longing to escape, the powerless disgust, the surrender, the hate."

He paused.

"Mind," he began again, lifting one arm from the elbow, the palm of the hand outwards, so that, with his legs folded before him, he had the pose of a Buddha preaching in European clothes and without a lotus-flower — "Mind, none of us would feel exactly like this. What saves us is efficiency — the devotion to efficiency.[1] But these chaps were not much account, really. They were no colonists; their administration was merely a squeeze, and nothing more, I suspect. They were conquerors, and for that you want only brute force — nothing to boast of, when you have it, since your strength is just an accident arising from the weakness of others. They grabbed what they could get for the sake of what was to be got. It was just robbery with violence, aggravated murder on a great scale, and men going at it blind — as is very proper for those who tackle a darkness. The conquest of the earth, which mostly means the taking it away from those who have a different complexion or slightly flatter noses than ourselves, is not a pretty thing when you look into it too much. What redeems it is the idea only. An idea at the back of it; not a sentimental pretence but an idea; and an unselfish belief in the idea — something you can set up, and bow down before, and offer a sacrifice to. . . ."

He broke off. Flames glided in the river, small green flames, red flames, white flames, pursuing, overtaking, joining, crossing each other — then separating slowly or hastily. The traffic of the great city went on in the deepening night upon the sleepless river. We looked on, waiting patiently — there was nothing else to do till the end of the flood; but it was only after a long silence,

[1] What does Marlow say devotion to efficiency saves us from?

when he said, in a hesitating voice, "I suppose you fellows remember I did once turn fresh-water sailor for a bit," that we knew we were fated, before the ebb began to run, to hear about one of Marlow's inconclusive experiences.

"I don't want to bother you much with what happened to me personally," he began, showing in this remark the weakness of many tellers of tales who seem so often unaware of what their audience would best like to hear; "yet to understand the effect of it on me you ought to know how I got out there, what I saw, how I went up that river to the place where I first met the poor chap. It was the farthest point of navigation and the culminating point of my experience. It seemed somehow to throw a kind of light on everything about me — and into my thoughts. It was sombre enough too — and pitiful — not extraordinary in any way — not very clear either. No, not very clear. And yet it seemed to throw a kind of light.

"I had then, as you remember, just returned to London after a lot of Indian Ocean, Pacific, China Seas — a regular dose of the East — six years or so, and I was loafing about, hindering you fellows in your work and invading your homes, just as though I had got a heavenly mission to civilise you. It was very fine for a time, but after a bit I did get tired of resting. Then I began to look for a ship — I should think the hardest work on

earth. But the ships wouldn't even look at me. And I got tired of that game too.

"Now when I was a little chap I had a passion for maps. I would look for hours at South America, or Africa, or Australia, and lose myself in all the glories of exploration. At that time there were many blank spaces on the earth, and when I saw one that looked particularly inviting on a map (but they all look that) I would put my finger on it and say, When I grow up I will go there. The North Pole was one of these places, I remember. Well, I haven't been there yet, and shall not try now. The glamour's off. Other places were scattered about the Equator, and in every sort of latitude all over the two hemispheres. I have been in some of them, and . . . well, we won't talk about that. But there was one yet — the biggest, the most blank, so to speak — that I had a hankering after.

"True, by this time it was not a blank space any more. It had got filled since my boyhood with rivers and lakes and names. It had ceased to be a blank space of delightful mystery — a white patch for a boy to dream gloriously over. It had become a place of darkness. But there was in it one river especially, a mighty big river, that you could see on the map, resembling an immense snake uncoiled, with its head in the sea, its body at rest curving afar over a vast country, and its tail lost in the depths of the land. And as I looked at the map of it in a shop-window, it fascinated me as a snake would a bird — a silly little bird. Then I remembered there was a big concern, a Company for trade on that river. Dash it all! I thought to myself, they can't trade without using some kind of craft on that lot of fresh water — steamboats! Why shouldn't I try to get charge of one? I went on along Fleet Street, but could not shake off the idea. The snake had charmed me.

"You understand it was a Continental concern, that Trading Society; but I have a lot of relations living on the Continent, because it's cheap and not so nasty as it looks, they say.

"I am sorry to own I began to worry them. This was already a fresh departure for me. I was not used to get things that way, you know. I always went my own road and on my own legs where I had a mind to go. I wouldn't have believed it of myself; but, then — you see — I felt somehow I must get there by hook or by crook. So I worried them. The men said, 'My dear fellow,' and did nothing. Then — would you believe it? — I tried the women. I, Charlie Marlow, set the women to work — to get a job. Heavens! Well, you see, the notion drove me. I had an aunt, a dear enthusiastic soul. She wrote: 'It will be delightful. I am ready to do anything, anything for you. It is a glorious idea. I know the wife of a very high personage in the Administration, and also a man who has lots of influence with,' etc. etc. She was determined to make no end of fuss to get me appointed skipper of a river steamboat, if such was my fancy.

"I got my appointment — of course; and I got it very quick. It appears the Company had received news that one of their captains had been killed in a scuffle with the natives. This was my chance, and it made me the more anxious to go. It was only months and months afterwards, when I made the attempt to recover what was left of the body, that I heard the original quarrel arose from a misunderstanding about some hens. Yes, two black hens. Fresleven — that was the fellow's name, a Dane — thought himself wronged somehow in the bargain, so he went ashore and started to hammer the chief of the village with a stick. Oh, it didn't surprise me in the least to hear this, and at the same time to be told that Fresleven was the gentlest, quietest creature that ever walked on two legs. No doubt he was; but he had been a couple of years already out there engaged in the noble cause, you know, and he probably felt the need at last of asserting his self-respect in some way. Therefore he whacked the old nigger mercilessly, while a big crowd of his people watched him, thunderstruck, till some man — I was told the chief's son — in desperation at hearing the old chap yell, made a tentative jab with a spear at the white man — and of course it went quite easy between the shoulder-blades. Then the whole population cleared into the forest, expecting all kinds of calamities to happen, while, on the other hand, the steamer Fresleven commanded left also in a bad panic, in charge of the engineer, I believe. Afterwards nobody seemed to trouble much about Fresleven's remains, till I got out and stepped into his shoes. I couldn't let it rest, though; but when an opportunity offered at last to meet my predecessor, the grass growing through his ribs was tall enough to hide his bones. They were all there. The supernatural being had not been touched after he fell. And the village was deserted, the huts gaped black, rotting, all askew within the fallen enclosures. A calamity had come to it, sure enough. The people had vanished. Mad terror had scattered them, men, women, and children, through the bush, and they had never returned. What became of the hens I don't know either. I should think the cause of progress got them, anyhow. However, through this glorious affair I got my appointment, before I had fairly begun to hope for it.

"I flew around like mad to get ready, and before forty-eight hours I was crossing the Channel to show myself to my employers, and sign the contract. In a very few hours I arrived in a city that always makes me think of a whited sepulchre.[1] Prejudice no doubt. I had no difficulty in finding the Company's offices. It was the biggest thing in the town, and everybody I met was full of it. They were going to run an over-sea empire, and make no end of coin by trade.

"A narrow and deserted street in deep shadow, high houses, innumerable windows with venetian blinds, a dead silence, grass sprouting between the stones, imposing carriage archways right and left, immense double doors standing ponderously ajar. I slipped through one of these cracks, went up a swept and ungarnished staircase, as arid as a desert, and opened the first door I came to. Two women, one fat and the other slim, sat on straw-bottomed chairs, knitting black wool. The slim one got up and walked straight at me — still knitting with downcast eyes — and only just as I began to think of getting out of her way, as you would for a somnambulist, stood still, and looked up. Her dress was as plain as an umbrella-cover, and she turned round without a word and preceded me into a waiting-room. I gave my name, and looked about.

[1] The words of Jesus Christ, as recorded in Matthew 23:27: "Woe unto you, scribes and Pharisees, hypocrites! for ye are like unto whited sepulchres, which indeed appear beautiful outward, but are within full of dead men's bones and of all uncleanness."

Deal table in the middle, plain chairs all round the walls, on one end a large shining map, marked with all the colours of a rainbow. There was a vast amount of red — good to see at any time, because one knows that some real work is done in there, a deuce of a lot of blue, a little green, smears of orange, and, on the East Coast, a purple patch, to show where the jolly pioneers of progress drink the jolly lager-beer. However, I wasn't going into any of these. I was going into the yellow.[1] Dead in the centre. And the river was there — fascinating — deadly — like a snake. Ough! A door opened, a white-haired secretarial head, but wearing a compassionate expression, appeared, and a skinny forefinger beckoned me into the sanctuary. Its light was dim, and a heavy writing-desk squatted in the middle. From behind that structure came out an impression of pale plumpness in a frock-coat. The great man himself. He was five feet six, I should judge, and had his grip on the handle-end of ever

[1] The colors on the map of Africa denoted areas ruled by the European colonial powers. Marlow (like Conrad) tends to approve of British colonial policy and says that it was "good to see" the "vast amount of red." The "yellow" into which Marlow was going was, of course, the Congo. In 1890, when Conrad went there, the Congo Free State, though technically independent, actually belonged to the Belgian King, Leopold II. It was formally annexed to Belgium in 1908.

so many millions. He shook hands, I fancy, murmured vaguely, was satisfied with my French. *Bon voyage.*

"In about forty-five seconds I found myself again in the waiting-room with the compassionate secretary, who, full of desolation and sympathy, made me sign some document. I believe I undertook amongst other things not to disclose any trade secrets. Well, I am not going to.

"I began to feel slightly uneasy. You know I am not used to such ceremonies, and there was something ominous in the atmosphere. It was just as though I had been let into some conspiracy — I don't know — something not quite right; and I was glad to get out. In the outer room the two women knitted black wool feverishly. People were arriving, and the younger one was walking back and forth introducing them. The old one sat on her chair. Her flat cloth slippers were propped up on a foot-warmer, and a cat reposed on her lap. She wore a starched white affair on her head, had a wart on one cheek, and silver-rimmed spectacles hung on the tip of her nose. She glanced at me above the glasses. The swift and indifferent placidity of that look troubled me. Two youths with foolish and cheery countenances were being piloted over, and she threw at them the same quick glance of unconcerned wisdom. She seemed to know all about them and about me too. An eerie feeling came over me. She seemed uncanny and fateful. Often far away there I thought of these two, guarding the door of Darkness, knitting black wool as for a warm pall, one introducing, introducing continuously to the unknown, the other scrutinising the cheery and foolish faces with unconcerned old eyes. *Ave!* Old knitter of black wool. *Morituri te salutant.*[1] Not many of those she looked at ever saw her again — not half, by a long way.

"There was yet a visit to the doctor. 'A simple formality,' assured me the secretary,[2] with an air of taking an immense part in all my sorrows. Accordingly a young chap wearing his hat over the left eyebrow, some clerk I suppose — there must have been clerks in the business, though the house was as still as a house in a city of the dead — came from somewhere upstairs, and led me forth. He was shabby and careless, with ink-stains on the sleeves of his jacket, and his cravat was large and billowy, under a chin shaped like the toe of an old boot. It was a little too early for the doctor, so I proposed a drink, and thereupon he developed a vein

[1] *Ave . . . Morituri te salutant:* "Hail, we who are about to die salute you." This was the formal greeting that Roman gladiators gave as they approached Cæsar's box in the amphitheater before they fought.

[2] assured . . . secretary: one of the few examples of unidiomatic English in this story. What would be the idiomatic English word order?

of joviality. As we sat over our vermuths he glorified the Company's business, and by and by I expressed casually my surprise at him not going out there. He became very cool and collected all at once. 'I am not such a fool as I look, quoth Plato to his disciples,' he said sententiously, emptied his glass with great resolution, and we rose.

"The old doctor felt my pulse, evidently thinking of something else the while. 'Good, good for there,' he mumbled, and then with a certain eagerness asked me whether I would let him measure my head. Rather surprised, I said Yes, when he produced a thing like callipers and got the dimensions back and front and every way, taking notes carefully. He was an unshaven little man in a threadbare coat like a gaberdine, with his feet in slippers, and I thought him a harmless fool. 'I always ask leave, in the interests of science, to measure the crania of those going out there,' he said. 'And when they come back too?' I asked. 'Oh, I never see them,' he remarked; 'and, moreover, the changes take place inside, you know.' He smiled, as if at some quiet joke. 'So you are going out there. Famous. Interesting too.' He gave me a searching glance, and made another note. 'Ever any madness in your family?' he asked, in a matter-of-fact tone. I felt very annoyed. 'Is that question in the interests of science too?' 'It would be,' he said, without taking notice of my irritation, 'interesting for science to watch the mental changes of individuals, on the spot, but . . .' 'Are you an alienist?'[1] I interrupted. 'Every doctor should be — a little,' answered that original imperturbably. 'I have a little theory which you Messieurs who go out there must help me to prove. This is my share in the advantages my country shall reap from the possession of such a magnificent dependency. The mere wealth I leave to others. Pardon my questions, but you are the first Englishman coming under my observation . . .' I hastened to assure him I was not in the least typical. 'If I were,' said I, 'I wouldn't be talking like this with you.' 'What you say is rather profound, and probably erroneous,' he said, with a laugh. 'Avoid irritation more than exposure to the sun. Adieu. How do you English say, eh? Good-bye. Ah! Good-bye. Adieu. In the tropics one must before everything keep calm.' . . . He lifted a warning forefinger. . . . '*Du calme, du calme.*[2] *Adieu.*'

"One thing more remained to do — say good-bye to my excellent aunt. I found her triumphant. I had a cup of tea — the last decent cup of tea for many days — and in a room that most soothingly looked just as you would expect a lady's drawing-room to look, we had a long quiet chat by the fireside. In the course of these confidences it

[1] alienist: psychiatrist.
[2] *Du . . . calme:* (idiomatic French) Keep calm, keep calm.

became quite plain to me I had been represented to the wife of the high dignitary, and goodness knows to how many more people besides, as an exceptional and gifted creature — a piece of good fortune for the Company — a man you don't get hold of every day. Good heavens! and I was going to take charge of a two-penny-halfpenny river-steamboat with a penny whistle attached! It appeared, however, I was also one of the Workers, with a capital — you know. Something like an emissary of light, something like a lower sort of apostle. There had been a lot of such rot let loose in print and talk just about that time, and the excellent woman, living right in the rush of all that humbug, got carried off her feet. She talked about 'weaning those ignorant millions from their horrid ways,' till, upon my word, she made me quite uncomfortable. I ventured to hint that the Company was run for profit.

"'You forget, dear Charlie, that the labourer is worthy of his hire,' she said brightly. It's queer how out of touch with truth women are. They live in a world of their own, and there had never been anything like it, and never can be. It is too beautiful altogether, and if they were to set it up it would go to pieces before the first sunset. Some confounded fact we men have been living contentedly with ever since the day of creation would start up and knock the whole thing over.

"After this I got embraced, told

to wear flannel, be sure to write often, and so on — and I left. In the street — I don't know why — a queer feeling came to me that I was an impostor. Odd thing that I, who used to clear out for any part of the world at twenty-four hours' notice, with less thought than most men give to the crossing of a street, had a moment — I won't say of hesitation, but of startled pause, before this commonplace affair. The best way I can explain it to you is by saying that, for a second or two, I felt as though, instead of going to the centre of a continent, I were about to set off for the centre of the earth.

"I left in a French steamer, and she called in every blamed port they have out there, for, as far as I could see, the sole purpose of landing soldiers and custom-house officers. I watched the coast. Watching a coast as it slips by the ship is like thinking about an enigma. There it is before you — smiling, frowning, inviting, grand, mean, insipid, or savage, and always mute with an air of whispering, Come and find out. This one was almost featureless, as if still in the making, with an aspect of monotonous grimness. The edge of a colossal jungle, so dark green as to be almost black, fringed with white surf, ran straight, like a ruled line, far, far away along a blue sea whose glitter was blurred by a creeping mist. The sun was fierce, the land seemed to glisten and drip with steam. Here and there greyish-whitish specks showed up clustered inside the white surf, with a flag flying above them perhaps — settlements some centuries old, and still no bigger than pin-heads on the untouched expanse of their background. We pounded along, stopped, landed soldiers; went on, landed custom-house clerks to levy toll in what looked like a God-forsaken wilderness, with a tin shed and a flag-pole lost in it; landed more soldiers — to take care of the custom-house clerks presumably. Some, I heard, got drowned in the surf; but whether they did or not, nobody seemed particularly to care. They were just flung out there, and on we went. Every day the coast looked the same, as though we had not moved; but we passed various places — trading places — with names like Gran' Bassam, Little Popo; names that seemed to belong to some sordid farce acted in front of a sinister back-cloth. The idleness of a passenger, my isolation amongst all these men with whom I had no point of contact, the oily and languid sea, the uniform sombreness of the coast, seemed to keep me away from the truth of things, within the toil of a mournful and senseless delusion. The voice of the surf heard now and then was a positive pleasure, like the speech of a brother. It was something natural, that had its reason, that had a meaning. Now and then a boat from the shore gave one a momentary contact with reality. It was paddled by black fellows.

You could see from afar the white of their eyeballs glistening. They shouted, sang; their bodies streamed with perspiration; they had faces like grotesque masks — these chaps; but they had bone, muscle, a wild vitality, an intense energy of movement, that was as natural and true as the surf along their coast. They wanted no excuse for being there. They were a great comfort to look at. For a time I would feel I belonged still to a world of straightforward facts; but the feeling would not last long. Something would turn up to scare it away. Once, I remember, we came upon a man-of-war anchored off the coast. There wasn't even a shed there, and she was shelling the bush. It appears the French had one of their wars going on thereabouts. Her ensign dropped limp like a rag; the muzzles of the long six-inch guns stuck out all over the low hull; the greasy, slimy swell swung her up lazily and let her down, swaying her thin masts. In the empty immensity of earth, sky, and water, there she was, incomprehensible, firing into a continent. Pop, would go one of the six-inch guns; a small flame would dart and vanish, a little white smoke would disappear, a tiny projectile would give a feeble screech — and nothing happened. Nothing could happen. There was a touch of insanity in the proceeding, a sense of lugubrious drollery in the sight; and it was not dissipated by somebody on board assuring me earnestly there was a camp of na-tives — he called them enemies! — hidden out of sight somewhere.

"We gave her her letters (I heard the men in that lonely ship were dying of fever at the rate of three a day) and went on. We called at some more places with farcical names, where the merry dance of death and trade goes on in a still and earthy atmosphere as of an overheated catacomb; all along the formless coast bordered by dangerous surf, as if Nature herself had tried to ward off intruders; in and out of rivers, streams of death in life, whose banks were rotting into mud, whose waters, thickened into slime, invaded the contorted mangroves, that seemed to writhe at us in the extremity of an impotent despair. Nowhere did we stop long enough to get a particularised impression, but the general sense of vague and oppressive wonder grew upon me. It was like a weary pilgrimage amongst hints for nightmares.

"It was upward of thirty days before I saw the mouth of the big river. We anchored off the seat of the government. But my work would not begin till some two hundred miles farther on. So as soon as I could I made a start for a place thirty miles higher up.

"I had my passage on a little seagoing steamer. Her captain was a Swede, and knowing me for a seaman, invited me on the bridge. He was a young man, lean, fair, and morose, with lanky hair and a shuffling gait. As we left the miserable little wharf, he tossed his head contemptuously at the shore. 'Been living there?' he asked. I said, 'Yes.' 'Fine lot these government chaps — are they not?' he went on, speaking English with great precision and considerable bitterness. 'It is funny what some people will do for a few francs a month. I wonder what becomes of that kind when it goes up country?' I said to him I expected to see that soon. 'So-o-o!' he exclaimed. He shuffled athwart, keeping one eye ahead vigilantly. 'Don't be too sure,' he continued. 'The other day I took up a man who hanged himself on the road. He was a Swede, too.' 'Hanged himself! Why, in God's name?' I cried. He kept on looking out watchfully. 'Who knows? The sun too much for him, or the country perhaps.'

"At last we opened a reach. A rocky cliff appeared, mounds of turned-up earth by the shore, houses on a hill, others with iron roofs, amongst a waste of excavations, or hanging to the declivity. A continuous noise of the rapids above hovered over this scene of inhabited devastation. A lot of people, mostly black and naked, moved about like ants. A jetty projected into the river. A blinding sunlight drowned all this at times in a sudden recrudescence of glare. 'There's your Company's station,' said the Swede, pointing to three wooden barrack-like structures on the rocky slope. 'I will send your things up. Four boxes did you say? So. Farewell.'

"I came upon a boiler wallowing in the grass, then found a path leading up the hill. It turned aside for the boulders, and also for an undersized railway truck lying there on its back with its wheels in the air. One was off. The thing looked as dead as the carcass of some animal. I came upon more pieces of decaying machinery, a stack of rusty nails. To the left a clump of trees made a shady spot, where dark things seemed to stir feebly. I blinked, the path was steep. A horn tooted to the right, and I saw the black people run. A heavy and dull detonation shook the ground, a puff of smoke came out of the cliff, and that was all. No change appeared on the face of the rock. They were building a railway. The cliff was not in the way or anything; but this objectless blasting was all the work going on.

"A slight clinking behind me made me turn my head. Six black men advanced in a file, toiling up the path. They walked erect and slow, balancing small baskets full of earth on their heads, and the clink kept time with their footsteps. Black rags were wound round their loins, and the short ends behind waggled to and fro like tails. I could see every rib, the joints of their limbs were like knots in a rope; each had an iron collar on his neck, and all were connected together with a chain whose bights swung between them, rhythmically clinking. Another report from the cliff made me think suddenly of that ship of war I had seen firing into a continent. It was the same kind of ominous voice; but these men could by no stretch of imagination be called enemies. They were called criminals, and the outraged law, like the bursting shells, had come to them, an insoluble mystery from the sea. All their meagre breasts panted together, the violently dilated nostrils quivered, the eyes stared stonily uphill. They passed me within six inches, without a glance, with that complete, deathlike indifference of unhappy savages. Behind this raw matter one of the reclaimed, the product of the new forces at work, strolled despondently, carrying a rifle by its middle. He had a uniform jacket with one button off, and seeing a white man on the path, hoisted his weapon to his shoulder with alacrity. This was simple prudence, white men being so much alike at a distance that he could not tell who I might be. He was speedily reassured, and with a large, white, rascally grin, and a glance at his charge, seemed to take me into partnership in his exalted trust. After all, I also was a part of the great cause of these high and just proceedings.[1]

"Instead of going up, I turned and descended to the left. My idea was to let that chain-gang get out of sight before I climbed the hill. You know I am not particularly tender; I've had to strike and to

fend off. I've had to resist and to attack sometimes — that's only one way of resisting — without counting the exact cost, according to the demands of such sort of life as I had blundered into. I've seen the devil of violence, and the devil of greed, and the devil of hot desire; but, by all the stars! these were strong, lusty, red-eyed devils, that swayed and drove men — men, I tell you. But as I stood on this hillside, I foresaw that in the blinding sunshine of that land I would become acquainted with a flabby, pretending, weak-eyed devil of a rapacious and pitiless folly. How insidious he could be, too, I was only to find out several months later and a thousand miles farther. For a moment I stood appalled, as though by a warning.[2] Finally I descended the hill, obliquely, towards the trees I had seen.

"I avoided a vast artificial hole somebody had been digging on the slope, the purpose of which I found it impossible to divine. It wasn't a quarry or a sandpit, anyhow. It was just a hole. It might have been connected with the philanthropic desire of giving the criminals something to do. I don't know. Then I nearly fell into a very narrow ravine, almost no more than a scar in the hillside. I discovered that a lot of imported drainage-pipes for the settlement had been tumbled in there. There wasn't one that was

[1] In what sense is Marlow "part of the great cause"? In what sense might everyone be considered part of it?

[2] Can these metaphorical devils be related to the personalities of Milton's fallen angels?

not broken. It was a wanton smash-up. At last I got under the trees. My purpose was to stroll into the shade for a moment; but no sooner within than it seemed to me I had stepped into the gloomy circle of some Inferno.[1] The rapids were near, and an uninterrupted, uniform, headlong, rushing noise filled the mournful stillness of the grove, where not a breath stirred, not a leaf moved, with a mysterious sound — as though the tearing pace of the launched earth had suddenly become audible.

"Black shapes crouched, lay, sat between the trees, leaning against the trunks, clinging to the earth, half coming out, half effaced within the dim light, in all the attitudes of pain, abandonment, and despair. Another mine on the cliff went off, followed by a slight shudder of the soil under my feet. The work was going on. The work! And this was the place where some of the helpers had withdrawn to die.

"They were dying slowly — it was very clear. They were not enemies, they were not criminals, they were nothing earthly now — nothing but black shadows of disease and starvation, lying confusedly in the greenish gloom. Brought from all the recesses of the coast in all the legality of time contracts, lost in uncongenial surroundings, fed on unfamiliar food, they sickened, became inefficient, and were then allowed to crawl away and rest. These moribund shapes were free as air — and nearly as thin. I began to distinguish the gleam of eyes under the trees. Then, glancing down, I saw a face near my hand. The black bones reclined at full length with one shoulder against the tree, and slowly the eyelids rose and the sunken eyes looked up at me, enormous and vacant, a kind of blind, white flicker in the depths of the orbs, which died out slowly. The man seemed young — almost a boy — but you know with them it's hard to tell. I found nothing else to do but to offer him one of my good Swede's ship's biscuits I had in my pocket. The fingers closed slowly on it and held — there was no other movement and no other glance. He had tied a bit of white worsted round his neck — Why? Where did he get it? Was it a badge — an ornament — a charm — a propitiatory act? Was there any idea at all connected with it? It looked startling round his black neck, this bit of white thread from beyond the seas.

"Near the same tree two more bundles of acute angles sat with their legs drawn up. One, with his chin propped on his knees, stared at nothing, in an intolerable and appalling manner: his brother phantom rested its forehead, as if overcome with a great weariness; and all about others were scattered

[1] **Inferno: Hell.** The reference is to that part of Dante Alighieri's great poem, the *Divine Comedy,* in which the poet visits the circles of Hell. Note how the diabolic image is sustained after Marlow's introduction of the devils.

in every pose of contorted collapse, as in some picture of a massacre or a pestilence. While I stood horror-struck, one of these creatures rose to his hands and knees, and went off on all-fours towards the river to drink. He lapped out of his hand, then sat up in the sunlight, crossing his shins in front of him, and after a time let his woolly head fall on his breastbone.

"I didn't want any more loitering in the shade, and I made haste towards the station. When near the buildings I met a white man, in such an unexpected elegance of get-up that in the first moment I took him for a sort of vision. I saw a high starched collar, white cuffs, a light alpaca jacket, snowy trousers, a clear necktie, and varnished boots. No hat. Hair parted, brushed, oiled, under a green-lined parasol held in a big white hand. He was amazing, and had a penholder behind his ear.

"I shook hands with this miracle, and I learned he was the Company's chief accountant, and that all the book-keeping was done at this station. He had come out for a moment, he said, 'to get a breath of fresh air.' The expression sounded wonderfully odd, with its suggestion of sedentary desk-life. I wouldn't have mentioned the fellow to you at all, only it was from his lips that I first heard the name of the man who is so indissolubly connected with the memories of that time. Moreover, I respected the fellow. Yes; I respected his collars, his vast cuffs, his brushed hair. His appearance was certainly that of a hairdresser's dummy; but in the great demoralisation of the land he kept up his appearance. That's backbone. His starched collars and got-up shirt-fronts were achievements of character. He had been out nearly three years; and, later, I could not help asking him how he managed to sport such linen. He had just the faintest blush, and said modestly, 'I've been teaching one of the native women about the station. It was difficult. She had a distaste for the work.' Thus this man had verily accomplished something. And he was devoted to his books, which were in apple-pie order.[1]

"Everything else in the station was in a muddle, — heads, things, buildings. Strings of dusty niggers with splay feet arrived and departed; a stream of manufactured goods, rubbishy cottons, beads, and brass-wire set into the depths of darkness, and in return came a precious trickle of ivory.

"I had to wait in the station for ten days — an eternity. I lived in a hut in the yard, but to be out of the chaos I would sometimes get into the accountant's office. It was built of horizontal planks, and so badly put together that, as he bent over his high desk, he was barred from neck to heels with narrow strips of sunlight. There was no need to open the big shutter to see.

[1] To what extent is Marlow's expressed respect for the chief accountant ironic?

It was hot there too; big flies buzzed fiendishly, and did not sting, but stabbed. I sat generally on the floor, while, of faultless appearance (and even slightly scented), perching on a high stool, he wrote, he wrote. Sometimes he stood up for exercise. When a truckle-bed with a sick man (some invalided agent from up-country) was put in there, he exhibited a gentle annoyance. 'The groans of this sick person,' he said, 'distract my attention. And without that it is extremely difficult to guard against clerical errors in this climate.'

"One day he remarked, without lifting his head, 'In the interior you will no doubt meet Mr. Kurtz.' On my asking who Mr. Kurtz was, he said he was a first-class agent; and seeing my disappointment at this information, he added slowly, laying down his pen, 'He is a very remarkable person.' Further questions elicited from him that Mr. Kurtz was at present in charge of a trading-post, a very important one, in the true ivory-country, at 'the very bottom of there. Sends in as much ivory as all the others put together . . .' He began to write again. The sick man was too ill to groan. The flies buzzed in a great peace.

"Suddenly there was a growing murmur of voices and a great tramping of feet. A caravan had come in. A violent babble of uncouth sounds burst out on the other side of the planks. All the carriers were speaking together, and in the midst of the uproar the lamentable voice of the chief agent was heard 'giving it up' tearfully for the twentieth time that day. . . . He rose slowly. 'What a frightful row,' he said. He crossed the room gently to look at the sick man, and returning, said to me, 'He does not hear.' 'What! Dead?' I asked, startled. 'No, not yet,' he answered, with great composure. Then, alluding with a toss of the head to the tumult in the station-yard, 'When one has got to make correct entries, one comes to hate those savages — hate them to the death.' He remained thoughtful for a moment. 'When you see Mr. Kurtz,' he went on, 'tell him from me that everything here' — he glanced at the desk — 'is very satisfactory. I don't like to write to him — with those messengers of ours you never know who may get hold of your letter — at that Central Station.' He stared at me for a moment with his mild, bulging eyes. 'Oh, he will go far, very far,' he began again. 'He will be a somebody in the Administration before long. They, above — the Council in Europe, you know — mean him to be.'

"He turned to his work. The noise outside had ceased, and presently in going out I stopped at the door. In the steady buzz of flies the homeward-bound agent was lying flushed and insensible; the other, bent over his books, was making correct entries of perfectly correct transactions; and fifty feet below the doorstep I could see the still tree-tops of the grove of death.

"Next day I left that station at last, with a caravan of sixty men, for a two-hundred-mile tramp.

"No use telling you much about that. Paths, paths, everywhere; a stamped-in network of paths spreading over the empty land, through long grass, through burnt grass, through thickets, down and up chilly ravines, up and down stony hills ablaze with heat; and a solitude, a solitude, nobody, not a hut. The population had cleared out a long time ago. Well, if a lot of mysterious niggers armed with all kinds of fearful weapons suddenly took to travelling on the road between Deal and Gravesend, catching the yokels right and left to carry heavy loads for them, I fancy every farm and cottage thereabouts would get empty very soon. Only here the dwellings were gone too. Still, I passed through several abandoned villages. There's something pathetically childish in the ruins of grass walls. Day after day, with the stamp and shuffle of sixty pair of bare feet behind me, each pair under a 60-pound load. Camp, cook, sleep, strike camp, march. Now and then a carrier dead in harness, at rest in the long grass near the path, with an empty water-gourd and his long staff lying by his side. A great silence around and above. Perhaps on some quiet night the tremor of far-off drums, sinking, swelling, a tremor vast, faint; a sound weird, appealing, suggestive, and wild — and perhaps with as profound a meaning as the sound of bells in a Christian country. Once a white man in an unbuttoned uniform, camping on the path with an armed escort of lank Zanzibaris, very hospitable and festive — not to say drunk. Was looking after the upkeep of the road, he declared. Can't say I saw any road or any upkeep, unless the body of a middle-aged Negro, with a bullethole in the forehead, upon which I absolutely stumbled three miles farther on, may be considered as a permanent improvement. I had a white companion too, not a bad chap, but rather too fleshy and with the exasperating habit of fainting on the hot hillsides, miles away from the least bit of shade and water. Annoying, you know, to hold your own coat like a parasol over a man's head while he is coming-to. I couldn't help asking him once what he meant by coming there at all. 'To make money, of course. What do you think?' he said scornfully. Then he got fever, and had to be carried in a hammock slung under a pole. As he weighed sixteen stone I had no end of rows with the carriers. They jibbed, ran away, sneaked off with their loads in the night — quite a mutiny. So, one evening, I made a speech in English with gestures, not one of which was lost to the sixty pairs of eyes before me, and the next morning I started the hammock off in front all right. An hour afterwards I came upon the whole concern wrecked in a bush — man, hammock, groans, blankets, horrors. The heavy pole had skinned his poor nose. He was very anxious for me to kill somebody, but there wasn't the shadow of a carrier near. I remembered the old doctor — 'It would be interesting for science to watch the mental changes of individuals, on the spot.' I felt I was becoming scientifically interesting.[1] However, all that is to no purpose. On the fifteenth day I came in sight of the big river again, and hobbled into the Central Station. It was on a back water surrounded by scrub and forest, with a pretty border of smelly mud on one side, and on the three others enclosed by a crazy fence of rushes. A neglected gap was all the gate it had, and the first glance at the place was enough to let you see the flabby devil was running that show. White men with long staves in their hands appeared languidly from amongst the buildings, strolling up to take a look at me, and then retired out of sight somewhere. One of them, a stout, excitable chap with black moustaches, informed me with great volubility and many digressions, as soon as I told him who I was, that my steamer was at the bottom of the river. I was thunderstruck. What, how, why? Oh, it was 'all right.' The 'manager himself' was there. All quite correct. 'Everybody had behaved splendidly! splendidly!' — 'You must,' he said in agitation, 'go and see the

general manager at once. He is waiting!'

"I did not see the real significance of that wreck at once. I fancy I see it now, but I am not sure — not at all. Certainly the affair was too stupid — when I think of it — to be altogether natural.[2] Still . . . But at the moment it presented itself simply as a confounded nuisance. The steamer was sunk. They had started two days before in a sudden hurry up the river with the manager on board, in charge of some volunteer skipper, and before they had been out three hours they tore the bottom out of her on stones, and she sank near the south bank. I asked myself what I was to do there, now my boat was lost. As a matter of fact, I had plenty to do in fishing my command out of the river. I had to set about it the very next day. That, and the repairs when I brought the pieces to the station, took some months.

"My first interview with the manager was curious. He did not ask me to sit down after my twenty-mile walk that morning. He was commonplace in complexion, in feature, in manners, and in voice. He was of middle size and of ordinary build. His eyes, of the usual blue, were perhaps remarkably cold, and he certainly could make

[1] ". . . the changes take place inside, you know. . . ." (page 728).

[2] Bear this in mind. Perhaps you will have some speculations on the real significance of the wreck as you read on. But, like Marlow, you will not be sure.

his glance fall on one as trenchant and heavy as an axe. But even at these times the rest of his person seemed to disclaim the intention. Otherwise there was only an indefinable, faint expression of his lips, something stealthy — a smile — not a smile — I remember it, but I can't explain. It was unconscious, this smile was, though just after he had said something it got intensified for an instant. It came at the end of his speeches like a seal applied on the words to make the meaning of the commonest phrase appear absolutely inscrutable. He was a common trader, from his youth up employed in these parts — nothing more. He was obeyed, yet he inspired neither love nor fear, nor even respect. He inspired uneasiness. That was it! Uneasiness. Not a definite mistrust — just uneasiness — nothing more. You have no idea how effective such a . . . a . . . faculty can be. He had no genius for organising, for initiative, or for order even. That was evident in such things as the deplorable state of the station. He had no learning, and no intelligence. His position had come to him — why? Perhaps because he was never ill . . . He had served three terms of three years out there . . . Because triumphant health in the general rout of constitutions is a kind of power in itself. When he went home on leave he rioted on a large scale — pompously. Jack [1] ashore —

[1] Jack: (also, *Jack-tar*) a sailor.

with a difference — in externals only. This one could gather from his casual talk. He originated nothing, he could keep the routine going — that's all. But he was great. He was great by this little thing that it was impossible to tell what could control such a man. He never gave that secret away. Perhaps there was nothing within him. Such a suspicion made one pause — for out there there were no external checks. Once when various tropical diseases had laid low almost every 'agent' in the station, he was heard to say, 'Men who come out here should have no entrails.' He sealed the utterance with that smile of his, as though it had been a door opening into a darkness he had in his keeping. You fancied you had seen things — but the seal was on. When annoyed at meal-times by the constant quarrels of the white men about precedence, he ordered an immense round table to be made, for which a special house had to be built. This was the station's mess-room. Where he sat was the first place — the rest were nowhere. One felt this to be his unalterable conviction. He was neither civil nor uncivil. He was quiet. He allowed his 'boy' — an overfed young Negro from the coast — to treat the white men, under his very eyes, with provoking insolence.

"He began to speak as soon as he saw me. I had been very long on the road. He could not wait. Had to start without me. The up-river stations had to be relieved. There had been so many delays already that he did not know who was dead and who was alive, and how they got on — and so on, and so on. He paid no attention to my explanations, and, playing with a stick of sealing-wax, repeated several times that the situation was 'very grave, very grave.' There were rumours that a very important station was in jeopardy, and its chief, Mr. Kurtz, was ill. Hoped it was not true. Mr. Kurtz was . . . I felt weary and irritable. Hang Kurtz, I thought, I interrupted him by saying I had heard of Mr. Kurtz on the coast. 'Ah! So they talk of him down there,' he murmured to himself. Then he began again, assuring me Mr. Kurtz was the best agent he had, an exceptional man, of the greatest importance to the Company; therefore I could understand his anxiety. He was, he said, 'very, very uneasy.' Certainly he fidgeted on his chair a good deal, exclaimed, 'Ah, Mr. Kurtz!' broke the stick of sealing-wax and seemed dumbfounded by the accident. Next thing he wanted to know 'how long it would take to' . . . I interrupted him again. Being hungry, you know, and kept on my feet too, I was getting savage. 'How can I tell?' I said. 'I haven't even seen the wreck yet — some months, no doubt.' All this talk seemed to me so futile. 'Some months,' he said. 'Well, let us say three months before we can make a start. Yes. That

ought to do the affair.' I flung out of his hut (he lived all alone in a clay hut with a sort of verandah) muttering to myself my opinion of him. He was a chattering idiot. Afterwards I took it back when it was borne in upon me startlingly with what extreme nicety he had estimated the time requisite for the 'affair.'

"I went to work the next day, turning, so to speak, my back on that station. In that way only it seemed to me I could keep my hold on the redeeming facts of life. Still, one must look about sometimes; and then I saw this station, these men strolling aimlessly about in the sunshine of the yard. I asked myself sometimes what it all meant. They wandered here and there with their absurd long staves in their hands, like a lot of faithless pilgrims bewitched inside a rotten fence. The word 'ivory' rang in the air, was whispered, was sighed. You would think they were praying to it. A taint of imbecile rapacity blew through it all, like a whiff from some corpse. By Jove! I've never seen anything so unreal in my life. And outside, the silent wilderness surrounding this cleared speck on the earth struck me as something great and invincible, like evil or truth, waiting patiently for the passing away of this fantastic invasion.

"Oh, these months! Well, never mind. Various things happened. One evening a grass shed full of calico, cotton prints, beads, and I don't know what else, burst into a blaze so suddenly that you would have thought the earth had opened to let an avenging fire consume all that trash. I was smoking my pipe quietly by my dismantled steamer, and saw them all cutting capers in the light, with their arms lifted high, when the stout man with moustaches came tearing down to the river, a tin pail in his hand, assured me that everybody was 'behaving splendidly, splendidly,' dipped about a quart of water and tore back again. I noticed there was a hole in the bottom of his pail.

"I strolled up. There was no hurry. You see the thing had gone off like a box of matches. It had been hopeless from the very first. The flame had leaped high, driven everybody back, lighted up everything — and collapsed. The shed was already a heap of embers glowing fiercely. A nigger was being beaten near by. They said he had caused the fire in some way; be that as it may, he was screeching most horribly. I saw him, later, for several days, sitting in a bit of shade looking very sick and trying to recover himself: afterwards he arose and went out — and the wilderness without a sound took him into its bosom again. As I approached the glow from the dark I found myself at the back of two men, talking. I heard the name of Kurtz pronounced, then the words, 'take advantage of this unfortunate acci-

dent.' One of the men was the manager. I wished him a good evening. 'Did you ever see anything like it — eh? it is incredible,' he said, and walked off. The other man remained. He was a first-class agent, young, gentlemanly, a bit reserved, with a forked little beard and a hooked nose. He was stand-offish with the other agents, and they on their side said he was the manager's spy upon them. As to me, I had hardly ever spoken to him before. We got into talk, and by and by we strolled away from the hissing ruins. Then he asked me to his room, which was in the main building of the station. He struck a match, and I perceived that this young aristocrat had not only a silver-mounted dressing-case but also a whole candle all to himself. Just at that time the manager was the only man supposed to have any right to candles. Native mats covered the clay walls; a collection of spears, assegais,[1] shields, knives, was hung up in trophies. The business entrusted to this fellow was the making of bricks — so I had been informed; but there wasn't a fragment of a brick anywhere in the station, and he had been there more than a year — waiting. It seems he could not make bricks without something, I don't know what — straw maybe. Anyway, it could not be found there, and as it was not likely to be sent from Eu-

[1] assegais: light thrusting spears of hardwood, usually iron-tipped.

rope, it did not appear clear to me what he was waiting for. An act of special creation perhaps. However, they were all waiting — all the sixteen or twenty pilgrims of them — for something; and upon my word it did not seem an uncongenial occupation, from the way they took it, though the only thing that ever came to them was disease — as far as I could see. They beguiled the time by backbiting and intriguing against each other in a foolish kind of way. There was an air of plotting about that station, but nothing came of it, of course. It was as unreal as everything else — as the philanthropic pretence of the whole concern,[1] as their talk, as their government, as their show of work. The only real feeling was a desire to get appointed to a trading-post where ivory was to be had, so that they could earn percentages. They intrigued and slandered and hated each other only on that account — but as to effectually lifting a little finger — oh no. By heavens! there is something after all in the world allowing one man to steal a horse while another must not look at a halter. Steal a horse straight out. Very well. He has done it. Perhaps he can ride. But there is a way of looking at a halter that would provoke the most charitable of saints into a kick.

"I had no idea why he wanted to be sociable, but as we chatted in there it suddenly occurred to me the fellow was trying to get at something — in fact, pumping me. He alluded constantly to Europe, to the people I was supposed to know there — putting leading questions as to my acquaintances in the sepulchral city,[2] and so on. His little eyes glittered like mica discs — with curiosity — though he tried to keep up a bit of superciliousness. At first I was astonished, but very soon I became awfully curious to see what he would find out from me. I couldn't possibly imagine what I had in me to make it worth his while. It was very pretty to see how he baffled himself, for in truth my body was full only of chills, and my head had nothing in it but that wretched steamboat business. It was evident he took me for a perfectly shameless prevaricator. At last he got angry, and, to conceal a movement of furious annoyance, he yawned. I rose. Then I noticed a small sketch in oils, on a panel, representing a woman, draped and blindfolded, carrying a lighted torch. The background was sombre — almost black. The movement of the woman was stately, and the effect of the torchlight on the face was sinister.

"It arrested me, and he stood by civilly, holding an empty half-pint champagne bottle (medical comforts) with the candle stuck in it. To my question he said Mr. Kurtz

[1] ". . . weaning those ignorant millions from their horrid ways. . . ." (page 729).

[2] Remember Marlow's earlier statement that Brussels always reminds him of a whited sepulchre.

had painted this [1] — in this very station more than a year ago — while waiting for means to go to his trading-post. 'Tell me, pray,' said I, 'who is this Mr. Kurtz?'

"'The chief of the Inner Station,' he answered in a short tone, looking away. 'Much obliged,' I said, laughing. 'And you are the brickmaker of the Central Station. Every one knows that.' He was silent for a while. 'He is a prodigy,' he said at last. 'He is an emissary of pity, and science, and progress, and devil knows what else. We want,' he began to declaim suddenly, 'for the guidance of the cause entrusted to us by Europe, so to speak, higher intelligence, wide sympathies, a singleness of purpose.' 'Who says that?' I asked. 'Lots of them,' he replied. 'Some even write that; and so *he* comes here, a special being, as you ought to know.' 'Why ought I to know?' I interrupted, really surprised. He paid no attention. 'Yes. To-day he is chief of the best station, next year he will be assistant-manager, two years more and . . . but I daresay you know what he will be in two years' time. You are of the new gang — the gang of virtue. The same people who sent him specially also recommended you. Oh, don't say no. I've my own eyes to trust.' Light dawned upon me. My dear aunt's

influential acquaintances were producing an unexpected effect upon that young man. I nearly burst into a laugh. 'Do you read the Company's confidential correspondence?' I asked. He hadn't a word to say. It was great fun. 'When Mr. Kurtz,' I continued severely, "is General Manager, you won't have the opportunity.'

"He blew the candle out suddenly, and we went outside. The moon had risen. Black figures strolled about listlessly, pouring water on the glow, whence proceeded a sound of hissing; steam ascended in the moonlight; the beaten nigger groaned somewhere. 'What a row the brute makes!' said the indefatigable man with the moustaches, appearing near us. 'Serve him right. Transgression — punishment — bang! Pitiless, pitiless. That's the only way. This will prevent all conflagrations for the future. I was just telling the manager . . .' He noticed my companion, and became crestfallen all at once. 'Not in bed yet,' he said, with a kind of servile heartiness; 'it's so natural. Ha! Danger — agitation.' He vanished. I went on to the river-side, and the other followed me. I heard a scathing murmur at my ear, 'Heap of muffs [2] — go to.' The pilgrims could be seen in knots gesticulating, discussing. Several had still their staves in their hands. I verily believe they took these sticks to bed with them. Beyond the fence the forest stood up spectrally in the

[1] Note that in Kurtz's painting the woman who is bearing light into the darkness is herself blindfolded. What symbolic meanings could be expressed in such a picture?

[2] muffs: bunglers, incompetents.

moonlight, and through the dim stir, through the faint sounds of that lamentable courtyard, the silence of the land went home to one's very heart — its mystery, its greatness, the amazing reality of it concealed life. The hurt nigger moaned feebly somewhere near by, and then fetched a deep sigh that made me mend my pace away from there. I felt a hand introducing itself under my arm. 'My dear sir,' said the fellow, 'I don't want to be misunderstood, and especially by you, who will see Mr. Kurtz long before I can have that pleasure. I wouldn't like him to get a false idea of my disposition. . . .'

"I let him run on, this papier-mâché Mephistopheles,[1] and it seemed to me that if I tried I could poke my forefinger through him, and would find nothing inside but a little loose dirt, maybe. He, don't you see, had been planning to be assistant-manager by and by under the present man, and I could see that the coming of that Kurtz had upset them both not a little. He talked precipitately, and I did not try to stop him. I had my shoulders against the wreck of my steamer, hauled up on the slope like a carcass of some big river animal. The smell of mud, of primeval mud, by Jove! was in my nostrils, the high stillness of primeval forest was before my eyes; there were shiny

---

[1] **Mephistopheles**: the suave demon who tempts Faust in *The Tragical History of Doctor Faustus* by Christopher Marlowe and in *Faust* by Goethe.

patches on the black creek. The moon had spread over everything a thin layer of silver — over the rank grass, over the mud, upon the wall of matted vegetation standing higher than the wall of a temple, over the great river I could see through a sombre gap glittering, glittering, as it flowed broadly by without a murmur. All this was great, expectant, mute, while the man jabbered about himself. I wondered whether the stillness on the face of the immensity looking at us two were meant as an appeal or as a menace. What were we who had strayed in here? Could we handle that dumb thing, or would it handle us? I felt how big, how confoundedly big, was that thing that couldn't talk and perhaps was deaf as well. What was in there? I could see a little ivory coming out from there, and I had heard Mr. Kurtz was in there. I had heard enough about it too — God knows! Yet somehow it didn't bring any image with it — no more than if I had been told an angel or a fiend was in there. I believed it in the same way one of you might believe there are inhabitants in the planet Mars. I knew once a Scotch sailmaker who was certain, dead sure, there were people in Mars. If you asked him for some idea how they looked and behaved, he would get shy and mutter something about 'walking on all-fours.' If you as much as smiled, he would — though a man of sixty — offer to fight you. I would not have gone so far as to fight for

Kurtz, but I went for him near enough to a lie. You know I hate, detest, and can't bear a lie, not because I am straighter than the rest of us, but simply because it appals me. There is a taint of death, a flavour of mortality in lies — which is exactly what I hate and detest in the world — what I want to forget. It makes me miserable and sick, like biting something rotten would do. Temperament, I suppose. Well, I went near enough to it by letting the young fool there believe anything he liked to imagine as to my influence in Europe. I became in an instant as much of a pretence as the rest of the bewitched pilgrims. This simply because I had a notion it somehow would be of help to that Kurtz whom at the time I did not see — you understand. He was just a word for me. I did not see the man in the name any more than you do. Do you see him? Do you see the story? Do you see anything? It seems to me I am trying to tell you a dream — making a vain attempt, because no relation of a dream can convey the dream-sensation, that commingling of absurdity, surprise, and bewilderment in a tremor of struggling revolt, that notion of being captured by the incredible which is of the very essence of dreams. . . ."

He was silent for a while.

". . . No, it is impossible; it is impossible to convey the life-sensation of any given epoch of one's existence — that which makes its truth, its meaning — its subtle and penetrating essence. It is impossible. We live, as we dream — alone. . . ."

He paused again as if reflecting, then added:

"Of course in this you fellows see more than I could then. You see me, whom you know. . . ."

It had become so pitch dark that we listeners could hardly see one another. For a long time already he, sitting apart, had been no more to us than a voice. There was not a word from anybody. The others might have been asleep, but I was awake. I listened, I listened on the watch for the sentence, for the word, that would give me the clue to the faint uneasiness inspired by this narrative that seemed to shape itself without human lips in the heavy night-air of the river.

". . . Yes — I let him run on," Marlow began again, "and think what he pleased about the powers that were behind me. I did! And there was nothing behind me! There was nothing but that wretched, old, mangled steamboat I was leaning against, while he talked fluently about 'the necessity for every man to get on.' 'And when one comes out here, you conceive, it is not to gaze at the moon.' Mr. Kurtz was a 'universal genius,' but even a genius would find it easier to work with 'adequate tools — intelligent men.' He did not make bricks — why, there was a physical impossibility in the way — as I was well aware; and if he did secretarial work for the manager, it was because 'no sensible man rejects wantonly the confidence of his superiors.' Did I see it? I saw it. What more did I want? What I really wanted was rivets, by heaven! Rivets. To get on with the work — to stop the hole. Rivets I wanted. There were cases of them down at the coast — cases — piled up — burst — split! You kicked a loose rivet at every second step in that station yard on the hillside. Rivets had rolled into the grove of death. You could fill your pockets with rivets for the trouble of stooping down — and there wasn't one rivet to be found where it was wanted. We had plates that would do, but nothing to fasten them with. And every week the messenger, a lone Negro, letter-bag on shoulder and staff in hand, left our station for the coast. And several times a week a coast caravan came in with trade goods — ghastly glazed calico that made you shudder only to look at it, glass beads, value about a penny a quart, confounded spotted cotton handkerchiefs. And no rivets. Three carriers could have brought all that was wanted to set that steamboat afloat.

"He was becoming confidential now, but I fancy my unresponsive attitude must have exasperated him at last, for he judged it necessary to inform me he feared neither God nor devil, let alone any mere man. I said I could see that very well, but what I wanted was a certain quantity of rivets — and rivets were what really Mr. Kurtz wanted, if

he had only known it. Now letters went to the coast every week. . . . 'My dear sir,' he cried, 'I write from dictation.' I demanded rivets. There was a way — for an intelligent man. He changed his manner [1]; became very cold, and suddenly began to talk about a hippopotamus; wondered whether sleeping on board the steamer (I stuck to my salvage night and day) I wasn't disturbed. There was an old hippo that had the bad habit of getting out on the bank and roaming at night over the station grounds. The pilgrims used to turn out in a body and empty every rifle they could lay hands on at him. Some even had sat up o' nights for him. All this energy was wasted, though. 'That animal has a charmed life,' he said; 'but you can say this only of brutes in this country. No man — you apprehend me? — no man here bears a charmed life.' He stood there for a moment in the moonlight with his delicate hooked nose set a little askew, and his mica eyes glittering without a wink, then, with a curt Good-night, he strode off. I could see he was disturbed and considerably puzzled, which made me feel more hopeful than I had been for days. It was a great comfort to turn from that chap to my influential friend, the battered, twisted, ruined, tin-pot steamboat. I clambered on board. She rang under my feet like an empty Huntley & Palmer biscuit-tin kicked along a gutter; she was nothing so solid

[1] Why?

in make, and rather less pretty in shape, but I had expended enough hard work on her to make me love her. No influential friend would have served me better. She had given me a chance to come out a bit — to find out what I could do. No, I don't like work. I had rather laze about and think of all the fine things that can be done. I don't like work — no man does — but I like what is in the work — the chance to find yourself. Your own reality — for yourself, not for others — what no other man can ever know. They can only see the mere show, and never can tell what it really means.

"I was not surprised to see somebody sitting aft, on the deck, with his legs dangling over the mud. You see I rather chummed with the few mechanics there were in that station, whom the other pilgrims naturally despised — on account of their imperfect manners, I suppose. This was the foreman — a boiler-maker by trade — a good worker. He was a lank, bony, yellow-faced man, with big intense eyes. His aspect was worried, and his head was as bald as the palm of my hand; but his hair in falling seemed to have stuck to his chin, and had prospered in the new locality, for his beard hung down to his waist. He was a widower with six young children (he had left them in charge of a sister of his to come out there), and the passion of his life was pigeon-flying. He was an enthusiast and a connoisseur. He would rave about pigeons.

After work hours he used sometimes to come over from his hut for a talk about his children and his pigeons; at work, when he had to crawl in the mud under the bottom of the steamboat, he would tie up that beard of his in a kind of white serviette he brought for the purpose. It had loops to go over his ears. In the evening he could be seen squatted on the bank rinsing that wrapper in the creek with great care, then spreading it solemnly on a bush to dry.

"I slapped him on the back and shouted 'We shall have rivets!' He scrambled to his feet exclaiming 'No! Rivets!' as though he couldn't believe his ears. Then in a low voice, 'You . . . eh?' I don't know why we behaved like lunatics. I put my finger to the side of my nose and nodded mysteriously. 'Good for you!' he cried, snapped his fingers above his head, lifting one foot. I tried a jig. We capered on the iron deck. A frightful clatter came out of that hulk, and the virgin forest on the other bank of the creek sent it back in a thundering roll upon the sleeping station. It must have made some of the pilgrims sit up in their hovels. A dark figure obscured the lighted doorway of the manager's hut, vanished, then, a second or so after, the doorway itself vanished too. We stopped, and the silence driven away by the stamping of our feet flowed back again from the recesses of the land. The great wall of vegetation, an exuberant and entangled mass of trunks, branches, leaves, boughs, festoons, motionless in the moonlight, was like a rioting invasion of soundless life, a rolling wave of plants, piled up, crested, ready to topple over the creek, to sweep every little man of us out of his little existence. And it moved not. A deadened burst of mighty splashes and snorts reached us from afar, as though an ichthyosaurus[1] had been taking a bath of glitter in the great river. 'After all,' said the boiler-maker in a reasonable tone, 'why shouldn't we get the rivets?' Why not, indeed! I did not know of any reason why we shouldn't. 'They'll come in three weeks,' I said confidently.

"But they didn't. Instead of rivets there came an invasion, an infliction, a visitation. It came in sections during the next three weeks, each section headed by a donkey carrying a white man in new clothes and tan shoes, bowing from that elevation right and left to the impressed pilgrims. A quarrelsome band of footsore sulky niggers trod on the heels of the donkey; a lot of tents, camp-stools, tin boxes, white cases, brown bales would be shot down in the courtyard, and the air of mystery would deepen a little over the muddle of the station. Five such instalments came, with their absurd air of disorderly flight with the loot of innumerable outfit shops and provision stores, that, one would think, they were lugging,

[1] ichthyosaurus: a prehistoric marine reptile.

after a raid, into the wilderness for equitable division. It was an inextricable mess of things decent in themselves but that human folly made look like the spoils of thieving.

"This devoted band called itself the Eldorado Exploring Expedition, and I believe they were sworn to secrecy. Their talk, however, was the talk of sordid buccaneers: it was reckless without hardihood, greedy without audacity, and cruel without courage; there was not an atom of foresight or of serious intention in the whole batch of them, and they did not seem aware these things are wanted for the work of the world. To tear treasure out of the bowels of the land was their desire, with no more moral purpose at the back of it than there is in burglars breaking into a safe. Who paid the expenses of the noble enterprise I don't know; but the uncle of our manager was leader of that lot.

"In exterior he resembled a butcher in a poor neighbourhood, and his eyes had a look of sleepy cunning. He carried his fat paunch with ostentation on his short legs, and during the time his gang infested the station spoke to no one but his nephew. You could see these two roaming about all day long with their heads close together in an everlasting confab.

"I had given up worrying myself about the rivets. One's capacity for that kind of folly is more limited than you would suppose. I said

Hang! — and let things slide. I had plenty of time for meditation, and now and then I would give some thought to Kurtz. I wasn't very interested in him. No. Still, I was curious to see whether this man, who had come out equipped with moral ideas of some sort, would climb to the top after all, and how he would set about his work when there."

II

"One evening as I was lying flat on the deck of my steamboat, I heard voices approaching — and there were the nephew and the uncle strolling along the bank. I laid my head on my arm again, and had nearly lost myself in a doze, when somebody said in my ear, as it were: 'I am as harmless as a little child, but I don't like to be dictated to. Am I the manager — or am I not? I was ordered to send him there. It's incredible.' . . . I became aware that the two were standing on the shore alongside the forepart of the steamboat, just below my head. I did not move; it did not occur to me to move: I was sleepy. 'It *is* unpleasant,' grunted the uncle. 'He has asked the Administration to be sent there,' said the other, 'with the idea of showing what he could do; and I was instructed accordingly. Look at the influence that man must have. Is it not frightful?' They both agreed it was frightful, then made several bizarre remarks: 'Make rain and fine weather — one man — the Council — by the nose' — bits of absurd sentences that got the better of my drowsiness, so that I had pretty near the whole of my wits about me when the uncle said, 'The climate may do away with this difficulty for you. Is he alone there?' 'Yes,' answered the manager; 'he sent his assistant down the river with a note to me in these terms: "Clear this poor devil out of the country, and don't bother sending more of that sort. I had rather be alone than have the kind of men you can dispose of with me." It was more than a year ago. Can you imagine such impudence?' 'Anything since then?' asked the other hoarsely. 'Ivory,' jerked the nephew; 'lots of it — prime sort — lots — most annoying, from him.' 'And with that?' questioned the heavy rumble. 'Invoice,' was the reply fired out, so to speak. Then silence. They had been talking about Kurtz.

"I was broad awake by this time, but, lying perfectly at ease, remained still, having no inducement to change my position. 'How did that ivory come all this way?' growled the elder man, who seemed very vexed. The other explained that it had come with a fleet of canoes in charge of an English half-caste clerk Kurtz had with him; that Kurtz had apparently intended to return himself, the station being by that time bare of goods and stores, but after coming three hundred miles, had suddenly decided to go back, which he started to do alone in a small dugout with four paddlers, leaving the half-caste to continue down the river with the ivory. The two fellows there seemed astounded at anybody attempting such a thing. They were at a loss for an adequate motive. As for me, I seemed to see Kurtz for the first time. It was a distinct glimpse: the dugout, four paddling savages, and the lone white man turning his back suddenly on the headquarters, on relief, on thoughts of home — perhaps; setting his face towards the depths of the wilderness, towards his empty and desolate station. I did not know the motive. Perhaps he was just simply a fine fellow who stuck to his work for its own sake. His name, you understand, had not been pronounced once. He was 'that man.' The half-caste, who, as far as I could see, had conducted a difficult trip with great prudence and pluck, was invariably alluded to as 'that scoundrel.' The 'scoundrel' had reported that the 'man' had been very ill — had recovered imperfectly. . . . The two below me moved away then a few paces, and strolled back and forth at some little distance. I heard: 'Military post — doctor — two hundred miles — quite alone now — unavoidable delays — nine months — no news — strange rumours.' They approached again, just as the manager was saying, 'No one, as far as I know, unless a species of wandering trader — a pestilential fellow, snapping ivory from the natives.' Who was it they were talking about now? I gathered in snatches that this was some man supposed to be in Kurtz's district, and of whom the manager did not approve. 'We will not be free from unfair competition till one of these fellows is hanged for an example, he said. 'Certainly,' grunted the other; 'get him hanged! Why not? Anything — anything can be done in this country. That's what I say; nobody here, you understand, *here,* can endanger your position. And why? You stand the climate — you outlast them all. The danger is in Europe; but there before I left I took care to — ' They moved off and whispered, then their voices rose again. 'The extraordinary series of delays is not my fault. I did my possible.' The fat man sighed, 'Very sad.' 'And the pestiferous absurdity of his talk,' continued the other; 'he bothered me enough when he was here. "Each station should be like a beacon on the road towards better things, a centre for trade of course, but also for humanising, improving, instructing." Conceive you — that ass! And he wants to be manager! No, it's — ' Here he got choked by excessive indignation, and I lifted my head the least bit. I was surprised to see how near they were — right under me. I could have spat upon their hats. They were looking on the ground, absorbed in thought. The manager was switching his leg with a slender twig: his sagacious relative lifted his head. 'You have been well since you came out this time?' he asked. The other gave a start. 'Who? I? Oh! Like a charm — like a charm. But the rest — oh, my goodness! All sick. They die so quick, too, that I haven't the time to send them out of the country — it's incredible!' 'H'm. Just so,' grunted the uncle. 'Ah! my boy, trust to this — I say, trust to this.'[1] I saw him extend his short flipper of an arm for a gesture that took in the forest, the creek, the mud, the river — seemed to beckon with a dishonouring flourish before the sunlit face of the land a treacherous appeal to the lurking death, to the hidden evil, to the profound darkness of its heart. It was so startling that I leaped to my feet and looked back at the edge of the forest, as though I had expected an answer of some sort to that black display of confidence. You know the foolish notions that come to one sometimes. The high stillness confronted these two figures with its ominous patience, waiting for the passing away of a fantastic invasion.

"They swore aloud together — out of sheer fright, I believe — then, pretending not to know anything of my existence, turned back to the station. The sun was low; and leaning forward side by side, they seemed to be tugging painfully uphill their two ridiculous shadows of unequal length, that trailed behind them slowly over the tall grass without bending a single blade.

"In a few days the Eldorado Ex-

[1] "Trust to this" for what?

pedition went into the patient wilderness, that closed upon it as the sea closes over a diver. Long afterwards the news came that all the donkeys were dead. I know nothing as to the fate of the less valuable animals. They, no doubt, like the rest of us, found what they deserved. I did not inquire. I was then rather excited at the prospect of meeting Kurtz very soon. When I say very soon I mean it comparatively. It was just two months from the day we left the creek when we came to the bank below Kurtz's station.

"Going up that river was like travelling back to the earliest beginnings of the world, when vegetation rioted on the earth and the big trees were kings. An empty stream, a great silence, an impenetrable forest. The air was warm, thick, heavy, sluggish. There was no joy in the brilliance of sunshine. The long stretches of the waterway ran on, deserted, into the gloom of overshadowed distances. On silvery sandbanks hippos and alligators sunned themselves side by side. The broadening waters flowed through a mob of wooded islands; you lost your way on that river as you would in a desert, and butted all day long against shoals, trying to find the channel, till you thought yourself bewitched and cut off for ever from everything you had known once — somewhere — far away — in another existence perhaps. There were moments when one's past came back to one, as it will sometimes when you have not a moment to spare to yourself; but it came in the shape of an unrestful and noisy dream, remembered with wonder amongst the overwhelming realities of this strange world of plants, and water, and silence. And this stillness of life did not in the least resemble a peace. It was the stillness of an implacable force brooding over an inscrutable intention. It looked at you with a vengeful aspect. I got used to it afterwards; I did not see it any more; I had no time. I had to keep guessing at the channel; I had to discern, mostly by inspiration, the signs of hidden banks; I watched for sunken stones; I was learning to clap my teeth smartly before my heart flew out, when I shaved by a fluke some infernal sly old snag that would have ripped the life out of the tin-pot steamboat and drowned all the pilgrims; I had to keep a look-out for the signs of dead wood we could cut up in the night for next day's steaming. When you have to attend to things of that sort, to the mere incidents of the surface, the reality — the reality, I tell you — fades. The inner truth is hidden — luckily, luckily. But I felt it all the same; I felt often its mysterious stillness watching me at my monkey tricks, just as it watches you fellows performing on your respective tight-ropes for — what is it? half a crown a tumble —"

"Try to be civil, Marlow," growled a voice, and I knew there was at least one listener awake besides myself.

"I beg your pardon. I forgot the heartache which makes up the rest of the price. And indeed what does the price matter, if the trick be well done? You do your tricks very well. And I didn't do badly either, since I managed not to sink that steamboat on my first trip. It's a wonder to me yet. Imagine a blindfolded man set to drive a van over a bad road. I sweated and shivered over that business considerably, I can tell you. After all, for a seaman, to scrape the bottom of the thing that's supposed to float all the time under his care is the unpardonable sin. No one may know of it, but you never forget the thump — eh? A blow on the very heart. You remember it, you dream of it, you wake up at night and think of it — years after — and go hot and cold all over. I don't pretend to say that steamboat floated all the time. More than once she had to wade for a bit, with twenty cannibals splashing around and pushing. We had enlisted some of these chaps on the way for a crew. Fine fellows — cannibals — in their place. They were men one could work with, and I am grateful to them. And, after all, they did not eat each other before my face: they had brought along a provision of hippo-meat which went rotten, and made the mystery of the wilderness stink in my nostrils. Phoo! I can sniff it now. I had the manager on board and three or four pilgrims with their staves — all complete. Sometimes we came upon a station close by the bank, clinging to the skirts of the unknown, and the white men rushing out of a tumble-down hovel, with great gestures of joy and surprise and welcome, seemed very strange — had the appearance of being held there captive by a spell. The word 'ivory' would ring in the air for a while — and on we went again into the silence, along empty reaches, round the still bends, between the high walls of our winding way, reverberating in hollow claps the ponderous beat of the stern-wheel. Trees, trees, millions of trees, massive, immense, running up high; and at their foot, hugging the bank against the stream, crept the little begrimed steamboat, like a sluggish beetle crawling on the floor of a lofty portico. It made you feel very small, very lost, and yet it was not altogether depressing, that feeling. After all, if you were small, the grimy beetle crawled on — which was just what you wanted it to do. Where the pilgrims imagined it crawled to I don't know. To some place where they expected to get something, I bet! For me it crawled towards Kurtz — exclusively; but when the steam-pipes started leaking we crawled very slow. The reaches opened before us and closed behind, as if the forest had stepped leisurely across the water to bar the way for our return. We penetrated deeper and

deeper into the heart of darkness. It was very quiet there. At night sometimes the roll of drums behind the curtain of trees would run up the river and remain sustained faintly, as if hovering in the air high over our heads, till the first break of day. Whether it meant war, peace, or prayer we could not tell. The dawns were heralded by the descent of a chill stillness; the woodcutters slept, their fires burned low; the snapping of a twig would make you start. We were wanderers on a prehistoric earth, on an earth that wore the aspect of an unknown planet. We could have fancied ourselves the first of men taking possession of an accursed inheritance, to be subdued at the cost of profound anguish and of excessive toil. But suddenly, as we struggled round a bend, there would be a glimpse of rush walls, of peaked grass-roofs, a burst of yells, a whirl of black limbs, a mass of hands clapping, of feet stamping, of bodies swaying, of eyes rolling, under the droop of heavy and motionless foliage. The steamer toiled along slowly on the edge of a black and incomprehensible frenzy. The prehistoric man was cursing us, praying to us, welcoming us — who could tell? We were cut off from the comprehension of our surroundings; we glided past like phantoms, wondering and secretly appalled, as sane men would be before an enthusiastic outbreak in a madhouse. We could not understand because we were too far and could not remember, because we were travelling in the night of first ages, of those ages that are gone, leaving hardly a sign — and no memories.

"The earth seemed unearthly. We are accustomed to look upon the shackled form of a conquered monster, but there — there you could look at a thing monstrous and free. It was unearthly, and the men were — No, they were not inhuman. Well, you know, that was the worst of it — this suspicion of their not being inhuman. It would come slowly to one. They howled and leaped, and spun, and made horrid faces; but what thrilled you was just the thought of their humanity — like yours — the thought of your remote kinship with this wild and passionate uproar. Ugly. Yes, it was ugly enough; but if you were man enough you would admit to yourself that there was in you just the faintest trace of a response to the terrible frankness of that noise, a dim suspicion of there being a meaning in it which you — you so remote from the night of first ages — could comprehend. And why not? The mind of man is capable of anything — because everything is in it, all the past as well as all the future. What was there after all? Joy, fear, sorrow, devotion, valour, rage — who can tell? — but truth — truth stripped of its cloak of time. Let the fool gape and shudder — the man knows, and can look on without a wink. But he must at least be as much of a man as these on the shore. He must meet that truth with his own true stuff — with his own inborn strength. Principles? Principles won't do. Acquisitions, clothes, pretty rags — rags that would fly off at the first good shake. No; you want a deliberate belief. An appeal to me in this fiendish row — is there? Very well; I hear; I admit, but I have a voice too, and for good or evil mine is the speech that cannot be silenced. Of course, a fool, what with sheer fright and fine sentiments, is always safe. Who's that grunting? You wonder I didn't go ashore for a howl and a dance? Well, no — I didn't. Fine sentiments, you say? Fine sentiments be hanged! I had no time. I had to mess about with white-lead and strips of woollen blanket helping to put bandages on those leaky steam-pipes — I tell you. I had to watch the steering, and circumvent those snags, and get the tin-pot along by hook or by crook. There was surface-truth enough in these things to save a wiser man. And between whiles I had to look after the savage who was fireman. He was an improved specimen; he could fire up a vertical boiler. He was there below me, and, upon my word, to look at him was as edifying as seeing a dog in a parody of breeches and a feather hat, walking on his hind legs. A few months of training had done for that really fine chap. He squinted at the steam-gauge and at the water-gauge with an evident effort of intrepidity — and he had filed teeth too, the poor devil, and the wool of his pate shaved into queer patterns, and three ornamental scars on each of his cheeks. He ought to have been clapping his hands and stamping his feet on the bank, instead of which he was hard at work, a thrall to strange witchcraft, full of improving knowledge. He was useful because he had been instructed; and what he knew was this — that should the water in that transparent thing disappear, the evil spirit inside the boiler would get angry through the greatness of his thirst, and take a terrible vengeance. So he sweated and fired up and watched the glass fearfully (with an impromptu charm, made of rags, tied to his arm, and a piece of polished bone, as big as a watch, stuck flatways through his lower lip), while the wooded banks slipped past us slowly, the short noise was left behind, the interminable miles of silence — and we crept on, towards Kurtz. But the snags were thick, the water was treacherous and shallow, the boiler seemed indeed to have a sulky devil in it, and thus neither that fireman nor I had any time to peer into our creepy thoughts.

"Some fifty miles below the Inner Station we came upon a hut of reeds, an inclined and melancholy pole, with the unrecognisable tatters of what had been a flag of some sort flying from it, and a neatly stacked wood-pile. This was unexpected. We came to the bank, and on the stack of firewood found a flat piece of board with some faded pencil-writing on it. When deciphered it said: 'Wood for you. Hurry up. Approach cautiously.' There was a signature, but it was illegible — not Kurtz — a much longer word. Hurry up. Where? Up the river? 'Approach cautiously.' We had not done so. But the warning could not have been meant for the place where it could be only found after approach. Something was wrong above. But what — and how much? That was the question. We commented adversely upon the imbecility of that telegraphic style. The bush around said nothing, and would not let us look very far, either. A torn curtain of red twill hung in the doorway of the hut, and flapped sadly in our faces. The dwelling was dismantled; but we could see a white man had lived there not very long ago. There remained a rude table — a plank on two posts; a heap of rubbish reposed in a dark corner, and by the door I picked up a book. It had lost its covers, and the pages had been thumbed into a state of extremely dirty softness; but the back had been lovingly stitched afresh with white cotton thread, which looked clean yet. It was an extraordinary find. Its title was, *An Inquiry into some Points of Seamanship,* by a man Towser, Towson — some such name — Master in His Majesty's Navy. The matter looked dreary reading enough, with illustrative diagrams and repulsive tables of figures, and the copy was sixty years old. I handled this amazing antiquity with the greatest possible tenderness, lest it should dissolve in my hands. Within, Towson or Towser was inquiring earnestly into the breaking strain of ships' chains and tackle, and other such matters. Not a very enthralling book; but at the first glance you could see there a singleness of intention, an honest concern for the right way of going to work, which made these humble pages, thought out so many years ago, luminous with another than a professional light. The simple old sailor, with his talk of chains and purchases, made me forget the jungle and the pilgrims in a delicious sensation of having come upon something unmistakably real. Such a book being there was wonderful enough; but still more astounding were the notes pencilled in the margin, and plainly referring to the text. I couldn't believe my eyes! They were in cipher! Yes, it looked like cipher. Fancy a man lugging with him a book of that description into this nowhere and studying it — and making notes — in cipher at that! It was an extravagant mystery.

"I had been dimly aware for some time of a worrying noise, and when I lifted my eyes I saw the wood-pile was gone, and the manager, aided by all the pilgrims, was shouting at me from the river-side. I slipped the book into my pocket. I assure you to leave off reading was like tearing myself away from the shelter of an old and solid friendship.

"I started the lame engine ahead. 'It must be this miserable trader — this intruder,' exclaimed the manager, looking back malevolently at the place we had left. 'He must be English,' I said. 'It will not save him from getting into trouble if he is not careful,' muttered the manager darkly. I observed with assumed innocence that no man was safe from trouble in this world.

"The current was more rapid now, the steamer seemed at her last gasp, the stern-wheel flopped languidly, and I caught myself listening on tiptoe for the next beat of the float, for in sober truth I expected the wretched thing to give up every moment. It was like watching the last flickers of a life. But still we crawled. Sometimes I would pick out a tree a little way ahead to measure our progress towards Kurtz by, but I lost it invariably before we got abreast. To keep the eyes so long on one thing was too much for human patience. The manager displayed a beautiful resignation. I fretted and fumed and took to arguing with myself whether or no I would talk openly with Kurtz; but before I could come to any conclusion it occurred to me that my speech or my silence, indeed any action of mine, would be a mere futility. What did it matter what any one knew or ignored? What did it matter who was manager? One gets sometimes such a flash of insight. The essentials of this affair lay deep under the surface, beyond my reach, and beyond my power of meddling.

"Towards the evening of the second day we judged ourselves about eight miles from Kurtz's station. I wanted to push on; but the manager looked grave, and told me the navigation up there was so dangerous that it would be advisable, the sun being very low already, to wait where we were till next morning. Moreover, he pointed out that if the warning to approach cautiously were to be followed, we must approach in daylight — not at dusk, or in the dark. This was sensible enough. Eight miles meant nearly three hours' steaming for us, and I could also see suspicious ripples at the upper end of the reach. Nevertheless, I was annoyed beyond expression at the delay, and most unreasonably too, since one night more could not matter much after so many months. As we had plenty of wood, and caution was the word, I brought up in the middle of the stream. The reach was narrow, straight, with high sides like a railway cutting. The dusk came gliding into it long before the sun had set. The current ran smooth and swift, but a dumb immobility sat on the banks. The living trees, lashed together by the creepers and every living bush of the undergrowth, might have been changed into stone, even to the slenderest twig, to the lightest leaf. It was not sleep — it seemed unnatural, like a state of trance. Not the faintest sound of any kind could be heard. You looked on amazed, and began to suspect yourself of being deaf — then the night came suddenly, and struck you blind as well. About three in the morning some large fish leaped, and the loud splash made me jump as though a gun had been fired. When the sun rose there was a white fog, very warm and clammy, and more blinding than the night. It did not shift or drive; it was just there, standing all round you like something solid. At eight or nine, perhaps, it lifted as a shutter lifts. We had a glimpse of the towering multitude of trees, of the immense matted jungle, with the blazing little ball of the sun hanging over it — all perfectly still — and then the white shutter came down again, smoothly, as if sliding in greased grooves. I ordered the chain, which we had begun to heave in, to be paid out again. Before it stopped running with a muffled rattle, a cry, a very loud cry, as of infinite desolation, soared slowly in the opaque air. It ceased. A complaining clamour, modulated in savage discords, filled our ears. The sheer unexpectedness of it made my hair stir under my cap. I don't know how it struck the others: to me it seemed as though the mist itself had screamed, so suddenly, and apparently from all sides at once, did this tumultuous and mournful uproar arise. It culminated in a hurried outbreak of almost intolerably excessive shrieking, which stopped short, leaving us stiffened in a variety of silly attitudes and obstinately listening to the nearly as appalling and excessive silence. 'Good God! What is the meaning — ?' stammered at my elbow one of the pilgrims — a little fat man, with sandy hair and red whiskers, who wore side-spring boots, and pink pyjamas tucked into his socks. Two others remained open-mouthed a whole minute, then dashed into the little cabin, to rush out incontinently and stand darting scared glances, with Winchesters [1] at 'ready' in their hands. What we could see was just the steamer we were on, her outlines blurred as though she had been on the point of dissolving, and a misty strip of water, perhaps two feet broad, around her — and that was all. The rest of the world was nowhere, as far as our eyes and ears were concerned. Just nowhere. Gone, disappeared; swept off without leaving a whisper or a shadow behind.

"I went forward, and ordered the chain to be hauled in short, so as to be ready to trip the anchor and move the steamboat at once if necessary. 'Will they attack?' whispered an awed voice. 'We will all be butchered in this fog,' murmured another. The faces twitched with the strain, the hands trembled slightly, the eyes forgot to wink. It was very curious to see the contrast of expressions of the white men and of the black fellows of our crew, who were as much strangers to that

part of the river as we, though their homes were only eight hundred miles away. The whites, of course greatly discomposed, had besides a curious look of being painfully shocked by such an outrageous row. The others had an alert, naturally interested expression; but their faces were essentially quiet, even those of the one or two who grinned as they hauled at the chain. Several exchanged short, grunting phrases, which seemed to settle the matter to their satisfaction. Their headman, a young, broad-chested black, severely draped in dark-blue fringed cloths, with fierce nostrils and his hair all done up artfully in oily ringlets, stood near me. 'Aha!' I said, just for good fellowship's sake. 'Catch 'im,' he snapped, with a bloodshot widening of his eyes and a flash of sharp teeth — 'catch 'im. Give 'im to us.' 'To you, eh?' I asked; 'what would you do with them?' 'Eat 'im!' he said curtly, and, leaning his elbow on the rail, looked out into the fog in a dignified and profoundly pensive attitude. I would no doubt have been properly horrified, had it not occurred to me that he and his chaps must be very hungry: that they must have been growing increasingly hungry for at least this month past. They had been engaged for six months (I don't think a single one of them had any clear idea of time, as we at the end of countless ages have. They still belonged to the beginnings of time — had no inherited experience to teach them,

[1] **Winchesters**: rifles.

as it were), and of course, as long as there was a piece of paper written over in accordance with some farcical law or other made down the river, it didn't enter anybody's head to trouble how they would live. Certainly they had brought with them some rotten hippo-meat, which couldn't have lasted very long, anyway, even if the pilgrims hadn't, in the midst of a shocking hullabaloo, thrown a considerable quantity of it overboard. It looked like a high-handed proceeding; but it was really a case of legitimate self-defence. You can't breathe dead hippo waking, sleeping, and eating, and at the same time keep your precarious grip on existence. Besides that, they had given them every week three pieces of brass wire, each about nine inches long; and the theory was they were to buy their provisions with that currency in river-side villages. You can see how *that* worked. There were either no villages, or the people were hostile, or the director, who like the rest of us fed out of tins, with an occasional old he-goat thrown in, didn't want to stop the steamer for some more or less recondite reasons. So, unless they swallowed the wire itself, or made loops of it to snare the fishes with, I don't see what good their extravagant salary could be to them. I must say it was paid with a regularity worthy of a large and honourable trading company. For the rest, the only thing to eat — though it didn't look eatable in the least — I saw in their possession was a few

lumps of some stuff like half-cooked dough, of a dirty lavender colour, they kept wrapped in leaves, and now and then swallowed a piece of, but so small that it seemed done more for the look of the thing than for any serious purpose of sustenance. Why in the name of all the gnawing devils of hunger they didn't go for us — they were thirty to five — and have a good tuck-in for once, amazes me now when I think of it. They were big powerful men, with not much capacity to weigh the consequences, with courage, with strength, even yet, though their skins were no longer glossy and their muscles no longer hard. And I saw that something restraining, one of those human secrets that baffle probability, had come into play there. I looked at them with a swift quickening of interest — not because it occurred to me I might be eaten by them before very long, though I own to you that just then I perceived — in a new light, as it were — how unwholesome the pilgrims looked, and I hoped, yes, I positively hoped, that my aspect was not so — what shall I say? — so — unappetising: a touch of fantastic vanity which fitted well with the dream-sensation that pervaded all my days at that time. Perhaps I had a little fever too. One can't live with one's finger everlastingly on one's pulse. I had often 'a little fever,' or a little touch of other things — the playful paw-strokes of the wilderness, the preliminary trifling before the more serious onslaught which came in due course. Yes; I looked at them as you would on any human being, with a curiosity of their impulses, motives, capacities, weaknesses, when brought to the test of an inexorable physical necessity. Restraint! What possible restraint? Was it superstition, disgust, patience, fear — or some kind of primitive honour? No fear can stand up to hunger, no patience can wear it out, disgust simply does not exist where hunger is; and as to superstition, beliefs, and what you may call principles, they are less than chaff in a breeze. Don't you know the devilry of lingering starvation, its exasperating torment, its black thoughts, its sombre and brooding ferocity? Well, I do. It takes a man all his inborn strength to fight hunger properly. It's really easier to face bereavement, dishonour, and the perdition of one's soul — than this kind of prolonged hunger. Sad, but true. And these chaps too had no earthly reason for any kind of scruple. Restraint! I would just as soon have expected restraint from a hyena prowling amongst the corpses of a battlefield. But there was the fact facing me — the fact dazzling, to be seen, like the foam on the depths of the sea, like a ripple on an unfathomable enigma, a mystery greater — when I thought of it — than the curious, inexplicable note of desperate grief in this savage clamour that had swept by us on the river-bank, behind the blind whiteness of the fog.

"Two pilgrims were quarrelling in hurried whispers as to which bank. 'Left.' 'No, no; how can you? Right, right, of course.' 'It is very serious,' said the manager's voice behind me; 'I would be desolated if anything should happen to Mr. Kurtz before we came up.' I looked at him, and had not the slightest doubt he was sincere. He was just the kind of man who would wish to preserve appearances. That was his restraint. But when he muttered something about going on at once, I did not even take the trouble to answer him. I knew, and he knew, that it was impossible. Were we to let go our hold of the bottom, we would be absolutely in the air — in space. We wouldn't be able to tell where we were going to — whether up or down stream, or across — till we fetched against one bank or the other — and then we wouldn't know at first which it was. Of course I made no move. I had no mind for a smash-up. You couldn't imagine a more deadly place for a shipwreck. Whether drowned at once or not, we were sure to perish speedily in one way or another. 'I authorise you to take all the risks,' he said, after a short silence. 'I refuse to take any,' I said shortly; which was just the answer he expected, though its tone might have surprised him. 'Well, I must defer to your judgment. You are captain,' he said, with marked civility. I turned my shoulder to him in sign of my appreciation, and looked into the fog. How long would it last? It was the most hopeless look-out.

The approach to this Kurtz grubbing for ivory in the wretched bush was beset by as many dangers as though he had been an enchanted princess sleeping in a fabulous castle. 'Will they attack, do you think?' asked the manager, in a confidential tone.

"I did not think they would attack, for several obvious reasons. The thick fog was one. If they left the bank in their canoes they would get lost in it, as we would be if we attempted to move. Still, I had also judged the jungle of both banks quite impenetrable — and yet eyes were in it, eyes that had seen us. The river-side bushes were certainly very thick; but the undergrowth behind was evidently penetrable. However, during the short lift I had seen no canoes anywhere in the reach — certainly not abreast of the steamer. But what made the idea of attack inconceivable to me was the nature of the noise — of the cries we had heard. They had not the fierce character boding of immediate hostile intention. Unexpected, wild, and violent as they had been, they had given me an irresistible impression of sorrow. The glimpse of the steamboat had for some reason filled those savages with unrestrained grief. The danger, if any, I expounded, was from our proximity to a great human passion let loose. Even extreme grief may ultimately vent itself in violence — but more generally takes the form of apathy. . . .

"You should have seen the pilgrims stare! They had no heart to grin, or even to revile me; but I believe they thought me gone mad — with fright, maybe. I delivered a regular lecture. My dear boys, it was no good bothering. Keep a look-out? Well, you may guess I watched the fog for the signs of lifting as a cat watches a mouse; but for anything else our eyes were of no more use to us than if we had been buried miles deep in a heap of cotton-wool. It felt like it too — choking, warm, stifling. Besides, all I said, though it sounded extravagant, was absolutely true to fact. What we afterwards alluded to as an attack was really an attempt at repulse. The action was very far from being aggressive — it was not even defensive, in the usual sense: it was undertaken under the stress of desperation, and in its essence was purely protective.

"It developed itself, I should say, two hours after the fog lifted, and its commencement was at a spot, roughly speaking, about a mile and a half below Kurtz's station. We had just floundered and flopped round a bend, when I saw an islet, a mere grassy hummock of bright green, in the middle of the stream. It was the only thing of the kind; but as we opened the reach more, I perceived it was the head of a long sandbank, or rather of a chain of shallow patches stretching down the middle of the river. They were discoloured, just awash, and the whole lot was seen just under the water, exactly as a man's backbone is seen running down the middle of his back under the skin. Now, as far as I did see, I could go to the right or to the left of this. I didn't know either channel, of course. The banks looked pretty well alike, the depth appeared the same; but as I had been informed the station was on the west side, I naturally headed for the western passage.

"No sooner had we fairly entered it than I became aware it was much narrower than I had supposed. To the left of us there was the long uninterrupted shoal, and to the right a high steep bank heavily overgrown with bushes. Above the bush the trees stood in serried ranks. The twigs overhung the current thickly, and from distance to distance a large limb of some tree projected rigidly over the stream. It was then well on in the afternoon, the face of the forest was gloomy, and a broad strip of shadow had already fallen on the water. In this shadow we steamed up — very slowly, as you may imagine. I sheered her well inshore — the water being deepest near the bank, as the sounding-pole informed me.

"One of my hungry and forbearing friends was sounding in the bows just below me. This steamboat was exactly like a decked scow. On the deck there were two little teak-wood houses, with doors and windows. The boiler was in the fore-end, and the machinery right astern. Over the whole there was a light roof, supported on stanchions. The funnel projected through that roof, and in front of the funnel a small cabin built of light planks served for a pilot-house. It contained a couch, two camp-stools, a loaded Martini-Henry [1] leaning in one corner, a tiny table, and the steering-wheel. It had a wide door in front and a broad shutter at each side. All these were always thrown open, of course. I spent my days perched up there on the extreme fore-end of that roof, before the door. At night I slept, or tried to, on the couch. An athletic black belonging to some coast tribe, and educated by my poor predecessor, was the helmsman. He sported a pair of brass earrings, wore a blue cloth wrapper from the waist to the ankles, and thought all the world of himself. He was the most unstable kind of fool I had ever seen. He steered with no end of a swagger while you were by; but if he lost sight of you, he became instantly the prey of an abject funk,[2] and would let that cripple of a steamboat get the upper hand of him in a minute.

"I was looking down at the sounding-pole, and feeling much annoyed to see at each try a little more of it stick out of that river, when I saw my poleman give up the business suddenly, and stretch himself flat on the deck, without even taking the trouble to haul his pole in. He kept hold on it though,

[1] **Martini-Henry:** a common military rifle of the time.
[2] **funk:** fear.

and it trailed in the water. At the same time the fireman, whom I could also see below me, sat down abruptly before his furnace and ducked his head. I was amazed. Then I had to look at the river mighty quick, because there was a snag in the fairway. Sticks, little sticks, were flying about — thick: they were whizzing before my nose, dropping below me, striking behind me against my pilot-house. All this time the river, the shore, the woods, were very quiet — perfectly quiet. I could only hear the heavy splashing thump of the stern-wheel and the patter of these things. We cleared the snag clumsily. Arrows, by Jove! We were being shot at! I stepped in quickly to close the shutter on the land-side. That fool-helmsman, his hands on the spokes, was lifting his knees high, stamping his feet, champing his mouth, like a reined-in horse. Confound him! And we were staggering within ten feet of the bank. I had to lean right out to swing the heavy shutter, and I saw a face amongst the leaves on the level with my own, looking at me very fierce and steady; and then suddenly, as though a veil had been removed from my eyes, I made out, deep in the tangled gloom, naked breasts, arms, legs, glaring eyes — the bush was swarming with human limbs in movement, glistening, of bronze colour. The twigs shook, swayed, and rustled, the arrows flew out of them, and then the shutter came to. 'Steer her straight,' I said to the helmsman. He held his head rigid, face forward; but his eyes rolled, he kept on lifting and setting down his feet gently, his mouth foamed a little. 'Keep quiet!' I said in a fury. I might just as well have ordered a tree not to sway in the wind. I darted out. Below me there was a great scuffle of feet on the iron deck; confused exclamations; a voice screamed, 'Can you turn back?' I caught sight of a V-shaped ripple on the water ahead. What? Another snag! A fusillade burst out under my feet. The pilgrims had opened with their Winchesters, and were simply squirting lead into that bush. A deuce of a lot of smoke came up and drove slowly forward. I swore at it. Now I couldn't see the ripple or the snag either. I stood in the doorway, peering, and the arrows came in swarms. They might have been poisoned, but they looked as though they wouldn't kill a cat. The bush began to howl. Our wood-cutters raised a warlike whoop; the report of a rifle just at my back deafened me. I glanced over my shoulder, and the pilot-house was yet full of noise and smoke when I made a dash at the wheel. The fool-nigger had dropped everything, to throw the shutter open and let off that Martini-Henry. We stood before the wide opening, glaring, and I yelled at him to come back, while I straightened the sudden twist out of that steamboat. There was no room to turn even if I had wanted to, the snag was somewhere very near ahead in that confounded smoke, there was no time to lose, so I just crowded her into the bank — right into the bank, where I knew the water was deep.

"We tore slowly along the overhanging bushes in a whirl of broken twigs and flying leaves. The fusillade below stopped short, as I had foreseen it would when the squirts got empty. I threw my head back to a glinting whizz that traversed the pilot-house, in at one shutter-hole and out at the other. Looking past that mad helmsman, who was shaking the empty rifle and yelling at the shore, I saw vague forms of men running bent double, leaping, gliding, distinct, incomplete, evanescent. Something big appeared in the air before the shutter, the rifle went overboard, and the man stepped back swiftly, looked at me over his shoulder in an extraordinary, profound, familiar manner, and fell upon my feet. The side of his head hit the wheel twice, and the end of what appeared a long cane clattered round and knocked over a little camp-stool. It looked as though after wrenching that thing from somebody ashore he had lost his balance in the effort. The thin smoke had blown away, we were clear of the snag, and looking ahead I could see that in another hundred yards or so I would be free to sheer off, away from the bank; but my feet felt so very warm and wet that I had to look down. The man had rolled on his back and stared straight up at me; both his hands clutched that cane. It was the shaft of a spear that, either thrown or lunged through the opening, had caught him in the side just below the ribs; the blade had gone in out of sight, after making a frightful gash; my shoes were full; a pool of blood lay very still, gleaming dark-red under the wheel; his eyes shone with an amazing lustre. The fusillade burst out again. He looked at me anxiously, gripping the spear like something precious, with an air of being afraid I would try to take it away from him. I had to make an effort to free my eyes from his gaze and attend to the steering. With one hand I felt above my head for the line of the steam whistle, and jerked out screech after screech hurriedly. The tumult of angry and warlike yells was checked instantly, and then from the depths of the woods went out such a tremulous and prolonged wail of mournful fear and utter despair as may be imagined to follow the flight of the last hope from the earth. There was a great commotion in the bush; the shower of arrows stopped, a few dropping shots rang out sharply — then silence, in which the languid beat of the stern-wheel came plainly to my ears. I put the helm hard a-starboard at the moment when the pilgrim in pink pyjamas, very hot and agitated, appeared in the doorway. 'The manager sends me — ' he began in an official tone, and stopped short. 'Good God!' he said, glaring at the wounded man.

"We two whites stood over him, and his lustrous and inquiring glance enveloped us both. I declare it looked as though he would presently put to us some question in an understandable language; but he died without uttering a sound, without moving a limb, without twitching a muscle. Only in the very last moment, as though in response to some sign we could not see, to some whisper we could not hear, he frowned heavily, and that frown gave to his black death-mask an inconceivably sombre, brooding, and menacing expression. The lustre of inquiring glance faded swiftly into vacant glassiness. 'Can you steer?' I asked the agent eagerly. He looked very dubious; but I made a grab at his arm, and he understood at once I meant him to steer whether or no. To tell you the truth, I was morbidly anxious to change my shoes and socks. 'He is dead,' murmured the fellow, immensely impressed. 'No doubt about it,' said I, tugging like mad at the shoe-laces. 'And by the way, I suppose Mr. Kurtz is dead as well by this time.'

"For the moment that was the dominant thought. There was a sense of extreme disappointment, as though I had found out I had been striving after something altogether without a substance. I couldn't have been more disgusted if I had travelled all this way for the sole purpose of talking with Mr. Kurtz. Talking with . . . I flung one shoe overboard, and became aware that that was exactly what I had been looking forward to — a talk with Kurtz. I made the strange discovery that I had never imagined him as doing, you know, but as discoursing. I didn't say to myself, 'Now I will never see him,' or 'Now I will never shake him by the hand,' but, 'Now I will never hear him.' The man presented himself as a voice. Not of course that I did not connect him with some sort of action. Hadn't I been told in all the tones of jealousy and admiration that he had collected, bartered, swindled, or stolen more ivory than all the other agents together? That was not the point. The point was in his being a gifted creature, and that of all his gifts the one that stood out pre-eminently, that carried with it a sense of real presence, was his ability to talk, his words — the gift of expression, the bewildering, the illuminating, the most exalted and the most contemptible, the pulsating stream of light, or the deceitful flow from the heart of an impenetrable darkness.

"The other shoe went flying unto the devil-god of that river. I thought, By Jove! it's all over. We are too late; he has vanished — the gift has vanished, by means of some spear, arrow, or club. I will never hear that chap speak after all — and my sorrow had a startling extravagance of emotion, even such as I had noticed in the howling sorrow of these savages in the bush. I couldn't have felt more of lonely desolation somehow, had I been robbed of a belief or had missed my destiny in life. . . . Why do you sigh in this beastly way, somebody? Absurd? Well, absurd. Good Lord! mustn't a man ever — Here, give me some tobacco." . . .

There was a pause of profound stillness, then a match flared, and Marlow's lean face appeared, worn, hollow, with downward folds and dropped eyelids, with an aspect of concentrated attention; and as he took vigorous draws at his pipe, it seemed to retreat and advance out of the night in the regular flicker of the tiny flame. The match went out.

"Absurd!" he cried. "This is the worst of trying to tell. . . . Here you all are, each moored with two good addresses, like a hulk with two anchors, a butcher round one corner, a policeman round another, excellent appetites, and temperature normal — you hear — normal from year's end to year's end. And you say, Absurd! Absurd be — exploded! Absurd! My dear boys, what can you expect from a man who out of sheer nervousness had just flung overboard a pair of new shoes? Now I think of it, it is amazing I did not shed tears. I am, upon the whole, proud of my fortitude. I was cut to the quick at the idea of having lost the inestimable privilege of listening to the gifted Kurtz. Of course I was wrong. The privilege was waiting for me. Oh

yes, I heard more than enough. And I was right, too. A voice. He was very little more than a voice. And I heard — him — it — this voice — other voices — all of them were so little more than voices — and the memory of that time itself lingers around me, impalpable, like a dying vibration of one immense jabber, silly, atrocious, sordid, savage, or simply mean, without any kind of sense. Voices voices — even the girl herself — now — "

He was silent for a long time.

"I laid the ghost of his gifts at last with a lie," he began suddenly. "Girl! What? Did I mention a girl? Oh, she is out of it — completely. They — the women I mean — are out of it — should be out of it. We must help them to stay in that beautiful world of their own, lest ours gets worse. Oh, she had to be out of it. You should have heard the disinterred body of Mr. Kurtz saying, 'My Intended.' You would have perceived directly then how completely she was out of it. And the lofty frontal bone of Mr. Kurtz! They say the hair goes on growing sometimes, but this — ah — specimen was impressively bald. The wilderness had patted him on the head, and, behold, it was like a ball — an ivory ball; it had caressed him, and — lo! — he had withered; it had taken him, loved him, embraced him, got into his veins, consumed his flesh, and sealed his soul to its own by the inconceivable ceremonies of some devilish initiation. He was its spoiled and pampered favourite. Ivory? I should think so. Heaps of it, stacks of it. The old mud shanty was bursting with it. You would think there was not a single tusk left either above or below the ground in the whole country. 'Mostly fossil,' the manager had remarked disparagingly. It was no more fossil than I am; but they call it fossil when it is dug up. It appears these niggers do bury the tusks sometimes — but evidently they couldn't bury this parcel deep enough to save the gifted Mr. Kurtz from his fate. We filled the steamboat with it, and had to pile a lot on the deck. Thus he could see and enjoy as long as he could see, because the appreciation of this favour had remained with him to the last. You should have heard him say, 'My ivory.' Oh yes, I heard him. 'My Intended, my ivory, my station, my river, my — ' everything belonged to him. It made me hold my breath in expectation of hearing the wilderness burst into a prodigious peal of laughter that would shake the fixed stars in their places. Everything belonged to him — but that was a trifle. The thing was to know what he belonged to, how many powers of darkness claimed him for their own. That was the reflection that made you creepy all over. It was impossible — it was not good for one either — trying to imagine. He had taken a high seat amongst the devils of the land — I mean literally. You can't understand. How could you? — with solid pavement under your feet, surrounded by kind neighbours ready to cheer you or to fall on you, stepping delicately between the butcher and the policeman, in the holy terror of scandal and gallows and lunatic asylums — how can you imagine what particular region of the first ages a man's untrammelled feet may take him into by the way of solitude — utter solitude without a policeman — by the way of silence — utter silence, where no warning voice of a kind neighbour can be heard whispering of public opinion? These little things make all the great difference. When they are gone you must fall back upon your own innate strength, upon your own capacity for faithfulness. Of course you may be too much of a fool to go wrong — too dull even to know you are being assaulted by the powers of darkness. I take it, no fool ever made a bargain for his soul with the devil: the fool is too much of a fool, or the devil too much of a devil — I don't know which. Or you may be such a thunderingly exalted creature as to be altogether deaf and blind to anything but heavenly sights and sounds. Then the earth for you is only a standing place — and whether to be like this is your loss or your gain I won't pretend to say. But most of us are neither one nor the other. The earth for us is a place to live in, where we must put up with sights, with sounds, with smells, too, by Jove! — breathe dead hippo, so to speak, and not be contaminated. And there, don't you see? your strength comes in, the faith in your ability for the digging of unostentatious holes to bury the stuff in — your power of devotion, not to yourself, but to an obscure, back-breaking business. And that's difficult enough. Mind, I am not trying to excuse or even explain — I am trying to account to myself for — for — Mr. Kurtz — for the shade of Mr. Kurtz. This initiated wraith from the back of Nowhere honoured me with its amazing confidence before it vanished altogether. This was because it could speak English to me. The original Kurtz had been educated partly in England, and — as he was good enough to say himself — his sympathies were in the right place. His mother was half-English, his father was half-French. All Europe contributed to the making of Kurtz; and by and by I learned that, most appropriately, the International Society for the Suppression of Savage Customs had entrusted him with the making of a report, for its future guidance. And he had written it too. I've seen it. I've read it. It was eloquent, vibrating with eloquence, but too high-strung, I think. Seventeen pages of close writing he had found time for! But this must have been before his — let us say — nerves went wrong, and caused him to preside at certain midnight dances ending with unspeakable rites, which — as far as I reluctantly gathered from what I heard at vari-

ous times — were offered up to him — do you understand? [1] — to Mr. Kurtz himself. But it was a beautiful piece of writing. The opening paragraph, however, in the light of later information, strikes me now as ominous. He began with the argument that we whites, from the point of development we had arrived at, 'must necessarily appear to them [savages] in the nature of supernatural beings — we approach them with the might as of a deity,' and so on, and so on. 'By the simple exercise of our will we can exert a power for good practically unbounded,' etc. etc. From that point he soared and took me with him. The peroration was magnificent, though difficult to remember, you know. It gave me the notion of an exotic Immensity ruled by an august Benevolence. It made me tingle with enthusiasm. This was the unbounded power of eloquence — of words — of burning noble words.[2] There were no practical hints to interrupt the magic current of phrases, unless a kind of note at the foot of the last page, scrawled evidently much later, in an unsteady hand, may be regarded as the exposition of a method. It was very simple, and at the end of that moving appeal to every altruistic sentiment it blazed at you, luminous and terrifying, like a flash of lightning in a serene sky: 'Exterminate all the brutes!' The curious

[1] Do *you* understand?
[2] Remember what Marlow has designated as Kurtz's principal gift.

part was that he had apparently forgotten all about that valuable postscriptum, because, later on, when he in a sense came to himself, he repeatedly entreated me to take good care of 'my pamphlet' (he called it), as it was sure to have in the future a good influence upon his career. I had full information about all these things, and, besides, as it turned out, I was to have the care of his memory. I've done enough for it to give me the indisputable right to lay it, if I choose, for an everlasting rest in the dustbin of progress, amongst all the sweepings and, figuratively speaking, all the dead cats of civilisation. But then, you see, I can't choose. He won't be forgotten. Whatever he was, he was not common. He had the power to charm or frighten rudimentary souls into an aggravated witch-dance in his honour; he could also fill the small souls of the pilgrims with bitter misgivings: he had one devoted friend at least, and he had conquered one soul in the world that was neither rudimentary nor tainted with self-seeking. No; I can't forget him, though I am not prepared to affirm the fellow was exactly worth the life we lost in getting to him. I missed my late helmsman awfully — I missed him even while his body was still lying in the pilot-house. Perhaps you will think it passing strange this regret for a savage who was no more account than a grain of sand in a black Sahara. Well, don't you see, he had done something, he had steered; for months I had him at my back — a help — an instrument. It was a kind of partnership. He steered for me — I had to look after him, I worried about his deficiencies, and thus a subtle bond had been created, of which I only became aware when it was suddenly broken. And the intimate profundity of that look he gave me when he received his hurt remains to this day in my memory — like a claim of distant kinship affirmed in a supreme moment.

"Poor fool! If he had only left that shutter alone. He had no restraint, no restraint — just like Kurtz — a tree swayed by the wind. As soon as I had put on a dry pair of slippers, I dragged him out, after first jerking the spear out of his side, which operation I confess I performed with my eyes shut tight. His heels leaped together over the little doorstep; his shoulders were pressed to my breast; I hugged him from behind desperately. Oh! he was heavy, heavy; heavier than any man on earth, I should imagine. Then without more ado I tipped him overboard. The current snatched him as though he had been a wisp of grass, and I saw the body roll over twice before I lost sight of it for ever. All the pilgrims and the manager were then congregated on the awning-deck about the pilot-house, chattering at each other like a flock of excited magpies, and there was a scandalised murmur at my heartless promptitude. What they wanted to keep that body hanging about for I can't guess. Embalm it, maybe. But I had also heard another, and a very ominous, murmur on the deck below. My friends the wood-cutters were likewise scandalised, and with a better show of reason — though I admit that the reason itself was quite inadmissible. Oh, quite! I had made up my mind that if my late helmsman was to be eaten, the fishes alone should have him. He had been a very second-rate helmsman while alive, but now he was dead he might have become a first-class temptation, and possibly cause some startling trouble. Besides, I was anxious to take the wheel, the man in pink pyjamas showing himself a hopeless duffer at the business.

"This I did directly the simple funeral was over. We were going half-speed, keeping right in the middle of the stream, and I listened to the talk about me. They had given up Kurtz, they had given up the station; Kurtz was dead, and the station had been burnt — and so on — and so on. The red-haired pilgrim was beside himself with the thought that at least this poor Kurtz had been properly revenged. 'Say! We must have made a glorious slaughter of them in the bush. Eh? What do you think? Say?' He positively danced, the bloodthirsty little gingery beggar. And he had nearly fainted when he saw the wounded man! I could not help saying, 'You made a glorious lot of smoke, anyhow.' I had seen, from the way the tops of the bushes rustled and flew,

that almost all the shots had gone too high. You can't hit anything unless you take aim and fire from the shoulder; but these chaps fired from the hip with their eyes shut. The retreat, I maintained — and I was right — was caused by the screeching of the steam-whistle. Upon this they forgot Kurtz, and began to howl at me with indignant protests.

"The manager stood by the wheel murmuring confidently about the necessity of getting well away down the river before dark at all events, when I saw in the distance a clearing on the river-side and the outlines of some sort of building. 'What's this?' I asked. He clapped his hands in wonder. 'The station!' he cried. I edged in at once, still going half-speed.

"Through my glasses I saw the slope of a hill interspersed with rare trees and perfectly free from undergrowth. A long decaying building on the summit was half buried in the high grass; the large holes in the peaked roof gaped black from afar; the jungle and the woods made a background. There was no enclosure or fence of any kind; but there had been one apparently, for near the house half a dozen slim posts remained in a row, roughly trimmed, and with their upper ends ornamented with round carved balls. The rails, or whatever there had been between, had disappeared. Of course the forest surrounded all that. The river-bank was clear, and on the

water side I saw a white man under a hat like a cart-wheel beckon-
ing persistently with his whole arm.
Examining the edge of the forest
above and below, I was almost certain I could see movements — human forms gliding here and there.
I steamed past prudently, then
stopped the engines and let her
drift down. The man on the shore
began to shout, urging us to land.
'We have been attacked,' screamed
the manager. 'I know — I know.
It's all right,' yelled back the other,
as cheerful as you please. 'Come
along. It's all right. I am glad.'

"His aspect reminded me of
something I had seen — something
funny I had seen somewhere. As
I manœuvred to get alongside, I
was asking myself, 'What does this
fellow look like?' Suddenly I got
it. He looked like a harlequin. His
clothes had been made of some
stuff that was brown holland
probably, but it was covered with
patches all over, with bright
patches, blue, red, and yellow — patches on the back, patches
on the front, patches on elbows, on
knees; coloured binding round his
jacket, scarlet edging at the bottom of his trousers; and the sunshine made him look extremely gay
and wonderfully neat withal, because you could see how beautifully all this patching had been
done. A beardless, boyish face, very
fair, no features to speak of, nose
peeling, little blue eyes, smiles and
frowns chasing each other over that
open countenance like sunshine and

shadow on the wind-swept plain.
'Look out, captain!' he cried;
'there's a snag lodged in here last
night.' What! Another snag? I confess I swore shamefully. I had
nearly holed my cripple, to finish
off that charming trip. The harlequin on the bank turned his little
pug nose up to me. 'You English?'
he asked, all smiles. 'Are you?' I
shouted from the wheel. The smiles
vanished, and he shook his head
as if sorry for my disappointment.
Then he brightened up. 'Never
mind!' he cried encouragingly. 'Are
we in time?' I asked. 'He is up
there,' he replied, with a toss of the
head up the hill, and becoming
gloomy all of a sudden. His face
was like the autumn sky, overcast
one moment and bright the next.

"When the manager, escorted by
the pilgrims, all of them armed to
the teeth, had gone to the house,
this chap came on board. 'I say, I
don't like this. These natives are
in the bush,' I said. He assured me
earnestly it was all right. 'They are
simple people,' he added; 'well, I
am glad you came. It took me all
my time to keep them off.' 'But you
said it was all right,' I cried. 'Oh,
they meant no harm,' he said; and
as I stared he corrected himself,
'Not exactly.' Then vivaciously,
'My faith, your pilot-house wants a
clean up!' In the next breath he
advised me to keep enough steam
on the boiler to blow the whistle
in case of any trouble. 'One good
screech will do more for you than
all your rifles. They are simple

people,' he repeated. He rattled away at such a rate he quite overwhelmed me. He seemed to be trying to make up for lots of silence, and actually hinted, laughing, that such was the case. 'Don't you talk with Mr. Kurtz?' I said. 'You don't talk with that man — you listen to him,' he exclaimed with severe exaltation. 'But now —' He waved his arm, and in the twinkling of an eye was in the uttermost depths of despondency. In a moment he came up again with a jump, possessed himself of both my hands, shook them continuously, while he gabbled: 'Brother sailor . . . honour . . . pleasure . . . delight . . . introduce myself . . . . Russian . . . son of an arch-priest . . . Government of Tambov . . . What? Tobacco! English tobacco; the excellent English tobacco! Now, that's brotherly. Smoke? Where's a sailor that does not smoke?'

"The pipe soothed him, and gradually I made out he had run away from school, had gone to sea in a Russian ship; ran away again; served some time in English ships; was now reconciled with the archpriest. He made a point of that. But when one is young one must see things, gather experience, ideas; enlarge the mind.' 'Here!' I interrupted. 'You can never tell! Here I met Mr. Kurtz,' he said, youthfully solemn and reproachful. I held my tongue after that. It appears he had persuaded a Dutch trading-house on the coast to fit him out with stores and goods, and

had started for the interior with a light heart, and no more idea of what would happen to him than a baby. He had been wandering about that river for nearly two years alone, cut off from everybody and everything. 'I am not so young as I look. I am twenty-five,' he said. 'At first old Van Shuyten would tell me to go to the devil,' he narrated with keen enjoyment; 'but I stuck to him, and talked and talked, till at last he got afraid I would talk the hind-leg off his favourite dog, so he gave me some cheap things and a few guns, and told me he hoped he would never see my face again. Good old Dutchman, Van Shuyten. I sent him one small lot of ivory a year ago, so that he can't call me a little thief when I get back. I hope he got it. And for the rest I don't care. I had some wood stacked for you. That was my old house. Did you see?'

"I gave him Towson's book. He made as though he would kiss me, but restrained himself. 'The only book I had left, and I thought I had lost it,' he said, looking at it ecstatically. 'So many accidents happen to a man going about alone, you know. Canoes get upset sometimes — and sometimes you've got to clear out so quick when the people get angry.' He thumbed the pages. 'You made notes in Russian?' I asked. He nodded. 'I thought they were written in cipher,' I said. He laughed, then became serious. 'I had lots of trouble to keep these people off,' he

said. 'Did they want to kill you?'
I asked. 'Oh no!' he cried, and
checked himself. 'Why did they attack us?' I pursued. He hesitated,
then said shamefacedly, 'They
don't want him to go.' 'Don't
they?' I said curiously. He nodded
a nod full of mystery and wisdom.
'I tell you,' he cried, 'this man has
enlarged my mind.' He opened his
arms wide, staring at me with his
little blue eyes that were perfectly
round." [1]

III

"I looked at him, lost in astonishment. There he was before me, in
motley,[2] as though he had ab-
sconded from a troupe of mimes,
enthusiastic, fabulous. His very existence was improbable, inexplicable, and altogether bewildering.
He was an insoluble problem. It
was inconceivable how he had existed, how he had succeeded in getting so far, how he had managed
to remain — why he did not instantly disappear. 'I went a little
farther,' he said, 'then still a little
farther — till I had gone so far that
I don't know how I'll ever get back.
Never mind. Plenty time. I can
manage. You take Kurtz away
quick — quick — I tell you.' The
glamour of youth enveloped his
particoloured rags, his destitution,

his loneliness, the essential desolation of his futile wanderings.
For months — for years — his life
hadn't been worth a day's purchase;
and there he was gallantly, thought-
lessly alive, to all appearance in-
destructible solely by the virtue of
his few years and of his unreflect-
ing audacity. I was seduced into
something like admiration — like
envy. Glamour urged him on,
glamour kept him unscathed. He
surely wanted nothing from the
wilderness but space to breathe in
and to push on through. His need
was to exist, and to move onwards
at the greatest possible risk, and
with a maximum of privation. If
the absolutely pure, uncalculating,
unpractical spirit of adventure had
ever ruled a human being, it ruled
this be-patched youth. I almost envied him the possession of this modest and clear flame. It seemed to
have consumed all thought of self
so completely, that, even while he
was talking to you, you forgot that
it was he — the man before your
eyes — who had gone through these
things. I did not envy him his devotion to Kurtz, though. He had
not meditated over it. It came to
him, and he accepted it with a sort
of eager fatalism. I must say that
to me it appeared about the most
dangerous thing in every way he
had come upon so far.
"They had come together un-
avoidably, like two ships becalmed
near each other, and lay rubbing
sides at last. I suppose Kurtz
wanted an audience, because on a

---

[1] Does Marlow's word picture of
the young Russian suggest anything
about the latter's mind?

[2] motley: the many-colored costume
of a court fool or jester.

certain occasion, when encamped in the forest, they had talked all night, or more probably Kurtz had talked. 'We talked of everything,' he said, quite transported at the recollection. 'I forgot there was such a thing as sleep. The night did not seem to last an hour. Everything! Everything! . . . Of love too.' 'Ah, he talked to you of love!' I said, much amused. 'It isn't what you think,' he cried, almost passionately. 'It was in general. He made me see things — things.'

"He threw his arms up. We were on deck at the time, and the headman of my wood-cutters, lounging near by, turned upon him his heavy and glittering eyes. I looked around, and I don't know why, but I assure you that never, never before, did this land, this river, this jungle, the very arch of this blazing sky, appear to me so hopeless and so dark, so impenetrable to human thought, so pitiless to human weakness. 'And, ever since, you have been with him, of course?' I said.

"On the contrary. It appears their intercourse had been very much broken by various causes. He had, as he informed me proudly, managed to nurse Kurtz through two illnesses (he alluded to it as you would to some risky feat), but as a rule Kurtz wandered alone, far in the depths of the forest. 'Very often coming to this station, I had to wait days and days before he would turn up,' he said. 'Ah, it was worth waiting for! — sometimes.' 'What was he doing? exploring or

what?' I asked. 'Oh yes, of course'; he had discovered lots of villages, a lake too — he did not know exactly in what direction; it was dangerous to inquire too much — but mostly his expeditions had been for ivory. 'But he had no goods to trade with by that time,' I objected. 'There's a good lot of cartridges left even yet,' he answered, looking away. 'To speak plainly, he raided the country,' I said. He nodded. 'Not alone, surely!' He muttered something about the villages round that lake. 'Kurtz got the tribe to follow him, did he?' I suggested. He fidgeted a little. 'They adored him,' he said. The tone of these words was so extraordinary that I looked at him searchingly. It was curious to see his mingled eagerness and reluctance to speak of Kurtz. The man filled his life, occupied his thoughts, swayed his emotions. 'What can you expect?' he burst out; 'he came to them with thunder and lightning, you know — and they had never seen anything like it — and very terrible. He could be very terrible. You can't judge Mr. Kurtz as you would an ordinary man. No, no, no! Now — just to give you an idea — I don't mind telling you, he wanted to shoot me too one day — but I don't judge him.' 'Shoot you!' I cried. 'What for?' 'Well, I had a small lot of ivory the chief of that village near my house gave me. You see I used to shoot game for them. Well, he wanted it, and wouldn't hear reason. He declared he would shoot me unless I gave him the ivory and then cleared out of the country, because he could do so, and had a fancy for it, and there was nothing on earth to prevent him killing whom he jolly well pleased. And it was true too. I gave him the ivory. What did I care! But I didn't clear out. No, no. I couldn't leave him. I had to be careful, of course, till we got friendly again for a time. He had his second illness then. Afterwards I had to keep out of the way; but I didn't mind. He was living for the most part in those villages on the lake. When he came down to the river, sometimes he would take to me, and sometimes it was better for me to be careful. This man suffered too much. He hated all this, and somehow he couldn't get away. When I had a chance I begged him to try and leave while there was time; I offered to go back with him. And he would say yes, and then he would remain; go off on another ivory hunt; disappear for weeks; forget himself amongst these people — forget himself — you know.' 'Why! he's mad,' I said. He protested indignantly. Mr. Kurtz couldn't be mad. If I had heard him talk, only two days ago, I wouldn't dare hint at such a thing. . . . I had taken up my binoculars while we talked, and was looking at the shore, sweeping the limit of the forest at each side and at the back of the house. The consciousness of there being people in that bush, so silent, so quiet — as silent and quiet as the

ruined house on the hill — made me uneasy. There was no sign on the face of nature of this amazing tale that was not so much told as suggested to me in desolate exclamations, completed by shrugs, in interrupted phrases, in hints ending in deep sighs. The woods were unmoved, like a mask — heavy, like the closed door of a prison — they looked with their air of hidden knowledge, of patient expectation, of unapproachable silence. The Russian was explaining to me that it was only lately that Mr. Kurtz had come down to the river, bringing along with him all the fighting men of that lake tribe. He had been absent for several months — getting himself adored, I suppose — and had come down unexpectedly, with the intention to all appearance of making a raid either across the river or down stream. Evidently the appetite for more ivory had got the better of the — what shall I say? — less material aspirations. However, he had got much worse suddenly. 'I heard he was lying helpless, and so I came up — took my chance,' said the Russian. 'Oh, he is bad, very bad.' I directed my glass to the house. There were no signs of life, but there was the ruined roof, the long mud wall peeping above the grass, with three little square window-holes, no two of the same size; all this brought within reach of my hand, as it were. And then I made a brusque movement, and one of the remaining posts of that vanished fence leaped up in the field of my glass. You remember I told you I had been struck at the distance by certain attempts at ornamentation, rather remarkable in the ruinous aspect of the place. Now I had suddenly a nearer view, and its first result was to make me throw my head back as if before a blow. Then I went carefully from post to post with my glass, and I saw my mistake. These round knobs were not ornamental but symbolic; they were expressive and puzzling, striking and disturbing — food for thought and also for the vultures if there had been any looking down from the sky; but at all events for such ants as were industrious enough to ascend the pole. They would have been even more impressive, those heads on the stakes, if their faces had not been turned to the house. Only one, the first I had made out, was facing my way. I was not so shocked as you may think. The start back I had given was really nothing but a movement of surprise. I had expected to see a knob of wood there, you know. I returned deliberately to the first I had seen — and there it was, black, dried, sunken, with closed eyelids — a head that seemed to sleep at the top of that pole, and, with the shrunken dry lips showing a narrow white line of the teeth, was smiling too, smiling continuously at some endless and jocose dream of that eternal slumber.

"I am not disclosing any trade secrets. In fact the manager said afterwards that Mr. Kurtz's methods had ruined the district. I have no opinion on that point, but I want you clearly to understand that there was nothing exactly profitable in these heads being there. They only showed that Mr. Kurtz lacked restraint in the gratification of his various lusts, that there was something wanting in him — some small matter which, when the pressing need arose, could not be found under his magnificent eloquence. Whether he knew of this deficiency himself I can't say. I think the knowledge came to him at last — only at the very last.[1] But the wilderness had found him out early, and had taken on him a terrible vengeance for the fantastic invasion. I think it had whispered to him things about himself which he did not know, things of which he had no conception till he took counsel with this great solitude — and the whisper had proved irresistibly fascinating. It echoed loudly within him because he was hollow at the core. . . . I put down the glass, and the head that had appeared near enough to be spoken to seemed at once to have leaped away from me into inaccessible distance.

"The admirer of Mr. Kurtz was a bit crestfallen. In a hurried, indistinct voice he began to assure me he had not dared to take these — say, symbols — down. He was not afraid of the natives; they would not stir till Mr. Kurtz gave the word. His ascendancy was ex-

[1] Bear this statement in mind when you come to Kurtz's last words.

traordinary. The camps of the people surrounded the place, and the chiefs came every day to see him. They would crawl . . . 'I don't want to know anything of the ceremonies used when approaching Mr. Kurtz,' I shouted. Curious, this feeling that came over me that such details would be more intolerable than those heads drying on the stakes under Mr. Kurtz's windows. After all, that was only a savage sight, while I seemed at one bound to have been transported into some lightless region of subtle horrors, where pure, uncomplicated savagery was a positive relief, being something that had a right to exist — obviously — in the sunshine. The young man looked at me with surprise. I suppose it did not occur to him that Mr. Kurtz was no idol of mine. He forgot I hadn't heard any of these splendid monologues on, what was it? on love, justice, conduct of life — or what not. If it had come to crawling before Mr. Kurtz, he crawled as much as the veriest savage of them all. I had no idea of the conditions, he said: these heads were the heads of rebels. I shocked him excessively by laughing. Rebels! What would be the next definition I was to hear? There had been enemies, criminals, workers — and these were rebels. Those rebellious heads looked very subdued to me on their sticks. 'You don't know how such a life tries a man like Kurtz,' cried Kurtz's last disciple. 'Well, and you?' I said. 'I! I! I am a simple man. I have no

great thoughts. I want nothing from anybody. How can you compare me to . . . ?' His feelings were too much for speech, and suddenly he broke down. 'I don't understand,' he groaned. 'I've been doing my best to keep him alive, and that's enough. I had no hand in all this. I have no abilities. There hasn't been a drop of medicine or a mouthful of invalid food for months here. He was shamefully abandoned. A man like this, with such ideas. Shamefully! Shamefully! I — I haven't slept for the last ten nights. . . .'

"His voice lost itself in the calm of the evening. The long shadows of the forest had slipped down hill while we talked, had gone far beyond the ruined hovel, beyond the symbolic row of stakes. All this was in the gloom, while we down there were yet in the sunshine, and the stretch of the river abreast of the clearing glittered in a still and dazzling splendour, with a murky and overshadowed bend above and below. Not a living soul was seen on the shore. The bushes did not rustle.

"Suddenly round the corner of the house a group of men appeared, as though they had come up from the ground. They waded waist-deep in the grass, in a compact body, bearing an improvised stretcher in their midst. Instantly, in the emptiness of the landscape, a cry arose whose shrillness pierced the still air like a sharp arrow flying straight to the very heart of the land; and, as if by enchantment, streams of human beings — of naked human beings — with spears in their hands, with bows, with shields, with wild glances and savage movements, were poured into the clearing by the dark-faced and pensive forest. The bushes shook, the grass swayed for a time, and then everything stood still in attentive immobility.

" 'Now, if he does not say the right thing to them we are all done for,' said the Russian at my elbow. The knot of men with the stretcher had stopped too, half-way to the steamer, as if petrified. I saw the man on the stretcher sit up, lank and with an uplifted arm, above the shoulders of the bearers. 'Let us hope that the man who can talk so well of love in general will find some particular reason to spare us this time,' I said. I resented bitterly the absurd danger of our situation, as if to be at the mercy of that atrocious phantom had been a dishonouring necessity.[1] I could not hear a sound, but through my glasses I saw the thin arm extended commandingly, the lower jaw moving, the eyes of that apparition shining darkly far in its bony head that nodded with grotesque jerks. Kurtz — Kurtz — that means 'short' in German — don't it? Well, the name was as true as everything else in his life — and death. He looked at least seven feet long. His covering had fallen off, and his body emerged

[1] Note Marlow's attitude toward Kurtz at this point.

from it pitiful and appalling as from a winding-sheet. I could see the cage of his ribs all astir, the bones of his arm waving. It was as though an animated image of death carved out of old ivory had been shaking its hand with menaces at a motionless crowd of men made of dark and glittering bronze. I saw him open his mouth wide — it gave him a weirdly voracious aspect, as though he had wanted to swallow all the air, all the earth, all the men before him. A deep voice reached me faintly. He must have been shouting. He fell back suddenly. The stretcher shook as the bearers staggered forward again, and almost at the same time I noticed that the crowd of savages was vanishing without any perceptible movement of retreat, as if the forest that had ejected these beings so suddenly had drawn them in again as the breath is drawn in a long aspiration.

"Some of the pilgrims behind the stretcher carried his arms — two shot-guns, a heavy rifle, and a light revolver-carbine — the thunderbolts of that pitiful Jupiter. The manager bent over him murmuring as he walked beside his head. They laid him down in one of the little cabins — just a room for a bedplace and a camp-stool or two, you know. We had brought his belated correspondence, and a lot of torn envelopes and open letters littered his bed. His hand roamed feebly amongst these papers. I was struck by the fire of his eyes and the composed languor of his expression. It was not so much the exhaustion of disease. He did not seem in pain. This shadow looked satiated and calm, as though for the moment it had had its fill of all the emotions.

"He rustled one of the letters, and looking straight in my face said, 'I am glad.' Somebody had been writing to him about me. These special recommendations were turning up again. The volume of tone he emitted without effort, almost without the trouble of moving his lips, amazed me. A voice! a voice! It was grave, profound, vibrating, while the man did not seem capable of a whisper. However, he had enough strength in him — factitious no doubt — to very nearly make an end of us, as you shall hear directly.

"The manager appeared silently in the doorway; I stepped out at once and he drew the curtain after me. The Russian, eyed curiously by the pilgrims, was staring at the shore. I followed the direction of his glance.

"Dark human shapes could be made out in the distance, flitting indistinctly against the gloomy border of the forest, and near the river two bronze figures, leaning on tall spears, stood in the sunlight under fantastic head-dresses of spotted skins, warlike and still in statuesque repose. And from right to left along the lighted shore moved a wild and gorgeous apparition of a woman.

"She walked with measured steps, draped in striped and fringed clothes, treading the earth proudly, with a slight jingle and flash of barbarous ornaments. She carried her head high; her hair was done in the shape of a helmet; she had brass leggings to the knee, brass wire gauntlets to the elbow, a crimson spot on her tawny cheek, innumerable necklaces of glass beads on her neck; bizarre things, charms, gifts of witch-men, that hung about her, glittered and trembled at every step. She must have had the value of several elephant tusks upon her. She was savage and superb, wild-eyed and magnificent; there was something ominous and stately in her deliberate progress. And in the hush that had fallen suddenly upon the whole sorrowful land, the immense wilderness, the colossal body of the fecund and mysterious life seemed to look at her, pensive, as though it had been looking at the image of its own tenebrous and passionate soul.

"She came abreast of the steamer, stood still, and faced us. Her long shadow fell to the water's edge. Her face had a tragic and fierce aspect of wild sorrow and of dumb pain mingled with the fear of some struggling, half-shaped resolve. She stood looking at us without a stir, and like the wilderness itself, with an air of brooding over an inscrutable purpose. A whole minute passed, and then she made a step forward. There was a low jingle, a glint of yellow metal, a sway of fringed draperies, and she stopped as if her heart had failed her. The young fellow by my side growled.

The pilgrims murmured at my back. She looked at us all as if her life had depended upon the unswerving steadiness of her glance. Suddenly she opened her bared arms and threw them up rigid above her head, as though in an uncontrollable desire to touch the sky, and at the same time the swift shadows darted out on the earth, swept around on the river, gathering the steamer into a shadowy embrace. A formidable silence hung over the scene.

"She turned away slowly, walked on, following the bank, and passed into the bushes to the left. Once only her eyes gleamed back at us in the dusk of the thickets before she disappeared.

"'If she had offered to come aboard I really think I would have tried to shoot her,' said the man of patches nervously. 'I had been risking my life every day for the last fortnight to keep her out of the house. She got in one day and kicked up a row about those miserable rags I picked up in the storeroom to mend my clothes with. I wasn't decent. At least it must have been that, for she talked like a fury to Kurtz for an hour, pointing at me now and then. I don't understand the dialect of this tribe. Luckily for me, I fancy Kurtz felt too ill that day to care, or there would have been mischief. I don't understand. . . . No — it's too much for me. Ah, well, it's all over now.'

"At this moment I heard Kurtz's deep voice behind the curtain: 'Save me! — save the ivory, you mean. Don't tell me. Save *me!* Why, I've had to save you. You are interrupting my plans now. Sick! Sick! Not so sick as you would like to believe. Never mind. I'll carry my ideas out yet — I will return. I'll show you what can be done. You with your little peddling notions — you are interfering with me. I will return. I . . .'

"The manager came out. He did me the honour to take me under the arm and lead me aside. 'He is very low, very low,' he said. He considered it necessary to sigh, but neglected to be consistently sorrowful. 'We have done all we could for him — haven't we? But there is no disguising the fact, Mr. Kurtz has done more harm than good to the Company. He did not see the time was not ripe for vigorous action. Cautiously, cautiously — that's my principle. We must be cautious yet. The district is closed to us for a time. Deplorable! Upon the whole, the trade will suffer. I don't deny there is a remarkable quantity of ivory — mostly fossil. We must save it, at all events — but look how precarious the position is — and why? Because the method is unsound.' 'Do you,' said I, looking at the shore, 'call it "unsound method"?' 'Without doubt,' he exclaimed hotly. 'Don't you?' . . . 'No method at all,' I murmured after a while. 'Exactly,' he exulted. 'I anticipated this. Shows a complete want of judgment. It is my duty to point it out in the proper quarter.'

'Oh,' said I, 'that fellow — what's his name? — the brickmaker, will make a readable report for you.' He appeared confounded for a moment. It seemed to me I had never breathed an atmosphere so vile, and I turned mentally to Kurtz for relief — positively for relief. 'Nevertheless, I think Mr. Kurtz is a remarkable man,' I said with emphasis. He started, dropped on me a cold heavy glance, said very quietly, 'He *was*,' and turned his back on me. My hour of favour was over; I found myself lumped along with Kurtz as a partisan of methods for which the time was not ripe: I was unsound! Ah! but it was something to have at least a choice of nightmares.[1]

"I had turned to the wilderness really, not to Mr. Kurtz, who, I was ready to admit, was as good as buried. And for a moment it seemed to me as if I also were buried in a vast grave full of unspeakable secrets. I felt an intolerable weight oppressing my breast, the smell of the damp earth, the unseen presence of victorious corruption, the darkness of an impenetrable night. . . . The Russian tapped me on the shoulder. I heard him mumbling and stammering something about 'brother seaman — couldn't conceal — knowledge of matters that would affect Mr. Kurtz's reputation.' I waited. For him evidently Mr. Kurtz was not in his grave; I suspect that for him

---
[1] What exactly is the moral dilemma in which Marlow finds himself?

Mr. Kurtz was one of the immortals. 'Well!' said I at last, 'speak out. As it happens, I am Mr. Kurtz's friend — in a way.'

"He stated with a good deal of formality that had we not been 'of the same profession,' he would have kept the matter to himself without regard to consequences. He suspected 'there was an active ill-will towards him on the part of these white men that — ' 'You are right,' I said, remembering a certain conversation I had overheard. 'The manager thinks you ought to be hanged.' He showed a concern at this intelligence which amused me at first. 'I had better get out of the way quietly,' he said earnestly. 'I can do no more for Kurtz now, and they would soon find some excuse. What's to stop them? There's a military post three hundred miles from here.' 'Well, upon my word,' said I, 'perhaps you had better go if you have any friends amongst the savages near by.' 'Plenty,' he said. 'They are simple people — and I want nothing, you know.' He stood biting his lip, then: 'I don't want any harm to happen to these whites here, but of course I was thinking of Mr. Kurtz's reputation — but you are a brother seaman and — ' 'All right,' said I after a time. 'Mr. Kurtz's reputation is safe with me.' I did not know how truly I spoke.

"He informed me, lowering his voice, that it was Kurtz who had ordered the attack to be made on the steamer. 'He hated sometimes the idea of being taken away — and then again . . . But I don't understand these matters. I am a simple man. He thought it would scare you away — that you would give it up, thinking him dead. I could not stop him. Oh, I had an awful time of it this last month.' 'Very well,' I said. 'He is all right now.' 'Ye-e-es,' he muttered, not very convinced apparently. 'Thanks,' said I; 'I shall keep my eyes open.' 'But quiet — eh?' he urged anxiously. 'It would be awful for his reputation if anybody here' — I promised a complete discretion with great gravity. 'I have a canoe and three black fellows waiting not very far. I am off. Could you give me a few Martini-Henry cartridges?' I could, and did, with proper secrecy. He helped himself, with a wink at me, to a handful of my tobacco. 'Between sailors — you know — good English tobacco.' At the door of the pilot-house he turned round — 'I say, haven't you a pair of shoes you could spare?' He raised one leg. 'Look.' The soles were tied with knotted strings sandal-wise under his bare feet. I rooted out an old pair, at which he looked with admiration before tucking it under his left arm. One of his pockets (bright red) was bulging with cartridges, from the other (dark blue) peeped 'Towson's Inquiry,' etc. etc. He seemed to think himself excellently well equipped for a renewed encounter with the wilderness. 'Ah! I'll never, never meet such a man again. You ought to have heard him recite poetry — his own too it was, he told me. Poetry!' He rolled his eyes at the recollection of these delights. 'Oh, he enlarged my mind!' 'Good-bye,' said I. He shook hands and vanished in the night. Sometimes I ask myself whether I had ever really seen him — whether is was possible to meet such a phenomenon! . . .

"When I woke up shortly after midnight his warning came to my mind with its hint of danger that seemed, in the starred darkness, real enough to make me get up for the purpose of having a look round. On the hill a big fire burned, illuminating fitfully a crooked corner of the station-house. One of the agents with a picket of a few of our blacks, armed for the purpose, was keeping guard over the ivory; but deep within the forest, red gleams that wavered, that seemed to sink and rise from the ground amongst confused columnar shapes of intense blackness, showed the exact position of the camp where Mr. Kurtz's adorers were keeping their uneasy vigil. The monotonous beating of a big drum filled the air with muffled shocks and a lingering vibration. A steady droning sound of many men chanting each to himself some weird incantation came out from the black, flat wall of the woods as the humming of bees comes out of a hive, and had a strange narcotic effect upon my half-awake senses. I believe I dozed off leaning over the rail, till an abrupt burst of yells, an overwhelming outbreak of a pent-up and mysterious frenzy, woke me up in a bewildered wonder. It was cut short all at once, and the low droning went on with an effect of audible and soothing silence. I glanced casually into the little cabin. A light was burning within, but Mr. Kurtz was not there.

"I think I would have raised an outcry if I had believed my eyes. But I didn't believe them at first — the thing seemed so impossible. The fact is I was completely unnerved by a sheer blank fright, pure abstract terror, unconnected with any distinct shape of physical danger. What made this emotion so overpowering was — how shall I define it? — the moral shock I received, as if something altogether monstrous, intolerable to thought and odious to the soul, had been thrust upon me unexpectedly. This lasted of course the merest fraction of a second, and then the usual sense of commonplace, deadly danger, the possibility of a sudden onslaught and massacre, or something of the kind, which I saw impending, was positively welcome and composing. It pacified me, in fact, so much, that I did not raise an alarm.

"There was an agent buttoned up inside an ulster and sleeping on a chair on deck within three feet of me. The yells had not awakened him; he snored very lightly; I left him to his slumbers and leaped ashore. I did not betray Mr. Kurtz — it was ordered I should never betray him — it was written I should be loyal to the nightmare of my choice. I was anxious to deal with this shadow by myself alone — and to this day I don't know why I was so jealous of sharing with any one the peculiar blackness of that experience.

"As soon as I got on the bank I saw a trail — a broad trail through the grass. I remember the exultation with which I said to myself, 'He can't walk — he is crawling on all-fours — I've got him.' The grass was wet with dew. I strode rapidly with clenched fists. I fancy I had some vague notion of falling upon him and giving him a drubbing. I don't know. I had some imbecile thoughts. The knitting old woman with the cat obtruded herself upon my memory as a most improper person to be sitting at the other end of such an affair. I saw a row of pilgrims squirting lead in the air out of Winchesters held to the hip. I thought I would never get back to the steamer, and imagined myself living alone and unarmed in the woods to an advanced age. Such silly things — you know. And I remember I confounded the beat of the drum with the beating of my heart, and was pleased at its calm regularity.

"I kept to the track though — then stopped to listen. The night was very clear; a dark blue space, sparkling with dew and starlight, in which black things stood very still. I thought I could see a kind of motion ahead of me. I was strangely cocksure of everything that night. I actually left the track and ran in a wide semicircle (I verily believe chuckling to myself) so as to get in front of that stir, of that motion I had seen — if indeed I had seen anything. I was circumventing Kurtz as though it had been a boyish game.

"I came upon him, and, if he had not heard me coming, I would have fallen over him too, but he got up in time. He rose, unsteady, long, pale, indistinct, like a vapour exhaled by the earth, and swayed slightly, misty and silent before me; while at my back the fires loomed between the trees, and the murmur of many voices issued from the forest. I had cut him off cleverly; but when actually confronting him I seemed to come to my senses, I saw the danger in its right proportion. It was by no means over yet. Suppose he began to shout? Though he could hardly stand, there was still plenty of vigour in his voice. 'Go away — hide yourself,' he said, in that profound tone. It was very awful. I glanced back. We were within thirty yards of the nearest fire. A black figure stood up, strode on long black legs, waving long black arms, across the glow. It had horns — antelope horns, I think — on its head. Some sorcerer, some witch-man no doubt: it looked fiend-like enough. 'Do you know what you are doing?' I whispered.[1] 'Perfectly,' he answered, raising his voice for that single word: it sounded to me far off and

[1] What do you think Kurtz is doing or planning to do? Why?

yet loud, like a hail through a speaking-trumpet. If he makes a row we are lost, I thought to myself. This clearly was not a case for fisticuffs, even apart from the very natural aversion I had to beat that Shadow — this wandering and tormented thing. 'You will be lost,' I said — 'utterly lost.' One gets sometimes such a flash of inspiration, you know. I did say the right thing, though indeed he could not have been more irretrievably lost than he was at this very moment, when the foundations of our intimacy were being laid — to endure — to endure — even to the end — even beyond.

"'I had immense plans,' he muttered irresolutely. 'Yes,' said I; 'but if you try to shout I'll smash your head with — ' There was not a stick or a stone near. 'I will throttle you for good,' I corrected myself. 'I was on the threshold of great things,' he pleaded, in a voice of longing, with a wistfulness of tone that made my blood run cold. 'And now for this stupid scoundrel — ' 'Your success in Europe is assured in any case,' I affirmed steadily. I did not want to have the throttling of him, you understand — and indeed it would have been very little use for any practical purpose. I tried to break the spell — the heavy, mute spell of the wilderness — that seemed to draw him to its pitiless breast by the awakening of forgotten and brutal instincts, by the memory of gratified and monstrous passions. This alone, I was convinced, had driven him out to the pilgrims looked upon me with disfavour. I was, so to speak, numbered with the dead. It is strange how I accepted this unforeseen partnership, this choice of nightmares forced upon me in the tenebrous land invaded by these mean and greedy phantoms.

"Kurtz discoursed. A voice! a voice! It rang deep to the very last. It survived his strength to hide in the magnificent folds of eloquence the barren darkness of his heart. Oh, he struggled! he struggled! The wastes of his weary brain were haunted by shadowy images now — images of wealth and fame revolving obsequiously round his unextinguishable gift of noble and lofty expression. My Intended, my station, my career, my ideas — these were the subjects for the occasional utterances of elevated sentiments. The shade of the original Kurtz frequented the bedside of the hollow sham, whose fate it was to be buried presently in the mould of primeval earth. But both the diabolic love and the unearthly hate of the mysteries it had penetrated fought for the possession of that soul satiated with primitive emotions, avid of lying fame, of sham distinction, of all the appearances of success and power.

"Sometimes he was contemptibly childish. He desired to have kings meet him at railway stations on his return from some ghastly Nowhere, where he intended to accomplish great things. 'You show them you have in you something that is really profitable, and then there will be no limits to the recognition of your ability,' he would say. 'Of course you must take care of the motives — right motives — always.' The long reaches that were like one and the same reach, monotonous bends that were exactly alike, slipped past the steamer with their multitude of secular trees looking patiently after this grimy fragment of another world, the forerunner of change, of conquest, of trade, of massacres, of blessings. I looked ahead — piloting. 'Close the shutter,' said Kurtz suddenly one day; 'I can't bear to look at this.' I did so. There was a silence. 'Oh, but I will wring your heart yet!' he cried at the invisible wilderness.

"We broke down — as I had expected — and had to lie up for repairs at the head of an island. This delay was the first thing that shook Kurtz's confidence. One morning he gave me a packet of papers and a photograph — the lot tied together with a shoe-string. 'Keep this for me,' he said. 'This noxious fool' (meaning the manager) 'is capable of prying into my boxes when I am not looking.' In the afternoon I saw him. He was lying on his back with closed eyes, and I withdrew quietly, but I heard him mutter, 'Live rightly, die, die . . .' I listened. There was nothing more. Was he rehearsing some speech in his sleep, or was it a fragment of a phrase from some newspaper article? He had been writing for the papers and meant to do so again, 'for the fur-thering of my ideas. It's a duty.'

"His was an impenetrable darkness. I looked at him as you peer down at a man who is lying at the bottom of a precipice where the sun never shines. But I had not much time to give him, because I was helping the engine-driver to take to pieces the leaky cylinders, to straighten a bent connecting-rod, and in other such matters. I lived in an infernal mess of rust, filings, nuts, bolts, spanners, hammers, ratchet-drills — things I abominate, because I don't get on with them. I tended the little forge we fortunately had aboard; I toiled wearily in a wretched scrap-heap — unless I had the shakes too bad to stand.

"One evening coming in with a candle I was startled to hear him say a little tremulously, 'I am lying here in the dark waiting for death.' The light was within a foot of his eyes. I forced myself to murmur, 'Oh, nonsense!' and stood over him as if transfixed.

"Anything approaching the change that came over his features I have never seen before, and hope never to see again. Oh, I wasn't touched. I was fascinated. It was as though a veil had been rent. I saw on that ivory face the expression of sombre pride, of ruthless power, of craven terror — of an intense and hopeless despair. Did he live his life again in every detail of desire, temptation, and surrender during that supreme moment of complete knowledge? He cried in a whisper at some image, at some vision —

he cried out twice, a cry that was no more than a breath:

" 'The horror! The horror!'

"I blew the candle out and left the cabin. The pilgrims were dining in the mess-room, and I took my place opposite the manager, who lifted his eyes to give me a questioning glance, which I successfully ignored. He leaned back, serene, with that peculiar smile of his sealing the unexpressed depths of his meanness. A continuous shower of small flies streamed upon the lamp, upon the cloth, upon our hands and faces. Suddenly the manager's boy put his insolent black head in the doorway, and said in a tone of scathing contempt:

" 'Mistah Kurtz — he dead.'

"All the pilgrims rushed out to see. I remained, and went on with my dinner. I believe I was considered brutally callous. However, I did not eat much. There was a lamp in there — light, don't you know — and outside it was so beastly, beastly dark. I went no more near the remarkable man who had pronounced a judgment upon the adventures of his soul on this earth. The voice was gone. What else had been there? But I am of course aware that next day the pilgrims buried something in a muddy hole.

"And then they very nearly buried me.

"However, as you see, I did not go to join Kurtz there and then. I did not. I remained to dream the nightmare out to the end, and to show my loyalty to Kurtz once

pilgrims looked upon me with disfavour. I was, so to speak, numbered with the dead. It is strange how I accepted this unforeseen partnership, this choice of nightmares forced upon me in the tenebrous land invaded by these mean and greedy phantoms.

"Kurtz discoursed. A voice! a voice! It rang deep to the very last. It survived his strength to hide in the magnificent folds of eloquence the barren darkness of his heart. Oh, he struggled! he struggled! The wastes of his weary brain were haunted by shadowy images now — images of wealth and fame revolving obsequiously round his unextinguishable gift of noble and lofty expression. My Intended, my station, my career, my ideas — these were the subjects for the occasional utterances of elevated sentiments. The shade of the original Kurtz frequented the bedside of the hollow sham, whose fate it was to be buried presently in the mould of primeval earth. But both the diabolic love and the unearthly hate of the mysteries it had penetrated fought for the possession of that soul satiated with primitive emotions, avid of lying fame, of sham distinction, of all the appearances of success and power.

"Sometimes he was contemptibly childish. He desired to have kings meet him at railway stations on his return from some ghastly Nowhere, where he intended to accomplish great things. 'You show them you have in you something that is really profitable, and then there will no limits to the recognition of yo ability,' he would say. 'Of cours you must take care of the motives — right motives — always.' The long reaches that were like one and the same reach, monotonous bends that were exactly alike, slipped past the steamer with their multitude of secular trees looking patiently after this grimy fragment of another world, the forerunner of change, of conquest, of trade, of massacres, of blessings. I looked ahead — piloting. 'Close the shutter,' said Kurtz suddenly one day; 'I can't bear to look at this.' I did so. There was a silence. 'Oh, but I will wring your heart yet!' he cried at the invisible wilderness.

"We broke down — as I had expected — and had to lie up for repairs at the head of an island. This delay was the first thing that shook Kurtz's confidence. One morning he gave me a packet of papers and a photograph — the lot tied together with a shoe-string. 'Keep this for me,' he said. 'This noxious fool' (meaning the manager) 'is capable of prying into my boxes when I am not looking.' In the afternoon I saw him. He was lying on his back with closed eyes, and I withdrew quietly, but I heard him mutter, 'Live rightly, die, die . . .' I listened. There was nothing more. Was he rehearsing some speech in his sleep, or was it a fragment of a phrase from some newspaper article? He had been writing for the papers and meant to do so again, 'for the fur-

thering of my ideas. It's a duty.'

"His was an impenetrable darkness. I looked at him as you peer down at a man who is lying at the bottom of a precipice where the sun never shines. But I had not much time to give him, because I was helping the engine-driver to take to pieces the leaky cylinders, to straighten a bent connecting-rod, and in other such matters. I lived in an infernal mess of rust, filings, nuts, bolts, spanners, hammers, ratchet-drills — things I abominate, because I don't get on with them. I tended the little forge we fortunately had aboard; I toiled wearily in a wretched scrap-heap — unless I had the shakes too bad to stand.

"One evening coming in with a candle I was startled to hear him say a little tremulously, 'I am lying here in the dark waiting for death.' The light was within a foot of his eyes. I forced myself to murmur, 'Oh, nonsense!' and stood over him as if transfixed.

"Anything approaching the change that came over his features I have never seen before, and hope never to see again. Oh, I wasn't touched. I was fascinated. It was as though a veil had been rent. I saw on that ivory face the expression of sombre pride, of ruthless power, of craven terror — of an intense and hopeless despair. Did he live his life again in every detail of desire, temptation, and surrender during that supreme moment of complete knowledge? He cried in a whisper at some image, at some vision —

he cried out twice, a cry that was no more than a breath:

"'The horror! The horror!'

"I blew the candle out and left the cabin. The pilgrims were dining in the mess-room, and I took my place opposite the manager, who lifted his eyes to give me a questioning glance, which I successfully ignored. He leaned back, serene, with that peculiar smile of his sealing the unexpressed depths of his meanness. A continuous shower of small flies streamed upon the lamp, upon the cloth, upon our hands and faces. Suddenly the manager's boy put his insolent black head in the doorway, and said in a tone of scathing contempt:

"'Mistah Kurtz — he dead.'

"All the pilgrims rushed out to see. I remained, and went on with my dinner. I believe I was considered brutally callous. However, I did not eat much. There was a lamp in there — light, don't you know — and outside it was so beastly, beastly dark. I went no more near the remarkable man who had pronounced a judgment upon the adventures of his soul on this earth. The voice was gone. What else had been there? But I am of course aware that next day the pilgrims buried something in a muddy hole.

"And then they very nearly buried me.

"However, as you see, I did not go to join Kurtz there and then. I did not. I remained to dream the nightmare out to the end, and to show my loyalty to Kurtz once

more. Destiny. My destiny! Droll thing life is — that mysterious arrangement of merciless logic for a futile purpose. The most you can hope from it is some knowledge of yourself — that comes too late — a crop of unextinguishable regrets. I have wrestled with death. It is the most unexciting contest you can imagine. It takes place in an impalpable greyness, with nothing underfoot, with nothing around, without spectators, without clamour, without glory, without the great desire of victory, without the great fear of defeat, in a sickly atmosphere of tepid scepticism, without much belief in your own right, and still less in that of your adversary. If such is the form of ultimate wisdom, then life is a greater riddle than some of us think it to be. I was within a hair's-breadth of the last opportunity for pronouncement, and I found with humiliation that probably I would have nothing to say. This is the reason why I affirm that Kurtz was a remarkable man. He had something to say. He said it. Since I had peeped over the edge myself, I understand better the meaning of his stare, that could not see the flame of the candle, but was wide enough to embrace the whole universe, piercing enough to penetrate all the hearts that beat in the darkness. He had summed up — he had judged. 'The horror!' He was a remarkable man. After all, this was the expression of some sort of belief; it had candour, it had conviction, it had a vibrating note of revolt in its whisper, it had the appalling face of a glimpsed truth — the strange commingling of desire and hate. And it is not my own extremity I remember best — a vision of greyness without form filled with physical pain, and a careless contempt for the evanescence of all things — even of this pain itself. No! It is his extremity that I seem to have lived through. True, he had made that last stride, he had stepped over the edge, while I had been permitted to draw back my hesitating foot. And perhaps in this is the whole difference; perhaps all the wisdom, and all truth, and all sincerity, are just compressed into that inappreciable moment of time in which we step over the threshold of the invisible. Perhaps! I like to think my summing-up would not have been a word of careless contempt. Better his cry — much better. It was an affirmation, a moral victory paid for by innumerable defeats, by abominable terrors, by abominable satisfactions. But it was a victory! That is why I have remained loyal to Kurtz to the last, and even beyond, when a long time after I heard once more, not his own voice, but the echo of his magnificent eloquence thrown to me from a soul as translucently pure as a cliff of crystal.

"No, they did not bury me, though there is a period of time which I remember mistily, with a shuddering wonder, like a passage through some inconceivable world that had no hope in it and no desire. I found myself back in the sepulchral city resenting the sight of people hurrying through the streets to filch a little money from each other, to devour their infamous cookery, to gulp their unwholesome beer, to dream their insignificant and silly dreams. They trespassed upon my thoughts. They were intruders whose knowledge of life was to me an irritating pretence, because I felt so sure they could not possibly know the things I knew. Their bearing, which was simply the bearing of commonplace individuals going about their business in the assurance of perfect safety, was offensive to me like the outrageous flauntings of folly in the face of a danger it is unable to comprehend. I had no particular desire to enlighten them, but I had some difficulty in restraining myself from laughing in their faces, so full of stupid importance. I daresay I was not very well at that time. I tottered about the streets — there were various affairs to settle — grinning bitterly at perfectly respectable persons. I admit my behaviour was inexcusable, but then my temperature was seldom normal in these days. My dear aunt's endeavours to 'nurse up my strength' seemed altogether beside the mark. It was not my strength that wanted nursing, it was my imagination that wanted soothing. I kept the bundle of papers given me by Kurtz, not knowing exactly what to do with it. His mother had died lately, watched over, as I was told, by his Intended.

A clean-shaved man, with an official manner and wearing gold-rimmed spectacles, called on me one day and made inquiries, at first circuitous, afterwards suavely pressing, about what he was pleased to denominate certain 'documents.' I was not surprised, because I had had two rows with the manager on the subject out there. I had refused to give up the smallest scrap out of that package, and I took the same attitude with the spectacled man. He became darkly menacing at last, and with much heat argued that the Company had the right to every bit of information about its 'territories.' And, said he, 'Mr. Kurtz's knowledge of unexplored regions must have been necessarily extensive and peculiar — owing to his great abilities and to the deplorable circumstances in which he had been placed: therefore — ' I assured him Mr. Kurtz's knowledge, however extensive, did not bear upon the problems of commerce or administration. He invoked then the name of science. 'It would be an incalculable loss if,' etc. etc. I offered him the report on the 'Suppression of Savage Customs,' with the postscriptum torn off. He took it up eagerly, but ended by sniffing at it with an air of contempt. 'This is not what we had a right to expect,' he remarked. 'Expect nothing else,' I said. 'There are only private letters.' He withdrew upon some threat of legal proceedings, and I saw him no more; but another fellow, calling himself Kurtz's cousin, appeared two days later, and was anxious to hear all the details about his dear relative's last moments. Incidentally he gave me to understand that Kurtz had been essentially a great musician. 'There was the making of an immense success,' said the man, who was an organist, I believe, with lank grey hair flowing over a greasy coat-collar. I had no reason to doubt his statement; and to this day I am unable to say what was Kurtz's profession, whether he ever had any — which was the greatest of his talents. I had taken him for a painter who wrote for the papers, or else for a journalist who could paint — but even the cousin (who took snuff during the interview) could not tell me what he had been — exactly. He was a universal genius — on that point I agreed with the old chap, who thereupon blew his nose noisily into a large cotton handkerchief and withdrew in senile agitation, bearing off some family letters and memoranda without importance. Ultimately a journalist anxious to know something of the fate of his 'dear colleague' turned up. This visitor informed me Kurtz's proper sphere ought to have been politics 'on the popular side.' He had furry straight eyebrows, bristly hair cropped short, an eyeglass on a broad ribbon, and, becoming expansive, confessed his opinion that Kurtz really couldn't write a bit — 'but heavens! how that man could talk! He electrified large meetings. He had faith — don't you see? —

he had the faith. He could get himself to believe anything — anything. He would have been a splendid leader of an extreme party.' 'What party?' I asked. 'Any party,' answered the other. 'He was an — an — extremist.' Did I not think so? I assented. Did I know, he asked, with a sudden flash of curiosity, 'what it was that had induced him to go out there?' 'Yes,' said I, and forthwith handed him the famous Report for publication, if he thought fit. He glanced through it hurriedly, mumbling all the time, judged 'it would do,' and took himself off with this plunder.

"Thus I was left at last with a slim packet of letters and the girl's portrait. She struck me as beautiful — I mean she had a beautiful expression. I know that the sunlight can be made to lie too, yet one felt that no manipulation of light and pose could have conveyed the delicate shade of truthfulness upon those features. She seemed ready to listen without mental reservation, without suspicion, without a thought for herself. I concluded I would go and give her back her portrait and those letters myself. Curiosity? Yes; and also some other feeling perhaps. All that had been Kurtz's had passed out of my hands: his soul, his body, his station, his plans, his ivory, his career. There remained only his memory and his Intended — and I wanted to give that up too to the past, in a way — to surrender personally all that remained of him with me to that oblivion which is the last word of our common fate. I don't defend myself. I had no clear perception of what it was I really wanted. Perhaps it was an impulse of unconscious loyalty, or the fulfilment of one of those ironic necessities that lurk in the facts of human existence. I don't know. I can't tell. But I went.

"I thought his memory was like the other memories of the dead that accumulate in every man's life — a vague impress on the brain of shadows that had fallen on it in their swift and final passage; but before the high and ponderous door, between the tall houses of a street as still and decorous as a well-kept alley in a cemetery, I had a vision of him on the stretcher, opening his mouth voraciously, as if to devour all the earth with all its mankind. He lived then before me; he lived as much as he had ever lived — a shadow insatiable of splendid appearances, of frightful realities; a shadow darker than the shadow of the night, and draped nobly in the folds of a gorgeous eloquence. The vision seemed to enter the house with me — the stretcher, the phantom-bearers, the wild crowd of obedient worshippers, the gloom of the forests, the glitter of the reach between the murky bends, the beat of the drum, regular and muffled like the beating of a heart — the heart of a conquering darkness. It was a moment of triumph for the wilderness, an invading and vengeful rush which, it seemed to me, I would have to keep back alone for the salvation of another soul. And the memory of what I had heard him say afar there, with the horned shapes stirring at my back, in the glow of fires, within the patient woods, those broken phrases came back to me, were heard again in their ominous and terrifying simplicity. I remembered his abject pleading, his abject threats, the colossal scale of his vile desires, the meanness, the torment, the tempestuous anguish of his soul. And later on I seemed to see his collected languid manner, when he said one day, 'This lot of ivory now is really mine. The Company did not pay for it. I collected it myself at a very great personal risk. I am afraid they will try to claim it as theirs though. H'm. It is a difficult case. What do you think I ought to do — resist? Eh? I want no more than justice.' . . . He wanted no more than justice — no more than justice. I rang the bell before a mahogany door on the first floor, and while I waited he seemed to stare at me out of the glassy panel — stare with that wide and immense stare embracing, condemning, loathing all the universe. I seemed to hear the whispered cry, 'The horror! The horror!'

"The dusk was falling. I had to wait in a lofty drawing-room with three long windows from floor to ceiling that were like three luminous and bedraped columns. The bent gilt legs and backs of the furniture shone in indistinct curves. The tall marble fireplace had a cold and monumental whiteness. A grand piano stood massively in a corner; with dark gleams on the flat surfaces like a sombre and polished sarcophagus. A high door opened — closed. I rose.

"She came forward, all in black, with a pale head, floating towards me in the dusk. She was in mourning. It was more than a year since his death, more than a year since the news came; she seemed as though she would remember and mourn for ever. She took both my hands in hers and murmured, 'I had heard you were coming.' I noticed she was not very young — I mean not girlish. She had a mature capacity for fidelity, for belief, for suffering. The room seemed to have grown darker, as if all the sad light of the cloudy evening had taken refuge on her forehead. This fair hair, this pale visage, this pure brow, seemed surrounded by an ashy halo from which the dark eyes looked out at me. Their glance was guileless, profound, confident, and trustful. She carried her sorrowful head as though she were proud of that sorrow, as though she would say, I — I alone know how to mourn for him as he deserves. But while we were still shaking hands, such a look of awful desolation came upon her face that I perceived she was one of those creatures that are not the playthings of Time. For her he had died only yesterday. And, by Jove! the impression was so powerful that for me too he seemed to have died only yesterday — nay, this very minute. I saw her and him in the same instant of time — his death and her sorrow — I saw her sorrow in the very moment of his death. Do you understand I saw them together — I heard them together. She had said, with a deep catch of the breath, 'I have survived'; while my strained ears seemed to hear distinctly, mingled with her tone of despairing regret, the summing-up whisper of his eternal condemnation. I asked myself what I was doing there, with a sensation of panic in my heart as though I had blundered into a place of cruel and absurd mysteries not fit for a human being to behold. She motioned me to a chair. We sat down. I laid the packet gently on the little table, and she put her hand over it. . . . 'You knew him well,' she murmured, after a moment of mourning silence.

"'Intimacy grows quickly out there,' I said. 'I knew him as well as it is possible for one man to know another.'

"'And you admired him,' she said. 'It was impossible to know him and not to admire him. Was it?'

"'He was a remarkable man,' I said unsteadily. Then before the appealing fixity of her gaze, that seemed to watch for more words on my lips, I went on, 'It was impossible not to —'

"'Love him,' she finished eagerly, silencing me into an appalled dumbness. 'How true! how true! But when you think that no one knew him so well as I! I had all his noble confidence. I knew him best.'

" 'You knew him best,' I repeated. And perhaps she did. But with every word spoken the room was growing darker, and only her forehead, smooth and white, remained illumined by the unextinguishable light of belief and love.

" 'You were his friend,' she went on. 'His friend,' she repeated, a little louder. 'You must have been, if he had given you this, and sent you to me. I feel I can speak to you — and oh! I must speak. I want you — you who have heard his last words — to know I have been worthy of him. . . . It is not pride. . . . Yes! I am proud to know I understood him better than any one on earth — he told me so himself. And since his mother died I have had no one — no one — to — to — '

"I listened. The darkness deepened. I was not even sure whether he had given me the right bundle. I rather suspect he wanted me to take care of another batch of his papers which, after his death, I saw the manager examining under the lamp. And the girl talked, easing her pain in the certitude of my sympathy; she talked as thirsty men drink. I had heard that her engagement with Kurtz had been disapproved by her people. He wasn't rich enough or something. And indeed I don't know whether he had not been a pauper all his life. He had given me some reason to infer that it was his impatience of comparative poverty that drove him out there.

" '. . . Who was not his friend who had heard him speak once?' she was saying. 'He drew men towards him by what was best in them.' She looked at me with intensity. 'It is the gift of the great,' she went on, and the sound of her low voice seemed to have the accompaniment of all the other sounds, full of mystery, desolation, and sorrow, I had ever heard — the ripple of the river, the soughing of the trees swayed by the wind, the murmurs of the crowds, the faint ring of incomprehensible words cried from afar, the whisper of a voice speaking from beyond the threshold of an eternal darkness. 'But you have heard him! You know!' she cried.

" 'Yes, I know,' I said with something like despair in my heart, but bowing my head before the faith that was in her, before that great and saving illusion that shone with an unearthly glow in the darkness, in the triumphant darkness from which I could not have defended her — from which I could not even defend myself.

" 'What a loss to me — to us!' — she corrected herself with beautiful generosity; then added in a murmur, 'To the world.' By the last gleams of twilight I could see the glitter of her eyes, full of tears — of tears that would not fall.

" 'I have been very happy — very fortunate — very proud,' she went on. 'Too fortunate. Too happy for a little while. And now I am un-happy for — for life.'

"She stood up; her fair hair seemed to catch all the remaining light in a glimmer of gold. I rose too.

" 'And of all this,' she went on mournfully, 'of all his promise, and of all his greatness, of his generous mind, of his noble heart, nothing remains — nothing but a memory. You and I — '

" 'We shall always remember him,' I said hastily.

" 'No!' she cried. 'It is impossible that all this should be lost — that such a life should be sacrificed to leave nothing — but sorrow. You know what vast plans he had. I knew of them too — I could not perhaps understand — but others knew of them. Something must re-main. His words, at least, have not died.'

" 'His words will remain,' I said.

" 'And his example,' she whis-pered to herself. 'Men looked up to him — his goodness shone in every act. His example — '

" 'True,' I said; 'his example too. Yes, his example. I forgot that.'

" 'But I do not. I cannot — I can-not believe — not yet. I cannot be-lieve that I shall never see him again, that nobody will see him again, never, never, never.'

"She put out her arms as if after a retreating figure, stretching them black and with clasped pale hands across the fading and narrow sheen of the window. Never see him! I saw him clearly enough then. I shall see this eloquent phantom as long as I live, and I shall see her too, a tragic and familiar Shade, resem-bling in this gesture another one, tragic also, and bedecked with powerless charms, stretching bare brown arms over the glitter of the infernal stream, the stream of dark-ness. She said suddenly very low, 'He died as he lived.'

" 'His end,' said I, with dull anger stirring in me, 'was in every way worthy of his life.'

" 'And I was not with him,' she murmured. My anger subsided be-fore a feeling of infinite pity.

" 'Everything that could be done — ' I mumbled.

" ' Ah, but I believed in him more than any one on earth — more than his own mother, more than — him-self. He needed me! Me! I would have treasured every sigh, every word, every sign, every glance.'

"I felt like a chill grip on my chest. 'Don't,' I said, in a muffled voice.

" 'Forgive me. I — I — have mourned so long in silence — in silence. . . . You were with him — to the last? I think of his loneliness. Nobody near to understand him as I would have understood. Perhaps no one to hear. . . .'

" 'To the very end,' I said shak-ily. 'I heard his very last words. . . .' I stopped in a fright.

" 'Repeat them,' she murmured in a heart-broken tone. 'I want — I want — something — something — to — to live with.'

"I was on the point of crying at

her, 'Don't you hear them?' The dusk was repeating them in a persistent whisper all around us, in a whisper that seemed to swell menacingly like the first whisper of a rising wind. 'The horror! The horror!'

" 'His last word—to live with,' she insisted. 'Don't you understand I loved him—I loved him—I loved him!'

"I pulled myself together and spoke slowly.

" 'The last word he pronounced was—your name.'

"I heard a light sigh and then my heart stood still, stopped dead short by an exulting and terrible cry, by the cry of inconceivable triumph and of unspeakable pain. 'I knew it—I was sure!' . . . She knew. She was sure. I heard her weeping; she had hidden her face in her hands. It seemed to me that the house would collapse before I could escape, that the heavens would fall upon my head. But nothing happened. The heavens do not fall for such a trifle. Would they have fallen, I wonder, if I had rendered Kurtz that justice which was his due? Hadn't he said he wanted only justice? But I couldn't. I could not tell her. It would have been too dark—too dark altogether. . . ."

Marlow ceased, and sat apart, indistinct and silent, in the pose of a meditating Buddha. Nobody moved for a time. "We have lost the first of the ebb," said the Director suddenly. I raised my head. The offing was barred by a black bank of clouds, and the tranquil waterway leading to the uttermost ends of the earth flowed sombre under an overcast sky—seemed to lead into the heart of an immense darkness.

For Study

1. From what is said about Marlow when he is aboard the *Nellie*, what do we learn about his background and experience?

2. What topic of conversation is suggested by the time and place of the *Nellie's* riding at anchor?

3. Why does Marlow want the job he takes with the Company? How does he get it?

4. Why does Brussels remind Marlow of a "whited sepulchre"?

5. What is the attitude of Marlow's excellent aunt toward her nephew? toward the Company?

6. "Avoid irritation more than exposure to the sun," says the eccentric doctor who gives Marlow his physical examination. What other details does Marlow note in Brussels that suggest the ominous quality of his new job?

7. What are Marlow's reflections on the natives he sees paddling out to the ship that brings him to Africa? How do these reflections contrast with his description of the warship that is shelling the bush (page 731)?

8. What does Marlow find happening to the natives at the first Company station he visits? What technological progress, the fruit of civilization, does he observe there?

9. Marlow first hears of Kurtz from the Company's immaculate chief ac-

countant at this station. The latter says, "He is a very remarkable person." This judgment of Kurtz is repeated in various ways later in the story. What does the accountant mean by it?

10. On his way to the Central Station, Marlow meets a drunken white man with an armed escort of Zanzibaris. What is the significance of what he finds on the trail three miles farther along?

11. When Marlow hobbles into the Central Station, in what state does he find the ship he is to command? How is the situation explained to him? What are his reactions?

12. What apparently are the real duties of the "brickmaker" at the Central Station? What duties occupy the "pilgrims" at the Central Station?

13. When that "papier-mâché Mephistopheles," the brickmaker, sneers jealously at "the new gang — the gang of virtue," to which he assumes that both Kurtz and Marlow belong, Marlow cuts him off by accusing him of reading official mail and adding, "When Mr. Kurtz is General Manager, you won't have the opportunity." What immediate effect does this treatment have on the brickmaker? Why?

14. What is the appearance of the Eldorado Exploring Expedition? Marlow notes that its members are reckless, greedy, and cruel, but these qualities are only part of the reason he holds them in contempt. What is the rest?

15. What of significance does Marlow overhear in the conversation near

the steamboat between the manager and his uncle?

16. Marlow becomes really interested in Kurtz when he learns that Kurtz, after coming three hundred miles toward headquarters by canoe, has turned back to return to his post. What is there in this news that stimulates Marlow's interest?

17. What is the nature of the tattered volume that Marlow finds at the empty hut? Why does this book impress Marlow so deeply?

18. When the steamboat is anchored in a dense fog about eight miles below Kurtz's station, the air is suddenly filled with eerie shrieks. How do the "pilgrims" react to these? What is the reaction of the savage crewmen?

19. In the fog, the manager says to Marlow, "I authorize you to take all risks" (in order to reach Mr. Kurtz before it is too late). What is the manager's real concern?

20. *Restraint* becomes a key word in the narrative as the steamboat nears Kurtz's station. From what are the cannibal crewmen mysteriously restrained? What principally restrains Marlow from going ashore for "a howl and a dance"?

21. The "pilgrims" and the native crew both resent Marlow's disposal of his dead helmsman, though for quite different reasons. What are these reasons?

22. After the helmsman is killed in the attack on the steamboat, Marlow assumes that Kurtz must be dead too. What special regret then occurs to Marlow?

23. What does the young Russian advance as the reason for the attack on the steamboat?

24. What facts about Kurtz's life in the interior does Marlow get from the young Russian sailor? What is the basis of the latter's attachment to Kurtz?

25. What does Marlow mean when he says that Kurtz "had taken a high seat amongst the devils of the land — I mean literally"? Why, according to Marlow, can his civilized friends aboard the *Nellie* not understand what Kurtz has done?

26. What is the manager's spoken reaction to Kurtz's "methods"? What is Marlow's?

27. After his conversation with the manager about Kurtz's methods, Marlow says ". . . but it was something to have at least a choice of night-mares." What does he mean? What nightmare does Marlow choose? Why does he choose it?

28. How does Marlow prevail on Kurtz to return to the steamboat after Kurtz's escape to shore?

29. On the voyage down the Congo, what does the dying Kurtz talk about in his conversations with Marlow? What are Kurtz's last words? What is Marlow's reactions to them?

30. What is the nature of Kurtz's report for the International Society for the Suppression of Savage Customs? In what spirit was it apparently undertaken? In what light does its author regard it on his deathbed? What is the significance of his scrawled postscript to the report?

31. What is the lie that Marlow tells Kurtz's "Intended"? Why does he tell it?

AFTERWORD

There are a good many ways of approaching this profound and complex tale. Though short, *Heart of Darkness* is about a surprising number of things: the rescue of a dying man who may not want to be rescued; a plot by jealous bureaucrats to get rid of a rival; the abuses of nineteenth-century colonial imperialism; powers of darkness; the adventurous Marlow's strange journey. Without overlooking these or other topics, let us here consider *Heart of Darkness* primarily as the study of two men: Marlow and Kurtz. They are individuals significantly distinct from the other people in the story; indeed, from the very first mentions of these two men, they are carefully and clearly set apart from the run of ordinary mankind.

True, Marlow is at ease with his friends aboard the *Nellie:* he shares the bond of the sea with them. But he is the only one among them who still follows the sea professionally, and he is the only one who apparently lives his life by his own rules rather than society's. Even as a sailor, Conrad notes, Marlow is unique. Sailors in general are "sedentary," home-loving (i.e., ship-loving) creatures who have little interest in the far places of the earth; Marlow is an adventurer.

Why does Marlow venture on the particular trip of the main story? A commonplace reason may occur to us first: he is out of work. But is it likely that the command of a steamboat in the heart of the Belgian Congo, obtained through family influence (repugnant to him), is Marlow's only alternative to unemployment and poverty? In any case, does Marlow care greatly about his social or economic state? No; Marlow's significant motive for going to Africa is found in the attraction that the map of Africa has for him. Marlow looks with hungry imagination at the great empty landmass represented; he is struck by the mysterious river curving through it like a snake. He is, he says, charmed by that snake. He is, in fact, so fascinated by the idea of life without civilization, by the darkness, as to want to risk its perils in an attempt to experience it.

As the story goes on, we see that there are other, more ordinary ways of being concerned with the darkness, and we see how little these attract him. He is repelled by the pharisaical atmosphere of "the sepulchral city" and is grimly amused at the business of signing a promise not to disclose "trade secrets." He knows very well that the function of the Company is exploitation, in spite of the platitudes of his excellent aunt. The medical examiner's oblique comments, as well as other details, make it clear that dealing with the darkness is a business that is dangerous both physically and psychologically.

What Marlow is *not* aware of in the sepulchral city is the *moral* peril of the undertaking that he, as an adventurer, has been attracted to for reasons alien to ordinary men. It is this moral peril that provides the ultimate stress to which Conrad exposes his characters and which indeed is the central theme of *Heart of Darkness*. All the white men who go to the Company's stations in Africa share ignorance of this danger. The ordinary sorts, such as the manager, the brickmaker, the accountant, and the pilgrims, maintain their ignorance; Marlow and Kurtz do not. The starting assumption for all is that the darkness they are entering is simply the darkness of uncivilization, of undeveloped country and of savages who may be brought the light of European progress. In the story, only Marlow and Kurtz learn the real nature and the enormous power of darkness. Only Marlow and Kurtz learn that darkness is not a simple matter of geography or technological progress, but a vast reservoir of lust and greed

— of inclinations and desires that are only fraily restrained by civilized customs and moral principles. What the dark African jungle and the dark natives provide is an opportunity for the darkness of the human heart to show itself.

The ordinary men who come to Africa simply to make money respond readily enough to the opportunity. The darkness within them answers the dark continent in their oppression and murder of natives, in their sloth and futility, in their covetous plots. But they are concerned so deeply with money (or ivory) and safety that they remain quite unaware of what is happening to themselves.

Marlow, unlike them, is impressed by the imbecilic "war" that is being carried on by the French warship against the African continent. In the course of his inspection of the first Company station he visits, he observes construction that produces futility and desolation, laws that enforce misery and death. He notes the statement of the freshly-dressed chief accountant, "When one has got to make correct entries, one comes to hate those savages — hate them to the death."

But it is only when Marlow knows Kurtz that he knows the ultimate danger of the darkness. To the manager and his colleagues, Kurtz is a highly effective ivory-collector, one of the "new gang of virtue," and a dangerous rival; but Marlow sees Kurtz truly as a man who has "taken a high seat among the devils of the land." Marlow sees that Kurtz has consciously given up all restraint and consciously met the darkness around him with a profounder darkness of his own. Without restraint, Kurtz has come to the point where he gratifies his every lust and whim — there is no one and nothing to deter him at the Inner Station. Paramount among these lusts and whims is the dark, diabolic desire that lurks beneath the restraints in our personalities: to be a god.

Kurtz, like Marlow, has come to Africa with ideas and motives that set him apart. As we learn from his report for the International Society for the Suppression of Savage Customs as well as from the comments of the other Company men, his aim has been to "exert a power for good practically unbounded," to bring light into the darkness. In his efforts to effect this moral aim, Kurtz reenacts the story of Dr. Faustus: needing unlimited power, he delivers himself to darkness. With the power of darkness, which is the power to break down all restraint, and with his courage and force of personality, he becomes the devil-god of the Inner Station. He commands property, life, and death as he wills, without the strictures of economy or fear that limit ordinary men, without the dedication to a job that restrains Marlow, and completely without the moral sentiments that were his original motivation. He pays the traditional price: the loss of his soul. But like Marlow he sees what is happening; and unlike the others he suffers, as shown by his final agonized cry, "The horror! The horror!" Marlow chooses Kurtz as his nightmare in preference to the nightmare of the careful little hollow men; and Kurtz chooses Marlow as his executor because Marlow understands.

Easter 1916

by William Butler Yeats

(1865-1939)

I have met them at close of day
Coming with vivid faces
From counter or desk among grey
Eighteenth-century houses.
I have passed with a nod of the head   5
Or polite meaningless words,
Or lingered awhile and said
Polite meaningless words,
And thought before I had done
Of a mocking tale or a gibe   10
To please a companion
Around the fire at the club,
Being certain that they and I
But lived where motley is worn:
All changed, changed utterly: 15
A terrible beauty is born.

That woman's° days were spent
In ignorant good-will,
Her nights in argument
Until her voice grew shrill.   20
What voice more sweet than hers
When, young and beautiful,
She rode to harriers?
This man° had kept a school
And rode our wingèd horse;   25
This other ° his helper and friend

17. **That woman:** Countess Markiewicz (before her marriage, Constance Gore-Booth) took an active part in the Easter insurrection and was sentenced to imprisonment for life. In her youth she had been famous for her beauty and riding ability. **24. This man:** Patrick Pearse, leader in the Gaelic language movement, founder of a bilingual school, and poet, commanded the rebel forces. **26. This other:** Thomas MacDonagh, whose writing Yeats had read and admired.

Was coming into his force;
He might have won fame in the end;
So sensitive his nature seemed,
So daring and sweet his thought.   30
This other man° I had dreamed
A drunken, vainglorious lout.
He had done most bitter wrong
To some who are near my heart,
Yet I number him in the song;   35
He, too, has resigned his part
In the casual comedy;
He, too, has been changed in his turn,
Transformed utterly:
A terrible beauty is born.   40

Hearts with one purpose alone
Through summer and winter seem
Enchanted to a stone
To trouble the living stream.
The horse that comes from the road,   45
The rider, the birds that range
From cloud to tumbling cloud,
Minute by minute they change;
A shadow of cloud on the stream
Changes minute by minute;   50
A horse-hoof slides on the brim,
And a horse plashes within it;
The long-legged moor-hens dive,
And hens to moor-cocks call;
Minute by minute they live: 55
The stone's in the midst of all.
Too long a sacrifice
Can make a stone of the heart.
O when may it suffice?
That is Heaven's part, our part   60
To murmur name upon name,
As a mother names her child
When sleep at last has come
On limbs that had run wild.
What is it but nightfall?   65

31. **This other man**: Major John MacBride, husband of a beautiful Irish patriot, Maud Gonne, whom Yeats loved.

No, no, not night but death;
Was it needless death after all?
For England may keep faith
For all that is done and said.
We know their dream; enough 70
To know they dreamed and are dead;
And what if excess of love
Bewildered them till they died?
I write it out in a verse —
MacDonagh and MacBride 75
And Connolly° and Pearse
Now and in time to be,
Wherever green is worn,
Are changed, changed utterly:
A terrible beauty is born. 80

September 25, 1916

76. Connolly: James Connolly was Pearse's partner in leading the insurrection.
(In the late 1890's Yeats and Maud Gonne had joined him in anti-English demonstrations.)

For Study and Writing

1. William Butler Yeats was an Irish poet who, after the fight for independence, became a member of the Irish Senate. His direct reference in this poem is to one of the first and most romantic events in "the troubles," the final and successful insurrections against English domination. Patrick Pearse and some comrades barricaded themselves in the Dublin post office, hoping that their resistance to the English troops quartered in the city would set off a general uprising. As for immediate results, the plot was a failure. On that Easter Monday there was no national revolution; business in Dublin went on much as usual. Many of the post office defenders were killed, and fifteen of the leaders, including the four men named in the poem, were executed after they surrendered. What can you infer to have been the attitude of Yeats, as he expresses it in "Easter 1916," to the uprising on that occasion? Why do you suppose that he himself was not among the fighters? What does he confess to have been his attitude towards these people before the event?

2. The line "A terrible beauty is born" with which each section of the poem ends is a statement about the tragic. Apply this statement to *King Lear* and *Oedipus*.

3. By what means does Yeats, in

the third section of the poem, express the importance of the unsuccessful attempt on Easter Monday?

4. What does the poet mean by these words: "But lived where motley is worn" (line 14) and "the casual comedy" (line 37)?

5. What does the poet conceive his own importance to be in the change from "casual comedy" to the birth of "a terrible beauty"?

6. What tragic catastrophe is the poet concerned with other than that of the death of the Irish patriots he mentions in the poem? Consider particularly the statement in lines 57 and 58 as well as the images which immediately precede these lines.

Tears, Idle Tears

by *Alfred, Lord Tennyson*

(*1809–1892*)

Tears, idle tears, I know not what they mean,
Tears from the depth of some divine despair
Rise in the heart, and gather to the eyes,
In looking on the happy autumn-fields,
And thinking of the days that are no more.   5

Fresh as the first beam glittering on a sail,
That brings our friends up from the underworld,
Sad as the last which reddens over one
That sinks with all we love below the verge;
So sad, so fresh, the days that are no more.   10

Ah, sad and strange as in dark summer dawns
The earliest pipe of half-awaken'd birds
To dying ears, when unto dying eyes
The casement slowly grows a glimmering square;
So sad, so strange, the days that are no more.   15

Dear as remember'd kisses after death,
And sweet as those by hopeless fancy feign'd
On lips that are for others; deep as love,
Deep as first love, and wild with all regret;
O Death in Life, the days that are no more!   20

1. In the first line of the poem, the poet says that he does not know what his tears mean. By the end of the poem, what does he reveal about their meaning?

2. How do the two similes used by the poet in the second stanza make vivid two responses to "the days that are no more"?

3. What does the poet mean by the phrase "Death in Life"?

4. What pattern of contrast is found in the last stanza of this poem that has been present since line 2?

5. Do you think the poet succeeds in transmuting the merely sentimental or pathetic into the tragic? Support your opinion.

Sonnet LXXIII

by William Shakespeare
(*1564–1616*)

That time of year thou may'st in me behold
When yellow leaves, or none, or few, do hang
Upon those boughs which shake against the cold,
Bare ruined choirs where late the sweet birds sang.
In me thou see'st the twilight of such day   5
As after sunset fadeth in the west,
Which by and by black night doth take away,
Death's second self, that seals up all in rest.
In me thou see'st the glowing of such fire,
That on the ashes of his youth doth lie,   10
As the death-bed whereon it must expire,
Consumed with that which it was nourished by.
   This thou perceiv'st, which makes thy love more strong,
   To love that well which thou must leave ere long.

For Study and Writing

1. Basic to any degree of the tragic mood is some element of inevitability, some sense of a destructive pattern beyond the comprehension and control, though not the vision, of man. How do the images with which the poet describes himself and his stage express this sense?

2. Is the reader in any way prepared for the introduction of the idea of *love* before it appears in the final couplet?

A PRACTICE TEST

I. Read the following poem *at least twice* before starting to answer the questions:

To Marguerite

by *Matthew Arnold*
(*1822–1888*)

Yes! in the sea of life enisled,
With echoing straits between us thrown,
Dotting the shoreless watery wild,
We mortal millions live *alone*.
The islands feel the enclasping flow   5
And then their endless bounds they know.

But when the moon their hollows lights,
And they are swept by balms of spring,
And in their glens, on starry nights,
The nightingales divinely sing;   10
And lovely notes, from shore to shore,
Across the sounds and channels pour —

Oh! then a longing like despair
Is to their farthest caverns sent;
For surely once, they feel, we were   15
Parts of a single continent!
Now round us spreads the watery plain —
Oh might our marges meet again!

Who ordered, that their longing's fire
Should be, as soon as kindled, cooled?   20
Who renders vain their deep desire? —
A God, a God their severance ruled!
And bade betwixt their shores to be
The unplumbed, salt, estranging sea.

   1. With what image does the poet express his sense of the isolation of human beings from one another? Discuss briefly the applicability of this image.

2. What qualification of, or exception to, this isolation does the poet introduce in the second stanza? What specifically does the image of the nightingales (line 10) suggest to you?

3. What, says the poet, is the *effect* of the exception introduced in the second stanza?

4. What question and what answer are offered by the poet in the final stanza? How are this question and this answer basic to the tragic view of the human situation in general?

II. In the preface to his play *Saint Joan* (1924), George Bernard Shaw writes that in tragedy there are no villains. He continues: "It is what men do at their best, with good intentions, and what normal men and women find that they must and will do in spite of their intentions, that really concern us."

In a well-organized essay, discuss Shaw's opinion as it applies not only to formal tragedy but to the tragic image of man.

III. Let us assume that in a given society the following lists show the major and the minor concerns of the people. Using the evidence of these lists, write a description of that society.

Major Concerns	*Minor Concerns*
1. Home-installed bomb shelters	1. Toys
2. Subscriptions to religious publications	2. Television sets
3. Travel	3. Subscriptions to magazines on current events
4. Romantic historical novels	4. Schools, colleges, and camps
5. Transistor radios	5. Science fiction
6. Retirement insurance	6. Inexpensive automobiles

Index of Authors and Titles

A 6
B 7
C 8
D 9
E 0
F 1
G 2
H 3
I 4
J 5